Troubleshooting TCP/IP

Third Edition

Troubleshooting TCP/IP

Third Edition

Mark A. Miller, P.E.

M&T Books

An Imprint of IDG Books Worldwide, Inc.

Foster City, CA ◆ Chicago, IL ◆ Indianapolis, IN ◆ New York, NY

Troubleshooting TCP/IP, Third Edition

Published by
M&T Books
An Imprint of IDG Books Worldwide, Inc.
An International Data Group Company
919 E. Hillsdale Blvd., Suite 400
Foster City, CA 94404
www.idgbooks.com (IDG Books Worldwide Web site)

ISBN: 0-7645-7012-9

Printed in the United States of America

10 9 8 7 6 5 4 3 2 1

3B/SZ/QW/ZZ/IN

Distributed in the United States by IDG Books Worldwide, Inc.

Distributed by CDG Books Canada Inc. for Canada; by Transworld Publishers Limited in the United Kingdom; by IDG Norge Books for Norway; by IDG Sweden Books for Sweden; by Woodslane Pty. Ltd. for Australia; by Woodslane (NZ) Ltd. for New Zealand; by TransQuest Publishers Pte Ltd. for Singapore, Malaysia, Thailand, Indonesia, and Hong Kong; by ICG Muse, Inc. for Japan; by Norma Comunicaciones S.A. for Colombia; by Intersoft for South Africa; by Eyrolles for France; by International Thomson Publishing for Germany, Austria and Switzerland; by Distribuidora Cuspide for Argentina; by Livraria Cultura for Brazil; by Ediciones ZETA S.C.R. Ltda. for Peru; by WS Computer Publishing Corporation, Inc., for the Philippines; by Contemporanea de Ediciones for Venezuela; by Express Computer Distributors for the Caribbean and West Indies; by Micronesia Media Distributor, Inc. for Micronesia; by Grupo Editorial Norma S.A. for Guatemala; by Chips Computadoras S.A. de C.V. for Mexico; by Editorial Norma de Panama S.A. for Panama; by American Bookshops for Finland. Authorized Sales Agent: Anthony Rudkin Associates for the Middle East and North Africa.

For general information on IDG Books Worldwide's books in the U.S., please call our Consumer Customer Service department at 800-762-2974. For reseller information, including discounts and premium sales, please call our Reseller Customer Service department at 800-434-3422.

For information on where to purchase IDG Books Worldwide's books outside the U.S., please contact our International Sales department at 317-596-5530 or fax 317-596-5692.

For consumer information on foreign language translations, please contact our Customer Service department at 800-434-3422, fax 317-596-5692, or e-mail rights@idgbooks.com.

For information on licensing foreign or domestic rights, please phone +1-650-655-3109.

For sales inquiries and special prices for bulk quantities, please contact our Sales department at 650-655-3200 or write to the address above.

For information on using IDG Books Worldwide's books in the classroom or for ordering examination copies, please contact our Educational Sales department at 800-434-2086 or fax 317-596-5499.

For press review copies, author interviews, or other publicity information, please contact our Public Relations department at 650-655-3000 or fax 650-655-3299.

For authorization to photocopy items for corporate, personal, or educational use, please contact Copyright Clearance Center, 222 Rosewood Drive, Danvers, MA 01923, or fax 978-750-4470.

Library of Congress Cataloging-in-Publication Data

Miller, Mark A., 1955-

Troubleshooting TCP/IP / Mark A. Miller. – 3rd ed.

p. cm.

Includes bibliographical references.

ISBN 0-7165-7012-9 (alk. paper)

1. TCP/IP (Computer network protocol) I. Title
TK5105.585.M558 1999

004.6'2–dc21 99-29515

CIP

ABOUT IDG BOOKS WORLDWIDE

Welcome to the world of IDG Books Worldwide.

IDG Books Worldwide, Inc., is a subsidiary of International Data Group, the world's largest publisher of computer-related information and the leading global provider of information services on information technology. IDG was founded more than 30 years ago by Patrick J. McGovern and now employs more than 9,000 people worldwide. IDG publishes more than 290 computer publications in over 75 countries. More than 90 million people read one or more IDG publications each month.

Launched in 1990, IDG Books Worldwide is today the #1 publisher of best-selling computer books in the United States. We are proud to have received eight awards from the Computer Press Association in recognition of editorial excellence and three from Computer Currents' First Annual Readers' Choice Awards. Our best-selling *...For Dummies®* series has more than 50 million copies in print with translations in 31 languages. IDG Books Worldwide, through a joint venture with IDG's Hi-Tech Beijing, became the first U.S. publisher to publish a computer book in the People's Republic of China. In record time, IDG Books Worldwide has become the first choice for millions of readers around the world who want to learn how to better manage their businesses.

Our mission is simple: Every one of our books is designed to bring extra value and skill-building instructions to the reader. Our books are written by experts who understand and care about our readers. The knowledge base of our editorial staff comes from years of experience in publishing, education, and journalism — experience we use to produce books to carry us into the new millennium. In short, we care about books, so we attract the best people. We devote special attention to details such as audience, interior design, use of icons, and illustrations. And because we use an efficient process of authoring, editing, and desktop publishing our books electronically, we can spend more time ensuring superior content and less time on the technicalities of making books.

You can count on our commitment to deliver high-quality books at competitive prices on topics you want to read about. At IDG Books Worldwide, we continue in the IDG tradition of delivering quality for more than 30 years. You'll find no better book on a subject than one from IDG Books Worldwide.

John Kilcullen
Chairman and CEO
IDG Books Worldwide, Inc.

Steven Berkowitz
President and Publisher
IDG Books Worldwide, Inc.

Eighth Annual Computer Press Awards 1992

Ninth Annual Computer Press Awards 1993

WINNER

Tenth Annual Computer Press Awards 1994

Eleventh Annual Computer Press Awards 1995

IDG is the world's leading IT media, research and exposition company. Founded in 1964, IDG had 1997 revenues of $2.05 billion and has more than 9,000 employees worldwide. IDG offers the widest range of media options that reach IT buyers in 75 countries representing 95% of worldwide IT spending. IDG's diverse product and services portfolio spans six key areas including print publishing, online publishing, expositions and conferences, market research, education and training, and global marketing services. More than 90 million people read one or more of IDG's 290 magazines and newspapers, including IDG's leading global brands — Computerworld, PC World, Network World, Macworld and the Channel World family of publications. IDG Books Worldwide is one of the fastest-growing computer book publishers in the world, with more than 700 titles in 36 languages. The "...For Dummies®" series alone has more than 50 million copies in print. IDG offers online users the largest network of technology-specific Web sites around the world through IDG.net (http://www.idg.net), which comprises more than 225 targeted Web sites in 55 countries worldwide. International Data Corporation (IDC) is the world's largest provider of information technology data, analysis and consulting, with research centers in over 41 countries and more than 400 research analysts worldwide. IDG World Expo is a leading producer of more than 168 globally branded conferences and expositions in 35 countries including E3 (Electronic Entertainment Expo), Macworld Expo, ComNet, Windows World Expo, ICE (Internet Commerce Expo), Agenda, DEMO, and Spotlight. IDG's training subsidiary, ExecuTrain, is the world's largest computer training company, with more than 230 locations worldwide and 785 training courses. IDG Marketing Services helps industry-leading IT companies build international brand recognition by developing global integrated marketing programs via IDG's print, online and exposition products worldwide. Further information about the company can be found at www.idg.com.

1/24/99

Credits

ACQUISITIONS EDITOR
Laura Lewin

DEVELOPMENT EDITOR
Elyn Wollensky

TECHNICAL EDITOR
Dr. John Thompson

COPY EDITORS
Annette S. Devlin
Anne Friedman
Marti Paul

PROJECT COORDINATOR
Tom Missler

BOOK DESIGNER
Catalin Dûlfû, Larry S. Willson

GRAPHICS AND PRODUCTION SPECIALIST
Laura Carpenter, Angela F. Hunckler, Anna Rohrer, Brent Savage, Kathie Schutte

COVER ART
© Nicholas Wilton/SIS

PROOFREADERS
Christine Berman, Rebecca Senninger, Robert Springer, Janet M. Withers, York Production Services, Inc.

INDEXER
York Production Services, Inc.

About the Author

Mark A. Miller, P.E. is the author of *The Network Troubleshooting Library* and *The IP Technologies Library*, both published by M&T Books. Other titles include: *LAN Troubleshooting Handbook,* 2nd Edition; *LAN Protocol Handbook; Internetworking,* 2nd Edition; *Troubleshooting Internetworks; Troubleshooting TCP/IP,* 3rd Edition, *Managing Internetworks with SNMP,* 2nd Edition; *Analyzing Broadband Networks,* 2nd Edition; *and Implementing IPv6*. He is President of DigiNet Corporation, a Denver-based data communications engineering firm specializing in the design of local area and wide area networks. Mr. Miller is a frequent speaker at industry events and has taught numerous tutorials on internetwork design and analysis at ComNet, Comdex, Networld+Interop, Next Generation Networks, and other conferences. He is a member of the IEEE and NSPE and a registered professional engineer in four states. For information on his many tutorials, including one that is based upon this text, contact him via `mark@diginet.com`.

To Buster, for his faithfulness

Preface

In today's harried environment, it is easy to wonder if you are *really* making any progress toward your goals. In the case of Internet technologies, however, you don't have to look too far back to remember when the World Wide Web did not exist, or when the vast majority of all data communication circuits operated over copper, not fiber optic lines. Now most of the Fortune 1000 companies have Web sites, e-mail is almost as prevalent as telephone communication, and a significant amount of our gross national product is produced via electronic commerce. So at least in this one area of technology, significant progress *has* been made.

But with that progress comes the second side of a two-edged sword: the more that technology improves, the more we depend on it. And the more that we depend on it, the more vulnerable we are if it fails. Hence, new troubleshooting and management techniques must keep up with the technologies themselves.

Who Should Read This Book

This book is written for network managers, administrators, and engineers who find themselves in this era of rapid technological change and want to have a deeper understanding of TCP/IP and the Internet suite of protocols. I assume that most readers have had some exposure to both local and wide area networks, and that their objective is to broaden their knowledge of networking protocols in general, and TCP/IP in particular. As such, this book discusses how TCP/IP is implemented over LANs, such as Ethernet and Token Ring, or over WANs, such as ATM or Frame Relay, but does not discuss the intricacies of those networks. (Other volumes in this series, such as the *LAN Troubleshooting Handbook,* 2nd Edition, or *Analyzing Broadband Networks*, 2nd Edition, provide those details).

How This Book Is Organized

In order to give the reader a more thorough understanding of the operation of TCP/IP, this book is organized into three major sections: technical chapters, reference appendixes, and a CD-ROM.

The chapters follow the architecture developed by the Advanced Research Project Agency (ARPA), a United States Government agency that sponsored, in part, the development of TCP/IP and the related Internet Protocols. Thus, following Chapters 1 and 2, which discuss the history and support for TCP/IP, respectively, are four chapters that examine the protocols that operate at the four layers of the ARPA model. In Chapters 3 through 6, technical information is reinforced by a number of case studies illustrating problems and solutions for that particular layer. These case studies are illustrated with output from the *Sniffer* protocol analyzer, developed by Network Associates, Inc. Chapter 7 discusses the Simple Network Management

Protocol, or SNMP, used to manage TCP/IP-based internetworks. Chapter 8 concludes with an overview of the next generation Internet Protocol, known as IPv6.

The appendixes provide a number of ready references for the reader, including contact information for standards organizations and vendors, Internet parameters, and definitions of acronyms and abbreviations.

The CD-ROM contains over 1,000 Request for Comments (RFC) and other documents that provide the information and standards on which the Internet suite of protocols has been built. This CD-ROM is a valuable reference to the documents that are discussed in each of the technical chapters.

What's New in the Third Edition

Information on recently-enhanced technologies, including Multiprotocol over ATM (MPOA), the Border Gateway Protocol (BGP), the Exterior Gateway Protocol (EGP), the Resource Reservation Protocol (RSVP), and the Hypertext Transfer Protocol (HTTP) is new to this edition. New case studies illustrate TCP/IP over ISDN, the operation of additional routing protocols, such as BGP and EGP, Web page access using HTTP, and more. The appendixes have also been updated with many additional pages of Internet-related parameters. The accompanying CD-ROM contains over 20 years of key Internet RFC, FYI and STD documents – a literal reference library of Internet technologies.

I trust that the information in this volume will assist you in managing your TCP/IP internetwork more effectively!

mark@diginet.com

April 1999

Preface to the Second Edition

I am pleased that you have added *Troubleshooting TCP/IP*, 2nd Edition to your technical library. Let me provide a brief summary of the revisions from the first edition.

First and foremost, the use of TCP/IP has migrated from the government and education sectors to general business applications. Chapters 1 and 2 illustrate some of the networks and operating systems that provide this application support.

Second, while the core functions of TCP and IP have remained stable for a number of years, a number of supporting protocols have been added or revised since the publication of the first edition. Examples would include support for ATM networks, which is new; revisions to the routing Information Protocol, known as RIP Version 2; updates to the Bootstrap Protocol, BOOTP, known as the Dynamic Host Configuration Protocol, DHCP; and security revisions to the second version of the Simple Network Management Protocol, SNMP. Chapters 3–7 discuss these, and other protocols, that have matured in the last few years.

But most important, at the time that the first edition was written, most of industry expected the TCP/IP suite to be replaced with Open Systems Interconnection (OSI)-based protocols. Current marketplace experience invalidates that prediction. Instead, the present Internet Protocol, now known as IP Version 4, is in the process of being replaced by a new version, known as IP Next Generation (IPng) or IP Version 6 (IPv6). It is expected that the migration from IPv4 to IPv6 will take several years, however these efforts may require extensive planning on the part of the network managers. To summarize, if your internetwork presently uses IPv4, at some time in the future, that internetwork will either directly or indirectly be impacted by IPv6. As a result, a brand new Chapter 8 that details the operation of IPv6 replaces the previous discussion on OSI migration.

The appendixes have been updated, and in addition, a CD-ROM containing over 1,000 Internet documents has been added for those readers that want to dig deeper into the various subjects.

As was the case in the first edition, a number of individuals contributed to this work. The management and staff at M&T Books, including Paul Farrell, Debra Williams Cauley, Annette S. Devlin, Anne Incao, and Joe McPartland provided editorial support. The insights of my technical editor, Dr. John Thompson, were especially appreciated. Karen Cope did much of the research on the appendixes, and David Hertzke of Integrated Graphic Communication produced all the figures.

Several individuals added their expertise to specific case studies and sections. In alphabetical order, there are: Ed Britton, Pat Burns, Brian Clark, Libby Fox, Paul Franchois, Derek Hodovance, Jack Jackson, Allen Kerr, Nick Lopez, Chip Mesec, Don Mulvey, Ken Pappas, Georgann Russo, Steve Stokes, and Ken Volpe.

As before, Holly, Nathan, and Nicholas added their support and encouragement, with Boomer and Brutus assisting as always. It is good to be surrounded by such a distinguished support team.

mark@diginet.com

May 1996

Preface to the First Edition

Writing the Preface or Foreword is something that I always look forward to for several reasons. First, it signals the end of numerous long hours, revisions, and telephone calls. Secondly, it provides a mechanism for me to present a road map for the reader, so that your navigation duties will be minimized. Finally, it provides an opportunity to say a few personal words about an otherwise very impersonal subject.

Presenting the Roadmap

This is the fifth volume of *The Network Troubleshooting Library,* and concentrates on the TCP/IP and related protocols. This book was inspired by the research that I did for the fourth volume, *Troubleshooting Internetworks* (M&T Books, 1991). In doing the research for the book, I wrote to a number of users of the Network General Corp. *Sniffer* Analyzer and asked them to contribute any interesting trace files that they may have saved. These submittals became the case studies that were used in the book. As I was surveying the numerous disks that I received, a trend emerged: There were more TCP/IP related submittals than any other protocol suite – even more than DECnet, SNA, or NetWare. A light came on, and the idea of devoting an entire volume to TCP/IP was born.

This book is structured like the other volumes in that it makes a somewhat orderly progression from the bottom to the top of the protocol architecture. In this case, however, that architecture is the Defense Advanced Research Projects Agency (DARPA) architecture – the architecture out of which these protocols were developed. In Chapter 1 we will look at the place these protocols occupy within the world of internetworking. In Chapter 2 we will survey the support for the protocols among mainframe, minicomputer, LAN, and analyzer manufacturers. In Chapters 3 through 6, we will study the Network Interface, Internet, Host-to-Host, and Application/Process Layers. Each of these chapters will present an overview of the protocols themselves, and then present a number of case studies that illustrate the protocols working (and not working!). Chapter 7 is devoted to the topic of the internetwork management, and Chapter 8 concludes with a glimpse into transition strategies for TCP/IP internetworks that may migrate to OSI protocols. Appendices A through H can be described as "useful information" – protocol parameters and documentation that I have needed to look up and that you may find handy as well.

A Few Personal Notes

As always, a number of people behind the scenes contributed to the volume that you are about to read. My editors at M&T Books, Brenda McLaughlin, Sarah Wadsworth, Tom Woolf, and Cheryl Goldberg spent many long hours to assure that the project would be completed on schedule.

Nancy Wright and Krystal Valdez did the word processing on the manuscript. David Hertzke of Integrated Graphic Communication took my hand-drawn scratchings and turned them into very legible figures. Thanks to the three of you for all your hard work.

On several occasions, specific tests were required to see how the protocols (running on live networks) would perform under "what if" conditions. Eural Authement, Chris Dutchyn, Ross Dunthorne, and Paul Franchois lent their expertise and time for these experiments.

I am indebted to several individuals who added their expertise to individual sections: Jay Allard, John Case, Dan Callahan, Bill Cohn, Michael Howard, Brian Meek, Larry Thomas, Ursula Sinkewicz, plus a host of folks from Banyan Systems Inc. Eural Authement, Paul Franchois, and Carl Shinn read the entire manuscript, making numerous suggestions for improvements. David Menges of the Colorado SuperNet, Inc. assisted with Internet-related questions and support issues.

The real heroes and heroines are the network managers throughout the world who shared their experiences via Network General *Sniffer* trace files that became the basis for the 29 case studies that you will read. It is one thing to discuss a protocol from an academic point of view, but something quite different to see those protocols in action. In alphabetical order, these individuals are: Rohit Aggarwal, Gerald Aster, Eural Authement, Joe Bardwell, Ross Dunthorne, Chris Dutchyn, Tony Farrow, Paul Franchois, Dave Heck, Dell Holmes, James Knights, Iwan Lie, Jeff Logullo, Dan Milligan, Tom Morocz, Marc Ryding, Bob Sherman, Mendy Valinsky, and Wayne Veilleux.

Ed Lucente and Bob Bessin of Network General Corporation provided me with a *Sniffer* Analyzer to study the various problems submitted for case studies. Juancho Forlanda located some unusual trace files when my normal sources failed. Their generosity is greatly appreciated.

I am grateful for three friends, Lloyd Boggs, Gordon England, and Marsh Riggs, who provided encouragement during the writing of the manuscript.

Most importantly, Holly, Nathan, and Nicholas provided the supportive environment that makes the undertaking of such a project possible. Boomer helped me get up for an early morning run, Brutus tried really hard not to bark when we did, and Buster was the ever-faithful sentry. Thanks to all of you for your love.

Mark A. Miller

June 1992

Acknowledgments

Many individuals made contributions to this new edition. The management and staff at IDG Books Worldwide, Inc., including Brenda McLaughlin, Steven Sayre, Elyn Wollensky, Laura Lewin, and Amy Barkat provided editorial support. My technical editor, Dr. John Thompson, drew upon his wealth of development experience, and provided many useful suggestions. Donna Mullen did most of the research on the appendixes and produced all of the figures.

Other individuals added their expertise for specific sections, figures and case studies. In alphabetical order, these are: Paula Cassano, Richard Ford, Paul Franchois, Janet Harrold, Dawn Herman, Derek Hodovance, Teresa Law, Barry Leiner, Juan Luciani, Sally Miller, Tracy Smith, Chip Sparling, Robert Watson, and Robert Zakon.

As always, Holly, Nathan, and Nicholas provided encouragement at the right time, with the able support of Boomer and Brutus.

Contents at a Glance

Contents

Table of Illustrations

Chapter 1

Using TCP/IP and the Internet Protocols

On the surface, the Transmission Control Protocol/Internet Protocol (TCP/IP) is just another networking buzzword. But dig deeper and you find one of the most popular solutions for internetworking and interoperability ever devised. More than simply two protocols, TCP/IP is an architecture that enables dissimilar hosts, such as a minicomputer from Digital Equipment Corp. (Maynard, Massachusetts, now part of Compaq Computer Corporation) and a workstation from Sun Microsystems Inc. (Mountain View, California), to communicate. This communication could be via Local Area Network (LAN), Metropolitan Area Network (MAN), Wide Area Network (WAN), or some hybrid internetwork technology – TCP/IP supports them all. You might call TCP/IP "the great communicator" or "the interoperability solution."

TCP/IP was developed, refined, and nurtured to meet the needs of the Internet. The Internet provides a worldwide mechanism for user-to-user, computer-to-computer communication that crosses corporate and national boundaries. The same TCP/IP protocols can meet any LAN or WAN connectivity requirements. But that's getting ahead of the story. We'll come back to the TCP/IP protocols in a little while. First, let's take a brief tour of the Internet.

1.1 The Challenge of the Internet

The word Internet means different things to different people. Some use it as a verb, as in "to internetwork an IBM SNA environment with a Digital DECnet environment." Others use it as a noun to mean a network comprised of two or more dissimilar networks, that is, an internet (or internetwork) between two Packet Switched Public Data Networks (PSPDNs). It is also a proper noun, the Internet, that refers to a collection of networks located around the world that interconnect for the purposes of user and computer communication.

Just as the word has diverse meanings, the Internet has diverse challenges. Let's assume you're connected to the Internet. Similar to the way you rely on the public telephone network, you depend on the Internet for communicating with your friends and associates. But what happens when there's a system failure? If the telephone network has a problem, you simply contact the Local Exchange Carrier (LEC) or InterExchange Carrier (IXC) responsible for your service. But when there's trouble with the Internet, service restoration is not as straightforward for several reasons. First, the Internet protocols are more complex than the telephone serving your home or business. Second, you're dealing with computer communication, which is more abstract than voice and more difficult to diagnose. Finally, because the Internet is an interconnected matrix of computer networks, identifying and diagnosing the problem is a greater challenge. Your Internet Service Provider (ISP) should certainly be able to diagnose problems within their network. However, that ISP's network likely connects to many other ISP networks, and no single entity or procedure (such as dialing "0" for the operator to connect you to telephone repair) is available to address these multinetwork problems. Thus, whoever ends up with the Internet problem will have to test and diagnose it him or herself. And, most likely, that person will be you.

That brings us to the purpose of this book. Since the mid-1970s, the TCP/IP suite has been the glue that holds the Internet together. Several ancillary protocols, such as the Address Resolution Protocol (ARP), Internet Control Message Protocol (ICMP), User Datagram Protocol (UDP), Routing Information Protocol (RIP), Open Shortest Path First (OSPF) Protocol, and many others, have also been developed along the way. And in the last few years of the twentieth century, significant enhancements, referred to as IPng, for Internet Protocol next generation, have been under development and deployment. The resulting mixture can be a challenge to troubleshoot; in many cases, it requires the help of a protocol analyzer. The purpose of this book is to demystify the process of troubleshooting TCP/IP-based internetworks. To do so, we will learn about the topology of the Internet, study the protocols used within the Internet, and examine case studies of actual Internet problems. But before going on to the mechanics, let's begin with a history lesson.

1.2 A Brief History of the Internet

The Internet with a capital I is one of the world's most interesting achievements in computer science and networking technology. It provides a worldwide mechanism for user-to-user, computer-to-computer communication that spans corporate and national boundaries. This achievement is even more amazing because the Internet is self-governing, run by committees comprised largely of volunteers. In the past, many government organizations, such as the U.S. Department of Defense and individual states, have subsidized the basic expenses. Much of the research into the Internet protocols is conducted at major U.S. research universities, such as the University of California, the University of Colorado, the University of Illinois, and the University of Texas. As the Internet has evolved, however, the expenses for Internet connectivity have been passed down to the individual users – those who benefit from access to this public resource. Let's see how this unique system evolved.

Today's Internet was born in 1969 as the Advanced Research Projects Agency Network (ARPANET) and was sponsored by the U.S. Defense Advanced Research Projects Agency (DARPA), now known as ARPA. The purpose of the ARPANET was to test and determine the viability of a communication technology known as *packet switching* [1-1]. The contract to build the original ARPANET was awarded to a firm known as Bolt, Baranek, and Newman (now BBN Communications, Inc., Cambridge, Massachusetts). ARPANET went online in September 1969 at four locations: Stanford Research Institute (SRI), the University of California at Santa Barbara (UCSB), the University of California at Los Angeles (UCLA), and the University of Utah. The original hosts were Honeywell minicomputers, known as Interface Message Processors (IMPs).

The initial test was successful, and the ARPANET grew quickly. At the same time, it became apparent that nonmilitary researchers could also benefit from access to a network of this type, so leaders in the university and industrial research communities made proposals to the National Science Foundation (NSF) for a cooperative network of computer science researchers [1-2]. The NSF approved funding for the Computer Science Network (CSNET) in 1981.

In 1984, the ARPANET was split into two different networks: MILNET (for unclassified military traffic) and ARPANET (for nonmilitary traffic and research). In 1984, the NSF established the Office of Advanced Scientific Computing (OASC) to further the development of supercomputers and to make access to them more widely available. The OASC developed the NSFNET to connect six supercomputing centers across the United States, using T-1 lines operating at 1.544 Mbps in 1987, and subsequently upgraded to the T-3 rate (44.736 Mbps) in 1990. NSFNET, with its higher transmission rates, was a resounding success; as a result, the U.S. Department of Defense declared the ARPANET obsolete and dismantled it in June 1990.

In the meantime, NSFNET connections encompassed a system of regional and state networks. The New England Academic and Research Network (NEARNET), the Southeastern Universities Research Association Network (SURAnet), and the California Education and Research Federation Network (CERFnet) were among the family of NSFNET-connected networks. Since these networks were designed, built, and operated, in part, with government funds, regulations called *Acceptable Use Policies,* or AUPs, governed the types of traffic that could traverse these networks. In general, traffic that was for "research or educational purposes" was deemed acceptable; other traffic was either discouraged or prohibited [1-3]. Few, if any, accounts of the "Internet Police" apprehending an AUP violator were recorded, however, again testifying to the self-governing nature of the Internet.

The business community, seeing the new opportunity for electronic commerce, began looking for ways to support general business traffic on the Internet without violating these regulations. As a result of this opportunity, the Commercial Internet Exchange Association (CIX) was formed in 1991 [1-4]. CIX is a nonprofit trade organization of Public Data Network service providers that promote and encourage the development of the public data communications internetworking services. Membership in CIX is open to organizations that offer TCP/IP or OSI public data internetworking services to the general public. CIX gives these service providers a neutral forum for the discussion and development of legislative, policy, and technology issues. Member networks agree to interconnect with all other CIX members, and to exchange traffic. There are no restrictions placed on the traffic routed between member networks. Nor are there "settlements," or traffic-based charges, as a result of these interconnections.

Another outgrowth of the Internet expansion was the founding of the nonprofit Internet Society (ISOC) in 1992. The Internet Society [1-5], headquartered in Reston, Virginia, is an international organization that strives for global cooperation and coordination for the Internet. Members of the ISOC include government agencies, nonprofit research and educational organizations, and for-profit corporations. The charter of the ISOC emphasizes support for the technical evolution of the Internet, educating the user community in the use and application of the Internet, and promoting the benefits of Internet technology for education at all grade levels.

In 1993, the NSF announced that it would no longer provide the traditional backbone architecture, but instead would specify a number of locations, called *Network Access Points* (NAPs), where various ISPs could interconnect and exchange traffic. This concept was based on the CIX concept, and specified four NAPs, located at San Francisco, Chicago, New York, and Washington, DC [1-6]. In addition to these four NAPs, two Federal Internet Exchange (FIX) points, one on each coast, were developed: FIX-East and FIX-West. Other NAPs, operated as commercial entities, also exist today.

In April 1995, the existing NSFNET backbone was retired and replaced by a new architecture that provides for very high speed connectivity. This new network is called the very high speed Backbone Network Service (vBNS). The vBNS is based on both Asynchonous Transfer Mode (ATM) and Synchronous Optical Network (SONET) technologies, and is designed as a noncommercial research network to develop and test high speed applications, routing, and switching technologies. We will explore the vBNS, and other successor NSFNET networks, in Section 1.4.

Figure 1-1 illustrates a timeline of significant events in the history of the Internet. Shown at the top of the figure are the various government organizations, starting with DARPA, that have participated in the development of the Internet. On the second line are the various organizations, starting with the ARPANET Working Group (WG) and then proceeding to the Internet Society (ISOC) and the World Wide Web Consortium (W3C), that have provided technical oversight into the development. At the lower portion of the figure are some of the significant milestones and their associated dates [1-7].

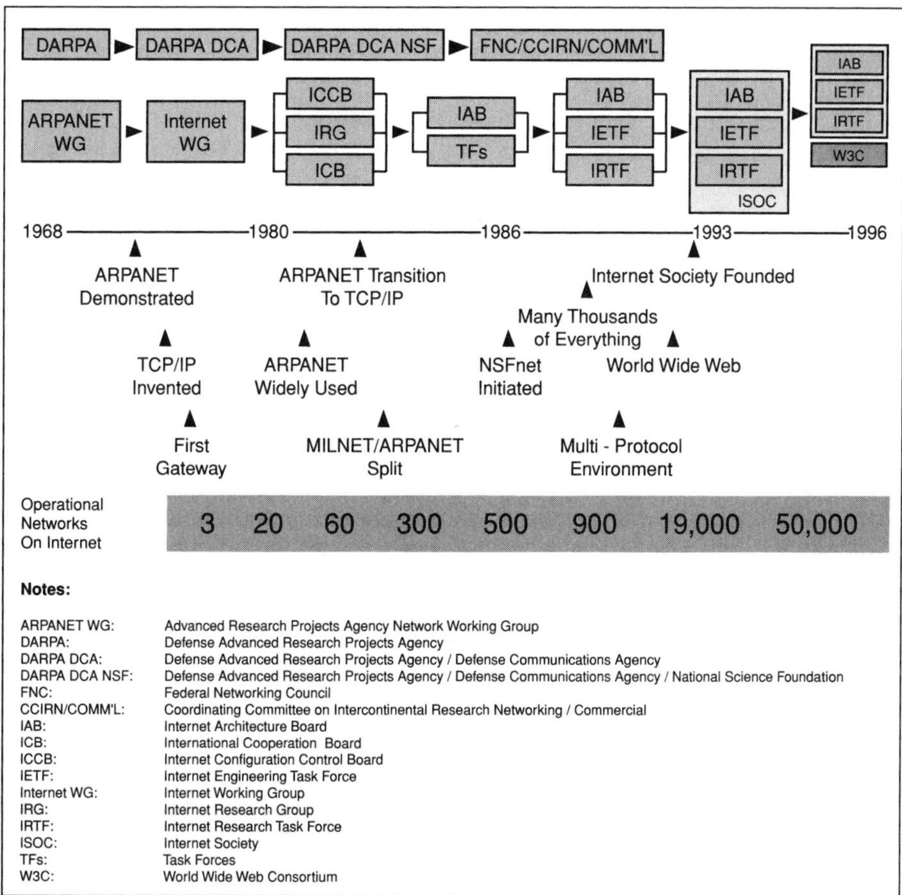

Figure 1-1 Internet Development Timeline
(Source: `http://www.isoc.org/internet/history/brief.html`**)**

Perhaps the most important aspect of Internet history is the Internet's astounding growth in the last few years. Figures 1-2 through 1-5, taken from Reference [1-8], illustrate the growth in Internet Hosts, Internet Domains, Internet Networks, and World Wide Web Servers, respectively. Note that in Figure 1-2 a new host counting mechanism, believed to be more accurate than the previous method, is shown for host statistics beginning in 1995. Reference [1-8] provides many references that detail these measurement methodologies and sources of Internet statistics.

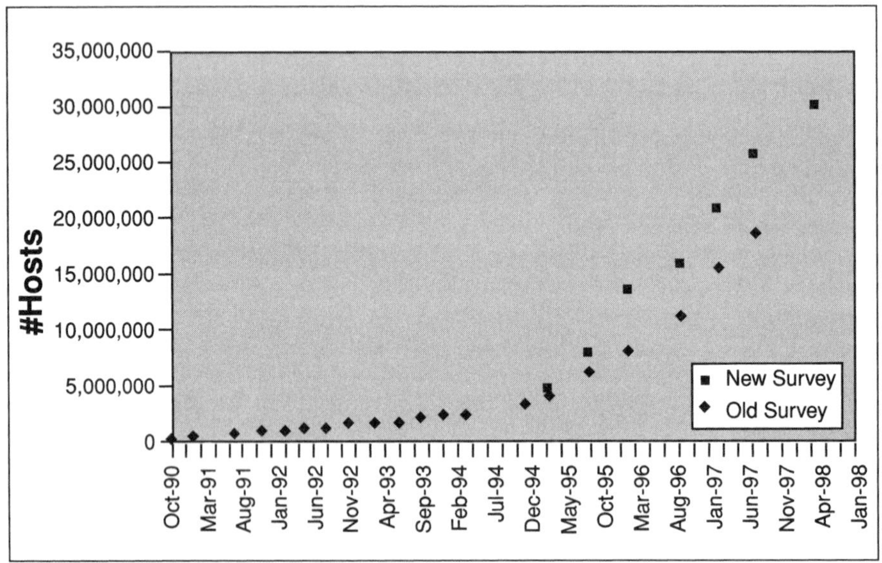

Figure 1-2 Internet Hosts
(Source: Hobbes' Internet Timeline,
`http://www.isoc.org/guest/zakon/Internet/History/HIT.html.`
Copyright 1998, Robert H. Zakon. Reprinted with permission.)

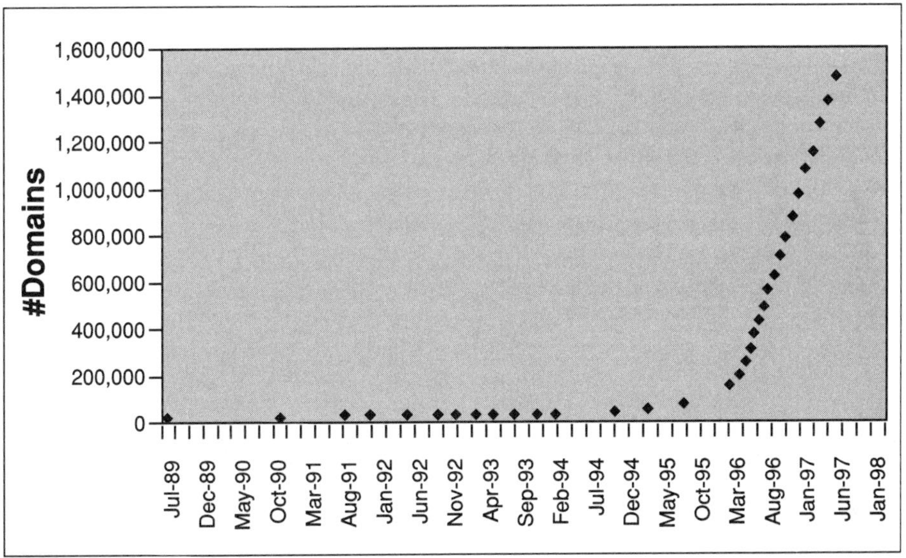

Figure 1-3 Internet Domains
(Source: Hobbes' Internet Timeline,
http://www.isoc.org/guest/zakon/Internet/History/HIT.html.
Copyright 1998, Robert H. Zakon. Reprinted with permission.)

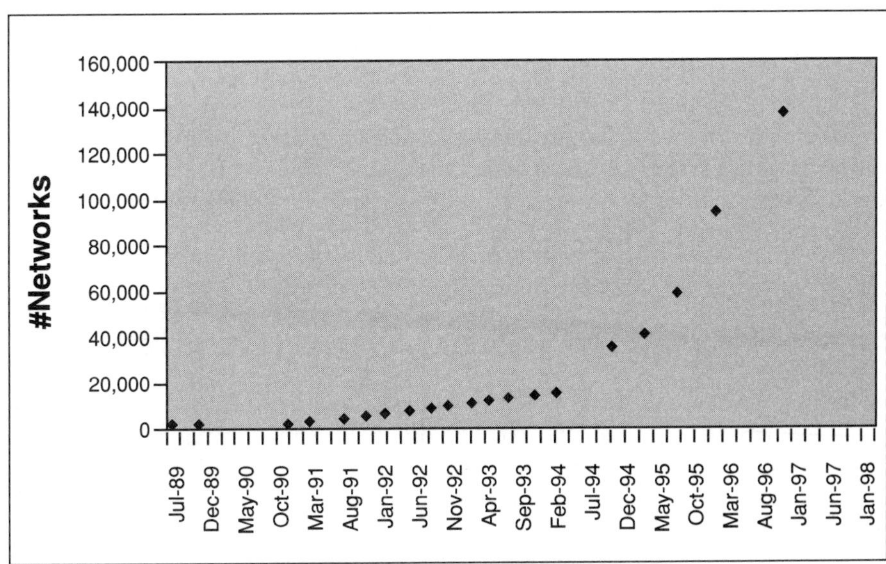

Figure 1-4 Internet Networks
(Source: Hobbes' Internet Timeline,
http://www.isoc.org/guest/zakon/Internet/History/HIT.html.
Copyright 1998, Robert H. Zakon. Reprinted with permission.)

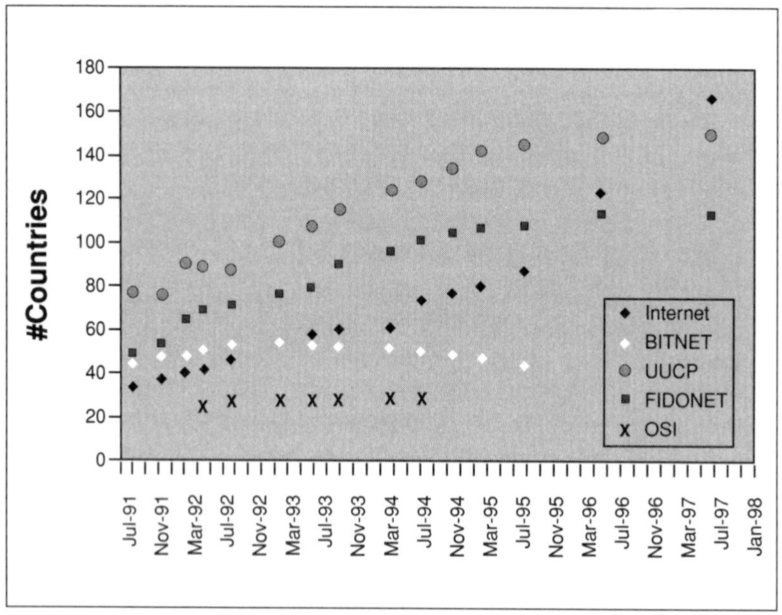

Figure 1-5 WWW Networks Growth
(Source: Hobbes' Internet Timeline,
`http://www.isoc.org/guest/zakon/Internet/History/HIT.html.`
Copyright 1998, Robert H. Zakon. Reprinted with permission.)

Lessons learned from the ARPANET have had a significant effect on a number of data communication technologies, such as LANs and packet switching. References [1-9] and [1-10] provide interesting historical information on these early networks. Now, let's open a different history book and study the development of the protocols used for internetwork communication.

1.3 The Protocols of the Internet

For its first decade, the ARPANET grew quickly, adding an average of one new host computer every 20 days [1-11]. The original protocol for internal network communications was known as the *Network Control Program* (NCP). When compared with the seven-layer Open Systems Interconnection Reference Model (OSI-RM), the NCP provided the functions of the third and fourth layers (Network and

Transport), managing the flow of messages between host computers and intermediate packet switches. NCP was designed with the assumption that the underlying communication subnetwork (i.e., OSI Physical, Data Link, and Network Layers) provided a perfect communication channel. Given ARPANET's mission to support government and military networks, which could include radio links under battlefield conditions, the assumption of a reliable communication channel needed reconsideration. In January 1973, ARPA made the Transmission Control Protocol (TCP) a standard for the Internet because of its proven performance. The ARPA internetwork architecture (Figure 1-6) consisted of networks connected by gateways [1-12]. (Note that in the OSI sense of the word, these devices were actually routers, operating at the OSI Network Layer. By current definition, gateways may operate at all seven layers of the OSI-RM. In this chapter, we will refer to these connectivity devices as *gateways,* however we will switch to the more appropriate term *router* when we begin our technical study in Chapter 2.) The ARPA model assumed that each network used packet switching technology and could connect to a variety of transmission media (LAN, WAN, radio, and so on).

The ARPA Internet architecture consisted of four layers (Figure 1-7). The lowest layer was called the *Network Interface Layer* (it was also referred to as the Local Network or Network Access Layer) and comprised the physical link (e.g., LAN) between devices. The Network Interface Layer existed in all devices, including hosts and gateways.

The *Internet Layer* insulated the hosts from network-specific details, such as addressing. The Internet Protocol (IP) was developed to provide end-to-end datagram service for this layer. (Datagram service is analogous to a telegram in which the information is sent as a package.) The Internet Layer (and, therefore, IP) existed only in hosts and gateways.

While the Internet Layer provided end-to-end delivery of datagrams, it did not guarantee their delivery. Therefore, a third layer, known as the *Service Layer* (now called the Host-to-Host Layer), was provided within the hosts. As its name implies, the Service Layer defined the level of service the host applications required. Two protocols were created for the Service Layer: the Transmission Control Protocol (TCP) for applications needing reliable end-to-end service, and the User Datagram Protocol (UDP) for applications with less-stringent reliability requirements. A third protocol, the Internet Control Message Protocol (ICMP), allowed hosts and gateways to exchange monitoring and control information.

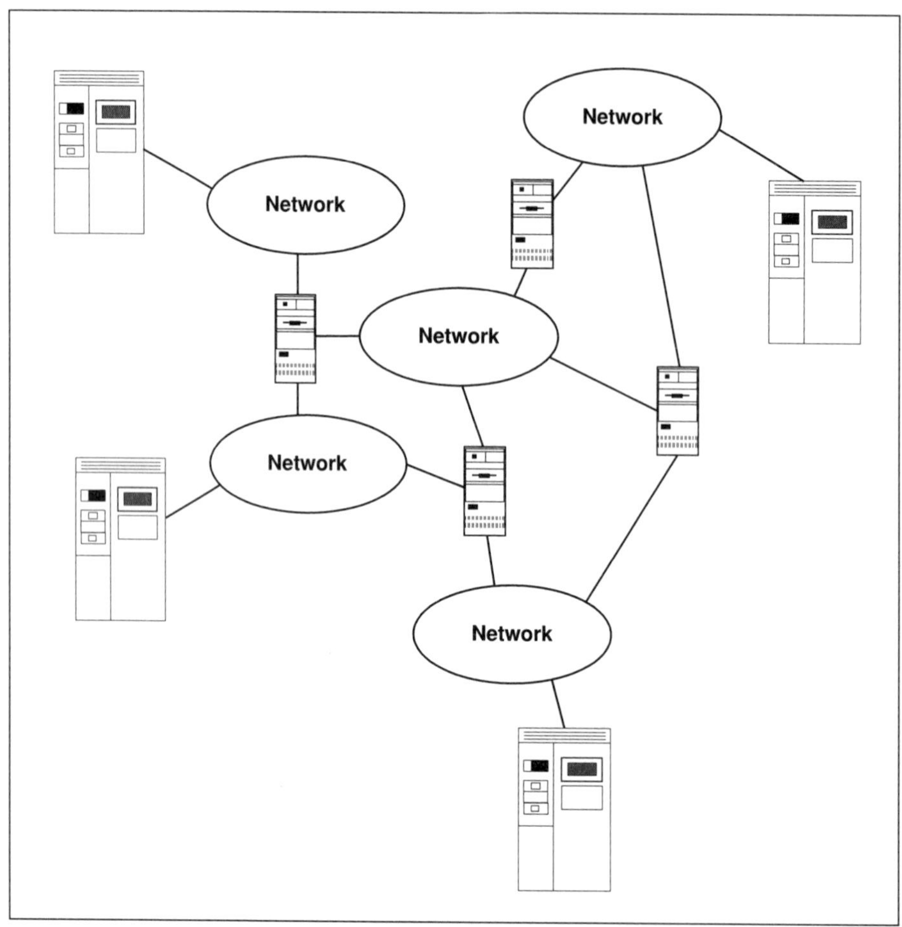

Figure 1-6 Networks Connected with Gateways to Form an Internetwork

The highest ARPA layer, the *Process/Application Layer,* resided only in hosts and supported user-to-host and host-to-host processing or applications. A variety of standard applications were developed. These included the Telecommunications Network (TELNET) for remote terminal access, the File Transfer Protocol (FTP) for file transfer, and the Simple Mail Transfer Protocol (SMTP) for electronic mail.

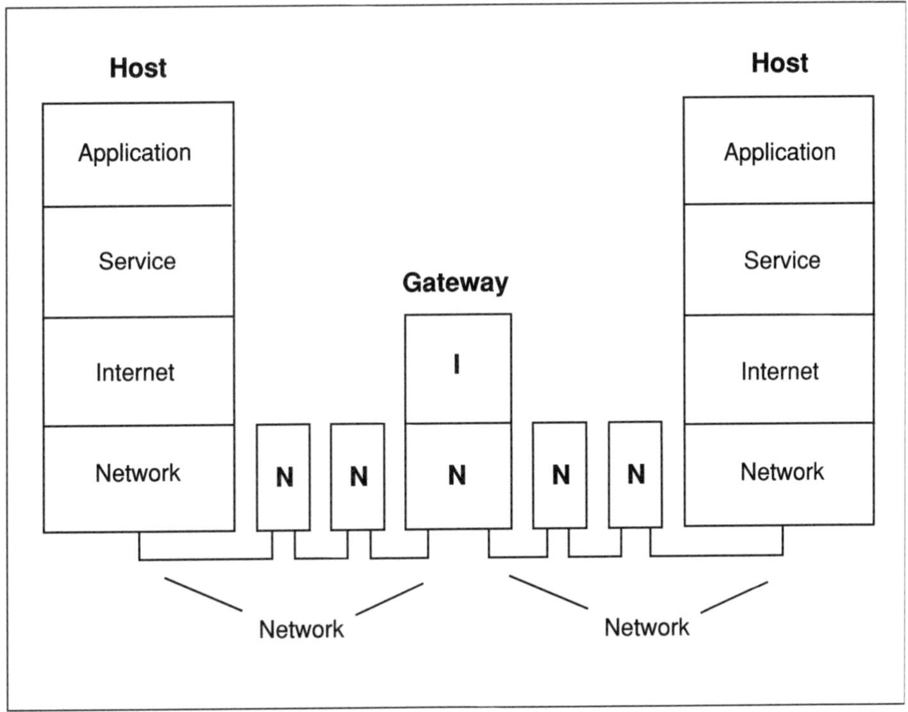

Figure 1-7 ARPA Layered Architecture

Figure 1-8 compares the OSI and ARPA architectures. Note that the OSI Physical and Data Link Layers represent the ARPA Network Interface (or Local Network) Layer; the OSI Network Layer corresponds to the Internet Layer; the OSI Transport Layer is functionally equivalent to the Host-to-Host (Service) Layer; and the OSI Session, Presentation, and Application Layers comprise the ARPA Process/Application Layer. References [1-13] through [1-15] describe the development of the ARPANET Reference Model and protocols.

With this background into the development of the IP and TCP protocols, let's look at the family of networks that use these protocols.

OSI Layer	ARPA Architecture
Application	Process / Application Layer
Presentation	
Session	
Transport	Host-to-Host Layer
Network	Internet Layer
Data Link	Network Interface or Local Network Layer
Physical	

Figure 1-8 Comparing OSI and ARPA Models

1.4 The Internet Family

A number of networks worldwide grew out of the ARPANET research to address nonmilitary requirements. Collectively, they became known as the Internet. The common denominator among these networks was their use of the TCP/IP and related protocols to build the underlying communication infrastructure. According to the organization Network Wizards [1-17], approximately 30,000,000 hosts are currently connected. John Quarterman's excellent reference *The Matrix* [1-18] describes these worldwide networks in exacting detail, and his firm's Web site provides current maps of Internet connectivity [1-19].

As we discussed in Section 1.2, much of the funding for the Internet was derived from U.S. government sources through the NSF. The NSFNET backbone service was operated by Merit Network, Inc., a partnership among ANS, IBM, MCI, and the state of Michigan. In May 1993, NSF proposed a new architecture for national networking, which became operational in April 1995. This architecture consists of four elements: a very high speed Backbone Network Service (vBNS), a Routing Arbiter (RA), Network Service Providers (NSPs), and Network Access Points (NAPs) [1-20].

The vBNS is a nationwide network that transmits at the OC-12 rate (622 Mbps) and is operated by MCI under a cooperative agreement with the National Science Foundation [1-21]. This network is designed for research projects that focus on noncommercial, high bandwidth applications and transmission technologies, and is not used for general Internet traffic, as shown in Figure 1-9. Connections to the vBNS are determined by the NSF, which awards grants under its high performance connection program. At the present time, connections include two NSF supercomputing centers and various research institutions. Some of the universities that have been awarded the high performance connection grants are participating in the Internet2 project, which is focusing on the development of advanced applications required to support academic research, teaching, and learning [1-22].

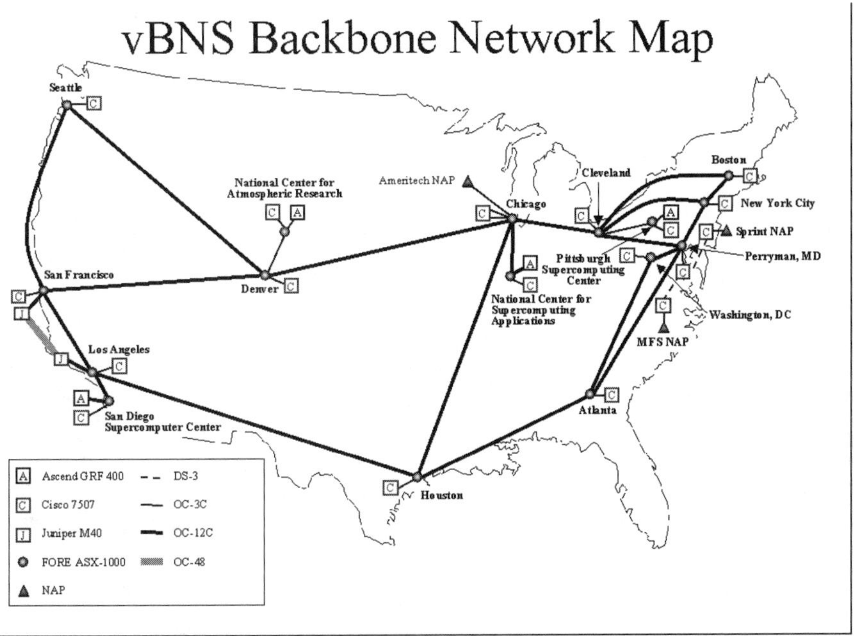

Figure 1-9 vBNS Backbone Network Map
(Source: http://www.vbns.net/backbone.html.
 This material is based on work supported by the National Science Foundation under Grant Number NCR 9321047. Any opinions, findings, and conclusions or recommendations expressed in this material are those of the author(s) and do not necessarily reflect the views of the National Science Foundation.)

Another outgrowth of this research is the Next Generation Internet (NGI) initiative, which is a cooperative project of a number of U.S. government agencies, including the National Aeronautics and Space Administration, the Departments of Defense, Energy, and Commerce, and the National Science Foundation. There are three stated goals for this new architecture [1-23]:

- To promote experimentation with next generation networking technologies
- To develop a testbed to demonstrate these technologies and support research
- To demonstrate new applications that support scientific research, education, environmental monitoring, and health care

The current architecture of the Next Generation Internet is shown in Figure 1-10; it incorporates a number of other networks, including the Defense Research and Engineering Network (DREN), the NASA Research and Education Network (NREN), the vBNS, and the SuperNet (Terabit Research Network from DARPA).

Further details on NASA's work on this project can be found in Reference [1-24].

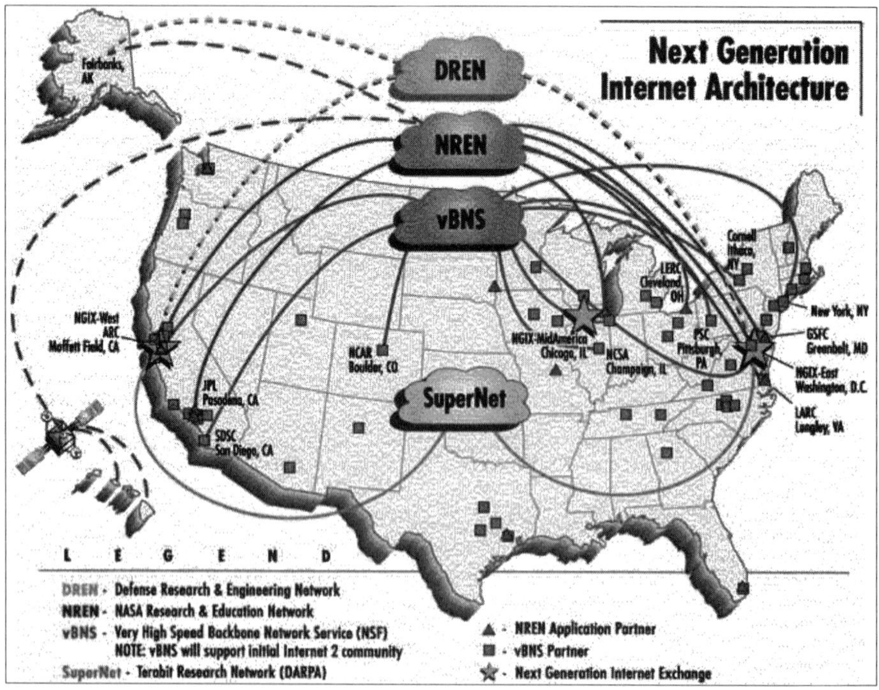

Figure 1-10 Next Generation Internet Architecture
(Source: http://www.nren.gov/ngiarc.html)

The *Routing Arbiter* manages the routing process for the Internet, including topology, connectivity, and routing table information. The RA project is a partnership of Merit Network, Inc., the University of Southern California Information Sciences Institute, IBM, and the University of Michigan. Like the vBNS, the RA is also funded by NSF [1-25].

The *Network Service Providers* (NSPs) provide both the backbone network and the end user service connections to the Internet. As we discussed in Section 1.2, ISPs exchange traffic at Network Access Points, or NAPs. *Boardwatch Magazine* divides Internet access into five different levels, moving from the traffic exchange point to the extensions of the Internet within a single LAN [1-26]:

- Level 1: Network Access Points (NAPs)
- Level 2: National Backbones
- Level 3: Regional Networks
- Level 4: Internet Service Providers (ISPs)
- Level 5: Consumer and Business Markets

An excellent directory of ISPs is also provided by *Boardwatch Magazine* [1-27]. With millions of people currently online, a number of networking journals research end user satisfaction with their providers. References [1-28] and [1-29] are two examples of recently-published articles on the subject. ISPs also have a forum, called the North American Network Operators' Group (NANOG), for the exchange of technical, business, and regulatory information [1-30].

An example of an NSP is ANSnet, operated by ANS Communications, Inc. (Purchase, New York), and acquired by America Online, Inc., in February 1995. The ANSnet backbone is a mesh of fiber-optic lines, operating at the DS-3 (44.736 Mbps) rate. These lines connect high-speed IP routers located in cities where ANSnet has a point of presence (POP). ANS also provides Virtual Private Networks, Web hosting, remote dial access, and network management functions for their customers.

An example of a regional provider is SuperNet, Inc., which serves Colorado and the metropolitan Denver area (Figure 1-11). SuperNet connects a number of the universities, public libraries, and high-technology companies such as Cray Computer Corp., Hewlett-Packard Co., McData Corp., and US West.

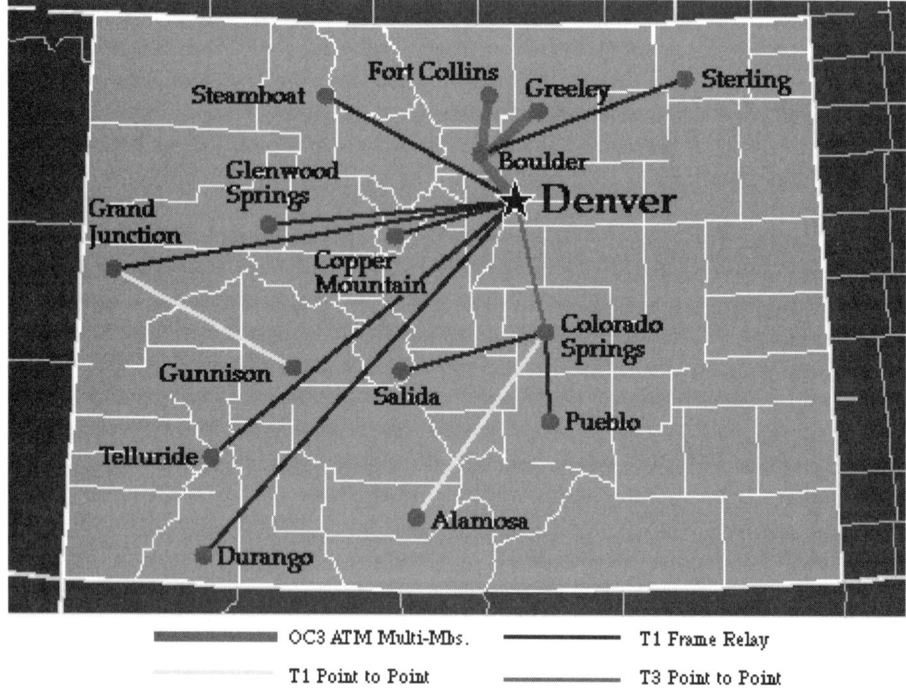

Figure 1-11 SuperNet Backbone Topology (Courtesy of SuperNet, Inc.)

1.5 Governing and Documenting the Internet

An amazing characteristic of the largely volunteer Internet community is how smoothly this rather avant-garde organization operates. To quote from RFC 1726 [1-31]: "A major contributor to the Internet's success is the fact that there is no single, centralized point of control or promulgator of policy for the entire network. This allows individual constituents of the network to tailor their own networks, environments and policies to suit their own needs. The individual constituents must cooperate only to the degree necessary to ensure that they interoperate."

But no organization, avant-garde or not, can operate without some degree of structure. The Internet Society provides some of that structure, and one of the Internet Society's components is the Internet Architecture Board (IAB), chartered in 1992. The IAB consists of 13 members: 12 full members plus the chair of the Internet Engineering Task Force (IETF). The IAB's responsibilities include [1-32]:

- Appointing a chair of the IETF and its subsidiary Internet Engineering Steering Group (IESG)
- Oversight of the architecture for the protocols and procedures used by the Internet
- Oversight of the process used to create Internet standards
- Editorial management and publication of the Request for Comment (RFC) document series and administration of the various Internet assigned numbers
- Representing the interests of the Internet Society to other organizations
- Providing guidance to the Internet Society regarding Internet technologies

Two task forces report to the IAB. The IETF coordinates the technical aspects of the Internet and its protocols and ensures that it functions effectively. The Internet Research Task Force (IRTF) researches new technologies.

The IAB produces numerous protocol standards and operational procedures that require dissemination and archiving. Most of these documents are known as Requests for Comments documents (RFCs) and are reviewed by the appropriate IETF or IRTF members. Many of the Internet protocols have become U.S. military standards and are assigned a MIL-STD number. For example, the Internet Protocol is described in both RFC 791 and MIL-STD-1777. Internet documents are published according to two tracks. Off-track specifications are labeled with one of three categories: experimental, informational, or historic. These documents contain information that is useful but not appropriate for an Internet standard. Specifications that are destined to become Internet standards evolve through several levels of testing and revision, known as the standards track, described in RFC 2026 [1-33]. Three "maturity levels" are defined. The first level of maturity is called a Proposed Standard. This standard is stable, well understood, has been reviewed by the community, and has sufficient interest to be considered valuable. A Draft Standard is one from which at least two independent and interoperable implementations have been developed and for which sufficient operational experience has been obtained. After significant implementation and operational experience is obtained, a Draft Standard may be elevated to an Internet Standard. The various organizations that are involved in this process are described in RFC 2028 [1-34].

Two key documents that provide information on Internet standards and parameters are published on a periodic basis. The Assigned Numbers document (currently RFC 1700 [1-35], with specific sections also updated online at `ftp://ftp.isi.edu/in-notes/iana/assignments`), documents protocol parameters, assigned addresses such as port numbers, and many others. This document is prepared by the Internet Assigned Numbers Authority, or IANA (email: `iana@isi.edu`). The Internet Official Protocol Standards document (currently RFC 2200 [1-36]) describes the standards track process and lists recently published RFCs and the current standardization status of the various protocols. Information on how to obtain Internet documentation is given in Appendix C.

With the explosive growth of the Internet within the last few years, a wealth of information is available. Throughout this text, we will make extensive use of the RFCs and other documents in our study. Readers needing details on the Internet itself could benefit from the following: RFC 1207, "FYI on Questions and Answers – Answers to Commonly Asked 'Experienced Internet User' Questions" [1-37]; RFC 1402, "There's Gold in Them Thar Networks! Or Searching for Treasure in All the Wrong Places" [1-38]; RFC 1580, "Guide to Network Resource Tools" [1-39]; RFC 1594, "FYI on Questions and Answers – Answers to Commonly Asked 'New Internet User' Questions" [1-40]; RFC 1738, "Uniform Resource Locators" [1-41]; RFC 1935, "FYI on 'What is the Internet'" [1-42]; RFC 1983, "Internet Users' Glossary" [1-43]; and RFC 2151, "A Primer on Internet and TCP/IP Tools" [1-44].

References [1-45] through [1-49] are excellent resources, available either online or in bookstores, as indicated in Section 1.8. Readers who like suspense will enjoy Cliff Stoll's *The Cuckoo's Egg* [1-50], which describes the author's true experience tracking a hacker through the Internet.

1.6 Applying the Technologies of the Internet

In the previous sections of this chapter, we took a short trip down TCP/IP's memory lane. We studied how the U.S. government sponsored the development of these protocols based on the research and development community's requirements. But what if you work for an organization that has nothing to do with research, the U.S. government, or the military? Can your organization benefit from TCP/IP and the Internet protocols? To find out, answer the following questions about your computing environment:

- Do you have a multivendor environment?
- Does your internetwork include LAN and WAN topologies?

- Do your users require file transfer, electronic mail, host terminal emulation, or network management?
- Is access to the World Wide Web and/or electronic commerce critical to business applications?

The bottom line is that the requirements for most organizations' internetworks do not differ appreciably from those of the 1969-vintage ARPANET. Most of us require a multivendor distributed architecture. We also need proven solutions and are eager to benefit from almost three decades of research and testing.

Even if you have no intention of connecting to the Internet, you can benefit from using TCP/IP. Those who implement these protocols will be in good company, as hundreds of vendors offer products to help configure, install, operate, and manage TCP/IP-based internetworks. (Appendix H lists a number of these vendors, although the list is growing so rapidly that it is impossible to ever be completely up-to-date.)

1.7 Looking Ahead

With this historical background, let's return to the present and take a practical approach. Chapter 2 will discuss the Internet protocols and support for them among Windows, Macintosh, DEC, IBM, and UNIX hosts. Chapters 3 through 7 will examine the Internet protocols, plus troubleshooting and management techniques. Our journey will coincide with the layers of the ARPA internetworking model, beginning with the Network Interface and ending with Process/Application Layers. In Chapter 7 we'll look at strategies for managing TCP/IP-based internetworks, and Chapter 8 will preview the next-generation Internet Protocol – IPng or IPv6. So warm up that protocol analyzer, and let's begin.

1.8 References

[1-1] Rosner, Roy D. *Packet Switching: Tomorrow's Communications Today.* Wadsworth, Inc., 1982.

[1-2] CSNET CIC. "A CSNET Retrospective." *CSNET News* (Summer 1985): 6–7.

[1-3] Miller, Mark A. "Get a Grip on Internet Access." *Network World* (July 19, 1993): 31–37.

[1-4] Information on the Commercial Internet Exchange may be obtained from:
CIX Association
1041 Sterling Road, Suite 104A
Herndon, VA 20170
Tel: +1 703 709 8200
Fax: +1 703 824 1611
Email: helpdesk@cix.org
http://www.cix.org

[1-5] The Internet Society may be contacted at:
12020 Sunrise Valley Drive, Suite 210
Reston, VA 22091
Tel: +1 703 648 9888 or +1 800 468 9507
Fax: +1 703 648 9887
Email: isoc@isoc.org
http://www.isoc.org

[1-6] Both Pacific Bell and Ameritech maintain Web sites that provide details on the operation of the San Francisco and Chicago NAPs, respectively. The Web sites are:
http://www.pacbell.com/products/business/fastrak/networking/nap/index.htm and
http//www.ameritech.com/products/data/nap.

[1-7] Leiner, Barry M., et al. *A Brief History of the Internet.* Available from: http://www.isoc.org/internet/history/brief.html.

[1-8] Zakon, Robert Hobbes. Hobbes' Internet Timeline. RFC 2235. Also available from
http://www.isoc.org/guest/zakon/Internet/History/HIT.html.

[1-9] Quarterman, John S., and Josiah C. Hoskins. "Notable Computer Networks." *Communications of the ACM* (October 1986): 932–971.

[1-10] Quarterman, John S. "The History of the Internet and the Matrix." *ConneXions* (April 1995): 13–25.

[1-11] Dern, Daniel P. "The ARPANET is Twenty: What We Have Learned and the Fun We Had." *ConneXions* (October 1989): 2–10.

[1-12] Leiner, B. M., et al. "The ARPA Internet Protocol Suite." RS-85-153, included in the *DDN Protocol Handbook,* Volume 2: 2-27-2-49.

[1-13] Cerf, V. G., and R. E. Kahn, "A Protocol for Packet Network Intercommunication." *IEEE Transactions on Communications* (May 1974): 637-648.

[1-14] Padlipsky, M. A. "A Perspective on the ARPANET Reference Model." RFC 871, The Mitre Corp., September 1982.

[1-15] Cerf, Vinton G., and Edward Cain. "The DoD Internet Architecture Model." *Computer Networks* (October 1983): 307-317.

[1-16] Cerf, Vint. "Requiem for the ARPANET." *ConneXions* (October 1991): 27.

[1-17] Network Wizards Internet Domain Survey is updated twice a year, and is available at `http://www.nw.com`.

[1-18] Quarterman, John S. *The Matrix – Computer Networks and Conferencing Systems Worldwide.* Digital Equipment Corp., 1990.

[1-19] Matrix Information and Directory Services, Inc. maintains maps that detail the composition of the Internet, which are available at `http://www.mids.org`.

[1-20] Merit Network, Inc. "Merit Retires NSFNET Backbone Service." *MichNet News,* Vol. 9, No. 2, 1995. Available from `http://www.merit.edu`.

[1-21] Information on the vBNS is available from `http://www.vbns.net`.

[1-22] Information on the Internet2 project is available from `http://www.internet2/edu`.

[1-23] Information on the Next Generation Internet initiative is available from `http://www.ngi.gov`.

[1-24] Information on NASA's involvement in the Next Generation Internet initiative is available from `http://www.nren.nasa.gov`.

[1-25] Information on the Routing Arbiter project is available from `http://www.ra.net`.

[1-26] Rickard, Jack. Internet Architecture. *Boardwatch Magazine,* 1996. Available from `http://www.boardwatch.com/isp/fall97/intarch.html`.

[1-27] Boardwatch Magazine Directory of Internet Service Providers. Available from `http://www.boardwatch.com/isp/index.html`.

[1-28] The 1997 ISP Survey. *Inter@ctive Week*, October 13, 1997: 47–60.

[1-29] Wetzel, Rebecca. "Customers Rate ISP Services." *PC Week* (November 10, 1997): 105–124.

[1-30] Information on the North American Network Operators' Group (NANOG) is available from `http://www.nanog.org`.

[1-31] Kastenholz, F., and C. Partridge. "Technical Criteria for Choosing IP: The Next Generation." RFC 1726, December 1994.

[1-32] Huitema, C. "Charter of the Internet Architecture Board." RFC 1601, March 1994.

[1-33] Bradner, S. "The Internet Standards Process – Revision 3." RFC 2026, October 1996.

[1-34] Hovey, R., and S. Bradner. "The Organizations Involved in the IETF Standards Process." RFC 2028, October 1996.

[1-35] Reynolds, J., and J. Postel. "Assigned Numbers." RFC 1700, October 1994. Individual sections of this document are updated periodically and archived at `ftp://ftp.isi.edu/in-notes/iana/assignments`.

[1-36] Postel, J., Editor. "Internet Official Protocol Standards." RFC 2200, June 1997.

[1-37] Malkin, G., et al. "FYI on Questions and Answers – Answers to Commonly Asked 'Experienced Internet User' Questions." RFC 1207, February 1991.

[1-38] Martin, J. "There's Gold in Them Thar Networks! Or Searching for Treasure in All the Wrong Places." RFC 1402, January 1993.

[1-39] EARN Staff. "Guide to Network Resource Tools." RFC 1580, March 1994.

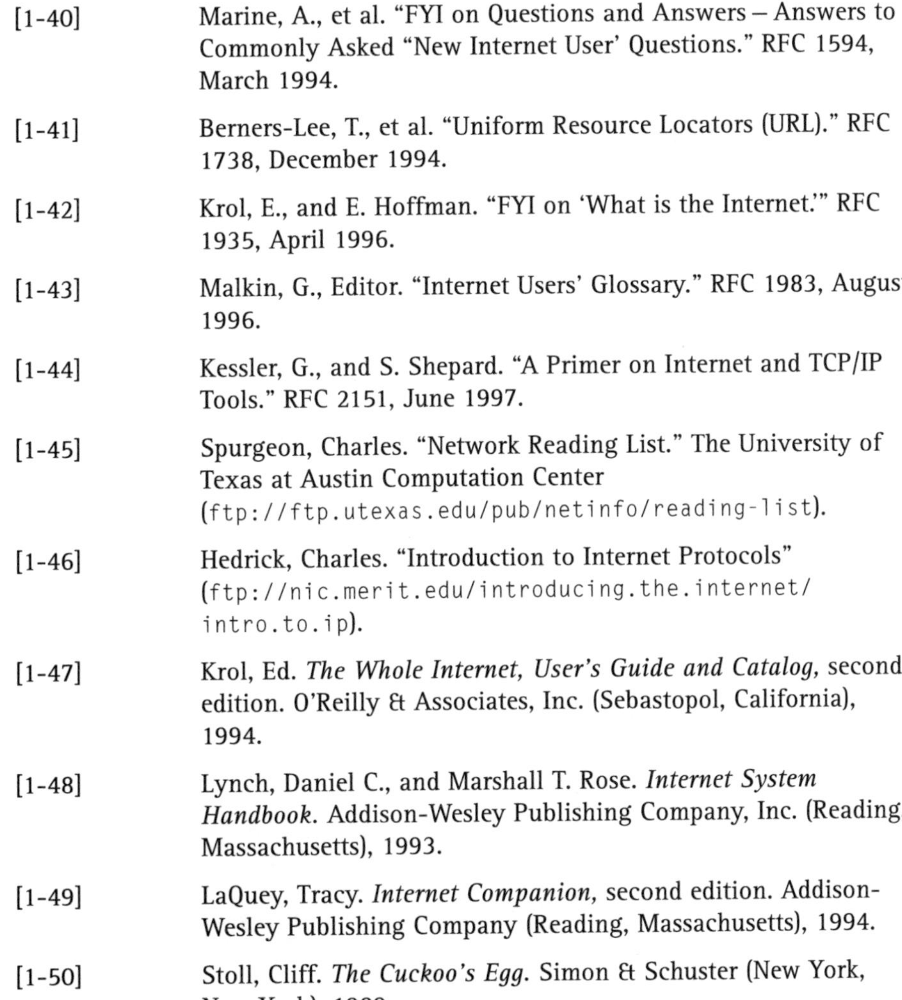

[1-40] Marine, A., et al. "FYI on Questions and Answers – Answers to Commonly Asked "New Internet User' Questions." RFC 1594, March 1994.

[1-41] Berners-Lee, T., et al. "Uniform Resource Locators (URL)." RFC 1738, December 1994.

[1-42] Krol, E., and E. Hoffman. "FYI on 'What is the Internet.'" RFC 1935, April 1996.

[1-43] Malkin, G., Editor. "Internet Users' Glossary." RFC 1983, August 1996.

[1-44] Kessler, G., and S. Shepard. "A Primer on Internet and TCP/IP Tools." RFC 2151, June 1997.

[1-45] Spurgeon, Charles. "Network Reading List." The University of Texas at Austin Computation Center (`ftp://ftp.utexas.edu/pub/netinfo/reading-list`).

[1-46] Hedrick, Charles. "Introduction to Internet Protocols" (`ftp://nic.merit.edu/introducing.the.internet/intro.to.ip`).

[1-47] Krol, Ed. *The Whole Internet, User's Guide and Catalog,* second edition. O'Reilly & Associates, Inc. (Sebastopol, California), 1994.

[1-48] Lynch, Daniel C., and Marshall T. Rose. *Internet System Handbook.* Addison-Wesley Publishing Company, Inc. (Reading, Massachusetts), 1993.

[1-49] LaQuey, Tracy. *Internet Companion,* second edition. Addison-Wesley Publishing Company (Reading, Massachusetts), 1994.

[1-50] Stoll, Cliff. *The Cuckoo's Egg.* Simon & Schuster (New York, New York), 1989.

Chapter 2

Supporting TCP/IP and the Internet Protocols

In Chapter 1, we discussed how TCP/IP and the Internet protocols were developed from requirements set forth by the U.S. government. Various hardware and software vendors have shown a great deal of interest in these protocols for several reasons. First, the U.S. government is a large customer and can generate a great deal of revenue with a single purchase order. Second, as the Internet and the number of connected hosts continue to grow, opportunities for products that support these popular connectivity solutions will increase as well. Finally, TCP/IP and the Internet protocols can serve any organization that needs to connect dissimilar hosts, such as an IBM mainframe to a UNIX workstation, Apple Macintosh, or PC on a LAN.

Of course, anyone who sets up an internet using these protocols is bound to run into problems sooner or later. When you have a problem with your internet connection, you need to first understand the TCP/IP protocols, and then you need a protocol analyzer that supports these protocols.

In this chapter, we'll provide the background you need to understand the TCP/IP protocols, plus various requirements to consider when shopping for an analyzer for your internet. First, we'll provide a general overview of the protocols themselves. Second, we'll discuss how different computing platforms support these protocols. Third, we'll survey the tools available for troubleshooting. We'll defer a detailed discussion of the protocols until Chapter 3.

2.1 The Internet Protocols

TCP/IP and the Internet protocols support the Advanced Research Projects Agency (ARPA) model of internetworking and its four defined layers: Network Interface, Internet, Host-to-Host, and Process/Application (see Figure 2-1a). Developed in the early 1970s, this model preceded the Open Systems Interconnection Reference Model (OSI-RM) by several years. Like ARPA, the OSI-RM was designed to internetwork dissimilar computer systems; however, the two models have different underlying assumptions. The ARPA model was designed to connect hosts serving the academic, research, government, and military populations, primarily in the United States. The OSI-RM was broader in scope. First, the OSI-RM was the product of an international standards body, the International Standards Organization (ISO). Thus, the OSI-RM received input from people in Europe and Asia as well as in North

America. Second, it had a much broader charter, the interconnection of Open Systems, and was not constrained by the type of system to be connected (e.g., academic, military, and so forth). To satisfy these two constraints, the ISO developed a seven-layer model in contrast to ARPA's four-layer model. To summarize, the ARPA world was more specific, the OSI world more general. The result was two architectures that are almost, but not quite, parallel. We will study these differences in greater detail in the following chapters. In the meantime, let's take a brief look at the protocols we will be analyzing.

The first layer of the ARPA model is the Network Interface Layer, sometimes called the Network Access Layer or Local Network Layer; it connects the local host to the local network hardware. As such, it comprises the functions of the OSI Physical and Data Link Layers: it makes the physical connection to the cable system, it accesses the cable at the appropriate time (e.g., using a Carrier Sense Multiple Access with Collision Detection (CSMA/CD) or token passing algorithm), and it places the data into a frame. The *frame* is a package that envelops the data with information, such as the hardware address of the local host and a check sequence to assure data integrity. The frame is defined by the hardware in use, such as an Ethernet LAN or a frame relay interface into a WAN. The ARPA model shows particular strength in this area – it includes a standard for virtually all popular connections to LANs, MANs, and WANs. (Recall that the Internet standards are defined in Request for Comments documents, or RFCs.) These include Ethernet (RFC 894); IEEE 802 LANs (RFC 1042); ARCNET (RFC 1201); Fiber Distributed Data Interface-FDDI (RFC 1103); serial lines using the Serial Line Internet Protocol or SLIP (RFC 1055); PSPDNs (RFC 877); frame relay (RFC 1490); Switched Multimegabit Data Service or SMDS (RFC 1209); and the Asynchronous Transfer Mode (ATM), defined in RFC 1438.

The Internet Layer transfers packets from one host (the computing device that runs application programs) to another host. Note that we said *packet* instead of frame. The packet differs from the frame in that it contains address information to facilitate its journey from one host to another through the internetwork; the address within the frame header gets the frame from host to host on the same local network. The protocol that operates the Internet Layer is known as the Internet Protocol (the IP in TCP/IP). Several other protocols are also required, however.

The *Address Resolution Protocol* (ARP) provides a way to translate between IP addresses and local network addresses, such as Ethernet, and is discussed in RFC 826. *The Reverse Address Resolution Protocol* (RARP), explained in RFC 903, provides the complementary function, translating from the local address (again, such as Ethernet) to IP addresses. (In some architectural drawings, ARP and RARP are shown slightly lower than IP to indicate their close relationship to the Network Interface Layer. In some respects, ARP/RARP overlap the Network Interface and Internet Layers.)

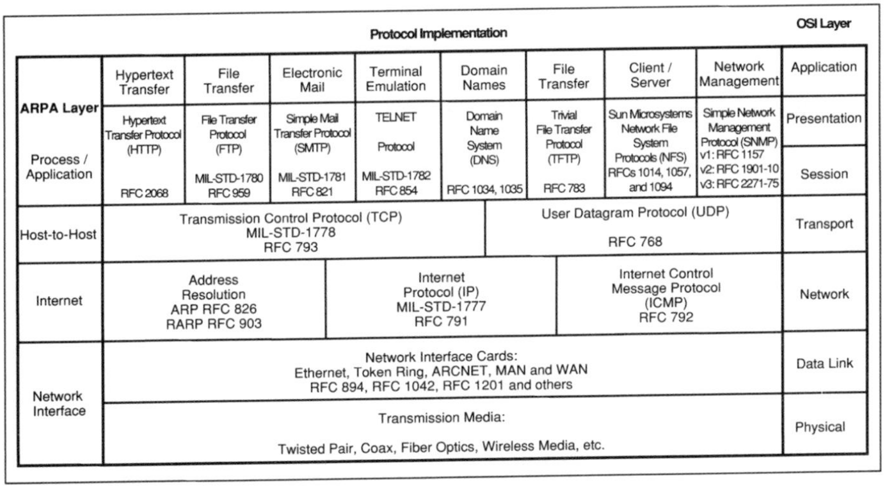

ARPA Layer	Protocol Implementation								OSI Layer
Process / Application	Hypertext Transfer	File Transfer	Electronic Mail	Terminal Emulation	Domain Names	File Transfer	Client / Server	Network Management	Application
	Hypertext Transfer Protocol (HTTP) RFC 2068	File Transfer Protocol (FTP) MIL-STD-1780 RFC 959	Simple Mail Transfer Protocol (SMTP) MIL-STD-1781 RFC 821	TELNET Protocol MIL-STD-1782 RFC 854	Domain Name System (DNS) RFC 1034, 1035	Trivial File Transfer Protocol (TFTP) RFC 783	Sun Microsystems Network File System Protocols (NFS) RFCs 1014, 1057, and 1094	Simple Network Management Protocol (SNMP) v1: RFC 1157 v2: RFC 1901-10 v3: RFC 2271-75	Presentation / Session
Host-to-Host	Transmission Control Protocol (TCP) MIL-STD-1778 RFC 793					User Datagram Protocol (UDP) RFC 768			Transport
Internet	Address Resolution ARP RFC 826 RARP RFC 903			Internet Protocol (IP) MIL-STD-1777 RFC 791			Internet Control Message Protocol (ICMP) RFC 792		Network
Network Interface	Network Interface Cards: Ethernet, Token Ring, ARCNET, MAN and WAN RFC 894, RFC 1042, RFC 1201 and others								Data Link
	Transmission Media: Twisted Pair, Coax, Fiber Optics, Wireless Media, etc.								Physical

Figure 2-1a Comparing ARPA Protocols with OSI and ARPA Architectures

The *Internet Control Message Protocol* (ICMP) provides a way for the IP software on a host or gateway to communicate with its peers on other machines about any problems it might have in routing IP datagrams. ICMP, which is explained in RFC 792, is a required part of the IP implementation. One of the most frequently used ICMP messages is the Echo Request, commonly called the *Ping*, which allows one device to test the communication path to another.

As the datagram traverses the Internet, it may pass through multiple gateways and their associated local network connections. Thus, there's a risk that packets may be lost or that a noisy communication circuit may corrupt data. The Host-to-Host Layer guards against these problems, however remote, and ensures the reliable delivery of a datagram sent from the source host to the destination host. (Recall that one of the major objectives of the ARPA project was military communication, which, by definition, must be ultra-reliable.)

The Host-to-Host Layer defines two protocols: the *User Datagram Protocol* (UDP) and the *Transmission Control Protocol* (TCP). The minimum security UDP, described in RFC 768, provides minimal protocol overhead. UDP restricts its involvement to higher-layer port addresses, defining the length, and a checksum. TCP, detailed in RFC 793, defines a much more rigorous error control mechanism. TCP (of the TCP/IP nomenclature) provides much of the strength of the Internet protocol suite. TCP provides reliable datastream transport between two host applications by providing a method of sequentially transferring every octet (8-bit quantity of data) passed between the two applications.

End users interact with the host via the Process/Application Layer. Because of the user interface, a number of protocols have been developed for this layer. As its name implies, the *File Transfer Protocol* (FTP) transfers files between two host systems. FTP is described in RFC 959. To guarantee its reliability, FTP is implemented over TCP. When economy of transmission is desired, you may use a simpler program, the *Trivial File Transfer Protocol* (TFTP), described in RFC 783. TFTP runs on top of UDP to economize the Host-to-Host Layer as well.

Electronic mail and terminal emulation are two of the more frequently used Internet applications. The *Simple Mail Transfer Protocol* (SMTP), given in RFC 821, sends mail messages from one host to another. When accessing a remote host via the Internet, one must emulate the type of terminal the host wishes to see. For example, a Digital host may prefer a VT-100 terminal while an IBM host would rather see a 3278 or 3279 display station. The *Telecommunications Network* (TELNET) protocol provides remote host access and terminal emulation.

As internetworks become more complex, system management requirements increase as well. A large number of vendors, including Hewlett-Packard, IBM, Microsoft, SunSoft, and others have developed network management systems that supply these needs. Common to all of these platforms is the use of a protocol, the *Simple Network Management Protocol* (SNMP), that was originally developed to meet the needs of TCP/IP-based internets. As its name implies, SNMP uses minimal overhead to communicate between the *Manager* (i.e., management console) and the *Agent* (i.e., the device, such as a router, being managed). There are presently three different versions of SNMP defined: version 1 (RFCs 1155, 1157, and 1213), version 2 (RFCs 1901–1910) and version 3 (RFCs 2271–2275).

Many other protocols are defined for the Internet suite that provide address resolution, control, and routing functions; they are illustrated in Figure 2-1b. Note that the address resolution protocols are functionally lower than the ARPA Internet Layer, and that the control and routing functions are functionally higher than the Internet Layer. We will explore these ancillary protocols in detail in Chapter 4.

With that background into the Internet protocols, let's turn our attention to the host systems that incorporate these protocols, starting with the large systems based on UNIX, Digital's DECnet, or IBM's SNA.

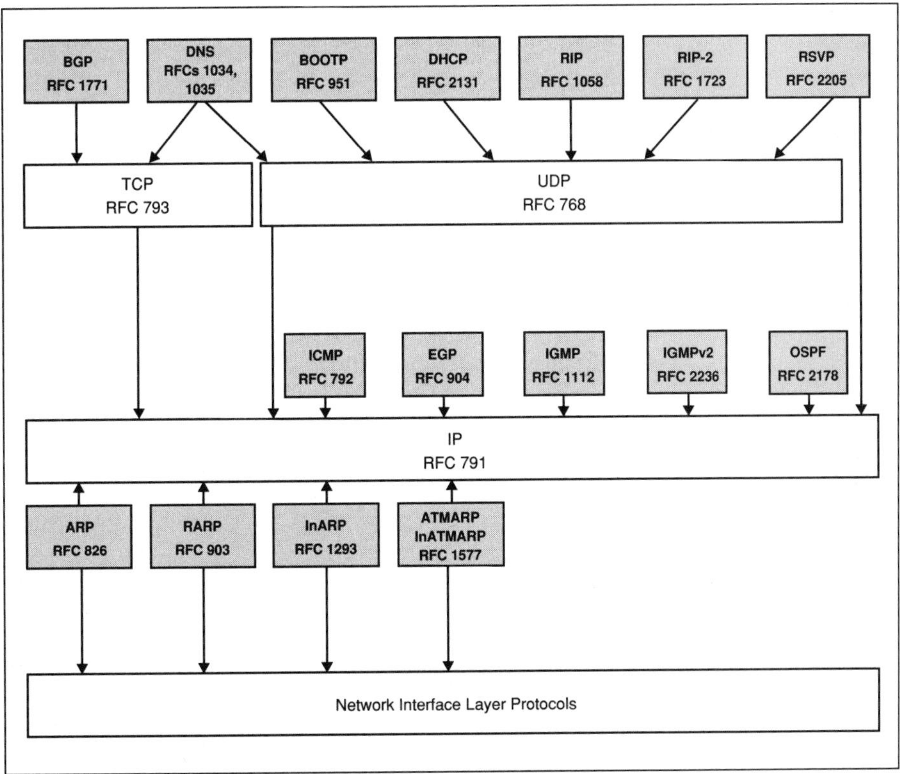

Figure 2-1b Internet Routing, Control, and Address Resolution Protocols

2.2 Internet Support within UNIX Environments

In the early 1980s, ARPA provided a grant to the University of California at Berkeley to modify the already robust UNIX operating system. One of the changes was support for the Internet protocols. The Berkeley Software Distribution version 4.2 (BSD 4.2) included support for the TCP, IP, SMTP, and ARP protocols. That version proved satisfactory for use on LANs and smaller internetworks.

BSD 4.3 offered support for larger internetworks that included routers and WAN transmission facilities (e.g., 56 Kbps leased lines). The changes included routines for ICMP redirect messages, retransmission algorithms, packet time-to-live parameters, and so on. BSD 4.4 was further enhanced to provide multicasting and other enhancements.

These releases have yielded a variety of implementations from a number of companies, including Hewlett-Packard (HP-UX), IBM (AIX), SunSoft (SunOS and Solaris), and the Santa Cruz Operation, or SCO (Xenix). When surveying this marketplace, it is easy to see why Reichard and Johnson in their book *UNIX in Plain English* [2-1] refer to these numerous variants as a "veritable Tower of Babel." Reference [2-2] discusses these UNIX releases from a user's perspective and Reference [2-3] deals with the programming requirements. Roosevelt Giles, in his paper "UNIX and PC Network Connectivity" [2-4], discusses the various options for connecting UNIX systems and PC networks. Last, John Foley discusses UNIX interoperability issues in Reference [2-5].

It should come as no surprise that UNIX environments have strong support for the Internet protocols, because their primary clientele are academic, scientific, and research users. Interest in the business community increased in the mid-1980s, coinciding with the rapid growth in LANs. We'll look at the two key players in the commercial sector, Digital and IBM, next.

2.3 Internet Support within Digital Environments

Compaq Computer Corp.'s (formerly Digital Equipment Corp., Maynard, Massachusetts) VAX and Alpha systems have been extremely well received among the scientific and engineering communities – computer users who have a strong interest in the Internet protocols. The Digital Network Architecture (DNA) and related DECnet products, the OpenVMS operating system, and Digital's version of UNIX, formerly known as Ultrix, are also popular choices for many internetworks. Solutions are available from both Digital and third-party vendors to integrate OpenVMS, DECnet, and the Internet protocols into one cohesive system.

First, consider the differences between the two most recent versions of the Digital Network Architecture, Phase IV and Phase V. Announced in 1982, DNA Phase IV provided a proprietary architecture for LAN and WAN connectivity. It supported industry-standard protocols such as Ethernet and ITU-T X.25 at the lower three OSI layers, but its upper layer protocols (Networks Services Protocol and Session Control Protocol) were proprietary. DECnet Phase IV users who wish to integrate OpenVMS-based systems into a UNIX environment have to install a TCP/IP software stack on OpenVMS. Digital's TCP/IP Services for OpenVMS is an example of such a product. Similar solutions are available from third-party vendors.

Announced in 1987, DNA Phase V combines the protocols from DNA Phase IV and OSI into a merged protocol stack (Figure 2-2a). The resulting "two-headed" protocol stack provides independent support for both DECnet and OSI applications. One half of the lower stack supports the proprietary DNA Phase IV protocols at the Transport Layer and below, and ensures backwards compatibility with older versions of DECnet. The other half supports the OSI protocols, such as the ISO 8248 (Connectionless Network Layer Protocol, or CLNP), the ISO 10589 (Intermediate Station-to-Intermediate Station, or IS-IS), which is used at the Network Layer, and the OSI 8073 Transport Protocol. Products based on DNA Phase V were shipped on OpenVMS and Digital UNIX in the early 1990s under the product name DECnet/OSI.

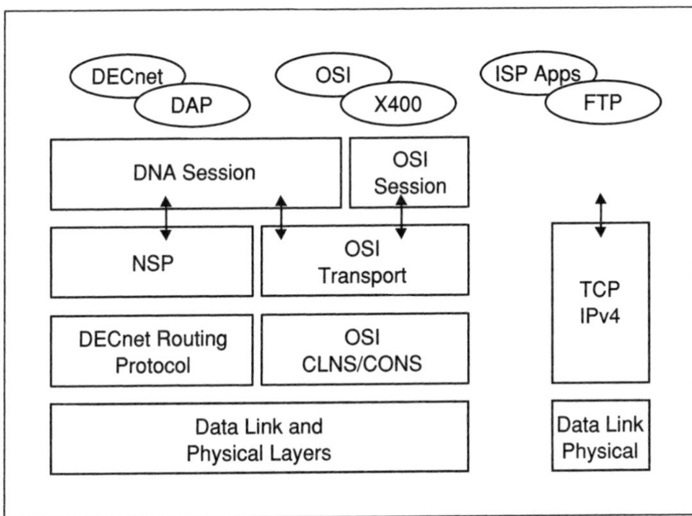

Figure 2-2a DECnet/OSI and TCP/IP
(Courtesy of Compaq Computer Corporation)

Users of DECnet/OSI have several additional options for TCP/IP connectivity. DECnet/OSI supports a number of Application Layer gateways between the DECnet, OSI, and Internet protocol stacks. These include an internal Data Access Protocol-to-File Transfer and Management (DAP-to-FTAM) gateway, which provides file transfers between DECnet Phase IV, DECnet/OSI and OSI systems, and an internal FTP-to-FTAM gateway, which facilitates file transfers from the TCP/IP-to-OSI sides. Other gateways between SMTP and X.400 (for electronic mail) and between TELNET and Virtual Terminal Protocol (for remote host access) are also part of DECnet/OSI.

Further enhancements to DECnet, announced in 1994, were achieved by the adoption of a third protocol stack to the architecture – the Internet protocols. These changes, known as "DECnet over TCP/IP," made it possible to run DECnet or OSI applications directly over TCP/IP as an alternative to using the traditional lower layer protocols (Figure 2-2b).

DECnet over TCP/IP is documented in RFC 1859 [2-7]. This informational RFC builds on RFC 1006 [2-6], published in 1987, which details how OSI applications can be run over TCP/IP transport. The concepts in RFCs 1006 and 1859 have been further developed and extended, and a resulting document, RFC 2126 [2-8], describes how to run DECnet or OSI-like applications over either IPv4 or IPv6.

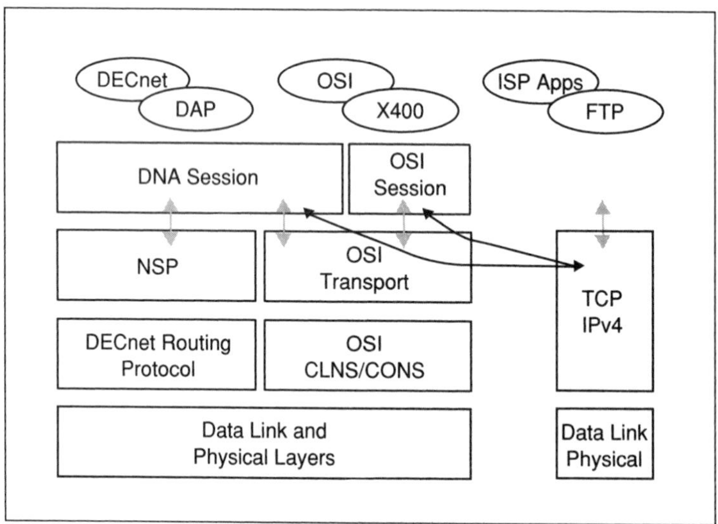

Figure 2-2b DECnet-Plus with DECnet over TCP/IP (Courtesy of Compaq Computer Corporation)

A consistent theme of Digital's Network Strategy is interoperability between DECnet, OSI, and the TCP/IP protocols. This theme runs through the OpenVMS, Digital UNIX, Windows 95, and Windows NT operating system level to the internetworking hardware. References [2-9] through [2-11] evaluate some of these internetworking options. Digital's Web site [2-12] contains up-to-date information on Digital products and their applications, and Malamud's *DECnet/OSI Phase V* presents a detailed study of the protocols [2-13].

2.4 Internet Support within IBM Environments

IBM mainframes, communication controllers, workstations, and minicomputers all support the Internet protocols, including TELNET, FTP, TFTP, NFS, and SMTP, as well as lower-layer protocols, such as IP, ICMP, and TCP. (An excellent reference is IBM's *TCP/IP Tutorial and Technical Overview* [2-14].) We'll look at each IBM platform separately.

At the mainframe level, IBM offers products that add support for the Internet protocols within the VM and MVS operating systems. These products are known as TCP/IP for VM and TCP/IP for MVS, respectively. Both products support the client/server nature of the Internet protocols. For example, the TN3270 function allows an IBM PC workstation running TCP/IP to remotely access a VM or MVS host via a LAN. The PC would appear as a client, that is, an IBM 3270-series terminal. Both VM and MVS implement FTP for host-to-host file transfers. The FTP Type command translates data between the mainframe's EBCDIC format and the PC's ASCII format. Both operating systems support SMTP for electronic mail service. IBM also offers an interface to exchange messages between SMTP and the IBM PROFS system. Other higher layer protocol functions available under VM and MVS include X-Windows, Sun Microsystem's NFS, SNMP, and remote printing.

The IBM 3172 Interconnect Controller, shown in Figure 2-3a, handles the hardware connection between the IBM host and the TCP/IP environment. The 3172 provides a hardware connection between the mainframe channel and Ethernet, FDDI, or token ring LANs, as well as DEC networks, although the DEC connection requires additional gateway software. Software that accompanies the 3172 controls the IBM channel, attached LAN hardware, and the software interface to the TCP/IP functions on the host. In addition to the model 3172 Controller, the model 3746 Controller also supports IP connections to a host.

In addition to the mainframe environment, IBM supports TCP/IP on a number of other platforms. IBM's version of UNIX, the AIX, Advanced Interactive Executive, runs on hardware such as the PS/2, RT, RISC System/6000, and 9370. IBM provides TCP/IP support for midrange computers such as the AS/400 and their operating systems (OS/400) as well. TCP/IP on workstations is supported by the *TCP/IP for DOS/Windows* and *TCP/IP for OS/2* products. Support among these products for specific protocols varies, however, so consult References [2-14] and [2-15] for complete details.

As a final example, consider the case in which a number of hosts are connected in a single internetwork that includes an SNA network (see Figure 2-3b). This application is known as SNAlink, and it transfers TCP/IP-related information via an SNA backbone. In this example, four hosts running VM, MVS, DOS, and AIX are connected. The DOS machine is connected via an Ethernet and 3172 Interconnect Controller to the MVS host, while the AIX and VM hosts are connected to a token ring. (Conversely, Data Link Switching on the 6611 network processor, a multiprotocol, multiport router and bridge, lets a TCP/IP backbone transport SNA traffic. We will investigate the Data Link Switching protocol in detail in Section 3.7.) A number of applications are possible using IBM's family of TCP/IP software products. Any user can log in to any of the remote hosts using TN3270. Files may be transferred between hosts using FTP or TFTP. Electronic mail may be transferred between any of the users. Finally, a user on the AIX host may use NFS to access files on either the VM or MVS hosts.

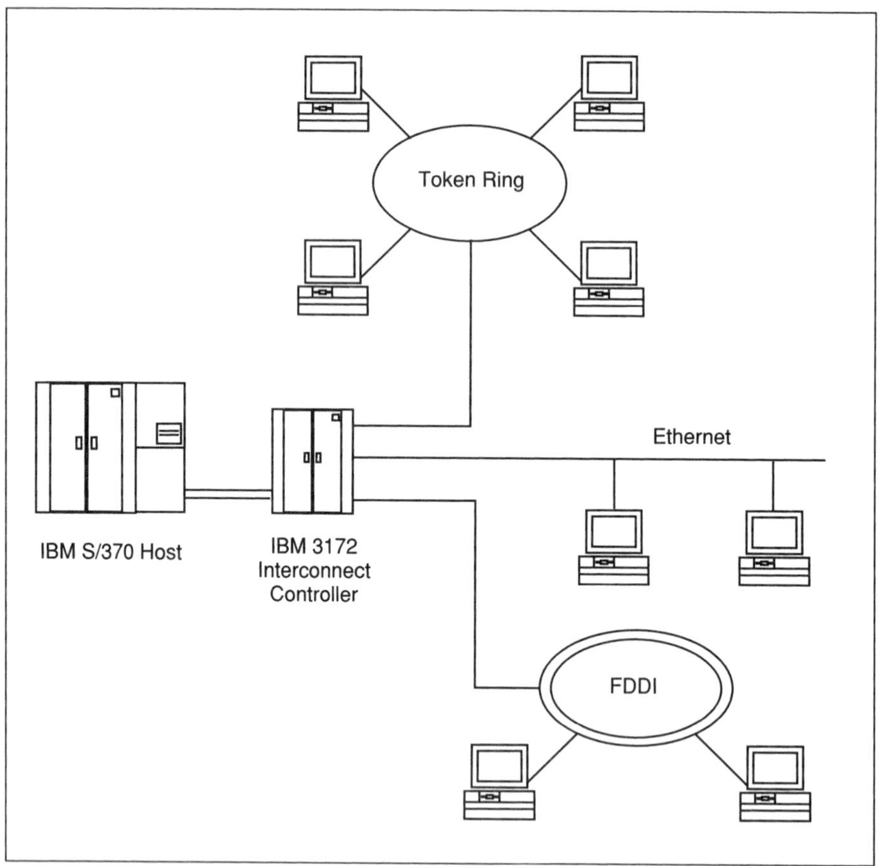

Figure 2-3a TCP/IP Connections Using the IBM 3172 Interconnect Controller (Reprinted by permission from TCP/IP Tutorial and Technical Overview GG24-3376-04 © by International Business Machines Corporation)

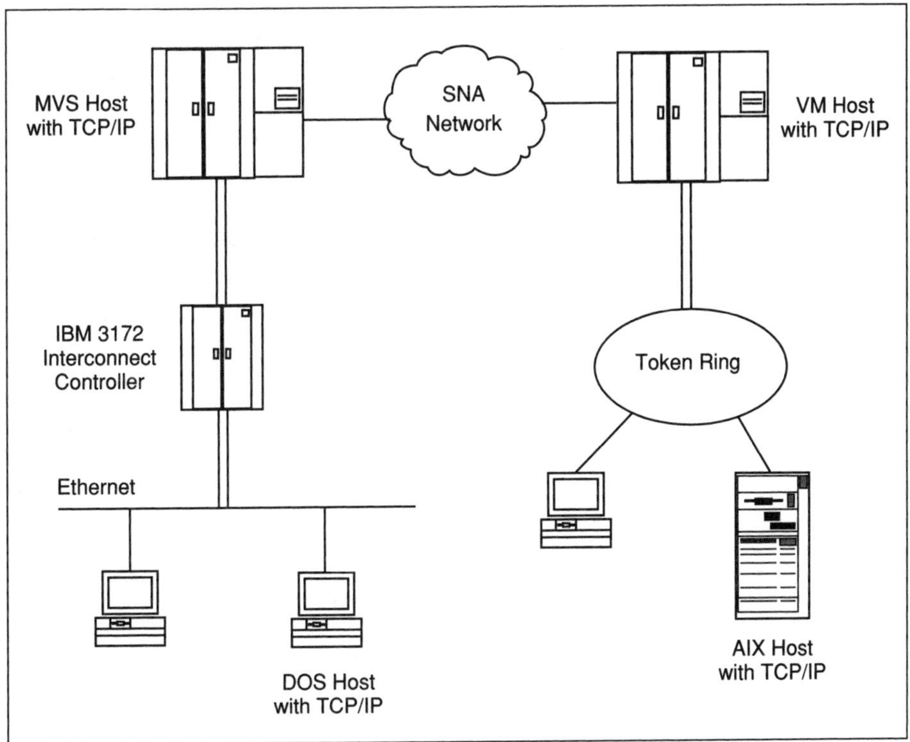

Figure 2-3b SNAlink Scenario
(Reprinted by permission from TCP/IP Tutorial and Technical Overview GG24-3376-04
© by International Business Machines Corporation)

2.5 Internet Support within DOS and Windows Environments

Recall from our history lesson in Chapter 1 that the TCP/IP protocols were developed in the early 1960s and that ARPANET came online in 1969. During the 1970s, ARPANET grew because of the addition of mainframe and minicomputer hosts. When the IBM PC was announced in 1981, a new market opened up for TCP/IP software developers – desktop PCs (as long as they were connected to the Internet via a LAN, dial-up link, etc.). Considering the popularity of PCs and the LANs connecting them, it's no wonder that a number of companies have developed TCP/IP connectivity software to support DOS, OS/2, and Windows-based workstations. And in addition to third-party solutions, many operating system developers, such as IBM and Microsoft, have incorporated support for the Internet protocols directly into their operating systems. In this section, we will look at the architecture of two sample products and discuss the features to consider when shopping.

One popular TCP/IP implementation for DOS is FTP Software, Inc.'s (now a subsidiary of NetManage, Inc.) PC/TCP Network Software for DOS. An extremely flexible product, PC/TCP works with each of the four standard network card interfaces: Novell's ODI, 3Com/Microsoft's Network Driver Interface Specification (NDIS), IBM's Adapter Support Interface (ASI), and the Packet Driver. (There will be more on these LAN interfaces in Section 2.7.) In fact, FTP Software wrote the Packet Driver Specification, which allowed the separation of the driver from the DOS protocol stack, and released it into the public domain in 1987. Using a Packet Driver, PC/TCP can concurrently support its TCP/IP protocol stack and a second stack, such as NetWare, VINES, DECNet, and others.

PC/TCP contains components – such as a driver, a kernel, and programs – that span from the Data Link Layer to the Application Layer of the OSI Reference Model (see Figure 2-4a). The components vary, depending on the physical medium and the simultaneous use of other network applications. In its most common configuration, the PC/TCP applications sit above the generic PC/TCP kernel, which in turn sits either on top of a Packet Driver, an NDIS-to-Packet Driver, or an ODI-to-Packet Driver conversion module.

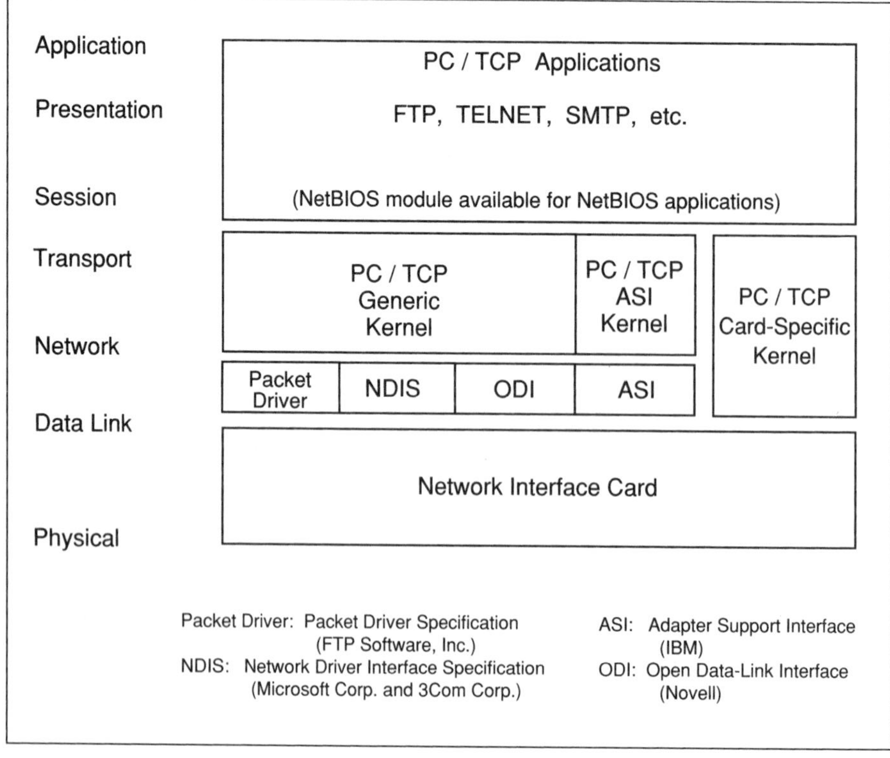

Figure 2-4a PC/TCP Support for Various Hardware Drivers
(Courtesy of FTP Software, Inc.)

Third-party developers can also use the PC/TCP kernel in their applications for network transport. Developers writing DOS applications can use a Native Mode API or a Berkeley Sockets emulation library, or they can access the TCP, UDP, and other application libraries. Developers writing Windows 3.x applications can use a Sockets Dynamic Link Library (DLL) and a Native Mode DLL. Other options include Remote Procedure Call (RPC) libraries.

Two other products, OnNet Kernel and OnNet Host Suite, support TCP/IP and IPv6 applications within Microsoft Windows 95/98 or Windows NT environments (Figure 2-4b).

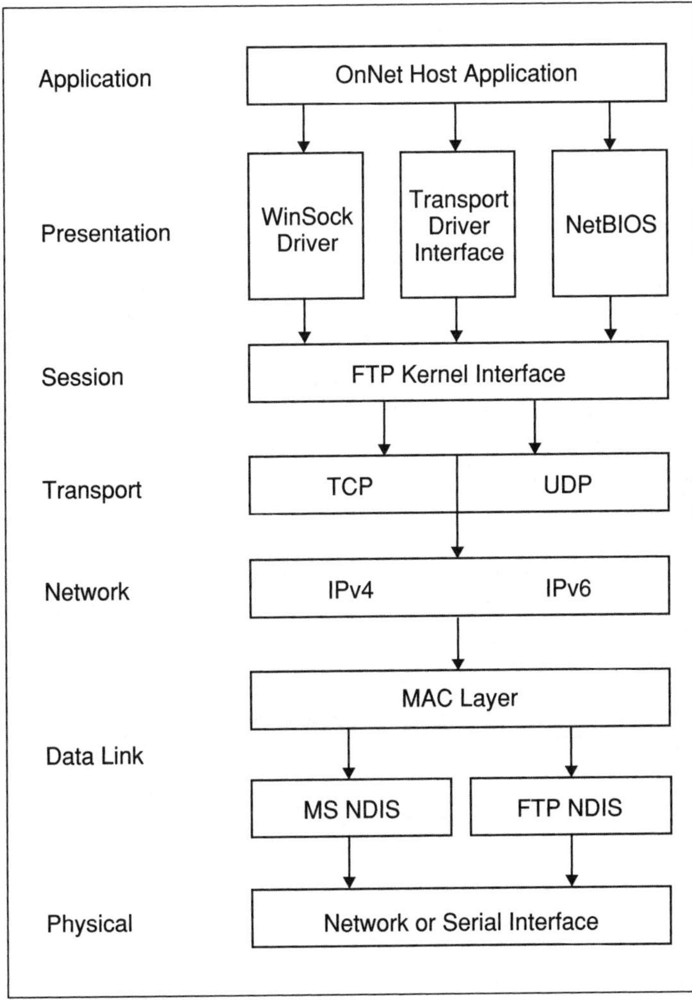

Figure 2-4b Kernel and OnNet Host Suite Architecture
(Courtesy of FTP Software, Inc.)

The OnNet Kernel and Host Suite may be installed together, or the Host Suite applications can be installed over other industry-standard TCP/IP stacks such as Windows 95 and Windows NT. The Kernel supports both IP version 4 and IP version 6, for users that are migrating to the next generation Internet Protocol. Some of the key features of the Host Suite include: full-featured TN3270, TN5250, and VT terminal emulators; an FTP server with both password and NIS authentication; an FTP client; the KEYview File Viewer, used to view, print, and convert popular file formats; InterDrive Client, an NFS version 3.0 client which connects from that workstation to Network File System servers for remote file and printer service; a Custom Install Manager, which allows the network administrator to easily install the network applications that are appropriate for each end user; plus network utilities such as IP Trace, Ping, Query, Retriever, and Network Time.

Since each network application is different, you should do some hands-on comparison shopping before committing to one of these TCP/IP software products on a company wide basis. In general, consider first the workstation software platform (e.g., DOS, OS/2, Windows, UNIX), then the support for your particular LAN hardware (e.g., IBM, 3Com, etc.). A closely related issue is the workstation software and hardware driver's support for your LAN operating system (e.g., VINES or NetWare). Next, look for specific features and the degree to which the product supports them. For file transfers using FTP, consider whether both FTP client and server functions are necessary and available. (Some products support the FTP client function, but not the FTP server.) For remote host access with terminal emulation requirements (TELNET), verify the type of terminal you need to emulate, such as DEC VT-100 or IBM 3278, then check the degree of support. For instance, does it offer a remappable keyboard, non-English characters, and so on. If electronic mail (SMTP) is necessary, look at the client/server capabilities. Most products offer client support, but few provide the host side. Other features that may be important include: developer's kits for writing custom applications; related products from the same manufacturer, such as an OS/2 or Windows version with a similar user interface; and ICMP network testing capabilities, such as the PING function. Table 2-1 provides a brief checklist to use when comparing different TCP/IP software packages.

TABLE 2-1 WORKSTATION INTERNET REQUIREMENTS

Workstation type ______________

Workstation operating system ______________ version ______________

Network interface type ______________

Network operating system ______________ version ______________

File Service Requirements

FTP client ______________

FTP server ______________

NFS client ______________

NFS server ______________

Electronic Mail Requirements

SMTP client ______________

SMTP server ______________

POP2/POP3 ______________

MIME ______________

Mail reader ______________

Remote Host Access Requirements

TELNET client ______________

TELNET server______________

DIGITAL emulation ______________ Terminal type ______________

IBM emulation ______________ Terminal type ______________

Network Diagnostic/Management Requirements

PING ______________

Finger ______________

SNMP agent ______________

SNMP manager ______________

Network Interface Requirements

NDIS ______________ Frame Relay ______________

ODI ______________ SMDS ______________

Packet Driver ______________ ATM ______________

SLIP ______________ Other ______________

PPP ______________

X.25 ______________

ISDN ______________

DSL ______________

2.6 Internet Support within Macintosh Workstations

A few years ago, because both the Macintosh and UNIX hosts existed in their own isolated worlds, it would have been hard to imagine connecting them. TCP/IP has solved that problem, however, as there are several alternatives that permit Mac and UNIX connectivity. One solution is to install the AppleTalk protocol suite on a UNIX platform. Another connectivity solution is to use a Datagram Delivery Protocol (DDP)-to-IP router. A third solution involves a combination of several packages: MacTCP from Apple Computer, Inc., application software from third-party developers, and the DDP-to-IP router.

MacTCP is a software driver written by Apple Computer for the Macintosh operating system (see Figure 2-5a). This package is recommended by Apple for systems with MacOS 6.*x* and 7.0.*x* installed, and for MacOS 7.1 installations in low RAM configurations. MacTCP provides functionality at the OSI Network and Transport layers, and relies on other vendor products for both the physical connectivity at the lower layers and the applications at the upper layers. MacTCP may also rely on the support of a DDP-to-IP router to send/receive the appropriate DDP packets or IP datagrams. MacTCP implements the following protocols: IP, ICMP, UDP, ARP, RARP, BOOTP, and TCP. These protocols provide the communication services that the higher layer Session, Presentation, and Application functions require. The product contains interfaces for C and assembly language to facilitate the writing of application programs. Reference [2-17] provides further details on MacTCP.

Apple's latest TCP/IP solution is called Open Transport, and it is recommended on all systems with MacOS 7.*x* that meet the minimum configuration requirements. Over time, Open Transport is designed to replace MacTCP.

Open Transport incorporates Mentat Portable STREAMS (MPS), developed by Mentat, Inc. (Los Angeles, California). MPS is a version of the UNIX System V Release 4 STREAMS environment (see Figure 2-5b). The incorporation of MPS into Open Transport provides a reliable platform for protocol development. MPS is the same implementation of STREAMS that is found in other industry-standard UNIX implementations, and it also allows easy porting of third-party protocols from other platforms.

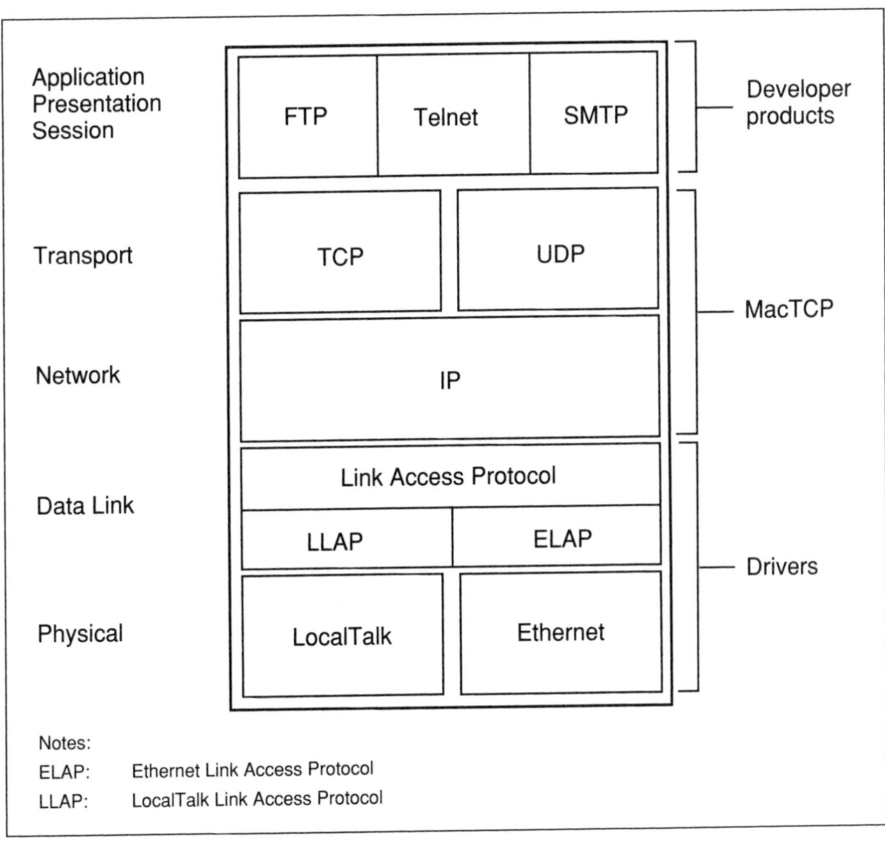

Figure 2-5a Comparing MacTCP with OSI
(Courtesy of Apple Computer, Inc.)

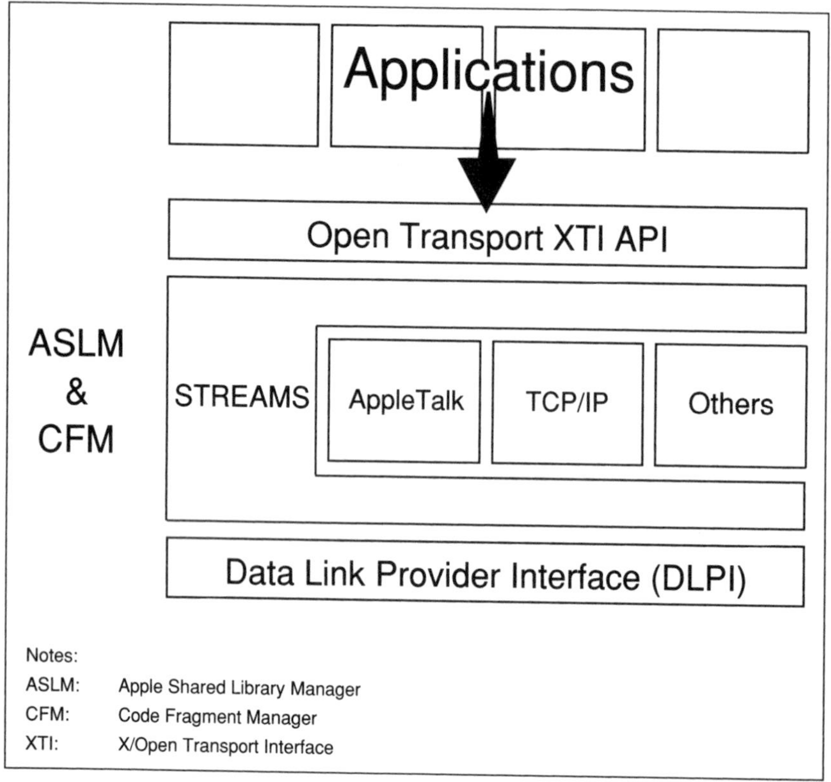

Figure 2-5b Open Transport Architecture (Courtesy of Apple Computer, Inc.)

Apple's Open Transport/TCP is a 32-bit stack that adds support for: dynamic path maximum transfer unit (MTU) discovery; the Dynamic Host Configuration Protocol (DHCP) for centralized address configuration management; IP multicast, which allows clients to participate on the MBone (multicast backbone); support for TCP Urgent Pointer semantics; support for both Ethernet version 2 and IEEE 802.3 framing; and other enhancements. References [2-18] and [2-19] provide details on Open Transport.

Apple Computer (Cupertino, California), Distinct Corporation (Saratoga, California), eSoft (Aurora, Colorado), FreeMail (Missoula, Montana), Mentat, Inc. (Los Angeles, California), Quarterdeck (Marina del Rey, California), Sonic Systems (Sunnyvale, California), and Synergy Software (Reading, Pennsylvania) are among the vendors that offer Macintosh-based TCP/IP solutions. Reference [2-20] provides details on Apple Computer's networking strategies.

2.7 Internet Support within LAN Operating Systems

Traditionally, LANs have been used for print and file sharing and, occasionally, for remote access to another system. The internetworking capabilities of those systems have only become significant in the last few years, and the TCP/IP protocols have become the solution to many connectivity challenges. Let's look at the effect this has had on the software architecture of the LAN.

If we consider the architecture of a typical LAN, we could divide the OSI Reference Model's seven layers into several functional groups (see Figure 2-6). To begin, the typical LAN consists of hardware (Layers 1 and 2) and the operating system (Layers 5 through 7). The Network and Transport layers in between provide internetwork connectivity. These functions include routing the packet through the internetwork (the Network Layer function) and ensuring that it gets there reliably (the Transport Layer function). If we only wanted a local network (not internetwork) function, we could design some mechanism to allow the operating system to communicate directly with the hardware. Developers of network operating systems, such as Banyan Systems Inc. (Westboro, Massachusetts), IBM (Austin, Texas), Novell Inc. (Provo, Utah), and Microsoft Corp. (Redmond, Washington), anticipated the need to internetwork LANs and built the required Network and Transport Layer functions into their operating systems. Banyan incorporates the VINES Internet Protocol (VIP) for the Network Layer and either the Sequenced Packet Protocol (SPP) or the VINES Interprocess Communications Protocol (VICP) at the Transport Layer of VINES. Novell built the internetworking capabilities of NetWare version 4.1 on the Internetwork Packet Exchange (IPX) Protocol and either the Sequenced Packet Exchange (SPX) or the NetWare Core Protocol (NCP) for the Transport Layer, and then migrated these proprietary protocols to IP in NetWare version 5. Microsoft's Windows NT uses the NetBIOS Extended User Interface (NetBEUI) for the Network and Transport Layer functions, with the option to use IP and TCP at these layers, respectively.

To run TCP/IP over a LAN, you can either replace the existing Network/Transport Layer software with TCP/IP or send the TCP/IP information inside existing Network and Transport Layer protocols, a process known as *encapsulation.* If you replace the existing protocols, you must devise a mechanism to allow higher layer protocols to communicate with the LAN hardware, such as the Ethernet board. A software interface that resides at the upper portion of the Data Link Layer provides this link. It also eliminates the need for each higher layer protocol stack to have its own hardware driver. In other words, the higher layers talk to the driver, and the driver talks to the hardware. Since the driver specifications are published, everyone's work is simpler.

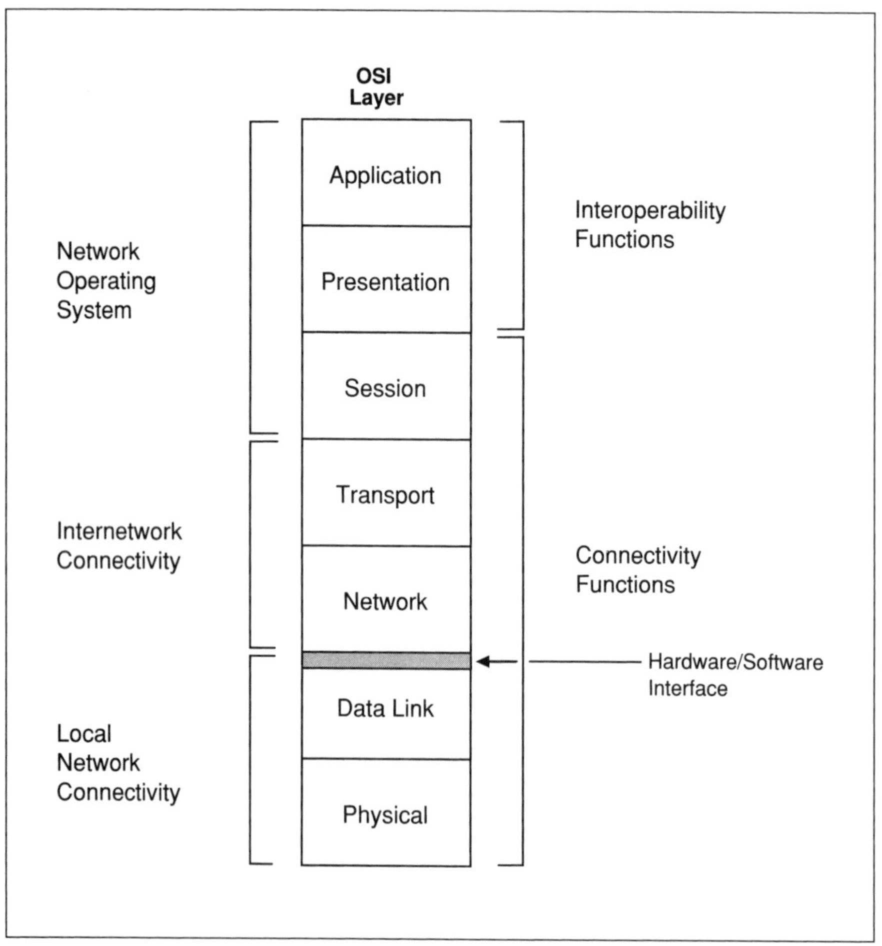

Figure 2-6 LAN and Internetwork Connectivity within the OSI Framework

Three such interfaces are widely used. The first is the Packet Drivers, which were originally specified by FTP Software and further developed at Brigham Young University (Provo, Utah), Clarkson University (Potsdam, New York), and Columbia University (New York, New York), among others. (Reference [2-21] discusses these drivers in detail. Some of these drivers are included in the Crynwr Packet Driver Collection; see Reference [2-22] for further information.)

The second interface is the Network Driver Interface Specification (NDIS) developed by 3Com Corp. (Santa Clara, California) and Microsoft and released as part of OS/2 LAN Manager [2-23]. The NDIS contains two components: a Medium Access Control (MAC) driver communicates with the LAN hardware and a protocol driver communicates with the higher layers. The NDIS insulates developers of higher layer software from the need to write drivers for each type of hardware in use. The third interface, the Open Data Link Interface (ODI), comes from Novell [2-24]. Similar to both the Crynwr drivers and the NDIS, ODI provides a logical link between hardware and software.

Returning to Figure 2-6, note the drivers' function. They reside at the upper portion of the Data Link Layer, providing a way for the Internet protocol stack (i.e., TCP/IP plus applications) or the network operating system (e.g., NetWare) to access the hardware.

The second way to use TCP/IP over a LAN is to use both the native NOS protocols and TCP/IP at the Network and Transport Layers. The NOS protocols (e.g., VINES VIP and VSPP) remain in place and the Internet information (e.g., FTP/TCP/IP) is encapsulated within the VINES packet. This process is known as *tunneling* since the native protocols create a tunnel through which the data from the other protocol stack (i.e., TCP/IP) can pass. This tunnel is created by treating the Internet protocols as data within the packet created by the native network OS protocols. We'll see an example of encapsulation in the next section.

Now that we have a background in the ways that LAN operating systems support the Internet protocols, let's study Banyan Systems' VINES, IBM's OS/2 WARP, Microsoft's Windows NT, and Novell's NetWare in more detail.

2.7.1 Banyan Systems' VINES

Banyan Systems Inc.'s VINES was one of the first network operating systems to incorporate both LAN and WAN protocols (see Figure 2-7a). VINES offers particularly strong support for these protocols at the OSI Physical and Data Link Layers. These layers offer the High-level Data Link Control (HDLC) protocol and ITU-T X.25 for access to Packet Switched Public Data Networks (PSPDNs), plus asynchronous transmission. The VINES applications include file access, printing, and electronic mail. A number of third-party products (shown on the left-hand side of the figure) are also available. VINES version 5.0 added the AppleTalk protocol stack (shown on the right-hand side of the figure). Another integral part of the VINES architecture is support for the Internet protocols, including ARP/RARP, IP, ICMP, TCP, and UDP. VINES also supports the usual applications, such as FTP, TELNET, and so on, using third-party packages.

Banyan offers two alternatives for TCP/IP and VINES integration [2-25]. The first is the TCP/IP Routing Option, which allows the VINES server to route TCP/IP traffic between non-VINES (i.e., foreign) hosts (see Figure 2-7b). In other words, the VINES server is acting as an IP router. In this case, the VINES server contains both the VINES and the TCP/IP protocol stacks and participates in the TCP/IP internetwork. To illustrate how this works, we'll trace a message from Host 1 to Host 2. Host 1 generates the message (shown as User Data), adds the appropriate IP and TCP headers, accesses LAN 1, then builds a transmission frame with the appropriate Data Link Layer (DLL) header and trailer. When that frame arrives at VINES Server 1, the server encapsulates the IP datagram within a VINES IP packet by adding the VINES IP header information necessary to route the packet through the VINES network. When the distant server (VINES Server 2) receives the packet, it removes the VINES IP header, and the IP header routes the packet to its destination host.

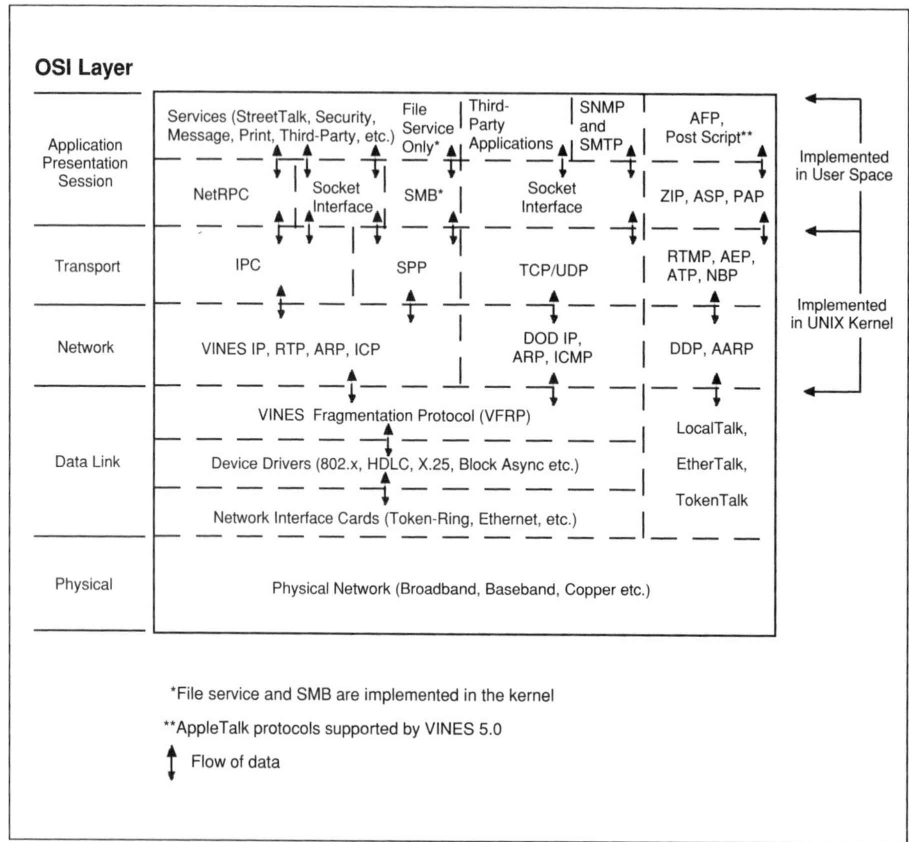

Figure 2-7a Banyan Elements (Server Side)
(Courtesy of Banyan Systems, Inc.)

The Routing Option is also capable of routing TCP/IP in and out of the server without any encapsulation. For example, suppose that a VINES server was the gateway to a Cisco Systems router used for access to the Internet. A user wishing to connect to the Internet could access the VINES server, which would communicate across the LAN to the Cisco router, which in turn would connect to the Internet service provider. In this case, all communication is native TCP/IP, and the VINES server is functioning solely as an IP router.

The second alternative is the VINES TCP/IP Server-to-Server option, shown in Figure 2-7c. This option allows VINES StreetTalk for Windows NT and Banyan ENS servers to route VINES traffic through an IP internetwork. (ENS is Banyan's Enterprise Network Services, which are services that are independent of VINES which run on other operating systems, such as IBM's AIX, Hewlett-Packard's HP-UX, Novell's NetWare, SunSoft's Solaris, and others.) In this case, the VINES server maps the VINES IP address of the desired destination host to an IP address that will

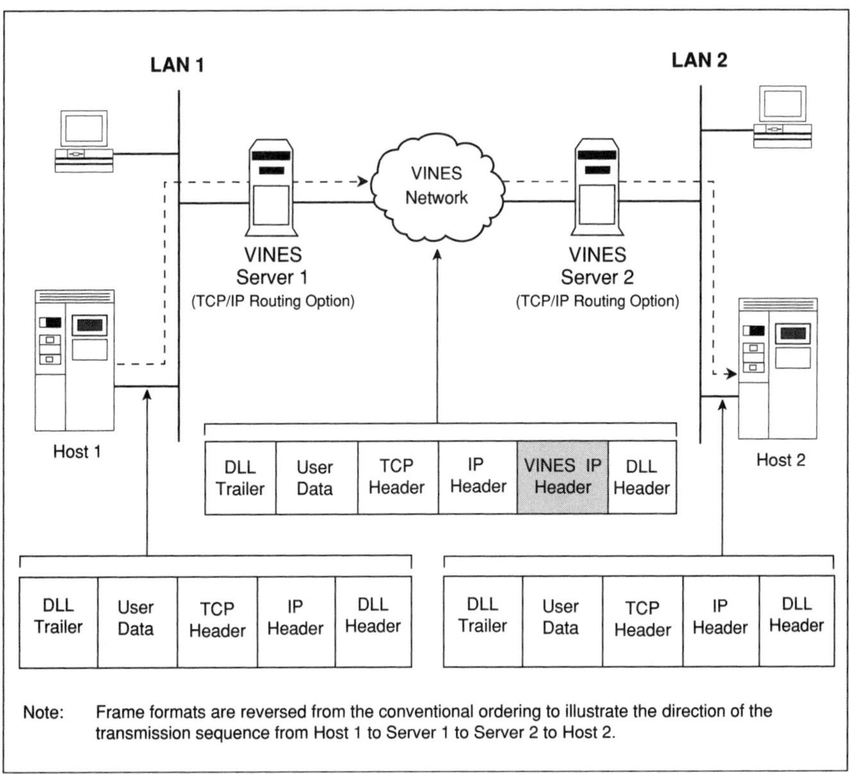

Figure 2-7b VINES TCP/IP Routing Option Encapsulation (Courtesy of Banyan Systems, Inc.)

allow for packet delivery. A message originating at VINES Server 1 would be in the VINES IP (proprietary) packet format. VINES Server 2 translates the VINES IP destination address to an ARPA IP destination address, adds the IP header, and sends the newly generated IP datagram to the IP internetwork. (In the case where one or both servers communicating via the Server-to-Server option is a StreetTalk for Windows NT server, the VINES IP packet is encapsulated with both UDP and IP. Reviewing Figure 2-7c, this configuration would add a UDP header between the IP header and the VINES IP header.) Once inside the IP internetwork, IP datagram may pass through a number of other routers. At the exit point from the IP internetwork, the VINES server (shown as Server 3) will remove the IP header (and also the UDP header, if StreetTalk for Windows NT was employed), and deliver the reconstructed VINES packet to its destination, VINES Server 4.

Reference [2-26] provides additional details on VINES protocols and their implementation, and Reference [2-27] provides further information on all Banyan products.

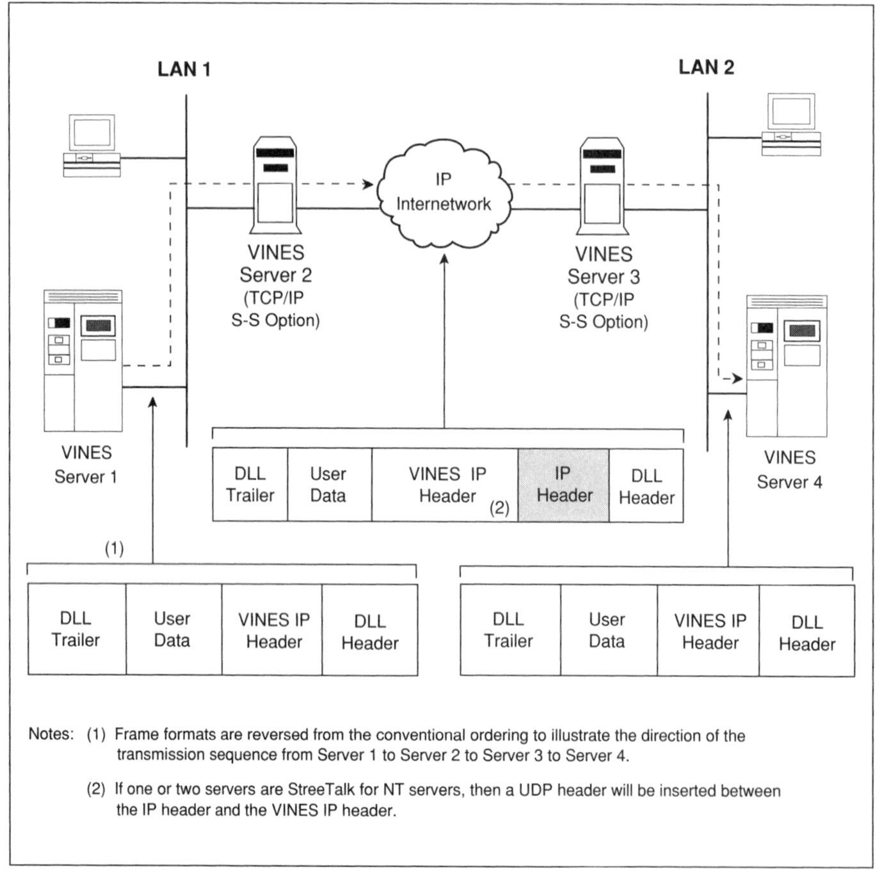

Figure 2-7c VINES TCP/IP Server-to-Server Option Encapsulation (Courtesy of Banyan Systems, Inc.)

2.7.2 IBM's LAN Server, OS/2 WARP, and OS/2 WARP Server

IBM's LAN Server 4.0, OS/2 WARP 4, and OS/2 WARP Server provide a TCP/IP protocol stack in a package called Multiple Protocols Transport Services (MPTS), shown in Figure 2-8a. In addition to the TCP/IP protocol, MPTS provides: NetBIOS, IEEE 802.2, LAN Virtual Device Driver (VDD), and NetWare Requester for OS/2 support.

MPTS provides a comprehensive solution to interconnecting LANs. The architecture is aimed at providing a general solution for interconnecting network applications by providing a protocol-independent transport interface for network applications, called Common Transport Semantics (CTS), and a hardware independent interface, called Network Driver Interface Specification (NDIS), for transport protocols.

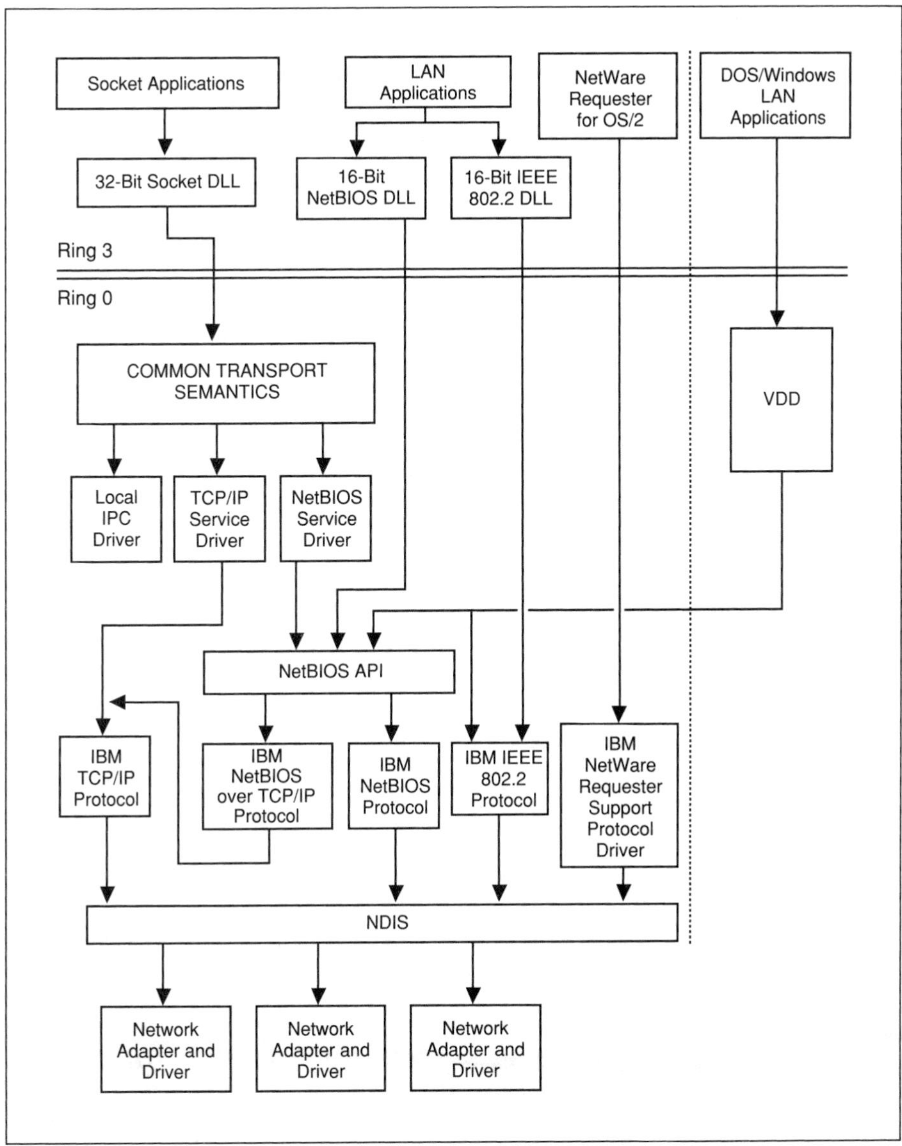

Figure 2-8a Functional Components of MPTS
(Reprinted by permission from MPTS Configuration Guide S10H-9693-00 © by International Business Machines Corporation)

CTS provides an interface so that applications and higher layer protocols written for a particular transport interface can be carried over another transport protocol with no apparent changes (see Figure 2-8b). This interface is provided via the socket programming interface and allows the socket applications to communicate using Local Inter-Process Communication (LIPC), TCP/IP, or NetBIOS protocols. A comprehensive introduction to MPTN is found in IBM's *Multi-Protocol Transport Networking Architecture, Tutorial and Product Implementations* [2-28].

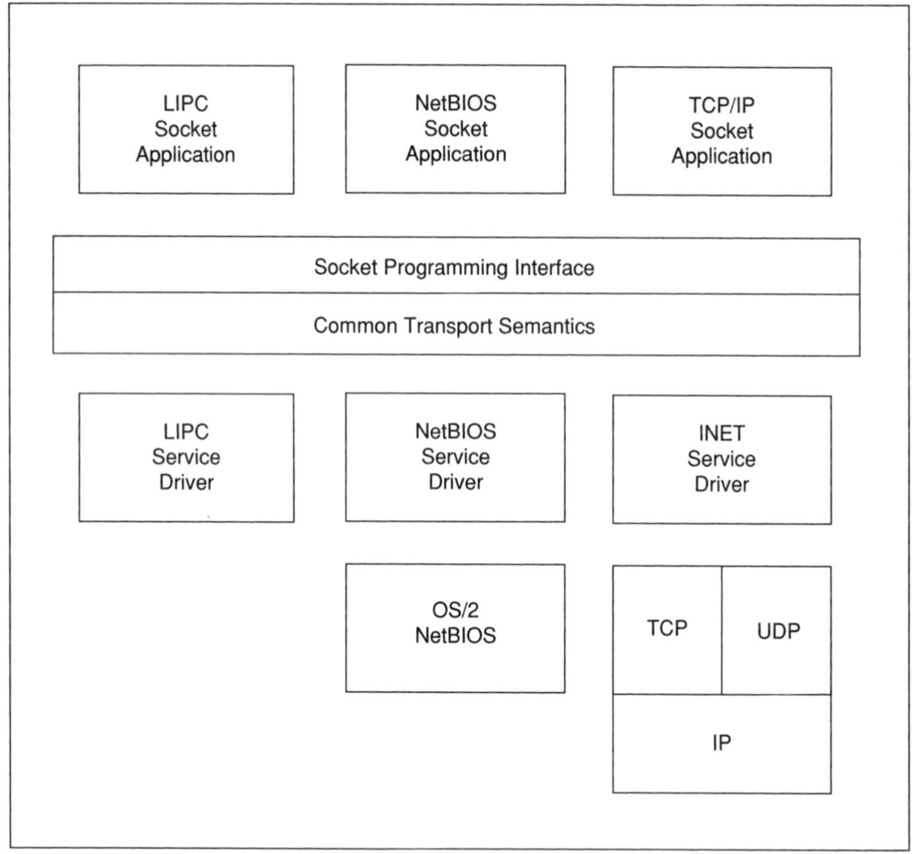

Figure 2-8b Common Transport Interface
(Reprinted by permission from MPTS Configuration Guide S10H-9693-00 © by International Business Machines Corporation)

The 3Com Corporation and Microsoft Corporation jointly developed NDIS as an interface that would allow any NDIS-compliant protocol stack to talk to any NDIS-compliant LAN or WAN adapter driver. NDIS has become an industry standard that provides a common open interface, allowing protocol stacks from different manufacturers to communicate with a variety of hardware adapters (review Figure 2-8a). The IBM NetWare Requester Support protocol driver allows an NDIS-compliant adapter driver to communicate with a protocol stack that complies with the Novell Open Data Link Interface (ODI) specification.

The MPTS provides the TCP/IP protocol suite and also those utilities necessary to configure and run TCP/IP applications. You will find TCP, UDP, IP, ARP, RARP, ICMP, and SNMP protocols in MPTS. There is support for SLIP, PPP, and LAN network interface connections. NetBIOS over TCP/IP (RFCs 1001, 1002) is supplied by MPTS for running NetBIOS applications across the Internet (see Figure 2-8c). The left-hand portion of that figure shows how NetBIOS is structured. ACSNETB.DLL provides the NetBIOS API for Ring 3 applications. NetBIOS.OS2 processes Ring 3 NetBIOS commands and also provides a Ring 0 interface for device drivers. (The terms Ring 0 and Ring 3 refer to Intel 286 and later CPU security levels, where Ring 0 is the most privileged level and Ring 3 is the least privileged level.) NETBEUI.OS2 is an LM10 (LAN Manager version 1.0) NetBIOS protocol driver, supporting this API and implementing the protocol. The right-hand portion of Figure 2-8c shows how this structure is easily modified to support NetBIOS over TCP/IP. TCPBEUI.OS2 is an LM10 protocol driver that transfers data using sockets rather than binding directly to a MAC driver for data transfers. Since NetBIOS.OS2 can bind to multiple LM10 API protocol drivers, it is an easy matter to configure both NETBEUI.OS2 and TCPBEUI.OS2 on your workstation.

TCP/IP Version 4.1 for OS/2 WARP provides a large portfolio of different TCP/IP tools and programs, and is available for the OS/2 WARP family of products. Its capabilities include: arp, assist, finger, host, hostname, ifconfig, ifolder, inetcfg, inetver, ipformat, iptrace, linkup, makeidx, netstat, nslookup, ping, ppp, route, sendmail, slattach, slcfg, slip, sliphold, slipkill, slipmsg, slipterm, tracerte, and update to name just some of them. FTP, FTPPM, TELNET, TN3270, PMANT, LPR, REXEC, and TFTP are there, and you'll also find more recent Internet applications for navigating and surfing the Web, such as the IBM WEB Explorer, NEWS/Reader, and Gopher. Good references for all of IBM's TCP/IP suite are Tyson's *Navigating the Internet with OS/2 Warp* [2-29], and IBM's "Redbook" series of publications [2-30].

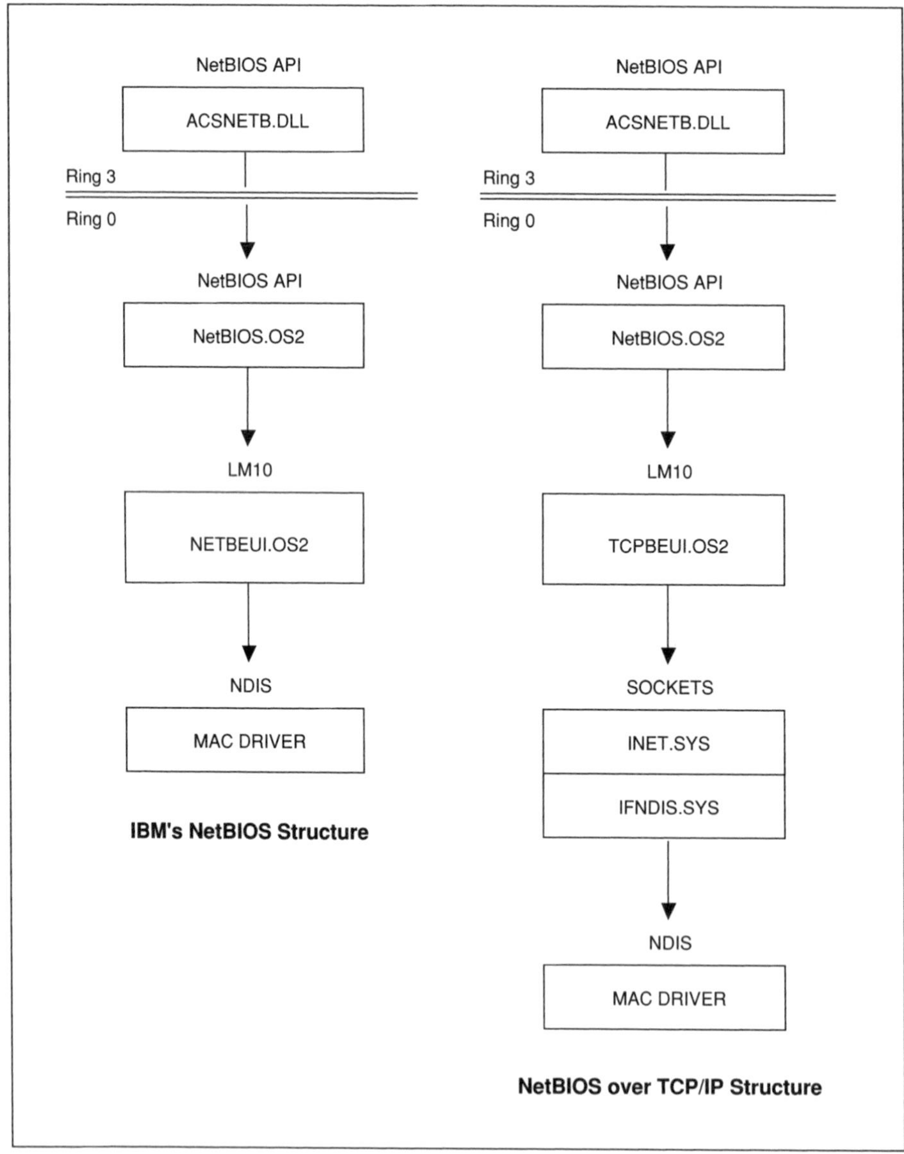

Figure 2-8c IBM's NetBIOS over TCP/IP
(Reprinted by permission from MPTS Configuration Guide S10H-9693-00 © by International Business Machines Corporation)

2.7.3 Microsoft's Windows NT

Microsoft Corporation of Redmond, Washington, perhaps best known for its desktop operating systems and applications, has developed a parallel strength in network operating systems. Microsoft included a TCP/IP protocol stack within LAN Manager 2.1 (shipped in 1991), and has continued to support the Internet protocols in the Windows 95/98 and the Windows NT Client and Server products.

The Microsoft TCP/IP architecture builds on the Windows NT networking model, which contains two key interfaces (Figure 2-9a). The NDIS interface isolates the network adapter cards or other network hardware from the transport protocols. This interface allows any NDIS-compatible transport protocol stack, such as TCP/IP, IPX/SPX (via Microsoft's NWLink software), or the NetBIOS Extended User Interface (NetBEUI), to communicate with a number of LAN or WAN hardware interfaces. Similarly, the Transport Driver Interface (TDI) provides an interface at the Session layer for upper layer protocols and application communication. Figure 2-9b illustrates how the various TCP/IP components use the Network Driver and Transport Device Interfaces for communication.

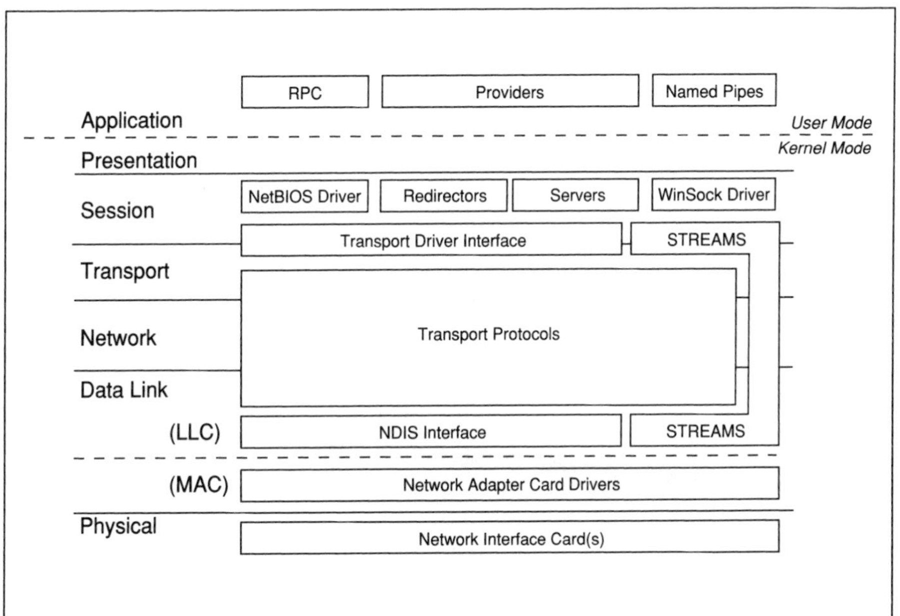

Figure 2-9a Windows NT Networking Model
(From Windows NT Server Networking Guide. Copyright ©1996, Microsoft Corporation. Reprinted with permission of Microsoft Press. All rights reserved.)

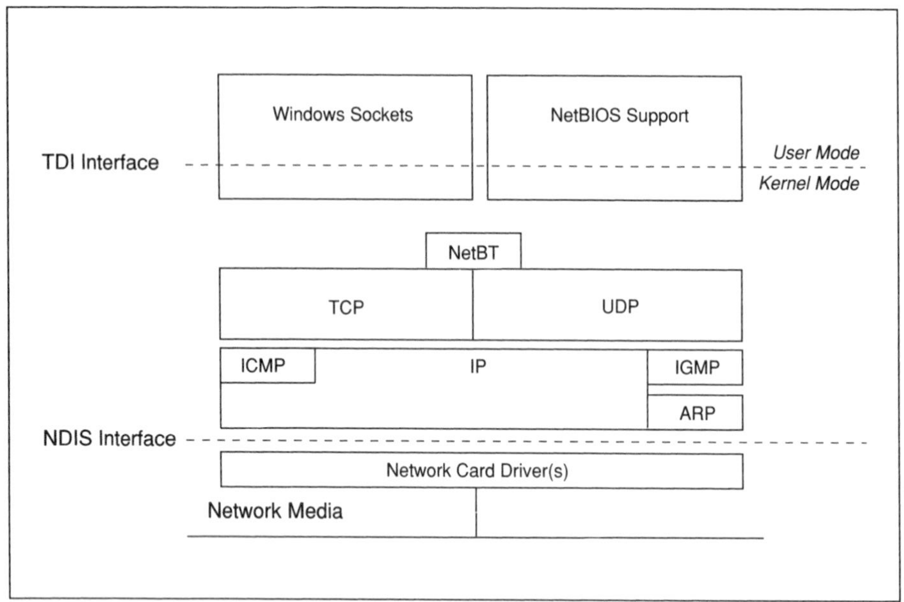

Figure 2-9b Architectural Model of Windows NT with TCP/IP
(From Windows NT Server Networking Guide. Copyright ©1996, Microsoft Corporation. Reprinted with permission of Microsoft Press. All rights reserved.)

Internet protocols that are included in the basic architecture are IP, ICMP, ARP, IGMP, TCP, and UDP. For remote access applications, the Point-to-Point Protocol (PPP) and Serial Line IP (SLIP) are also included, and for virtual private remote networks, the Point-to-Point Tunneling Protocol (PPTP) is used. Support for Application Programming Interfaces (APIs) includes NetBIOS support over TCP/IP (NetBT) and Windows Sockets for network programming. Connectivity services include support for FTP, TFTP, TELNET, FINGER, RCP, REXEC, and RSH. Diagnostic utilities include ARP, HOSTNAME, IPCONFIG, NBSTAT, NETSTAT, NSLOOKUP, PING, ROUTE, and TRACERT. Other key functions include: the Windows Internet Name Service (WINS), used for NetBIOS name resolution services; the Domain Name System (DNS) for host and domain name resolution; and the Dynamic Host Configuration Protocol (DHCP). An SNMP agent is also available to facilitate the management of the Windows NT workstation by a network management console.

Support for DHCP and WINS, two Windows NT functions, lessens certain administrative burdens associated with managing a large TCP/IP-based internet. With DHCP, IP addresses are managed by a server, which leases them to clients for a specified duration of time. When a client workstation boots, it broadcasts a DHCP DISCOVER message on the local network. DHCP servers respond with a DHCP OFFER message, which contains proposed configuration information. A response from the client with a DHCP REQUEST message to one of the servers acknowledges the parameters, with the selected server then finalizing the transaction with the DHCP ACK message. WINS is also designed for administrative purposes. It provides a distributed database for registering and querying mappings of computer names and IP addresses. Thus, administration, allocation, and configuration of IP addresses is more automated, relieving the human network administrator of these tasks.

A great deal of literature has been published detailing the capabilities of Windows NT. Reference [2-31] is available from Microsoft, and the Microsoft Developer Network (MSDN) [2-32] is an online source of further information.

2.7.4 Novell's NetWare

In releasing NetWare version 5 in mid-1998, Novell, Inc. has recognized the importance of the Internet protocols in a significant way. Previous versions of NetWare incorporated Novell's Internetwork Packet Exchange (IPX) and Sequenced Packet Exchange (SPX) protocols, which were based on the Xerox Network Systems (XNS) protocol suite. In contrast, NetWare 5 makes the Internet Protocol its transport of choice, while still allowing backward compatibility for IPX-based applications from previous versions of NetWare. Novell offered several reasons for the significant change in their architecture [2-33], such as:

- For routed environments, consolidating into one protocol (such as IP) instead of several (IP, IPX, etc.) saves on both hardware and software expenses.
- Bandwidth can be used more efficiently (for example, broadcast messages from multiple protocols are no longer necessary).
- Support for only one client protocol is required, thus reducing operating costs.
- Connectivity with other IP-based solutions, such as remote access products, is facilitated.

Recognizing that its clients are not likely to migrate from an IPX-based internetwork to an IP-based internetwork immediately, Novell has developed the Compatibility Mode architecture (see Figure 2-10a) which enables previous and current versions of NetWare to coexist. Three different technologies are incorporated into Compatibility Mode. First, all existing NetWare Core Protocol (NCP) applications have been moved to run over IP (shown in the center of Figure 2-10a). Thus, NCP messages will be encapsulated within IP datagrams, not within IPX packets as before. Second, a Bindery Gateway allows for backward compatibility with the NetWare bindery (shown on the right-hand side of Figure 2-10a). Third, a technology called the Migration Gateway, which is a NetWare Loadable Module that runs on a NetWare 5 server, provides for required protocol translations (see Figure 2-10b).

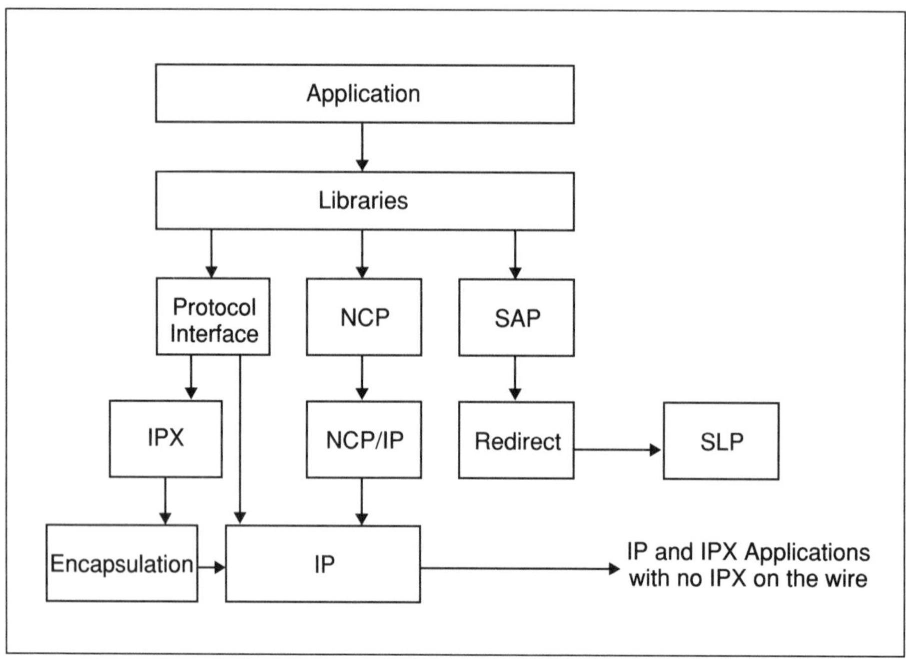

Figure 2-10a IP Compatibility Mode
(Courtesy of Novell, Inc.)

The Migration Gateway provides two types of protocol translations. The first translation converts between IPX packets and IP packets. When an IPX packet needs to be sent on an IP segment, the IPX packet is encapsulated inside IP. The second translation converts between the different naming and discovery services: the Service Advertising Protocol (SAP), which runs on the IPX segment; and the Service Location Protocol (SLP), which runs on the IP segment. The Migration Gateway uses both IPX and IP addresses, as well as routing information that is contained in the IPX packets, to ensure correct packet delivery.

Other key features within NetWare 5 that support the Internet protocols include the Dynamic Host Configuration Protocol (DHCP), the Domain Name Services (DNS), the Network Time Protocol (NTP), IP Security (IPSec), the Secure Socket Layer, and support for IP version 6. Thus, Novell customers can continue to use their installed base of existing NetWare applications while migrating to the Internet Protocol that is incorporated into many other local and wide area network configurations. References [2-34] through [2-36] are additional sources of information on Novell's support for TCP/IP within NetWare.

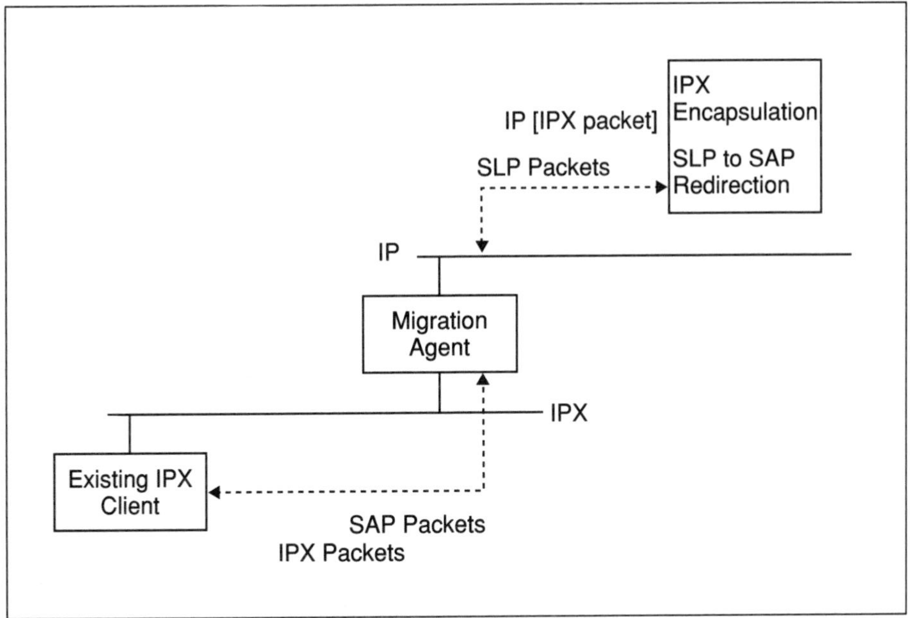

Figure 2-10b Migration Gateway
(Courtesy of Novell, Inc.)

2.8 Internetwork Analysis Tools

In the previous sections of this chapter, we examined the way networks, such as SNA and DECnet, or LAN operating systems, such as NetWare and VINES, support the Internet protocol suite. From such discussions, we can conclude that we're dealing with complex scenarios, such as encapsulating an IP datagram within a VINES packet and transmitting that packet over an X.25 link to another VINES network. When all goes well, the internetwork manager is a hero. But what happens when something fails?

Internetwork failures call for three things: well-trained analysts, the correct analysis tool, and a quick response. Fortunately, the TCP/IP protocol suite is considered "standard equipment" among analyzer vendors, as testimony to the popularity of these protocols. The key task for the analyst is to review the various products available and select one that satisfies both technical and budgetary constraints. As a starting point, RFC 1470 [2-37] presents a number of these tools for consideration. Readers wishing to solicit bids from various analyzer manufacturers can use Table 2-2 to survey vendors about their support for available LAN, MAN, and WAN interfaces and Internet protocols.

TABLE 2-2 EVALUATING TCP/IP PROTOCOL ANALYZERS

Date ____________________

Vendor ____________________

Address ____________________

City, State, Zip ____________________

Phone ____________________

Fax ____________________

Contact Person ____________________

Model Number ____________________

Base Price ____________________

Price as Optioned ____________________

Interfaces Supported

AppleTalk ______	Frame Relay ______
ARCNET ______	IEEE 802.3 ______
ATM ______	IEEE 802.5 ______
Ethernet ______	SMDS ______
FDDI ______	Other ______

Internet Protocols Supported

ARP/RARP ______	NetBIOS ______
BGP ______	NFS ______
BOOTP ______	OSPF ______
CMIP/CMOT ______	RIP ______
DHCP ______	SMTP ______
DNS ______	SNAP ______
FTP ______	SNMP ______
IPv4 ______	TCP ______
IPv6 ______	TELNET ______
ICMP ______	UDP ______

2.9 Looking Ahead

So far, we've surveyed the Internet protocols, studied how different vendors implement them, and looked at analysis tools. In subsequent chapters, we will study the protocols in more depth and will look at case studies of the protocols in use taken from actual internetworks. For consistency, we've detailed all case studies using trace files from the Network Associates, Inc. (Menlo Park, CA) *Sniffer* protocol analyzer. We will structure our discussion along the lines of the ARPA Internet model. Thus, Chapter 3 will consider the Network Interface Layer, Chapter 4 the Internet Layer, and so on. Now the real work begins.

2.10 References

[2-1] Reichard, Kevin, and Eric F. Johnson. *UNIX in Plain English.* MIS Press (New York, NY), 1994.

[2-2] Krol, E. "The Hitchhiker's Guide to the Internet." RFC 1118, September 1989.

[2-3] Frost, Lyle. "Bridging Networks." *UNIX Review* (May 1991): 46–52.

[2-4] Giles, Roosevelt. "UNIX and PC Network Connectivity." *Network VAR* (October 1995): 40–46.

[2-5] Foley, John. "The Unix World." *Information Week* (October 16, 1995): 52–61.

[2-6] Rose, Marshall T., and Dwight E. Cass. "ISO Transport Service on Top of the TCP – Version 3." RFC 1006, May 1987.

[2-7] Pouffary, Y. "ISO Transport Class 2 Non-use of Explicit Flow Control over TCP – RFC 1006 Extension." RFC 1859, October 1995.

[2-8] Pouffary, Y., and A. Young. "ISO Transport Service on Top of TCP (ITOT)." RFC 2126, March 1997.

[2-9] Gasiewski, Donna. "DECnet, Revised and Revisited." *Digital Age* (formerly *DEC Professional*), (May 1995): 24–30.

[2-10] Cini, Al. "DECnet and TCP/IP: Over Easy." *Digital Age* (formerly *DEC Professional*) (April 1995): 37–39.

[2-11] Pouffary, Yanick, and Robert Watson. "DECnet over TCP/IP: Avoiding the Applications vs. Network Traps." Digital Systems Report (Fall 1997): 9–14. (This report is published by Computer Economics, Inc., `http://www.computereconomics.com`.)

[2-12] Current information on Compaq Computer Corp.'s line of Digital Equipment Corp. products may be found on `http://www.digital.com`.

[2-13] Malamud, Carl. *Analyzing DECnet/OSI Phase V.* Van Nostrand Reinhold (New York, NY), 1991.

[2-14] IBM. *TCP/IP Tutorial and Technical Overview,* Fifth edition, Document number GG24-3376-04. Prentice Hall (Upper Saddle River, NJ), 1995.

[2-15] Current information on IBM's desktop software offerings is available at: `http://www.software.ibm.com/os/warp/swchoice`.

[2-16] Current information on FTP Software Inc.'s products is available at: `http://www.ftp.com`.

[2-17] Apple Computer, Inc. *Apple MacTCP Administrator's Guide,* 1989.

[2-18] Apple Computer, Inc. *Apple Open Transport Reference Q & A. Version 2.3*, October 1996.

[2-19] Apple Computer, Inc. *Open Transport User's Guide.* Document U95600-024A, 1996.

[2-20] Kohlhepp, Robert J. "Apple's Mac OS 8.1: Networking Per Usual." Network Computing (March 1, 1998): 44.

[2-21] Romkey, John, and Sharon Fisher. "Under the Hood: Packet Drivers." BYTE (May 1991): 297–303.

[2-22] For information on the Crynwr packet drivers, contact `info@crynwr.com`. The packet drivers are archived at: `ftp://ftp.crnwr.com/drivers`.

[2-23] Richer, Mark. "Who Needs Universal Network Interface Standards?" Data Communications (September 21, 1990): 71–72.

[2-24] Breidenbach, Susan. "Network Driver Wars: It's NDIS vs. ODI." LAN Times (January 21, 1991): 35.

[2-25] Banyan Systems, Inc. *VINES TCP/IP Option.* Document number 001891, 1992.

[2-26] Banyan Systems, Inc. *VINES Protocol Definition.* Document number 003673, June 1993.

[2-27] Many VINES documents are available on line from the Banyan Systems' Web site: `http://www.banyan.com`.

[2-28] IBM. *Multi-Protocol Transport Networking Architecture, Tutorial and Product Implementations.* Document GG24-4170-00, January 1994.

[2-29] Tyson, Herb. *Navigating the Internet with OS/2 Warp.* SAMS Publishing, 1995.

[2-30] Much of IBM's documentation is contained in the "Red Book" series of publications, available at: `http://www.redbooks.ibm.com`.

[2-31] Microsoft Corp. *Windows NT Server Networking Guide.* Microsoft Press, 1996.

[2-32] Much of the information on Microsoft's networking products is available from the Microsoft Developer Network Web site: http://www.microsoft.com/msdn.

[2-33] Novell, Inc. "Pure IP: Delivering NetWare Services on TCP/IP." January 1998, available at http://www.novell.com/whitepapers/nw5/pureip.html.

[2-34] Mosbarger, Myron. "Comparing Novell's IPX-to-IP Connectivity Solutions: IP Tunneling, NetWare/IP and IP Relay." Novell Application Notes (September 1995): 53–69.

[2-35] Meek, Brian. "Novell TCP/IP Technology." Novell Brainshare 1995 Presentation Book (Volume 9): 52–54.

[2-36] Stearns, Tom. "Novell's IP Gets Real." *Information Week* (March 16, 1998): 52–56.

[2-37] Enger, R., and J. Reynolds. "FYI on a Network Management Tool Catalog: Tools for Monitoring and Debugging TCP/IP Internets and Interconnected Devices." RFC 1470, June 1993.

Chapter 3

Troubleshooting the Network Interface Connection

We will begin our study of TCP/IP analysis by examining problems that can occur at the ARPA architectural model's Network Interface Layer, which makes the connection to local, metropolitan-area, or wide-area networks (as discussed in Section 2.1). The popularity of the Internet protocols has produced RFC (Request for Comments) documents detailing implementations over virtually every type of LAN, MAN, and WAN, including ARCNET, Ethernet, IEEE 802, FDDI, Packet Switched Public Data Networks (PSPDNs) using the ITU-T X.25 protocol, Integrated Services Digital Networks (ISDN) connections, frame relay, Asynchronous Transfer Mode (ATM), and many others.

To connect to LANs, the Network Interface Layer must exist in all hosts and routers, although its implementation may change across the internetwork (see Figure 3-1a). Thus Host A must have a consistent attachment to Router B, but the destination Host Z may be of a different type. In other words, you can start with an Ethernet, traverse a frame relay network, and end with a token ring as long as you maintain pair-wise consistencies.

Figure 3-1b shows the options for the Network Interface Layer and their supporting RFCs. Recall that the higher layer information (e.g., IP, TCP, and so on) is treated as data inside the transmitted frame (see Figure 3-1c). The headers and trailers are defined by the particular LAN or WAN in use, for example, ARCNET, token ring, and so on. Immediately following the Local Network header is the IP header, then the TCP header, and finally, the higher layer application data, which might be FTP, TELNET, and so forth.

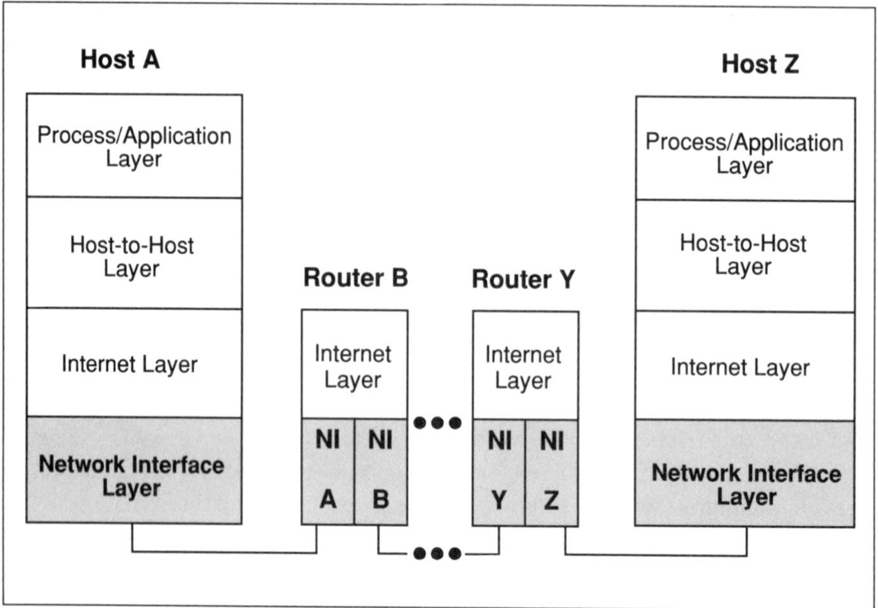

Figure 3-1a The Network Interface Connection

In summary, the TCP segment comprises the TCP header plus the application data. The IP process treats the TCP segment as data, adds the IP header, and produces the IP datagram. The Local Network process adds the frame header and trailer and transmits that frame on the physical network, such as the Ethernet cable or the X.25 link.

In this chapter, we'll study how various Network Interface Layer options support TCP/IP and the constraints on those implementations when they transmit TCP/IP-related information. The case studies in Section 3.13 will illustrate these protocol interactions in detail. A good reference about support for the Network Interface Layer is RFC 1122, "Requirements for Internet Hosts: Communication Layers" [3-1]. We'll begin by examining how ARCNET networks support TCP/IP.

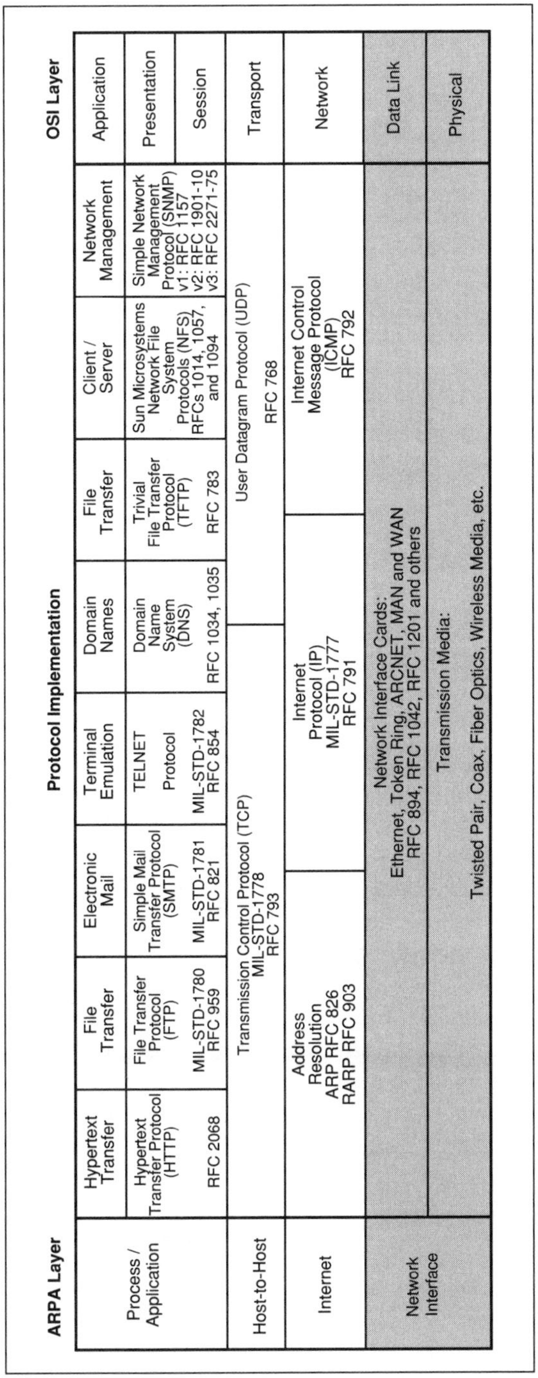

ARPA Layer	Protocol Implementation								OSI Layer
Process / Application	Hypertext Transfer	File Transfer	Electronic Mail	Terminal Emulation	Domain Names	File Transfer	Client / Server	Network Management	Application
	Hypertext Transfer Protocol (HTTP) RFC 2068	File Transfer Protocol (FTP) MIL-STD-1780 RFC 959	Simple Mail Transfer Protocol (SMTP) MIL-STD-1781 RFC 821	TELNET Protocol MIL-STD-1782 RFC 854	Domain Name System (DNS) RFC 1034, 1035	Trivial File Transfer Protocol (TFTP) RFC 783	Sun Microsystems Network File System Protocols (NFS) RFCs 1014, 1057, and 1094	Simple Network Management Protocol (SNMP) v1: RFC 1157 v2: RFC 1901-10 v3: RFC 2271-75	Presentation / Session
Host-to-Host	Transmission Control Protocol (TCP) MIL-STD-1778 RFC 793					User Datagram Protocol (UDP) RFC 768			Transport
Internet	Address Resolution ARP RFC 826 RARP RFC 903		Internet Protocol (IP) MIL-STD-1777 RFC 791			Internet Control Message Protocol (ICMP) RFC 792			Network
Network Interface	Network Interface Cards: Ethernet, Token Ring, ARCNET, MAN and WAN RFC 894, RFC 1042, RFC 1201 and others								Data Link
	Transmission Media: Twisted Pair, Coax, Fiber Optics, Wireless Media, etc.								Physical

Figure 3-1b ARPA Network Interface Layer Protocols

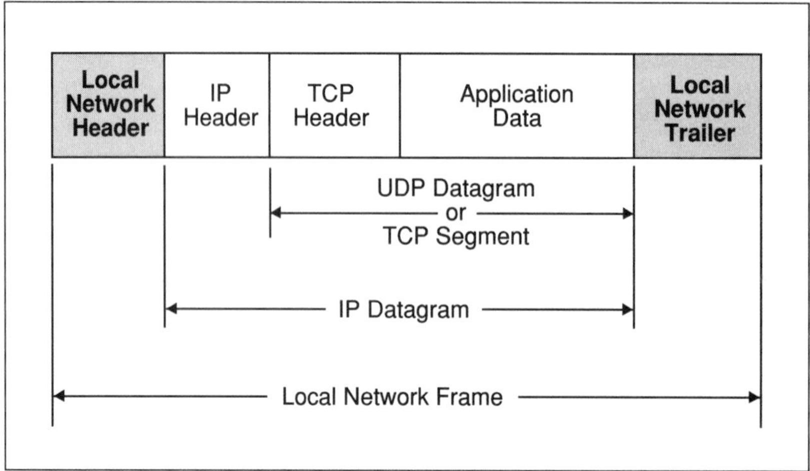

Figure 3-1c The Internet Transmission Frame

3.1 ARCNET

ARCNET, which stands for Attached Resource Computer Network, was developed by Datapoint Corp. in 1977. ARCNET is a token passing architecture that supports a number of Physical Layer alternatives, including a linear bus, a star, or a branching tree [3-2]. The original version supported a transmission rate of 2.5 Mbps and up to 255 workstations. It is standardized as ANSI 878.1. An enhancement to the architecture, known as ARCNETPLUS, operates at 20 Mbps. While it would be rare to see a new network design that specified ARCNET hardware, the significant installed base of these systems, especially for smaller networks, justifies the following discussion.

The Internet standard for ARCNET, RFC 1201 [3-3], suggests methods for encapsulating both IP and ARP datagrams within the ARCNET frame. Three frame formats are available, as shown in Figure 3-2. (Note that this RFC supercedes the older version (RFC 1051) and makes a number of protocol enhancements that have improved TCP/IP support.) The short frame format (Figure 3-2a) limits transmitted client data to 249 octets (an *octet* represents 8 bits of information). The long frame (Figure 3-2b) allows between 253 and 504 octets of client data. An exception frame (Figure 3-2c) is used with frames having between 250 and 252 octets of client data.

(Note that Figure 3-2 shows the frame formats that appear in the software buffers; the hardware transmits formats that duplicate the Destination ID (DID), that do not send the Unused and Protocol ID fields, and that add some hardware framing.)

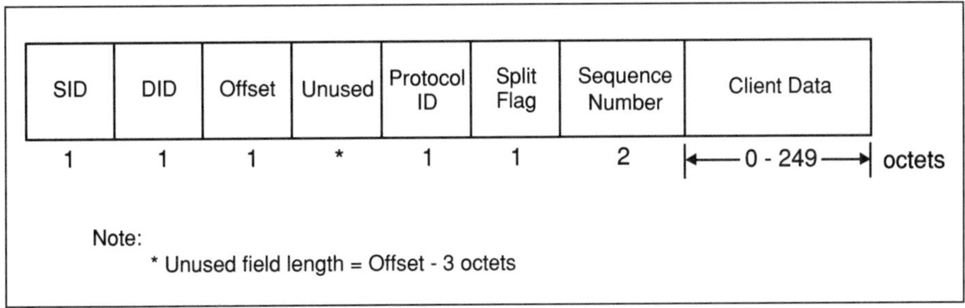

Figure 3-2a ARCNET Short Frame Format

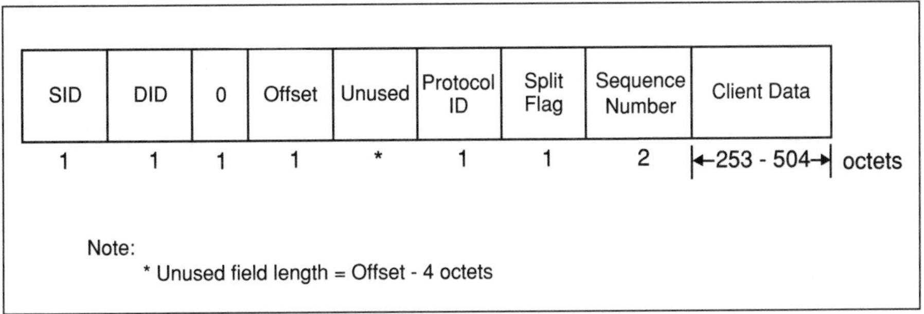

Figure 3-2b ARCNET Long Frame Format

The ARCNET frame may contain up to 512 octets, of which 504 octets may be client data. The sender fragments larger packets, using the Split Flag and Sequence Number fields for identification. The Split Flag takes on one of three values depending on the fragmentation required. Unfragmented packets use Split Flag = 0. The first fragment of a fragmented packet uses Split Flag = ((T-2)*2)+1, where T is the total number of expected fragments. Subsequent fragments use Split Flag = ((N-1)*2), where N is the number of this fragment.

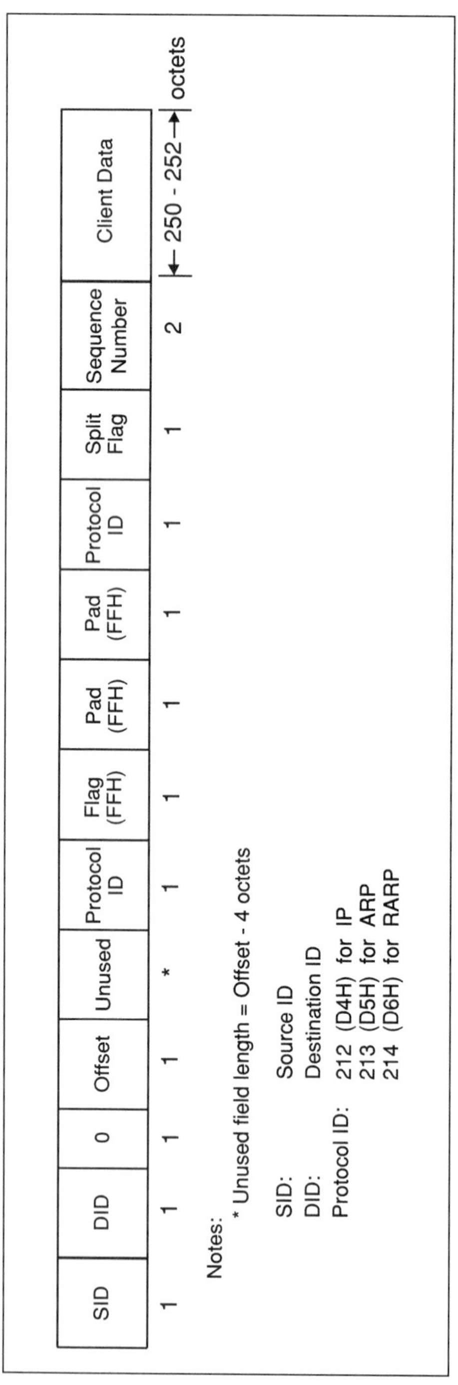

Figure 3-2c ARCNET Exception Frame Format

For example, assume that a packet requires eight fragments. The Split Flag values would be:

Fragment	Split Flag (decimal)
1	13
2	2
3	4
4	6
5	8
6	10
7	12
8	14

The ARCNET frame may contain up to 120 fragments, yielding a maximum value of 238 decimal (or EE in hexadecimal; throughout this text, we will use an uppercase h (H) to represent hexadecimal numbers). This allows up to 60,480 octets per packet (120 * 504 = 60,480). All fragments belonging to the same packet use an identical 2-octet sequence number.

Another unique characteristic of ARCNET is the addressing structure it uses to define an 8-bit address field. This structure allows 255 unique hardware addresses, plus a broadcast designation (address = 0). (This address is implemented with an 8-position DIP switch that you set manually on each ARCNET card. An error in duplicating these switch settings can cause a complete network failure, so use caution when setting the address and other options on the ARCNET card.)

To correlate the 8-bit ARCNET address with the 32-bit IP address RFC 1201 considers three scenarios: Unicast, Broadcast, and Multicast. (Section 4.2 will discuss the IP addresses in detail.) Unicast IP addresses may be mapped to an ARCNET address using the Address Resolution Protocol (ARP), which we will discuss in Section 4.3.1. Broadcast IP addresses are mapped to the ARCNET broadcast address of 0. Multicast IP addresses must also be mapped to the ARCNET broadcast address since ARCNET has no provision for multicasting.

RFC 1201 also discusses the transmission of ARP and Reverse Address Resolution Protocol (RARP) packets that may be required to support the more common IP datagrams. When ARP is used, the ARP packet will indicate ARCNET hardware by setting the ARP Hardware Type = 7. RARP packets are transmitted in a similar fashion.

3.2 Ethernet

Developed by Digital Equipment Corporation (Digital), Intel, and Xerox (sometimes referred to as DIX) in 1973, Ethernet was the first LAN to achieve widespread acceptance. The first version, known as Experimental Ethernet, operated at 3 Mbps and used 8-bit addresses. It was later upgraded to Ethernet version 1 and finally to the Ethernet version 2 that we use today, which transmits at 10 Mbps and uses 48-bit addresses. Much of Ethernet's development coincided with research into the Internet protocols. As a result, many TCP/IP-based internetworks contain Ethernet segments.

A word of caution is necessary at this point. In the early 1980s, Digital, Intel, and Xerox turned over the Ethernet Standard [3-4] to the IEEE as a model for today's IEEE 802.3, Carrier Sense Multiple Access Bus with Collision Detection (CSMA/CD) network. The IEEE made improvements in the DIX version and published IEEE 802.3 in 1983 [3-5]. Thus, the Ethernet and IEEE 802.3 standards are not identical. Section 3.3 will discuss examples of these differences. In this section we will examine Ethernet, and in Section 3.3 we will discuss IEEE 802.3.

The Ethernet frame format (Figure 3-3) defines a length between 64 and 1,518 octets including the header, data, and trailer. The header consists of Destination and Source addresses that are 6 octets (48 bits) each and a 2-octet field known as the Type (or EtherType) field. ARP or RARP perform any address mapping between the 32-bit IP address and the 48-bit Ethernet address, which we will explore in Section 4.2. The Ethernet-designated Destination Address for Broadcast frames is all ONEs (FFFFFFFFFFFFH). The Type designates the higher layer protocol in use within the Data field. Appendix I defines and gives a number of these Ethernet protocol types. Examples relevant to the Internet protocols include 0800H (IP), 0805H (X.25 Level 3), and 0806H (ARP).

The Data field itself must be between 46 and 1,500 octets in length. Should an extremely short IP datagram be transmitted (i.e., fewer than 46 octets), the IP process must pad the Data field with zeros to reach the minimum length. (This padding is not considered part of the IP datagram length and is not counted in the Total Length field within the IP header.) The maximum length of the Ethernet Data field is 1,500 octets, which also constrains the IP datagram length. Recall that the default IP datagram Maximum Transmission Unit (MTU) is 576 octets (4,608 bits), which easily fits inside one Ethernet frame. The information within the IP datagram is transmitted as a series of octets in numerical order (i.e., first octet transmitted first, second octet transmitted second, and so on). The Internet Standard for Ethernet networks, RFC 894 [3-6], and Appendix B of the IP specification (RFC 791) provide further details on the specific data formats.

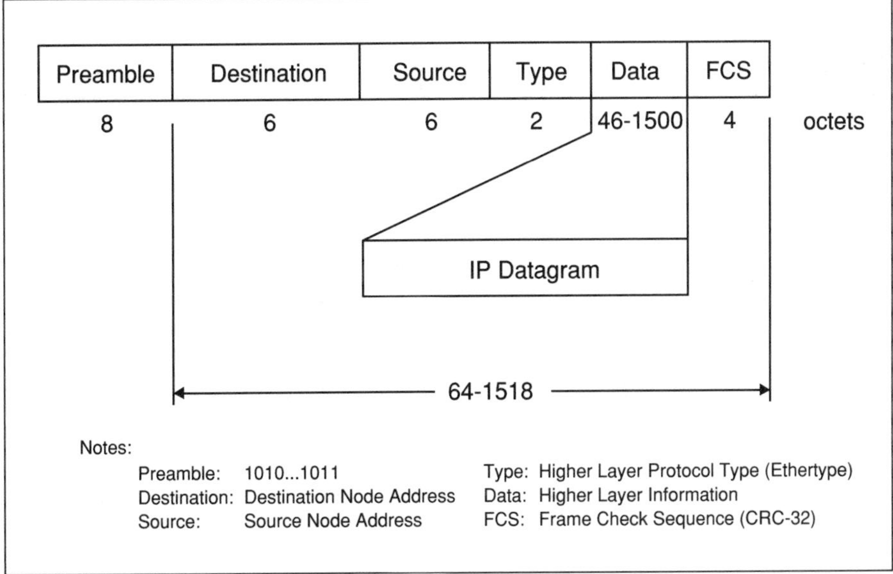

Figure 3-3 Ethernet Frame with IP Datagram
(Courtesy of Digital Equipment Corp.)

3.3 IEEE 802.3

The IEEE project 802 is concerned with internetworking between LANs and MANs. All of the IEEE 802 series of LANs (802.3, 802.4, and 802.5) are covered by the same Internet standard, RFC 1042 [3-7]. These LANs, therefore, exhibit similar characteristics, notably a common addressing format and the use of the IEEE 802.2 Logical Link Control mechanism, that facilitate their interconnection. The primary differences are in the Medium Access Control (MAC) header formats, which are unique to each transmission frame type as dictated by the requirements of the topology. We will point out these differences and similarities as we proceed through our discussion of the IEEE 802 LANs.

As we discussed in the last section, the IEEE 802.3 standard is similar but not identical to the DIX Ethernet. Figure 3-4 shows the IEEE 802.3 frame format. Several differences between the IEEE 802.3 and the Ethernet frames are readily apparent. First, the IEEE 802.3 Destination and Source address fields may have a length of 2 or 6 octets, although the 6-octet length (matching the Ethernet address lengths) is more common. ARP maps the IP address (32 bits) to the IEEE 802.3 address (48 bits). The ARP hardware code for IEEE 802 networks is 6. Broadcast addresses for both Ethernet and IEEE 802 networks are consistent, however, and use all ones.

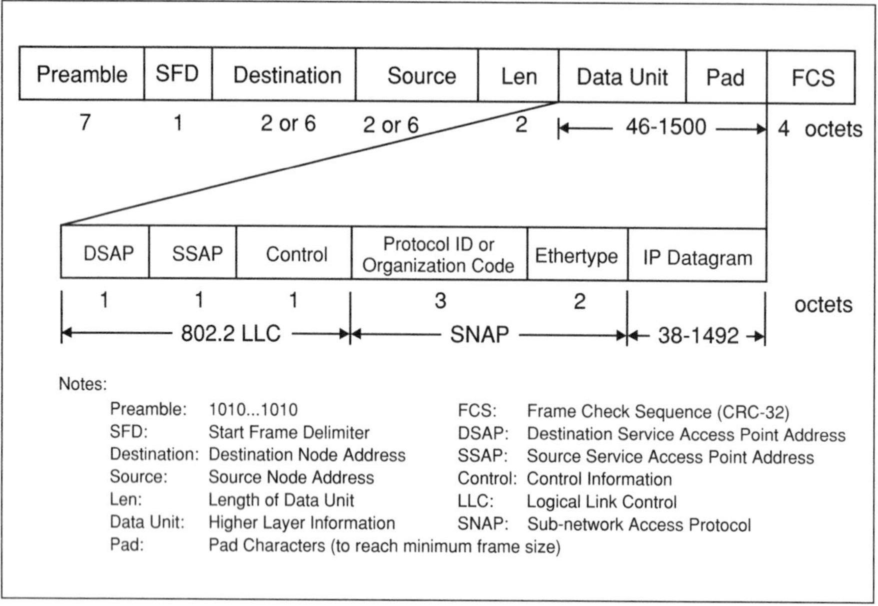

Figure 3-4 IEEE 802.3 Frame Including 802.2 LLC and SNAP Headers, plus IP Datagram (Courtesy of the IEEE, Inc.)

Next, the IEEE 802.3 frame defines a Length field, which specifies the length of the Data unit. Recall that in the Ethernet frame this position was the Type, indicating the higher layer protocol in use. These 2 octets (the Type or Length fields) distinguish the frame format – Ethernet or IEEE 802.3, respectively. If the Data Link Layer driver mixes these up, confusion results. For example, a destination host expecting an Ethernet frame with a Type field will be unable to respond to an IEEE 802.3 frame that contains the Length field. This is because the destination host's higher layer software can recognize only a finite number of Types, such as IP (0800H), ARP (0806H), DECnet Phase IV (6003H), and DEC LAT (6004H). Suppose that the transmitting host had an IEEE 802.3 driver and the Data field was 1,500 octets (05DCH) long. The transmitting host would insert 05DCH in the Length field, which the destination host would be unable to recognize. We will look at an example of this confusion in Section 3.13.4.

The Data field contains the information from the higher layers, plus two IEEE-defined headers. The first header is the Logical Link Control (LLC) header, defined by IEEE 802.2 [3-8]. The LLC header includes Destination and Source Service Access Point addresses (DSAP and SSAP, respectively) and a Control field. The second header is the Sub-Network Access Protocol (SNAP), described in

Reference [3-9]. The SNAP header includes a Protocol ID or Organization Code field (3 octets) and an Ethernet Type field, or EtherType (2 octets). The combination of the LLC and SNAP headers allows the higher layer protocol to be identified with both a SAP and a Type designation. The balance of the Data field contains the higher layer information, such as an IP datagram.

3.4 IEEE 802.5

Another IEEE 802 network of interest is the token ring, described in the IEEE Standard 802.5 [3-10]. The token ring's popularity is due partially to strong support from major networking companies, and is also due to its built-in internetworking. This provision is known as Source Routing [3-11]; it uses the Routing Information (RI) field to connect rings via bridges. The RI field specifies the path the frame must take from its source to its destination. The mechanism for determining that path is called Route Discovery. (Chapter 6 of *Troubleshooting Internetworks* [3-12] discusses the Source Routing protocol and gives several internetwork examples.)

Figure 3-5 shows the token ring frame format. An IP datagram occupies the Information field of the token ring frame. Any necessary routing information precedes the Information field. The Information field contains the IEEE 802.2 LLC header (3 octets), SNAP header (5 octets), and the IP datagram. Given a minimum IP datagram header of 20 octets, the protocol overhead (LLC + SNAP + IP) is, thus, 28 octets per IP datagram. The maximum length of the Information field (and, thus, the encapsulated IP datagram) varies, depending on a parameter known as the Token Holding time. This parameter specifies the length of time any one node may hold the token before it must pass the token to its downstream neighbor. RFC 1042 gives an example for a Token Holding time of nine milliseconds that results in a maximum length of the IP header plus datagram of 4,464 octets.

When bridges connect multiple rings, the Largest Frame (LF) parameter within the RI field controls the maximum frame size and, thus, the maximum IP datagram length. The LF parameter ensures that a source station does not transmit a frame length that exceeds an intermediate bridge's processing or memory capabilities. If an intermediate bridge cannot handle a particular frame length, all devices along that transmission path must use a shorter frame. Currently defined LF lengths are between 516 and 62,543 octets.

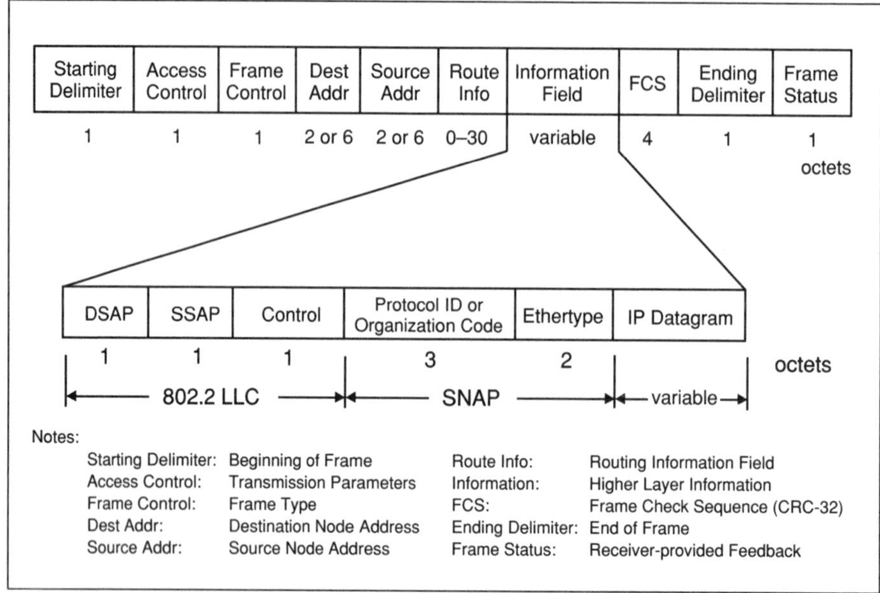

Figure 3-5 IEEE 802.5 Frame Including IEEE 802.2 LLC and SNAP Headers, plus IP Datagram (Courtesy of the IEEE, Inc.)

As a final note, RFC 1042 clarifies the differences between the IEEE and Internet procedures for transmitting the data on the cable. The IEEE specifies numbers in bit-wise little-endian order, that is, the way they are transmitted on the cable [3-9]. The Internet specifies numbers in byte-wise big-endian order. The following table shows examples of commonly used numbers:

Usage	IEEE HEX	IEEE Binary	Internet Binary	Internet Decimal
LLC UI Op Code	C0	11000000	00000011	3
LLC SAP for SNAP	55	01010101	10101010	170
LLC XID	F5	11110101	10101111	175
LLC XID, P	FD	11111101	10111111	191
LLC TEST	C7	11000111	11100011	227
LLC TEST, P	CF	11001111	11110011	243
LLC XID Info	818000			129.1.0

3.5 FDDI

The Fiber Distributed Data Interface (FDDI) is a standard for fiber optic data transmission developed by the American National Standards Institute (ANSI) and defined in Reference [3-13]. FDDI is a token passing ring architecture operating at 100 Mbps. (The actual data rate for FDDI is 125 Mbps, but one out of five bits is used for overhead.) Because of its transmission rate, FDDI may emerge as an important alternative to Ethernet or token ring for local TCP/IP data transport.

The FDDI frame structure (Figure 3-6) is similar to that for IEEE 802.5. The maximum frame size is 4,500 octets (or 9,000 symbols, with 4 bits/symbol). When 6-octet addressing (the most common) is used, the MAC-Layer header (Preamble through Source address) uses 16 octets, and the MAC-Layer trailer uses 6 octets. Subtracting the headers from the maximum frame size leaves 4,478 octets for data. As we saw in the last section, the IEEE 802.2 LLC header requires 3 octets and the SNAP header requires 5 octets. Subtracting these yields the maximum IP datagram length of 4,470 octets.

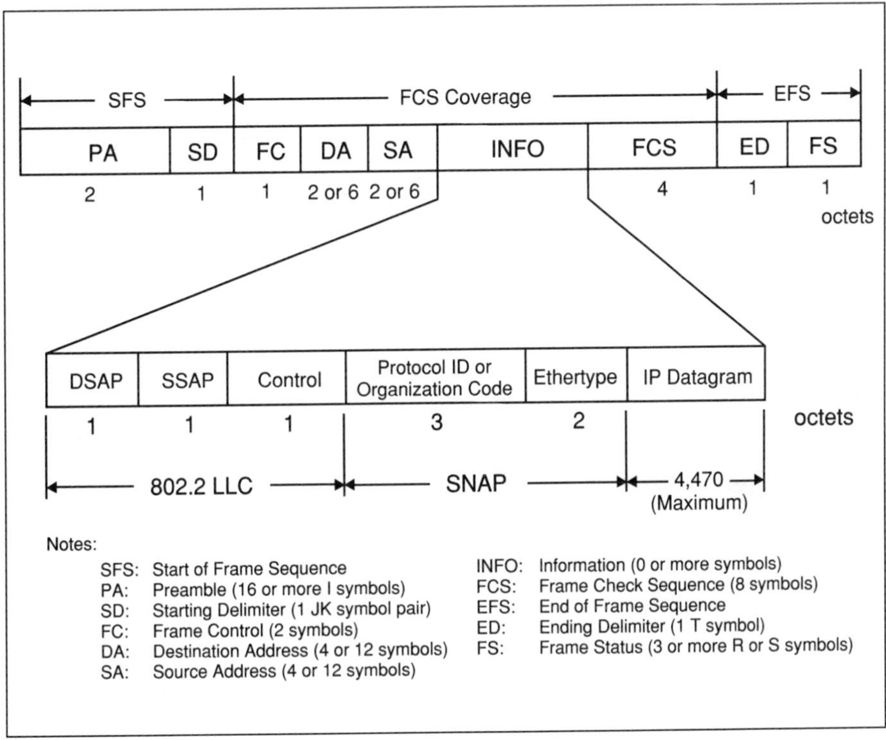

Figure 3-6 FDDI Frame Including IEEE 802.2 LLC and SNAP Headers, plus IP Datagram (Courtesy of the American National Standards Institute)

Like IEEE 802 networks, FDDI networks use ARP to map the 32-bit Internet addresses to the 48-bit FDDI addresses [3-14]. An ARP Hardware Type = 1 designates the FDDI hardware used to provide interoperability with bridged Ethernet networks. Readers needing further information on FDDI should consult Reference [3-15].

3.6 Serial Lines

For years, digital and analog leased lines have been the mainstay of host-to-host and LAN-to-LAN connections. As TCP/IP-based internets grew larger, leased lines became a natural solution for the WAN connection. Two protocols have been developed to support TCP/IP-based data transmission over those topologies: the Serial Line IP (SLIP) and the Point-to-Point Protocol (PPP).

3.6.1 Serial Line IP

Serial Line IP (SLIP), described in RFC 1055 [3-16], frames IP datagrams on a serial line. SLIP is not an Internet standard, but it is included in BSD 4.3 UNIX. As the RFC describes, SLIP performs no other protocol functions.

SLIP defines two characters: END (C0H or octal 300 or decimal 192) and ESC (DBH or octal 333 or decimal 219). To transmit, the SLIP host begins sending the IP datagram (see Figure 3-7). It replaces any data octet equivalent to the END character with the 2-octet sequence of ESC plus octal 334 (DB DCH). It replaces any octet equal to the ESC character with the 2-octet sequence of ESC plus octal 335 (DB DDH). After completing the datagram transmission, it sends an END character. (Note that the ESC character used with SLIP is not the ASCII escape character.)

Because SLIP is nonstandard, it has no maximum packet size. Many systems adhere to the maximum packet size used by the Berkeley UNIX SLIP of 1,006 octets (excluding the SLIP framing characters). Because of its nonstandard status, any SLIP implementation must ensure that the packet size is compatible at both ends of the link before transmitting data.

An enhancement to SLIP, known as Compressed SLIP or CSLIP, compresses the TCP/IP header for transmission over low speed serial lines. CSLIP is defined in RFC 1144 and is often referred to as Van Jacobson header compression. This technique minimizes the protocol overhead being sent, thus partially compensating for the lower speed of the transmission system.

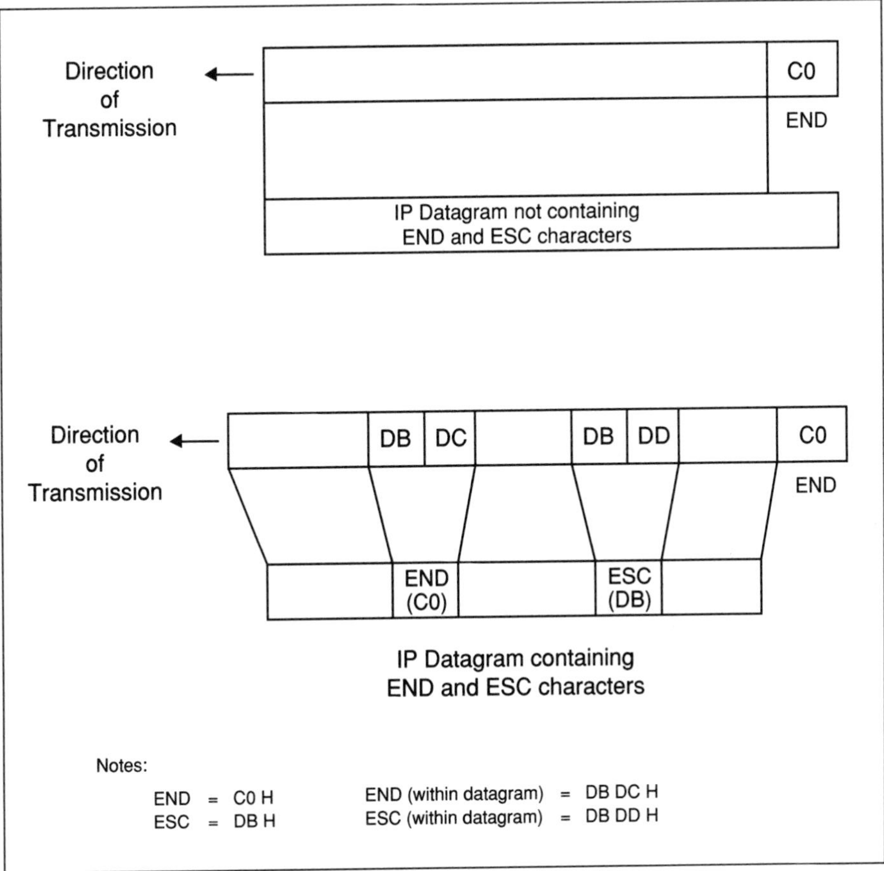

Figure 3-7 Serial Line IP (SLIP) Frame Format

3.6.2 Point-to-Point Protocol

The Point-to-Point Protocol (PPP), described in RFC 1661 [3-17], is the second protocol used for serial line connections. Unlike SLIP, PPP is a standard protocol for use over asynchronous or synchronous serial lines. RFC 1661 describes three main components of PPP: a method of encapsulating multiprotocol datagrams, a Link Control Protocol (LCP), and a family of Network Control Protocols (NCPs). LCP packets initialize the Data Link Layer of the communicating devices. NCP packets negotiate the Network Layer connection between the two endpoints. Once the LCP and NCP configuration is complete, datagrams may be transmitted over the link. Let's look at the PPP frame structure in detail.

The PPP frame is based on the ISO High Level Data Link Control (HDLC) protocol (known as ISO 3309) which has been implemented by itself and has also been incorporated into many other protocol suites, including X.25, Frame Relay, and ISDN. (The 1979 HDLC standard addresses synchronous environments; the 1984 modification extends the usage to asynchronous environments. When asynchronous transmission is used, all octets are transmitted with 1 start bit, 8 data bits, and 1 stop bit.) The PPP frame (see Figure 3-8a) includes fields for beginning and ending Flags (set to 07H); an Address (set to FFH, the all-stations address); Control (set to 03H, for Unnumbered Information); Protocol (a one- or two-octet field identifying the higher layer protocol in use); Information (the higher layer information, with a default maximum length of 1,500 octets); and a Frame Check Sequence (2 octets). RFC 1662 describes the details of the HDLC-like framing.

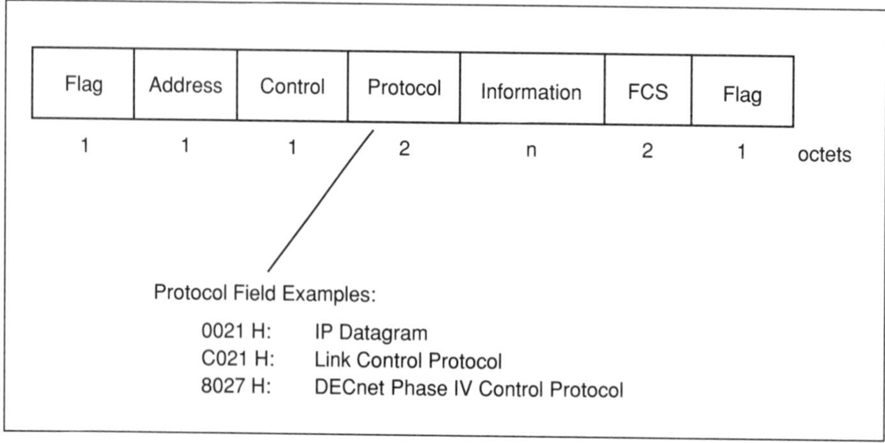

Figure 3-8a Point-to-Point Protocol Frame

The Protocol field is used to distinguish multiprotocol datagrams, with the value contained in that field identifying the datagram encapsulated in the Information field of the packet. RFC 1661 specifies values for the Protocol field that are reserved; the Assigned Numbers document (currently RFC 1700) contains specific Protocol field assignments.

The Protocol field is 2 octets (or 4 hex characters) in length, with possible values from 0000–FFFFH. Values in the 0xxx–3xxx range identify the Network Layer protocol of specific packets, and values in the 8xxx–Bxxx range identify packets belonging to the associated Network Control Protocols (NCPs), if any. Protocol Field values in the 4xxx–7xxx range are used for protocols with low volume traffic that have no associated NCP. Protocol field values in the Cxxx–Fxxx range identify packets as link layer Control Protocols (such as LCP). Examples include:

Value	Protocol
0021H	Internet Protocol (IPv4)
0023	ISO CLNP
0027	DECnet Phase IV
0029	AppleTalk
002B	Novell IPX
0035	Banyan VINES
003D	PPP Multilink
003F	NetBIOS Framing
0201	802.1D Hello Packets
0203	IBM Source Routing BPDUs
C021	Link Control Protocol (LCP)
C023	Password Authentication Protocol
C025	Link Quality Report
C223	Challenge Handshake Authentication Protocol

PPP's second component is the Link Control Protocol (LCP), which deals with Data Link Layer issues. LCP defines five steps for link control. The process begins with the Link Dead phase, which indicates that the Physical Layer is not ready. When the Physical Layer is ready to be used, the process proceeds with the Link Establishment phase. In the Link Establishment phase, the Link Control Protocol (LCP) is used to establish the connection through the exchange of Configure packets between the two ends of the link. The Authentication Phase, which is optional, allows the peer at the other end of the link to authenticate itself prior to exchanging Network Layer protocol packets. In the Network Layer Protocol Phase, each Network Layer in operation, such as IP, Novell's IPX, or AppleTalk, is configured by the Network Control Protocol (NCP). The final step, the Link Termination Phase, uses LCP to close the link.

PPP's third objective is to develop a family of NCPs to transmit Network Layer information. A number of NCPs have been defined, each addressing a particular Network Layer protocol. These include DECnet Phase IV, defined in RFC 1762; Banyan VINES, defined in RFC 1763; and Xerox Network Systems (XNS) Internet Datagram Protocol (IDP), defined in RFC 1764. Each of these protocols would be defined by a distinct value of the Protocol field:

Value (hex)	Protocol
8025	XNS IDP Protocol
8027	DECnet Phase IV Control Protocol
Banyan VINES Control Protocol	

Consult the current Assigned Numbers document, under the PPP section, for additional NCP assignments.

3.6.3 PPP Multilink Protocol

In some cases, a WAN may provide multiple logical links available to the end-user applications. One example of this is ISDN, in which multiple bearer (or B) channels are provided that carry application data. In the case of an ISDN Basic Rate Interface (BRI) line, the end user sees two B channels, each with a 64 Kbps bandwidth, for a total of 128 Kbps bandwidth. Other WAN architectures that include similar multiplexing capabilities are X.25 and frame relay.

A high speed application can use these multiple links if a mechanism for alternating packets delivered to the individual links, plus a mechanism for recombining these individual data streams for delivery to the single receiver, is provided. The goal of the PPP Multilink Protocol (MP), as stated in RFC 1990 [3-18], is "a method for splitting, recombining and sequencing datagrams across multiple logical data links."

That coordination function is accomplished through the addition of a two- or four-octet sequencing header inside the PPP frame. Two formats are defined, supporting either short sequence numbers or long sequence numbers (see Figure 3-8b). Note that for either case, the Protocol field of the PPP frame contains the value 003DH, identifying the PPP Multilink protocol. Both the two – and four – octet sequencing headers contain two single-bit flags that indicate if that fragment begins (B) or ends (E) a PPP packet. When the fragment is the beginning of sequence, B = 1, and when the fragment is the end of a sequence, E = 1. A 12- or 24-bit sequence number then completes the header. The four-octet header (with a 24-bit sequence number) is the default case, however the four-octet header may be replaced with the two-octet version upon negotiation with the other end of the link. Details regarding this negotiation process, as well as implementation specifics, are provided in RFC 1990.

3.7 Data Link Switching

Many internetworks, especially those that support banking, insurance, and other financial business operations, operate as two parallel networks: one internetwork supporting IBM Systems Network Architecture (SNA) functions, and a second supporting TCP/IP. SNA networks are connection oriented, and are based on protocols such as the Synchronous Data Link Control (SDLC), IEEE Logical Link Control 2 (LLC2), or Network Basic Input/Output System (NetBIOS). In direct contrast, TCP/IP networks are connectionless, and based on the Internet Protocol we will study in Chapter 4.

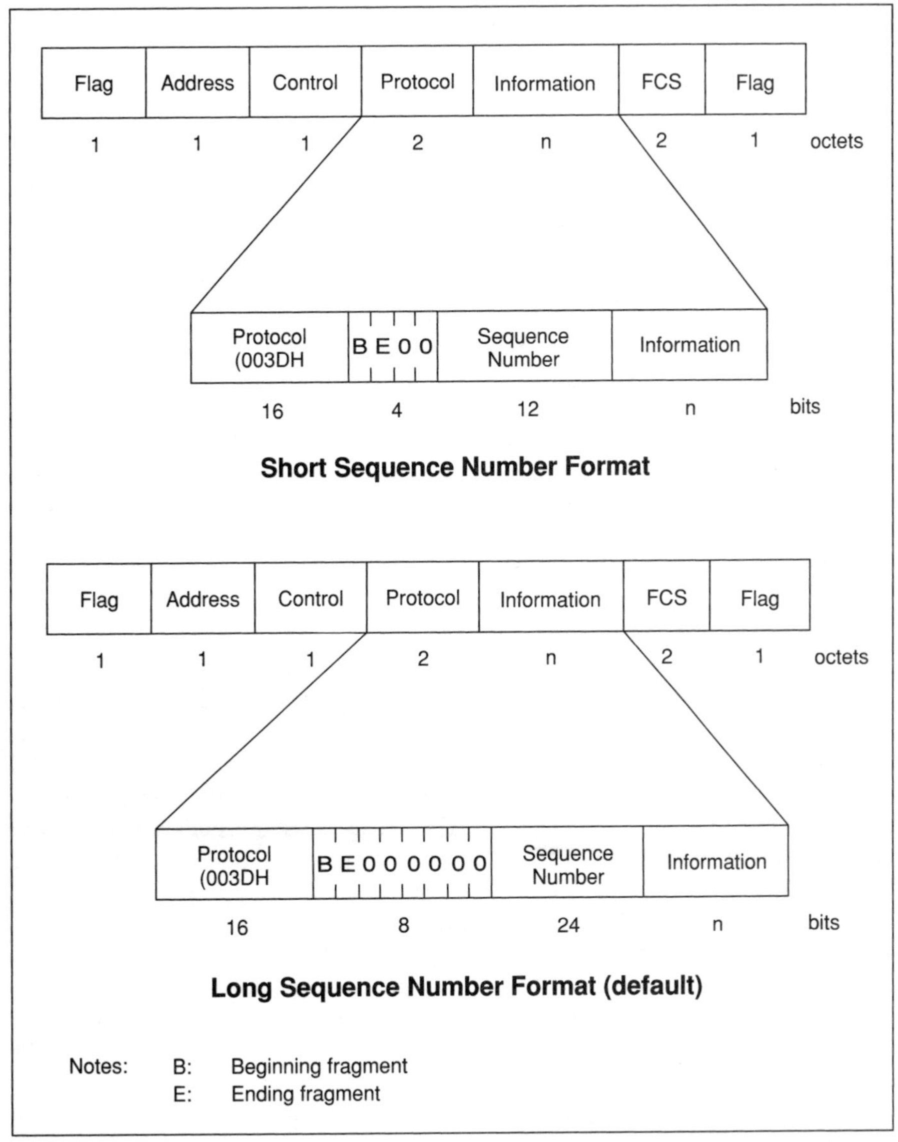

Figure 3-8b PPP Multilink Frame

In many cases these two internetworks operate in parallel, connecting the same locations, which increases the total cost of operation. Tunneling the SNA traffic inside TCP/IP packets would solve the issue of dissimilar protocols; however, the connection-oriented nature of SNA must still be addressed. This connection orientation, inherent in both the SDLC and LLC2 protocols, requires that data be acknowledged within a certain period of time, or the sender will retransmit. If multiple retransmissions occur, the upper protocol layers conclude that the logical connection (or session) is no longer active, and drop that connection. We know this as a *session timeout.*

To solve this problem, IBM developed a process known as Data Link Switching (abbreviated DLSw), a technique that maintains the connection-oriented nature of the connection while tunneling SNA traffic inside TCP/IP packets. Support for DLSw comes from the Advanced Peer-to-Peer Networking Implementers Workshop (AIW) Data Link Switching Related Interest Group, or AIW DLSw RIG for short. The AIW DLSw RIG has published RFC 1795 [3-19], which defines the methods and procedures for DLSw operation.

As defined in RFC 1795, DLSw is a forwarding mechanism for SNA and NetBIOS protocols. The DLSw Switch-to-Switch Protocol (SSP) defines a method for switching at the Data Link Layer, and then for the encapsulation of that data inside TCP/IP packets. When used within token ring based LAN internetworks, the Data Link Switch (DLS) appears as a source-routed token ring bridge. Problems associated with bridged internetworks that DLSw is designed to solve include: Data Link Control (DLC) timeouts; DLC acknowledgments over the WAN (which consume scarce bandwidth); flow and congestion control; broadcast control of token ring search (or discovery) frames; and the hop count limits associated with source route bridging environments.

The operation of a DLSw-based internetwork is illustrated in Figure 3-9. Note that the protocol flows are divided into two major sections: interaction between the host and the Data Link Switch and end-to-end control across the TCP/IP internetwork. At the local and remote ends, the DLSs acknowledge the data sent from the connected hosts, without requiring that those acknowledgments traverse the WAN and be returned from the receiving device. A connection-oriented transport protocol, such as TCP or OSI Transport Class 4 (TP4), ensures reliable delivery of the data. This technique is known as *spoofing,* as the local host is "spoofed" into thinking that the acknowledgments come from the distant receiver, when in reality they are coming from the other end of that data link. This design limits the LLC2 communication to the local networks, which limits the timeouts and reduces the amount of traffic traversing the WAN link. The DLSs control the broadcast of token ring discovery frames, further limiting the amount of extraneous traffic. In addition, the DLSs can provide flow or congestion control to the host systems as required by the current status of the WAN link.

A number of router vendors, including Ascom Timeplex, Bay Networks, Cisco Systems, IBM, and 3Com, have added DLSw capabilities to their products. Further details regarding the DLSw architecture and protocol are found in RFC 1795.

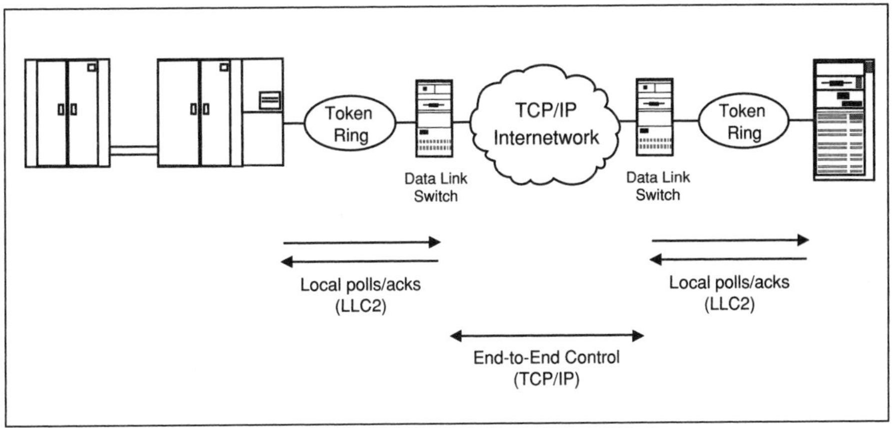

Figure 3-9 Data Link Switching Architecture

3.8 Public Data Networks Using X.25

Much of the early work that produced TCP/IP and the Internet protocols was also applicable to the development of packet switching technologies. Some of the most popular WANs are Packet Switched Public Data Networks (PSPDNs) that use the X.25 protocol. X.25 can, therefore, be considered a by-product of much of this research and is frequently used in conjunction with the TCP/IP protocols for the WAN element of an internetwork.

The X.25 standard encompasses three layers of protocols for the Physical Layer, the Frame Layer, and the Packet Layer. The Physical Layer defines the X.21 protocol, a digital interface that is primarily used in Europe. In North America, the X.21 bis (equivalent to EIA-232) is used. The Frame (or Data Link) Layer protocol is known as the Link Access Procedure Balanced (LAPB) protocol. The Packet (or Network) Layer protocol is simply called the Packet Layer Protocol (PLP).

In previous sections, we discussed the transmission of IP datagrams within the Data Link Layer frames, such as Ethernet or token ring. The X.25 protocols transmit the IP datagram within a PLP packet, which in turn carries the IP datagram. Figure 3-10 shows the LAPB frame structure, which is identical to the HDLC or Synchronous Data Link Control (SDLC) formats that are familiar to many readers. The LAPB frame begins and ends with a Flag character (01111110 binary or 7EH). It contains separate fields for address and control information and a Frame Check Sequence (FCS). The PLP packet is carried inside the frame's Information field.

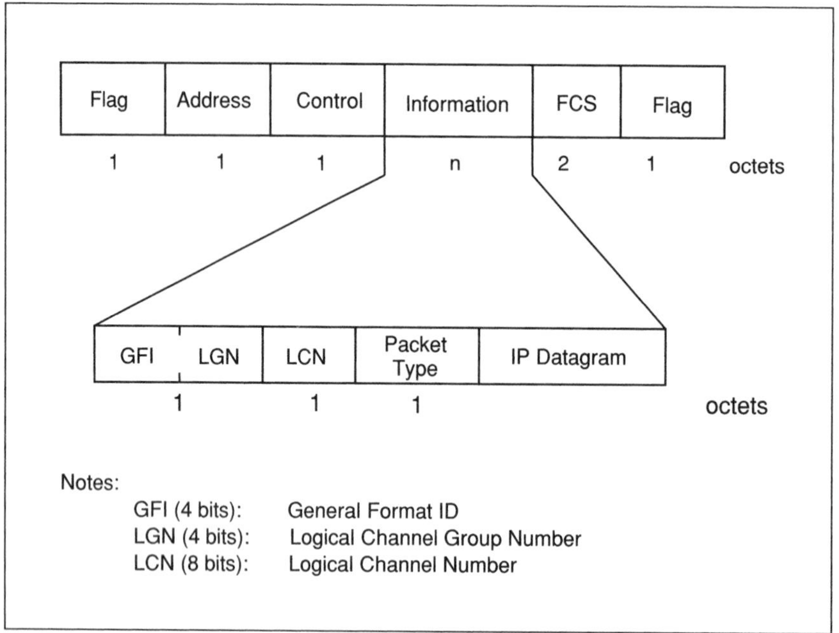

Figure 3-10 X.25 LAPB Frame with IP Datagram (Courtesy of ITU-T X.25-1988)

When the virtual circuit (i.e., WAN connection) is first established, the Call Request packet specifies a Network Layer Protocol Identifier (NLPID) with a value of CCH (binary 11001100 or decimal 204) to indicate that IP will be encapsulated over the X.25 virtual circuit. The IP datagram is then placed within a PLP data packet for transmission. A 4-octet PLP header precedes the IP datagram and specifies the General Format ID (GFI) used for control purposes, the Logical Channel Group Number (LGN) and Logical Channel Number (LCN) that identify the logical channel, and a Packet Type field containing packet sequence numbers and flags. The maximum size of the IP datagram transmitted over X.25 is 1600 octets, unless both sender and receiver negotiate otherwise. RFC 1356 [3-20] also describes procedures for encapsulating other protocols, such as the ISO Connectionless Network Protocol (CLNP), End System-to-Intermediate System (ES-IS) and Intermediate System-to-Intermediate System (IS-IS) over X.25 or over the packet mode of ISDN. *Inside X.25: A Manager's Guide* [3-21] is an excellent handbook for network administrators needing further details on X.25 protocol operation.

3.9 Frame Relay

Frame Relay (FR) was developed by the International Telecommunications Union – Telecommunications Standards Sector (ITU-T), and derived from earlier work on Integrated Services Digital Networks (ISDNs). As such, the FR protocol is similar to ISDN's Link Access Protocol for the D-Channel (LAPD). FR is also a packet switching technology, similar to X.25, designed to transport data over a WAN link. FR improves on its X.25 predecessor primarily through its faster processing speed.

FR has cranked up its processing speed by streamlining the way it deals with information. Most protocols, such as X.25, that operate within the communications subnetwork (i.e., the OSI Physical, Data Link, and Network Layers) process information at all three layers: the Physical Layer decodes the bits, the Data Link Layer decodes the frame, and the Network Layer decodes the packet. Both frames and packets perform error checks to ensure reliable communication. While this method increases the reliability of the data transmission, it also increases overhead in the number of bits transmitted and in the time required to process the bits. FR eliminates the Network Layer (i.e., packet) processing and performs only a few Data Link Layer functions. For example, FR checks the frame for errors, but it does not automatically request a retransmission if it discovers one. Should an error occur, the processes within the sender and receiver take responsibility for that function.

Note that FR operates based ontwo assumptions. The first is that the underlying communications subnet is more reliable than the networks of years ago. Considering the trend within telephone networks of replacing copper circuits with fiber optic cable, this is a valid argument. If the communication subnetwork is reliable, why bother with all the rigorous error control? Second, FR technology assumes that if an error does sneak by, the sending and receiving devices are usually computers with the intelligence to diagnose and cure the problem. For example, they can ask for a retransmission and simply try again.

The FR frame structure is shown in Figure 3-11; it resembles the X.25 frame shown in Figure 3-10. You can see the differences in the formats of the first 2 octets following the Flag character. In the X.25 LAPB frame, these 2 octets are used for the Address and Control fields. The Information field would contain the X.25 packet. For FR, the first 2 octets comprise the FR header and are followed by the higher layer information, such as an IP datagram.

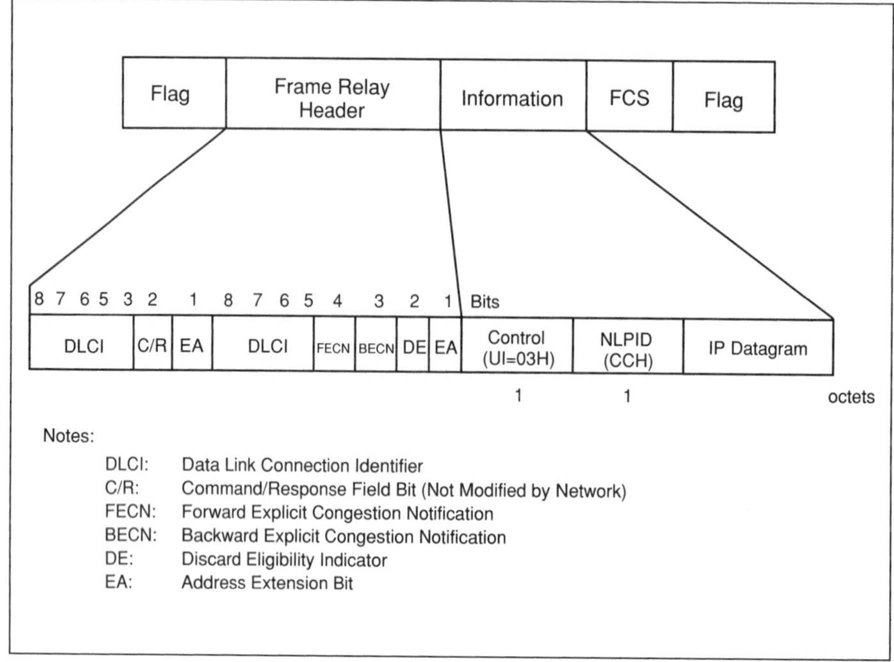

Figure 3-11 Frame Relay Frame with IP Datagram

The FR header contains a number of subfields. The longest of these is the Data Link Connection Identifier (DLCI), which identifies the virtual circuit used for any particular communication path. (A virtual circuit is a logical communication channel between the end-user equipment, or Data Terminal Equipment (DTE), and the FR network, or Data Circuit-Terminating Equipment (DCE). In most cases, the DTE is called a Frame Relay Access Device, or FRAD, and the DCE is called a Frame Relay Network Device, or FRND. The FR network interface, called the User Network Interface, or UNI, is defined at the physical communication line between the FRAD and the FRND.) Multiple virtual circuits may exist at this interface. For example, if a router is the FRAD, it may serve 50 workstations on a LAN, which could each conceivably have a virtual circuit (identified with the DLCI field) into the FR network. The DLCI field (10 bits in length when the default two-octet FR header is used) allows up to 1,024 virtual circuits, although some are reserved for network diagnostic purposes. These circuits are further defined as Permanent Virtual Circuits (PVCs) and are established when the FRAD is attached to the FR network.

When a frame enters the FR network, the FRND examines the Frame Check Sequence (FCS) at the end of the frame for errors. If an error is present, the frame is discarded. If the FCS passes, the FRND examines the DLCI field and a table lookup determines the correct outgoing link. If a table entry does not exist for a particular frame, the frame is discarded. (By now, you should appreciate why FR is a streamlined protocol – if the frame contains any errors or if there is any confusion over how to process the frame, the frame is simply discarded. The higher layer protocols within the machines at either end of the link must recover from the problem.)

The FR header contains 3 bits to indicate congestion on the FR network. The first 2 bits are known as Explicit Congestion Notification (ECN) bits. Any node within the FR network can send an ECN bit in two directions: downstream using the Forward ECN (or FECN) bit and upstream using the Backward ECN (or BECN) bit. The third bit used for congestion control is the Discard Eligibility (DE) bit. The DE bit indicates which frames should be discarded to relieve congestion. ANSI T1.617a discusses these congestion management principles.

Returning to Figure 3-11, the Command/Response (C/R) and Extended Address (EA) complete the FR Header. The C/R bit was defined for LAPD, but is not used with FR networks. The EA bits allow the FR Header to extend to 3 or 4 octets in length to accommodate more DLCI addresses. The Internet standard for frame relay support is RFC 1490 [3-22], which provides specifics for implementing multiprotocol traffic over FR networks. The key word in RFC 1490's title is "multiprotocol" since the FR Information field has several variations. Consistent among all the variants, are the Control field and the Network Level Protocol ID (NLPID). The Control field may either specify Unnumbered Information (UI) with a field value of 03H or Exchange Identification (XID) with a field value of AF or BFH. ISO and ITU-T administer the NLPID and identify the type of protocol used within the Information field. RFC 1490 gives the following examples:

NLPID	Usage
00H	Null Network Layer (not used with Frame Relay)
80	SNAP
81	ISO CLNP
82	ISO ES-IS
83	ISO IS-IS
CC	Internet IP
CE	EtherType (unofficial temporary use)

Of particular interest to Internet designers is NLPID = CCH, which indicates that the frame contains an IP datagram. If a protocol does not have an NLPID, the 1-octet NLPID field is replaced with a 6-octet field. That field includes NLPID = 80H (indicating the SNAP), followed by the 5-octet SNAP header. The EtherType within the SNAP header would then identify the higher layer protocol in use. An ARP packet is an example of a SNAP-encoded frame. The first 6 octets of the Information field (i.e., NLPID plus SNAP) would contain 80-00-00-00-08-06H. The

80 identifies NLPID = SNAP, the 00-00-00 is the SNAP Organization ID, and the 08-06 is the EtherType for ARP. Inverse ARP performs the conversion between DLCIs and protocol addresses, and is described in RFC 1293 [3-23]. Other formats for routed and bridged frames have been defined as well; consult RFC 1490 for specific details.

A number of carrier and equipment vendors joined together in 1991 to establish the Frame Relay Forum. The purpose of the Forum was to promote FR technology from an implementation and user perspective. On the standards side, ANSI T1.606 [3-24] describes the service; standards such as T1.617, T1.618, and others deal with signaling, core aspects, congestion management, and so on. The Frame Relay Forum publishes a newsletter, provides information on upcoming conferences and the status of standards, and produces implementation agreements which describe agreed-upon methods for implementing the published standards. Reference [3-25] provides contact information for the Frame Relay Forum.

Both users and carriers have demonstrated great interest in FR services. Like other data transport services – and as is especially important when using new technologies – FR networks must be designed with careful consideration for the end-user application. Users need to understand where FR fits into their WAN strategies along with existing technologies, such as X.25 packet switching, and network technologies, such as ATM. Uyless Black's *Frame Relay Networks* [3-26] provides further details on the Frame Relay protocols. Hume and Seaman's "X.25 and Frame Relay: Packet Switched Technologies for Wide Area Connectivity" [3-27] offers an interesting perspective on WAN connectivity.

3.10 Switched Multimegabit Data Service

The IEEE 802.6 standard describes a network topology known as a Distributed Queue Dual Bus (DQDB) [3-28]. The Switched Multimegabit Data Service (SMDS) is a technology based on the IEEE 802.6 standard. As its name implies, DQDB consists of two buses arranged in a loop topology. It is intended for metropolitan- or wide-area use, such as a loop around metropolitan Denver, Colorado. (Strictly speaking, SMDS has no distance limitations.) When one organization needs to transmit data to another, it can use SMDS as the connection between the two LANs.

Bell Communication Research, Inc. (Bellcore, which is now known as Telecordia Technologies, Inc.) developed SMDS as a data transport standard for use by the Regional Bell Operating Companies (RBOCs). SMDS is a packet switched data transport mechanism that provides connectionless service. Bellcore describes SMDS in Technical Report TR-TSV-000772 [3-29], which defines the Subscriber Network Interface (SNI) and the SMDS Interface Protocol (SIP). The SMDS SNI resembles other network interfaces, such as ISDN or X.25, in that it functions as a point of data ingress and egress between the user and the transmission facility; by conforming to the interface specification, both the user and the network can communicate efficiently.

SIP is a three-layer protocol. SIP Level 1 provides physical data transport and is usually implemented at the DS-1 (1.544 Mbps) or DS-3 (44.736 Mbps) rates. SIP Level 2 defines the frame format, including the header and trailer, for data transmission. Level 2 functions include detecting errors and segmenting and reassembling the variable length SIP Level 3 Protocol Data Unit (PDU). The length of the SIP Level 2 frame is fixed at 53 octets. The Level 3 PDU includes the additional address and control information needed to reliably transfer the user information from source to destination via the SMDS network. The SIP Level 3 PDU may contain up to 9,188 octets of data.

The Bellcore specification [3-29] suggests a scenario for interconnecting TCP/IP end systems using SMDS (see Figure 3-12a). End System A includes the higher layers, TCP, IP, and the MAC layer specific to the attached LAN. End System B also includes the higher TCP and IP layers, but the lower layers connect to the SMDS network using SIP. A router ties together the LAN and SMDS network, connecting to the LAN MAC layer on one side and the SMDS SIP layers on the other.

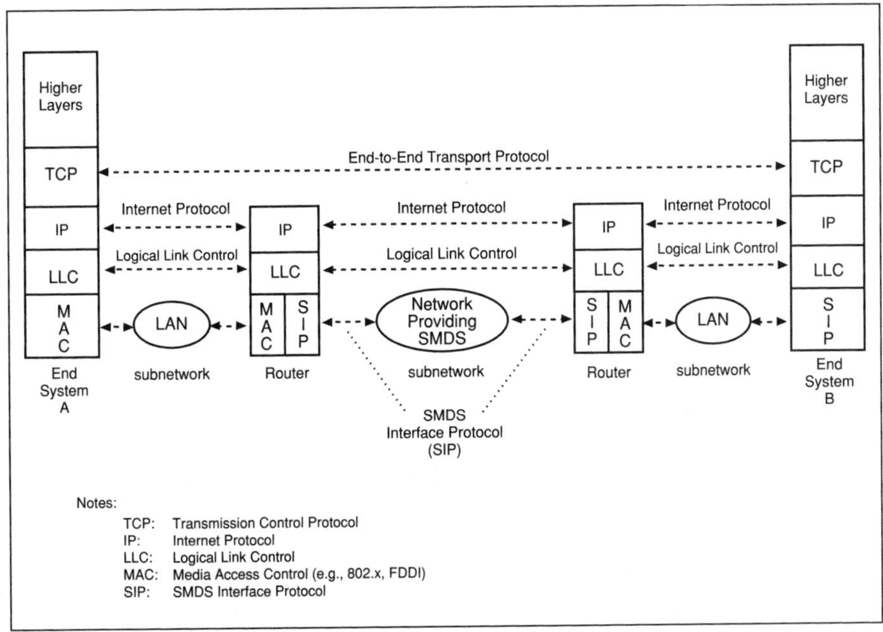

Figure 3-12a Using SMDS with the Internet Protocols
(Reprinted with permission from TR-TSV-000772, Copyright © 1991 Bellcore.)

The Internet community has also defined scenarios for internetworking between LANs and SMDS for the transmission of IP and ARP packets [3-30]. The resulting packet structure incorporates the SMDS SIP headers, the IEEE 802.2 header, the SNAP header, and the IP/ARP information (see Figure 3-12b). For efficient transmission on the SMDS network, the Level 3 PDU is segmented into many smaller SIP Level 2 frames. The SIP L3 PDU may contain up to 9,188 octets of data, but the SIP L2 PDU may contain only 44 octets. Thus, one L3 PDU may generate a number of L2 frames. The data structure in Figure 3-12b shows the order of the fields and the IP/ARP data as it would be assembled prior to the fragmentation process that occurs at SIP L2.

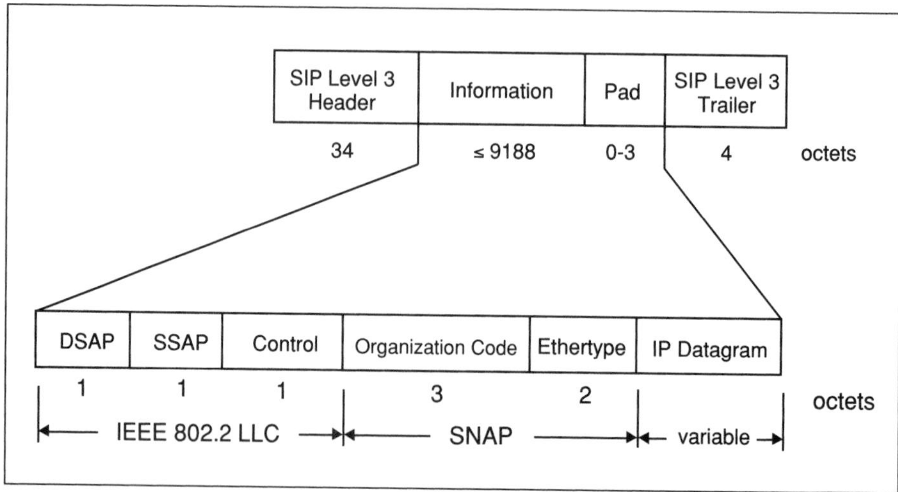

Figure 3-12b SMDS SIP Level 3 PDU Including IEEE 802.2 LLC and SNAP Headers, plus IP Datagram
(Reprinted with permission from TR-TSV-000772, Copyright © 1991 Bellcore.)

Within the SIP Level 3 header, the Higher Layer Protocol ID (HLPI) field must be set to a value of 1, indicating IEEE 802.2 LLC. The SMDS Information field then begins with the IEEE 802.2 LLC header, which includes the DSAP and SSAP fields (set to AAH) and the Control field, set to 3 (Type 1 Unnumbered Information). The next fields include the SNAP header, which contains the Organization Code (set to zero) and an EtherType. The EtherType for IP packets is 0800H and for ARP is 0806H. The total length of the SIP Level 3 PDU may not exceed 9,188 octets, thus allowing an IP datagram to have an MTU of up to 9,180 octets.

SMDS enhances the speed, reliability, and subscriber services for metropolitan-area and wide-area data transport services. These services come out of the addressing features (such as Source and Destination address screening) incorporated in the SMDS standard. One such subscriber benefit is the ability to use the SMDS 8-octet addressing scheme to create Logical IP Subnetworks (LISs), also known as closed user groups. (ARP translates Internet addresses to/from SMDS addresses. The ARP Hardware Address length is eight (HA = 8) and the Hardware Type is 14.) Within an LIS, the hosts may communicate with each other directly via the SMDS. When communicating to a host outside of that LIS, an IP router performs the network address translation.

SMDS is a technology that meets the requirements for high-speed data transport, especially within metropolitan areas. More importantly, it provides an excellent transition to the next major level of high speed networking, ATM. Information on the SMDS Interest Group, or SIG, an industry consortium of SMDS users, service providers, and equipment vendors, is noted in Reference [3-31].

3.11 Asynchronous Transfer Mode

Asynchronous Transfer Mode, or ATM, is a very high speed transmission technology designed for LAN, MAN, and WAN applications. It operates over a wide range of transmission rates, as currently defined from 1.5 Mbps (DS-1) to 622 Mbps (OC-12), with higher rates under development. The ATM architecture is connection oriented and based on high speed switches which direct the 53-octet cells of information from their source to the ultimate destination. ATM technology, which is generally considered to be the next generation of high speed networking, is actively supported by the ATM Forum [3-32], a consortium of users, vendors, and carriers who have joined together to further develop the technology. The principle document from the ATM Forum is known as the *User-Network Interface* [3-33], which defines the interaction between user devices and an ATM network.

ATM is based on a four layer architecture: the Physical Layer, which handles bit timing and transmission-related issues; the ATM layer, responsible for the transfer of the 53-octet cells; the ATM Adaptation layer, which supports the transport of higher layer information by dividing that information into 53-octet cells and incorporating appropriate error control mechanisms; and the Higher layers, containing user information. A thorough study of ATM is beyond the scope of this text. However, readers interested in an in-depth study of ATM and its protocols are referred to a companion text, *Analyzing Broadband Networks* [3-34].

In this section we will survey four related alternatives for TCP/IP internetworking with ATM: Multiprotocol Encapsulation over AAL5 (defined in RFC 1483), Classical IP and ARP over ATM (defined in RFC 1577), LAN Emulation – LANE (defined by the ATM Forum), and Multiprotocol over ATM – MPOA (defined by the ATM Forum).

3.11.1 Multiprotocol Encapsulation over ATM

As ATM technology has developed, a number of documents have been written to address the need for sending TCP/IP information over ATM connections. RFC 1483, "Multiprotocol Encapsulation over ATM Adaptation Layer 5" [3-35], describes two encapsulation techniques for carrying network interconnect traffic over ATM AAL5: LLC encapsulation and VC-based multiplexing. The LLC encapsulation method allows multiplexing of multiple protocols over a single ATM virtual circuit. The receiver uses information contained within LLC and SNAP headers to identify the protocol carried within that PDU. The LLC encapsulation method is used when it is not feasible to have a separate VC for each protocol or when network charges are based on the number of active VCs. Support for this method is required per RFC 1577. The VC-based multiplexing technique uses ATM VCs to implicitly provide higher layer protocol multiplexing. In other words, each protocol is carried on a separate VC. This method is used when it is feasible and economical to dynamically create large numbers of virtual circuits.

The LLC encapsulation method is shown in Figure 3-13a. Information contained within an IEEE 802.2 LLC header and an IEEE 802.1a SNAP header identifies the protocol carried within that PDU.

Within the LLC header, the DSAP address (1 octet) and the Source Service Access Point (SSAP) address (1 octet) both contain a value of AAH, which indicates that a SNAP header follows. The Control field (1 octet) has a value of 03H, indicating an Unnumbered Information (UI) field. The SNAP header (5 octets) contains two fields, a 3-octet Organizationally Unique Identifier, or OUI, and a 2-octet Protocol Identifier, or PID. The OUI has a value of 00 00 00H indicating a routed PDU. The PID is a 2-octet EtherType, which for IP would have a value of 08 00H. Following the header is the AAL5-CPCS-PDU, which can contain up to 65,527 octets of higher layer information, such as an IP datagram.

RFC 1483 provides further details on this encapsulation format.

3.11.2 Classical IP and ARP over ATM

RFC 1577, "Classical IP and ARP over ATM" [3-36], considers the application of ATM as a direct replacement for the physical transmission technologies (such as cables and routers) that have heretofore been employed.

In this case, the network is assumed to be configured as a Logical IP Subnetwork (LIS). RFC 1577, section 3, defines the following requirements for members of a LIS: all members must have the same IP network/subnet number and address mask; all members within a LIS must be directly connected to the ATM network; all members outside of the LIS must be accessed via a router; all members of the LIS must have a mechanism for resolving IP addresses to ATM addresses using ATMARP; all members must have a mechanism for resolving virtual circuits (VCs) to IP addresses using InATMARP; and all members of a LIS must be able to communicate with all other members of the same LIS using ATM. Each LIS operates and communicates independently of other LISs on the same ATM network. Hosts connected to ATM communicate directly to other hosts within the same LIS. To communicate with a host outside of the local LIS requires an IP router. Figure 3-13b illustrates such a LIS, where all members have a consistent IP network and subnet address [N.S.x] and use a router for communication outside of the LIS.

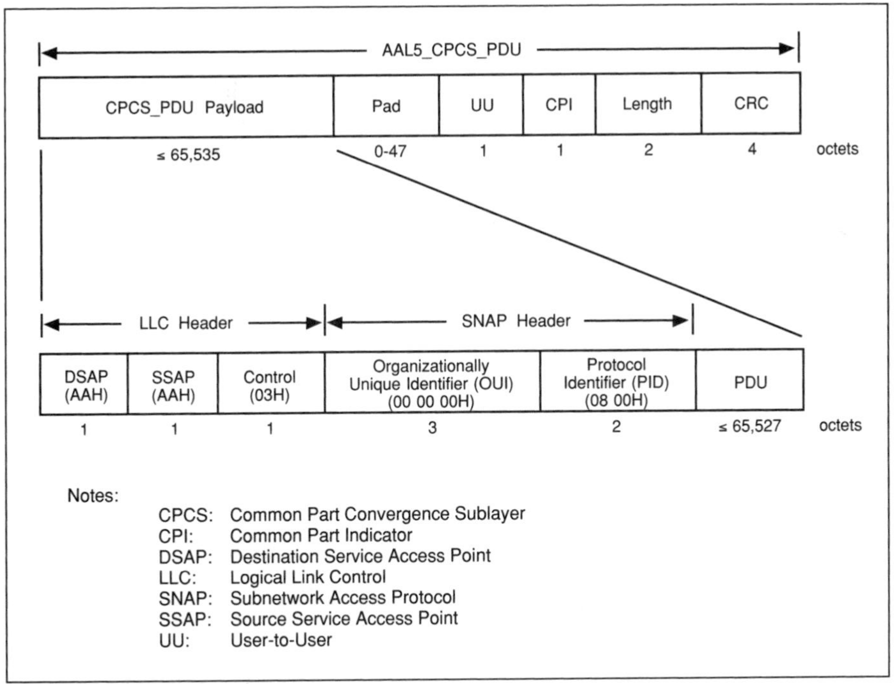

Figure 3-13a IP Datagram Encapsulation over AAL5

For two LIS members to communicate, they must know each other's IP and ATM addresses. IP over ATM uses an enhanced version of the Address Resolution Protocol (ARP) called ATMARP to provide translation between ATM and IP addresses. ATMARP runs on a server that exists at an ATM address that all LIS members are aware of. To communicate with another member requires the establishment of an ATM connection using the resources of the ATMARP server (see Figure 3-13c). As LIS clients are initialized, they register with the ATMARP server, which allows the server to build an address table. If Client A needs to resolve a destination IP address, it sends an ATMARP Request to the server, which responds with an ATMARP Reply containing the needed ATM address. A connection may then be established with remote Client B. A similar process occurs at Client B if it needs the ATM address of Client A. After all addresses have been resolved, Clients A and B communicate directly. We will look at the packet structure of ATMARP in Section 4.3.4.

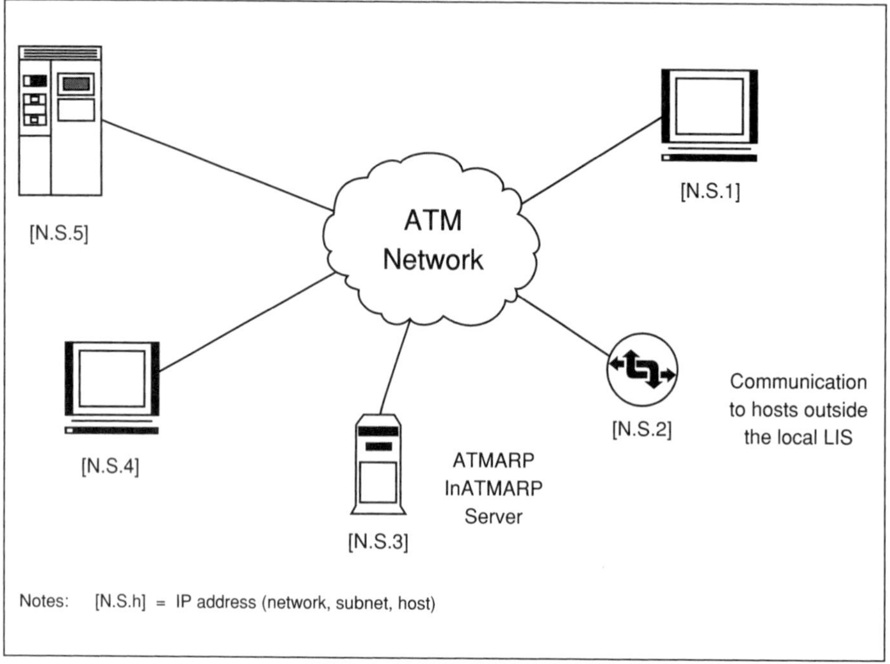

Figure 3-13b Logical IP Subnetwork

The IP datagram is encapsulated within an ATM Adaptation Layer 5 (AAL5) message, and is then further subdivided into cells for transmission over the ATM network. IEEE 802.2 LLC and SNAP headers precede the IP datagram for higher layer protocol identification. The default maximum transmission unit (MTU) for the AAL5 PDU is 9,188 octets, which allows 8 octets for the LLC and SNAP headers, and 9,180 octets for the IP datagram, as discussed in RFC 1626, "Default UP MTU for use over ATM AAL5." Further details on IP over ATM are found in RFC 1755, "ATM Signaling Support for IP over ATM."

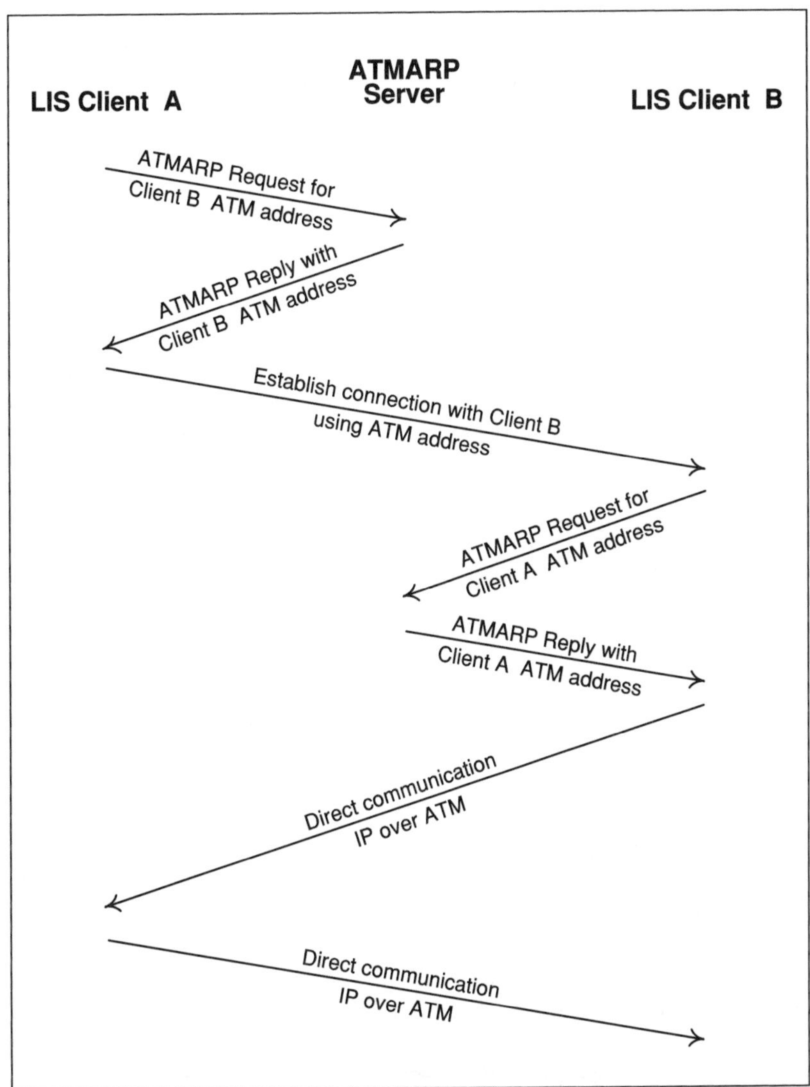

Figure 3-13c LIS Client/ATMARP Server Operation

3.11.3 LAN Emulation

LAN Emulation, or LANE as it is commonly known, is a service that allows existing end-user applications to access an ATM network. More importantly, this access appears to the application as if it were using more traditional protocols, such as TCP/IP or Novell's Internetwork Packet Exchange (IPX), and as if it were running over more traditional LANs such as Ethernet or token ring. One of the design constraints is to account for the differences in protocol design – ATM is connection oriented, whereas IP and IPX are connectionless. A number of functions, including setting up the ATM connection and translating LAN to ATM addresses, must be hidden from the upper layers, thus making the application think it is operating over a traditional network.

The ATM Forum has defined two different interfaces for LAN Emulation: a LAN Emulation User to Network Interface, called LUNI; and a LAN Emulation Network to Network Interface, called LENNI. Current work has focused on the LUNI.

The ATM Forum's LAN Emulation version 2.0 specification [3-37] defines two scenarios that are applicable. In the first, an ATM network may be used to interconnect Ethernets to Ethernets, an Ethernet to an ATM device, or an ATM device to another ATM device. The second scenario replaces Ethernet LANs with token ring LANs under similar conditions. To make either of these systems operate requires the LAN Emulation protocol stack, shown in Figure 3-13d. Notice that the LAN host and its applications operate over traditional protocols, such as TCP/IP and IPX, and that a driver, such as NDIS or ODI, provides an interface between the upper layer software and the MAC layer hardware. The ATM-to-LAN converter sits at the edge of the network, running dual protocol stacks: one that communicates with the LAN (on the right) and another that communicates with the ATM switch (on the left). Note that this ATM-to-LAN converter is functioning as a bridge, operating independently of the Network and higher layer protocols. The ATM switch (or switches) do not participate in LAN Emulation other than to switch the ATM connections, as would be the case with any other ATM-based network scenario. An element of LAN Emulation is also active on the ATM host (the left side of Figure 3-13d), masking the ATM functions from the higher layer processes. In summary, the LAN Emulation function maps the Ethernet or token ring MAC layer functions into ATM virtual connections, while shielding the application from the connection setup and handshaking functions that the ATM switch requires.

The LANE architecture is designed around a client/server paradigm, such that the LAN Emulation Client (LEC) derives information that it needs from one of several servers: the Configuration Server, the LAN Emulation Server (LES), or the Broadcast and Unknown (BUS) Server. The LEC software may be incorporated into workstation drivers, or it could be incorporated into other internetworking devices such as routers or switches.

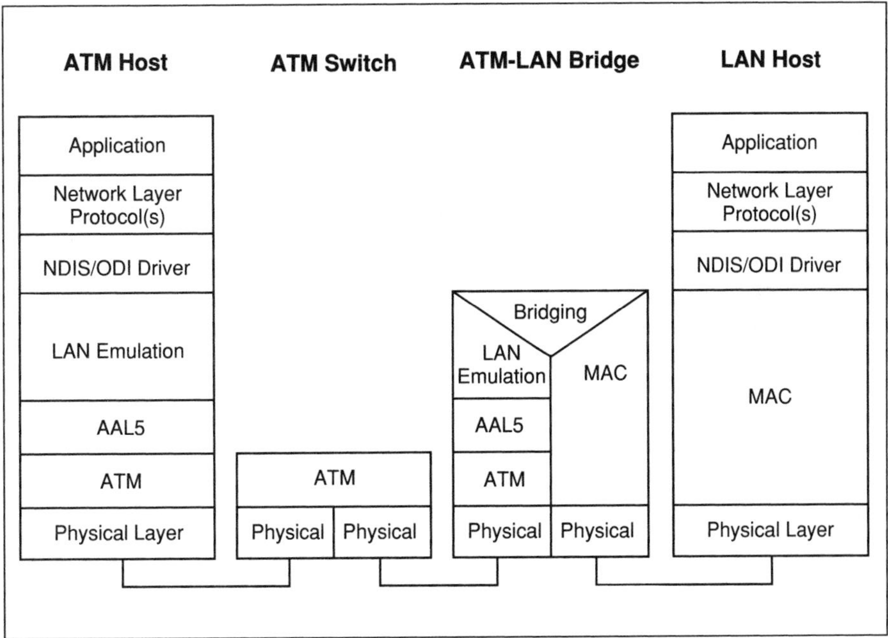

Figure 3-13d LAN Emulation Architecture
(From 3TECH. Copyright © 1995.
Reprinted with permission of 3Com Corporation. All rights reserved)

Several steps are required to establish an emulated LAN connection. The control functions (shown in the upper portion of Figure 3-13e) occur prior to any data transfer (shown in the lower portion of Figure 3-13e). First, the LEC is initialized by learning the ATM address of the LAN Emulation Configuration Server (LECS). (The Configuration Server resides at a well-known address, making this task easier.) The LEC next obtains configuration information, sending the LECS its ATM and MAC addresses, plus the LAN type and frame size requested. The LECS returns the address of the LAN Emulation Server (LES), plus the LAN type and frame size to use. The connection between the LEC and the LECS is transient; once the required information is obtained, the connection is torn down. When the LEC has the required configuration information, it requests to join the emulated LAN by sending a message to the LAN Emulation Server (LES). The LES maps the MAC-to-ATM addresses, allowing a switch (or switches) to establish a connection to the correct destination. The LES may be implemented in a number of devices, including switches, routers, or file servers; however, only one LES is used per configuration. The LES also supplies the LEC with the ATM address of the Broadcast and Unknown Server (BUS), which relays multicast or broadcast frames to all emulated LAN clients. A bidirectional connection is established with the BUS, and then data transfer is allowed.

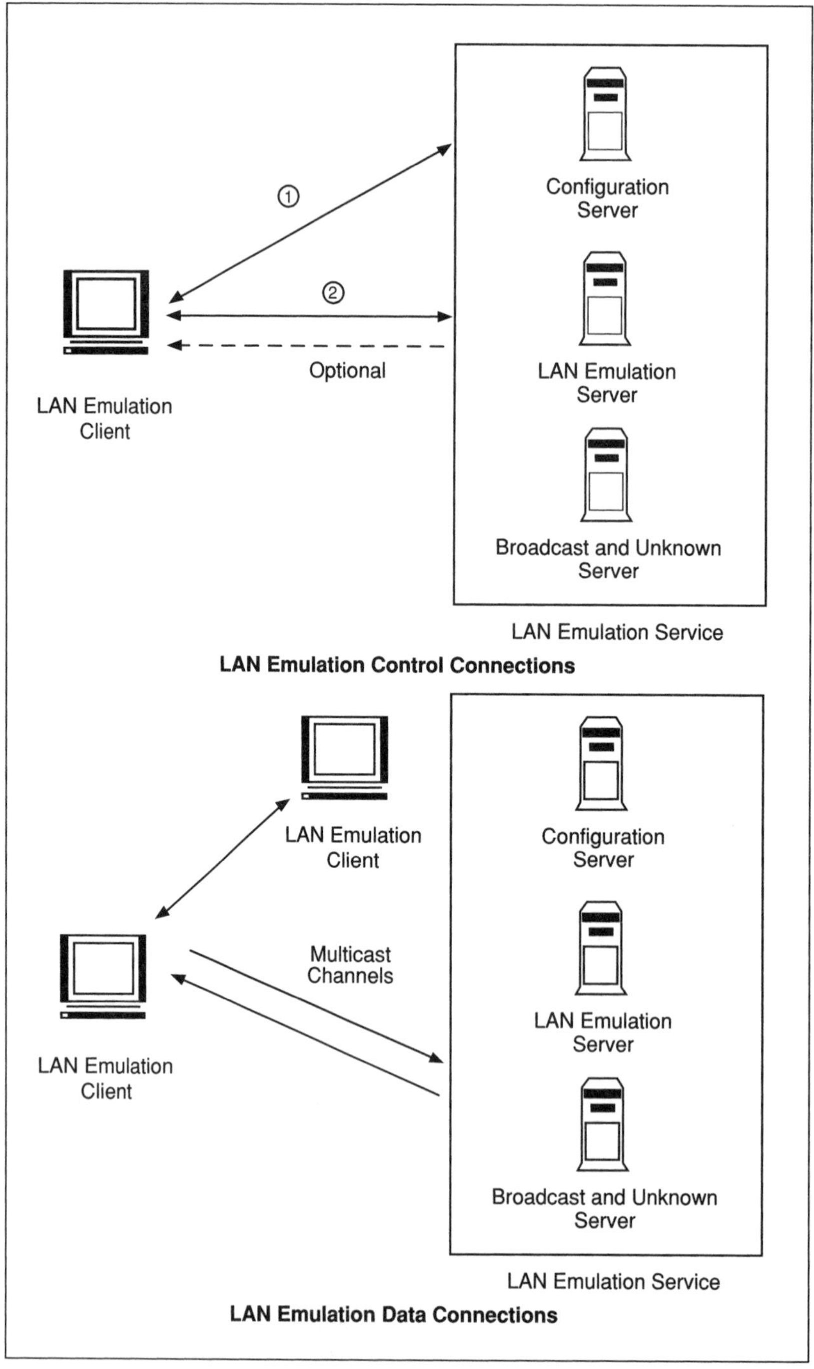

Figure 3-13e LAN Emulation Operation

When communication with another LEC is required, the sending LEC will first check its internal address cache to see if the destination address is known. If it is not known, it consults with the LES. After the ATM address is available, a direct connection with the remote LEC is established, streamlining that subsequent communication.

As is evident in Figure 3-13d, LANE is essentially a bridging function, independent of Network or higher layer protocols. Another technique – Multiprotocol over ATM (or MPOA) – addresses the routing scenario, and will be investigated next.

3.11.4 Multiprotocol over ATM

The ATM Forum has developed a process known as Multiprotocol over ATM (MPOA) [3-38], which is an evolution of the LAN Emulation work. While LANE operates at the MAC layer (OSI Data Link Layer), MPOA operates at the OSI Network layer. MPOA is designed to integrate with LAN Emulation, and to support the traditional routing functions of protocol filtering plus enhanced security through firewalls, while handling both Data Link and Network layer operations.

MPOA is designed with a client/server architecture, with the MPOA Client (MPC) residing in an edge device or MPOA host, and the MPOA Server (MPS) residing in an MPOA router (Figure 3-13f). Both the MPC and the MPS contain a LAN Emulation Client (LEC) function. The MPC includes a Layer 3 forwarding function, but it does not run internetwork routing protocols. The primary function of the MPC is to act as the initiation and termination points (source and sink, respectively) of internetwork shortcuts. When the MPC recognizes a data flow that could benefit from a shorter path, or shortcut, it uses an NHRP-based request to establish that shortcut to the destination. The MPS provides forwarding information to the MPCs. It also contains a Next Hop Server (NHS) as defined for the Next Hop Routing Protocol (NHRP), which aids the path selection process.

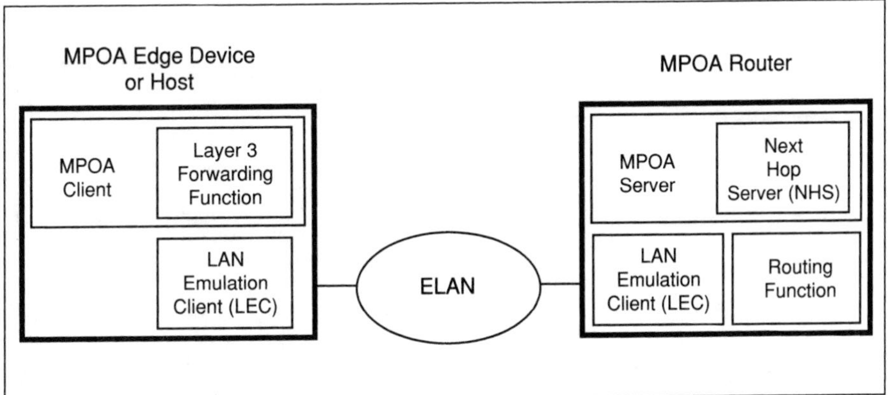

Figure 3-13f MPOA Components
(Copyright 1997, The ATM Forum)

The paths that a data packet can take from its source to its destination are illustrated in Figure 3-13g. Assume that the data packet enters the MPOA System at MPOA Client 1, where that packet is bridged via LANE to the first MPOA Server (its default router), and thereafter to other emulated LANs or Logical IP Subnets (LISs) on its way to the destination, MPOA Client 2. If a shortcut path from MPOA Client 1 to MPOA Client 2 has been established, then the shortcut path is used. If no data flow from Client 1 to Client 2 has been previously detected, then the number of packets sent between that particular source and destination are tallied. When that packet tally exceeds a threshold, the MPC initiates procedures to establish a shortcut path, which would result in an ATM SVC between Client 1 and Client 2. When the shortcut (or pre-established) path is used, performance gains should result, especially for stream-based transmissions such as video.

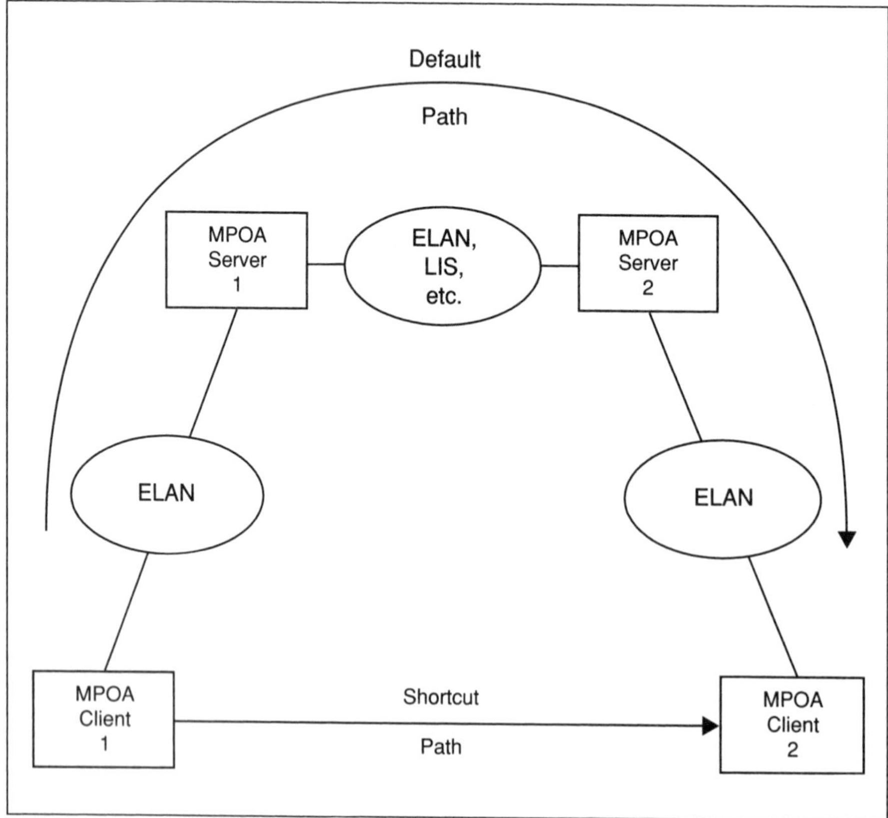

Figure 3-13g MPOA Data Paths
(Copyright 1997, The ATM Forum)

In the next two sections of this chapter, we will consider some typical problems that occur at the Network Interface Layer, along with solutions.

3.12 Troubleshooting the Network Interface Connection

So far in this chapter, we have explored the hardware configurations upon which a TCP/IP-based internetwork may operate, including options for LANs (Ethernet or token ring), MANs (SMDS), and WANs (serial lines or PSPDNs). The large number of available and documented alternatives attests to the popularity of the protocols. Reviewing Figure 3-1b, notice that we are still discussing the physical, not the logical, communication path.

If you're like most TCP/IP administrators, you'll spend as much (if not more) time troubleshooting the hardware (i.e., the Network Interface Layer) as the higher layer software. If a connector is bad or a network interface card is defective, you must troubleshoot and repair those elements before moving up the protocol stack to analyze the TCP/IP protocols. A companion volume to this book, the *LAN Troubleshooting Handbook*, second edition [3-39], discusses LAN hardware troubleshooting in detail. Here are some key points to consider:

- First, check the basic communication path between devices. Broken cables, loose connectors, and so on can cause what appear to be more complex problems.
- Check for compliance with standards. For example, verify that all workstations on an Ethernet are transmitting Ethernet, not IEEE 802.3 frames. Or verify that all segments have the correct cable type, such as the RG58A/U used with IEEE 802.3 10BASE2 networks, not the RG59A/U used with video systems such as VCRs.
- Systematically isolate the problem to a single LAN, MAN, or WAN segment. It is rare for two segments to fail simultaneously.

In our next section, we will examine case studies that demonstrate Network Interface Layer problems typical for TCP/IP-based internetworks.

3.13 Case Studies

In light of our previous discussion of the protocols used at the ARPA Network Interface Layer, let's look at some case studies of actual situations that illustrate the operation of the protocols. For consistency, we captured all data with the Network General Sniffer protocol analyzer.

3.13.1 Initializing a Token Ring Workstation

In our first case study, we'll look at how a workstation becomes an active member of a token ring network, prior to initiating any higher layer service such as a file transfer using FTP (see Figure 3-14). In general, the workstation must complete two steps before TCP/IP or any higher layer protocols can be activated. First, the workstation must make the physical (electrical) connection to the token ring network. Second, it must make the logical connection into the token passing system, ensuring its proper standing among its peers. Let's examine these processes in detail.

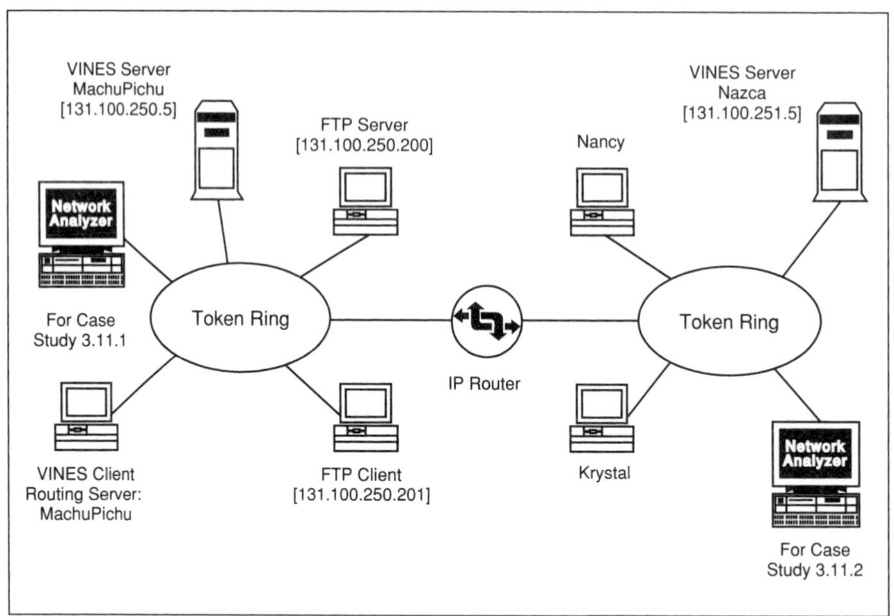

Figure 3-14 IEEE 802.5 Network with Banyan VINES and TCP/IP

The token ring standard (IEEE 802.5) defines two types of transmission frames. A Logical Link Control (LLC) frame carries user data, such as an electronic mail message. A Medium Access Control (MAC) frame transmits network management information. (These frame types are distinguished by the first two bits of the Frame Control field: 00 = MAC and 01 = LLC.) The MAC frames are always transmitted first (because one of their functions is network initialization), then a combination of MAC and LLC frames may be transmitted. The IEEE 802.5 standard defines a total of 25 MAC frames, which perform a number of network management functions.

Two examples of MAC-related functions are the Active Monitor (AM) and the Standby Monitor (SM). All token ring controller chips (such as Texas Instruments'

TMS380) can perform these functions. The AM function observes the overall health of the network, making sure that the token circulates properly, that transmitted frames circle the ring only once, and so on. The workstation with the highest address (the 48-bit address stored in a ROM on the network interface card) is selected to be the AM. All other workstations assume an SM function and assure the proper operation of the AM. (This is somewhat akin to parents leaving their children with a sitter. The sitter watches the children, but the children also report any unusual actions, such as excessive telephone use, of the sitter.) The AMs and SMs identify themselves by periodically transmitting the Active Monitor Present (AMP) and Standby Monitor Present (SMP) frames.

In this example (see Trace 3.13.1 at the end of this section), a workstation (designated FTP Client) wishes to enter the token ring network on the left-hand side of the TCP/IP Router. The network analyzer is placed on the left-hand ring, network [131.100.250.x], to capture the data. Only the network analyzer and the server (designated FTP Server) are currently active. The server is the AM and transmits an AMP frame approximately every seven seconds. When the TR client is turned on, its NIC actuates the relay connected to its port within the token ring wiring hub, known as the Multistation Access Unit (MSAU). Because the relay actuation momentarily disrupts the signal transmission, the AM transmits a Ring Purge MAC frame to test the transmission path.

Next, the FTP client transmits a frame to itself (see Frame 6, the MAC Duplicate Address Test (DAT)) to determine whether another workstation with the same address is active on the ring. If two identical addresses existed, both stations might respond to a transmission and would confuse the recipient. Thus, if the new station received a response to the DAT frame, it would abort its login.

Each workstation maintains a register containing the address of its nearest upstream neighbor. When this address changes (or is entered for the first time) the workstation reports a change in the Stored Upstream Address (SUA) to the Configuration Report Server (CRS). (The CRS is a functional address that maintains the logical topology of the ring for purposes of network management.) Notice that a second DAT frame is sent in Frame 8, followed by a Report SUA Change in Frame 9. In Frame 11, the server also reports an SUA change. As a passive device, the network analyzer does not participate in these logical ring transmissions.

In Frames 12 through 15 the client requests its parameters from another functional address, the Ring Parameter Server (RPS). The RPS is not active; therefore, the FTP Client uses its default parameters and continues. The AM station has been keeping track of the transmission interruptions caused by the new workstation's MSAU relay actuation and transmits an error report to another functional address, the Ring Error Monitor (REM), in Frame 16.

Finally, the new workstation participates in a Ring Poll, which verifies its status as an SM, since the AM (FTP Server) is already selected. Frames 17 and 18 (AMP then SMP) show this Ring Poll, which repeats every seven seconds (Frames 23–24 and 25–26). The Internet protocols become active in Frame 19, when the FTP Client uses ARP to determine a hardware address that matches internet address

131.100.250.200. ICMP and TCP information is also transmitted (Frames 21–22 and 27–29, respectively) before an FTP session begins in Frame 30. The TCP sequence is known as a three-way handshake, which we will look at in detail in Section 5.5.5.

To summarize, the FTP Client underwent the following MAC-Layer functions to make the physical and logical connection to the token ring network:

Event 1	The relay actuation triggers the transmission of a Ring Purge frame.
Event 2	The new node transmits one or two Duplicate Address Test frames.
Event 3	The new node and its downstream neighbor report a Stored Upstream Address change to the Configuration Report server.
Event 4	The new node requests Initialization parameters from Ring Parameter server (maximum 4 tries).
Event 5	The new node's downstream neighbor transmits a Report Error frame.
Event 6	The new node participates in a Ring Poll.

TRACE 3.13.1. TOKEN RING STATION INITIALIZATION

Sniffer Network Analyzer data 16-Jan at 14:54:28, file FTPXCHNG.TRC Pg 1

SUMMARY	Delta T	Destination	Source	Summary
M 1		LAN Manager	NwkGnlE00E1A	IBMNM Trace Tool Present
2	2.009	Broadcast	FTP Server	MAC Active Monitor Present
3	6.998	Broadcast	FTP Server	MAC Active Monitor Present
4	6.998	Broadcast	FTP Server	MAC Active Monitor Present
5	2.900	Broadcast	FTP Server	MAC Ring Purge
6	0.001	FTP Client	FTP Client	MAC Duplicate Address Test
7	0.000	Broadcast	FTP Server	MAC Active Monitor Present
8	0.001	FTP Client	FTP Client	MAC Duplicate Address Test
9	0.001	Config Srv	FTP Client	MAC Report SUA Change
10	0.017	Broadcast	FTP Client	MAC Standby Monitor Present
11	0.000	Config Srv	FTP Server	MAC Report SUA Change
12	0.000	Param Server	FTP Client	MAC Request Initialization
13	0.000	Param Server	FTP Client	MAC Request Initialization
14	0.000	Param Server	FTP Client	MAC Request Initialization
15	0.000	Param Server	FTP Client	MAC Request Initialization
16	2.166	Error Mon.	FTP Server	MAC Report Soft Error
17	4.798	Broadcast	FTP Server	MAC Active Monitor Present

18	0.017	Broadcast	FTP Client	MAC Standby Monitor Present
19	4.032	Broadcast	FTP Client	ARP C PA=[131.100.250.200] PRO=IP
20	0.003	FTP Client	FTP Server	ARP R PA=[131.100.250.200] HA=10005A2502CE PRO=IP
21	0.003	FTP Server	FTP Client	ICMP Echo
22	0.003	FTP Client	FTP Server	ICMP Echo reply
23	2.937	Broadcast	FTP Server	MAC Active Monitor Present
24	0.016	Broadcast	FTP Client	MAC Standby Monitor Present
25	6.981	Broadcast	FTP Server	MAC Active Monitor Present
26	0.016	Broadcast	FTP Client	MAC Standby Monitor Present
27	0.903	FTP Server	FTP Client	TCP D=21 S=3592 SYN SEQ=82509567 LEN=0 WIN=1800
28	0.005	FTP Client	FTP Server	TCP D=3592 S=21 SYN ACK=82509568 SEQ=48955135 LEN=0 WIN=1800
29	0.003	FTP Server	FTP Client	TCP D=21 S=3592 ACK=48955136 WIN=1800
30	0.042	FTP Client	FTP Server	FTP R PORT=3592 220-hewey PC/TCP 2.0 FTP Server by FTP Software re...
31	0.150	FTP Server	FTP Client	TCP D=21 S=3592 ACK=48955253 WIN=1683
32	3.461	FTP Server	FTP Client	FTP C PORT=3592 USER anonymous<0D><0A>
33	0.003	FTP Client	FTP Server	TCP D=3592 S=21 ACK=82509584 WIN=1784
34	0.032	FTP Client	FTP Server	FTP R PORT=3592 230 User OK, no password<0D><0A>
35	0.125	FTP Server	FTP Client	TCP D=21 S=3592 ACK=48955279 WIN=1774
36	2.252	Broadcast	FTP Server	MAC Active Monitor Present
37	0.015	Broadcast	FTP Client	MAC Standby Monitor Present
38	3.428	FTP Server	FTP Client	FTP C PORT=3592 PWD<0D><0A>
39	0.004	FTP Client	FTP Server	TCP D=3592 S=21 509589 WIN=1795
40	0.009	FTP Client	FTP Server	FTP R PORT=3592 250 Current working directory is C:\MIKES\PCTCP<0D>...

In our next example, we'll see how information passes from one server to another within an IP tunnel.

3.13.2 Transmitting Banyan VINES Packets through the Internet

In Section 2.7, we discussed the concept of tunneling or encapsulation. Recall that in this process, a LAN operating system, such as NetWare or VINES, uses the Internet protocols to transmit data over a WAN connection. The process is often referred to as an IP tunnel.

Figure 3-14 illustrates the tunneling process using a VINES internetwork. The VINES client is connected to network 131.100.250.X and must access a server (Nazca) on another network, 131.100.251.X. An IP-based internetwork connects the two rings. Several steps are necessary to complete the connection. First, the client must attach to its routing server (MachuPichu) on the local ring. Next, the local server encapsulates the VINES packets in an IP datagram for transmission on the internetwork. Finally, the distant server (Nazca) receives the token ring frame, strips off the token ring header, IP header, and token ring trailer, and returns the VINES packet to the way it was before encapsulation in the IP datagram. Let's use the analyzer to examine this process.

The placement of the analyzer is vital to understanding the protocol interaction. In this example, we located the analyzer on the distant ring (review Figure 3-14). If the analyzer were on the local ring, it would only be able to see the traffic going into the router; by locating the analyzer on the distant ring you can verify the data coming out of the router and the communication line in between. The analyzer is capturing both VINES and IP packets. The VINES packets represent traffic between the client and the routing server, MachuPichu. The IP packets represent traffic (via the IP Router) between the routing server, MachuPichu, and the server on the client's ring, Nazca.

In Trace 3.13.2a, we observe several interactions, including a MAC AMP frame (sent from IP Router in Frame 4) and the MAC SMP frames sent from the other ring stations (Frames 5 and 6). In Frame 7, the router and server begin exchanging IP packets that come from node 131.100.250.5 (MachuPichu, the client's routing server) to the target server (Nazca), node 131.100.251.5. The IP packets contain the requests from, and the responses to, the client for file service.

Trace 3.13.2b shows the details of Frame 7, the client's request for a file search. (Frame 8 contains the server's reply, which is not shown in Trace 3.13.2b.) Note that the token ring header also contains the SNAP header (IEEE 802.2 LLC plus EtherType) shown in Figure 3-5. The SNAP header uses DSAP = AAH, SSAP = AAH, and Control = 03H (Unnumbered Information or UI). The Protocol ID = 000000H (not indicated in the trace file, but available in the hexadecimal decode), with an EtherType = 0800H (IP). The 20-octet IP header is transmitted next. It identifies source network address 131.100.250.5 (MachuPichu) and destination network address 131.100.251.5 (Nazca). These addresses confirm the communication between the two VINES servers. Note that IP datagrams in both directions are given an ID number (e.g. 20253 in Frame 7) from the originating node. The final portion of the IP datagram is the VINES packet itself.

We may derive two conclusions from this example. First, the placement of the analyzer has a dramatic effect on the data that is captured during encapsulation. (Move the analyzer to either side of an encapsulating server and observe the results for yourself.) Second, multiple protocols, such as IP and VINES, may exist on an internetwork simultaneously. This requires a number of protocol interpreters within the analyzer. Make sure that your analyzer can analyze all of your protocols.

TRACE 3.13.2A. VINES PACKET TUNNELING SUMMARY

Sniffer Network Analyzer data 15-Jan at 19:40:38, file TCPTUNEL.TRC Pg 1

SUMMARY	Delta T	Destination	Source	Summary
M 1	Nazca	IP Router	VMATCH Call	Port=00C0 (Unknown) ID=0 Procedure=100 Arguments=<0006>
2	0.004	Nazca	IP Router	 Port=00C0 (Unknown) ID=0 Procedure=100 Arguments=<0007>
3	0.009	Nazca	IP Router	VSTRTK C NewIncome IncomeType=Detail
4	2.701	Broadcast	IP Router	MAC Active Monitor Present
5	0.014	Broadcast	IBM 38235C	MAC Standby Monitor Present
6	0.019	Broadcast	Nazca	MAC Standby Monitor Present
7	1.214	Nazca	IP Router	SMB C Search \TEMP\????????.???
8	0.013	IP Router	Nazca	SMB R 1 entry found
9	0.081	Nazca	IP Router	SMB C Search \TEMP\????????.???
10	0.037	IP Router	Nazca	SMB R 15 entries found
11	0.024	Nazca	IP Router	SMB C Check dir \TEMP
12	0.013	IP Router	Nazca	SMB R OK
13	0.359	Nazca	IP Router	VSPP Ack NS=854 NR=875 Window=879 RID=0027 LID=0011
14	0.086	Nazca	IP Router	SMB too short to decode
15	0.012	IP Router	Nazca	SMB R Got Disk Attributes
16	0.341	Nazca	IP Router	VSPP Ack NS=855 NR=876 Window=880 RID=0027 LID=0011
17	3.093	Nazca	IP Router	VSTRTK C NewIncome IncomeType=Detail

18	1.694	Broadcast	IP Router	MAC Active Monitor Present
19	0.014	Broadcast	IBM 38235C	MAC Standby Monitor Present
20	0.018	Broadcast	Nazca	MAC Standby Monitor Present

TRACE 3.13.2B. VINES PACKET TUNNELING DETAILS

Sniffer Network Analyzer data 15-Jan at 19:40:38, file TCPTUNEL.TRC Pg 1

```
- - - - - - - - - - - - - - - Frame 7 - - - - - - - - - - - - - - - - -

DLC: — DLC Header —
DLC:
DLC: Frame 7 arrived at 19:40:44.533; frame size is 140 (008C hex) bytes.
DLC: AC: Frame priority 0, Reservation priority 0, Monitor count 0
DLC: FC: LLC frame, PCF attention code: None
DLC: FS: Addr recognized indicators: 00, Frame copied indicators: 00
DLC: Destination = Station IBM   11A83D, Nazca
DLC: Source      = Station IBM   39078A, IP Router
DLC:
LLC: — LLC Header —
LLC:
LLC: DSAP = AA, SSAP = AA, Command, Unnumbered frame: UI
LLC:
SNAP: — SNAP Header —
SNAP:
SNAP: Type = 0800 (IP)
SNAP:
IP: — IP Header —
IP:
IP: Version = 4, header length = 20 bytes
IP: Type of service = 00
IP:      000. .... = routine
IP:      ...0 .... = normal delay
IP:      .... 0... = normal throughput
IP:      .... .0.. = normal reliability
IP: Total length = 118 bytes
IP: Identification = 20253
IP: Flags = 0X
IP: .0.. .... = may fragment
IP: ..0. .... = last fragment
IP: Fragment offset = 0 bytes
IP: Time to live = 254 seconds/hops
IP: Protocol = 83 (VINES)
IP: Header checksum = 7143 (correct)
```

```
IP: Source address = [131.100.250.5]
IP: Destination address = [131.100.251.5]
IP: No options
IP:
VFRP: — VINES FRP Header —
VFRP:
VFRP: Fragmentation byte = 03
VFRP:       0000 00.. = Unused
VFRP:       .... ..1. = End of packet
VFRP:       .... ...1 = Beginning of packet
VFRP:
VFRP: Sequence number = 186
VFRP:
VIP: — VINES IP Header —
VIP:
VIP: Checksum = A7D8
VIP: Packet length = 96
VIP:
VIP: Transport control = 5E
VIP:      0... .... = Unused
VIP:      .1.. .... = Contains RTP redirect message
VIP:      ..0. .... = Do not return metric notification packet
VIP:      ...1 .... = Return exception notification packet
VIP:      .... 1110 = Hop count remaining (14)
VIP:
VIP: Protocol type = 2 (Sequenced Packet Protocol - VSPP)
VIP:
VIP: Destination network.subnetwork = 0000067A.0001
VIP: Source network.subnetwork      = 00000384.8001
VIP:
VSPP: — VINES SPP Header —
VSPP:
VSPP: Source port      = 0203
VSPP: Destination port = 0253
VSPP:
VSPP: Packet type = 1 (Data)
VSPP:
VSPP: Control = 60
VSPP: 0... .... = Unused
VSPP: .1.. .... = End of message
VSPP: ..1. .... = Beginning of message
VSPP: ...0 .... = Do not abort current message
VSPP: .... 0000 = Unused
VSPP:
```

```
VSPP: Local connection ID  = 0011
VSPP: Remote connection ID  = 0027
VSPP:
VSPP: Sequence number      = 852
VSPP: Acknowledgment number = 872
VSPP: Window              = 876
VSPP:
SMB:            — SMB Search Directory Command —
SMB:
SMB: Function = 81 (Search Directory)
SMB: Tree id     (TID) = 002A
SMB: Process id  (PID) = 0E67
SMB: File pathname = "\TEMP\????????.???"
SMB: Maximum number of search entries to return = 25
SMB: Attribute flags = 0008
SMB: .... ....  ..0. .... = File(s) not changed since last archive
SMB: .... ....  ...0 .... = No directory file(s)
SMB: .... ....  .... 1... = Volume label info
SMB: .... ....  .... .0.. = No system file(s)
SMB: .... ....  .... ..0. = No hidden file(s)
SMB: .... ....  .... ...0 = No read only file(s)
SMB:
```

3.13.3 Collisions on an Ethernet

Ethernet and IEEE 802.3 networks operate under a principle known as Carrier Sense, Multiple Access with Collision Detection (CSMA/CD). This means that any station wishing to transmit must first listen to the cable (i.e., carrier sense) to detect whether any other station is transmitting. If the station hears no other signals, it may proceed. Otherwise, it must repeat the carrier sense process later. During periods of heavy traffic, several stations may be waiting for a station to complete its transmission. If those stations make the carrier sense test simultaneously, different stations may conclude that the cable is not in use and that it's OK to proceed. When this happens, signals from the two stations collide, neither transmits data, and precious bandwidth is wasted (Figure 3-15). In short, everyone loses. Collisions also become self-perpetuating; as more stations collide, more bandwidth is wasted, more stations need to transmit, and so on. These collisions may occur on any Ethernet or 802.3 network, regardless of the higher layer protocol in use, because they are a hardware or electrical signal phenomenon.

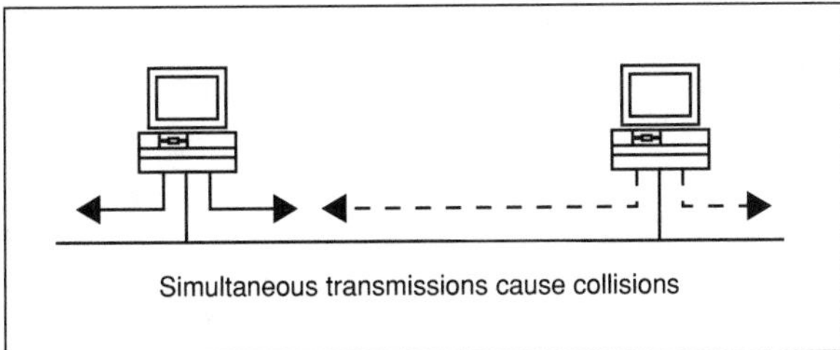

Figure 3.15 Collisions on an Ethernet

In this case study, an Ethernet is running a mixture of DECnet and Internet protocols, such as TCP (see Trace 3.13.3a). We chose this protocol/hardware combination because when the TCP/IP protocols were developed in the 1970s, Ethernet networks were by far the most common LAN solution; therefore, TCP/IP and Ethernet are frequently associated. Thus, if you have TCP/IP you probably have some Ethernet networks (and vice versa), and you'll probably see collisions.

Let's see how such collisions would appear on a network analyzer. Without warning, frames appear with no identifiable Source or Destination address (see Frames 5, 9, 12, 14, 18, 19, etc.). The network analyzer places question marks (????????????) in place of the normal 12 hexadecimal characters since it cannot decode that information. The summary of the frame (on the right-hand side of the trace) indicates that the highest layer within that frame is the Data Link Control (DLC) Layer. This means that the analyzer was also unable to decode any data from the frame's Information field. Note the BAD FRAME indication in the summary.

The details of Frames 18 and 19 (see Trace 3.13.3b) yield little additional information. Both frames are fragments (less than the required 64 octets in length) and have bad alignment, which indicates that the frame does not contain an integral number of octets. There are two clues, however. The first is in the hexadecimal decode of the Address fields. In Frame 18, the decoded data is all ONEs (FF FF FF. . .), indicating that it may have been a Broadcast frame with the Destination address intended to be FFFFFFFFFFFFH. In Frame 19, part of the Destination address is 01 04 80H. Unfortunately, neither of the fragments contains enough information to decode the Source address. If you know the Source address, you might be able to fix the problem by swapping in a new network interface card (assuming the collisions were caused by a faulty CSMA/CD controller chip on the card). The second clue is the time stamp at the top of the trace file (10:18:08). This indicates that the collisions occurred at 10:18 AM. On most networks the heavy traffic periods are between 10:00 and 11:00 AM and between 2:00 and 3:00 PM. The network administrator could study the network for several days and determine whether the collisions were more prevalent during these peak periods. If so, the administrator could logically segment the network with a bridge to isolate the traffic between the bridged segments. Such bridging would improve overall network performance and would reduce collisions.

TRACE 3.13.3A. ETHERNET COLLISION SUMMARY

Sniffer Network Analyzer data 26-Jan at 10:18:08, file COLSN.ENC, Pg 1

SUMMARY	Delta T	Destination	Source	Summary
M 1		DECnet002130	DECnet001F30	Ethertype=6007 (DEC LAVC)
2	0.0334	01048003C04D	820D00008000	Ethertype=825E (Unknown)
3	0.0312	Sun 0A508D	3Com02D383	TCP D=3184 S=6000 ACK=191069101 SEQ=1600831189 LEN=32 WIN=11557
4	0.0001	01048003C04D	821100008000	Ethertype=825E (Unknown)
5	0.0318	????????????	????????????	DLC, BAD FRAME, size=8 bytes
6	0.0094	01048003C04D	820A00008000	Ethertype=825E (Unknown)
7	0.0116	3Com 02D383	Sun 0A508D	TCP D=6000 S=3184 ACK=1600831221 SEQ=191069101 LEN=40 WIN=4096
8	0.0014	Sun0A508D	3Com02D383	TCP D=3184 S=6000 ACK=191069141 WIN=11517
9	0.0161	????????????	????????????	DLC, BAD FRAME, size=7 bytes
10	0.0087	DECnet000130	0000C9007311	LAT C Data D=9301 S=7E13 NR=92 NS=62 Len=2
11	0.0654	3Com05D2DB	0080D3004852	ATP C ID=2196 LEN=6
12	0.0201	????????????	????????????	DLC, BAD FRAME, size=2 bytes
13	0.0083	3Com 05D2DB	0080D3004852	ATP D ID=2196
14	0.0656	????????????	????????????	DLC, BAD FRAME, size=5 bytes
15	0.0051	0000C9007311	DECnet000130	LAT R Data D=7E13 S=9301 NR=64 NS=95 Len=15
16	0.0758	KinetxA09827	3Com 4DE473	NBP C Request ID=31
17	0.0013	DECnet000130	0000C9007311	LAT C Data D=9301 S=7E13 NR=95 NS=65 Len=3
18	0.0223	????????????	????????????	DLC, BAD FRAME, size=5 bytes
19	0.0292	????????????	????????????	DLC, BAD FRAME, size=3 bytes
20	0.0168	0000C9007311	Cisco 006A04	Telnet R PORT=5112 u
21	0.0051	01048003C04D	820A00008000	Ethertype=825E (Unknown)
22	0.0039	????????????	????????????	RI Invalid length
23	0.0191	A5B191A5B99D	80D0A195818C	Ethertype=BDC9 (Unknown)
24	0.0281	01048003C04D	820A00008000	Ethertype=825E (Unknown)
25	0.0190	Sun0A508D	3Com02D383	TCP D=3184 S=6000 ACK=191069141 SEQ=1600831221 LEN=32 WIN=11557

26	0.0088	Sun0A508D	3Com02D383	TCP D=3184 S 6000 ACK=191069181 WIN=11517
27	0.0054	DECnet000130	0000C9007311	LAT C Data D=9301 S=7E13 NR=97 NS=67 Len=3
28	0.0244	????????????	????????????	DLC, BAD FRAME, size=11 bytes

TRACE 3.13.3B. ETHERNET COLLISION DETAILS

Sniffer Network Analyzer data 26-Jan at 10:18:08, file COLSN.ENC, Pg 1

```
- - - - - - - - - - - - - - - - Frame 18 - - - - - - - - - - - - - - - - -
DLC:        —DLC Header —
DLC:
DLC:        Frame 18 arrived at  10:18:09.6937; frame size is 5 (0005 hex) bytes.
DLC:        FRAME ERROR= Fragment  Bad alignment
DLC:
ADDR HEX    ASCII
0000          FF FF FF FF FF.....
- - - - - - - - - - - - - - - - Frame 19 - - - - - - - - - - - - - - - - -
DLC:        —DLC Header —
DLC:
DLC:        Frame 19 arrived at  10:18:09.7229; frame size is 3 (0003 hex) bytes.
DLC:        FRAME ERROR= Fragment  Bad alignment
DLC:
ADDR HEX    ASCII
0000   01 04 80...
```

3.13.4 Incompatibilities between Ethernet and IEEE 802.3 Frames

Technical standards ensure that all parties involved with a project or procedure can communicate accurately. This "communication" could be a bolt communicating with a nut (adhering to the same number of threads per inch) or a terminal communicating with a host computer (adhering to the same character set, such as ASCII). Unfortunately, the Ethernet world has two separate standards that are both loosely termed "Ethernet." The original Ethernet, last published in 1982 by DEC, Intel, and Xerox, is called the Blue Book. The second standard, IEEE 802.3, accommodates elements of the other IEEE LAN standards, such as the IEEE 802.2 Logical Link Control header.

In this case study, a user tries to access some higher layer TCP/IP functions, TCP-CON, but can't because the lower layer connection fails due to the confusion of the two Ethernets on the internet. Let's see what happened.

In Section 2.7.4 we discussed Novell's NetWare operating system and its TCP/IP Transport facility. TCPCON, which is one of TCP/IP's functions, provides SNMP-based management functions through the server's console. To access TCPCON, the user logs into the server from his workstation, executes the remote console (RCONSOLE) command, then loads TCPCON.

The internetwork topology consists of several Ethernet segments that connect a number of devices. The NetWare server doubles as an IP router and connects to both local and remote hosts (see Figure 3-16). The network administrator (David, shown in Trace 3.13.4a) wishes to access TCPCON to check some SNMP statistics at the remote host. He must first log into his NetWare server. Looking for the nearest file server, he broadcasts a NetWare Service Advertisement Protocol (SAP) packet in Frame 1, then repeats the request every 0.6 seconds. But he receives no response.

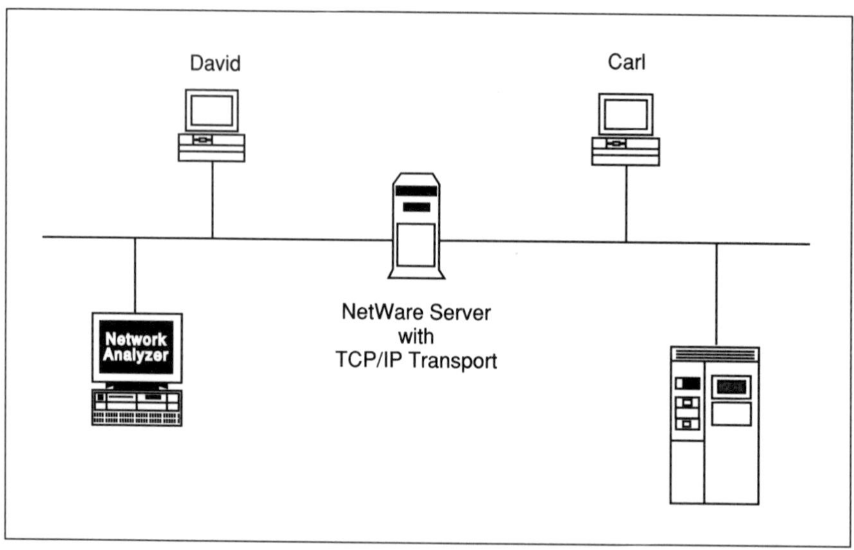

Figure 3-16 IEEE 802.3 Network with Novell NetWare and TCP/IP

Trace 3.13.4b shows the details of the SAP Nearest Service Query and indicates that David's workstation (address H-P 06CA73) was transmitting an Ethernet frame. We know this because the frame header contains an EtherType (8137H) instead of a Length field. David realizes that the server was configured for IEEE 802.3 framing and speculates that the problem might be a frame incompatibility. He reconfigures the workstation by editing the Protocol.ini file to include a driver (IPXDRV.DOS) that accepts the IEEE 802.3 frame type.

A second attempt (Trace 3.13.4c) proves successful. David's workstation requests the nearest server and receives a response from five servers: NW Svr 2, NW Svr 3, H-P 133A5B, NW Svr 1, and H-P 136A06 (Frames 2 through 6). The NetWare Core Protocol (NCP) algorithm then selects the first responding server (NW Svr 2, shown in Frame 2) and creates a connection to that server in Frame 9. The connection is confirmed and a buffer size accepted in Frames 10 through 12. David is now logged into the server and can finish gathering the SNMP statistics. Trace 3.13.4d examines the NCP Nearest Service Query packet after the workstation reconfiguration. Note that the EtherType field has been replaced with the 802.3 length = 34 octets. All other aspects of the frame are identical. Reviewing Figures 3-3 and 3-4, note that the only difference between the Ethernet and IEEE 802.3 frame formats is the field following the Source Address: Ethernet specifies the Type (the higher layer protocol type, in this case, NetWare) while IEEE 802.3 counts the length of the Data field (in this example, 34 octets). The receiving station cannot tolerate a mistake in the frame format. If it is expecting a length (0022H) and it receives an EtherType (8137H), it rejects the frame because that frame is outside of the range of valid 802.3 length fields (0000–05DCH or 46–1500 decimal). Now that David has successfully logged into the server, he can complete his business with RCONSOLE and TCPCON. The moral of the story: If a newly configured "Ethernet" workstation cannot communicate with its server (but appears to be functioning otherwise), check the frame format. Until the lower layers can communicate, you cannot transmit or receive any TCP/IP-related information.

TRACE 3.13.4A. ATTEMPTED TCPCON LOGIN SUMMARY

Sniffer Network Analyzer data 31-Jan at 4:54:50, file ETHERNET.ENC, Pg 1

SUMMARY	Delta T	Destination	Source	Summary
M 1		Broadcast	David	SAP C Find nearest file server
2	0.5503	Broadcast	David	SAP C Find nearest file server
3	0.6042	Broadcast	David	SAP C Find nearest file server
4	0.6042	Broadcast	David	SAP C Find nearest file server
5	0.6042	Broadcast	David	SAP C Find nearest file server
6	0.6042	Broadcast	David	SAP C Find nearest file server
7	0.6042	Broadcast	David	SAP C Find nearest file server
8	0.6042	Broadcast	David	SAP C Find nearest file server
9	0.6042	Broadcast	David	SAP C Find nearest file server
10	0.6042	Broadcast	David	SAP C Find nearest file server
11	0.6042	Broadcast	David	SAP C Find nearest file server
12	0.6042	Broadcast	David	SAP C Find nearest file server

TRACE 3.13.4B. ATTEMPTED NETWARE SERVER TCPCON LOGIN DETAILS

Sniffer Network Analyzer data 31-Jan at 4:54:50 file ETHERNET.ENC, Pg 1

```
- - - - - - - - - - - - - - - - Frame 1 - - - - - - - - - - - - - - - - -

DLC:     --- DLC Header ---
DLC:
DLC:     Frame 1 arrived at  14:54:52.9662; frame size is 60 (003C hex) bytes.
DLC:     Destination = BROADCAST FFFFFFFFFFFF, Broadcast
DLC:     Source      = Station H-P  06CA73, David
DLC:     Ethertype  = 8137 (Novell)
DLC:
IPX:     --- XNS Header ---
IPX:
IPX:     Checksum = FFFF
IPX:     Length = 34
IPX:     Transport control = 00
IPX:             0000 .... = Reserved
IPX:             .... 0000 = Hop count
IPX:     Packet type = 17 (Novell NetWare)
IPX:
IPX:     Dest   net = 00000000, host = FFFFFFFFFFFF,
         socket = 1106 (NetWare Service Advertising)
IPX:     Source net = 00000000, host = 08000906CA73, socket = 16390 (4006)
IPX:
NSAP:    --- NetWare Nearest Service Query ---
NSAP:
NSAP:    Server type = 0004 (file server)
```

TRACE 3.13.4C. SUCCESSFUL NETWARE SERVER LOGIN SUMMARY

Sniffer Network Analyzer data 31-Jan at 4:47:46, file IEEE802.ENC, Pg 1

SUMMARY	Delta T	Destination	Source	Summary
M 1		Broadcast	David	SAP C Find nearest file server
2	0.0008	David	NW Svr 2	SAP R ISD
3	0.0003	David	NW Svr 3	SAP R HR
4	0.0004	David	H-P 133A5B	SAP R GL
5	0.0002	David	NW Svr 1	SAP R IC2
6	0.0001	David	H-P 136A06	SAP R ICTEMP
7	0.0018	Broadcast	David	IPX RIP request: find 1 network, 00133ADE
8	0.0005	David	NW Svr 2	IPX RIP response: 1 network, 00133ADE at 1 hop
9	0.0012	NW Svr 2	David	NCP C Create Connection

10	0.0034	David	NW Svr 2	NCP NCP R OK2
11	0.0013	NW Svr 2	David	NCP C Propose buffer size of 1024
12	0.0004	David	NW Svr 2	NCP R OK Accept buffer size of 1024
13	0.0300	David	H-P 11D4BD	SAP R H20
14	0.0016	David	H-P 133A76	SAP R BOOKS
15	0.00272	NW Svr 2	David	NCP C Logout
16	0.0023	David	H-P 133AAA	SAP R OLD
17	0.0008	David	NW Svr 2	NCP R OK
18	0.0012	NW Svr 2	David	NCP R C Get server's clock
19	0.0004	David	NW Svr 2	NCP R OK

TRACE 3.13.4D. SUCCESSFUL NETWARE SERVER LOGIN DETAILS

Sniffer Network Analyzer data 31-Jan at 4:47:46, file IEEE802.ENC, Pg 1

```
---------------- Frame 1 -----------------

DLC: — DLC Header —
DLC:
DLC: Frame 1 arrived at  14:48:13.7824; frame size is 60 (003C hex) bytes.
DLC: Destination = BROADCAST FFFFFFFFFFFF, Broadcast
DLC: Source      = Station H-P   06CA73, David
DLC: 802.3 length = 34
DLC:
IPX: — IPX Header —
IPX:
IPX: Checksum = FFFF
IPX: Length = 34
IPX: Transport control = 00
IPX:         0000 .... = Reserved
IPX:         .... 0000 = Hop count
IPX: Packet type = 17 (Novell NetWare)
IPX:
IPX: Dest   net = 00000000, host = FFFFFFFFFFFF,
                    socket = 1106 (NetWare Service Advertising)
IPX: Source net = 00000000, host = 08000906CA73, socket = 16390 (4006)
IPX:
NSAP: — NetWare Nearest Service Query —
NSAP:
NSAP: Server type = 0004 (file server)
```

3.13.5 Encapsulating IP Packets inside AppleTalk Packets

In this example, we will discuss another alternative for multiprotocol Internet connectivity: an AppleTalk gateway. As we discussed in Section 2.6, Apple developed the AppleTalk protocol suite, which is described in *Inside AppleTalk* [3-40]. Apple supports the Internet protocols via a product called MacTCP, which supports the Network and Transport Layers over LocalTalk (the 230 Kbps twisted pair network), Ethernet/IEEE 802.3, or token ring. In the internetwork shown in Figure 3-17, a FastPath DDP-to-IP gateway from Shiva Corp. (Cambridge, Massachusetts) connects a LocalTalk and an Ethernet network. The FastPath supports AppleTalk, TCP/IP, and DECnet protocols, plus SNMP network management.

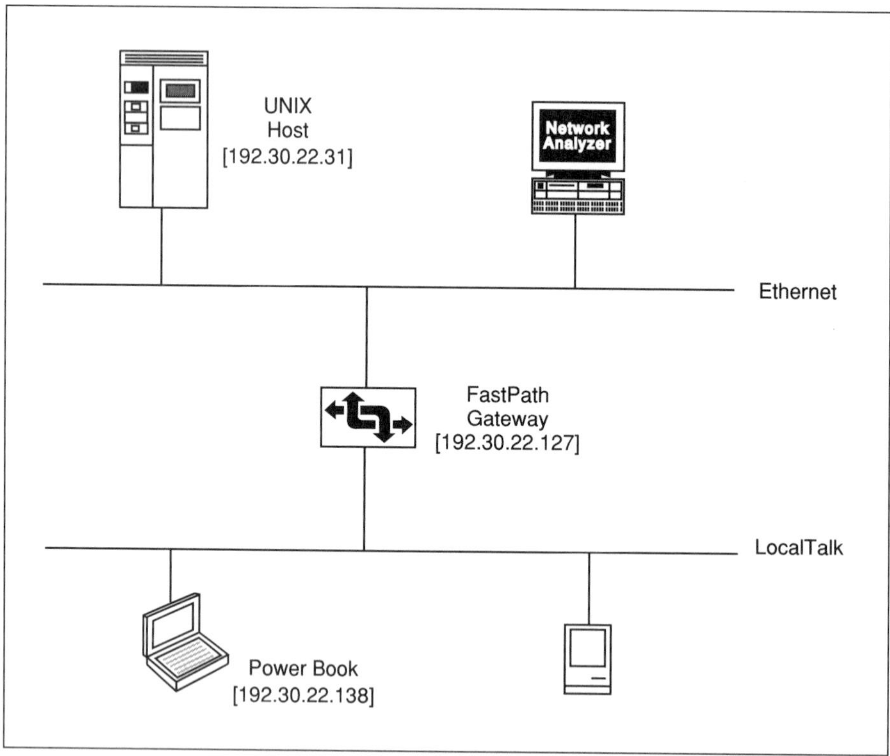

Figure 3-17 AppleTalk to Internet Gateway

In this case study, a network manager (whom we will call Jeff) is using an Apple PowerBook computer on the LocalTalk network, Apple's MacTCP software, and Intercon's TCP/Connect II application package. Jeff wishes to access a UNIX host on the Ethernet network. The process for the protocols is for Jeff's workstation to communicate with the FastPath using the AppleTalk protocols. The FastPath then converts the AppleTalk to Internet protocols, and then communicates to the UNIX host via the Ethernet network. If we were to place the network analyzer on the LocalTalk side, we would observe LocalTalk frames containing AppleTalk data; with the analyzer on the Ethernet side, we observe Ethernet frames containing TCP/IP data. Let's look and see.

With the analyzer on the Ethernet side, we can capture the communication between the Ethernet network card inside the FastPath and the Ethernet network card inside the UNIX host. Trace 3.13.5a shows a summary of these frames; extraneous traffic on the Ethernet network was filtered out for clarity. Beginning in Frame 9, Jeff initializes a TCP connection to the TELNET port on the remote host. The initialization is a three-way handshake, with Jeff asking for a connection (Frame 9), the host responding (Frame 10), and Jeff confirming the arrangement (Frame 11). Looking at the details of those frames (Trace 3.13.5b), the IP header contains the source of the data (Internet address 192.30.22.138, the PowerBook) and the designated destination (192.30.22.31, the UNIX host). The TCP header addresses the destination process (Destination Port = 23 [TELNET]). The only clue that another protocol suite is in use is in the TCP options contained in Frame 9. Note that the originating station (Jeff) requires a maximum TCP segment size of 536 octets, a constraint imposed by MacTCP. When the TCP segment size is added to the TCP header (20 octets) and the IP header (also 20 octets), a maximum IP datagram size of 576 octets results.

Returning to Trace 3.13.5a, we see the host begin the TELNET options negotiation process, first asking for Jeff's terminal type (Frame 12). Jeff's workstation requests a suppress go-ahead (Frame 15) and responds to the terminal type (Frame 18), plus other parameters (Frames 19 through 26). Jeff then signals the host to log in by hitting the carriage return and linefeed in succession <CR><LF>, which is represented in hexadecimal by <0D><0A> in Frame 29. The Host responds by asking for Jeff's login (Frame 30), and Jeff's workstation responds by sending the login (Guest) one character at a time (Frames 41 through 55). Note that the Host echoes each character (e.g., Frame 42) and that the workstation sends a TCP acknowledgment between each successive character (e.g., Frame 43). Jeff's workstation sends another <CR><LF> in Frame 57, prompting the host to request his password. The password (apple) is transferred one character at a time in Frames 71 through 87, but this time the host does not echo the password characters to the workstation. We only see a TCP acknowledgment from the host to Jeff between password characters. Now that the login and password are validated, Jeff may go about his business on the UNIX host.

TRACE 3.13.5A. APPLETALK TO INTERNET GATEWAY SUMMARY

Sniffer Network Analyzer data 5-Feb at 16:54:54, file DDPIP.ENC, Pg 1

SUMMARY	Delta T	Destination	Source	Summary
9		UNIX Host	FastPath	TCP D=23 S=28529 SYN SEQ=3613179760 LEN=0 WIN=10843
10	0.0012	FastPath	UNIX Host	TCP D=28529 S=23 SYN ACK=3613179761 SEQ=724864001 LEN=0 WIN=4096
11	0.0170	UNIX Host	FastPath	TCP D=23 S=28529 ACK=724864002 WIN=10843
12	0.0508	FastPath	UNIX Host	Telnet R PORT=28529 IAC Do Terminal type
13	0.0166	UNIX Host	FastPath	TCP D=23 S=28529 ACK=724864005 WIN=10840
15	0.2170	UNIX Host	FastPath	Telnet C PORT=28529 IAC Do Suppress go-ahead
16	0.0013	FastPath	UNIX Host	Telnet R PORT=28529 IAC Will Suppress go-ahead
17	0.0178	UNIX Host	FastPath	TCP D=23 S=28529 ACK=724864008 WIN=10837
18	0.0143	UNIX Host	FastPath	Telnet C PORT=28529 IAC Will Terminal type
19	0.0012	FastPath	UNIX Host	Telnet R PORT=28529 IAC SB ...
20	0.0165	UNIX Host	FastPath	TCP D=23 S=28529 ACK=724864014 WIN=10831
21	0.0809	UNIX Host	FastPath	Telnet C PORT=28529 IAC SB ...
22	0.1126	FastPath	UNIX Host	TCP D=28529 S=23 ACK=3613179782 WIN=4096
23	0.0018	FastPath	UNIX Host	Telnet R PORT=28529 IAC Will Echo
24	0.0233	UNIX Host	FastPath	TCP D=23 S=28529 ACK=724864059 WIN=10798
25	0.0232	UNIX Host	FastPath	Telnet C PORT=28529 IAC Do Echo
26	0.1514	FastPath	UNIX Host	TCP D=28529 S=23 ACK=3613179785 WIN=4096
29	0.6094	UNIX Host	FastPath	Telnet C PORT=28529 <0D><0A>

30	0.0036	FastPath	UNIX Host	Telnet R PORT=28529 <0D><0A>login:
32	0.0193	UNIX Host	FastPath	TCP D=23 S=28529 ACK=724864068 WIN=10834
41	0.5279	UNIX Host	FastPath	Telnet C PORT=28529 G
42	0.0026	FastPath	UNIX Host	Telnet R PORT=28529 G
43	0.0169	UNIX Host	FastPath	TCP D=23 S=28529 ACK=724864069 WIN=10842
44	0.2052	UNIX Host	FastPath	Telnet C PORT=28529 u
45	0.0025	FastPath	UNIX Host	Telnet R PORT=28529 u
46	0.0171	UNIX Host	FastPath	TCP D=23 S=28529 ACK=724864070 WIN=10842
47	0.0831	UNIX Host	FastPath	Telnet C PORT=28529 e
48	0.0025	FastPath	UNIX Host	Telnet R PORT=28529 e
49	0.0171	UNIX Host	FastPath	TCP D=23 S=28529
51	0.1882	UNIX Host	FastPath	Telnet C PORT=28529 s
52	0.0026	FastPath	UNIX Host	Telnet R PORT=28529 s
53	0.0170	UNIX Host	FastPath	TCP D=23 S=28529 ACK=724864072 WIN=10842
54	0.2058	UNIX Host	FastPath	Telnet C PORT=28529 t
55	0.0026	FastPath	UNIX Host	Telnet R PORT=28529 t
56	0.0163	UNIX Host	FastPath	TCP D=23 S=28529 ACK=724864073 WIN=10842
57	0.3692	UNIX Host	FastPath	Telnet C PORT=28529 <0D><0A>
58	0.0077	FastPath	UNIX Host	Telnet R PORT=28529 <0D><0A>
59	0.0166	UNIX Host	FastPath	TCP D=23 S=28529 ACK=724864075 WIN=10841
64	0.2520	FastPath	UNIX Host	Telnet R PORT=28529 Password:
65	0.0170	UNIX Host	FastPath	TCP D=23 S=28529 ACK=724864084 WIN=10834
71	0.3686	UNIX Host	FastPath	Telnet C PORT=28529 a
72	0.0282	FastPath	UNIX Host	TCP D=28529 S=23 ACK=3613179795 WIN=4096
73	0.1660	UNIX Host	FastPath	Telnet C PORT=28529 p
74	0.0339	FastPath	UNIX Host	TCP D=28529 S=23 ACK=3613179796 WIN=4096
75	0.1594	UNIX Host	FastPath	Telnet C PORT=28529 p
76	0.0405	FastPath	UNIX Host	TCP D=28529 S=23 ACK=3613179797 WIN=4096
85	0.1536	UNIX Host	FastPath	Telnet C PORT=28529 l
86	0.0463	FastPath	UNIX Host	TCP D=28529 S=23 ACK=3613179798 WIN=4096

87	0.1245	UNIX Host	FastPath	Telnet C PORT=28529 e
91	0.0754	FastPath	UNIX Host	TCP D=28529 S=23 ACK=3613179799 WIN=4096
92	0.0850	UNIX Host	FastPath	Telnet C PORT=28529 <0D><0A>
93	0.0048	FastPath	UNIX Host	Telnet R PORT=28529 <0D><0A>
94	0.0164	UNIX Host	FastPath	TCP D=23 S=28529 ACK=724864086 WIN=10841
95	0.5532	FastPath	UNIX Host	Telnet R PORT=28529 <0D><0A>
96	0.0309	UNIX Host	FastPath	TCP D=23 S=28529 ACK=724864495 WIN=10434
97	0.7618	FastPath	UNIX Host	Telnet R PORT=28529 TERM = (vt100)
98	0.0172	UNIX Host	FastPath	TCP D=23 S=28529 ACK=724864510 WIN=10828

TRACE 3.13.5B. APPLETALK TO INTERNET GATEWAY DETAILS

Sniffer Network Analyzer data 5-Feb at 16:54:54, file DDPIP.ENC, Pg 1

```
- - - - - - - - - - - - - - - - Frame 9 - - - - - - - - - - - - - - - - -

DLC:  — DLC Header —
DLC:
DLC:  Frame 9 arrived at  16:54:58.1627; frame size is 60 (003C hex) bytes.
DLC:  Destination = Station 1000E0019B07, UNIX Host
DLC:  Source      = Station KinetxA13296, FastPath
DLC:  Ethertype  = 0800 (IP)
DLC:
IP:   — IP Header —
IP:
IP:   Version = 4, header length = 20 bytes
IP:   Type of service = 00
IP:   000. .... = routine
IP:   ...0 .... = normal delay
IP:   .... 0... = normal throughput
IP:   .... .0.. = normal reliability
IP:   Total length = 44 bytes
IP:   Identification = 352
IP:   Flags = 0X
IP:   .0.. .... = may fragment
IP:   ..0. .... = last fragment
```

```
IP:   Fragment offset = 0 bytes
IP:   Time to live = 59 seconds/hops
IP:   Protocol = 6 (TCP)
IP:   Header checksum = D186 (correct)
IP:   Source address = [192.30.22.138]
IP:   Destination address = [192.30.22.31]
IP:   No options
IP:
TCP:  — TCP header —
TCP:
TCP:  Source port = 28529
TCP:  Destination port = 23 (Telnet)
TCP:  Initial sequence number = 3613179760
TCP:  Data offset = 24 bytes
TCP:  Flags = 02
TCP:  ..0. .... = (No urgent pointer)
TCP:  ...0 .... = (No acknowledgment)
TCP:  .... 0... = (No push)
TCP:  .... .0.. = (No reset)
TCP:  .... ..1. = SYN
TCP:  .... ...0 = (No FIN)
TCP:  Window = 10843
TCP:  Checksum = BE2B (correct)
TCP:
TCP:  Options follow
TCP:  Maximum segment size = 536
TCP:

- - - - - - - - - - - - - - - - Frame 10 - - - - - - - - - - - - - - - - -

DLC:  — DLC Header —
DLC:
DLC:  Frame 10 arrived at  16:54:58.1640; frame size is 60 (003C hex) bytes.
DLC:  Destination = Station KinetxA13296, FastPath
DLC:  Source      = Station 1000E0019B07, UNIX Host
DLC:  Ethertype  = 0800 (IP)
DLC:
IP:   — IP Header —
IP:
IP:   Version = 4, header length = 20 bytes
IP:   Type of service = 00
IP:   000. .... = routine
IP:   ...0 .... = normal delay
IP:   .... 0... = normal throughput
```

```
IP:   .... .0.. = normal reliability
IP:   Total length = 44 bytes
IP:   Identification = 2082
IP:   Flags = 0X
IP:   .0.. .... = may fragment
IP:   ..0. .... = last fragment
IP:   Fragment offset = 0 bytes
IP:   Time to live = 30 seconds/hops
IP:   Protocol = 6 (TCP)
IP:   Header checksum = E7C4 (correct)
IP:   Source address = [192.30.22.31]
IP:   Destination address = [192.30.22.138]
IP:   No options
IP:
TCP:  — TCP header —
TCP:
TCP:  Source port = 23 (Telnet)
TCP:  Destination port = 28529
TCP:  Initial sequence number = 724864001
TCP:  Acknowledgment number = 3613179761
TCP:  Data offset = 24 bytes
TCP:  Flags = 12
TCP:  ..0. .... = (No urgent pointer)
TCP:  ...1 .... = Acknowledgment
TCP:  .... 0... = (No push)
TCP:  .... .0.. = (No reset)
TCP:  .... ..1. = SYN
TCP:  .... ...0 = (No FIN)
TCP:  Window = 4096
TCP:  Checksum = 1F58 (correct)
TCP:
TCP:  Options follow
TCP:  Maximum segment size = 1024
TCP:

- - - - - - - - - - - - - - - - Frame 11 - - - - - - - - - - - - - - - - -

DLC:  — DLC Header —
DLC:
DLC:  Frame 11 arrived at  16:54:58.1810; frame size is 60 (003C hex) bytes.
DLC:  Destination = Station 1000E0019B07, UNIX Host
DLC:  Source      = Station KinetxA13296, FastPath
DLC:  Ethertype  = 0800 (IP)
DLC:
```

```
IP:   — IP Header —
IP:
IP:   Version = 4, header length = 20 bytes
IP:   Type of service = 00
IP:   000. .... = routine
IP:   ...0 .... = normal delay
IP:   .... 0... = normal throughput
IP:   .... .0.. = normal reliability
IP:   Total length = 40 bytes
IP:   Identification = 353
IP:   Flags = 0X
IP:   .0.. .... = may fragment
IP:   ..0. .... = last fragment
IP:   Fragment offset = 0 bytes
IP:   Time to live = 59 seconds/hops
IP:   Protocol = 6 (TCP)
IP:   Header checksum = D189 (correct)
IP:   Source address = [192.30.22.138]
IP:   Destination address = [192.30.22.31]
IP:   No options
IP:
TCP:  — TCP header —
TCP:
TCP:  Source port = 28529
TCP:  Destination port = 23 (Telnet)
TCP:  Sequence number = 3613179761
TCP:  Acknowledgment number = 724864002
TCP:  Data offset = 20 bytes
TCP:  Flags = 10
TCP:  ..0. .... = (No urgent pointer)
TCP:  ...1 .... = Acknowledgment
TCP:  .... 0... = (No push)
TCP:  .... .0.. = (No reset)
TCP:  .... ..0. = (No SYN)
TCP:  .... ...0 = (No FIN)
TCP:  Window = 10843
TCP:  Checksum = 1B06 (correct)
TCP:  No TCP options
TCP:
```

3.13.6 Transmitting IP Datagrams over a PSPDN

In Section 3.8, we discussed the principles behind sending IP datagrams over a Packet Switched Public Data Network (PSPDN) using the X.25 protocol. In this case study (see Figure 3-18), we will examine the interactions between TCP/IP and the Internet protocols with the X.25 protocol.

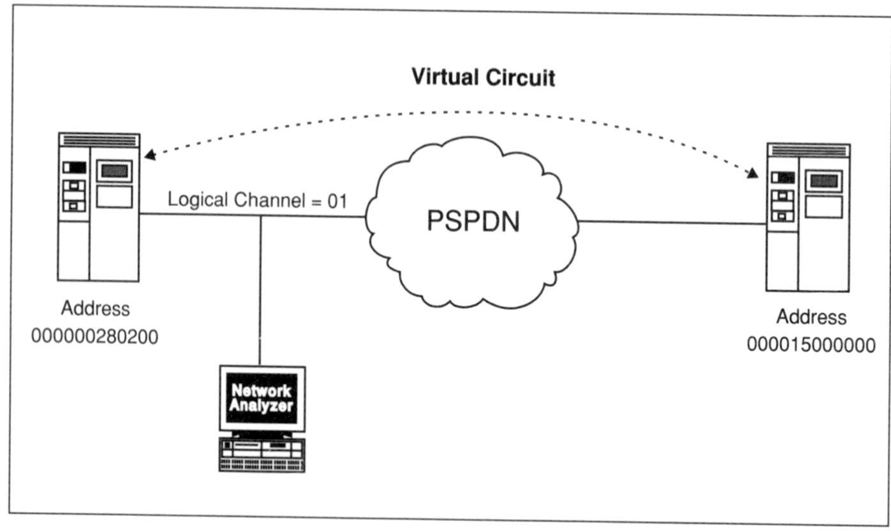

Figure 13-18 Internet Protocols over a PSPDN

To begin, recall that X.25 defines an interface between a packet mode DTE (the user) and a DCE (the network). To capture the internetwork transmission, you must place the analyzer at the DTE/DCE interface. Before any higher layer (e.g., IP) data can be transmitted, an X.25 Virtual Call must be established end to end between the two hosts via the network. Trace 3.13.6a reveals that this occurs in Frame 79; it is an X.25 Call Request packet, transmitted on Logical Channel 001 and destined for remote host 000015000000. The X.25 packet, shown in Trace 3.13.6b, contains a Protocol Identification field within the Call User Data field that identifies the higher layer protocol in use. The value of CCH in the Protocol Identification field tells the destination address (000015000000) that the sender (000000280200) will be using IP. Frame 80 contains a Data Link Layer response. (The response is from LAPB, but is shown as HDLC in the trace. LAPB is a derivative of HDLC, so the Sniffer has given it the generic name.) The destination node's Packet Level response is received in Frame 81 (Call Accepted). The DCE Link Level sends an acknowledgment in Frame 83, and data transfer begins in Frame 84. The data is transmitted on Logical Channel 01 as a single packet (More data bit = 0). Note that the total length of the IP datagram is 46 octets, so it fits completely within the X.25 default packet length of 128 octets. The IP header identifies the protocol within that datagram as the

Interior Gateway Protocol (IGP). The internet source address (XXX.YYY.165.2) is broadcasting the IGP information to all hosts on this network (destination address 255.255.255.255). Frame 85 contains a Packet Level acknowledgment (Receive Ready), indicating receipt of the packet at the local X.25 interface. We know that this acknowledgment did not come from the distant host because the Delivery Confirmation bit within the Packet Level header = 0. The value (0) indicates local acknowledgments; a positive value (1) would indicate remote (i.e., distant host) acknowledgments.

Returning to the data summary (Trace 3.13.6a), we can observe a communication problem between the Source and Destination hosts. In Frame 87, the local host requests a file using the Trivial File Transfer Protocol (TFTP) described in Chapter 6 (Read Request File = network-confg). Three seconds later, it repeats the request (Frame 89). The DTE process appears to be functioning properly since the packet sequence counter is incrementing correctly (PS = 2 in Frame 87; PS = 3 in Frame 89). The local DCE's Packet Level process acknowledges the request with PR = 4 in Frame 90, but never responds with the requested file. The DTE makes a third and a fourth attempt for the file in Frames 92 and 94, with equally disappointing results (Frame 95). Undaunted, the DTE requests a different file (cyg-x1-confg) in Frame 97. Several tries later (Frame 104) this file has also not been received.

The local DTE makes a second Call Request, this time using Logical Channel 002 (Frame 107). By now the local DCE is completely confused and responds with a Clear Request (Frame 109), which is confirmed by the DTE in Frame 111.

The trace file does not identify the exact source of the problem, but it appears to be at the local DTE/DCE interface. The DTE is not the likely culprit since its processes appear to know what they want and have demonstrated patience in their repeated requests. At this point, the network administrator should enlist the aid of the PSPDN analysis center to isolate the problem with the DCE side of the X.25 interface.

TRACE 3.13.6A. X.25 CALL REQUEST AND IP DATA TRANSFER

Sniffer Network Analyzer data 19-Oct at 15:09:24, file CISX251.SYC Pg 1

SUMMARY	Delta T	From DCE	From DTE
79	6.7309		HDLC R I NR=1 NS=1 P/F=0 X.25 001 Call Req Dst:000015000000 Src:000000280200 TCP_IP
80	0.0085	HDLC C RR NR=2 P/F=0	
81	0.0099	HDLC R I NR=2 NS=1 P/F=0 X.25 001 Call Acc	
82	0.0583		HDLC R I NR=2 NS=2 P/F=0 X.25 001 Data PR=0 PS=0 IP D=[255.255.255.255]

			S=[131.100.165.2] LEN=26 ID=0
83	0.0086	HDLC C RR NR=3 P/F=0	
84	1.3943		HDLC R I NR=2 NS=3 P/F=0 X.25 001 Data PR=0 PS=1 IP D=[255.255.255.255] S=[131.100.165.2] LEN=26 ID=0
85	0.0112	HDLC R I NR=4 NS=2 P/F=0 X.25 001 RR PR=2	
86	0.0087		HDLC C RR NR=3 P/F=0
87	36.4935		HDLC R I NR=3 NS=4 P/F=0 X.25 001 Data PR=0 PS=2 IP D=[255.255.255.255] S=[131.100.165.2] LEN=33
ID=0			
			UDP D=69 S=28624 LEN=33 TFTP Read request File=network-confg
88	0.0092	HDLC C RR NR=5 P/F=0	
89	3.0128		HDLC R I NR=3 NS=5 P/F=0 X.25 001 Data PR=0 PS=3 IP D=[255.255.255.255] S=[131.100.165.2] LEN=33 ID=1 UDP D=69 S=28624 LEN=33 TFTP Read request File=network-confg
90	0.0122	HDLC R I NR=6 NS=3 P/F=0 X.25 001 RR PR=4	
91	0.0087		HDLC C RR NR=4 P/F=0
92	2.983		HDLC R I NR=4 NS=6 P/F=0 X.25 001 Data PR=0 PS=4 IP D=[255.255.255.255] S=[131.108.165.2] LEN=33 ID=2 UDP D=69 S=28624 LEN=33 TFTP Read request File=network-confg
93	0.0091	HDLC C RR NR=7 P/F=0	
94	2.9939		R I NR=4 NS=7 P/F=0 X.25 001 Data PR=0 PS=5 IP D=[255.255.255.255] S=[131.108.165.2]

			LEN=33 ID=3 UDP D=69 S=28624 LEN=33 TFTP Read request File=network-confg
95	0.0121	HDLC R I NR=0 NS=4 P/F=0 X.25 001 RR PR=6	
96	0.0088		HDLC C RR NR=5 P/F=0
97	3.0330		HDLC R I NR=5 NS=0 P/F=0 X.25 001 Data PR=0 PS=6 IP D=[255.255.255.255] S=[131.108.165.2] LEN=32 ID=0 UDP D=69 S=40712 LEN=32 TFTP Read request File=cyg-x1-confg
98	0.0081	HDLC C RR NR=1 P/F=0	
99	3.0149		HDLC R I NR=5 NS=1 P/F=0 X.25 001 Data PR=0 PS=7 IP D=[255.255.255.255] S=[131.108.165.2] LEN=32 ID=1 UDP D=69 S=40712 LEN=32 TFTP Read request File=cyg-x1-confg
100	0.0122	HDLC R I NR=2 NS=5 P/F=0 X.25 001 RR PR=0	
101	0.0087		HDLC C RR NR=6 P/F=0
102	2.9820		HDLC R I NR=6 NS=2 P/F=0 X.25 001 Data PR=0 PS=0 IP D=[255.255.255.255] S=[131.108.165.2] LEN=32 ID=2 UDP D=69 S=40712 LEN=32 TFTP Read request File=cyg-x1-confg
103	0.0082	HDLC C RR NR=3 P/F=0	
104	2.9958		HDLC R I NR=6 NS=3 P/F=0 X.25 001 Data PR=0 PS=1 IP D=[255.255.255.255] S=[131.108.165.2] LEN=32 ID=3 UDP D=69 S=40712 LEN=32 TFTP Read request File=cyg-x1-confg

105	0.0112	HDLC R I NR=4 NS=6 P/F=0 X.25 001 RR PR=2	
106	0.0087		HDLC C RR NR=7 P/F=0
107	35.8026		HDLC R I NR=7 NS=4 P/F=0 X.25 002 Call Req Dst:000015000000 Src:000000280200 ISO_CLNP
108	0.0082	HDLC C RR NR=5 P/F=0	
109	0.0120	HDLC R I NR=5 NS=7 P/F=0 X.25 002 Clr Req DTE originated	
110	0.0087		HDLC C RR NR=0 P/F=0
111	0.0099		HDLC R I NR=0 NS=5 P/F=0 X.25 002 Clr Conf

TRACE 3.13.6B. X.25 CALL REQUEST DETAILS

```
Sniffer Network Analyzer data 19-Oct at 15:09:24 file CISX251.SYC Pg 1

- - - - - - - - - - - - - - - - Frame 79 - - - - - - - - - - - - - - - - -

DLC:  — DLC Header —
DLC:
DLC:  Frame 79 arrived at  15:21:44.3950; frame size is 23 (0017 hex) bytes.
DLC:  Destination = DCE
DLC:  Source      = DTE
DLC:
HDLC: — High Level Data Link Control (HDLC) —
HDLC:
HDLC: Address = 03 (Response)
HDLC: Control field = 22
HDLC: 001. .... = N(R) = 1
HDLC: ...0 .... = Poll/Final bit
HDLC: .... 001. = N(S) = 1
HDLC: .... ...0 = I (Information transfer)
HDLC:
X.25:  — X.25 Packet Level —
X.25:
X.25:  General format id = 10
X.25:  .0.. .... = Delivery confirmation bit
X.25:  ..01 .... = Sequence numbering modulo 8
X.25:  .... 0000 = Logical channel group number = 0
X.25:  Logical channel number = 01
X.25:  Packet type identifier = 0B (Call request)
X.25:  Address length field = CC
X.25:  1100 .... = Source length = 12 digits
```

```
X.25: .... 1100 = Destination length = 12 digits
X.25: Destination address = 000015000000
X.25: Source address = 000000280200
X.25: Facility length = 0
X.25: Protocol identification = CC (TCP_IP)
X.25:
X.25: [4 bytes of user data = CC000000]
X.25:

- - - - - - - - - - - - - - - - Frame 80 - - - - - - - - - - - - - - - - -

DLC:  — DLC Header —
DLC:
DLC:  Frame 80 arrived at  15:21:44.4036; frame size is 2 (0002 hex) bytes.
DLC:  Destination = DTE
DLC:  Source      = DCE
DLC:
HDLC: — High Level Data Link Control (HDLC) —
HDLC:
HDLC: Address = 03 (Command)
HDLC: Control field = 41
HDLC: 010. .... = N(R) = 2
HDLC: ...0 .... = Poll/Final bit
HDLC: .... 0001 = RR  (Receive ready)
HDLC:

- - - - - - - - - - - - - - - - Frame 81 - - - - - - - - - - - - - - - - -

DLC:  — DLC Header —
DLC:
DLC:  Frame 81 arrived at  15:21:44.4135; frame size is 5 (0005 hex) bytes.
DLC:  Destination = DTE
DLC:  Source      = DCE
DLC:
HDLC: — High Level Data Link Control (HDLC) —
HDLC:
HDLC:Address = 01 (Response)
HDLC:Control field = 42
HDLC:010. .... = N(R) = 2
HDLC:...0 .... = Poll/Final bit
HDLC:.... 001. = N(S) = 1
HDLC:.... ...0 = I (Information transfer)
HDLC:
X.25:  — X.25 Packet Level —
```

```
X.25:
X.25: General format id = 10
X.25: .0.. .... = Delivery confirmation bit
X.25: ..01 .... = Sequence numbering modulo 8
X.25: .... 0000 = Logical channel group number = 0
X.25: Logical channel number = 01
X.25: Packet type identifier = 0F (Call accepted)
X.25:

---------------- Frame 82 -----------------

DLC: — DLC Header —
DLC:
DLC: Frame 82 arrived at  15:21:44.4719; frame size is 51 (0033 hex) bytes.
DLC: Destination = DCE
DLC: Source      = DTE
DLC:
HDLC:--- High Level Data Link Control (HDLC) ---
HDLC:
HDLC:Address = 03 (Response)
HDLC:Control field = 44
HDLC:010. .... = N(R) = 2
HDLC:...0 .... = Poll/Final bit
HDLC:.... 010. = N(S) = 2
HDLC:.... ...0 = I (Information transfer)
HDLC:
X.25: — X.25 Packet Level —
X.25:
X.25: General format id = 10
X.25: 0... .... = Qualifier bit
X.25: .0.. .... = Delivery confirmation bit
X.25: ..01 .... = Sequence numbering modulo 8
X.25: .... 0000 = Logical channel group number = 0
X.25: Logical channel number = 01
X.25: Data packet info = 00
X.25: 000. .... = P(R) = 0
X.25: ...0 .... = More bit
X.25: .... 000. = P(S) = 0
X.25: .... ...0 = Packet type identifier (Data)
X.25:
IP: — IP Header —
IP:
IP: Version = 4, header length = 20 bytes
IP: Type of service = 00
```

```
IP: 000. .... = routine
IP: ...0 .... = normal delay
IP: .... 0... = normal throughput
IP: .... .0.. = normal reliability
IP: Total length = 46 bytes
IP: Identification = 0
IP: Flags = 0X
IP: .0.. .... = may fragment
IP: ..0. .... = last fragment
IP: Fragment offset = 0 bytes
IP: Time to live = 2 seconds/hops
IP: Protocol = 9 (IGP)
IP: Header checksum = 9059 (correct)
IP: Source address = [131.100.165.2]
IP: Destination address = [255.255.255.255]
IP: No options
IP: [26 byte(s) of data]

- - - - - - - - - - - - - - - - Frame 83 - - - - - - - - - - - - - - - - -

DLC:   — DLC Header —
DLC:
DLC:   Frame 83 arrived at  15:21:44.4805; frame size is 2 (0002 hex) bytes.
DLC:   Destination = DTE
DLC:   Source      = DCE
DLC:
HDLC:  — High Level Data Link Control (HDLC) —
HDLC:
HDLC:  Address = 03 (Command)
HDLC:  Control field = 61
HDLC:  011. .... = N(R) = 3
HDLC:  ...0 .... = Poll/Final bit
HDLC:  .... 0001 = RR  (Receive ready)
HDLC:

- - - - - - - - - - - - - - - - Frame 84 - - - - - - - - - - - - - - - - -

DLC:   — DLC Header —
DLC:
DLC:   Frame 84 arrived at  15:21:45.8748; frame size is 51 (0033 hex) bytes.
DLC:   Destination = DCE
DLC:   Source      = DTE
DLC:
```

```
HDLC: — High Level Data Link Control (HDLC) —
HDLC:
HDLC: Address = 03 (Response)
HDLC: Control field = 46
HDLC: 010. .... = N(R) = 2
HDLC: ...0 .... = Poll/Final bit
HDLC: .... 011. = N(S) = 3
HDLC: .... ...0 = I (Information transfer)
HDLC:
X.25: — X.25 Packet Level —
X.25:
X.25: General format id = 10
X.25: 0... .... = Qualifier bit
X.25: .0.. .... = Delivery confirmation bit
X.25: ..01 .... = Sequence numbering modulo 8
X.25: .... 0000 = Logical channel group number = 0
X.25: Logical channel number = 01
X.25: Data packet info = 02
X.25: 000. .... = P(R) = 0
X.25: ...0 .... = More bit
X.25: .... 001. = P(S) = 1
X.25: .... ...0 = Packet type identifier (Data)
X.25:
IP: — IP Header —
IP:
IP: Version = 4, header length = 20 bytes
IP: Type of service = 00
IP: 000. .... = routine
IP: ...0 .... = normal delay
IP: .... 0... = normal throughput
IP: .... .0.. = normal reliability
IP: Total length = 46 bytes
IP: Identification = 0
IP: Flags = 0X
IP: .0.. .... = may fragment
IP: ..0. .... = last fragment
IP: Fragment offset = 0 bytes
IP: Time to live = 2 seconds/hops
IP: Protocol = 9 (IGP)
IP: Header checksum = 9059 (correct)
IP: Source address = [131.100.165.2]
IP: Destination address = [255.255.255.255]
IP: No options
IP: [26 byte(s) of data]
```

```
---------------- Frame 85 -----------------

DLC:  — DLC Header —
DLC:
DLC:  Frame 85 arrived at  15:21:45.8861; frame size is 5 (0005 hex) bytes.
DLC:  Destination = DTE
DLC:  Source      = DCE
DLC:
HDLC:— High Level Data Link Control (HDLC) —
HDLC:
HDLC:Address = 01 (Response)
HDLC:Control field = 84
HDLC: 100. .... = N(R) = 4
HDLC:...0 .... = Poll/Final bit
HDLC:.... 010. = N(S) = 2
HDLC:.... ...0 = I (Information transfer)
HDLC:
X.25:  — X.25 Packet Level —
X.25:
X.25:  General format id = 10
X.25:  ..01 .... = Sequence numbering modulo 8
X.25:  .... 0000 = Logical channel group number = 0
X.25:  Logical channel number = 01
X.25:  Flow control info = 41
X.25:  010. .... = P(R) = 2
X.25:  ...0 0001 = Packet type identifier (Receive ready)
X.25:
```

3.13.7 File Transfers over Frame Relay Networks

Extending our illustration of using TCP/IP over wide-area networks, this example will demonstrate how the File Transfer Protocol operates over a frame relay network. In this case, a user at a branch office needs access to a file that is resident on a host at the headquarters location (see Figure 3-19). A frame relay network connects the various locations, with two permanent virtual connections (PVCs) between the two sites in question. These PVCs operate over a 56 Kbps leased line, transmitting both IPX and IP traffic. The IP traffic is of greater interest to our discussion; this traffic is carried on the PVC identified by Data Link Connection Identifier (DLCI) 140.

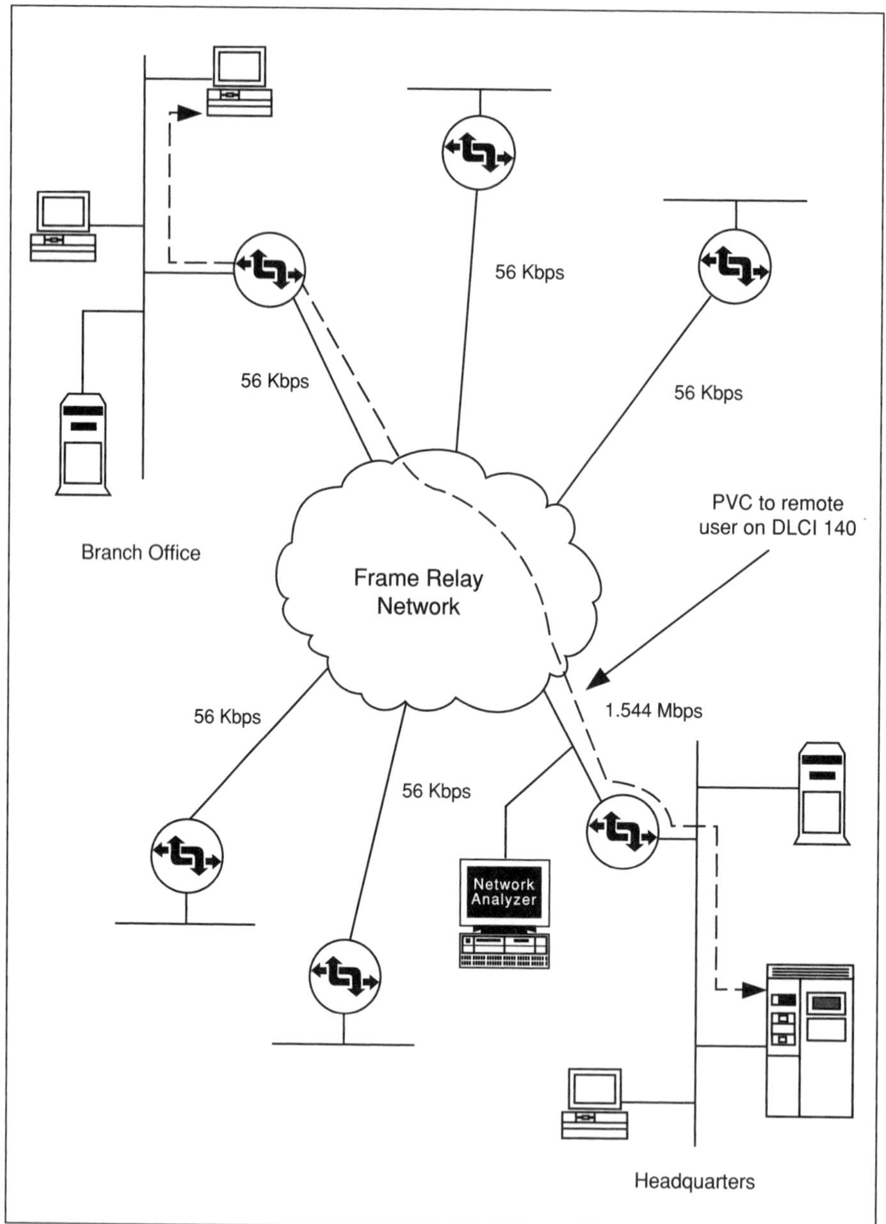

Figure 3-19 TCP/IP over Frame Relay

Note from Figure 3-19 and Trace 3.13.7a that the data was captured at the host end (or headquarters side) of the connection. As a result, careful attention to the Source/Destination address designations is necessary to avoid confusion. For example, in Frame 1078, the destination specified is the DTE, which is actually the host at headquarters. The source of the data in Frame 1078 is the DCE (the network), which is actually the data coming from the remote user, via the network. (As in previous examples, this trace has been filtered to only show frames relevant to our discussion.)

The remote user initiates the file transfer process in Frame 1078 by entering TYPE A at his workstation to indicate to the headquarters host that an ASCII file transfer is being requested. The host confirms the TYPE A transfer in Frame 1079. The ports to be used are defined in Frame 1082 and confirmed in Frame 1083. The user indicates the file to be retrieved in Frame 1088 (Otherlinks.html). The host opens the data connection in Frame 1092, and begins the file transfer in Frame 1093. An acknowledgment from the remote user is seen in Frame 1105, and the host completes the file transfer in Frame 1107 (shown in Trace 3.13.7b).

TRACE 3.13.7A. FILE TRANSFER SUMMARY

Sniffer Internetwork Analyzer data from 8-Mar at 12:44:38, file FR1.SYC, Pg 1

SUMMARY	Delta T	Destination	Source	Summary
1078	2.5111	DTE	DCE	FTP C PORT=1214 TYPE A<0D0A>
1079	0.0128	DCE	DTE	FTP R PORT=1214 200 Type set to A.<0D0A>
1082	0.0751	DTE		DCE FTP C PORT=1214 PORT 161,69,133,72,4,254<0D0A>
1083	0.0110	DCE	DTE	FTP R PORT=1214 200 PORT command successful.<0D0A>
1088	0.0491	DTE	DCE	FTP C PORT=1214 RETR Otherlinks.html<0D0A>
1092	0.0552	DCE	DTE	FTP R PORT=1214 150 Opening ASCII mode data connection for Oth...
1107	0.2048	DCE	DTE	FTP R PORT=1214 226 Transfer complete.<0D0A>

The details of the file transfer illustrate how FTP operates over frame relay connections (see Trace 3.13.7b). In Frame 1078, note that the frame relay header (the lines designated FRELAY in Trace 3.13.7b) identifies the DLCI in use (140), the absence of any congestion (either forward or backward), and other details. The IP header identifies the protocol inside the IP datagram (Protocol = 6 (TCP)), along with the IP addresses of the source and destination (the remote workstation and the headquarters host, respectively), indicating that they are on different IP subnetworks. The TCP header defines the host port that will be accessed (Destination Port = 21, the FTP Control port), along with the TCP connection-related information such as sequence and acknowledgment numbers and flags. The FTP layer decode identifies the eight octets of data that were transmitted (TYPE A <0D0A>, where the 0D is a carriage return character, and the 0A is a line feed character).

Readers studying subsequent frames can trace the consistency of the source and destination IP addresses, the orderly progression of the TCP sequence and acknowledgment numbers, and the details of the FTP process at both the remote and host ends of the connection. In the following chapters, we will study these protocol intricacies in greater detail.

TRACE 3.13.7B. FILE TRANSFER DETAILS

```
Sniffer Internetwork Analyzer data 8-Mar at 12:44:38, file FR1.SYC, Pg 1

---------------- Frame 1078 -----------------

DLC: — DLC Header —
DLC:
DLC: Frame 1078 arrived at  15:07:45.5908; frame size is 52 (0034 hex) bytes.
DLC: Destination = DTE
DLC: Source = DCE
DLC:
FRELAY: — Frame Relay v
FRELAY:
FRELAY: Address word = 20C1
FRELAY: 0010 00.. 1100 .... = DLCI 140
FRELAY: .... ..0. .... .... = Response
FRELAY: .... .... .... 0... = No forward congestion
FRELAY: .... .... .... .0.. = No backward congestion
FRELAY: .... .... .... ..0. = Not eligible for discard
FRELAY: .... .... .... ...1 = Not extended address
FRELAY:
ETYPE:  Ethertype  = 0800 (IP)
ETYPE:
IP: — IP Header —
IP:
IP: Version = 4, header length = 20 bytes
IP: Type of service = 00
IP:       000. .... = routine
IP:       ...0 .... = normal delay
IP:       .... 0... = normal throughput
IP:       .... .0.. = normal reliability
IP: Total length    = 48 bytes
IP: Identification  = 12828
IP: Flags           = 4X
IP:       .1.. .... = don't fragment
```

```
IP:       ..0. .... = last fragment
IP:  Fragment offset = 0 bytes
IP:  Time to live    = 31 seconds/hops
IP:  Protocol        = 6 (TCP)
IP:  Header checksum = F1B8 (correct)
IP:  Source address      = [XXX.YYY.133.72]
IP:  Destination address = [XXX.YYY.81.1]
IP:  No options
IP:
TCP:  — TCP header —
TCP:
TCP:  Source port            = 1214
TCP:  Destination port       = 21 (FTP)
TCP:  Sequence number        = 3275985
TCP:  Acknowledgment number  = 725589307
TCP:  Data offset            = 20 bytes
TCP:  Flags                  = 18
TCP:             ..0. .... = (No urgent pointer)
TCP:             ...1 .... = Acknowledgment
TCP:             .... 1... = Push
TCP:             .... .0.. = (No reset)
TCP:             .... ..0. = (No SYN)
TCP:             .... ...0 = (No FIN)
TCP:  Window                 = 8065
TCP:  Checksum               = BC15 (correct)
TCP:  No TCP options
TCP:  [8 byte(s) of data]
TCP:
FTP:  —  FTP data —
FTP:
FTP:  TYPE A<0D0A>
FTP:

- - - - - - - - - - - - - - - - Frame 1079 - - - - - - - - - - - - - - - -

DLC:  — DLC Header —
DLC:
DLC:  Frame 1079 arrived at  15:07:45.6037; frame size is 64 (0040 hex) bytes.
DLC:  Destination = DCE
DLC:  Source = DTE
DLC:
FRELAY:  — Frame Relay —
FRELAY:
FRELAY:  Address word = 20C1
```

```
FRELAY:  0010 00..  1100 .... = DLCI 140
FRELAY:  .... ..0.  .... .... = Response
FRELAY:  .... ....  .... 0... = No forward congestion
FRELAY:  .... ....  .... .0.. = No backward congestion
FRELAY:  .... ....  .... ..0. = Not eligible for discard
FRELAY:  .... ....  .... ...1 = Not extended address
FRELAY:
ETYPE:   Ethertype  = 0800 (IP)
ETYPE:
IP:   — IP Header —
IP:
IP:   Version = 4, header length = 20 bytes
IP:   Type of service = 00
IP:        000. .... = routine
IP:        ...0 .... = normal delay
IP:        .... 0... = normal throughput
IP:        .... .0.. = normal reliability
IP:   Total length    = 60 bytes
IP:   Identification  = 7358
IP:   Flags           = 0X
IP:        .0.. .... = may fragment
IP:        ..0. .... = last fragment
IP:   Fragment offset = 0 bytes
IP:   Time to live    = 51 seconds/hops
IP:   Protocol        = 6 (TCP)
IP:   Header checksum = 330B (correct)
IP:   Source address      = [XXX.YYY.81.1]
IP:   Destination address = [XXX.YYY.133.72]
IP:   No options
IP:
TCP:  — TCP header —
TCP:
TCP:  Source port            = 21 (FTP)
TCP:  Destination port       = 1214
TCP:  Sequence number        = 725589307
TCP:  Acknowledgment number  = 3275993
TCP:  Data offset            = 20 bytes
TCP:  Flags                  = 18
TCP:             ..0. .... = (No urgent pointer)
TCP:             ...1 .... = Acknowledgment
TCP:             .... 1... = Push
TCP:             .... .0.. = (No reset)
TCP:             .... ..0. = (No SYN)
TCP:             .... ...0 = (No FIN)
```

```
TCP:  Window              = 4096
TCP:  Checksum            = 1289 (correct)
TCP:  No TCP options
TCP:  [20 byte(s) of data]
TCP:
FTP:  — FTP data —
FTP:
FTP:  200 Type set to A.<0D0A>
FTP:

- - - - - - - - - - - - - - - - Frame 1082 - - - - - - - - - - - - - - - - -

DLC:  — DLC Header —
DLC:
DLC:  Frame 1082 arrived at  15:07:45.6787; frame size is 70 (0046 hex) bytes.
DLC:  Destination = DTE
DLC:  Source = DCE
DLC:
FRELAY:  — Frame Relay —
FRELAY:
FRELAY:  Address word = 20C1
FRELAY:  0010 00..  1100 .... = DLCI 140
FRELAY:  .... ..0.  .... .... = Response
FRELAY:  .... ....  .... 0... = No forward congestion
FRELAY:  .... ....  .... .0.. = No backward congestion
FRELAY:  .... ....  .... ..0. = Not eligible for discard
FRELAY:  .... ....  .... ...1 = Not extended address
FRELAY:
ETYPE: Ethertype  = 0800 (IP)
ETYPE:
IP:  — IP Header —
IP:
IP:  Version = 4, header length = 20 bytes
IP:  Type of service = 00
IP:        000. .... = routine
IP:        ...0 .... = normal delay
IP:        .... 0... = normal throughput
IP:        .... .0.. = normal reliability
IP:  Total length    = 66 bytes
IP:  Identification  = 13084
IP:  Flags           = 4X
IP:        .1.. .... = don't fragment
IP:        ..0. .... = last fragment
IP:  Fragment offset = 0 bytes
```

```
IP:  Time to live   = 31 seconds/hops
IP:  Protocol       = 6 (TCP)
IP:  Header checksum = F0A6 (correct)
IP:  Source address    = [XXX.YYY.133.72]
IP:  Destination address = [XXX.YYY.81.1]
IP:  No options
IP:
TCP:  — TCP header —
TCP:
TCP:  Source port          = 1214
TCP:  Destination port       = 21 (FTP)
TCP:  Sequence number        = 3275993
TCP:  Acknowledgment number  = 725589327
TCP:  Data offset          = 20 bytes
TCP:  Flags               = 18
TCP:              ..0. .... = (No urgent pointer)
TCP:              ...1 .... = Acknowledgment
TCP:              .... 1... = Push
TCP:              .... .0.. = (No reset)
TCP:              .... ..0. = (No SYN)
TCP:              .... ...0 = (No FIN)
TCP:  Window               = 8045
TCP:  Checksum              = F946 (correct)
TCP:  No TCP options
TCP:  [26 byte(s) of data]
TCP:
FTP:  — FTP data —
FTP:
FTP:  PORT 161,69,133,72,4,254<0D0A>
FTP:

- - - - - - - - - - - - - - - - Frame 1083 - - - - - - - - - - - - - - - - -

DLC:   — DLC Header —
DLC:
DLC:   Frame 1083 arrived at  15:07:45.6897; frame size is 74 (004A hex) bytes.
DLC:   Destination = DCE
DLC:   Source = DTE
DLC:
FRELAY:  — Frame Relay —
FRELAY:
FRELAY:  Address word = 20C1
FRELAY:  0010 00..  1100 .... = DLCI 140
FRELAY:  .... ..0.  .... .... = Response
```

```
FRELAY: .... .... .... 0... = No forward congestion
FRELAY: .... .... .... .0.. = No backward congestion
FRELAY: .... .... .... ..0. = Not eligible for discard
FRELAY: .... .... .... ...1 = Not extended address
FRELAY:
ETYPE: Ethertype = 0800 (IP)
ETYPE:
IP: — IP Header —
IP:
IP: Version = 4, header length = 20 bytes
IP: Type of service = 00
IP:       000. .... = routine
IP:       ...0 .... = normal delay
IP:       .... 0... = normal throughput
IP:       .... .0.. = normal reliability
IP: Total length = 70 bytes
IP: Identification = 7396
IP: Flags = 0X
IP:       .0.. .... = may fragment
IP:       ..0. .... = last fragment
IP: Fragment offset = 0 bytes
IP: Time to live = 51 seconds/hops
IP: Protocol = 6 (TCP)
IP: Header checksum = 32DB (correct)
IP: Source address = [XXX.YYY.81.1]
IP: Destination address = [XXX.YYY.133.72]
IP: No options
IP:
TCP: — TCP header —
TCP:
TCP: Source port = 21 (FTP)
TCP: Destination port = 1214
TCP: Sequence number = 725589327
TCP: Acknowledgment number = 3276019
TCP: Data offset = 20 bytes
TCP: Flags = 18
TCP:          ..0. .... = (No urgent pointer)
TCP:          ...1 .... = Acknowledgment
TCP:          .... 1... = Push
TCP:          .... .0.. = (No reset)
TCP:          .... ..0. = (No SYN)
TCP:          .... ...0 = (No FIN)
TCP: Window = 4096
TCP: Checksum = E04C (correct)
```

```
TCP: No TCP options
TCP: [30 byte(s) of data]
TCP:
FTP: — FTP data —
FTP:
FTP: 200 PORT command successful.<0D0A>
FTP:

- - - - - - - - - - - - - - - - Frame 1088 - - - - - - - - - - - - - - - - -

DLC: — DLC Header —
DLC:
DLC: Frame 1088 arrived at  15:07:45.7388; frame size is 66 (0042 hex) bytes.
DLC: Destination = DTE
DLC: Source = DCE
DLC:
FRELAY: — Frame Relay —
FRELAY:
FRELAY: Address word = 20C1
FRELAY: 0010 00.. 1100 .... = DLCI 140
FRELAY: .... ..0. .... .... = Response
FRELAY: .... .... .... 0... = No forward congestion
FRELAY: .... .... .... .0.. = No backward congestion
FRELAY: .... .... .... ..0. = Not eligible for discard
FRELAY: .... .... .... ...1 = Not extended address
FRELAY:
ETYPE: Ethertype  = 0800 (IP)
ETYPE:
IP:  — IP Header —
IP:
IP:  Version = 4, header length = 20 bytes
IP:  Type of service = 00
IP:       000. .... = routine
IP:       ...0 .... = normal delay
IP:       .... 0... = normal throughput
IP:       .... .0.. = normal reliability
IP:  Total length    = 62 bytes
IP:  Identification  = 13340
IP:  Flags           = 4X
IP:       .1.. .... = donít fragment
IP:       ..0. .... = last fragment
IP:  Fragment offset = 0 bytes
IP:  Time to live    = 31 seconds/hops
IP:  Protocol        = 6 (TCP)
```

```
IP:   Header checksum = EFAA (correct)
IP:   Source address      = [XXX.YYY.133.72]
IP:   Destination address = [XXX.YYY.81.1]
IP:   No options
IP:
TCP:  — TCP header —
TCP:
TCP:  Source port            = 1214
TCP:  Destination port       = 21 (FTP)
TCP:  Sequence number        = 3276019
TCP:  Acknowledgment number  = 725589357
TCP:  Data offset            = 20 bytes
TCP:  Flags                  = 18
TCP:              ..0. .... = (No urgent pointer)
TCP:              ...1 .... = Acknowledgment
TCP:              .... 1... = Push
TCP:              .... .0.. = (No reset)
TCP:              .... ..0. = (No SYN)
TCP:              .... ...0 = (No FIN)
TCP:  Window                 = 8576
TCP:  Checksum               = B9EE (correct)
TCP:  No TCP options
TCP:  [22 byte(s) of data]
TCP:
FTP:  — FTP data —
FTP:
FTP:  RETR Otherlinks.html<0D0A>
FTP:

- - - - - - - - - - - - - - - - Frame 1092 - - - - - - - - - - - - - - - - -

DLC:  — DLC Header —
DLC:
DLC:  Frame 1092 arrived at  15:07:45.7940; frame size is 118 (0076 hex) bytes.
DLC:  Destination = DCE
DLC:  Source = DTE
DLC:
FRELAY:  — Frame Relay —
FRELAY:
FRELAY:  Address word = 20C1
FRELAY:  0010 00..  1100 .... = DLCI 140
FRELAY:  .... ..0.  .... .... = Response
FRELAY:  .... ....  .... 0... = No forward congestion
FRELAY:  .... ....  .... .0.. = No backward congestion
```

```
FRELAY: .... .... .... ..0. = Not eligible for discard
FRELAY: .... .... .... ...1 = Not extended address
FRELAY:
ETYPE:  Ethertype = 0800 (IP)
ETYPE:
IP:  — IP Header —
IP:
IP:  Version = 4, header length = 20 bytes
IP:  Type of service = 00
IP:      000. .... = routine
IP:      ...0 .... = normal delay
IP:      .... 0... = normal throughput
IP:      .... .0.. = normal reliability
IP:  Total length    = 114 bytes
IP:  Identification  = 7442
IP:  Flags           = 0X
IP:      .0.. .... = may fragment
IP:      ..0. .... = last fragment
IP:  Fragment offset = 0 bytes
IP:  Time to live    = 51 seconds/hops
IP:  Protocol        = 6 (TCP)
IP:  Header checksum = 3281 (correct)
IP:  Source address      = [XXX.YYY.81.1]
IP:  Destination address = [XXX.YYY.133.72]
IP:  No options
IP:
TCP: — TCP header —
TCP:
TCP: Source port          = 21 (FTP)
TCP: Destination port     = 1214
TCP: Sequence number      = 725589357
TCP: Acknowledgment number = 3276041
TCP: Data offset          = 20 bytes
TCP: Flags                = 18
TCP:          ..0. .... = (No urgent pointer)
TCP:          ...1 .... = Acknowledgment
TCP:          .... 1... = Push
TCP:          .... .0.. = (No reset)
TCP:          .... ..0. = (No SYN)
TCP:          .... ...0 = (No FIN)
TCP: Window               = 4096
TCP: Checksum             = AB7B (correct)
TCP: No TCP options
TCP: [74 byte(s) of data]
```

```
TCP:
FTP:  — FTP data —
FTP:
FTP:  150 Opening ASCII mode data connection for Otherlinks.html (1081 bytes).<0D0A>
FTP:

- - - - - - - - - - - - - - - - Frame 1093 - - - - - - - - - - - - - - - - -

DLC:  — DLC Header —
DLC:
DLC:  Frame 1093 arrived at  15:07:45.8005; frame size is 556 (022C hex) bytes.
DLC:  Destination = DCE
DLC:  Source = DTE
DLC:
FRELAY:  — Frame Relay v
FRELAY:
FRELAY:  Address word = 20C1
FRELAY:  0010 00..  1100 .... = DLCI 140
FRELAY:  .... ..0.  .... .... = Response
FRELAY:  .... ....  .... 0... = No forward congestion
FRELAY:  .... ....  .... .0.. = No backward congestion
FRELAY:  .... ....  .... ..0. = Not eligible for discard
FRELAY:  .... ....  .... ...1 = Not extended address
FRELAY:
ETYPE:   Ethertype  = 0800 (IP)
ETYPE:
IP:   — IP Header —
IP:
IP:   Version = 4, header length = 20 bytes
IP:   Type of service = 00
IP:         000. .... = routine
IP:         ...0 .... = normal delay
IP:         .... 0... = normal throughput
IP:         .... .0.. = normal reliability
IP:   Total length    = 552 bytes
IP:   Identification  = 7443
IP:   Flags           = 0X
IP:         .0.. .... = may fragment
IP:         ..0. .... = last fragment
IP:   Fragment offset = 0 bytes
IP:   Time to live    = 51 seconds/hops
IP:   Protocol        = 6 (TCP)
IP:   Header checksum = 30CA (correct)
IP:   Source address      = [XXX.YYY.81.1]
```

```
IP:   Destination address = [XXX.YYY.133.72]
IP:   No options
IP:
TCP:  — TCP header —
TCP:
TCP:  Source port            = 20 (FTP data)
TCP:  Destination port       = 1278
TCP:  Sequence number        = 1306944001
TCP:  Acknowledgment number  = 4105807
TCP:  Data offset            = 20 bytes
TCP:  Flags                  = 10
TCP:              ..0. .... = (No urgent pointer)
TCP:              ...1 .... = Acknowledgment
TCP:              .... 0... = (No push)
TCP:              .... .0.. = (No reset)
TCP:              .... ..0. = (No SYN)
TCP:              .... ...0 = (No FIN)
TCP:  Window                 = 4096
TCP:  Checksum               = 69D3 (correct)
TCP:  No TCP options
TCP:  [512 byte(s) of data]
TCP:

- - - - - - - - - - - - - - - - Frame 1105 - - - - - - - - - - - - - - - - -

DLC:  — DLC Header —
DLC:
DLC:  Frame 1105 arrived at  15:07:45.9879; frame size is 50 (0032 hex) bytes.
DLC:  Destination = DTE
DLC:  Source = DCE
DLC:
FRELAY: — Frame Relay —
FRELAY:
FRELAY: Address word = 20C1
FRELAY: 0010 00..  1100 .... = DLCI 140
FRELAY: .... ..0.  .... .... = Response
FRELAY: .... ....  .... 0... = No forward congestion
FRELAY: .... ....  .... .0.. = No backward congestion
FRELAY: .... ....  .... ..0. = Not eligible for discard
FRELAY: .... ....  .... ...1 = Not extended address
FRELAY:
ETYPE:  Ethertype  = 0800 (IP)
ETYPE:
IP:    — IP Header —
```

```
IP:
IP:  Version = 4, header length = 20 bytes
IP:  Type of service = 00
IP:       000. .... = routine
IP:       ...0 .... = normal delay
IP:       .... 0... = normal throughput
IP:       .... .0.. = normal reliability
IP:  Total length   = 40 bytes
IP:   Identification  = 14108
IP:   Flags          = 4X
IP:       .1.. .... = donít fragment
IP:       ..0. .... = last fragment
IP:   Fragment offset = 0 bytes
IP:   Time to live   = 31 seconds/hops
IP:   Protocol       = 6 (TCP)
IP:   Header checksum = ECC0 (correct)
IP:   Source address     = [XXX.YYY.133.72]
IP:   Destination address = [XXX.YYY.81.1]
IP:   No options
IP:
TCP:  — TCP header —
TCP:
TCP:  Source port            = 1278
TCP:  Destination port        = 20 (FTP data)
TCP:  Sequence number         = 4105807
TCP:  Acknowledgment number   = 1306944513
TCP:  Data offset            = 20 bytes
TCP:  Flags                  = 10
TCP:              ..0. .... = (No urgent pointer)
TCP:              ...1 .... = Acknowledgment
TCP:              .... 0... = (No push)
TCP:              .... .0.. = (No reset)
TCP:              .... ..0. = (No SYN)
TCP:              .... ...0 = (No FIN)
TCP:  Window                 = 8064
TCP:  Checksum                = FAD9 (correct)
TCP:  No TCP options
TCP:

- - - - - - - - - - - - - - - - Frame 1107 - - - - - - - - - - - - - - - - -

DLC: — DLC Header —
DLC:
DLC: Frame 1107 arrived at  15:07:45.9987; frame size is 68 (0044 hex) bytes.
```

```
DLC: Destination = DCE
DLC: Source = DTE
DLC:
FRELAY: — Frame Relay —
FRELAY:
FRELAY: Address word = 20C1
FRELAY: 0010 00.. 1100 .... = DLCI 140
FRELAY: .... ..0. .... .... = Response
FRELAY: .... .... .... 0... = No forward congestion
FRELAY: .... .... .... .0.. = No backward congestion
FRELAY: .... .... .... ..0. = Not eligible for discard
FRELAY: .... .... .... ...1 = Not extended address
FRELAY:
ETYPE: Ethertype = 0800 (IP)
ETYPE:
IP: — IP Header —
IP:
IP: Version = 4, header length = 20 bytes
IP: Type of service = 00
IP:      000. .... = routine
IP:      ...0 .... = normal delay
IP:      .... 0... = normal throughput
IP:      .... .0.. = normal reliability
IP:   Total length    = 64 bytes
IP:   Identification  = 7543
IP:   Flags           = 0X
IP:      .0.. .... = may fragment
IP:      ..0. .... = last fragment
IP:   Fragment offset = 0 bytes
IP:   Time to live    = 51 seconds/hops
IP:   Protocol        = 6 (TCP)
IP:   Header checksum = 324E (correct)
IP:   Source address      = [XXX.YYY.81.1]
IP:   Destination address = [XXX.YYY.133.72]
IP:   No options
IP:
TCP: — TCP header —
TCP:
TCP: Source port              = 21 (FTP)
TCP: Destination port         = 1214
TCP: Sequence number          = 725589431
TCP: Acknowledgment number    = 3276041
TCP: Data offset              = 20 bytes
TCP: Flags                    = 18
```

```
TCP:            ..0. .... = (No urgent pointer)
TCP:            ...1 .... = Acknowledgment
TCP:            .... 1... = Push
TCP:            .... .0.. = (No reset)
TCP:            .... ..0. = (No SYN)
TCP:            .... ...0 = (No FIN)
TCP: Window               = 4096
TCP: Checksum             = CDC6 (correct)
TCP: No TCP options
TCP: [24 byte(s) of data]
TCP:
FTP:  — FTP data —
FTP:
FTP:  226 Transfer complete.<0D0A>
FTP:
```

3.13.8 Internet Access via ISDN

The final example in this chapter will consider the transmission of TCP/IP and related protocols over an ISDN line connecting to an Internet Services Provider (ISP). The scenario described in this case study is similar to one used everyday by telecommuters who are accessing the Internet or their corporate intranetwork via ISDN connections. In this example, the end user's workstation connects to an ISDN bridge/router via an IEEE 802.3 10BASE-T link, and from there to the ISDN, and eventually to the Internet and both email and Web servers (Figure 3-20).

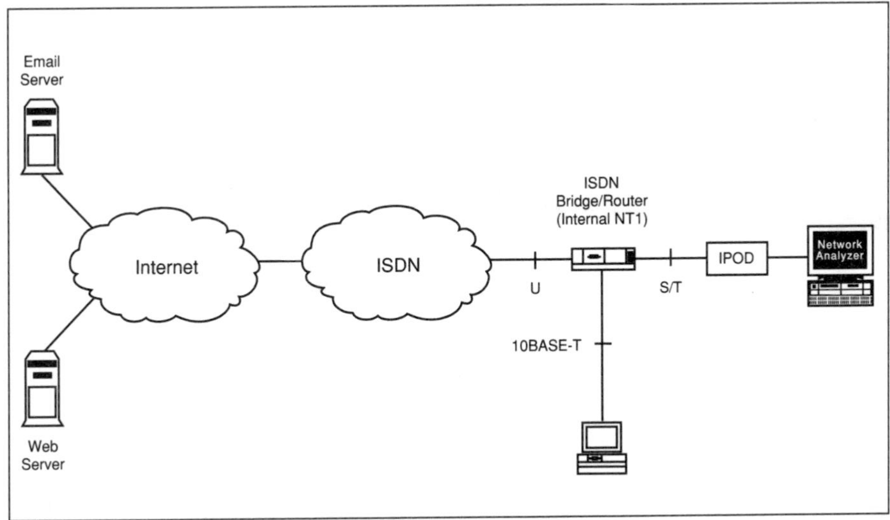

Figure 3-20 TCP/IP over ISDN

Most data communication operations can be divided into three phases: connection establishment, data transfer, and connection termination. In this case, there are two steps involved in the connection establishment phase: the first establishes the ISDN link (the physical connection), and the second establishes the TCP/IP connection with the remote server (the virtual connection). Referring to Trace 3.13.8a, note the various protocol processes that occur:

Frames	Protocol Process
1–18	ISDN connection setup
19–39	Link and router maintenance traffic
40–48	TCP connection setup
49–59	Data transfer (email server query)
60–62	TCP connection termination

TRACE 3.13.8A. TCP/IP OVER ISDN SUMMARY

Sniffer Internetwork Analyzer data 16-Feb at 20:36:02, file DEMOBRI.SYC, Pg 1

SUMMARY	Delta T	Destination	Source	Summary
M 1		DTE.ISDN.7F	DCE.ISDN.7F	ISDN Setup Speech None
2	3.5556	DCE.TEI.127	DTE.TEI.127	TEI C Request ID
3	0.0103	DTE.TEI.127	DCE.TEI.127	TEI R ID=112 assigned
4	0.0433	DCE.TEI.112	DTE.TEI.112	LAPD C SAPI=0 TEI=112 SABME
5	0.0069	DTE.TEI.112	DCE.TEI.112	LAPD R SAPI=0 TEI=112 UA
6	0.0491	DTE.ISDN	DCE.ISDN	ISDN Information
7	0.0189	DCE.TEI.112	DTE.TEI.112	LAPD R SAPI=0 TEI=112 RR NR=1
8	0.0107	DTE.ISDN	DCE.ISDN	ISDN Information
9	0.0178	DCE.TEI.112	DTE.TEI.112	LAPD R SAPI=0 TEI=112 RR NR=2
10	29.9619	DCE.TEI.112	DTE.TEI.112	LAPD C SAPI=0 TEI=112 RR NR=2
11	0.0067	DTE.TEI.112	DCE.TEI.112	LAPD R SAPI=0 TEI=112 RR NR=0
12	10.5554	DCE.ISDN.01	DTE.ISDN.01	ISDN Setup UNRestricted digital Any Keypad= 16505551212
13	0.0073	DTE.TEI.112	DCE.TEI.112	LAPD R SAPI=0 TEI=112 RR NR=1

14	0.1573	DTE.ISDN.01	DCE.ISDN.01	ISDN Call proceeding B1
15	0.0202	DCE.TEI.112	DTE.TEI.112	LAPD R SAPI=0 TEI=112 RR NR=3
16	2.6684	DTE.ISDN.01	DCE.ISDN.01	ISDN Connect
17	0.0227	DCE.TEI.112	DTE.TEI.112	LAPD R SAPI=0 TEI=112 RR NR=4
18	0.0689	DCE.ISDN.01	DTE.ISDN.01	ISDN Connect acknowledge
19	0.0075	DTE.TEI.112	DCE.TEI.112	LAPD R SAPI=0 TEI=112 RR NR=2
20	0.1817	DCE.B1	DTE.B1	Router Combinet In-band
21	0.0170	DTE.B1	DCE.B1	Router Combinet In-band
22	0.0197	DCE.B1	DTE.B1	Router Combinet In-band
23	0.4587	[XXX.YYY.0.10]	[XXX.YYY.10.1]	IGRP Request AS=53638 Subnets=0 AS network=0 AS exterior=0
24	0.3785	10.FFFFFFFFFFFF	APPLE_LWbd3636	SAP R APPLE_LWbd3636
25	2.8501	0.FFFFFFFFFFFF	0.00C04FDCFF18	SAP C Find nearest File server
26	0.7469	[XXX.YYY.10.255]	[XXX.YYY.10.253]	RIP R Routing entries=25
27	0.0691	[XXX.YYY.10.255]	[XXX.YYY.10.253]	RIP R Routing entries=25
28	0.0691	[XXX.YYY.10.255]	[XXX.YYY.10.253]	RIP R Routing entries=25
29	0.0614	[XXX.YYY.10.255]	[XXX.YYY.10.253]	RIP R Routing entries=22
30	0.8140	[XXX.YYY.0.10]	[XXX.YYY.10.1]	IGRP Request AS=53638 Subnets=0 AS network=0 AS exterior=0
31	1.1453	10.FFFFFFFFFFFF	10.cisco 368BA1	IPX RIP response: 50 networks, 00000101 at 3 hops, 00000001 at 3 hops, ...
32	0.0566	10.FFFFFFFFFFFF	10.cisco 368BA1	IPX RIP response: 50 networks, 00000533 at 2 hops, 00000037 at 2 hops,
33	0.0159	10.FFFFFFFFFFFF	10.cisco 368BA1	IPX RIP response: 9 networks, C9067F13 at 4 hops, 000008B8 at 4 hops,
34	0.9927	DTE.ISDN.01	DCE.ISDN.01	ISDN Status enquiry
35	0.0174	DCE.TEI.112	DTE.TEI.112	LAPD R SAPI=0 TEI=112 RR NR=5
36	0.0107	DCE.ISDN.01	DTE.ISDN.01	ISDN Status Response to status enquiry
37	0.0075	DTE.TEI.112	DCE.TEI.112	LAPD R SAPI=0 TEI=112 RR NR=3

38	2.3361	DCE.B1	DTE.B1	Router Combinet In-band
39	0.0330	[XXX.YYY.0.10]	[XXX.YYY.10.1]	IGRP Request AS=53638 Subnets=0 AS network=0 AS exterior=0
40	1.8700	FFFFFFFFFFFF	00C04FDCFF18	ARP C PA=[XXX.YYY.6.254] PRO=IP
41	0.0217	00C04FDCFF18	cisco 368BA1	ARP R PA=[XXX.YYY.6.254] HA=00000C368BA1 PRO=IP
42	0.0182	[XXX.YYY.2.1]	[XXX.YYY.10.222]	DNS C ID=1 OP=QUERY NAME= postoffice.pacbell.net
43	0.0446	[XXX.YYY.10.222]	[XXX.YYY.2.1]	DNS R ID=1 STAT=OK NAME= postoffice.pacbell.net
44	0.0257	[XXX.YYY.2.1]	[XXX.YYY.10.222]	DNS C ID=2 OP=QUERY NAME=www.cnet.com
45	0.0088	pacbell.net	[XXX.YYY.10.222]	TCP D=110 S=1091 SYN SEQ=2063918 LEN=0 WIN=8192
46	0.0390	[XXX.YYY.10.222]	[XXX.YYY.2.1]	DNS R ID=2 STAT=OK NAME=www.cnet.com
47	0.0082	[XXX.YYY.10.222]	pacbell.net	TCP D=1091 S=110 SYN ACK=2063919 SEQ=1413986716 LEN=0 WIN=17520
48	0.0154	pacbell.net	[XXX.YYY.10.222]	TCP D=110 S=1091 ACK=1413986717 WIN=8760
49	0.7565	[XXX.YYY.10.222]	pacbell.net	TCP D=1091 S=110 ACK=2063919 SEQ=1413986717 LEN=67 WIN=17520
50	0.0414	pacbell.net	[XXX.YYY.10.222]	TCP D=110 S=1091 ACK=1413986784 SEQ=2063919 LEN=14 WIN=8693
51	0.0766	[XXX.YYY.10.222]	pacbell.net	TCP D=1091 S=110 ACK=2063933 WIN=17520

52	0.2596	[XXX.YYY.10.222]	pacbell.net	TCP D=1091 S=110 ACK=2063933 SEQ=1413986784 LEN=36 WIN=17520
53	0.0174	pacbell.net	[XXX.YYY.10.222]	TCP D=110 S=1091 ACK=1413986820 SEQ=2063933 LEN=14 WIN=8657
54	0.0717	[XXX.YYY.10.222]	pacbell.net	TCP D=1091 S=110 ACK=2063947 WIN=17520
55	0.0978	[XXX.YYY.10.222]	pacbell.net	TCP D=1091 S=110 ACK=2063947 SEQ=1413986820 LEN=40 WIN=17520
56	0.0163	pacbell.net	[XXX.YYY.10.222]	TCP D=110 S=1091 ACK=1413986860 SEQ=2063947 LEN=6 WIN=8617
57	0.0330	[XXX.YYY.10.222]	pacbell.net	TCP D=1091 S=110 ACK=2063953 SEQ=1413986860 LEN=9 WIN=17520
58	0.0197	pacbell.net	[XXX.YYY.10.222]	TCP D=110 S=1091 ACK=1413986869 SEQ=2063953 LEN=6 WIN=8608
59	0.0406	[XXX.YYY.10.222]	pacbell.net	TCP D=1091 S=110 ACK=2063959 SEQ=1413986869 LEN=41 WIN=17520
60	0.0082	[XXX.YYY.10.222]	pacbell.net	TCP D=1091 S=110 FIN ACK=2063959 SEQ=1413986910 LEN=0 WIN=17520
61	0.0150	pacbell.net	[XXX.YYY.10.222]	TCP D=110 S=1091 ACK=1413986911 WIN=8567
62	0.0163	pacbell.net	[XXX.YYY.10.222]	TCP D=110 S=1091 RST WIN=0

The details of selected frames are shown in Trace 3.13.8b. Note the various ISDN messages that are involved in the establishment of the ISDN connection between the workstation and the network:

Frames	ISDN Protocol Process
1	SETUP message (circuit mode speech at 64 Kbps)
2–3	Request for, and assignment of, Terminal Endpoint Identifier (TEI = 112)
3–4	Establish LAPD mode (Set Asynchronous Balanced Mode Extended – SABME)
5–11	LAPD Information and Receive Ready messages
12–13	SETUP message (circuit mode data at 64 Kbps, called number 16505551212), LSPD acknowledgment
14–15	CALL Proceeding message (selecting B1 channel), acknowledgment
16–18	CONNECT and CONNECT ACKNOWLEDGE messages

Note the number of messages that are involved in the establishment of the ISDN connection and the details that are included in those messages, such as the data rate to be used and the destination telephone number being requested. Once the ISDN connection is established, the Address Resolution Protocol (ARP) is used to locate the bridge/router that provides access off of the end user's local network (Frames 40–41); the Domain Name System (DNS) locates the IP address of the email server of interest, postoffice.pacbell.net (Frames 42–43); and the TCP connection is then established using a three-way handshake (Frames 45, 47, and 48). At the conclusion of Frame 48, the first phase of the data communication process (connection establishment) is complete.

TRACE 3.13.8B. TCP/IP OVER ISDN DETAILS

```
Sniffer Internetwork Analyzer data 16-Feb at 20:36:02, file DEMOBRI.SYC, Pg 1

---------------- Frame 1 -----------------

ISDN:  —— ISDN Call Control (Generic Q.931 Primary Rate) ——
ISDN:
ISDN:  Protocol discriminator = 08 (Q.931 user-network call control messages)
ISDN:  Length of call reference = 1 byte
ISDN:  Call reference field = FF
ISDN:          1... .... = Message to call reference originator
ISDN:          .111 1111 = Call reference value = 7F
ISDN:  Message type = 05 (Setup)
ISDN:
```

```
ISDN:  Info element id = 04 (Bearer capability)
ISDN:  Length of information element = 3 byte(s)
ISDN:  Octet 3 value = 80
ISDN:     1... .... = Extension bit
ISDN:     .00. .... = Coding standard (CCITT)
ISDN:     ...0 0000 = Information transfer capability (Speech)
ISDN:  Octet 4 value = 90
ISDN:     1... .... = Extension bit
ISDN:     .00. .... = Transfer mode (Circuit mode)
ISDN:     ...1 0000 = Information transfer rate (64 kbit/s)
ISDN:  Octet 5 value = A2
ISDN:     1... .... = Extension bit
ISDN:     .01. .... = Layer 1 identification
ISDN:     ...0 0010 = Layer 1 protocol (G.711 u-law)
ISDN:
ISDN:  Info element id = 18 (Channel identification)
ISDN:  Length of information element = 1 byte(s)
ISDN:  Octet 3 value = 88
ISDN:     1... .... = Extension bit
ISDN:     .0.. .... = Interface implicitly identified
ISDN:     ..0. .... = Basic interface
ISDN:     .... 1... = Only the indicated channel is acceptable
ISDN:     .... .0.. = Not the D-channel
ISDN:     .... ..00 = Information channel selection (No channel)
ISDN:
ISDN:  Info element id = 96 (Shift)
ISDN:  Shift = X6
ISDN:  .... 0... = Locking shift
ISDN:  .... .110 = Codeset (Network-specific information elements)
ISDN:
ISDN:  Info element id = 25 (Network-specific: ?)
ISDN:  Length of information element = 1 byte(s)
ISDN:  *** 1 unknown byte (01)
ISDN:

- - - - - - - - - - - - - - - - Frame 2 - - - - - - - - - - - - - - - - -

TEI: — TEI Management —
TEI:
TEI: Management entity identifier = 15
TEI: Reference number = 64398
TEI: Message type = 1 (Identity request)
TEI: Action indicator = FF
TEI:       1111 111. = Action = 127 (Any TEI value acceptable)
```

```
TEI:    .... ...1 = Extention bit
TEI:

- - - - - - - - - - - - - - - - Frame 3 - - - - - - - - - - - - - - - - -

TEI: — TEI Management —
TEI:
TEI: Management entity identifier = 15
TEI: Reference number = 64398
TEI: Message type = 2 (Identity assigned)
TEI: Action indicator = E1
TEI:     1110 000. = Action = 112 (Assigned TEI value)
TEI:     .... ...1 = Extention bit
TEI:

- - - - - - - - - - - - - - - - Frame 4 - - - - - - - - - - - - - - - - -

LAPD: — Link Access Procedure D (LAPD) v
LAPD:
LAPD: Address byte #1 = 00
LAPD:     0000 00.. = SAPI = 0
LAPD:     .... ..0. = Command/Response bit
LAPD:     .... ...0 = EA
LAPD: Address byte #2 = E1
LAPD:     1110 000. = TEI = 112
LAPD:     .... ...1 = EA
LAPD: Control field = 7F
LAPD:   ...1 .... = Poll/Final bit
LAPD:   011. 1111 = SABME (Set asynchronous balanced mode extended)
LAPD:

- - - - - - - - - - - - - - - - Frame 5 - - - - - - - - - - - - - - - - -

LAPD: — Link Access Procedure D (LAPD) —
LAPD:
LAPD: Address byte #1 = 00
LAPD:     0000 00.. = SAPI = 0
LAPD:     .... ..0. = Command/Response bit
LAPD:     .... ...0 = EA
LAPD: Address byte #2 = E1
LAPD:     1110 000. = TEI = 112
LAPD:     .... ...1 = EA
LAPD: Control field = 73
LAPD:   ...1 .... = Poll/Final bit
```

```
LAPD:     011. 0011 = UA (Unnumbered acknowledgement)
LAPD:

- - - - - - - - - - - - - - - - Frame 6 - - - - - - - - - - - - - - - - -

ISDN: — ISDN Call Control (Generic Q.931 Primary Rate) —
ISDN:
ISDN: Protocol discriminator = 08 (Q.931 user-network call control messages)
ISDN: Length of call reference = 0 bytes
ISDN: Message type = 7B (Information)
ISDN:
ISDN: Info element id = 96 (Shift)
ISDN: Shift = X6
ISDN: .... 0... = Locking shift
ISDN: .... .110 = Codeset (Network-specific information elements)
ISDN:
ISDN: Info element id = 39 (Network-specific: ?)
ISDN: Length of information element = 2 byte(s)
ISDN: *** 2 unknown bytes (C701)
ISDN:

- - - - - - - - - - - - - - - - Frame 7 - - - - - - - - - - - - - - - - -

LAPD: — Link Access Procedure D (LAPD) —
LAPD:
LAPD: Address byte #1 = 02
LAPD:     0000 00.. = SAPI = 0
LAPD:     .... ..1. = Command/Response bit
LAPD:     .... ...0 = EA
LAPD: Address byte #2 = E1
LAPD:     1110 000. = TEI = 112
LAPD:     .... ...1 = EA
LAPD: Control byte #1 = 1 (RR: Receive ready)
LAPD: Control byte #2 = 02
LAPD:     0000 001. = N(R) = 1
LAPD:     .... ...0 = Poll/Final bit
LAPD:

- - - - - - - - - - - - - - - - Frame 8 - - - - - - - - - - - - - - - - -

ISDN: — ISDN Call Control (Generic Q.931 Primary Rate) —
ISDN:
ISDN: Protocol discriminator = 08 (Q.931 user-network call control messages)
ISDN: Length of call reference = 0 bytes
```

```
ISDN: Message type = 7B (Information)
ISDN:
ISDN: Info element id = 96 (Shift)
ISDN: Shift = X6
ISDN: .... 0... = Locking shift
ISDN: .... .110 = Codeset (Network-specific information elements)
ISDN:
ISDN: Info element id = 22 (Network-specific: ?)
ISDN: Length of information element = 1 byte(s)
ISDN: *** 1 unknown byte (01)
ISDN:

- - - - - - - - - - - - - - - - Frame 9 - - - - - - - - - - - - - - - - -

LAPD: — Link Access Procedure D (LAPD) —
LAPD:
LAPD: Address byte #1 = 02
LAPD:      0000 00.. = SAPI = 0
LAPD:      .... ..1. = Command/Response bit
LAPD:      .... ...0 = EA
LAPD: Address byte #2 = E1
LAPD:      1110 000. = TEI = 112
LAPD:      .... ...1 = EA
LAPD: Control byte #1 = 1 (RR: Receive ready)
LAPD: Control byte #2 = 04
LAPD:      0000 010. = N(R) = 2
LAPD:      .... ...0 = Poll/Final bit
LAPD:

- - - - - - - - - - - - - - - - Frame 10 - - - - - - - - - - - - - - - - -

LAPD: — Link Access Procedure D (LAPD) —
LAPD:
LAPD: Address byte #1 = 00
LAPD:      0000 00.. = SAPI = 0
LAPD:      .... ..0. = Command/Response bit
LAPD:      .... ...0 = EA
LAPD: Address byte #2 = E1
LAPD:      1110 000. = TEI = 112
LAPD:      .... ...1 = EA
LAPD: Control byte #1 = 1 (RR: Receive ready)
LAPD: Control byte #2 = 05
LAPD:      0000 010. = N(R) = 2
LAPD:      .... ...1 = Poll/Final bit
LAPD:
```

```
---------------- Frame 11 ----------------

LAPD:— Link Access Procedure D (LAPD) —
LAPD:
LAPD:Address byte #1 = 00
LAPD:     0000 00.. = SAPI = 0
LAPD:     .... ..0. = Command/Response bit
LAPD:     .... ...0 = EA
LAPD:Address byte #2 = E1
LAPD:     1110 000. = TEI = 112
LAPD:     .... ...1 = EA
LAPD:Control byte #1 = 1 (RR: Receive ready)
LAPD:Control byte #2 = 01
LAPD:     0000 000. = N(R) = 0
LAPD:     .... ...1 = Poll/Final bit
LAPD:

---------------- Frame 12 ----------------

ISDN: — ISDN Call Control (Generic Q.931 Primary Rate) —
ISDN:
ISDN: Protocol discriminator = 08 (Q.931 user-network call control messages)
ISDN: Length of call reference = 1 byte
ISDN: Call reference field = 01
ISDN:         0... .... = Message from call reference originator
ISDN:         .000 0001 = Call reference value = 01
ISDN: Message type = 05 (Setup)
ISDN:
ISDN: Info element id = 04 (Bearer capability)
ISDN: Length of information element = 2 byte(s)
ISDN: Octet 3 value = 88
ISDN:    1... .... = Extension bit
ISDN:    .00. .... = Coding standard (CCITT)
ISDN:    ...0 1000 = Information transfer capability (Unrestricted digital)
ISDN: Octet 4 value = 90
ISDN:    1... .... = Extension bit
ISDN:    .00. .... = Transfer mode (Circuit mode)
ISDN:    ...1 0000 = Information transfer rate (64 kbit/s)
ISDN:
ISDN: Info element id = 18 (Channel identification)
ISDN: Length of information element = 1 byte(s)
ISDN: Octet 3 value = 83
ISDN:    1... .... = Extension bit
ISDN:    .0.. .... = Interface implicitly identified
```

```
ISDN:   ..0. .... = Basic interface
ISDN:   .... 0... = Indicated channel is preferred
ISDN:   .... .0.. = Not the D-channel
ISDN:   .... ..11 = Information channel selection (Any channel)
ISDN:
ISDN: Info element id = 2C (Keypad facility)
ISDN: Length of information element = 11 byte(s)
ISDN: Information = "16505551212"
ISDN:

- - - - - - - - - - - - - - - - Frame 13 - - - - - - - - - - - - - - - - -

LAPD: — Link Access Procedure D (LAPD) —
LAPD:
LAPD: Address byte #1 = 00
LAPD:     0000 00.. = SAPI = 0
LAPD:     .... ..0. = Command/Response bit
LAPD:     .... ...0 = EA
LAPD: Address byte #2 = E1
LAPD:     1110 000. = TEI = 112
LAPD:     .... ...1 = EA
LAPD: Control byte #1 = 1 (RR: Receive ready)
LAPD: Control byte #2 = 02
LAPD:     0000 001. = N(R) = 1
LAPD:     .... ...0 = Poll/Final bit
LAPD:

- - - - - - - - - - - - - - - - Frame 14 - - - - - - - - - - - - - - - - -

ISDN: — ISDN Call Control (Generic Q.931 Primary Rate) —
ISDN:
ISDN: Protocol discriminator = 08 (Q.931 user-network call control messages)
ISDN: Length of call reference = 1 byte
ISDN: Call reference field = 81
ISDN:        1... .... = Message to call reference originator
ISDN:        .000 0001 = Call reference value = 01
ISDN: Message type = 02 (Call proceeding)
ISDN:
ISDN: Info element id = 18 (Channel identification)
ISDN: Length of information element = 1 byte(s)
ISDN: Octet 3 value = 89
ISDN:   1... .... = Extension bit
ISDN:   .0.. .... = Interface implicitly identified
ISDN:   ..0. .... = Basic interface
```

```
ISDN:    .... 1... = Only the indicated channel is acceptable
ISDN:    .... .0.. = Not the D-channel
ISDN:    .... ..01 = Information channel selection (B1 channel)
ISDN:

---------------- Frame 15 ----------------

LAPD: — Link Access Procedure D (LAPD) —
LAPD:
LAPD: Address byte #1 = 02
LAPD:     0000 00.. = SAPI = 0
LAPD:     .... ..1. = Command/Response bit
LAPD:     .... ...0 = EA
LAPD: Address byte #2 = E1
LAPD:     1110 000. = TEI = 112
LAPD:     .... ...1 = EA
LAPD: Control byte #1 = 1 (RR: Receive ready)
LAPD: Control byte #2 = 06
LAPD:     0000 011. = N(R) = 3
LAPD:     .... ...0 = Poll/Final bit
LAPD:

---------------- Frame 16 ----------------

ISDN: — ISDN Call Control (Generic Q.931 Primary Rate) —
ISDN:
ISDN: Protocol discriminator = 08 (Q.931 user-network call control messages)
ISDN: Length of call reference = 1 byte
ISDN: Call reference field = 81
ISDN:         1... .... = Message to call reference originator
ISDN:         .000 0001 = Call reference value = 01
ISDN: Message type = 07 (Connect)
ISDN:

---------------- Frame 17 ----------------

LAPD: — Link Access Procedure D (LAPD) —
LAPD:
LAPD: Address byte #1 = 02
LAPD:     0000 00.. = SAPI = 0
LAPD:     .... ..1. = Command/Response bit
LAPD:     .... ...0 = EA
LAPD: Address byte #2 = E1
LAPD:     1110 000. = TEI = 112
```

```
LAPD:       .... ...1 = EA
LAPD:  Control byte #1 = 1 (RR: Receive ready)
LAPD:  Control byte #2 = 08
LAPD:       0000 100. = N(R) = 4
LAPD:       .... ...0 = Poll/Final bit
LAPD:

- - - - - - - - - - - - - - - - Frame 18 - - - - - - - - - - - - - - - - -

ISDN: — ISDN Call Control (Generic Q.931 Primary Rate) —
ISDN:
ISDN: Protocol discriminator = 08 (Q.931 user-network call control messages)
ISDN: Length of call reference = 1 byte
ISDN: Call reference field = 01
ISDN:         0... .... = Message from call reference originator
ISDN:         .000 0001 = Call reference value = 01
ISDN: Message type = 0F (Connect acknowledge)
ISDN:
```

The hexadecimal decode of the information (and the resulting ASCII translation) that is transferred over the ISDN physical connection (and the resulting TCP/IP logical connection) contains interesting details (Trace 3.13.8c):

Frame	Hexadecimal Protocol Process
49	Email server prompt message
50	Login from user
51–52	Acknowledgment from server and request for password
53	Password from user
54–55	Acknowledgment and number of messages from server
56	"STAT" request from user
57	"OK" response from user
58	"QUIT" message from user
59-60	Signoff message from server

Returning to Trace 3.13.8a, note that frames 60–61 close the TCP/IP logical connection to the email server, allowing the ISDN physical connection to be reused for another application, such as Web server access. Also note that the user's account code and password were sent without encryption, making that information vulnerable to capture with the protocol analyzer.

TRACE 3.13.8C. TCP/IP OVER ISDN HEXADECIMAL DATA

Sniffer Internetwork Analyzer data 16-Feb at 20:36:02, file DEMOBRI.SYC, Pg 1

--------------------------- Frame 49 ---------------------------

ADDR	HEX		ASCII
0000	10 00 00 C0 4F DC FF 18	00 00 0C 36 8B A1 08 00	...@O\ ....6.!..
0010	45 00 00 6B B0 F2 40 00	F3 06 40 42 CE 0D 1C 27	E..kOr@.s.@BN.'
0020	A1 45 0A DE 00 6E 04 43	54 47 B9 9D 00 1F 7E 2F	!E.^.n.CTG9...~/
0030	50 18 44 70 68 21 00 00	2B 4F 4B 20 50 42 49 2D	P.Dph!..+OK PBI-
0040	70 72 6F 78 79 20 50 4F	50 33 20 73 65 72 76 65	proxy POP3 serve
0050	72 20 76 31 2E 30 36 20	72 65 61 64 79 20 61 74	r v1.06 ready at
0060	20 4D 6F 6E 20 46 65 62	20 31 36 20 32 30 3A 33	Mon Feb 16 20:3
0070	32 3A 35 38 20 31 39 39	38 0D 0A	2:58 1998..

--------------------------- Frame 50 ---------------------------

ADDR	HEX		ASCII
0000	06 00 00 00 0C 36 8B A1	00 C0 4F DC FF 18 08 00	.....6.!.@O\ ...
0010	45 00 00 36 19 02 40 00	20 06 AB 68 A1 45 0A DE	E..6..@. .+h!E.^
0020	CE 0D 1C 27 04 43 00 6E	00 1F 7E 2F 54 47 B9 E0	N.'C.n..~/TG9`
0030	50 18 21 F5 6E D4 00 00	55 53 45 52 20 73 62 72	P.!unT..USER sbr
0040	5F 6E 6D 72 0D 0A		_nmr..

--------------------------- Frame 51 ---------------------------

ADDR	HEX		ASCII
0000	11 00 00 C0 4F DC FF 18	00 00 0C 36 8B A1 08 00	...@O\ ....6.!..
0010	45 00 00 28 B0 F3 40 00	F3 06 40 84 CE 0D 1C 27	E..(Os@.s.@.N.'
0020	A1 45 0A DE 00 6E 04 43	54 47 B9 E0 00 1F 7E 3D	!E.^.n.CTG9`..~=
0030	50 10 44 70 43 D7 00 00	55 55 55 55 55 55	P.DpCW..UUUUUU

--------------------------- Frame 52 ---------------------------

ADDR	HEX		ASCII
0000	12 00 00 C0 4F DC FF 18	00 00 0C 36 8B A1 08 00	...@O\ ....6.!..
0010	45 00 00 4C B0 F4 40 00	F3 06 40 5F CE 0D 1C 27	E..L0t@.s.@_N.'
0020	A1 45 0A DE 00 6E 04 43	54 47 B9 E0 00 1F 7E 3D	!E.^.n.CTG9`..~=
0030	50 18 44 70 A1 C8 00 00	2B 4F 4B 20 50 61 73 73	P.Dp!H..+OK Pass
0040	77 6F 72 64 20 72 65 71	75 69 72 65 64 20 66 6F	word required fo
0050	72 20 73 62 72 5F 6E 6D	72 2E 0D 0A	r sbr_nmr...

--------------------------- Frame 53 ---------------------------

ADDR	HEX		ASCII
0000	07 00 00 00 0C 36 8B A1	00 C0 4F DC FF 18 08 00	.....6.!.@O\ ...
0010	45 00 00 36 1A 02 40 00	20 06 AA 68 A1 45 0A DE	E..6..@. .*h!E.^
0020	CE 0D 1C 27 04 43 00 6E	00 1F 7E 3D 54 47 BA 04	N..'C.n..~=TG:.
0030	50 18 21 D1 88 0A 00 00	50 41 53 53 20 39 36 74	P.!Q....PASS 96t
0040	61 72 75 73 0D 0A		arus..

--------------------------- Frame 54 ---------------------------

ADDR	HEX		ASCII
0000	13 00 00 C0 4F DC FF 18	00 00 0C 36 8B A1 08 00	...@O\ ....6.!..
0010	45 00 00 28 B0 F5 40 00	F3 06 40 82 CE 0D 1C 27	E..(Ou@.s.@.N..'
0020	A1 45 0A DE 00 6E 04 43	54 47 BA 04 00 1F 7E 4B	!E.^.n.CTG:...~K
0030	50 10 44 70 43 A5 00 00	55 55 55 55 55 55	P.DpC%..UUUUUU

--------------------------- Frame 55 ---------------------------

ADDR	HEX		ASCII
0000	14 00 00 C0 4F DC FF 18	00 00 0C 36 8B A1 08 00	...@O\ ....6.!..
0010	45 00 00 50 B0 F6 40 00	F3 06 40 59 CE 0D 1C 27	E..POv@.s.@YN..'
0020	A1 45 0A DE 00 6E 04 43	54 47 BA 04 00 1F 7E 4B	!E.^.n.CTG:...~K
0030	50 18 44 70 74 A3 00 00	2B 4F 4B 20 73 62 72 5F	P.Dpt#..+OK sbr_
0040	6E 6D 72 20 68 61 73 20	30 20 6D 65 73 73 61 67	nmr has 0 messag
0050	65 73 20 28 30 20 6F 63	74 65 74 73 29 2E 0D 0A	es (0 octets)...

--------------------------- Frame 56 ---------------------------

ADDR	HEX		ASCII
0000	08 00 00 00 0C 36 8B A1	00 C0 4F DC FF 18 08 00	.....6.!.@O\ ...
0010	45 00 00 2E 1B 02 40 00	20 06 A9 70 A1 45 0A DE	E.....@. .)p!E.^
0020	CE 0D 1C 27 04 43 00 6E	00 1F 7E 4B 54 47 BA 2C	N..'C.n..~KTG:,
0030	50 18 21 A9 C4 83 00 00	53 54 41 54 0D 0A	P.!)D...STAT..

--------------------------- Frame 57 ---------------------------

ADDR	HEX		ASCII
0000	15 00 00 C0 4F DC FF 18	00 00 0C 36 8B A1 08 00	...@O\ ....6.!..
0010	45 00 00 31 B0 F7 40 00	F3 06 40 77 CE 0D 1C 27	E..1Ow@.s.@wN..'
0020	A1 45 0A DE 00 6E 04 43	54 47 BA 2C 00 1F 7E 51	!E.^.n.CTG:,..~Q
0030	50 18 44 70 62 C9 00 00	2B 4F 4B 20 30 20 30 0D	P.Dpbl..+OK 0 0.
0040	0A		

```
---------------- Frame 58 -----------------

ADDR   HEX                                                ASCII
0000   09 00 00 00 0C 36 8B A1   00 C0 4F DC FF 18 08 00  .....6.!.@O\ ...
0010   45 00 00 2E 1C 02 40 00   20 06 A8 70 A1 45 0A DE  E.....@. .(p!E.^
0020   CE 0D 1C 27 04 43 00 6E   00 1F 7E 51 54 47 BA 35  N..'C.n..~QTG:5
0030   50 18 21 A0 BE 7C 00 00   51 55 49 54 0D 0A         P.! >|..QUIT..

---------------- Frame 59 ----------------

ADDR   HEX                                                ASCII
0000   16 00 00 C0 4F DC FF 18   00 00 0C 36 8B A1 08 00  ...@O\ ....6.!..
0010   45 00 00 51 B0 F8 40 00   F3 06 40 56 CE 0D 1C 27  E..Q0x@.s.@VN..'
0020   A1 45 0A DE 00 6E 04 43   54 47 BA 35 00 1F 7E 57  !E.^.n.CTG:5..~W
0030   50 18 44 70 9C 66 00 00   2B 4F 4B 20 50 6F 70 20  P.Dp.f..+OK Pop
0040   73 65 72 76 65 72 20 61   74 20 6D 61 69 6C 2D 73  server at mail-s
0050   66 32 20 73 69 67 6E 69   6E 67 20 6F 66 66 2E 0D  f2 signing off..
0060   0A                                                 .
```

3.14 Looking Ahead

In this chapter we have laid the foundation for internetworking by looking into the many ways that the ARPA Network Interface Layer may be implemented on LANs, MANs, and WANs. In the next chapter we will study the layer responsible for routing and addressing, the Internet Layer.

3.15 References

[3-1] Braden, R. "Requirements for Internet Hosts: Communication Layers." RFC 1122, October 1989.

[3-2] *ARCNET Designer's Handbook*, second edition. Document 61610, Datapoint Corp., 1988.

[3-3] Provan, D. "Transmitting IP Traffic over ARCNET Networks." RFC 1201, February 1991.

[3-4] *The Ethernet, A Local Area Network-Data Link Layer and Physical Layer Specification*, version 2.0, November 1982. Published by DEC, Intel, and Xerox, DEC document number AA-K759B-TK.

[3-5] Institute of Electrical and Electronics Engineers. *Information Technology – Local and Metropolitan Area Networks – Part 3: Carrier sense multiple access with collision detection (CSMA/CD) access method and physical layer specifications.* ISO/IEC 8802-3: 1996 (ANSI/IEEE Std 802.3-1996).

[3-6] Horning, Charles. "A Standard for the Transmission of IP Datagrams over Ethernet Networks." RFC 894, April 1984.

[3-7] Postel, J., and J. Reynolds. "A Standard for the Transmission of IP Datagrams over IEEE 802 Networks." RFC 1042, February 1988.

[3-8] Institute of Electrical and Electronics Engineers. *Information Technology – Telecommunications and information exchange between systems – Local and metropolitan area networks – Specific requirements – Part 2: Logical Link Control.* ISO/IEC 8802-2: 1994 (ANSI/IEEE Std 802.2-1994).

[3-9] Institute of Electrical and Electronics Engineers. *Standards for Local and Metropolitan Area Networks: Overview and Architecture.* IEEE Std 802-1990, December 1990.

[3-10] Institute of Electrical and Electronics Engineers. *Information Technology – Telecommunications and information exchange between systems – Local and Metropolitan Area Networks – Specific requirements – Part 5: Token ring access method and physical layer specification.* ISO/IEC 8802-5:1995 (ANSI/IEEE Std 802.5, 1995).

[3-11] Institute of Electrical and Electronics Engineers. *Information Technology – Telecommunications and information exchange between systems – Local area networks – Media Access Control (MAC) bridges.* ISO/IEC 10038:1993 (ANSI/IEEE Std 802.1D, 1993).

[3-12] Miller, Mark A. *Troubleshooting Internetworks.* M&T Books, Inc. (New York, NY), 1992.

[3-13] American National Standards Institute. *Fiber Distributed Data Interface (FDDI) – Token Ring Media Access Control (MAC).* ANSI X3.139 1987.

[3-14] Katz, D. "A Proposed Standard for the Transmission of IP Datagrams over FDDI Networks." RFC 1188, October 1990.

[3-15] Sherman, Doug. "Understanding FDDI: Standards, Features, and Applications." *3TECH, the 3Com Technical Journal* (Winter 1992): 18–31.

[3-16] Romkey, J. "A Nonstandard for Transmission of IP Datagrams Over Serial Lines: SLIP." RFC 1055, June 1988.

[3-17] Simpson, W., Editor. "The Point-to-Point Protocol (PPP)." RFC 1661, July 1994.

[3-18] Sklower, K. et al. "The PPP Multilink Protocol (MP)." RFC 1990, August 1996.

[3-19] Wells, L., Chair, and A. Bartky, Editor. "Data Link Switching: Switch-to-Switch Protocol AIW DLSw RIG: DLSw Closed Pages, DLSw Standard Version 1.0," RFC 1795, April 1995.

[3-20] Malis, A., et al. "Multiprotocol Interconnect on X.25 and ISDN in the Packet Mode." RFC 1356, August 1992.

[3-21] Schlar, Sherman K. *Inside X.25: A Manager's Guide.* McGraw Hill (New York, NY), 1990.

[3-22] Bradley, T., et al. "Multiprotocol Interconnect over Frame Relay." RFC 1490, January 1992.

[3-23] Bradley, T. et al. "Inverse Address Resolution Protocol." RFC 1293, January 1992.

[3-24] American National Standards Institute. *Integrated Services Digital Network (ISDN) – Architectural Framework and Service Description for Frame-Relaying Bearer Service.* T1.606, 1990.

[3-25] The Frame Relay Forum may be contacted at:
Frame Relay Forum North American Office
39355 California Street, Suite 307
Fremont, CA 94538
Tel: (510) 608-5920
Fax: (510) 608-5917
Email: `frf@frforum.com`
`http://www.frforum.com`

[3-26] Black, Ulyess. *Frame Relay Networks,* second edition. McGraw-Hill (New York, NY), 1996.

[3-27] Hume, Sharon, and Alison Seaman. "X.25 and Frame Relay: Packet Switched Technologies for Wide Area Connectivity." *3Tech, the 3Com Technical Journal* (Winter 1992): 33–45.

[3-28] Institute of Electrical and Electronics Engineers. *Information Technology – Telecommunications and information exchange between systems – Local and metropolitan area networks – Specific requirements – Part 6: Distributed Queue Dual Bus (DQDB) Subnetwork of a Metropolitan Area Network (MAN).* ISO/IEC 8802-6: 1994 (ANSI/IEEE 802.6 1994).

[3-29] Bell Communications Research, Inc. *Generic System Requirements in Support of Switched Multi-megabit Data Service.* TR-TSV-000772, May 1991.

[3-30] Piscitello, D., and J. Lawrence. "The Transmission of IP Datagrams over the SMDS Service." RFC 1209, March 1991.

[3-31] The SMDS Interest Group documents may be obtained from: `ftp://ftp.acc.com/pub/protocols/smds`

[3-32] The ATM Forum may be contacted at:
ATM Forum Worldwide Headquarters
2570 W. El Camino Rio, Suite 304
Mountain View, CA 94440
Tel: (650) 949-6700
Fax: (650) 949-6705
Email: `info@atmforum.com`
`http://www.atmforum.com`

[3-33] The ATM Forum. ATM User-Network Interface Specification Version 3.1, September 1994. (Many ATM Forum documents are available from `http://www.atmforum.com`.)

[3-34] Miller, Mark A. *Analyzing Broadband Networks,* second edition. M&T Books, Inc. (New York, NY), 1997.

[3-35] Heinanen, Juha. "Multiprotocol Encapsulation over ATM Adaptation Layer 5." RFC 1483, July 1993.

[3-36] Laubach, M. "Classical IP and ARP over ATM." RFC 1577, January 1994.

[3-37] The ATM Forum. *LAN Emulation Over ATM Version 2 – LUNI Specification,* document AF-LANE-00084.000, July 1997.

[3-38] The ATM Forum. *Multiprotocol over ATM (MPOA) Specification 1.0,* document AF-MPOA-0087.000, July 1997.

[3-39] Miller, Mark A. *LAN Troubleshooting Handbook,* second edition. M&T Books, Inc. (New York, NY), 1993.

[3-40] Sidhu, Gursharan, et al. *Inside AppleTalk,* second edition. Addison-Wesley Publishing Company, Inc. (New York, NY), 1990.

Chapter 4

Troubleshooting the Internet Connection

In the previous chapter, we discussed the options for the ARPA Network Interface (or Local Network) Layer, ranging from ATM to SMDS. In this chapter, we move up one layer in the ARPA architectural model and explore the Internet Layer. This layer is analogous to the OSI Network Layer and is responsible for delivering a package of data (known as a *datagram*) from its source to its destination via the internetwork. Note that this internetwork may include the Internet, a corporate internet, or any of the LAN and WAN transmission channels that we studied in Chapter 3.

One of the principal functions of the Network Interface Layer is *routing*. Routing gets a data packet from one host to another via the internetwork. Several steps occur during the routing process. First, each device must have a Logical address that uniquely identifies it within the internetwork. This internet address is independent of any Hardware or Physical address, such as the 48-bit Data Link Layer address of an Ethernet or token ring workstation. A mechanism is also necessary to associate the Logical address within the datagram with the Physical address within the LAN, MAN, or WAN frame. The Address Resolution Protocol (ARP) and the Reverse Address Resolution Protocol (RARP) handle this translation.

Second, you may set up the logical address to identify individual hosts and/or subnetworks (such as LANs) within a network. Third, you must distribute intelligent devices, known as *routers,* throughout the internetwork to guide the packets to their destination. Routers decide on the appropriate path for the packets to take by comparing address information from within the packet with information they have accumulated about the internetwork topology. The Routing Information Protocol (RIP) and the Open Shortest Path First (OSPF) protocol are two of the interior gateway protocols (IGP) that routers use to communicate among themselves. Reference [4-1] is an excellent overview of internetworking hardware; [4-2] discusses routing principles in general.

Finally, the Internet Control Message Protocol (ICMP) establishes a mechanism for performance feedback and communication within the internetwork. ICMP permits tests, diagnostic procedures, and flow control among various devices.

IP switching technologies, such as the Multiprotocol over ATM (MPOA) topology standardized by the ATM Forum (review Section 3.11.4), are architectural alternatives to IP routing. These switches are designed to integrate into an existing routing infrastructure and provide some type of shortcut or cut-through path via switches for end stations that are communicating large volumes of packets. Some IP switching solutions are in the early stages of product deployment, therefore vendor-proprietary implementations may exist before industry standards become widely accepted. References [4-3] and [4-4] provide analyses of representative products.

We'll begin our study of the Internet Layer by investigating the current version of the Internet Protocol, IPv4. In Chapter 8 we will study the next-generation Internet Protocol, IPv6.

4.1 Internet Protocol

The Internet Protocol (IP) was developed to "provide the functions necessary to deliver a package of bits (an internet datagram) from a source to a destination over an interconnected system of networks" [4-5]. IP is primarily concerned with delivery of the datagram. Equally important, however, are the issues that IP does not address, such as the end-to-end reliable delivery of data or the sequential delivery of data. IP leaves those issues for the Host-to-Host Layer and the implementations of TCP and UDP that reside there. (As mentioned previously, a new version of IP, called IP Version 6 (IPv6) or IP Next Generation (IPng), has been developed and is being implemented. In this text, we will refer to the older version (IP Version 4 or IPv4) as just IP, and the newer version as IPv6.)

The term datagram refers to a package of data transmitted over a connectionless network. *Connectionless* means that no connection between source and destination is established prior to data transmission. Datagram transmission is analogous to mailing a letter. With both a letter and a datagram, you write a Source and Destination address on the envelope, place the information inside, and drop the package into a mailbox for pickup. But while the post office uses blue or red mailboxes, the Internet uses your network node as the pickup point.

Another type of data transmission is a *virtual circuit connection,* which uses a connection-oriented network. A virtual circuit is analogous to a telephone call, where the Destination address is contacted and a path defined through the network prior to transmitting data. IP is an example of a datagram-based protocol, TCP of a virtual circuit-based protocol.

In the process of delivering datagrams, IP must deal with *addressing* and *fragmentation.* The address ensures that the datagram arrives at the correct destination, whether it's across town or across the world. Notice from Figure 4-1a that, unlike the Network Interface Layer, the Internet Layer must be implemented with a consistent protocol, such as the Internet Protocol, on an end-to-end basis for addressing consistency. Figure 4-1b illustrates the protocols implemented at the Internet Layer, while Figure 4-1c illustrates the various routing, control, and address resolution protocols that will also be considered in this chapter.

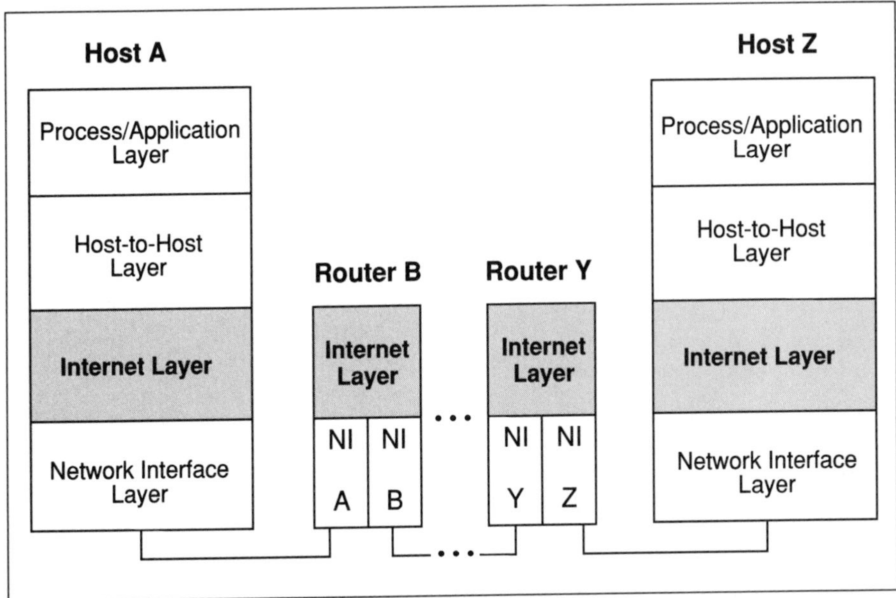

Figure 4-1a The Internet Connection

Fragmentation is necessary because the LANs and WANs that any datagram may traverse can have differing frame sizes, and the IP datagram must always fit within the frame, as shown in Figure 4-1d. (We saw this explicitly in the frame structures illustrated in Chapter 3. For example, an ARCNET frame can accommodate only up to 504 octets of data, while FDDI carries up to 4,470 octets.) Specific fields within the IP header handle the addressing and fragmentation functions (see Figure 4-2). Note from the figure that each horizontal group of bits (called a *word*) is 32 bits wide.

ARPA Layer	Protocol Implementation								OSI Layer
Process / Application	Hypertext Transfer	File Transfer	Electronic Mail	Terminal Emulation	Domain Names	File Transfer	Client / Server	Network Management	Application
	Hypertext Transfer Protocol (HTTP) RFC 2068	File Transfer Protocol (FTP) MIL-STD-1780 RFC 959	Simple Mail Transfer Protocol (SMTP) MIL-STD-1781 RFC 821	TELNET Protocol MIL-STD-1782 RFC 854	Domain Name System (DNS) RFC 1034, 1035	Trivial File Transfer Protocol (TFTP) RFC 783	Sun Microsystems Network File System Protocols (NFS) RFCs 1014, 1057, and 1094	Simple Network Management Protocol (SNMP) v1: RFC 1157 v2: RFC 1901-10 v3: RFC 2271-75	Presentation / Session
Host-to-Host	Transmission Control Protocol (TCP) MIL-STD-1778 RFC 793					User Datagram Protocol (UDP) RFC 768			Transport
Internet	Address Resolution ARP RFC 826 RARP RFC 903			Internet Protocol (IP) MIL-STD-1777 RFC 791			Internet Control Message Protocol (ICMP) RFC 792		Network
Network Interface	Network Interface Cards: Ethernet, Token Ring, ARCNET, MAN and WAN RFC 894, RFC 1042, RFC 1201 and others								Data Link
	Transmission Media: Twisted Pair, Coax, Fiber Optics, Wireless Media, etc.								Physical

Figure 4-1b ARPA Internet Layer Protocols

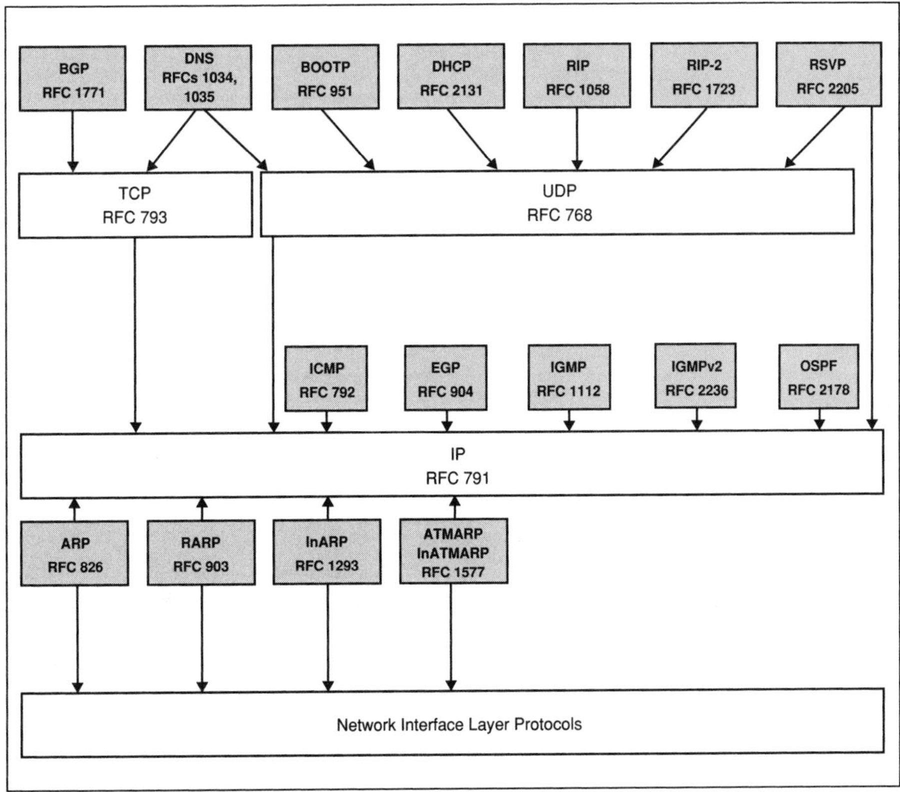

Figure 4-1c Internet Routing, Control, and Address Resolution Protocols

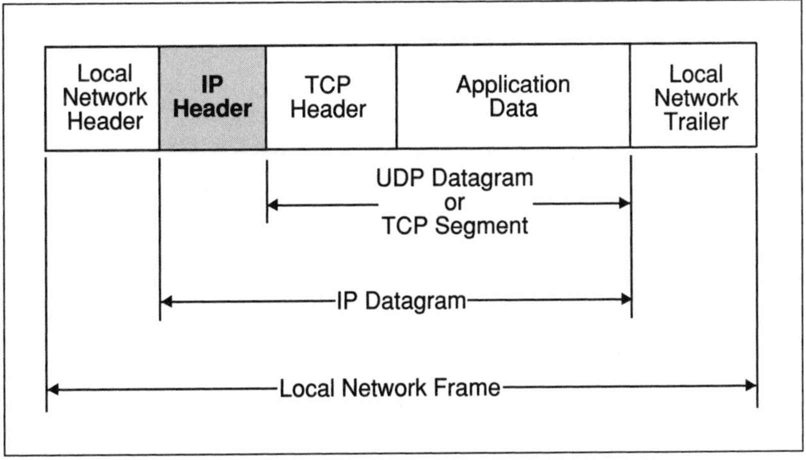

Figure 4-1d The Internet Transmission Frame and IP Header Position

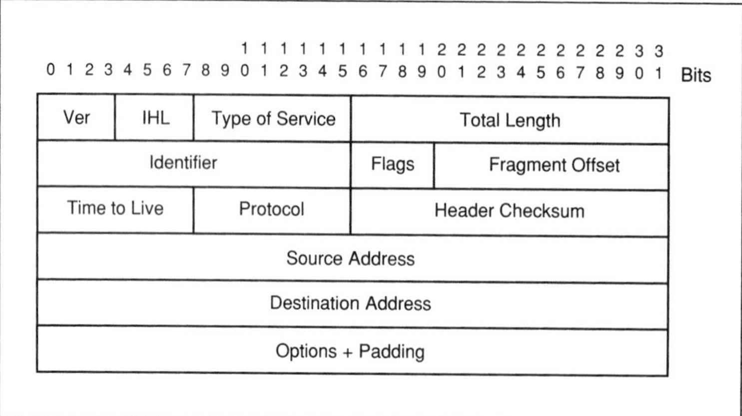

Figure 4-2 Internet Protocol (IPv4) Header Format

The IP header contains a minimum of 20 octets of control information. Version (4 bits) defines the current version of the IP protocol and should equal 4. Internet Header Length (IHL, 4 bits) measures the length of the IP header in 32-bit words. (The minimum value would be five 32-bit words, or 20 octets.) The IHL also provides a measurement (or offset) where the higher layer information, such as the TCP header, begins within that datagram. The Type of Service (8 bits) indicates the quality of service requested for the datagram. Values include:

Bits 0–2:	**Precedence (or relative importance of this datagram)**
	111 - Network Control
	110 - Internetwork Control
	101 - CRITIC/ECP
	100 - Flash Override
	011 - Flash
	010 - Immediate
	001 - Priority
	000 - Routine
Bit 3:	Delay, 0 = Normal Delay, 1 = Low Delay
Bit 4:	Throughput, 0 = Normal Throughput, 1 = High Throughput
Bit 5:	Reliability, 0 = Normal Reliability, 1 = High Reliability
Bits 6–7:	Reserved for future use (set to 0)

The Total Length field (16 bits) measures the length, in octets, of the IP datagram (IP header plus higher layer information). The 16-bit field allows for a datagram of up to 65,535 octets, although all hosts must be able to handle datagrams of at least 576 octets.

The next 32-bit word contains three fields that deal with datagram fragmentation/reassembly. Recall that the IP datagram may be up to 65,535 octets long. What happens if the endpoint of a WAN that handles such a datagram is attached to an IEEE 802.3 LAN with a maximum data field size of 1,500 octets? IP fragments the large IP datagram into smaller pieces (i.e., fragments) that will fit. The Destination node reassembles all the fragments (sort of the antithesis of Humpty Dumpty). The sender assigns the Identification field (16 bits) to help reassemble the fragments into the datagram. Three flags indicate how the fragmentation process will be handled:

Bit 0:	Reserved (set to 0)
Bit 1:	(DF) 0 = May fragment, 1 = Don't fragment
Bit 2:	(MF) 0 = Last fragment, 1 = More fragments

The last field in this word is a 13-bit fragment offset, which indicates where a fragment belongs in the complete message. This offset is measured in 64-bit units. The case study in Section 4.10.2 will illustrate the fragmentation process.

The next word in the IP header contains a Time-to-Live (TTL) measurement, which is the maximum amount of time the datagram can live within the internet. When TTL = 0, the datagram is destroyed. This field is a failsafe measure, preventing misaddressed datagrams from wandering the internet forever. TTL may be measured in either router hops or seconds. If the measurement is in seconds, the maximum is 255 seconds, or 4.25 minutes (a long time to be lost in today's high-speed internetworks). The Assigned Numbers document (currently RFC 1700 [4-6]) specifies a default TTL = 64.

The Protocol field (8 bits) following the IP header identifies the higher layer protocol in use. Examples include:

Decimal	**Keyword**	**Description**
1	ICMP	Internet Control Message Protocol
6	TCP	Transmission Control Protocol
17	UDP	User Datagram Protocol

The Assigned Numbers document (currently RFC 1700 [4-6]) and Appendix I provide a more detailed listing of the protocols defined. A 16-bit header checksum completes the third 32-bit word.

The fourth and fifth words of the IP header contain the Source and Destination addresses, respectively. Recall that we discussed Hardware addresses for the ARPA Network Interface Layer (or OSI Data Link Layer) in Chapter 3. The addresses within the IP header are the Internet Layer (or OSI Network Layer) addresses. The Internet address is a Logical address that gets the IP datagram through the Internet to the correct host and network (LAN, MAN, or WAN). Reference [4-7] is an excellent analysis of addressing schemes used within different LAN and WAN topologies, including X.25, IEEE 802, and IP. In the next section we will study IP addressing in detail.

Options and Padding, if present, may complete the IP header. The Options field, which may be of variable length, carries options within this datagram. Examples of options, as defined in RFC 791, include security, source routing, stream identifier, and timestamp information. Another option, called the Router Alert Option, is defined in RFC 2113 and is also mentioned in conjunction with the Internet Group Management Protocol (IGMP), which we will study in Section 4.6. This option acts as a flag to transit routers, causing them to closely examine the contents of a particular IP datagram while not causing performance penalties for all datagrams going through that router. Finally, the Padding field adds a variable number of zeros to ensure that the IP header ends on a 32-bit boundary.

4.2 Internetwork Addressing

Each 32-bit IP address is divided into Host ID and Network ID sections and may take one of five formats ranging from Class A to Class E, as shown in Figure 4-3. The formats differ in the number of bits they allocate to the Host IDs and Network IDs and are identified by the first four bits.

4.2.1 Address Classes

Class A addresses are designed for very large networks with many hosts. They are identified by Bit 0 = 0. Bits 1 through 7 identify the network, and Bits 8 through 31 identify the host. With a 7-bit Network ID, only 128 Class A network addresses are available. Of these, addresses 0 and 127 are reserved [4-8].

The majority of organizations that have distributed processing systems including LANs and hosts use Class B addresses. Class B addresses are identified with the first 2 bits having a value of 10 (binary). The next 14 identify the network. The remaining 16 bits identify the host. A total of 16,384 Class B network addresses are possible; however, addresses 0 and 16,383 are reserved.

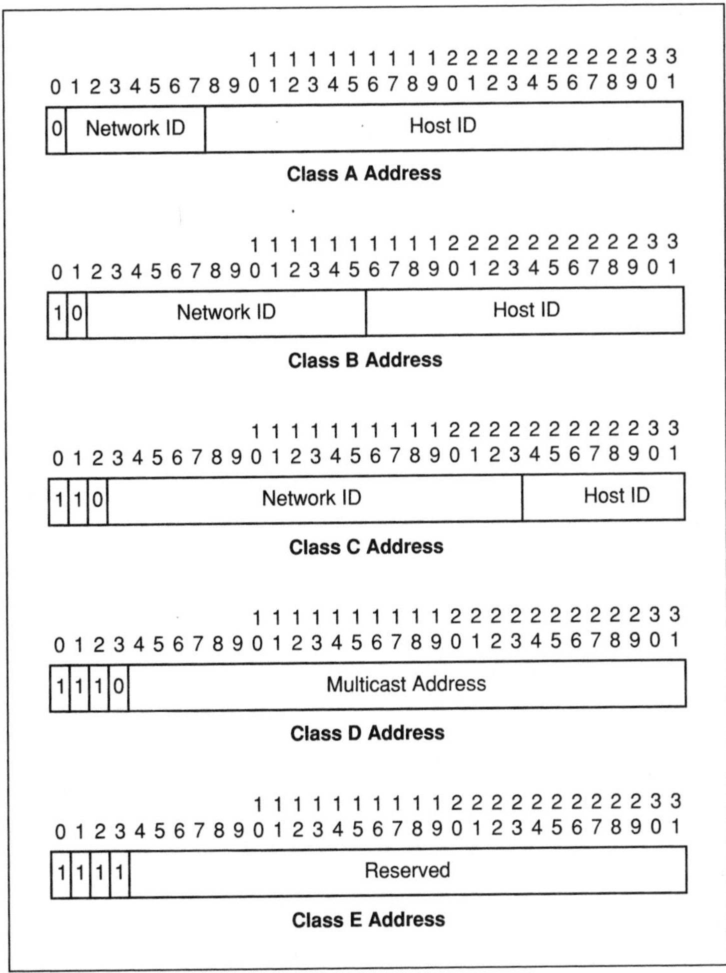

Figure 4-3 IPv4 Address Formats

Class C addresses are generally used for smaller networks, such as LANs. They begin with a binary 110. The next 21 bits identify the network. The remaining 8 bits identify the host. A total of 2,097,152 Class C network addresses are possible, with addresses 0 and 2,097,151 reserved.

Class D addresses begin with a binary 1110 and are intended for multicasting. Class E addresses begin with a binary 1111 and are reserved for future use.

All IP addresses are written in dotted decimal notation, in which each octet is assigned a decimal number from 0 to 255. For example, network [10.55.31.84] is represented in binary as 00001010 00110111 00011111 1010100. The first bit (0) indicates a Class A address, the next 7 bits (0001010) represent the Network ID (decimal 10), and the last 24 bits (00110111 00011111 1010100) represent the Host ID.

Class A addresses begin with 1–127, Class B with 128–191, Class C with 192–223, and Class D with 224–239. Thus, an address of [150.100.200.5] is easily identified as a Class B address.

4.2.2 Multicast Addresses

Class D addresses are reserved to support multicast applications, and range in value from 224.0.0.0 through 239.255.255.255. Of these values, the Internet Assigned Numbers Authority (IANA) has assigned specific values for particular multicast functions. For example, the range of addresses between 224.0.0.0 and 224.0.0.255, inclusive, is used for routing protocols and other topology and maintenance functions. Within this range, address 224.0.0.1 identifies "all systems on this subnet" and 224.0.0.2 identifies "all routers on this subnet." Other values have been specified RIP2 routers (224.0.0.9), DHCP Server/Relay Agents (224.0.0.12), audio and video transport, and others. Addresses in the range from 239.0.0.0 through 239.255.255.255 are reserved for local applications. A complete listing of the assigned multicast addresses is available in the Assigned Numbers document (currently RFC 1700 [4-6]), and also in Appendix I.

4.2.3 Subnetting

As discussed above, the IP addresses are divided into two fields that identify a network and a host. A central authority assigns the Network ID and the local network administrator assigns the Host ID. Routers send packets to a particular network using the Network ID, and that network completes the delivery to the host. If an organization has two networks, it could request two Network ID assignments from the central authority. But this would cause the routing tables within hosts and routers to expand considerably. The popularity of LANs in the mid-1980s, therefore, inspired the Internet community to revise the IP address structure. The new structure allows for an additional field to identify a *subnetwork* within an assigned Network ID. Thus the [Network, Host] address format is replaced with the [Network, Subnetwork, Host] format. The space for the Subnetwork field comes from reducing the Host field. The central authority assigns the Network ID, and the individual organization assigns the Subnetwork IDs and the Host IDs on each subnetwork.

The Address Mask differentiates between various subnetworks. A Subnet Mask is a 32-bit number that has ones in the Network ID and Subnetwork ID fields and zeros in the Host ID field. The router or the host implements a mathematical function that performs a logical AND function between the Subnet Mask and a particular IP address to determine whether a datagram can be delivered on the same subnet, or whether it must go through an IP router to another subnet.

A host or router that needs to make a routing decision uses the Subnet Mask for assistance and the logical AND function to arrive at its conclusion. For example, suppose the Destination address is D and my address is M. Further suppose that the Subnet Mask is [255.255.255.0]. Two calculations are made: Subnet Mask AND Address D, plus Subnet Mask AND Address M. The result of the AND function strips off the host portion of the address, leaving only the network and subnet portions. (Recall that the Host ID field is filled with zeros and that any number AND zero is still zero.) From the calculations, we have two results, each representing a Network ID and a Subnet ID. The two results are then compared and used to make a routing decision. When the two results are identical, Addresses M and D are on the same subnetwork. If Addresses M and D are not equal, the two addresses are on different subnetworks, and the datagram must go to a router for delivery.

Subnet Masks may be either a fixed length (sometimes called static subnetting), as described above, or a variable length. With the static case, all subnets in that network use the same Subnet Mask. With variable length subnetting, the subnets that comprise that network may use different Subnet Masks. In that way, if a particular subnet only has a small number of hosts, the Subnet Mask can be adjusted to allow fewer bits for the host portion of the mask, thus conserving IP addresses. Likewise, if a particular subnet had a large number of hosts, the host portion could be similarly increased in response. However, some hosts and routers, and some routing protocols, such as RIP version 1, do not support variable length Subnet Masks. (As we will see in Section 4.4, RIP version 2 does support variable-length Subnet Masks.)

If the host doesn't know which Subnet Mask to use, it uses ICMP to discover the right one. The host broadcasts an ICMP Address Mask Request message and waits for an ICMP Address Mask Reply from a neighboring router. If an Address Mask is used improperly and a datagram is sent to a router erroneously, the router that identifies the misdirected packet returns an ICMP Redirect message. We will look at this scenario in Section 4.10.5.

RFC 950, "Internet Standard Subnetting Procedure" [4-9], was written to cover subnet-related issues. Steve Steinke's "IP Addresses and Subnet Masks" [4-10] discuss the topic from an implementation perspective. RFC 1118, "The Hitchhiker's Guide to the Internet" [4-11], discusses UNIX-related subnetting issues.

4.2.4 Reserved Addresses

Several addresses are reserved to identify special purposes ([4-6, page 4], [4-12, Sections 4.2.2.11 and 4.2.3.1]):

Address	Interpretation
[Net = 0, Host = 0]	This host on this network
[Net = 0, Host = H]	Specific Host H on this network (Source address only)
[Net = all ones, Host = all ones]	Limited broadcast (within the source's subnetwork)
[Net = N, Host = all ones]	Directed broadcast to network (Destination address only)
[Net = N, Sub = all ones, Host = all ones]	Directed broadcast to all subnets on Network N (Destination address only)

Continued

Continued

Address	Interpretation
[Net = N, Sub = S, Host = all ones]	Directed broadcast to all hosts on Subnet S, Network N (Destination address only)
[Net = 127, Host = any]	Internal host loopback address
The following two numbers are used for network numbers, but not IP addresses:	
[Net = N, Host = 0]	Network N, No Host
[Net = N, Sub = S, Host = 0]:	Subnet S, No Host

Abbreviations:
Net = Network ID
Sub = Subnet ID
Host = Host ID

RFC 1118 [4-11] issues two cautions about IP addresses. First, it notes that BSD 4.2 UNIX systems require additional software for subnetting; BSD 4.3 systems do not. Second, some machines use an IP address of all zeros to specify a broadcast, instead of the more common all ones. BSD 4.3 requires the system administrator to choose the broadcast address. Use caution, since many problems, such as broadcast storms, can result when the broadcast address is not implemented consistently over the network. RFC 1812 [4-12] also discusses cautions in this area.

4.2.5 Network Address Translation (NAT)

In some circumstances, having a globally unique IP address is not required or desired. For example, stations in a test lab, or those that never communicate to the global Internet, would not need a unique address that is assigned by a central authority. In other cases, perhaps for security reasons, advertising a private network's IP address to the world may not be desired. In either case, assigning a private (or nonglobal) IP address is necessary. This issue is addressed in RFC 1918, "Address Allocation for Private Internets" [4-13]. The IANA has reserved the following blocks of IP addresses for private internets:

```
[10.0.0.0] – [10.255.255.255]       (A single Class A number)
[172.16.0.0] – [172.31.255.255      (16 contiguous Class B numbers)
[192.168.0.0] – [192.168.255.255]   (256 contiguous Class C numbers)
```

Thus, a network administrator could number his network internally using network number 10, and as long as no routing information regarding network number 10 was propagated to the outside world, no confusion would exist. In addition, there could be multiple private networks, all using network number 10. Again, if no routing information was propagated to the outside world, there would be no confusion.

However, communication with the outside world requires translation from the internal (private) network address to a global (or universally known) address. This process is called Network Address Translation, or NAT, and is defined in RFC 1631 [4-14]. The NAT process may be performed at a border router between a private internet and some regional router (such as within the Internet), as shown in Figure 4-4. In this example, taken from RFC 1631, two private networks, designated A and B, are both internally numbered with network address 10. Each of these networks is attached to a router with NAT capabilities, which has a globally unique Class C address assigned: [198.76.29.0] for the Network A case, and [198.76.28.0] for the Network B case. These NAT routers, in turn, connect to a regional router.

Suppose that Workstation 1 in Network A wishes to communicate with Workstation 2 in Network B. Workstation 1 would compose an IP datagram using its source address [10.33.96.5] and the globally unique address for Workstation 2 [198.76.28.4]. This packet is then passed to the NAT router, which translates the internal source address of Workstation 1 [10.33.96.5] to a globally unique address [198.76.29.7] that can be forwarded through the regional router. In a similar fashion, the NAT process at Network B translates the globally unique destination address of the datagram [198.76.28.4] to the private destination address [10.81.13.22] used internally within Network B. In a similar fashion, datagrams from Network B to Network A would also go through address translations.

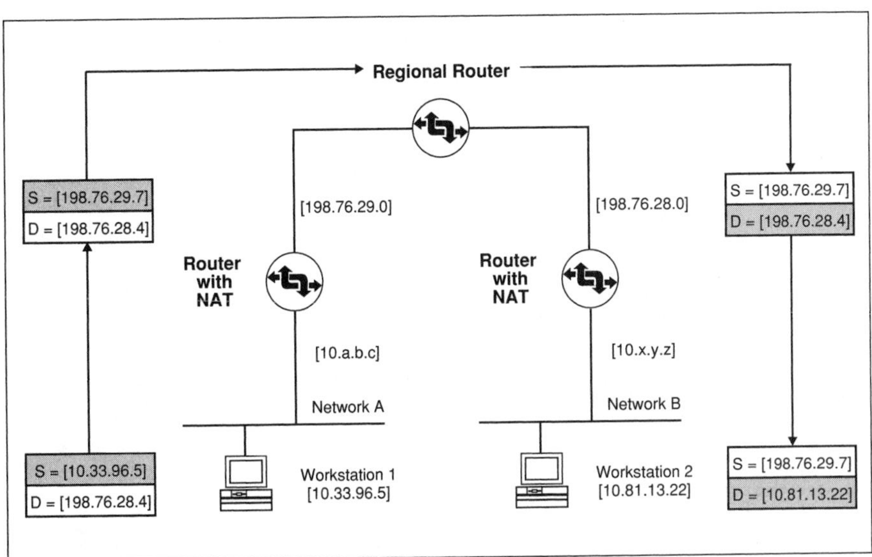

Figure 4-4 Network Address Translation Example

For further details on private addresses and address translation, see RFCs 1918 and 1631, or William Dutcher's paper, "IP Addressing – Playing the Numbers" [4-15], which discusses Network Address Translation implementation.

4.2.6 Classless Inter-Domain Routing (CIDR)

Thus far in our discussion, we have assumed that a device is identified by one of the three classes of IP addresses: A, B, or C. Those three address formats have fixed boundaries between the Network ID and the Host ID fields. For example, with a Class A address, there are seven bits in the Network ID field, so there are a maximum of 128 (2^7) theoretical networks. Likewise, there are 24 bits in the Host ID field, so 16,777,216 (2^{24}) hosts can be uniquely identified. (For the purpose of this discussion, we will not consider any reserved addresses that could further reduce the maximum number of theoretical network addresses.) In a similar fashion, Class B addresses can accommodate 16,384 (2^{14}) unique networks, each with 65,536 (2^{16}) unique hosts, and Class C addresses can accommodate 2,097,152 (2^{21}) unique networks, each with 256 (2^8) unique hosts.

But what happens if a network needs addresses for 260 hosts? You immediately exceed the capacity of a Class C address, and must use a Class B. To further complicate matters, what if the Internet community is running out of Class B addresses? Is it reasonable to assign a Class B address to your organization, just because you need a few more addresses beyond what a Class C address can supply?

This is the problem that has faced the Internet community in the past few years; it has been addressed with the address process called Classless Inter-Domain Routing, or CIDR for short. The technical and implementation aspects of CIDR are addressed in a series of RFC documents: RFCs 1517 through 1520 [4-16]. With CIDR, the problem stated above would be solved by assigning two *contiguous* Class C addresses to the end user's network, thus enabling 512 (2 256) unique host addresses to be assigned. In effect, then, the user has a nine-bit Host ID field.

Thus, CIDR does not determine the route based on the class of network (A, B, or C) and the resulting Network ID field, but instead on a variable number of high-order bits in the IP address. These bits are referred to as the *address prefix*. When multiple Class C addresses are assigned to an organization, they are assigned contiguously, which forces them to have the same address prefix. These multiple Class C addresses can then be grouped together into a single routing table entry, which is a process known as *address aggregation*. This route aggregation also minimizes the number of routing table entries that are needed to identify a single CIDR-based route.

Further details on CIDR may be found in RFCs 1517 through 1520.

4.2.7 Mobile IP

Thus far, we have discussed addressing schemes that assume that the IP-addressable device is at a fixed location. But with many end users employing a nomadic lifestyle for their business operations, changes to some of the previous assumptions are necessary. The technical side of Mobile IP is addressed in RFC 2002 [4-17], "IP Mobility Support."

To implement Mobile IP, each node is identified by two addresses: its home address and a care-of address. A mobile node is always identified by its home address, independent of its current attachment to the Internet. When it is away from its home location, the node is also associated with a care-of address, which provides information regarding its current attachment point. Operating at the home location is a Home Agent, where the node can register a care-of address. Similarly, operating at the remote location is a Foreign Agent. When datagrams arrive for a node, and that node is not at its home location, the Home Agent encapsulates that datagram within a new IP header and sends it to the Foreign Agent, which decapsulates the packet and is responsible for ultimate packet delivery.

Mobile IP is a complex and still evolving work, involving issues such as packet loss during relocation, security, and communication across firewalls. Readers needing further details on this subject should study RFC 2002.

4.3 Address Resolution

In the last two sections, we looked at the differences between the Internet address, used by IP, and the Local address, used by the LAN or WAN hardware. We observed that the IP address was a 32-bit Logical address, but that the Physical address depends on the hardware. For example, ARCNET has an 8-bit and Ethernet a 48-bit Hardware address. Since we may know one of these addresses but not the other, protocols are provided to map the Logical and Physical addresses to each other. Since two translations may be necessary (Logical to Physical or Physical to Logical), two protocols have been developed. The Address Resolution Protocol (ARP) described in RFC 826 [4-18] translates from an IP address to a Hardware address. The Reverse Address Resolution Protocol (RARP) detailed in RFC 903 [4-19] does the opposite, as its name implies. Let's look at these protocols separately.

4.3.1 Address Resolution Protocol

Let's assume that a device, Host X, on an Ethernet wishes to deliver a datagram to another device on the same Ethernet, Host Y. Host X knows Host Y's Destination Protocol (IP) address, but does not know its Hardware (Ethernet) address. It would, therefore, broadcast an ARP packet within an Ethernet frame to determine Host Y's Hardware address. The ARP packet is shown in Figure 4-5a. The packet consists of 28 octets, primarily addresses, which are contained within the Data field of a LAN frame. The sender broadcasts an ARP packet within a LAN frame requesting the information that it lacks. The device that recognizes its own Protocol address responds with the sought-for Hardware address. The individual fields of the ARP message show how the protocol operates.

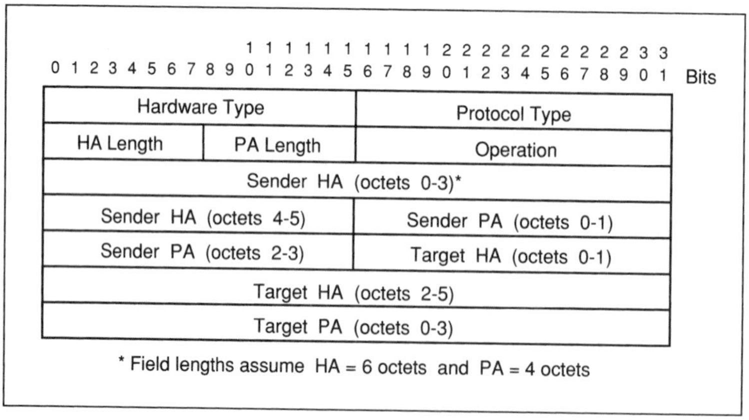

Bits 0–31

Bits 0–7	Bits 8–15	Bits 16–31
Hardware Type		Protocol Type
HA Length	PA Length	Operation
Sender HA (octets 0-3)*		
Sender HA (octets 4-5)		Sender PA (octets 0-1)
Sender PA (octets 2-3)		Target HA (octets 0-1)
Target HA (octets 2-5)		
Target PA (octets 0-3)		

* Field lengths assume HA = 6 octets and PA = 4 octets

Figure 4-5a Address Resolution Protocol (ARP) and Reverse Address Resolution Protocol (RARP) Packet Formats

The first field, Hardware (2 octets), defines the type of hardware in use. Current values are listed in the Assigned Numbers document (currently RFC 1700). Examples include Hardware = 1 (Ethernet), 6 (IEEE 802 Networks), 7 (ARCNET), 11 (LocalTalk), 14 (SMDS), 15 (Frame Relay), and 16 (ATM). The second field, Protocol (2 octets), identifies the Protocol address in use. For example, protocol = 0800H would identify IP addresses.

The second word allows the ARP packet to be used with a variety of address structures rather than restricting its use to only two, such as IP (32 bits) and IEEE 802 (48 bits). This makes the protocol more adaptive. The Hardware Length (HLEN), 1 octet, and Protocol Length (PLEN), 1 octet, specify the lengths, in octets, of the addresses to be used. Figure 4-5a represents the most common scenario. The Hardware Address (HA) requires 6 octets or 48 bits (HLEN = 6); the Protocol Address (PA) needs 4 octets or 32 bits (PLEN = 4). The Operation field (2 octets) defines an ARP Request = 1 and ARP Reply = 2.

The next fields contain the addresses themselves. With an ARP Request message, the target Hardware address field is unknown and is sent filled with zeros. The ARP Reply packet from the target host will insert the requested address in that field. When it receives the ARP Reply, the originating station records that information in a table, called the ARP cache. The ARP cache reduces internetwork traffic asking to resolve the same address on multiple occasions. Routers' ARP caches have a finite lifetime, which prevents the table from growing too large.

4.3.2 Reverse Address Resolution Protocol

Most hosts on networks are smart enough to remember their own Hardware and Protocol addresses. But diskless workstations rely on the server for much of their intelligence. Such a workstation would know its Hardware address, which is coded into ROM, but the server might assign a Protocol address of which the workstation was unaware. The Reverse Address Resolution Protocol (RARP) can discover an unknown Protocol address given a known Hardware address and a RARP server to supply the answer. Note that the sought-for address is the sender's own IP address, and that the presence of the RARP server is critical to the operation of this protocol.

The process of determining an unknown Protocol address is similar to that of finding an unknown Hardware address. The same packet structure is used (review Figure 4-5a) with only minor modifications to the field values. The Operation field adds two new values: 3 (RARP Request) and 4 (RARP Reply). When the RARP Request is made, the Sender Hardware address, Sender Protocol address, and Target Hardware address are transmitted. The RARP Reply contains the sought-after Target Protocol address.

4.3.3 Inverse ARP

ARP allows a Protocol address, such as an IP address, to be associated with a Hardware address, such as Ethernet. In some cases, however, a virtual address identifies the endpoint of the connection, replacing the Hardware address. Two examples of this are frame relay and ATM, where a virtual circuit address identifies the connection endpoint. In the case of frame relay, a permanent or switched virtual circuit (PVC or SVC) is identified by a Data Link Connection Identifier (DLCI) as we studied in Section 3.9. When a new PVC or SVC is provisioned (with its associated DLCI), the end user devices know of the PVC's or SVC's existence, but not the IP address associated with that circuit. For these applications, it is necessary to provide a mechanism to discover the Protocol address associated with that particular virtual circuit. The Inverse Address Resolution Protocol (InARP), defined in RFC 1293 [4-20], provides the details of these protocol operations.

Inverse ARP is an extension to ARP, and therefore uses the same packet format (review Figure 4-5a). The Hardware address field length may be different from the LAN case; for example, frame relay would use a Hardware address length of 2, 3, or 4 octets. Two new operation codes are defined: InARP Request and InArp Reply.

InARP operates in a similar fashion to ARP, with the exception that requests are not broadcast, because the Hardware address (such as a DLCI) of the destination station is already known. Instead, the requesting station fills in the sending and target Hardware addresses plus the sending Protocol address, and sends the InARP Request to the distant station which fills in the missing target Protocol address. For further details on InARP, consult RFC 1293.

4.3.4 ATMARP

Another extension to ARP is provided for IP traffic over ATM-based internetworks, and is defined in RFC 1577, "Classical IP and ARP over ATM" [4-21]. The ATMARP protocol is based on both ARP (RFC 826) and Inverse ARP (RFC 1293), discussed above. ATMARP provides a mechanism for associating IP and ATM addresses for communication within a Logical IP Subnetwork, or LIS, as we discussed in Section

3.11.2. The ATMARP packet format expands on the ARP packet format, and is illustrated in Figure 4-5b. The first two fields, Hardware Type (2 octets) and Protocol Type (2 octets), are used identically to the original ARP usage. The Hardware address assigned to the ATM Forum address family is 19 decimal (0013H); however, the Protocol Address field value for IP remains the same (0800H). Four new 1-octet fields define the type and length of the Sender ATM number (SHTL), the Sender ATM subaddress (SSTL), the Target ATM number (THTL), and the Target ATM subaddress (TSTL). The Operation Code (2 octets) defines five operation codes:

Operation Code	Operation
1	ARP Request
2	ARP Reply
8	InARP Request
9	InARP Reply
10	ARP NAK

Two 1-octet fields are also included in the third word that specify the Sender Protocol Address (SPA) length and the Target Protocol Address (TPA) length. The four addresses, Sender ATM, Sender Protocol, Target ATM, and Target Protocol, complete the packet. (Note that the format shown in Figure 4-5b assumes ATM address lengths of 20 octets and a Protocol Address length of 4 octets.) For further details on ATMARP and InATMARP, consult RFC 1577.

4.3.5 Proxy ARP

When IP is run on a LAN, special attention to the addressing scheme is required. In most cases, it is not desirable for each segment to have a distinct network number; instead, subnetting a single network number is the preferred approach for distinguishing individual LAN segments. The details of this subnetted configuration need not be relevant to those outside the LAN, as long as a packet destined for a host on a particular LAN segment can be delivered correctly. RFC 925, "Multi-LAN Address Resolution" [4-22], addresses these issues; it defines a variation on the ARP process, known as Proxy ARP or promiscuous ARP, to handle these operations.

Bits 0–7	Bits 8–15	Bits 16–23	Bits 24–31
Hardware Type		Protocol Type	
SHTL	SSTL	Operation	
SPA Length	THTL	TSTL	TPA Length
Sender ATM Address (octets 0-3)			
Sender ATM Address (octets 4-7)			
Sender ATM Address (octets 8-11)			
Sender ATM Address (octets 12-15)			
Sender ATM Address (octets 16-19)			
Sender PA			
Target ATM Address (octets 0-3)			
Target ATM Address (octets 4-7)			
Target ATM Address (octets 8-11)			
Target ATM Address (octets 12-15)			
Target ATM Address (octets 16-19)			
Target PA			

* Field lengths assume ATM Address = 20 octets and PA = 4 octets

Figure 4-5b ATM Address Resolution Protocol (ATMARP) and Inverse ATM Address Resolution Protocol (InATMARP) Packet Formats

A proxy is a person or device that acts on behalf of another person or device. Suppose that two networks use the same IP network address, and that we call these two networks A and B. Router R, running ARP, connects these two networks. Router R will become the proxy device. Now suppose that a host on Network A wishes to communicate with another host on Network B, but doesn't know its Hardware address. The host on Network A would broadcast an ARP Request seeking the Hardware address of the remote host. Router R would intercept the request and reply with HA = R, which would be stored in the host's ARP cache. Subsequent communication between the two hosts would go via R, with Router R using its own lookup table to forward the packet to Network B. In effect, Proxy ARP allows the router to respond to an ARP request that came from one of its attached networks with the information concerning another one of its attached networks. In essence, the router deceives the originating host into thinking that it (i.e. the router) is the correct destination Hardware address. In this way, the outside world is insulated from that LAN's address resolution operation. Black [4-23] and Comer [4-24] discuss the advantages and disadvantages of Proxy ARP in further detail.

4.3.6 Bootstrap Protocol

The Bootstrap Protocol (BOOTP), described in RFC 951 [4-25], is an alternative to ARP/RARP. The protocol gets it name from the fact that it is meant to be contained within a bootstrap ROM. BOOTP is designed for diskless clients that need information from a server, such as their own IP address, the server's IP address, or the name of a file (i.e., the boot file) to be loaded into memory and then executed. The client broadcasts a Boot Request packet, which is answered by a Boot Reply packet from the server.

One of the significant differences between ARP/RARP and BOOTP is the layer of protocol they address. ARP/RARP packets are contained within local network frames and are transmitted on the local network. BOOTP packets are contained within IP datagrams, contain a UDP header, and are transmitted on the internetwork. The designated server can, therefore, be several router hops away from the client. Two reserved port numbers are used: port 67 for the BOOTP Server and port 68 for the BOOTP Client.

The individual fields of the BOOTP packet are shown in Figure 4-6a. The OpCode (Op, 1 octet) specifies a BOOTREQUEST (Op = 1) or BOOTREPLY (Op = 2). Hardware address Type (Htype, 1 octet) and Hardware address Length (Hlen, 1 octet) are similar to those fields in the ARP/RARP packet. The Hops field (1 octet) is optional for use in cross-router booting. The Transaction ID (4 octets) correlates the boot requests and responses. The Seconds field (2 octets) allows the client to count the elapsed time since it started the bootup sequence. Two unused octets complete the third word of the BOOTP packet.

The next four words designate the various IP addresses. The client states the addresses it knows and the server fills in the rest. These include the Client IP address (filled in by client), Your IP address (filled in by the server if the client does not know its own address), Server IP address, and Gateway router IP address. The Client HA (16 octets), Boot File Name (128 octets), and a Vendor-Specific Area (64 octets), containing information to be sent from the server to the client, complete the packet. RFC 1497 discusses implementation of that vendor-specific field. In summary, BOOTP improves on the ARP concept by allowing the address resolution process to occur across routers. Although it uses IP/UDP, it is small enough to fit within a bootstrap ROM on the client workstation.

RFC 1542 [4-26] provides clarifications and extensions to BOOTP, such as its use with IEEE 802.5 token ring networks. RFC 2132 [4-27] discusses extensions to BOOTP, plus a related protocol, the Dynamic Host Configuration Protocol, which will be discussed in further detail in the next section. Jeffrey Mogul's "Booting Diskless Hosts: The BOOTP Protocol" [4-28] describes the client/server interaction in further detail.

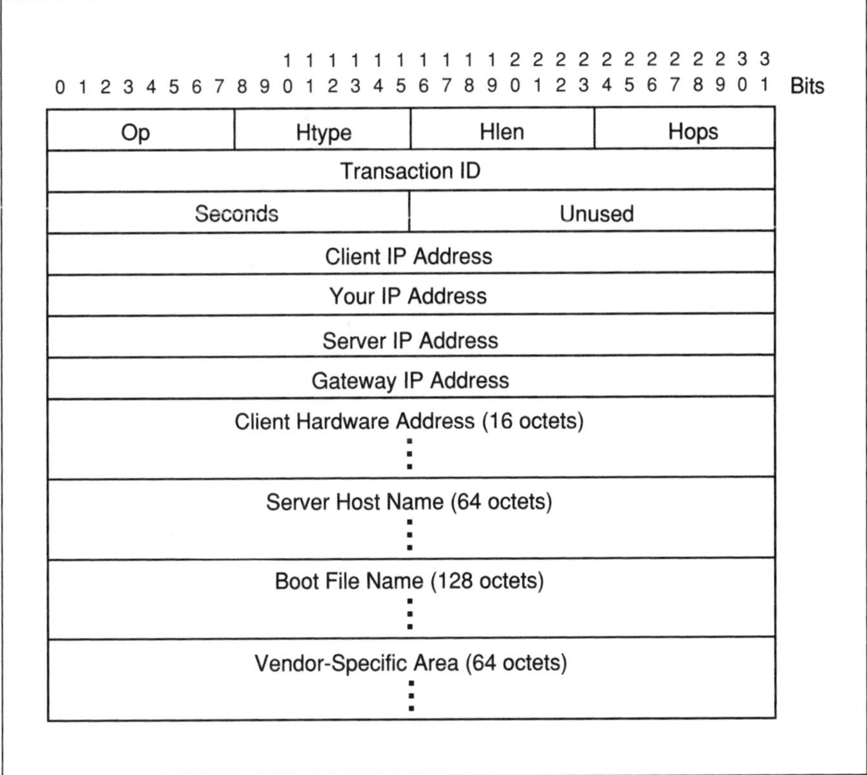

Figure 4-6a Bootstrap Protocol (BOOTP) Packet Format

4.3.7 Dynamic Host Configuration Protocol

The Dynamic Host Configuration Protocol (DHCP) provides a superset of BOOTP capabilities to include additional configuration options and automatic allocation of reusable network addresses. DHCP defines a mechanism to transmit configuration parameters to hosts using the ARPA protocol suite, with a message format based on the format of BOOTP. DHCP is defined in RFC 2131 [4-29], and the interoperation between DHCP and BOOTP is discussed in RFC 1534 [4-30].

DHCP is built on a client-server model in which the designated DHCP server allocates network addresses and delivers configuration information to the requesting client (another host). Examples of configuration information include: a default TTL, IP address, subnet mask, maximum transmission unit (MTU), list of default routers, list of static routes, ARP cache timeouts, and others. Two components are therefore included in DHCP: a mechanism for allocating network addresses to clients, and a protocol for delivering these host-specific configuration parameters to a dynamically configured host.

Seven types of DHCP messages are defined in RFC 2131:

1. DHCPDISCOVER: client broadcast to locate available servers.
2. DHCPOFFER: server to client response to the DHCPDISCOVER message, with an offer of configuration parameters.
3. DHCPREQUEST: client broadcast to servers, either:
   a. Requesting offered parameters from one server and implicitly declining offers from all others,
   b. Confirming correctness of previously allocated address after, for example, a system reboot, or
   c. Extending the lease on a particular network address.
4. DHCPACK: server to client with configuration parameters, including committed network address.
5. DHCPNAK: server to client refusing request for configuration parameters.
6. DHCPDECLINE: client to server indicating configuration parameters invalid.
7. DHCPRELEASE: client to server relinquishing network address and canceling remaining lease.

The DHCP message format is based on the BOOTP message format and is illustrated in Figure 4-6b. The first word contains four 1-octet fields: Op, Htype, Hlen, and Hops. The Op Code (Op) defines the message type, with 1 = BOOTREQUEST and 2 = BOOTREPLY. The Hardware Type (Htype) and Hardware Address Length (Hlen) fields define the hardware type and address, respectively, similar to the fields used in the ARP/RARP messages. The Hops field is optionally used by relay-agents when booting via a relay-agent. A client would set the Hops field to zero. The Transaction ID (also called XID) is a 32-bit random number chosen by the client; it is used by the client and the server to associate messages and responses between a client and a server. The Seconds field (2 octets) is filled in by the client, noting the seconds elapsed since the client started to boot. The Flags field (2 octets) contains a one-bit flag, called the broadcast flag, with all other bits set to zero. Details of the use of this flag are discussed in RFC 2131.

The Client IP Address field (4 octets) is set by the client, with its known address or all zeros. The Your IP Address field (4 octets) is set by the server if the Client IP Address field contains all zeros. The Server IP Address field (4 octets) is set by the server, and the Gateway (or router) IP Address is set by the relay-agent. The Client Hardware Address (16 octets) is set by the client. The Server Name is an optional server host name. The Boot File Name (128 octets) is used by the server to return a fully qualified directory path name to the client. Finally, the Options field (variable length) may contain DHCP options as defined in RFC 2132.

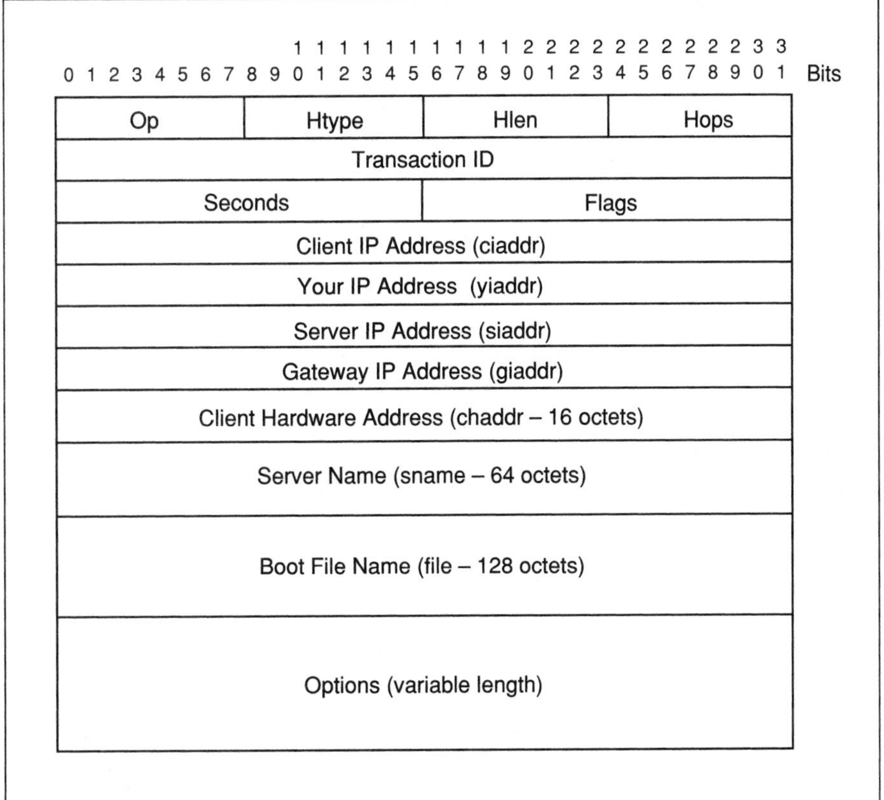

Figure 4-6b Dynamic Host Configuration Protocol (DHCP) Message Format

For further details on DHCP, study RFC 2131, J. Allard's article "DHCP – TCP/IP Network Configuration Made Easy" [4-31], Kirk Demaree's article "DHCP and DNS: A Dynamic Duo" [4-32], or visit the DHCP resource Web site noted in [4-33].

4.4 Datagram Routing

So far, we've learned that hosts transmit datagrams and use a 32-bit address to identify the source and destination of the datagram. The host drops the datagram into the internetwork, and the datagram somehow finds its way to its destination. That "somehow" is the work of routers, which examine the Destination address, compare that address with their internal routing tables, and send the datagram on the correct outgoing communication circuit.

Router operation involves several processes [4-2, page 5]. First, the router creates a routing table to gather information from other routers about the optimum path for each packet. This table may be *static* (i.e., manually built) and fixed for all network conditions, or *dynamic* (i.e., constructed by the router according to the current topology and conditions). Dynamic routing is considered the better technique because it adapts to changing network conditions. The router uses a *metric*, or measurement, of the shortest distance between two endpoints to help determine the optimum path. It determines the metric using a number of factors, including the shortest distance, or least cost path, to the destination. The router plugs the metric into one of two algorithms to make a final decision on the correct path. A *Distance Vector* algorithm makes its choice based on the distance to a remote node. A *Link State* algorithm also includes information about the status of the various links connecting the nodes and the topology of the network.

The various routers within the network use the Distance Vector or Link State algorithms to inform each other of their current status. Because routers use them for intra-network communication, the protocols that make use of these algorithms are referred to as Interior Gateway Protocols (IGPs). The Routing Information Protocol (RIP) is an IGP based on a Distance Vector algorithm. The Open Shortest Path First (OSPF) protocol is an IGP based on a Link State algorithm. We'll look at these two algorithms separately in the following sections. If one network wishes to communicate routing to another network, it uses an Exterior Gateway Protocol (EGP). An example of an EGP is the Border Gateway Protocol (BGP).

4.4.1 Routing Information Protocol

The Routing Information Protocol, described in RFC 1058 [4-34], is used for inter-router (or inter-gateway) communications. RIP is based on a Distance Vector algorithm, sometimes referred to as a Ford-Fulkerson algorithm after its developers L. R. Ford, Jr. and D. R. Fulkerson. A Distance Vector algorithm is one in which the routers periodically exchange information from their routing tables. The routing decision is based on the best path between two devices, which is often the path with the fewest hops or router transversals. The Internet standard warns that many LAN operating systems have their own RIP implementations. Therefore, it is important to adhere to the Internet standard to alleviate interoperability problems. There are, however, enhancements to RIP that are in the Internet Standards track. One example is RFC 2091 [4-35], "Triggered Extensions to RIP to Support Demand Circuits," which discusses the use of RIP over WAN links such as X.25 and ISDN.

RFC 1058 acknowledges several limitations to RIP. RIP allows a path length of 15 hops, which may be insufficient for large internetworks. Routing loops are possible for internetworks containing hundreds of networks, because of the time required to transmit updated routing table information. Finally, the metrics used to choose the routing path are fixed and do not allow for dynamic conditions, such as a measured delay or a variable traffic load.

RIP assumes that all devices (hosts and routers) contain a routing table. This table contains several entries: the IP address of the destination; the metric, or cost, to get a datagram from the host to the destination; the address of the next router in the path to the destination; a flag indicating whether the routing information has been recently updated; and timers.

Routing information is exchanged via RIP packets, shown in Figure 4-7a, which are transmitted to/from UDP port number 520. The packet begins with a 32-bit header and may contain as many as 25 messages giving details on specific networks. The first field of the header is 1 octet long and specifies a unique command. Values include:

Command	Meaning
1	Request for routing table information
2	Response containing routing table information
3	Traceon (obsolete)
4	Traceoff (obsolete)
5	Reserved for Sun Microsystems
9	Update Request (from RFC 2091)
10	Update Response (from RFC 2091)
11	Update Acknowledge (from RFC 2091)

The second octet contains a RIP Version Number. Octets 3 and 4 are set equal to zero. The next 2 octets identify the Address Family being transmitted within that RIP packet; RFC 1058 only defines a value for IP with Address Family ID = 2.

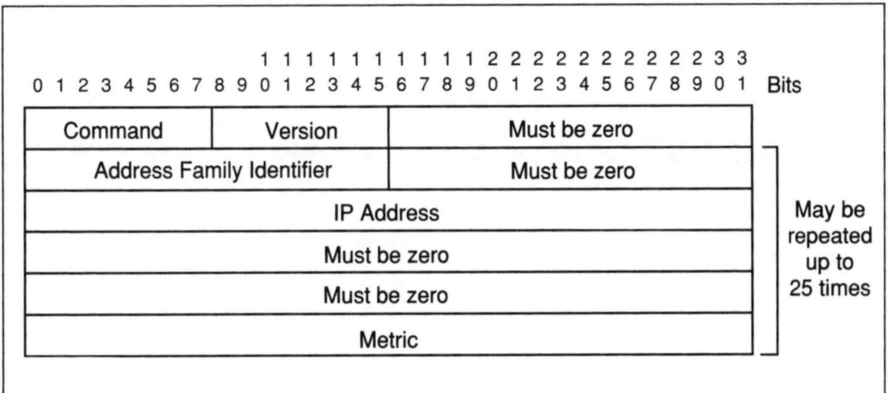

Figure 4-7a Routing Information Protocol (RIP) Packet Format

The balance of the RIP packet contains entries for routing information. Each entry includes the destination IP Address and the Metric to reach that destination. Metric values must be between 1 and 15, inclusive. A metric of 16 indicates that the desired destination is unreachable. Up to 25 of these entries (from the Address Family Identifier through the Metric) may be contained within the datagram. We will see an example of RIP in Section 4.10.8.

An extension to the Routing Information Protocol, called RIP version 2, is defined in RFC 1723 [4-36]. This enhancement expands the amount of useful information carried in RIP messages and also adds a measure of security to those messages.

The RIP version 2 packet format is very similar to the original format, containing a four-octet header and up to 25 route entries of 20 octets each in length (see Figure 4-7b). Within the header, the Command, Address Family Identifier, IP Address, and Metric fields are identical to their counterparts used with the original RIP packet format. The Version field specifies version number 2, and the two-octet unused field (filled with all zeros) is ignored. The Route Tag field carries an attribute assigned to a route that must be preserved and readvertised with a route, such as information defining the routing information's origin (either intra- or internetwork). Within each route entry, the Subnet Mask field (four octets) defines the subnet mask associated with a routing entry. The Next Hop field (also four octets) provides the immediate next hop IP address for the packets specified by this routing entry. The spaces now occupied by the Subnet Mask and Next Hop fields were previously filled with all zeros.

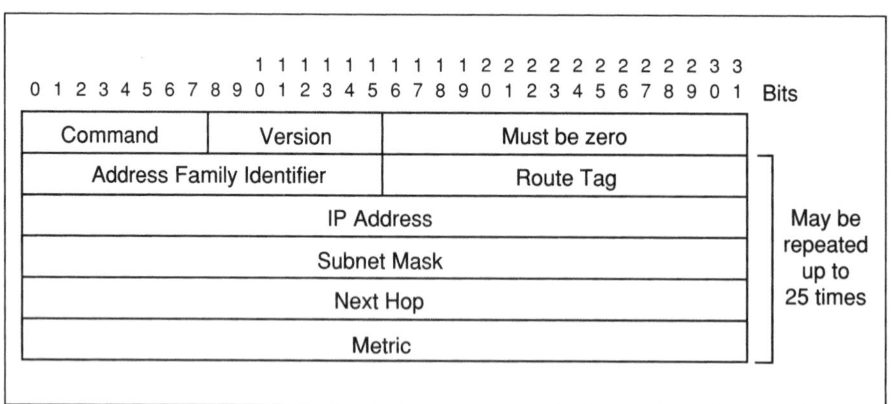

Figure 4-7b Routing Information Protocol Version 2 (RIPv2) Packet Format

The first routing entry in a RIP version 2 packet may contain authentication information to identify the origin of the subsequent data. If that authentication information is included in the packet, the maximum number of routing entries is reduced to 24 (from 25). To use this option, the Address Family Identifier is set for FFFFH, the Route Tag field specifies an Authentication Type, and the remaining 16 octets contain the authentication, such as a password, as shown in Figure 4-7c.

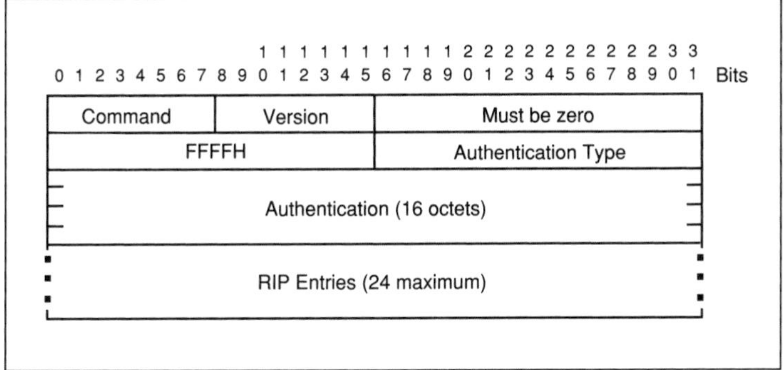

Figure 4-7c Authenticated RIPv2 Packet Format

For further details on RIP version 2, consult RFC 1723 or the companion documents RFC 1721 ("RIP version 2 Protocol Analysis"), RFC 1722 ("RIP version 2 Applicability Statement"), or RFC 1724 ("RIP version 2 Management Information Base – MIB"). Information on migration from RIP to OSPF is found in Eddie Rabinovitch's paper "Migration to OSPF is not a Luxury" [4-37].

Many WAN circuits are established based on traffic demand, and are disconnected when that traffic subsides or ceases. If routing information was periodically transmitted on that connection (say every 30 seconds), the connection would never be closed, and WAN circuit costs would increase. With fixed-bandwidth WAN circuits, such as a point-to-point leased line, the periodic transmission of routing updates may significantly impact the amount of end-user data that can be conveyed. As a result of these limitations, RFC 2091 [4-35] was written as a modification to RIP and RIPv2 so that routing information would only be sent on the WAN when a significant change had occurred, such as an update to the routing database or a change in the reachability of a next-hop router. The protocol modification is known as Triggered RIP, in which routing updates are transmitted (or triggered) by one of the following actions:

- When a specific request for a routing update has been received.
- When the routing database is modified by new information from another interface.
- When the circuit manager indicates that a destination has changed from an unreachable to a reachable state.
- When the unit is first powered on (and thus becoming reachable).

To support the Triggered RIP updates, three new packet types are defined: Update Request, Update Response, and Update Acknowledge. The Update Request packet, a request to send all appropriate elements from its routing system, is transmitted when a router is first powered on or a circuit changes from an unreachable to a reachable state. The Update Response is transmitted in response to an Update

Request packet, and is sent at periodic intervals until an Update Acknowledge packet is received.

An Update Header is added to the RIP or RIPv2 packet, and it precedes any routing-specific information in that packet, as shown in Figure 4-7d. This header may take on one of two forms. The first is an Update Request Header which includes a header Version (currently 1), followed by 24 bits of zero, as shown in Figure 4-7e. The second form is used for an Update Response or Update Acknowledge Header, as shown in Figure 4-7f. This header includes the header Version, a Flush field, which is set to 1 in Response headers when the peer is required to start timing out its entries, and a Sequence Number field, which is incremented for every new Update Response packet transmitted.

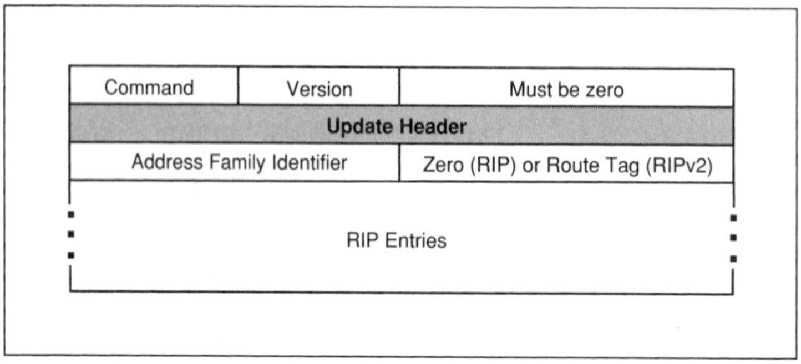

Command	Version	Must be zero
Update Header		
Address Family Identifier		Zero (RIP) or Route Tag (RIPv2)
RIP Entries		

Figure 4-7d Header Location within the RIP and RIPv2 Packet

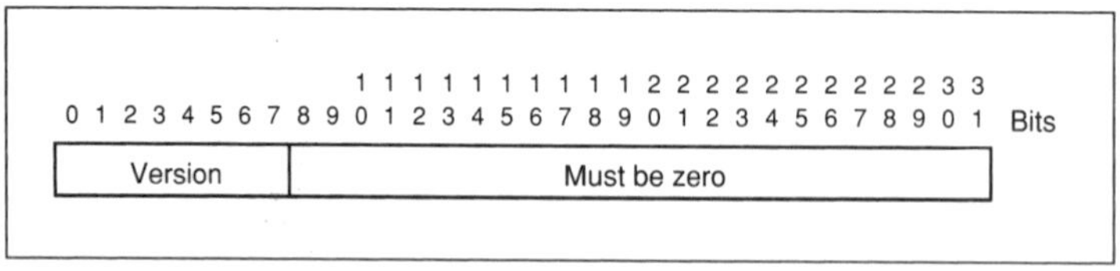

Bits 0–7	Bits 8–31
Version	Must be zero

Figure 4-7e Update Request Header for RIP and RIPv2

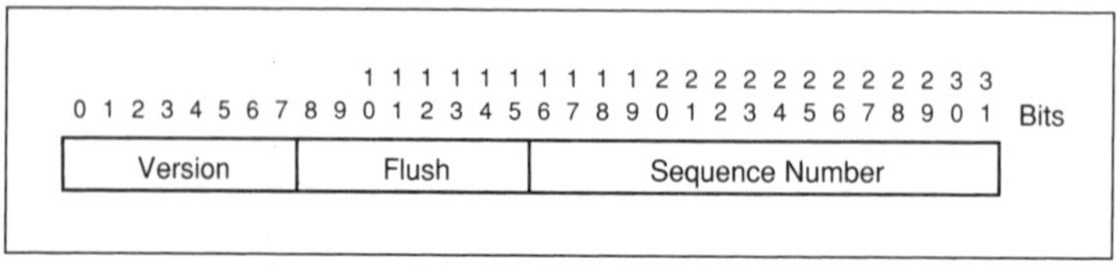

Bits 0–7	Bits 8–15	Bits 16–31
Version	Flush	Sequence Number

Figure 4-7f Update Response and Acknowledge Headers for RIP and RIPv2

4.4.2 Open Shortest Path First Protocol

The Open Shortest Path First protocol is a Link State algorithm that offers several advantages over RIP's Distance Vector algorithm. These advantages include: the ability to configure hierarchical (instead of flat) topologies; to quickly adapt to changes within the internet; to allow for large internetworks; to calculate multiple minimum-cost routes that allow traffic load to be balanced over several paths; to authenticate the exchange of routing table information; and to permit the use of variable-length subnet masks. The protocol uses the IP address and Type of Service field of each datagram (review Figure 4-2) for its operation. An optimum path can be calculated for each Type of Service.

The Internet standard for OSPF version 2 is RFC 2178 [4-38]. OSPF protocol analysis and experience are discussed in RFC 1245 and RFC 1246, respectively. The OSPF version 2 Management Information Base (MIB) is discussed in RFC 1850, and the Applicability Statement for OSPF is found in RFC 1370. References [4-39] through [4-41] are articles that discuss OSPF implementation.

4.4.2.1 COMPARING ROUTING ALGORITHMS

OSPF, a Link State algorithm (LSA), improves on RIP, a Distance Vector algorithm (DVA), in several ways. Before considering the improvements, let's review some of the characteristics of Distance Vector algorithms. First, a DVA routes its packets based on the distance, measured in router hops, from the source to the destination. With RIP the maximum hop count is 16, which is a possible limitation for large networks. A DVA-based network is a flat network topology, without a defined hierarchy to subdivide the network into smaller, more manageable pieces. In addition, the hop count measurement does not account for other factors in the communication link, such as the speed of that link or its associated cost. Furthermore, RIP broadcasts its complete routing table to every other router every 30 seconds. As we saw in Figure 4-7a, the RIP packet may contain information for up to 25 routes. If a router's table contains more entries, say 100 routes, then transmitting all of these routes would require a total of four RIP packets. This requires considerable overhead at each router for packet processing, and it consumes valuable bandwidth on the WAN links in between these routers.

The improvements obtained with a Link State algorithm come in several areas. First, an LSA is based on type of service routing, not hop counts. This allows the network manager to define the least-cost path between two network points based on the actual cost, delay characteristics, reliability factors, and so on. Secondly, OSPF defines a hierarchical, not a flat, network topology. This allows the routing information to be distributed to only a relevant subset of the routers in the internetwork instead of to all of the routers. As Eddie Rabinovitch states: "a distance vector algorithm tells all neighbors about the world, while a link state router tells the world about the neighbors" [4-37]. This hierarchical structure reduces both the router processing time and the bandwidth consumed on the WAN links.

An *autonomous system* (AS), used with an LSA, is defined as a group of routers that exchange routing information via a common routing protocol. The AS is subdivided into areas, which are collections of contiguous routers and hosts that are grouped together, much like the telephone network is divided into area codes. The topology of an area is invisible from outside that area, and routers within a particular area do not know the details of the topology outside of that area. When the AS is partitioned into areas, it is no longer likely (as was the case with a DVA) that all routers in the AS are storing identical topological information in their databases. A router would have a separate topological database for each area it is connected to; however, two routers in the same area would have identical topological databases. A backbone is also defined, which connects the various areas and is used to route a packet between two areas.

Different types of routers are used to connect the various areas. *Internal routers* operate within a single area, connect to other routers within that area, and maintain information about that area only. An *area border router* attaches to multiple areas, runs multiple copies of the basic routing algorithm, and condenses the topological information about its attached areas for distribution to the backbone. A *backbone router* is one that has an interface to the backbone, but it does not have to be an area border router. Lastly, an *AS router* is one that exchanges information with routers that belong to other Autonomous Systems.

4.4.2.2 OSPF OPERATION AND PACKET FORMATS

The basic routing algorithm for OSPF provides several sequential functions, as defined in RFC 2178, Section 4: discovering a router's neighbors and electing a Designated Router for the network using the OSPF Hello protocol; forming adjacencies between pairs of routers and synchronizing the databases of these adjacent routers; performing calculations of routing tables; and flooding the area with link state advertisements.

These protocol operations are performed using one of five OSPF packets. The OSPF packets are carried within IP datagrams and are designated as IP protocol = 89. If the datagram requires fragmentation, the IP process handles that function. The five OSPF packet types have a common 24-octet header as shown in Figure 4-8a. The first 32-bit word includes fields defining a Version Number (1 octet), an OSPF Packet Type (1 octet), and a Packet Length (2 octets), which measures the length of the OSPF packet including the header. The five packet types defined are:

Type	Packet Name	Protocol Function
1	Hello	Discover/maintain neighbors
2	Database Description	Summarize database contents
3	Link State Request	Database download
4	Link State Update	Database update
5	Link State Acknowledgment	Flooding acknowledgment

The next two fields define the Router ID of the source of that packet (4 octets) and the Area ID (4 octets) that the packet came from. The balance of the OSPF packet header contains a Checksum (2 octets), an Authentication Type (AuType, 2 octets), and an Authentication field (8 octets), used to validate the packet.

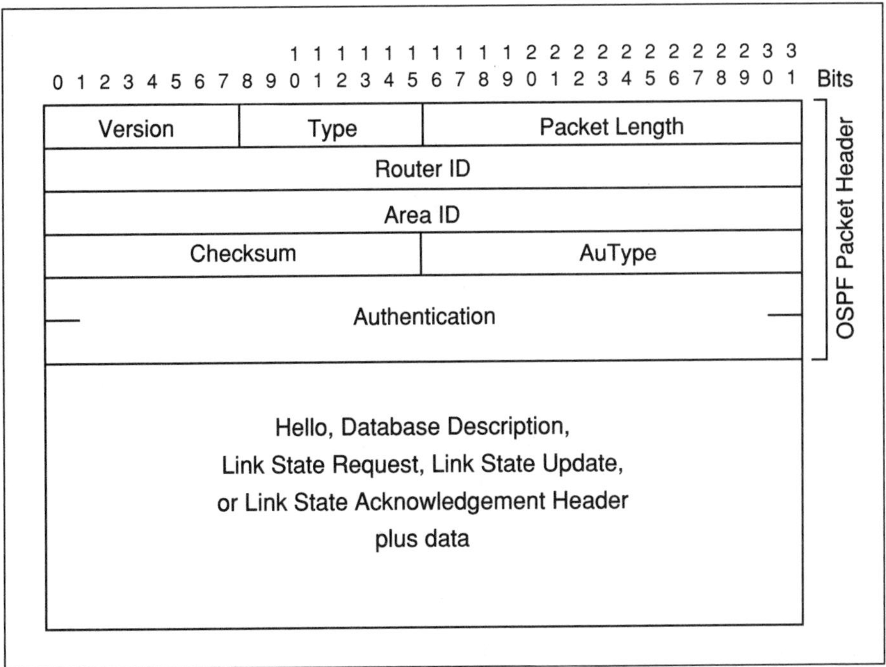

Figure 4-8a Open Shortest Path First (OSPF) Packet Header Format

Following the OSPF packet header is another header specific to the routing information being conveyed. Hello packets (OSPF Packet Type = 1) are periodic transmissions that convey information about neighboring routers (see Figure 4-8b). Fields within the Hello packet include: a Network Mask (4 octets), the network mask associated with this interface; a Hello Interval (2 octets), the number of seconds between this router's Hello packets; Options (1 octet), this router's optional capabilities, as described in RFC 1583, Section A.2; Router Priority (Rtr Pri, 1 octet), this router's router priority, used in Designated (or backup) router election; Router Dead Interval (4 octets), the number of seconds before declaring a silent router down; Designated Router (4 octets), the identity of the Designated Router for this network; Backup Designated Router (4 octets), the identity of the Backup Designated Router for this network; and Neighbor (4 octets), the Router IDs of each router from whom valid Hello packets have been seen recently (i.e. in the last Router Dead Interval seconds) on the network.

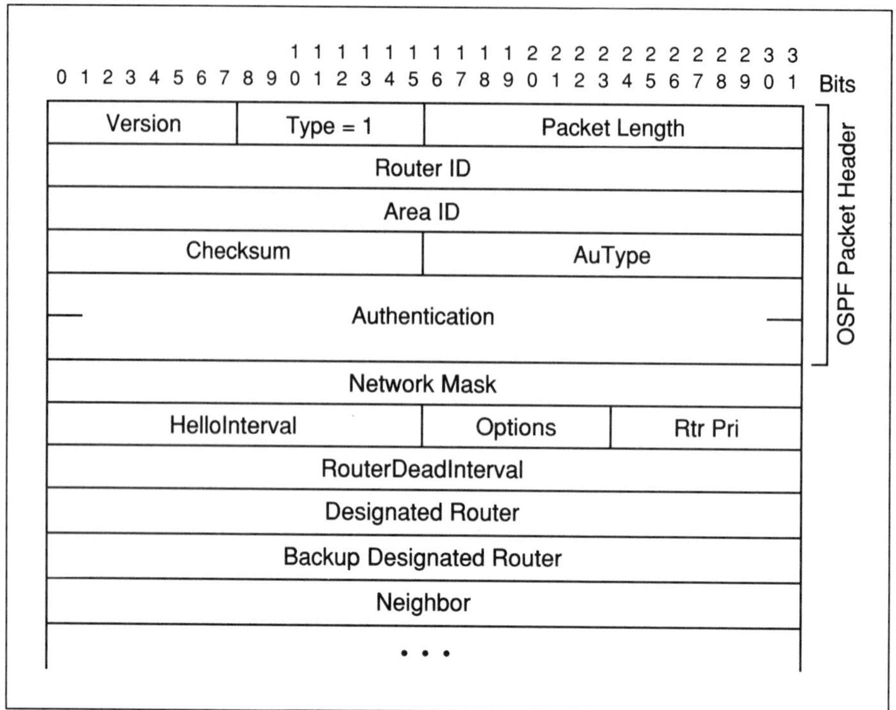

Figure 4-8b OSPF Hello Packet Format

Database Description packets (OSPF Packet Type = 2) convey information needed to initialize the topological databases of adjacent devices (see Figure 4-8c). Fields within the Database Description packet include: Interface MTU (2 octets), the size, in octets, of the largest IP datagram that can be sent over the associated interface without fragmentation; Options (1 octet), this router's optional capabilities, as described in RFC 2178, Section A.2; I-bit, the Init bit (when set to one, this packet is the first in the sequence of Database Description packets); M-bit, the More bit (when set to one, it indicates that more Database Description packets are to follow); the MS-bit, the Master/Slave bit (when set to one, it indicates that the router is the master during the Database Exchange process; otherwise the router is the slave); Database Description Sequence Number (DD Sequence Number, 4 octets), used to sequence the collection of Database Description Packets. The remainder of the packet consists of a list of the topological database's pieces. Each link state advertisement in the database is described by its link state advertisement header (described below).

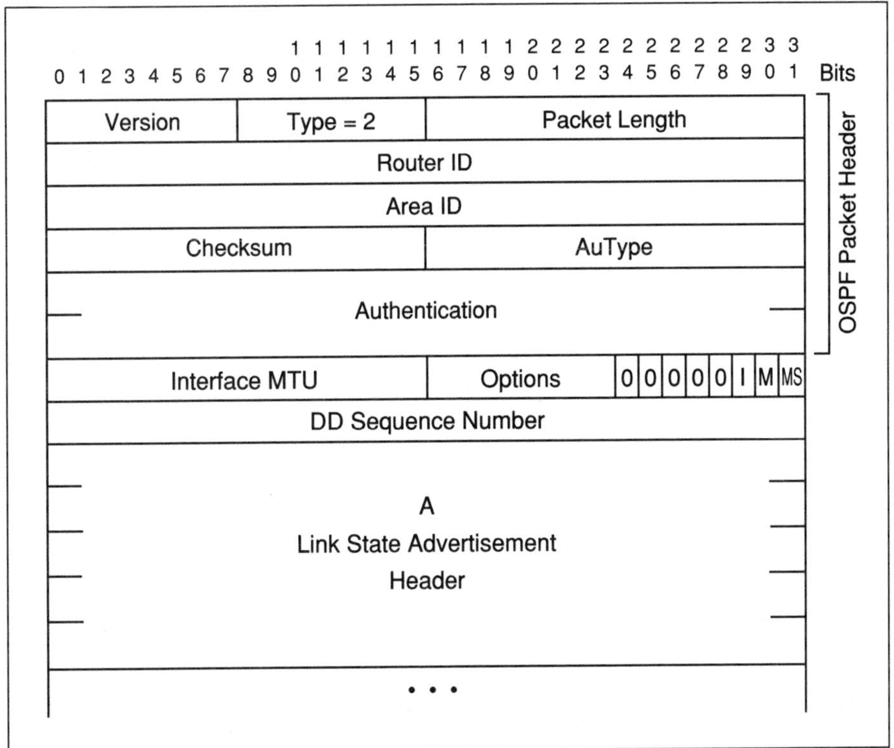

Figure 4-8c OSPF Database Description Packet Format

Link State Request packets (OSPF Packet Type = 3) obtain current database information from a neighboring router (see Figure 4-8d). Fields within the Link State Request packet include the Link State type (4 octets), which defines the type of the Link State advertisement and is more fully described below. The Link State ID (4 octets) is a unique identification for the advertisement, and the Advertising Router (4 octets) is the identification of the router that originated the link state advertisement.

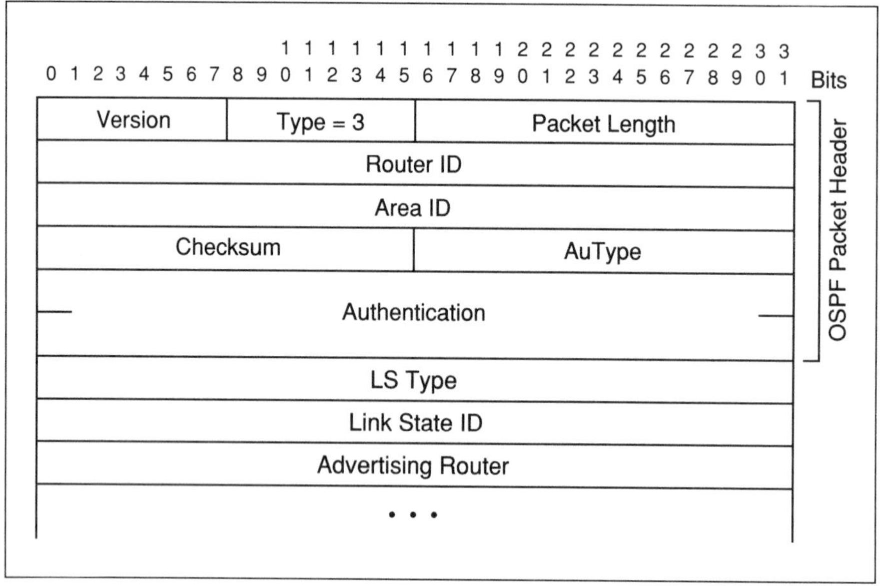

Figure 4-8d OSPF Link State Request Packet Format

Link State Update packets (OSPF Packet Type = 4) advertise the status of various links within the internet (see Figure 4-8e). Several link state advertisements may be included in a single packet. The Number advertisements field (# Advertisements, 4 octets) defines the number of link state advertisements included in this update. The body of the Link State Update packet consists of a list of link state advertisements. Each of these advertisements begins with a common 20-octet header, followed by one of five link state advertisements:

LS Type	Advertisement Name	Advertisement Description
1	Router link	Describes the states of the router's interfaces to an area
2	Network link	Lists the routers connected to the network
3	Summary link	Describes a route to a network destination outside the area
4	Summary link	Describes a route to an AS boundary router destination outside the area
5	AS external link	Describes a route to a destination in another Autonomous System

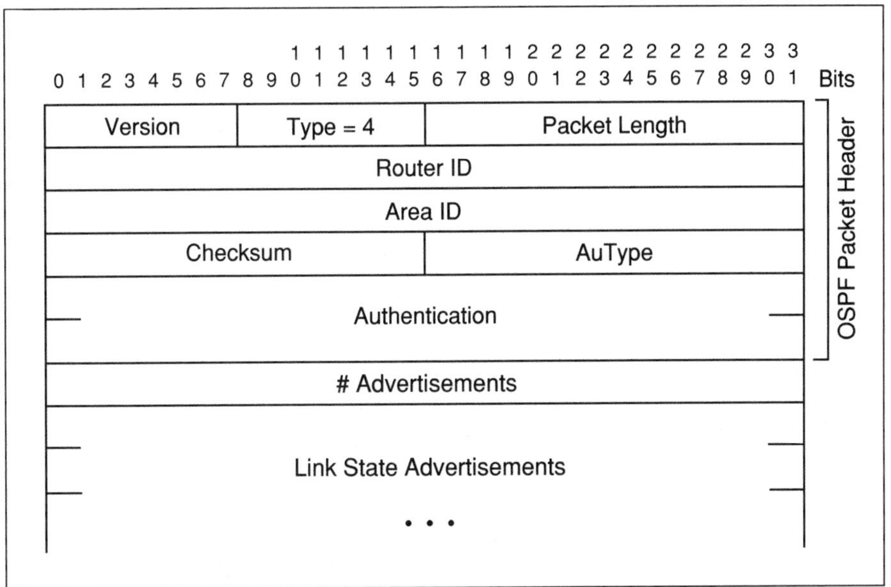

Figure 4-8e OSPF Link State Update Packet Format

The Link State header contains enough information to uniquely identify the advertisement (see Figure 4-8f). Fields within the Link State header include: Link State Age (LS Age, 2 octets), the time in seconds since the link state advertisement was originated; Options (1 octet), the optional capabilities supported by the described portion of the routing domain and defined in RFC 1583, Section A.2; Link State type (LS Type, 1 octet), the type of link state advertisement, as described in the table above; Link State ID (4 octets), an identifier of the portion of the internet environment that is being described by the advertisement, with the contents of this field dependent on the advertisement's link state type (as above); Advertising Router (4 octets), the Router ID of the router that originated the link state advertisement; Link State Sequence Number (LS Sequence Number, 4 octets), which detects old or duplicate link state advertisements; Link State Checksum (LS Checksum, 2 octets), a checksum for the Link State advertisement; and Length (2 octets), the length, in octets, of the link state advertisement.

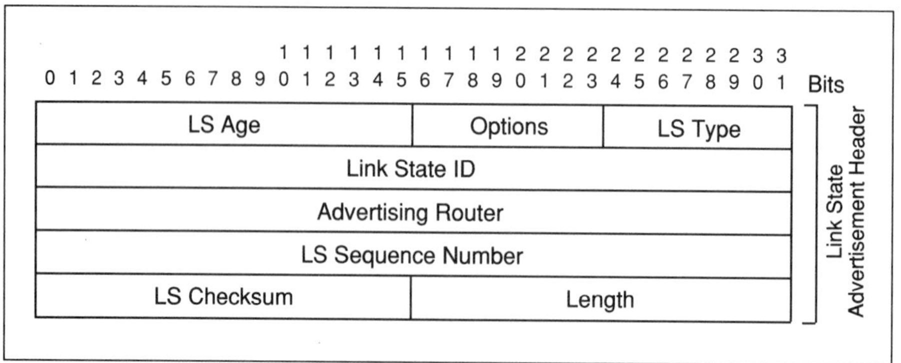

Figure 4-8f OSPF Link State Advertisement Header Format

The Router Links Advertisement packet (the Type 1 link state advertisement) describes the state and cost of the router's links (or interfaces) to the area (see Figure 4-8g). This packet begins with the Link State advertisement header (20 octets, described above). Other fields within this packet include: V-bit, which, when set, indicates that the router is an endpoint of an active virtual link that is using the described area; E-bit, which, when set, indicates that the router is an external (or AS boundary) router; B-bit, which, when set, indicates that the router is an area border router; Number of Links (# Links, 2 octets), the number of router links described by this advertisement.

Seven fields, consuming 16 octets, are then used to describe each router link. The third descriptive field, Type (1 octet), provides a description of the router link, which may be one of the following:

Type	Description
1	Point-to-point connection to another router
2	Connection to a transit network
3	Connection to a stub network
4	Virtual link

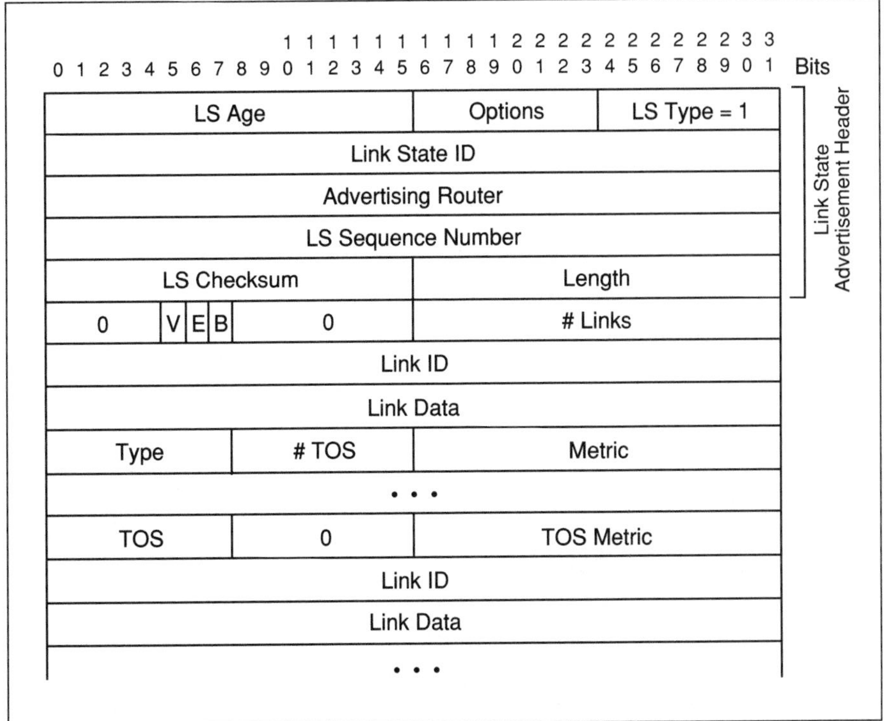

Figure 4-8g OSPF Router Links Advertisement Packet Format

The first descriptive field, Link ID (4 octets), identifies the object that this router link connects to; it depends on the link's Type, described above. The values of the Link ID are:

Type	Link ID
1	Neighboring router's Router ID
2	IP address of Designated Router
3	IP network/subnet number
4	Neighboring router's Router ID

The contents of the Link Data field (4 octets) also depend on the Type field. For example, for connections to stub networks, this field specifies the network's IP address mask. For each link, separate metrics may be specified for each Type of Service (TOS). The Number of TOS field (# TOS, 1 octet) provides the number of different TOS metrics given for this link, not counting the required metric for TOS 0.

The Metric field (1 octet) provides the cost for using this router link. The Type of Service field (TOS, 1 octet) indicates the IP Type of Service that this metric refers to, while the TOS Metric field (2 octets) indicates TOS-specific metric information.

The Network Links Advertisement packet (the Type 2 link state advertisement) describes all routers attached to the network, including the Designated Router (see Figure 4-8h). There are two fields in addition to the Link State Advertisement header: Network Mask (4 octets), the IP address mask for the network; and Attached Router (4 octets), the Router IDs of each of the routers attached to the network.

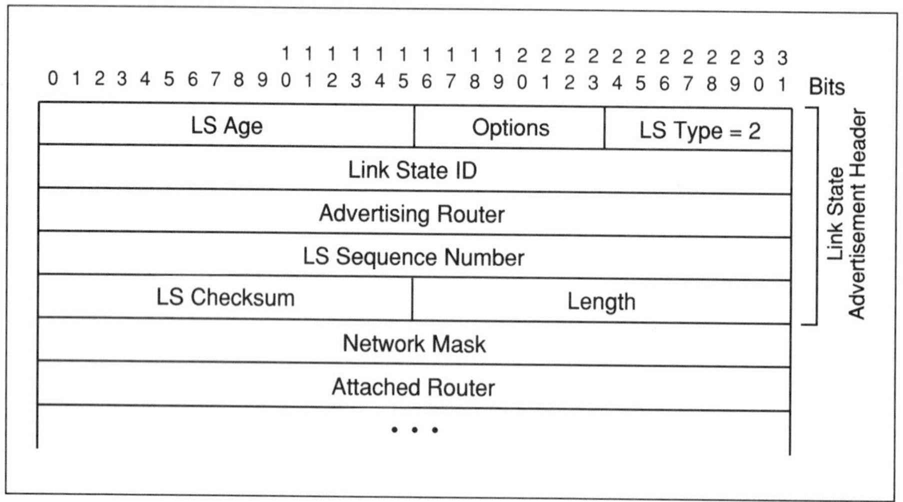

Figure 4-8h OSPF Network Links Advertisement Packet Format

The Summary Links Advertisements are originated by area border routers and describe destination links outside of the area. Type 3 link state advertisements are used when the destination is an IP network; when the destination is an AS boundary router, a Type 4 Summary Links Advertisement is used (see Figure 4-8i). There are three fields in addition to the Link State Advertisement header: Network Mask (4 octets) indicates the destination network's IP address mask for Type 3, and is not meaningful and is set to zero for Type 4; Type of Service (TOS, 1 octet) indicates the type of service that the following cost concerns; and Metric (3 octets) indicates the cost of this route, expressed in the same units as the interface costs in the Router Links advertisements.

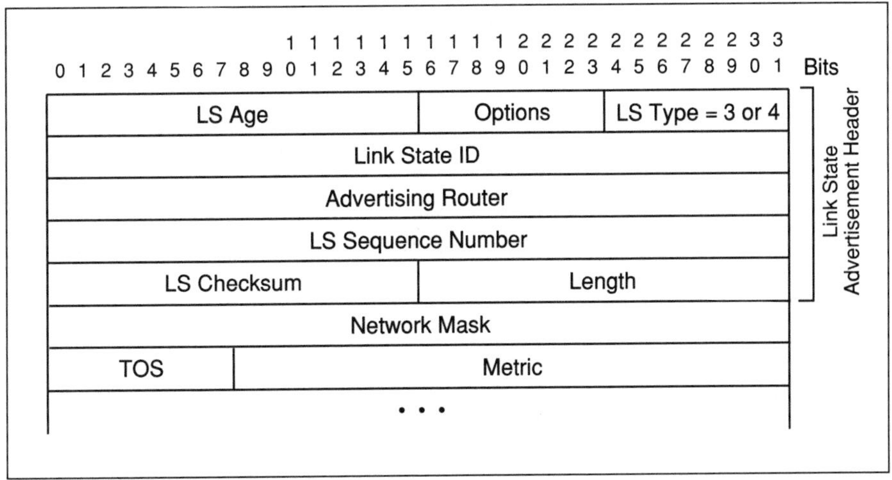

Figure 4-8i OSPF Summary Links Advertisement Packet Format

AS External Links Advertisements are originated by AS boundary routers and advertise destinations which are external to the AS (see Figure 4-8j). Fields within the AS External Links Advertisement Packet include: Network Mask (4 octets), the IP address mask for the advertised destination; E-bit, which indicates the type of external metric; Metric (3 octets), the cost of this route; Type of Service (TOS, 7 bits), the type of service that the following cost concerns; TOS Metric (3 octets), which provides TOS-specific metric information; Forwarding Address (4 octets), which specifies where data traffic for the advertised destination will be forwarded to; and External Route Tag (4 octets), a field attached to each external route, which is not used by the OSPF protocol itself but which may be used to communicate information between AS boundary routers.

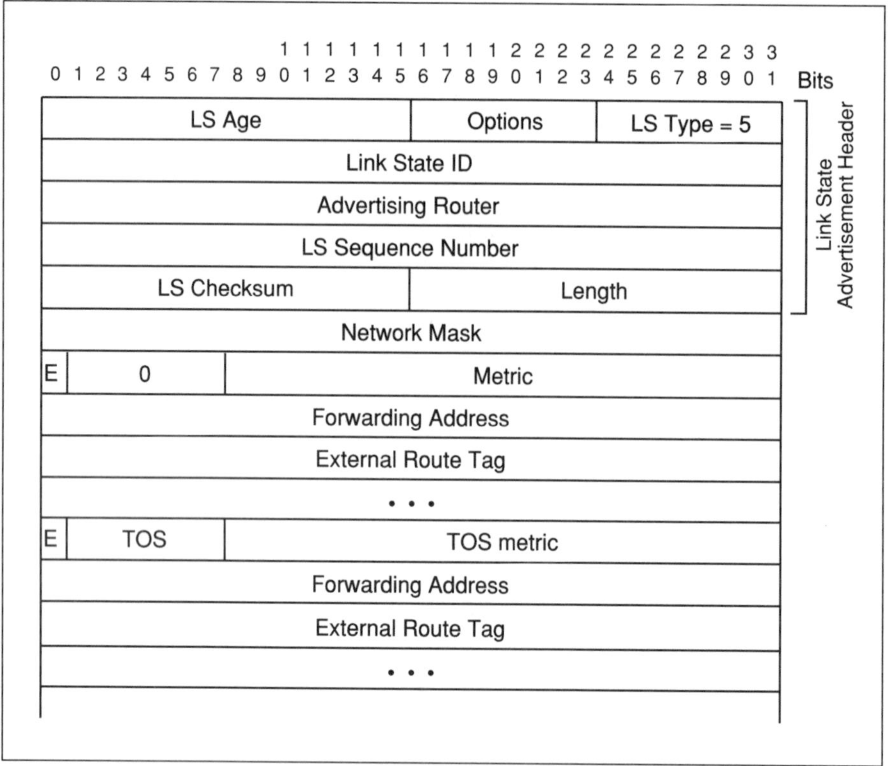

Figure 4-8j OSPF External Links Advertisement Packet Format

Finally, Link State Acknowledgment packets (OSPF Type = 5) verify the receipt of database information (see Figure 4-8k). The format of this packet is similar to that of the Database Description packet, and contains a list of Link State advertisement headers.

4.4.3 Exterior Gateway Protocol (EGP)

Recall from our earlier discussion that there are two general categories of routing protocols: Interior Gateway Protocols and Exterior Gateway Protocols. In short, *interior protocols* are concerned with routing within a network. *Exterior protocols* are concerned with routing between Autonomous Systems, which are generally described as groups of routers that all fall within a single administrative domain. In other words, exterior protocols facilitate your communication with networks outside of your router's domain. In this section, we will briefly study the Exterior Gateway Protocol (EGP), defined in RFC 904 [4-42]. In the next section, we will go into greater detail on the Border Gateway Protocol (BGP), defined in RFC 1771 [4-43]. BGP is a higher function replacement for EGP.

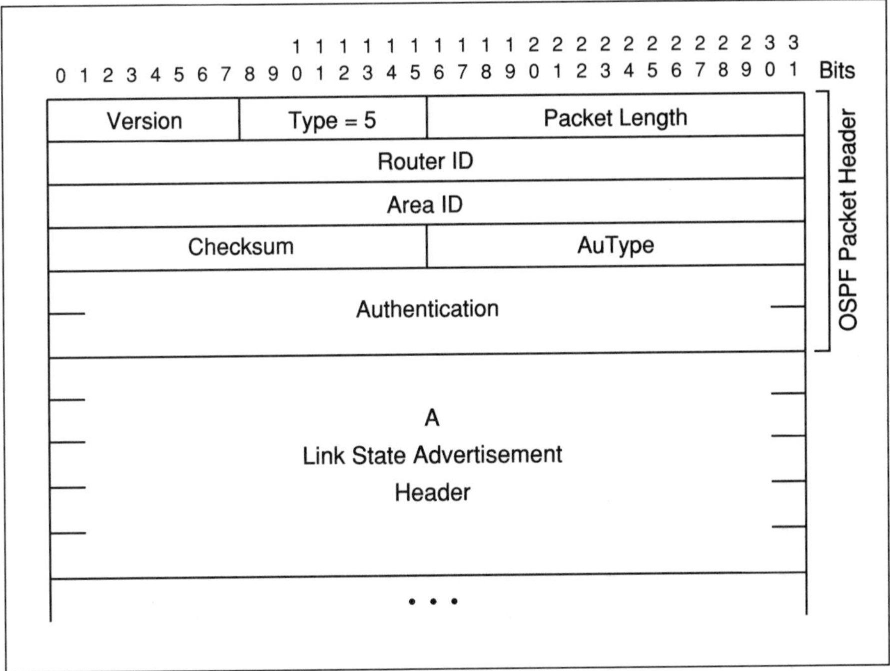

Figure 4-8k OSPF Link State Acknowledgment Packet Format

EGP is used to convey network reachability information between neighboring gateways (or routers) that are in different Autonomous Systems. EGP runs over IP and is assigned IP protocol number 8. Three key mechanisms are present in the protocol. The Neighbor Acquisition mechanism allows two neighbors to begin exchanging information using the Acquisition Request and Acquisition Confirm messages. The Neighbor Reachability mechanism maintains real-time information regarding the reachability of its neighbors, using the Hello and I Hear You (I-H-Y) messages. Finally, Update messages are exchanged that carry routing information.

The specific messages, as defined in RFC 904, are:

Message	Function
Request	Request acquisition of neighbor and/or initialize polling variables
Confirm	Confirm acquisition of neighbor and/or initialize polling variables
Refuse	Refuse acquisition of neighbor
Cease	Request deacquisition of neighbor
Cease-ack	Confirm deacquisition of neighbor

Continued

Continued

Message	Function
Hello	Request neighbor reachability
I-H-U	Confirm neighbor reachability
Poll	Request net-reachability update
Update	Net-reachability update
Error	Error

The general structure of the EGP messages is shown in Figure 4-9. A common message header precedes each message type. The header consists of the EGP Version Number field (one octet); the Type field (one octet), which identifies the message type; the Code field (one octet), which identifies a subtype; the Status field (one octet), which contains message-specific status information; the Checksum field (two octets), used for error control; the Autonomous System Number (two octets), which is an assigned number that identifies the particular autonomous system; and the Sequence Number (two octets), which maintains state variables.

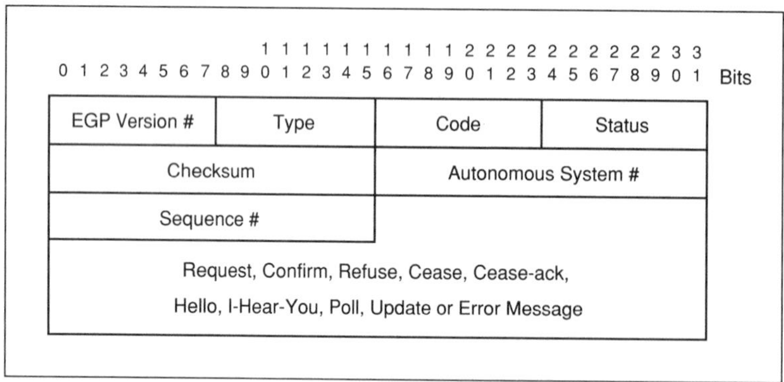

Figure 4-9 EGP Message Format

Further details on the use and specific formats of the various messages can be found in RFC 904.

4.4.4 Border Gateway Protocol (BGP)

The Border Gateway Protocol, currently in its fourth version (BGP-4), is defined in RFC 1771 [4-43]. BGP is an inter-Autonomous System (AS) protocol which builds upon and enhances the capabilities of EGP. For example, where EGP runs on IP, BGP runs on TCP, thus ensuring a connection-oriented data flow and greater reliability. BGP is assigned TCP port number 179 (more on TCP port numbers in the next chapter). BGP also supports Classless Domain Routing (CIDR) and the aggregation of routes.

The system running BGP is called a *BGP speaker.* Connections between BGP speakers in different Autonomous Systems are called *external links,* while connections between BGP speakers in the same Autonomous System are called *internal links.* In a similar fashion, a BGP peer in another AS is referred to as an *external peer,* while a peer within the same AS is called an *internal peer.* After the TCP connection has been established in support of BGP, the two BGP systems exchange their entire routing tables. Updates are then sent as those routing tables change. As a result, the BGP speaker will maintain the current version of the routing tables for all of its peers. That routing information is stored within a Routing Information Base, or RIB.

The BGP message consists of a fixed message header that is 19 octets in length, followed by one of four messages: OPEN, UPDATE, NOTIFICATION, or KEEPALIVE. The OPEN, UPDATE, and NOTIFICATION messages add additional information to the BGP message header, while the KEEPALIVE consists of only the annotated message header.

The BGP message header is shown in Figure 4-10a, and consists of three fields plus message-specific information. The Marker field (16 octets) contains a value that the receiver can predict. For example, an OPEN message would use a Marker of all ones. Otherwise the Marker can be incorporated into some authentication mechanism. The Length field (2 octets) indicates the total length of the message, including the header, given in octets. The valid range of the Length field is 19–4,096 octets. The Type field (one octet) specifies the type of the message as follows:

Type	Message	Function
1	OPEN	The first message sent after transport connection is established
2	UPDATE	Transfers routing information between BGP peers
3	NOTIFICATION	Indicates detection of an error and closure of the connection
4	KEEPALIVE	Periodic confirmation of reachability

The OPEN message (message Type = 1) is the first message that is sent by each side following the establishment of the transport (TCP) connection. If the OPEN message is acceptable, then a KEEPALIVE message is returned, confirming the connection. After the OPEN has been confirmed, then UPDATE, KEEPALIVE, and NOTIFICATION messages may be exchanged.

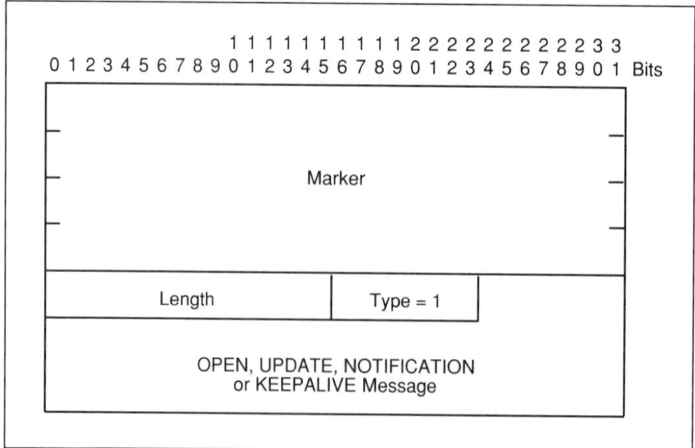

Figure 4-10a BGP-4 Message Header

The OPEN message adds five fields, plus optional parameters, to the BGP header (Figure 4-10b). The Version field (1 octet) defines the protocol version of the message (currently 4). The My Autonomous System field (2 octets) indicates the Autonomous System number of the sender. The Hold Time field (2 octets) is the number of seconds that the sender proposes for the value of the Hold Timer. The BGP Identifier field (4 octets) indicates the BGP identifier of the sender. The Optional Parameters Length field (1 octet) indicates the length of any optional parameters, such as Authentication Information, that may be included in this message. If no parameters are present, then the value of this field is zero. The Optional Parameters field may contain a list of optional parameters, encoded as a triplet of <Parameter Type, Parameter Length, Parameter Value>.

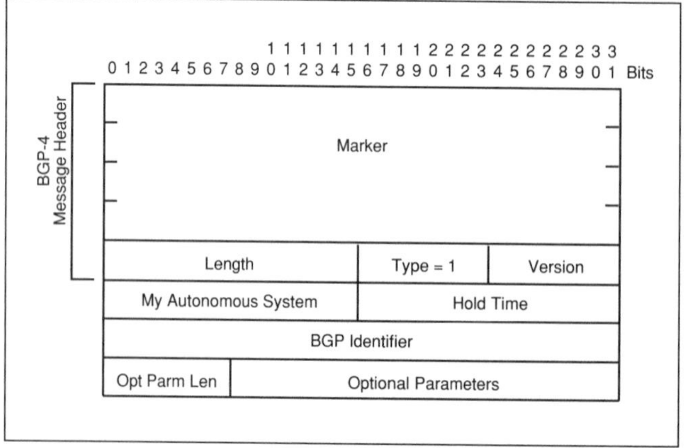

Figure 4-10b BGP OPEN Message Format

The UPDATE message (message Type = 2) is used to transfer routing information between BGP peers. It is used to advertise a single feasible route to a peer, and/or to withdraw multiple feasible routes from service.

The UPDATE message adds five fields to the BGP header (Figure 4-10c). The Unfeasible Routes Length field (2 octets) indicates the total length of the Withdrawn Routes field in octets. A value of zero indicates that no Withdrawn Routes are present in this UPDATE message. The Withdrawn Routes field (variable length) contains a list of IP address prefixes for the routes that are being withdrawn from service. The Total Path Attribute Length field (2 octets) indicates the total length of the Path Attributes field in octets. A value of zero indicates that no Network Layer Reachability Information is present in this UPDATE message. The Path Attributes field (variable length) is a sequence of path attributes that are present in every UPDATE message. Each Path Attribute is a variable length triple <Attribute Type, Attribute Length, Attribute Value>. The Network Layer Reachability Information field (variable length) contains a list of IP address prefixes indicating reachability.

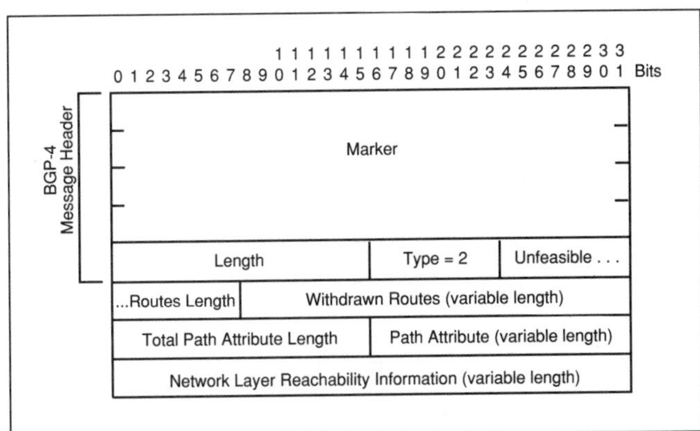

Figure 4-10c BGP UPDATE Message Format

The NOTIFICATION message (message Type = 3) is sent when an error condition is detected. The BGP connection is closed immediately after sending the NOTIFICATION message.

The NOTIFICATION message adds three fields to the BGP header (Figure 4-10d). The Error Code field (1 octet) indicates the types of errors that have been defined. The Error Subcode field (1 octet) provides more specific information on the type of error. The Data field (variable length) is used to diagnose the reason for this NOTIFICATION, and is dependent upon the contents of the Error Code and Error Subcode fields. Specific values for these fields are delineated in RFC 1771.

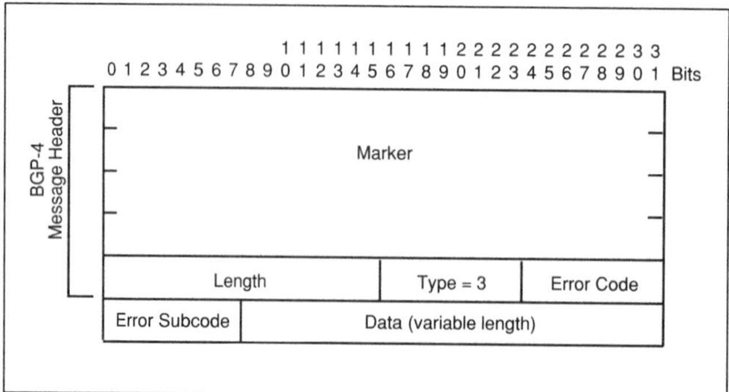

Figure 4-10d BGP NOTIFICATION Message Format

The KEEPALIVE message (message Type = 4) is used to determine reachability between peers. KEEPALIVE messages are exchanged often enough so that the Hold Timer does not expire, but they are not sent more frequently than one per second. The KEEPALIVE message (Figure 4-10e) consists of the BGP message header only, without any additional information.

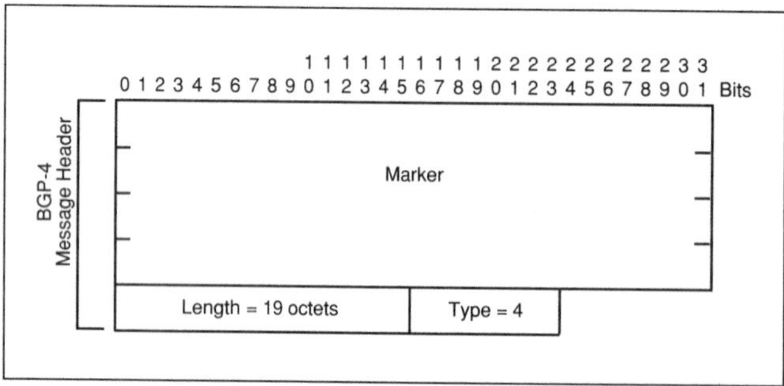

Figure 4-10e BGP KEEPALIVE Message Format

Further details on the operation of BGP-4 can be found in RFC 1771.

4.5 Intra-Network Communications

If the Internet were flawless, it would always route datagrams to their intended destination without errors, excessive delays, or retransmissions. Unfortunately, this is not the case. (If it were, you wouldn't be reading a book on troubleshooting!) As we studied in Section 4.1, IP provides a connectionless service to the attached hosts but requires an additional module, known as the Internet Control Message Protocol

(ICMP), to report errors that may have occurred in processing those datagrams. Examples of errors include undeliverable datagrams or incorrect routes. Other uses for the protocol include testing the path to a distant host (known as a PING) or requesting an Address Mask for a particular subnet. ICMP is considered an integral part of IP and must be implemented in IP modules contained in both hosts and routers. The standard for ICMP is RFC 792 [4-44].

ICMP messages are contained within IP datagrams. In other words, ICMP is a user (client) of IP, and the IP header precedes the ICMP message. Thus, the datagram would include the IP header, the ICMP header, and ICMP data. Protocol = 1 identifies ICMP within the IP header. A Type field within the ICMP header further identifies the purpose and format of the ICMP message. Any data required to complete the ICMP message would then follow the ICMP header.

The standard defines thirteen ICMP message formats, each with a specific ICMP header format. Two of these formats (Information Request/Reply) are considered obsolete and several others share a common message structure. The result is six unique message formats, shown in Figure 4-11. The first three fields are common to all headers. The Type field (1 octet) identifies one of the thirteen unique ICMP messages. These include:

Type Code	ICMP Messages
0	Echo Reply
3	Destination Unreachable
4	Source Quench
5	Redirect
8	Echo
11	Time Exceeded
12	Parameter Problem
13	Timestamp
14	Timestamp Reply
15	Information Request (obsolete)
16	Information Reply (obsolete)
17	Address Mask Request
18	Address Mask Reply

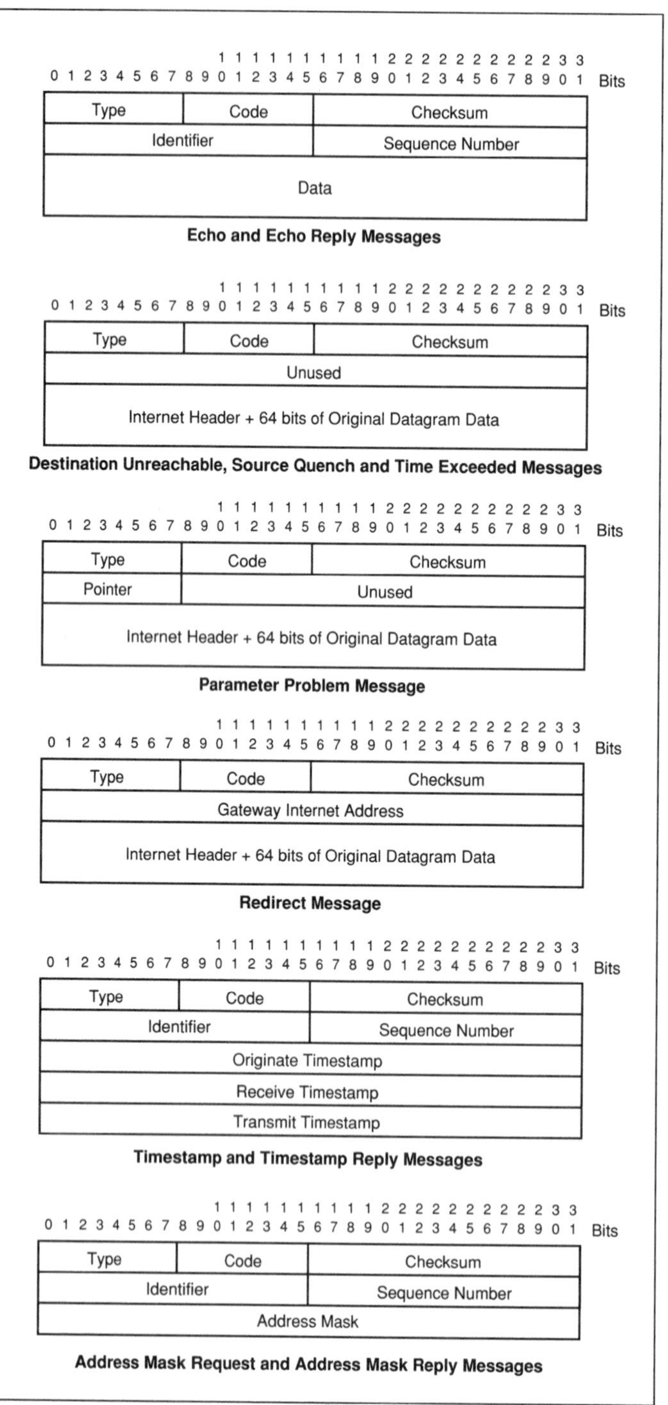

Figure 4-11 Internet Control Message Protocol (ICMP) Message Formats

The second field is labeled Code (1 octet), and it elaborates on specific message types. For example, the Code field for the Destination Unreachable message indicates whether the network, host, protocol, or port was the unreachable entity. The third field is the Checksum (2 octets) on the ICMP message. Because ICMP messages are of great value in internetwork troubleshooting, we will look at all of the ICMP messages in detail. Internet standards describing ICMP formats and usage include the original standard, RFC 792; implementing congestion control, RFC 896 [4-45]; use of source quench messages, RFC 1016 [4-46]; and Subnet Mask Messages, RFC 950 [4-9].

The Echo message (ICMP Type = 8) tests the communication path from a sender to a receiver via the internet. On many hosts, this function is called PING. The sender transmits an Echo message, which may also contain an Identifier (2 octets) and a Sequence Number (2 octets). Data may be sent with the message. When the destination receives the message, it reverses the Source and Destination addresses, recomputes the Checksum, and returns an Echo Reply (ICMP Type = 0). The contents of the Data field (if any) would also be returned to the sender.

The Destination Unreachable message (ICMP Type = 3) is used when the router or host is unable to deliver the datagram. This message is returned to the Source host of the datagram in question and describes the reason for the delivery problem in the Code field:

Code	Meaning
0	Net Unreachable
1	Host Unreachable
2	Protocol Unreachable
3	Port Unreachable
4	Fragmentation Needed and DF Set
5	Source Route Failed

Routers may use codes 0, 1, 4, or 5. Hosts may use codes 2 or 3. For example, when a datagram arrives at a router, it will do a table lookup to determine the outgoing path to use. If the router determines that the Destination network cannot be reached (i.e., a distance of infinite hops away), a Net Unreachable message will be returned. Similarly, if a host cannot process a datagram because the requested protocol or port is inactive, a Protocol Unreachable or Port Unreachable message, respectively, would be returned. Included in the Destination Unreachable message is the IP header plus the first 64 bits (8 octets) of the datagram in question. This returned data should help the host diagnose the failure in the transmission process.

The advantage of connectionless datagram transmission is its simplicity. The disadvantage is its inability to regulate the traffic on the network. (For an analogy, consider the problem that your local post office faces. To handle the maximum number of letters, it should install enough boxes to handle the holiday rush. However, this might be considered wasteful because many of the boxes are only partially used during the summer.) If a router or host gets congested, it may send a Source Quench message (ICMP Type = 4) to the source of the datagrams asking it to reduce its output. This mechanism is similar to traffic signals that regulate the flow of cars onto a freeway. The Source Quench message does not use the second 32-bit word of the ICMP header, but fills it with zeros. The rest of the message contains the IP header and the first 8 octets of the datagram that triggered the request.

Hosts do not always choose the correct Destination address for a particular datagram and occasionally send one to the wrong router. This is most likely to occur when the host is initialized and its routing tables are incomplete. When such a routing mistake occurs, the router that improperly received the datagram will return a Redirect message to the host identifying a better route. The Code field would contain the following information:

Code	Message
0	Redirect datagrams for the network
1	Redirect datagrams for the host
2	Redirect datagrams for the type of service and network
3	Redirect datagrams for the type of service and host

The Redirect message (ICMP Type = 5) contains the correct router (gateway) address to reach the desired destination. In addition, the IP header plus the first 8 octets of the datagram in question are returned to the source host to aid in the diagnostic process.

Another potential problem of connectionless networks is that datagrams can get lost within the network and can wander for an excessive amount of time. Alternatively, congestion could prevent all fragments of a datagram from being reassembled within the host's required time. Either of these situations can trigger an ICMP Time Exceeded message (ICMP Type = 11). The message defines two codes: Time-to-Live Exceeded in Transmit (code = 0) and Fragment Reassembly Time Exceeded (code = 1). The balance of the message has the same format as the Source Quench message: the second word contains all zeros, and the rest of the message contains the IP header and the first 8 octets of the offending datagram.

Higher layer processes, such as TCP, recognize datagrams that cannot be processed because of errors and discard them, relying on a higher layer process to recognize the problem and take corrective action. Parameter problems within an IP datagram header (such as an incorrect Type of Service field) may send an ICMP Parameter Problem message (ICMP Type = 12) to the source of the datagram, identifying the location of the problem. The message contains a pointer that identifies the octet with the error. The rest of the message contains the IP datagram header plus the first 8 octets of data, as before.

The Timestamp (ICMP Type = 13) and Timestamp Reply (ICMP Type = 14) messages measure the round-trip transit time between two machines and synchronize their clocks. The first two words of the Timestamp and Timestamp Reply messages are similar to the Echo and Echo Reply messages. The next three fields contain timestamps measured in milliseconds since midnight, Universal Time (UT). The Timestamp Requester fills in the Originate field upon transmission; the recipient fills in the Receive Timestamp when it receives the request. The recipient fills in the Transmit Timestamp when it sends the Timestamp Reply message. The Requester may now estimate the remote processing and round-trip transit times. (Note that these are only estimates because network delay is a highly dynamic and variable measurement.) The remote processing time is the Received Timestamp minus the Transmit Timestamp. The round-trip transit time will be the Timestamp Reply message arrival time minus the Originate Timestamp. With these two calculations, the two clocks can be synchronized.

Finally, Address Mask Request (ICMP Type = 17) and Address Mask Reply (ICMP Type = 18) were added to the ICMP message in response to subnetting requirements (RFC 950). It is assumed that the requesting host knows its own Internet address. (If it doesn't, it uses RARP to discover the Internet address.) It then broadcasts the Address Mask Request message to the Destination address [255.255.255.255]. The Address Mask field of the ICMP message would be filled with all zeros. The IP router that knows the correct address mask would respond. For example, the response for a Class B network (without subnetting) would be [255.255.0.0]. A Class B network using an 8-bit subnet field would be [255.255.255.0]. Barry Gerber's article "IP Routing: Learn to Follow the Yellow Brick Road" [4-47] contains additional examples of Subnet Mask usage. Section 4.10.5 will show how an incorrect Subnet Mask can hinder network communication.

4.6 Internet Group Management Protocol (IGMP)

The Internet Group Management Protocol, or IGMP, is an adjunct protocol to the Internet Protocol, and is required to be implemented on all hosts that wish to receive IP multicasts (review Section 4.2.2 on multicast addressing). IGMP is used by IP hosts to report their group memberships to any immediately neighboring multicast routers. The protocol was originally specified in RFC 1112; IGMP version 2 is documented in RFC 2236 [4-48].

The IGMP message is encapsulated within an IP datagram and identified with protocol number = 2. It is sent with TTL = 1 and includes the IP Router Alert option defined in RFC 2113 [4-49]. The message format is very similar to the ICMP message structure, and is shown in Figure 4-12. The message has four fields. The Type field (1 octet) specifies one of four different types of messages. In the case of the Membership Query message, there are two subtype messages, which are distinguished by the group address used. The Type field values and their functions are:

Type Field (hex)	Message	Function
11	Membership Query	To learn about members and groups. Subtype: General Query message, used to learn which groups have members on an attached network, sent to the All Systems Group, [224.0.0.1]. Subtype: Group-Specific Query message, used to learn if a particular group has any members on an attached network.
12	Version 1 Membership Report	For backwards compatibility with IGMPv1.
16	Version 2 Membership Report	To indicate that a host has joined a group.
17	Leave Group	To indicate that a host is leaving a group, sent to the All Routers Group, [224.0.0.2].

The Max Response Time field (1 octet) is only meaningful in Membership Query Messages, and specifies the maximum time allowed before sending responding Report messages. The unit of measure is in tenths (1/10) of a second. For all other messages, this field is set to 0 and ignored by the receiver. The Checksum field (2 octets) is used for error control purposes. The Group Address field (4 octets) contains an IP address of a type that depends on the message type being transmitted. For a General Query message, this field is set to 0; for a Group-Specific Query, this field is set to the group address of the group being queried; for the Membership Report or Leave Group messages, this field is set to the IP multicast group address of the group being reported or left.

Further details on the state diagrams and other specifics of IGMP operation can be found in RFC 2236.

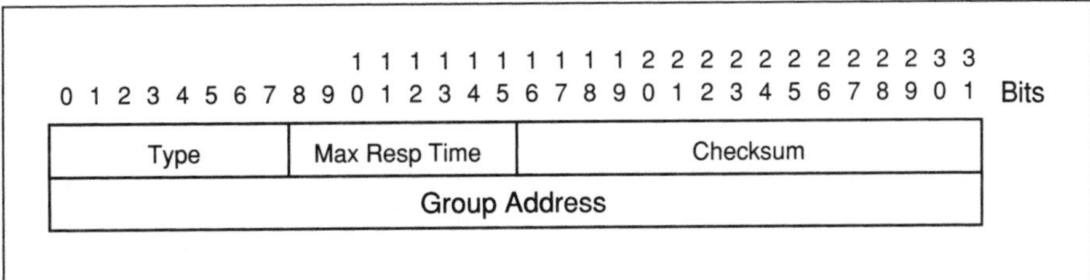

Figure 4-12 Internet Group Management Protocol (IGMP) Message Format

4.7 Domain Name System (DNS)

The 32-bit IP addresses and the various classes defined for these addresses provide an extremely efficient way to identify devices on an internetwork. Unfortunately, remembering all of those addresses can be overwhelming. To solve that problem, a system of hierarchical naming known as the Domain Name System was developed. DNS is described in RFCs 1034 [4-50] and 1035 [4-51].

DNS is based on several premises. First, it arranges the names hierarchically, like the numbering plan devised for the telephone network. Just as a telephone number is divided into a country code, an area code, an exchange code, and finally a line number, the DNS root is divided into a number of top-level domains, defined in RFC 920. These are:

Domain	Purpose
MIL	U.S. Military
GOV	Other U.S. Government
EDU	Educational
COM	Commercial
NET	NICs and NOCs
ORG	Nonprofit Organizations
CON	Two-letter Country Code, e.g. US represents the United States, CA represents Canada, and so on.

As with many other addressing-related issues, the rapid growth of the Internet has stressed the number of available domain names. At the time of this writing, a number of additional top-level domains have been proposed, including: .firm, .shop, .web, .arts, .rec, .info, and .nom. The assignment and administration of these new top-level domains has been the subject of much debate, both in the United

States and in the international community. A Web site, `www.gtld-mou.org` (the Generic Top Level Domain Memorandum of Understanding), has been devoted to these issues.

Returning to our discussion of the currently approved top-level domains, specific sites would be under each top-level domain. For example, the University of Ferncliff could use the edu domain designation (using the traditional lowercase letters), and it would be shown as ferncliff.edu. The University could then designate names for its departments, such as cs.ferncliff.edu (Computer Science) or ee.ferncliff.edu (Electrical Engineering). A particular host in the Electrical Engineering department could be named voltage.ee.ferncliff.edu. A user with a login on that host could be identified as boomer@voltage.ee.ferncliff.edu. Note that the @ sign separates the user from the remainder of the Host address.

The second DNS premise is that devices are not expected to remember the IP addresses of remote hosts. Rather, Name Servers throughout the internetwork provide this information. The requesting device thus assumes the role of a client, and the Name Server provides the necessary information, known as a *resource record,* or RR. RRs provide a mapping between domain names and network objects, such as IP addresses. Many different types of RRs are defined in RFCs 1034 and 1035, and types that are used for ISO NSAP addresses are defined in RFC 1706. Examples of RRs include: the A record, which is used to map a host address; the MX record, which provides a mail exchange for the domain, and is used with the SMTP; the NS record, which defines the Name Server for a domain; and the PTR record, which is a pointer to another part of the domain name space.

The format for client/server interaction is a DNS message, shown in Figure 4-13. The message header is 12 octets long and describes the type of message. The next four sections provide the details of the query or response.

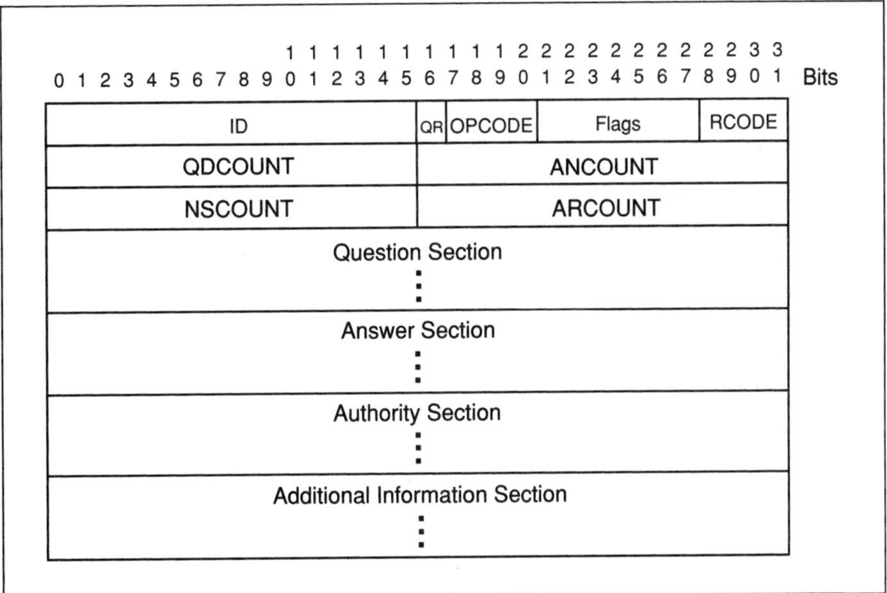

Figure 4-13 Domain Name System (DNS) Message Format

The first field within the header is an Identifier (16 bits) that correlates the queries and responses. The QR bit identifies the message type as a Query (QR = 0) or a Response (QR = 1). An OPCODE field (4 bits) further defines a Query:

OPCODE	Meaning
0	Standard Query (QUERY)
1	Inverse Query (IQUERY)
2	Server Status request (STATUS)
3–15	Reserved

Four Flags are then transmitted to further describe the message:

Bit Number	Meaning
5	Authoritative Answer (AA)
6	Truncation (TC)
7	Recursion Desired (RD)

Continued

Continued

8	Recursion Available (RA)
9–11	Reserved (set to 0)

A Response Code (RCODE) completes the first word:

Field	Meaning
0	No error
1	Format error
2	Server error
3	Name error
4	Not implemented
5	Refused
6–15	Reserved for future use

The balance of the header contains fields that define the lengths of the remaining four sections:

Field	Meaning
QDCOUNT	Number of Question entries
ANCOUNT	Number of resource records in the Answer section
NSCOUNT	Number of Name Server resource records in the Authority section
ARCOUNT	Number of resource records in the Additional Records section

Following the header is the Question section and the Answer sections (Answer, Authority, or Additional Information).

The DNS was designed during a time when there were fewer Internet hosts, and these hosts were devices whose addresses were typically statically assigned, and infrequently changed. In contrast, today's hosts may be laptop or notebook computers, which have an IP address that is dynamically assigned, possibly using a DHCP server. Unfortunately, the current version of DHCP, as defined in RFC 1541, does not provide a mechanism for updating the DNS Resource Records (RRs) that associate the host's domain name with its IP address. In other words, a host's current RR may not match the IP address that has been assigned by the DHCP server.

A partial solution to this problem is found in RFC 2136, "Dynamic Updates in the Domain Name System (DNS UPDATE)" [4-52], and RFC 2137, "Secure Domain Name System Dynamic Update" [4-53], which discuss methods for updating DNS information over a network. The UPDATE message format is defined in RFC 2136, which specifies the zone to be updated, the resource records (RRs) or resource record sets (RRsets) being added or deleted by this operation, plus additional data that is required. To make these updates secure, RFC 2137 describes the use of digital signatures to ensure that only authorized entities perform the DNS updates required.

A more complete solution is currently under development and is documented in an Internet Draft entitled "Interaction Between DHCP and DNS" [4-54]. When the host with a particular domain name is assigned an IP address by the DHCP server, the Dynamic DNS UPDATE message would be used to update the A resource record (RR) associated with that new address. In a similar manner, when an IP address is assigned to a host with a particular domain name, the PTR RR associated with this address is updated (again using the Dynamic DNS UPDATE message) to reflect the new domain name. Thus, the assignment of an address to a DHCP client requires updates to two RRs: the A RR (to update the domain name) and the PTR RR (to update the acquired address). These protocol operations are detailed in Reference [4-54].

We will look at an example of a DNS message in Section 4.10.1. A good resource on DNS is Kirk Demaree's article "DNS Gets an Update" [4-55], or pay a visit to the DNS Resources Directory Web site [4-56].

4.8 Resource Reservation Protocol (RSVP)

As more time-sensitive applications have been developed for the Internet, the need to define a Quality of Service (QoS), and the mechanisms to provide that QoS, have become requirements. The Resource Reservation Protocol (RSVP), defined in RFC 2205 [4-57], is designed to address those requirements. When a host has an application, such as real-time video or multimedia, it may use RSVP to request an appropriate level of service from the network in support of that application. But for RSVP to be effective, every router in that path must support that protocol – something that some router vendors and ISPs are not yet equipped to do. In addition, RSVP is a control protocol, and therefore works in collaboration with – not instead of – traditional routing protocols. In other words, the routing protocol, such as RIP or OSPF, determines *which* datagrams are forwarded, while RSVP is concerned with the *QoS* of those datagrams that are forwarded.

RSVP requests that network resources be reserved to support data flowing on a simplex path, and that reservation is initiated and maintained by the receiver of the information. Using this model, it can support both unicast and multicast applications. Reviewing Figure 2-1b, RSVP messages may be sent directly inside IP datagrams (using IP Protocol = 46), or encapsulated inside UDP datagrams, using Ports 1698 and 1699. RSVP defines two basic message types: Reservation Request (or Resv) messages and Path messages. A receiver sends Path messages downstream, following the paths prescribed by the routing protocols that follow the paths of the data, which store path state information along the way.

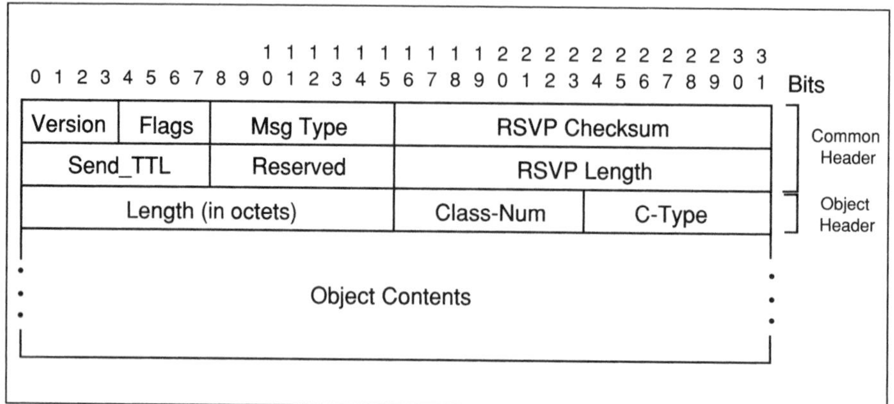

Figure 4-14 RSVP Message Format

The RSVP message consists of three sections: a Common Header (8 octets), an Object Header (4 octets), and Object Contents (variable length), as shown in Figure 4-14. The Version field (4 bits) contains the protocol version (currently 1). The Flags field (4 bits) is reserved for future definition. The Message Type field (1 octet) defines one of seven currently defined RSVP messages:

Message Type	Message Name	Function
1	Path	Path message, from sender to receiver, along same path used for the data packets.
2	Resv	Reservation message with reservation requests, carried hop-by-hop from receivers to senders.
3	PathErr	Path error message, reports errors in processing Path messages, and travels upstream toward senders.
4	ResvErr	Reservation error message, reports errors in processing Resv messages, and sent downstream toward receivers.

Message Type	Message Name	Function
5	PathTear	Path teardown message, initiated by senders or by a timeout, and sent downstream to all receivers.
6	ResvTear	Reservation teardown message, initiated by receivers or by a timeout, and sent upstream to all matching senders.
7	ResvConf	Reservation confirmation message, acknowledges reservation requests.

The RSVP Checksum field (2 octets) provides error control. The Send_TTL field (1 octet) is the IP Time to Live field value with which the message was sent. The RSVP Length field (2 octets) is the total length of the RSVP message, given in octets.

Every object consists of one or more 32-bit words with a 1-octet Object Header. This second header includes a Length field (2 octets) that is the total length of the object (with a minimum of 4 octets, and also a multiple of 4 octets), a Class Number (1 octet) which defines the object class, and a C-Type field (1 octet), which is an object type that is unique with the Class Number. The Object Contents complete the message. Currently defined object classes (which, by convention, are always capitalized), include:

Class-Num	Object Class	Object Function
0	NULL	Null.
1	SESSION	Defines the specific session for other objects that follow, and is required in every RSVP message.
3	RSVP_HOP	The IP address of the RSVP-capable sending node.
4	INTEGRITY	Carries cryptographic data to authenticate the originating node and verify contents of the message.
5	TIME_VALUES	The value of the refresh period used by the message creator; it is required in every Path and Resv message.
6	ERROR_SPEC	Specifies an error in a PathErr, ResvErr, or a confirmation in a ResvConf message.

Continued

Continued

Class-Num	Object Class	Object Function
7	SCOPE	Carries a list of sender hosts to which the information in the message is to be forwarded, and may appear in a Resv, ResvErr, or ResvTear message.
8	STYLE	Defines the reservation style, and is required in every Resv message.
9	FLOW_SPEC	Defines a desired QoS, and is used in a Resv message.
10	FILTER_SPEC	Defines a subset of session data packets to receive the desired QoS, and is used in a Resv message.
11	SENDER_TEMPLATE	Contains the sender's IP address, and is required in a Path message.
12	SENDER_TSPEC	Defines the traffic characteristics of a sender's data flow, and is required in a Path message.
13	ADSPEC	Carries One Pass with advertising (OPWA) data, and is used in a Path message.
14	POLICY_DATA	Determines if an associated reservation is administratively permitted, and may be used in Path, Resv, PathErr, or ResvErr messages.
15	RESV_CONFIRM	Carries the IP address of the receiver that requested a confirmation, and may appear in a Resv or ResvConf message.

Details on the operation of RSVP can be found in RFC 2205. References [4-58] and [4-59] provide additional resources on RSVP.

4.9 Troubleshooting the Internetwork Connection

When planning a strategy to diagnose internetwork-related problems, it is important to reconsider the functions of the ARPA Internet Layer discussed in Section 4.1. Recall that its principle function is routing, with the desired result being connectivity between two hosts. Associated with routing are the issues of addressing, subnet assignments, and masks. Because addresses are not always known, protocols such as ARP/RARP and BOOTP may be used. The Domain Name System may also assist in this process.

Intelligent devices known as routers use the addresses to guide the datagram through the internet. Those routers communicate with each other using an IGP, such as RIP or OSPF. Because the routing mechanism doesn't always function properly, another protocol, ICMP, helps the hosts determine what went wrong.

One frequently used test is the ICMP Echo (PING) message, which verifies connectivity between internet devices. The PING can be used in a sequential manner to isolate a problem. For example, first PING a host on your subnet, then PING a router, then PING a host on the other side of that router, and so on until the faulty connection is identified. Another maintenance utility known as *traceroute* is available with some host operating systems. Traceroute uses ICMP messages to verify each segment along a path to a distant host. Traceroute must be used with some caution, however, as it can generate large amounts of internetwork (and/or Internet) traffic.

To summarize, if a problem occurs in the internet and the Network Interface Layer looks healthy (review Section 3.12), look for the significant events at the Internet Layer. These events relate to datagram delivery. The processes of address discovery, address assignment, communication between routers, and notification of router errors may offer clues about the reason for a problem with the delivery of your datagram. Carl Auerbach's paper "Trouble-Busters" [4-60] discusses TCP/IP network troubleshooting and suggests various tools that come in handy. The following case studies will show examples of these clues.

4.10 Case Studies

We have studied a number of protocols in this chapter, including ARP, IP, ICMP, RIP, and OSPF. We have also looked at IP addressing schemes and Subnet Masks. Next, let's look at some case studies that illustrate these protocols in action.

4.10.1 Login to a Remote Host

In our first example, we'll look at the processes necessary to log into a remote host using the UNIX TELNET utility (see Trace 4.10.1a). The network administrator, Paul, resides on an Ethernet segment (Network 132) in one location, and the remote host that he needs to access resides on a different segment (Network 129) in another part of the country (see Figure 4-15).

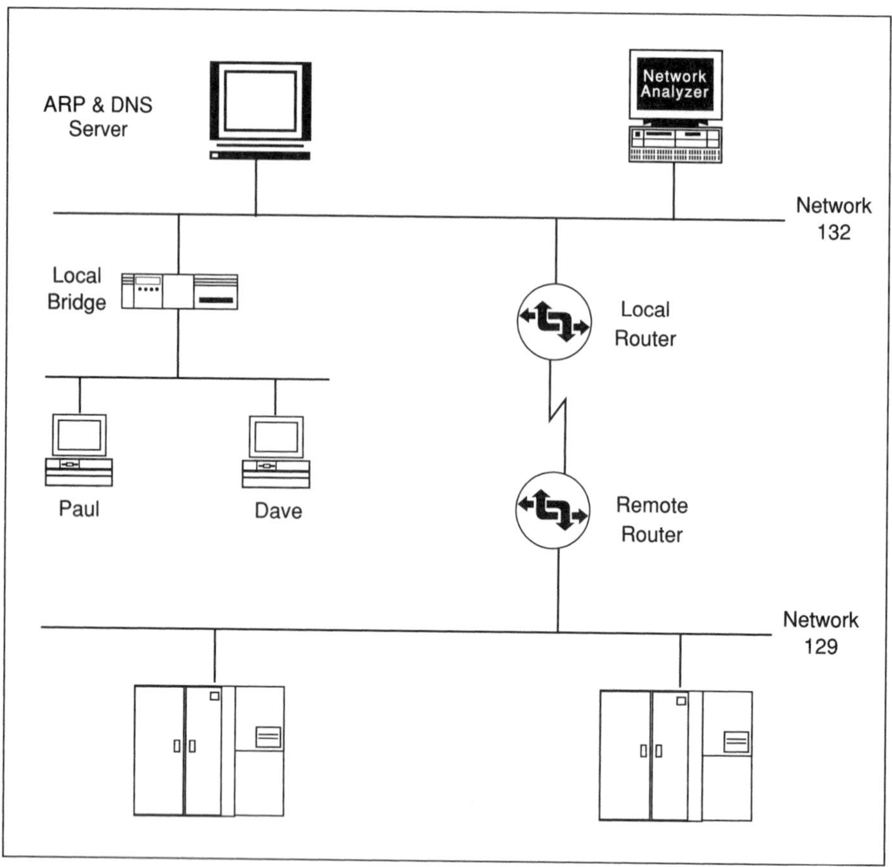

Figure 4-15 Login to Remote Host

First, Paul must find the Domain Name System (DNS) Server. To do so, he broadcasts an ARP Request packet within an Ethernet frame identifying the Protocol Address, PA = [132.XXX.128.1], for the Internet Protocol (IP), but with an unknown Hardware Address (HA = 0) as shown in Frame 1 of Trace 4.10.1b. The Name Server responds in Frame 2, identifying its HA = 08002006B501H. Paul now knows how to reach the Name Server. (Expert analysts will note a subtle difference between the address representations in Frame 2 of Trace 4.10.1a (Summary) and Frame 2 of Trace 4.10.1b (Details). In the Summary trace, the entire hardware address is represented: HA = 08002006B501. In the Detail trace, the Sniffer decodes the Manufacturer ID portion of the Sender's hardware address (080020) and substitutes the manufacturer's name (Sun). The balance of the address (06B501) remains the same. The substituted name (Name Svr) comes from the Sniffer's manually entered database of node names.)

Paul next locates the address for the remote host fs1.cam.nist.gov that he wishes to log into. The DNS request is transmitted in Frame 3, with a response given in Frame 4 of Trace 4.10.1c indicating that fs1.cam.nist.gov is located at [129.XXX.80.33]. Recall that Paul is located on Network 132 and the Name Server says that his desired destination is located on another network (Network 129). A router must now spring into action. Paul broadcasts an ARP Request packet looking for the router (address [132.XXX.1.1] in Frame 5 of Trace 4.10.1a). The router responds with its hardware address in Frame 6 (HA = 000093E0807BH).

Paul now has all the information he needs. In Frame 7 he initiates a TCP connection (via a three-way handshake, which we will study in Chapter 5) with the remote host. The details of the Connection Establishment message verify that Paul knows where to find his desired host (see Trace 4.10.1d). In the Data Link Control (DLC, or frame) header, Paul addresses this message to the Proteon router (address ProteonE0807B). We know that this frame is transmitted on a DIX Ethernet (not an IEEE 802.3) LAN, because of the EtherType field identified IP = 0800 H. (Had it been an IEEE 802.3 frame, a Length field would have been shown instead of the EtherType field.) The IP header identifies Paul's workstation as the source of the datagram [132.XXX.129.15], with the destination address of the remote host on a different network [129.XXX.80.33]. The TCP header specifies that the Destination Port = 23 (TELNET). The TCP flags indicate that Paul wants to establish a connection, since the Synchronize flag is set (SYN = 1). Paul also specifies that he can accept a maximum segment size of 512 octets.

In the subsequent frames (8 through 20 of Trace 4.10.1a), Paul's workstation and the remote host negotiate various TELNET parameters, such as the Terminal Type (Frames 10 through 12), Echo (Frames 15 and 16), and Login (Frames 17 through 20). Once Paul is logged in, he can complete his business with the remote host.

To summarize, Paul's workstation undertakes the following steps:

1. Identify DNS Name Server (ARP).
2. Identify remote host address (DNS).
3. Identify required router (ARP).
4. Establish connection with remote host (TCP).
5. Negotiate parameters with remote host (TELNET).
6. Initiate remote terminal session (TELNET).

In the next case study, we will examine how IP fragments long messages.

TRACE 4.10.1A. LOGIN TO REMOTE HOST SUMMARY

Sniffer Network Analyzer data 21-Jun at 13:37:00, LOGIN.ENC, Pg 1

SUMMARY	Delta T	Destination	Source	Summary
M 1		Broadcast	Paul	ARP C PA=[132.XXX.128.1] PRO=IP
2	0.0006	Paul	Name Svr	ARP R PA=[132.XXX.128.1] HA=08002006B501 PRO=IP
3	0.0016	Name Svr	Paul	DNS C ID=3 OP=QUERY NAME=fs1.cam.nist.gov
4	0.0026	Paul	Name Svr	DNS R ID=3 STAT=OK NAME=fs1.cam.nist.gov
5	0.0088	Broadcast	Paul	ARP C PA=[132.XXX.1.1] PRO=IP
6	0.0010	Paul	Router	ARP R PA=[132.XXX.1.1] HA=000093E0807B PRO=IP
7	0.0016	Router	Paul	TCP D=23 S=3133 SYN SEQ=9947492 LEN=0 WIN=1024
8	0.1081	Paul	Router	TCP D=3133 S=23 SYN ACK=9947493 SEQ=80448000 LEN=0 WIN=4096
9	0.0032	Router	Paul	TCP D=23 S=3133 ACK=80448001 WIN=1024
10	2.1818	Paul	Router	Telnet R PORT=3133 IAC Do Terminal type
11	0.0029	Router	Paul	TCP D=23 S=3133 ACK=80448004 WIN=1021
12	0.0027	Router	Paul	Telnet C PORT=3133 IAC Will Terminal type
13	0.1134	Paul	Router	Telnet R PORT=3133 IAC SB ...
14	0.0070	Router	Paul	Telnet C PORT=3133 IAC SB ...
15	0.1912	Paul	Router	Telnet R PORT=3133 IAC Will Echo
16	0.0053	Router	Paul	Telnet C PORT=3133 IAC Do Echo
17	0.2566	Paul	Router	Telnet R PORT=3133 login:
18	0.0033	Router	Paul	Telnet C PORT=3133 IAC Do Suppress go-ahead
19	0.1113	Paul	Router	Telnet R PORT=3133 IAC Don't Echo
20	0.2591	Router	Paul	TCP D=23 S=3133 ACK=80448057 WIN=968

TRACE 4.10.1B. LOGIN TO REMOTE HOST ARP/RARP DETAILS

```
Sniffer Network Analyzer data 21-Jun at 13:37:00, file LOGIN.ENC, Pg 1

- - - - - - - - - - - - - - - Frame 1 - - - - - - - - - - - - - - - - -

DLC:  ——DLC Header——
DLC:
DLC:  Frame 1 arrived at  13:37:06.3280; frame size is 60 (003C hex) bytes.
DLC:  Destination = BROADCAST FFFFFFFFFFFF, Broadcast
DLC:  Source = Station 3Com  1AB9BE, Paul
DLC:  Ethertype = 0806 (ARP)
DLC:
ARP:  ——ARP/RARP frame——
ARP:
ARP:  Hardware type = 1 (10Mb Ethernet)
ARP:  Protocol type = 0800 (IP)
ARP:  Length of hardware address = 6 bytes
ARP:  Length of protocol address = 4 bytes
ARP:  Opcode 1 (ARP request)
ARP:  Sender's hardware address = 3Com  1AB9BE, Paul
ARP:  Sender's protocol address = [132.XXX.129.15]
ARP:  Target hardware address = 000000000000, 000000000000
ARP:  Target protocol address = [132.XXX.128.1]
ARP:

- - - - - - - - - - - - - - - Frame 2 - - - - - - - - - - - - - - - - -

DLC:  ——DLC Header——
DLC:
DLC:  Frame 2 arrived at  13:37:06.3287; frame size is 60 (003C hex) bytes.
DLC:  Destination = Station 3Com  1AB9BE, Paul
DLC:  Source      = Station Sun   06B501, Name Svr
DLC:  Ethertype  = 0806 (ARP)
DLC:
ARP:  ——ARP/RARP frame——
ARP:
ARP:  Hardware type = 1 (10Mb Ethernet)
ARP:  Protocol type = 0800 (IP)
ARP:  Length of hardware address = 6 bytes
ARP:  Length of protocol address = 4 bytes
ARP:  Opcode 2 (ARP reply)
ARP:  Sender's hardware address = Sun   06B501, Name Svr
ARP:  Sender's protocol address = [132.XXX.128.1]
ARP:  Target hardware address = 3Com  1AB9BE, Paul
```

```
ARP:  Target protocol address = [132.XXX.129.15]
ARP:
```

TRACE 4.10.1C. LOGIN TO REMOTE HOST DNS DETAILS

Sniffer Network Analyzer data 21-Jun at 13:37:00, LOGIN.ENC, Pg 1

```
- - - - - - - - - - - - - - - - Frame 3 - - - - - - - - - - - - - - - - -

DLC:  —— DLC Header ——
DLC:
DLC:  Frame 3 arrived at  13:37:06.3304; frame size is 76 (004C hex) bytes.
DLC:  Destination = Station Sun   06B501, Name Svr
DLC:  Source      = Station 3Com  1AB9BE, Paul
DLC:  Ethertype  = 0800 (IP)
DLC:
IP:   —— IP Header ——
IP:
IP:   Version = 4, header length = 20 bytes
IP:   Type of service = 20
IP:         001. .... = priority
IP:         ...0 .... = normal delay
IP:         .... 0... = normal throughput
IP:         .... .0.. = normal reliability
IP:   Total length = 62 bytes
IP:   Identification = 30
IP:   Flags = 0X
IP:   .0.. .... = may fragment
IP:   ..0. .... = last fragment
IP:   Fragment offset = 0 bytes
IP:   Time to live = 64 seconds/hops
IP:   Protocol = 17 (UDP)
IP:   Header checksum = 701A (correct)
IP:   Source address = [132.XXX.129.15]
IP:   Destination address = [132.XXX.128.1]
IP:   No options
IP:
UDP:  —— UDP Header ——
UDP:
UDP:  Source port = 1116 (Domain)
UDP:  Destination port = 53
UDP:  Length = 42
UDP:  Checksum = 54EF (correct)
UDP:
```

```
DNS: — Internet Domain Name Service header —
DNS:
DNS: ID = 3
DNS: Flags = 01
DNS: 0... .... = Command
DNS: .000 0... = Query
DNS: .... ..0. = Not truncated
DNS: .... ...1 = Recursion desired
DNS: Flags = 0X
DNS: ...0 .... = Unicast packet
DNS: Question count = 1, Answer count = 0
DNS: Authority count = 0, Additional record count = 0
DNS:
DNS: Question section:
DNS:     Name = fs1.cam.nist.gov
DNS:     Type = Host address (A,1)
DNS:     Class = Internet (IN,1)
DNS:
DNS: [Normal end of ìInternet Domain Name Service headerî.]
DNS:

- - - - - - - - - - - - - - - - Frame 4 - - - - - - - - - - - - - - - - -

DLC: — DLC Header —
DLC:
DLC: Frame 4 arrived at 13:37:06.3330; frame size is 92 (005C hex) bytes.
DLC: Destination = Station 3Com 1AB9BE, Paul
DLC: Source      = Station Sun  06B501, Name Svr
DLC: Ethertype = 0800 (IP)
DLC:
IP: — IP Header —
IP:
IP: Version = 4, header length = 20 bytes
IP: Type of service = 00
IP:      000. .... = routine
IP:      ...0 .... = normal delay
IP:      .... 0... = normal throughput
IP:      .... .0.. = normal reliability
IP: Total length = 78 bytes
IP: Identification = 60111
IP: Flags = 0X
IP: .0.. .... = may fragment
IP: ..0. .... = last fragment
IP: Fragment offset = 0 bytes
```

```
IP:  Time to live = 30 seconds/hops
IP:   Protocol = 17 (UDP)
IP:   Header checksum = A778 (correct)
IP:  Source address = [132.XXX.128.1]
IP:  Destination address = [132.XXX.129.15]
IP:  No options
IP:
UDP:  —— UDP Header ——
UDP:
UDP:  Source port = 53 (Domain)
UDP:  Destination port = 1116
UDP:  Length = 58
UDP:  No checksum
UDP:
DNS:  —— Internet Domain Name Service header ——
DNS:
DNS:  ID = 3
DNS:  Flags = 85
DNS:  1... .... = Response
DNS:  .... .1.. = Authoritative answer
DNS:  .000 0... = Query
DNS:  .... ..0. = Not truncated
DNS:  Flags = 8X
DNS:  ...0 .... = Unicast packet
DNS:  1... .... = Recursion available
DNS:  Response code = OK (0)
DNS:  Question count = 1, Answer count = 1
DNS:  Authority count = 0, Additional record count = 0
DNS:
DNS:  Question section:
DNS:      Name = fs1.cam.nist.gov
DNS:      Type = Host address (A,1)
DNS:      Class = Internet (IN,1)
DNS:  Answer section:
DNS:      Name = fs1.cam.nist.gov
DNS:      Type = Host address (A,1)
DNS:      Class = Internet (IN,1)
DNS:      Time-to-live = 2589119 (seconds)
DNS:      Address = [129.XXX.80.33]
DNS:
DNS:  [Normal end of "Internet Domain Name Service header".]
DNS:
```

TRACE 4.10.1D. LOGIN TO REMOTE HOST TCP DETAILS

```
Sniffer Network Analyzer data 21-Jun at 13:37:00, LOGIN.ENC, Pg 1

- - - - - - - - - - - - - - - - Frame 7 - - - - - - - - - - - - - - - - -

DLC:  —— DLC Header ——
DLC:
DLC:  Frame 7 arrived at  13:37:06.3445; frame size is 60 (003C hex) bytes.
DLC:  Destination = Station PrteonE0807B, Router
DLC:  Source      = Station 3Com  1AB9BE, Paul
DLC:  Ethertype  = 0800 (IP)
DLC:
IP:   —— IP Header ——
IP:
IP:   Version = 4, header length = 20 bytes
IP:   Type of service = 00
IP:         000. .... = routine
IP:         ...0 .... = normal delay
IP:         .... 0... = normal throughput
IP:         .... .0.. = normal reliability
IP:   Total length = 44 bytes
IP:   Identification = 31
IP:   Flags = 0X
IP:   .0.. .... = may fragment
IP:   ..0. .... = last fragment
IP:   Fragment offset = 0 bytes
IP:   Time to live = 64 seconds/hops
IP:   Protocol = 6 (TCP)
IP:   Header checksum = A3D3 (correct)
IP:   Source address = [132.XXX.129.15]
IP:   Destination address = [129.XXX.80.33]
IP:   No options
IP:
TCP:  —— TCP header ——
TCP:
TCP:  Source port = 3133
TCP:  Destination port = 23 (Telnet)
TCP:  Initial sequence number = 9947492
TCP:  Data offset = 24 bytes
TCP:  Flags = 02
TCP:  ..0. .... = (No urgent pointer)
TCP:  ...0 .... = (No acknowledgment)
TCP:  .... 0... = (No push)
TCP:  .... .0.. = (No reset)
```

```
TCP: .... ..1. = SYN
TCP: .... ...0 = (No FIN)
TCP: Window = 1024
TCP: Checksum = EAAF (correct)
TCP:
TCP: Options follow
TCP: Maximum segment size = 512
TCP:
```

4.10.2 Fragmenting Long Messages

In this case study, we will investigate how a host fragments a long message into multiple IP datagrams for transmission on a TCP/IP-based internetwork. In this example, the source is a station (DEC 029487) that wishes to send a large SUN RPC file to another station (Intrln 00027C0) on the same LAN. Three frames are needed to transmit the message (see Trace 4.10.2 and Figure 4-16). The message requires a User Datagram Protocol (UDP) header to identify the source and destination ports at the communicating hosts.

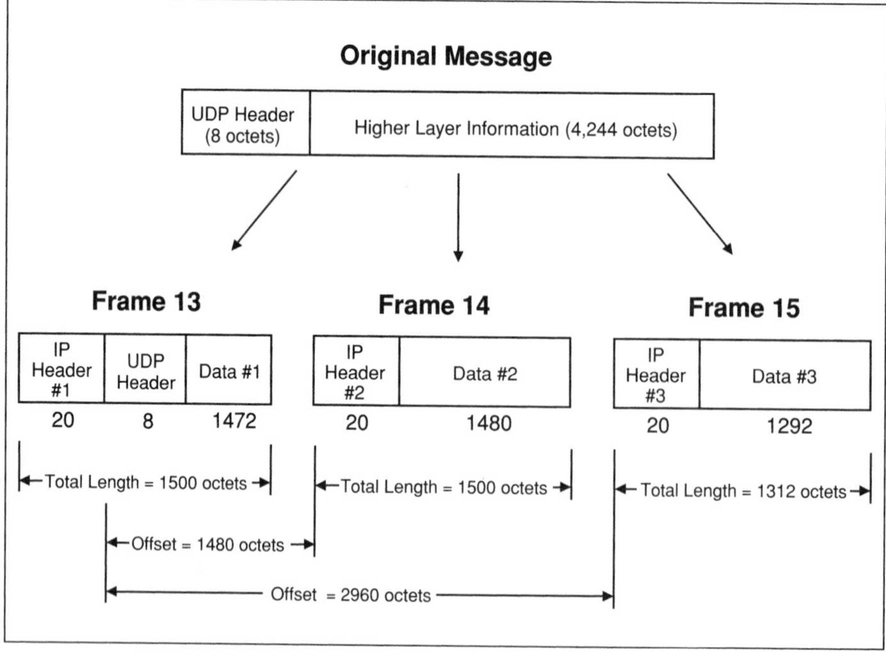

Figure 4-16 IPv4 Fragments

The message contains 4,244 octets of data plus an 8-octet UDP header, for a total of 4,252 octets. The message is divided into three frames, with 1,472, 1,480, and 1,292 octets of data each (Frames 13, 14, and 15, respectively). Frame 13 has a total length of 1,500 octets (matching the maximum Ethernet frame size) and indicates that more fragments, associated with message ID = 59738, are on the way. The next higher layer protocol within the first fragment is UDP (Protocol = 17, UDP). The Source and Destination addresses [XXX.YYY.0.33] and [XXX.YYY.0.10] identify the network. The UDP header indicates that the total message length is 4,252 octets. This includes the UDP header (8 octets) plus the data (4,244 octets). Thus, the 1,500 octets of Frame 13 consist of the IP header (20 octets), the UDP header (8 octets), and the first data fragment (1,472 octets).

The second frame also contains 1,514 octets of information (14 octets of Ethernet frame header plus 1,500 octets of data). The IP header indicates that this fragment is 1,500 octets in length and that more fragments associated with message ID = 59738 are coming. The fragment offset is 1,480, indicating that the data within Frame 14 starts 1,480 octets after the beginning of the original datagram. Note that the second IP header comprises 20 octets of Frame 14's data, but it does not count in the offset calculation because the IP header is not part of the original message.

The third fragment (Frame 15) contains 1,312 octets of information, consisting of a 20-octet IP header and 1,292 octets of data. This third IP header uses the same message ID = 59738 but indicates that no more fragments are coming (the More Fragments bit = 0). This fragment belongs 2,960 octets after the beginning of the original message.

Now let's see if the IP module in the Source host was working properly. The UDP header in Frame 13 says that the total length of this message is 4,252 octets. This is divided into the UDP header (8 octets), Data Fragment 1 (1,472 octets), Data Fragment 2 (1,480 octets), and Data Fragment 3 (1,292 octets). Each fragment requires a 20-octet IP header, which does not count in the total. Each frame requires 14 octets of Ethernet header, which also does not count in the total. Reviewing Figure 4-16, we can see that the fragment offsets are also correct: 1,480 (8 + 1,472) for Fragment 2, and 2,960 (8 + 1,472 + 1,480) for Fragment 3. We can therefore conclude that the IP module within station DEC 029487 was functioning properly.

TRACE 4.10.2. IP FRAGMENTS

```
Sniffer Network Analyzer data 10-Dec at 11:20:38, file TCPIP.ENC, Pg 1

---------------- Frame 13 -----------------

SUMMARY    Delta T    Destination     Source       Summary
13         0.0152     Intrln0027C0    DEC029487    DLC Ethertype=0800,
                                                   size=1514 bytes
```

```
                                                    IP D=[XXX.YYY.0.10]
                                                     S=[XXX.YYY.0.33]
                                                     LEN=1480 ID=59738
                                                    UDP D=2049 S=1026
LEN=4252

DLC:  —— DLC Header ——
DLC:
DLC:  Frame 13 arrived at  11:20:35.9514; frame size is 1514 (05EA hex) bytes.
DLC:  Destination = Station Intrln0027C0
DLC:  Source      = Station DEC   029487
DLC:  Ethertype  = 0800 (IP)
DLC:
IP:   —— IP Header ——
IP:
IP:   Version = 4, header length = 20 bytes
IP:   Type of service = 00
IP:         000. .... = routine
IP:         ...0 .... = normal delay
IP:         .... 0... = normal throughput
IP:        .... .0.. = normal reliability
IP:   Total length = 1500 bytes
IP:   Identification = 59738
IP:   Flags = 2X
IP:   .0.. .... = may fragment
IP:   ..1. .... = more fragments
IP:   Fragment offset = 0 bytes
IP:  Time to live = 255 seconds/hops
IP:   Protocol = 17 (UDP)
IP:   Header checksum = 6421 (correct)
IP:   Source address = [XXX.YYY.0.33]
IP:   Destination address = [XXX.YYY.0.10]
IP:   No options
IP:
UDP:  —— UDP Header ——
UDP:
UDP:  Source port = 1026
UDP:  Destination port = 2049 (Sun RPC)
UDP:  Length = 4252 (not all data contained in this fragment)
UDP:  No checksum
UDP:
UDP:  [1472 byte(s) of data]
UDP:
```

```
- - - - - - - - - - - - - - - - Frame 14 - - - - - - - - - - - - - - - - -

SUMMARY   Delta T   Destination    Source      Summary
14        0.0022    Intrln0027C0   DEC029487   DLC Ethertype=0800,
                                                size=1514 bytes
                                               IP D=[XXX.YYY.0.10]
                                                S=[XXX.YYY.0.33]
                                                LEN=1480 ID=59738
                                               UDP continuation ID=59738

DLC: —— DLC Header ——
DLC:
DLC: Frame 14 arrived at  11:20:35.9536; frame size is 1514 (05EA hex) bytes.
DLC: Destination = Station Intrln0027C0
DLC: Source      = Station DEC  029487
DLC: Ethertype  = 0800 (IP)
DLC:
IP: —— IP Header ——
IP:
IP:  Version = 4, header length = 20 bytes
IP:  Type of service = 00
IP:       000. .... = routine
IP:       ...0 .... = normal delay
IP:       .... 0... = normal throughput
IP:       .... .0.. = normal reliability
IP:  Total length = 1500 bytes
IP:  Identification = 59738
IP:   Flags = 2X
IP:  .0.. .... = may fragment
IP:  ..1. .... = more fragments
IP:   Fragment offset = 1480 bytes
IP:   Time to live = 255 seconds/hops
IP:   Protocol = 17 (UDP)
IP:   Header checksum = 6368 (correct)
IP:   Source address = [XXX.YYY.0.33]
IP:   Destination address = [XXX.YYY.0.10]
IP:   No options
IP:
UDP:  [1480 byte(s) of data, continuation of IP ident=59738]
```

```
---------------- Frame 15 -----------------

SUMMARY    Delta T    Destination    Source       Summary
15         0.0019     Intrln0027C0   DEC029487    DLC Ethertype=0800,
                                       size=1326 bytes
                                       IP D=[XXX.YYY.0.10]
                                       S=[XXX.YYY.0.33]
                                       LEN=1292 ID=59738
                                       UDP continuation ID=59738

DLC:  — DLC Header —
DLC:
DLC:  Frame 15 arrived at  11:20:35.9556; frame size is 1326 (052E hex) bytes.
DLC:  Destination = Station Intrln0027C0
DLC:  Source      = Station DEC  029487
DLC:  Ethertype   = 0800 (IP)
DLC:
IP:   — IP Header —
IP:
IP:   Version = 4, header length = 20 bytes
IP:   Type of service = 00
IP:        000. .... = routine
IP:        ...0 .... = normal delay
IP:        .... 0... = normal throughput
IP:        .... .0.. = normal reliability
IP:   Total length = 1312 bytes
IP:   Identification = 59738
IP:   Flags = 0X
IP:   .0.. .... = may fragment
IP:   ..0. .... = last fragment
IP:   Fragment offset = 2960 bytes
IP:   Time to live = 255 seconds/hops
IP:   Protocol = 17 (UDP)
IP:   Header checksum = 836B (correct)
IP:   Source address = [XXX.YYY.0.33]
IP:   Destination address = [XXX.YYY.0.10]
IP:   No options
IP:
UDP: [1292 byte(s) of data, continuation of IP ident=59738]
```

4.10.3 Measuring the Aging of ARP Tables

One of the router parameters that network managers must determine is the time period for aging the ARP tables. If the tables age too quickly, the network devices must resend ARP messages to discover the correct Hardware address of an intended destination. Retransmitting ARPs needlessly consumes internetwork bandwidth. Conversely, if the tables age out too slowly (or not at all), the transmission might go to an obsolete (or incorrect) address. Router manufacturers allow the administrator to tailor the ARP table's aging period to respond to local traffic patterns. After you set the time period, it is useful to test the aging with a protocol analyzer to verify proper operation. Let's see how to do this.

First we filter the data to show only the ARP messages (Trace 4.10.3a). From this we see that several devices are active, including Bay Networks Inc.'s Link Node routers (shown as Router LN1 and Router LN2), a Cisco Systems Inc.'s IGS router (shown as Router IGS), and a Sun SPARCstation (shown as Sparcstn). For a consistent test, all of the ARP Request messages ask for a device on the same subnet [192.92.168.X]. The Delta T column gives the time between transmissions in seconds and measures the delay between ARP Requests and Replies.

To determine whether the ARP table of a particular device is operating properly, the analyzer further filters the data to show only the transmission to and from that device. Trace 4.10.3b shows a Bay Networks Link Node router. Frame 4 is set as the baseline for all time measurements. By adding the Delta T measurements, we can determine the time between the transmission of any two frames. Router LN1 broadcasts an ARP message in Frame 4 looking for the Hardware address associated with [192.92.168.3]. Router LN2 responds almost immediately in Frame 6. The next time this Hardware address is requested is almost 158 seconds (about 2.5 minutes) later in Frame 142 (we calculate this by adding the significant Delta T measurements: 11.0 + 1.9 + 14.1 + 130.7 = 157.7 seconds). Another Bay Networks router responds (Frame 144). The ARP cache timer within the Bay Networks routers was set to age out after two minutes. We note that the ARP Request is retransmitted after 2.5 minutes, thus verifying the proper operation of the timer. From this we can also conclude that the ARP tables in both LN1 and LN2 are functioning properly, since the same values are used for ARP requests and replies on several occasions. Consider implementing a similar test any time you install a new router to verify its proper operation and to eliminate the possibility of excessive traffic due to unnecessary ARP Requests.

TRACE 4.10.3A. ARP MESSAGES FROM VARIOUS ROUTERS

Sniffer Network Analyzer data 17-Feb at 13:25:20, ARPTST1.ENC, Pg 1

SUMMARY	Delta T	Destination	Source	Summary
M 4		Broadcast	Router LN1	ARP C PA=[192.92.168.3] PRO=IP
5	0.0001	Broadcast	Router LN1	ARP C PA=[192.92.168.3] PRO=IP
6	0.0005	Router LN1	Router LN2	ARP R PA=[192.92.168.3] HA=0000A2009459 PRO=IP
7	0.0010	Router LN1	Router LN2	ARP R PA=[192.92.168.3] HA=0000A2009459 PRO=IP
17	11.0782	Broadcast	Router IGS	ARP R PA=[192.92.168.1] HA=00000C0079AF PRO=IP

21	1.9512	Broadcast	Router LN2	ARP C PA=[192.92.168.6] PRO=IP
22	0.0002	Broadcast	Router LN2	ARP C PA=[192.92.168.6] PRO=IP
23	0.0001	Router LN2	SparcStn	ARP R PA=[192.92.168.6] HA=080020103170 PRO=IP
36	14.1529	Broadcast	Router IGS	ARP C PA=[192.92.168.3] PRO=IP
37	0.0006	Router IGS	Router LN2	ARP R PA=[192.92.168.3] HA=0000A2009459 PRO=IP
142	130.7503	Broadcast	Router LN1	ARP C PA=[192.92.168.3] PRO=IP
143	0.0001	Broadcast	Router LN1	ARP C PA=[192.92.168.3] PRO=IP
144	0.0005	Router LN1	Router LN2	ARP R PA=[192.92.168.3] HA=0000A2009459 PRO=IP
145	0.0010	Router LN1	Router LN2	ARP R PA=[192.92.168.3] HA=0000A2009459 PRO=IP
154	6.2799	Broadcast	Router LN2	ARP C PA=[192.92.168.6] PRO=IP
155	0.0002	Broadcast	Router LN2	ARP C PA=[192.92.168.6] PRO=IP
156	0.0001	Router LN2	SparcStn	ARP R PA=[192.92.168.6] HA=080020103170 PRO=IP
165	7.9092	Broadcast	Router LN2	ARP C PA=[192.92.168.1] PRO=IP
166	0.0001	Broadcast	Router LN2	ARP C PA=[192.92.168.1] PRO=IP
167	0.0015	Router LN2	Router IGS	ARP R PA=[192.92.168.1] HA=00000C0079AF PRO=IP
168	0.0009	Router LN2	Router IGS	ARP R PA=[192.92.168.1] HA=00000C0079AF PRO=IP

TRACE 4.10.3B. ARP MESSAGES FROM A BAY NETWORKS LINK NODE ROUTER

Sniffer Network Analyzer data 17-Feb at 13:25:20, ARPTST1.ENC, Pg 1

SUMMARY	Delta T	Rel Time	Destination	Source	Summary
M 4		0.0000	Broadcast	Router LN1	ARP C PA=[192.92.168.3] PRO=IP
5	.0001	0.0001	Broadcast	Router LN1	ARP C PA=[192.92.168.3] PRO=IP
6	0.0005	0.0007	Router LN1	Router LN2	ARP R PA=[192.92.168.3] HA=0000A2009459 PRO=IP
7	0.0010	0.0018	Router LN1	Router LN2	ARP R PA=[192.92.168.3] HA=0000A2009459 PRO=IP

142	157.9338	157.9357	Broadcast	Router LN1	ARP C PA=[192.92.168.3] PRO=IP
143	0.0001	157.9359	Broadcast	Router LN1	ARP C PA=[192.92.168.3] PRO=IP
144	0.0005	157.9365	Router LN1	Router LN2	ARP R PA=[192.92.168.3] HA=0000A2009459 PRO=IP
145	0.0010	157.9375	Router LN1	Router LN2	ARP R PA=[192.92.168.3] HA=0000A2009459 PRO=IP

4.10.4 Duplicate IP Addresses

In Section 4.1, we looked at the differences between the Physical (Hardware) address and the Logical (Internet Protocol) address on any internet node. Recall that a ROM on the network interface card (Ethernet, token ring, and so on) normally contains the Physical address, while the network administrator assigns the Logical address. Let's see what happens when human error affects address assignments.

In this scenario, two engineers, Wayne and Benoit, wish to establish TELNET sessions with a router. The router's TELNET capabilities allow administrators to access its configuration files for network management. Wayne establishes his session first (see Trace 4.10.4a). The TCP connection is established in Frames 1 through 3, and the TELNET session initiates beginning in Frame 5. Wayne's session appears to be proceeding normally until Benoit starts to transmit in Frame 43. Benoit sends an ARP broadcast looking for the same router (Frame 43), and the router responds in Frame 44. Benoit then establishes his TCP connection in Frames 45 through 48, and, like Wayne, initiates a TELNET session beginning in Frame 49. Benoit doesn't realize, however, that his presence on the internetwork has caused Wayne's connection to fail. Let's see why.

Details of Wayne's TCP connection message (Frame 1) are shown in Trace 4.10.4b. Note that Wayne is communicating to the router using IP source address [131.195.116.250] on the same Class B network. Wayne is accessing the TELNET port on the router, and is using Sequence Number = 265153482. The router acknowledges the use of this sequence number in its response, shown in Frame 2.

In Trace 4.10.4c, Benoit's TCP connection message looks similar (Frame 45). Benoit claims that his Source Address = [131.195.116.250] (the same as Wayne's) and that the Destination Address = [131.195.116.42]. The TCP header also identifies the same Destination Port (23, for TELNET), but uses a different Sequence Number (73138176).

We can now see why Wayne's TELNET connection failed. When Benoit established a connection with the router using the same IP source address as Wayne's, confusion resulted. The router was examining the IP source address, not the Hardware (Data Link Layer) address. As a result, it was unable to differentiate between the duplicate IP addresses.

We traced the problem to a duplicate entry on the network manager's address database. Unknowingly, he had given both Wayne and Benoit the same IP address for their workstations. After discovering this mistake, Wayne changed his workstation configuration file to incorporate a unique IP address and no further problems occurred.

TRACE 4.10.4A. DUPLICATE IP ADDRESS SUMMARY

Sniffer Network Analyzer data 11-Oct at 10:49:04, IPDUPLIC.ENC, Pg 1

SUMMARY	Delta T	Destination	Source	Summary
M 1		Router	Wayne	TCP D=23 S=2588 SYN SEQ=265153482 LEN=0 WIN=1024
2	0.0014	Wayne	Router	TCP D=2588 S=23 SYN ACK=265153483 SEQ=331344504 LEN=0 WIN=0
3	0.0016	Router	Wayne	TCP D=23 S=2588 ACK=331344505 WIN=1024
4	0.0019	Wayne	Router	TCP D=2588 S=23 ACK=265153483 WIN=2144
5	0.0048	Wayne	Router	Telnet R PORT=2588 IAC Will Echo
6	0.0304	Wayne	Router	Telnet R PORT=2588 <0D><0A>
7	0.0896	Router	Wayne	Telnet C PORT=2588 IAC Do Echo
8	0.3010	Wayne	Router	TCP D=2588 S=23 ACK=265153486 WIN=2141
9	0.0312	Router	Wayne	Telnet C PORT=2588 IAC Do Suppress go-ahead
10	0.3005	Wayne	Router	TCP D=2588 S=23 ACK=265153489 WIN=2138
11	0.4320	Router	Wayne	Telnet C PORT=2588 c
12	0.3000	Wayne	Router	TCP D=2588 S=23 ACK=265153490 WIN=2137
13	0.0016	Router	Wayne	Telnet C PORT=2588 d
14	0.2984	Wayne	Router	TCP D=2588 S=23 ACK=265153491 WIN=2136

15	0.0016	Router	Wayne	Telnet C PORT=2588 2
16	0.2985	Wayne	Router	TCP D=2588 S=23 ACK=265153492 WIN=2135
17	0.0016	Router	Wayne	Telnet C PORT=2588 <0D><0A>
18	0.0024	Wayne	Router	Telnet R PORT=2588 <0D><0A>CD_BAS1_2>
19	0.1206	Router	Wayne	TCP D=23 S=2588 ACK=331344857 WIN=1012
20	0.7757	Router	Wayne	Telnet C PORT=2588 s
21	0.0025	Wayne	Router	Telnet R PORT=2588 s
22	0.1552	Router	Wayne	TCP D=23 S=2588 ACK=331344858 WIN=1023
23	0.1939	Router	Wayne	Telnet C PORT=2588 h
24	0.0030	Wayne	Router	Telnet R PORT=2588 h
25	0.1326	Router	Wayne	TCP D=23 S=2588 ACK=331344859 WIN=1023
26	0.0158	Router	Wayne	Telnet C PORT=2588
27	0.0030	Wayne	Router	Telnet R PORT=2588
28	0.1458	Router	Wayne	TCP D=23 S=2588 ACK=331344860 WIN=1023
29	0.0410	Router	Wayne	Telnet C PORT=2588 i
30	0.0026	Wayne	Router	Telnet R PORT=2588 i
31	0.1212	Router	Wayne	TCP D=23 S=2588 ACK=331344861 WIN=1023
32	0.1134	Router	Wayne	Telnet C PORT=2588 n
33	0.0034	Wayne	Router	Telnet R PORT=2588 n
34	0.1575	Router	Wayne	TCP D=23 S=2588 ACK=331344862 WIN=1023
35	0.2039	Router	Wayne	Telnet C PORT=2588 t
36	0.0027	Wayne	Router	Telnet R PORT=2588 t
37	0.1229	Router	Wayne	TCP D=23 S=2588 ACK=331344863 WIN=1023
38	0.1116	Router	Wayne	Telnet C PORT=2588 <0D><0A>
39	0.0332	Wayne	Router	Telnet R PORT=2588 <0D><0A><0D><0A>Ethernet 0 line protocol is...
40	0.0026	Router	Wayne	TCP D=23 S=2588 ACK=331345399 WIN=1024
41	0.0165	Wayne	Router	Telnet R PORT=2588 ute output rate 9325 bits/sec, 2 packets/sec<0D>...

42	0.2203	Router	Wayne	TCP D=23 S=2588 ACK=331345750 WIN=649
43	41.4005	Broadcast	Benoit	ARP C PA=[131.195.116.42] PRO=IP
44	0.0007	Benoit	Router	ARP R PA=[131.195.116.42] HA=00000C00A145 PRO=IP
45	0.0013	Router	Benoit	TCP D=23 S=15165 SYN SEQ=73138176 LEN=0 WIN=2048
46	0.0015	Benoit	Router	TCP D=15165 S=23 SYN ACK=73138177 SEQ=331390708 LEN=0 WIN=0
47	0.0031	Router	Benoit	TCP D=23 S=15165 ACK=331390709 WIN=2048
48	0.0018	Benoit	Router	TCP D=15165 S=23 ACK=73138177 WIN=2144
49	0.0068	Benoit	Router	Telnet R PORT=15165 IAC Will Echo
50	0.0297	Benoit	Router	Telnet R PORT=15165 <0D><0A>
51	0.2341	Router	Benoit	Telnet C PORT=15165 IAC DoEcho
52	0.2997	Benoit	Router	TCP D=15165 S=23 ACK=73138180 WIN=2141
53	0.0323	Router	Benoit	Telnet C PORT=15165 IAC Do Suppress go-ahead
54	0.2995	Benoit	Router	TCP D=15165 S=23 ACK=73138183 WIN=2138

TRACE 4.10.4B. DUPLICATE IP ADDRESS DETAILS (ORIGINAL STATION)

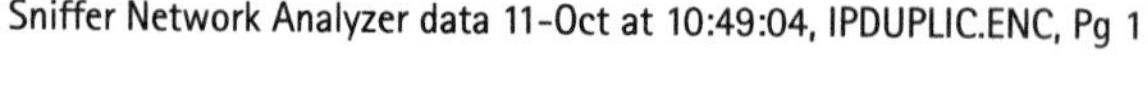

Sniffer Network Analyzer data 11-Oct at 10:49:04, IPDUPLIC.ENC, Pg 1

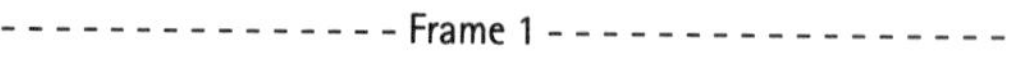

```
- - - - - - - - - - - - - - - Frame 1 - - - - - - - - - - - - - - - - -

DLC:  —— DLC Header ——
DLC:
DLC:  Frame 1 arrived at  10:49:08.4044; frame size is 60 (003C hex) bytes.
DLC:  Destination = Station Cisco 00A145, Router
DLC:  Source      = Station Intrln06C202, Wayne
```

```
DLC:  Ethertype = 0800 (IP)
DLC:
IP:   —— IP Header ——
IP:
IP:   Version = 4, header length = 20 bytes
IP:   Type of service = 00
IP:        000. .... = routine
IP:        ...0 .... = normal delay
IP:        .... 0... = normal throughput
IP:        .... .0.. = normal reliability
IP:   Total length = 44 bytes
IP:   Identification = 13
IP:   Flags = 0X
IP:   .0.. .... = may fragment
IP:   ..0. .... = last fragment
IP:   Fragment offset = 0 bytes
IP:   Time to live = 64 seconds/hops
IP:   Protocol = 6 (TCP)
IP:   Header checksum = 8A14 (correct)
IP:   Source address = [131.195.116.250]
IP:   Destination address = [131.195.116.42]
IP:   No options
IP:
TCP:  —— TCP header ——
TCP:
TCP:  Source port = 2588
TCP:  Destination port = 23 (Telnet)
TCP:  Initial sequence number = 265153482
TCP:  Data offset = 24 bytes
TCP:  Flags = 02
TCP:  ..0. .... = (No urgent pointer)
TCP:  ...0 .... = (No acknowledgment)
TCP:  .... 0... = (No push)
TCP:  .... .0.. = (No reset)
TCP:  .... ..1. = SYN
TCP:  .... ...0 = (No FIN)
TCP:  Window = 1024
TCP:  Checksum = 9DAF (correct)
TCP:
TCP:  Options follow
TCP:  Maximum segment size = 1460
TCP:
```

```
---------------- Frame 2 -----------------

DLC: —— DLC Header ——
DLC:
DLC: Frame 2 arrived at  10:49:08.4059; frame size is 60 (003C hex) bytes.
DLC: Destination = Station Intrln06C202, Wayne
DLC: Source      = Station Cisco 00A145, Router
DLC: Ethertype  = 0800 (IP)
DLC:
IP:   —— IP Header ——
IP:
IP:   Version = 4, header length = 20 bytes
IP:  Type of service = 00
IP:         000. .... = routine
IP:         ...0 .... = normal delay
IP:         .... 0... = normal throughput
IP:        .... .0.. = normal reliability
IP:   Total length = 44 bytes
IP:   Identification = 0
IP:   Flags = 0X
IP:   .0.. .... = may fragment
IP:   ..0. .... = last fragment
IP:   Fragment offset = 0 bytes
IP:   Time to live = 255 seconds/hops
IP:   Protocol = 6 (TCP)
IP:  Header checksum = CB20 (correct)
IP:  Source address = [131.195.116.42]
IP:  Destination address = [131.195.116.250]
IP:  No options
IP:
TCP:   —— TCP header ——
TCP:
TCP:  Source port = 23 (Telnet)
TCP:  Destination port = 2588
TCP:  Initial sequence number = 331344504
TCP:  Acknowledgment number = 265153483
TCP:  Data offset = 24 bytes
TCP:  Flags = 12
TCP:  ..0. .... = (No urgent pointer)
TCP:  ...1 .... = Acknowledgment
TCP:  .... 0... = (No push)
TCP:  .... .0.. = (No reset)
TCP:  .... ..1. = SYN
TCP:  .... ...0 = (No FIN)
```

```
TCP:  Window = 0
TCP:  Checksum = A367 (correct)
TCP:
TCP:  Options follow
TCP:  Maximum segment size = 1460
TCP:
```

TRACE 4.10.4C. DUPLICATE IP ADDRESS DETAILS (DUPLICATE STATION)

```
Sniffer Network Analyzer data 11-Oct at 10:49:04, IPDUPLIC.ENC, Pg 1

- - - - - - - - - - - - - - - - Frame 45 - - - - - - - - - - - - - - - - -

DLC:  —— DLC Header ——
DLC:
DLC:  Frame 45 arrived at  10:49:54.6082; frame size is 60 (003C hex) bytes.
DLC:  Destination = Station Cisco 00A145, Router
DLC:  Source      = Station Intrln05E253, Benoit
DLC:  Ethertype  = 0800 (IP)
DLC:
IP:   —— IP Header ——
IP:
IP:   Version = 4, header length = 20 bytes
IP:   Type of service = 10
IP:        000. .... = routine
IP:        ...1 .... = low delay
IP:        .... 0... = normal throughput
IP:        .... .0.. = normal reliability
IP:   Total length = 44 bytes
IP:   Identification = 1
IP:   Flags = 0X
IP:   .0.. .... = may fragment
IP:   ..0. .... = last fragment
IP:   Fragment offset = 0 bytes
IP:   Time to live = 64 seconds/hops
IP:   Protocol = 6 (TCP)
IP:   Header checksum = 8A10 (correct)
IP:   Source address = [131.195.116.250]
IP:   Destination address = [131.195.116.42]
IP:   No options
IP:
TCP: —— TCP header ——
TCP:
TCP: Source port = 15165
```

```
TCP:  Destination port = 23 (Telnet)
TCP:  Initial sequence number = 73138176
TCP:  Data offset = 24 bytes
TCP:  Flags = 02
TCP:  ..0. .... = (No urgent pointer)
TCP:  ...0 .... = (No acknowledgment)
TCP:  .... 0... = (No push)
TCP:  .... .0.. = (No reset)
TCP:  .... ..1. = SYN
TCP:  .... ...0 = (No FIN)
TCP:  Window = 2048
TCP:  Checksum = 5FCA (correct)
TCP:
TCP:  Options follow
TCP:  Maximum segment size = 1460
TCP:

- - - - - - - - - - - - - - - - Frame 46 - - - - - - - - - - - - - - - - -

DLC:  —— DLC Header ——
DLC:
DLC:  Frame 46 arrived at  10:49:54.6097; frame size is 60 (003C hex) bytes.
DLC:  Destination = Station Intrln05E253, Benoit
DLC:  Source      = Station Cisco 00A145, Router
DLC:  Ethertype   = 0800 (IP)
DLC:
IP:   —— IP Header ——
IP:
IP:   Version = 4, header length = 20 bytes
IP:   Type of service = 00
IP:        000. .... = routine
IP:        ...0 .... = normal delay
IP:        .... 0... = normal throughput
IP:        .... .0.. = normal reliability
IP:   Total length = 44 bytes
IP:   Identification = 0
IP:   Flags = 0X
IP:   .0.. .... = may fragment
IP:   ..0. .... = last fragment
IP:   Fragment offset = 0 bytes
IP:   Time to live = 255 seconds/hops
IP:   Protocol = 6 (TCP)
IP:   Header checksum = CB20 (correct)
IP:   Source address = [131.195.116.42]
```

```
IP:   Destination address = [131.195.116.250]
IP:   No options
IP:
TCP:  —— TCP header ——
TCP:
TCP:  Source port = 23 (Telnet)
TCP:  Destination port = 15165
TCP:  Initial sequence number = 331390708
TCP:  Acknowledgment number = 73138177
TCP:  Data offset = 24 bytes
TCP:  Flags = 12
TCP:  ..0. .... = (No urgent pointer)
TCP:  ...1 .... = Acknowledgment
TCP:  .... 0... = (No push)
TCP:  .... .0.. = (No reset)
TCP:  .... ..1. = SYN
TCP:  .... ...0 = (No FIN)
TCP:  Window = 0
TCP:  Checksum = B505 (correct)
TCP:
TCP:  Options follow
TCP:  Maximum segment size = 1460
TCP:
```

4.10.5 Incorrect Address Mask

As discussed in Section 4.2.3, system implementors can use subnetworks to form a hierarchical routing structure within an internetwork. Subnet addressing works as follows: A 32-bit IP address is comprised of a Network ID plus a Host ID. For example, a Class B network uses 16 bits for the network portion and 16 bits for the host portion. If an internet has multiple physical networks (e.g., LANs), the 16-bit host portion of the address can be further divided into a subnetwork address (representing the particular physical network, such as an Ethernet) and a host address (representing a particular device on that Ethernet). Class B addresses commonly use 8-bit subnetting. This would give a Network ID of 16 bits, a Subnetwork ID of 8 bits, and a Host ID of 8 bits. Thus, it could uniquely identify up to 254 subnetworks (i.e., LANs), each having up to 254 hosts (i.e., workstations, servers, and so on). Recall that the all zeros and all ones addresses are not allowed, thus reducing the theoretical limit of 256 subnetworks and 256 hosts to 254 of each (256 - 2 = 254). The first 16 bits (the Network ID) would deliver the datagram to the access point for the network (the router). The router would then decide which of the 254 subnetworks this datagram was destined for. The router uses a Subnet Mask to make that decision. Subnet Masks are stored within the host and are obtained using the ICMP

Address Mask Request message. This case study will show what happens when the host uses an incorrect Subnet Mask.

In this example, a network manager, Paul, wishes to check the status of a host on a different segment but connected via a bridge (see Figure 4-15). Paul's workstation software stores a number of parameters, including the Subnet Mask. The network in question is a Class B network, without subnetting. The Subnet Mask should be set for [255.255.0.0], corresponding with a Network ID of 16 bits and a Host ID of 16 bits. Since subnetting is not used, all datagrams for the local network should be delivered directly, but datagrams destined for another network should go through the router. Paul uses the ICMP Echo (PING) command to check the status of his host (a Sun 4 Server), but there's a delay in the ICMP Echo Reply. Let's see what happened.

Paul's workstation first broadcasts an ARP message looking for a router (Frames 1–2 in Trace 4.10.5a). This step is unexpected, since a router is not required for this transaction. Next, it attempts an ICMP Echo message (Frame 3). If all systems are functioning properly, an ICMP Echo Reply should follow the ICMP Echo immediately. In Paul's case, however, the ICMP Redirect message in Frame 4 follows the ICMP Echo. The Redirect message (see Trace 4.10.5b) indicates that it is redirecting datagrams for the host (ICMP Code = 1), and that the correct router (gateway) for this operation is [132.XXX.132.12]. Paul's workstation then sends another ARP Request, looking for address [132.XXX.132.12] in Frame 5. The Sun 4 Server responds with HA = 0800200C1DC3H (Frame 6). The ICMP Echo and Echo Reply then proceed as expected in Frames 7 and 8. The question remains: Why did Paul's workstation access the router, causing the ICMP Redirect Message?

The second ICMP Echo (Frame 7) sent from Paul's workstation [132.XXX.129.15] to the Sun 4 Server [132.XXX.132.12] provides a clue. Note that both devices are on the same network [132.XXX]. Since this is a Class B network without subnetting, the Subnet Mask should be [255.255.0.0]. When Paul examined the Subnet Mask in his workstation parameters, he found that it had been set for a Class B network with an 8-bit subnet address field, that is [255.255.255.0]. When his workstation calculated the Subnet Mask, it came up with:

```
Subnet Mask         11111111  11111111  11111111  00000000
AND
Source Address      10000100  XXXXXXXX  10000001  00001111
[132.XXX.129.15]
Result #1           10000100  XXXXXXXX  10000001  00000000
Subnet Mask         11111111  11111111  11111111  00000000
    AND
Destination Address 1000100   XXXXXXXX  10000100  00001100
[132.XXX.132.12]
Result #2           1000100   XXXXXX    10000100  00000000
```

Because the workstation found that Result #1 and Result #2 were different, it incorrectly concluded that the two devices were on different subnetworks, requiring the assistance of the router. When Paul reconfigured his workstation's Subnet Mask to [255.255.0.0], the ICMP Echo and Echo Replies proceeded without router intervention.

TRACE 4.10.5A. SUBNET MASK MISCONFIGURATION SUMMARY

Sniffer Network Analyzer data 13-Feb at 14:50:26, SUBNETC.ENC, Pg 1

SUMMARY	Delta T	Destination	Source	Summary
M 1		Broadcast	Paul	ARP C PA=[132.XXX.1.1] PRO=IP
2	0.0011	Paul	Router	ARP R PA=[132.XXX.1.1] HA=000093E0A0BF PRO=IP
3	0.0022	Router	Paul	ICMP Echo
4	0.0021	Paul	Router	ICMP Redirect (Redirect datagrams for the host)
5	11.7626	Broadcast	Paul	ARP C PA=[132.XXX.132.12] PRO=IP
6	0.0008	Paul	Sun4Svr	ARP R PA=[132.XXX.132.12] HA=0800200C1DC3 PRO=IP
7	0.0023	Sun4Svr	Paul	ICMP Echo
8	0.0016	Paul	Sun4Svr	ICMP Echo reply

TRACE 4.10.5B. SUBNET MASK MISCONFIGURATION ICMP DETAILS

Sniffer Network Analyzer data 13-Feb at 14:50:26, SUBNETC.ENC, Pg 1

```
- - - - - - - - - - - - - - - - Frame 3 - - - - - - - - - - - - - - - - -

ICMP:  —— ICMP header ——
ICMP:
ICMP:  Type = 8 (Echo)
ICMP:  Code = 0
ICMP:  Checksum = 719E (correct)
ICMP:  Identifier = 1315
ICMP:  Sequence number = 1
ICMP:  [256 bytes of data]
ICMP:
ICMP:  [Normal end of ìICMP headerî.]
ICMP:
- - - - - - - - - - - - - - - - Frame 4 - - - - - - - - - - - - - - - - -
ICMP:  —— ICMP header ——
```

```
ICMP:
ICMP:  Type = 5 (Redirect)
ICMP:  Code = 1 (Redirect datagrams for the host)
ICMP:  Checksum = 738C (correct)
ICMP:  Gateway internet address = [132.XXX.132.12]
ICMP:  IP header of originating message (description follows)
ICMP:
IP:  — IP Header —
IP:
IP:  Version = 4, header length = 20 bytes
IP:  Type of service = 00
IP:        000. .... = routine
IP:        ...0 .... = normal delay
IP:        .... 0... = normal throughput
IP:        .... .0.. = normal reliability
IP:  Total length = 284 bytes
IP:  Identification = 2
IP:  Flags = 0X
IP:  .0.. .... = may fragment
IP:  ..0. .... = last fragment
IP:  Fragment offset = 0 bytes
IP:  Time to live = 63 seconds/hops
IP:  Protocol = 1 (ICMP)
IP:  Header checksum = 6C7D (correct)
IP:  Source address = [132.XXX.129.15]
IP:  Destination address = [132.XXX.132.12]
IP:  No options
ICMP:
ICMP:  [First 8 byte(s) of data of originating message]
ICMP:
ICMP:  [Normal end of ìICMP headerî.]
ICMP:

- - - - - - - - - - - - - - - - Frame 7 - - - - - - - - - - - - - - - - -

ICMP:  — ICMP header —
ICMP:
ICMP:  Type = 8 (Echo)
ICMP:  Code = 0
ICMP:  Checksum = 4070 (correct)
ICMP:  Identifier = 13905
ICMP:  Sequence number = 1
ICMP:  [256 bytes of data]
ICMP:
```

```
ICMP: [Normal end of "ICMP header".]
ICMP:

- - - - - - - - - - - - - - - - Frame 8 - - - - - - - - - - - - - - - - -

ICMP: —— ICMP header ——
ICMP:
ICMP: Type = 0 (Echo reply)
ICMP: Code = 0
ICMP: Checksum = 4870 (correct)
ICMP: Identifier = 13905
ICMP: Sequence number = 1
ICMP: [256 bytes of data]
ICMP:
ICMP: [Normal end of "ICMP header".]
ICMP:
```

4.10.6 Using ICMP Echo Messages

ICMP messages can answer many questions about the health of the network. The ICMP Echo/Echo Reply messages, commonly known as the PING, are probably the most frequently used. You invoke PING from your host operating system to test the path to a particular host. If all is well, a message will return verifying the existence of the path to the host or network. One caution is in order, however: unpredictable results can occur if you PING an improper destination address. For example, PINGing address [255.255.255.255] (limited broadcast within this subnet) may cause excessive internetwork traffic. Let's look at an example.

One lonely weekend, a network administrator decides to test the paths to some of the hosts on his internet. He has two ways to accomplish this. He could send an ICMP Echo message to each host separately, or he could send a directed broadcast to all hosts on his network and subnetwork. He decides to enter the Destination address [129.99.23.255] that PINGs all of the hosts on Class B network 129.99, subnet 23. Trace 4.10.6a shows the result. Frame 683 is the ICMP Echo (PING); the network administrator receives 27 frames containing ICMP Echo Reply messages. Note that all of the reply messages are directed to the originator of the ICMP Echo message, workstation 020C5D. Also note that the Bay Networks routers on this network did not respond to the PING because their design protects against such a transmission. Other hosts or routers may be designed with such a safeguard in place as well.

Details of the ICMP Echo (Frame 683) and the first ICMP Echo Reply (Frame 684) are given in Trace 4.10.6b. The Echo's Destination address is set for broadcast, and it indicates that the Echo Replies come back to the originating station. As the trace shows, the message originator [129.99.23.146] has specified that all hosts on subnet 23 should respond by setting the Destination address to [129.99.23.255]. The first response (Frame 684) is from device [129.99.23.17], followed by responses from 26 other hosts (Frames 685 through 712). Also note that the ICMP header contains an Identifier (18501) that correlates Echo and Echo Reply messages in case PINGs to/from different hosts occur simultaneously. The 56 octets of data transmitted with the Echo message are returned with the Echo Reply.

We can draw one clear conclusion from this exercise: The ICMP Echo message can be a very valuable troubleshooting tool, but make sure of your destination before you initiate the command. A PING to a broadcast address could have a great impact on the internetwork traffic.

TRACE 4.10.6A. ICMP ECHO TO IP ADDRESS [X.X.X.255] SUMMARY

Sniffer Network Analyzer data 17-Feb at 15:31:08, PINGTST4.ENC, Pg 1

SUMMARY	Delta T	Destination	Source	Summary
683		Broadcast	SilGrf 020C5D	ICMP Echo
684	0.0004	SilGrf020C5D	SilGrf 060C44	ICMP Echo reply
685	0.0004	SilGrf020C5D	SilGrf 020FF9	ICMP Echo reply
686	0.0003	SilGrf020C5D	Sun 106604	ICMP Echo reply
687	0.0003	SilGrf020C5D	Sun 0F5DC2	ICMP Echo reply
688	0.0002	SilGrf020C5D	Sun 08FE6B	ICMP Echo reply
689	0.0003	SilGrf020C5D	SilGrf 021193	ICMP Echo reply
690	0.0001	SilGrf020C5D	SilGrf 02137B	ICMP Echo reply
691	0.0004	SilGrf020C5D	Sun 094668	ICMP Echo reply
692	0.0003	SilGrf020C5D	Prteon1064D6	ICMP Echo reply
693	0.0002	SilGrf020C5D	Sun 062A16	ICMP Echo reply
694	0.0002	SilGrf020C5D	Sun 00DAFF	ICMP Echo reply
695	0.0002	SilGrf020C5D	CMC A00666	ICMP Echo reply
696	0.0002	SilGrf020C5D	Sun 00E849	ICMP Echo reply
697	0.0003	SilGrf020C5D	Sun 005513	ICMP Echo reply
698	0.0001	SilGrf020C5D	NSC 010212	ICMP Echo reply
699	0.0002	SilGrf020C5D	00802D0020F8	ICMP Echo reply
700	0.0001	SilGrf020C5D	Excelnt+231835	ICMP Echo reply
701	0.0002	SilGrf020C5D	00802D002202	ICMP Echo reply
702	0.0001	SilGrf020C5D	DEC++0A136F	ICMP Echo reply
703	0.0001	SilGrf020C5D	DECnet00F760	ICMP Echo reply
704	0.0001	SilGrf020C5D	Sun++0045AD	ICMP Echo reply
705	0.0001	SilGrf020C5D	Intel++0361A8	ICMP Echo reply
706	0.0001	SilGrf020C5D	Sun++0A73A2	ICMP Echo reply
707	0.0001	SilGrf020C5D	DEC++0D0B05	ICMP Echo reply
708	0.0001	SilGrf020C5D	Sun++00F725	ICMP Echo reply
709	0.0001	SilGrf020C5D	SilGrf++020C38	ICMP Echo reply
712	0.0211	SilGrf020C5D	Intrlnt+008248	ICMP Echo reply

TRACE 4.10.6B. ICMP ECHO TO IP ADDRESS [X.X.X.255] DETAILS

```
Sniffer Network Analyzer data 17-Feb at 15:31:08, PINGTST4.ENC, Pg 1

- - - - - - - - - - - - - - - - Frame 683 - - - - - - - - - - - - - - - - -

DLC:  —— DLC Header ——
DLC:
DLC:  Frame 683 arrived at  15:31:50.3581; frame size is 102 (0066 hex) bytes.
DLC:  Destination = BROADCAST FFFFFFFFFFFF, Broadcast
DLC:  Source      = Station SilGrf020C5D
DLC:  Ethertype   = 0800 (IP)
DLC:
IP:  —— IP Header ——
IP:
IP:   Version = 4, header length = 20 bytes
IP:   Type of service = 00
IP:         000. .... = routine
IP:         ...0 .... = normal delay
IP:         .... 0... = normal throughput
IP:         .... .0.. = normal reliability
IP:   Total length = 84 bytes
IP:   Identification = 16898
IP:   Flags = 0X
IP:   .0.. .... = may fragment
IP:   ..0. .... = last fragment
IP:   Fragment offset = 0 bytes
IP:   Time to live = 255 seconds/hops
IP:   Protocol = 1 (ICMP)
IP:   Header checksum = 474F (correct)
IP:   Source address = [129.99.23.146]
IP:   Destination address = [129.99.23.255]
IP:   No options
IP:
ICMP:  —— ICMP header ——
ICMP:
ICMP:  Type = 8 (Echo)
ICMP:  Code = 0
ICMP:  Checksum = 851E (correct)
ICMP:  Identifier = 18501
ICMP:  Sequence number = 0
ICMP:  [56 bytes of data]
ICMP:
ICMP:  [Normal end of "ICMP header".]
ICMP:
```

```
---------------- Frame 684 -----------------

DLC:  —— DLC Header ——
DLC:
DLC:  Frame 684 arrived at  15:31:50.3585; frame size is 98 (0062 hex) bytes.
DLC:  Destination = Station SilGrf020C5D
DLC:  Source      = Station SilGrf060C44
DLC:  Ethertype  = 0800 (IP)
DLC:
IP:  —— IP Header ——
IP:
IP:  Version = 4, header length = 20 bytes
IP:  Type of service = 00
IP:        000. .... = routine
IP:        ...0 .... = normal delay
IP:        .... 0... = normal throughput
IP:        .... .0.. = normal reliability
IP:  Total length = 84 bytes
IP:  Identification = 985
IP:  Flags = 0X
IP:  .0.. .... = may fragment
IP:  ..0. .... = last fragment
IP:  Fragment offset = 0 bytes
IP:  Time to live = 255 seconds/hops
IP:  Protocol = 1 (ICMP)
IP:  Header checksum = 8666 (correct)
IP:  Source address = [129.99.23.17]
IP:  Destination address = [129.99.23.146]
IP:  No options
IP:
ICMP:  —— ICMP header ——
ICMP:
ICMP:  Type = 0 (Echo reply)
ICMP:  Code = 0
ICMP:  Checksum = 8D1E (correct)
ICMP:  Identifier = 18501
ICMP:  Sequence number = 0
ICMP:  [56 bytes of data]
ICMP:
ICMP:  [Normal end of "ICMP header".]
ICMP:
```

4.10.7 Misdirected Datagrams

In Section 4.5, we studied the operation of the Internet Control Message Protocol (ICMP) and saw how the ICMP Redirect message (ICMP Type = 5) corrects routing problems. A unique code within the ICMP message specifies the datagrams to be redirected (review Figure 4-11).

In this example, a workstation wishes to communicate with a remote host on another subnetwork (see Figure 4-17). Unfortunately, the workstation's configuration file is incorrect, and its initial attempt to communicate with the remote host fails (see Trace 4.10.7a). From out of the internet comes an intelligent router to the rescue! Router 234 (the workstation's default router) recognizes the error and issues an ICMP Redirect in Frame 4. The workstation obliges, switches its transmissions to the correct path (Router 235) in Frame 5, and successfully establishes a TELNET session with the remote host (Frames 6 through 20). Let's look inside the ICMP messages and see what happened (Trace 4.10.7b).

The workstation's initial transmission (Frame 3) is directed to Router 234, with the datagram destined for the remote Host address [XXX.YYY.0.154]. We know that a router will be involved in the communication because the Source address (the workstation address) [XXX.YYY.0.152] and the Host address [XXX.YYY.0.154] are on different subnetworks. Router 234 responds to this initial transmission by issuing an ICMP Redirect in Frame 4. We can now identify the IP address of Router 234 (the Source address [XXX.YYY.0.234] of the ICMP Redirect). The ICMP header indicates a Redirect for the host (ICMP Code = 1) and the correct path, which is via Router 235, address [XXX.YYY.0.235].

The workstation sees the error of its ways and changes the Destination hardware address to be Router 235 (Frame 5). Note that the Source and Destination IP addresses did not change between Frame 3 and Frame 5. In other words, the workstation knew who it wanted to communicate with, it just didn't know how to get there. Frame 6 shows the confirmation of the redirected path; that datagram is a response from the remote host (IP Source address = [XXX.YYY.0.154]).

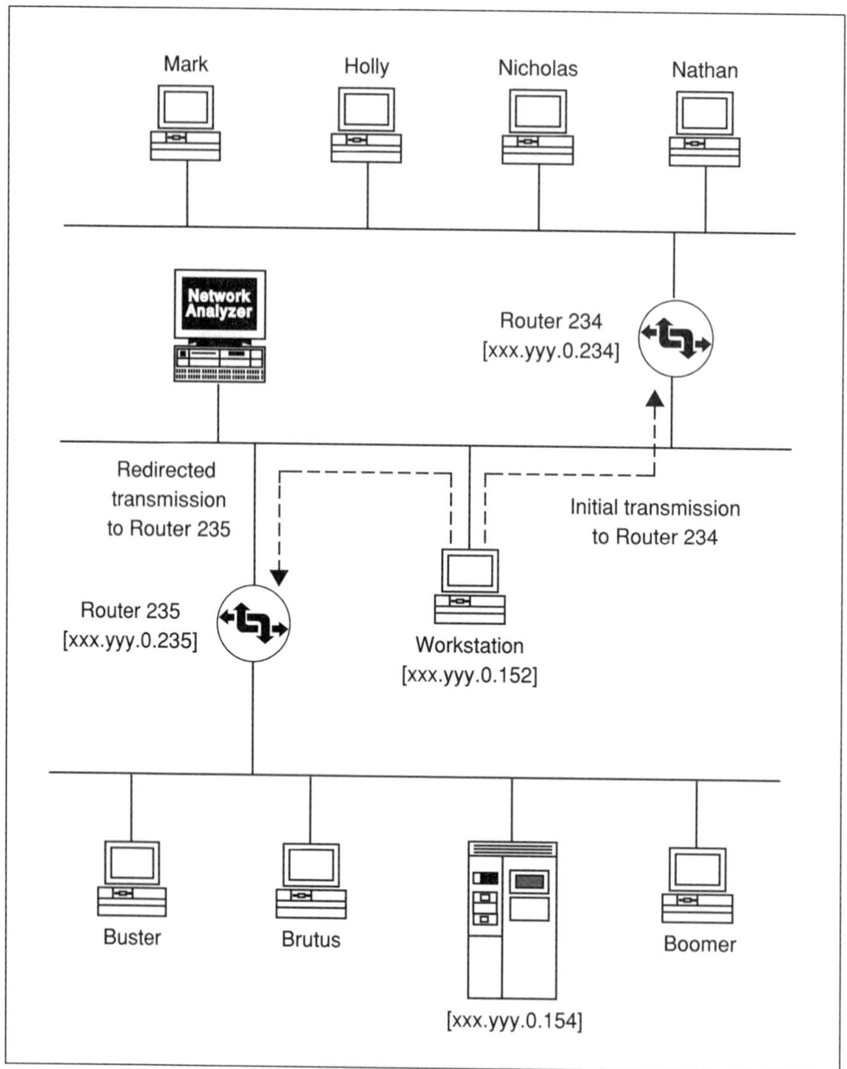

Figure 4-17 Misdirected Datagram Topology

Upon further study, the network manager discovered that the workstation's default gateway had been set incorrectly. When this parameter was changed to reflect Router 235 (instead of Router 234) the problem did not reoccur.

TRACE 4.10.7A. MISDIRECTED DATAGRAM SUMMARY

Sniffer Network Analyzer data 2-Mar at 10:17:44, RICMP.ENC, Pg 1

SUMMARY	Delta T	Destination	Source	Summary
3	0.0162	Router 234	Workstation	Telnet R PORT=2909 <0D><0A>
4	0.0029	Workstation	Router 234	ICMP Redirect (Redirect datagrams for the host)
5	0.0118	Router 235	Workstation	Telnet R PORT=2909 $
6	0.0941	Workstation	Router 235	TCP D=23 S=2909 ACK=813932917 WIN=4096
7	3.7848	Workstation	Router 235	Telnet C PORT=2909 p
8	0.0088	Router 235	Workstation	Telnet R PORT=2909 p
9	0.0065	Workstation	Router 235	TCP D=23 S=2909 ACK=813932918 WIN=4096
10	0.3042	Workstation	Router 235	Telnet C PORT=2909 s
11	0.0082	Router 235	Workstation	Telnet R PORT=2909 s
12	0.0881	Workstation	Router 235	TCP ACK=813932919 WIN=4096
13	0.0053	Workstation	Router 235	Telnet C PORT=2909
14	0.0080	Router 235	Workstation	Telnet R PORT=2909
15	0.1858	Workstation	Router 235	TCP D=23 S=2909 ACK=813932920 WIN=4096
16	0.5343	Workstation	Router 235	Telnet C PORT=2909 -
17	0.0078	Router 235	Workstation	Telnet R PORT=2909 -
18	0.0577	Workstation	Router 235	TCP D=23 S=2909 ACK=813932921 WIN=4096
19	0.1744	Workstation	Router 235	Telnet C PORT=2909 a
20	0.0078	Router 235	Workstation	Telnet R PORT=2909 a

TRACE 4.10.7B. MISDIRECTED DATAGRAM DETAILS

Sniffer Network Analyzer data 2-Mar at 10:17:44, RICMP.ENC, Pg 1

```
- - - - - - - - - - - - - - - - Frame 3 - - - - - - - - - - - - - - - - -

DLC:  —— DLC Header ——
DLC:
DLC:  Frame 3 arrived at  10:21:01.5697; frame size is 74 (004A hex) bytes.
DLC:  Destination = Station XXXXXX 002461, Router 234
DLC:  Source      = Station XXXXXX 01BB41, Workstation
DLC:  Ethertype   = 0800 (IP)
DLC:
IP:   —— IP Header ——
IP:
```

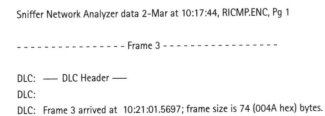

```
IP: Version = 4, header length = 20 bytes
IP: Type of service = 00
IP:     000. .... = routine
IP:     ...0 .... = normal delay
IP:     .... 0... = normal throughput
IP:     .... .0.. = normal reliability
IP: Total length = 42 bytes
IP: Identification = 2931
IP: Flags = 0X
IP: .0.. .... = may fragment
IP: ..0. .... = last fragment
IP: Fragment offset = 0 bytes
IP: Time to live = 30 seconds/hops
IP: Protocol = 6 (TCP)
IP: Header checksum = 31A8 (correct)
IP: Source address = [XXX.YYY.0.152]
IP: Destination address = [XXX.YYY.0.154]
IP: No options
IP:
TCP:  —— TCP header ——
TCP:
TCP:  Source port = 23 (Telnet)
TCP:  Destination port = 2909
TCP:  Sequence number = 813932913
TCP:  Acknowledgment number = 63520058
TCP:  Data offset = 20 bytes
TCP:  Flags = 18
TCP:  ..0. .... = (No urgent pointer)
TCP:  ...1 .... = Acknowledgment
TCP:  .... 1... = Push
TCP:  .... .0.. = (No reset)
TCP:  .... ..0. = (No SYN)
TCP:  .... ...0 = (No FIN)
TCP:  Window = 9116
TCP:  Checksum = 0105 (correct)
TCP:  No TCP options
TCP:  [2 byte(s) of data]
TCP:
Telnet:   —— Telnet data ——
Telnet:
Telnet:   <0D><0A>
Telnet:
```

```
---------------- Frame 4 -----------------

DLC:  —— DLC Header ——
DLC:
DLC:  Frame 4 arrived at  10:21:01.5726; frame size is 70 (0046 hex) bytes.
DLC:  Destination = Station XXXXXX 01BB41, Workstation
DLC:  Source      = Station XXXXXX 002461, Router 234
DLC:  Ethertype  = 0800 (IP)
DLC:
IP:  —— IP Header ——
IP:
IP:  Version = 4, header length = 20 bytes
IP:  Type of service = 00
IP:        000. .... = routine
IP:        ...0 .... = normal delay
IP:        .... 0... = normal throughput
IP:        .... .0.. = normal reliability
IP:   Total length = 56 bytes
IP:   Identification = 0
IP:   Flags = 0X
IP:   .0.. .... = may fragment
IP:   ..0. .... = last fragment
IP:   Fragment offset = 0 bytes
IP:   Time to live = 255 seconds/hops
IP:   Protocol = 1 (ICMP)
IP:   Header checksum = 5CA3 (correct)
IP:   Source address = [XXX.YYY.0.234]
IP:   Destination address = [XXX.YYY.0.152]
IP:   No options
IP:
ICMP:  —— ICMP header ——
ICMP:
ICMP:  Type = 5 (Redirect)
ICMP:  Code = 1 (Redirect datagrams for the host)
ICMP:  Checksum = EE0C (correct)
ICMP:  Gateway internet address = [XXX.YYY.0.235]
ICMP:  IP header of originating message (description follows)
ICMP:
IP:  —— IP Header ——
IP:
IP:  Version = 4, header length = 20 bytes
IP:  Type of service = 00
IP:        000. .... = routine
IP:        ...0 .... = normal delay
IP:        .... 0... = normal throughput
IP:        .... .0.. = normal reliability
```

```
IP:   Total length = 42 bytes
IP:   Identification = 2931
IP:   Flags = 0X
IP:   .0.. .... = may fragment
IP:   ..0. .... = last fragment
IP:  Fragment offset = 0 bytes
IP:  Time to live = 29 seconds/hops
IP:  Protocol = 6 (TCP)
IP:  Header checksum = 32A8 (correct)
IP:  Source address = [XXX.YYY.0.152]
IP:  Destination address = [XXX.YYY.0.154]
IP:  No options
ICMP:
ICMP:  [First 8 byte(s) of data of originating message]
ICMP:
ICMP:  [Normal end of "ICMP header".]
ICMP:

- - - - - - - - - - - - - - - - Frame 5 - - - - - - - - - - - - - - - - -

DLC:  —— DLC Header ——
DLC:
DLC:  Frame 5 arrived at  10:21:01.5845; frame size is 74 (004A hex) bytes.
DLC:  Destination = Station XXXXXX 00244F, Router 235
DLC:  Source      = Station XXXXXX 01BB41, Workstation
DLC:  Ethertype  = 0800 (IP)
DLC:
IP:  —— IP Header ——
IP:
IP:  Version = 4, header length = 20 bytes
IP:  Type of service = 00
IP:        000. .... = routine
IP:        ...0 .... = normal delay
IP:        .... 0... = normal throughput
IP:        .... .0.. = normal reliability
IP:   Total length = 42 bytes
IP:   Identification = 2932
IP:   Flags = 0X
IP:  .0.. .... = may fragment
IP:  ..0. .... = last fragment
IP:   Fragment offset = 0 bytes
IP:   Time to live = 30 seconds/hops
IP:   Protocol = 6 (TCP)
IP:   Header checksum = 31A7 (correct)
```

```
IP:  Source address = [XXX.YYY.0.152]
IP:  Destination address = [XXX.YYY.0.154]
IP:  No options
IP:
TCP:  —— TCP header ——
TCP:
TCP:  Source port = 23 (Telnet)
TCP:  Destination port = 2909
TCP:  Sequence number = 813932915
TCP:  Acknowledgment number = 63520058
TCP:  Data offset = 20 bytes
TCP:  Flags = 18
TCP:  ..0. .... = (No urgent pointer)
TCP:  ...1 .... = Acknowledgment
TCP:  .... 1... = Push
TCP:  .... .0.. = (No reset)
TCP:  .... ..0. = (No SYN)
TCP:  .... ...0 = (No FIN)
TCP:  Window = 9116
TCP:  Checksum = E9EC (correct)
TCP:  No TCP options
TCP:  [2 byte(s) of data]
TCP:
Telnet:  —— Telnet data ——
Telnet:
Telnet:  $
Telnet:

- - - - - - - - - - - - - - - - Frame 6 - - - - - - - - - - - - - - - - -

DLC:  ——DLC Header ——
DLC:
DLC:  Frame 6 arrived at  10:21:01.6787; frame size is 60 (003C hex) bytes.
DLC:  Destination = Station XXXXXX 01BB41, Workstation
DLC:  Source      = Station XXXXXX 00244F, Router 235
DLC:  Ethertype  = 0800 (IP)
DLC:
IP:                    —— IP Header ——
IP:
IP:  Version = 4, header length = 20 bytes
IP:                    Type of service = 00
IP:        000. .... = routine
IP:        ...0 .... = normal delay
IP:        .... 0... = normal throughput
```

```
IP:      .... .0.. = normal reliability
IP:   Total length = 40 bytes
IP:   Identification = 37695
IP:   Flags = 0X
IP:   .0.. .... = may fragment
IP:   ..0. .... = last fragment
IP:   Fragment offset = 0 bytes
IP:   Time to live = 58 seconds/hops
IP:   Protocol = 6 (TCP)
IP:   Header checksum = 8DDD (correct)
IP:   Source address = [XXX.YYY.0.154]
IP:   Destination address = [XXX.YYY.0.152]
IP:   No options
IP:
TCP:  — TCP header —
TCP:
TCP:  Source port = 2909
TCP:  Destination port = 23 (Telnet)
TCP:  Sequence number = 63520058
TCP:  Acknowledgment number = 813932917
TCP:  Data offset = 20 bytes
TCP:  Flags = 10
TCP:  ..0. .... = (No urgent pointer)
TCP:  ...1 .... = Acknowledgment
TCP:  .... 0... = (No push)
TCP:  .... .0.. = (No reset)
TCP:  .... ..0. = (No SYN)
TCP:  .... ...0 = (No FIN)
TCP:  Window = 4096
TCP:  Checksum = 21B1 (correct)
TCP:  No TCP options
TCP:
```

4.10.8 Confused Routers

For our next example, we'll consider a case of false advertising by a router (see Figure 4-18). This internetwork consists of a number of Ethernet segments and one Apollo token ring connected by routers. Workstations wishing to communicate with other hosts are getting confused because two routers want their datagrams. As a result, the two routers become locked in a battle, with the workstation coming out the loser. Let's see what happened.

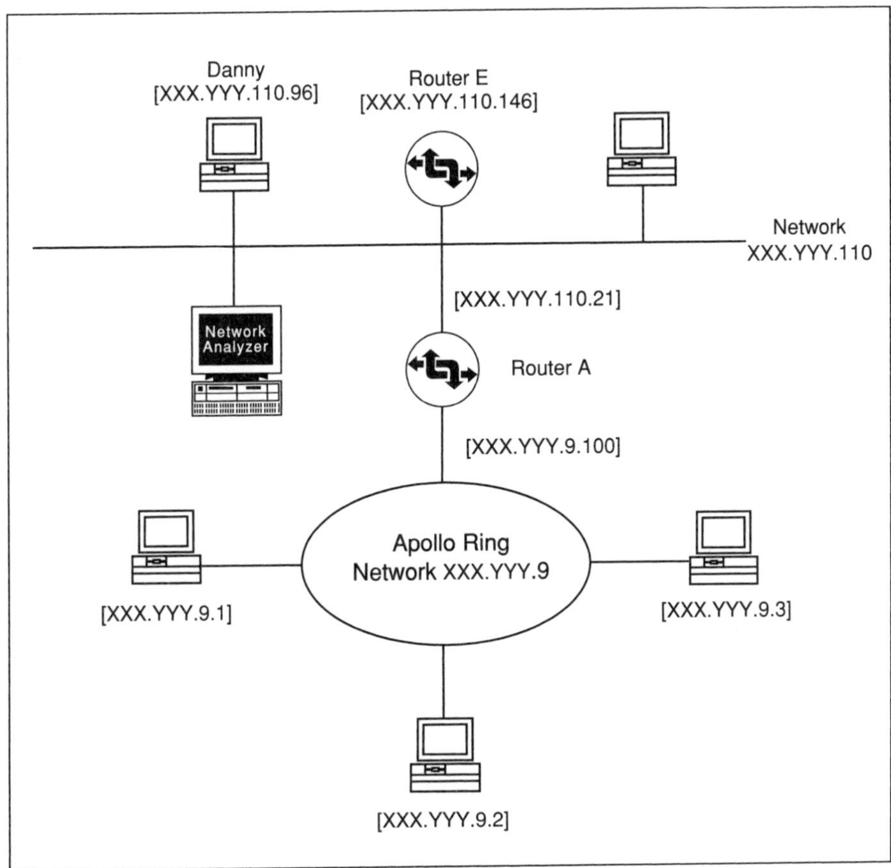

Figure 4-18 Confused Router Topology

In this scenario, a router (designated Router A in Figure 4-18) connects an Ethernet segment and an Apollo token ring. (The Apollo token ring is a proprietary network designed by Apollo Computer, now part of Hewlett-Packard, to connect Apollo workstations.) Confusion occurs between Router A and Router E, which is also connected to the Ethernet segment.

The network manager, Danny, address [XXX.YYY.110.96], has a workstation on the Ethernet segment and wishes to communicate with Router E, address [XXX.YYY.110.146], shown in Trace 4.10.8a. Danny sends an ARP message in Frame 13, and Router E responds in Frame 14 with its Hardware address, 0000A200226CH. Next, Danny initiates a TCP connection in Frame 15 via Router E, asking for a host on an Ethernet 3 hops away. Instead of the expected TCP handshake, Router E tells Danny to redirect his datagrams to Router A (Frame 16), and then passes Danny's TCP connect request to Router A (Frame 17).

Unfortunately, Router A does not agree, and tells Danny to redirect his datagrams back to Router E (Frame 18). Router A then passes the same TCP connect request back to Router E (Frame 19). Router E now disagrees and sends a redirect to Router A, along with the same TCP connect request (Frames 20 and 21). Note the identical Sequence Number in Frames 15, 17, 19, and 21: SEQ = 170068605. The routers are passing the same TCP message back and forth because neither knows what to do with it. The scenario repeats for some time (Frames 22 through 35). Danny's TCP connect request is stuck in a routing loop.

An examination of the RIP broadcasts from both Router A and Router E yields a clue to the problem. Router E's RIPs (Trace 4.10.8b) include 17 routing messages. Danny scrutinized all of the network addresses, along with the number of router hops (the metric) required to reach those other networks. All of the information looked correct except for the Routing data in Frame 16. The IP address of [P.P.9.0] (the Apollo token ring network) showed a metric of 16, or unreachable. This metric was clearly incorrect, since the Apollo network was only one hop away – via Router A. The desired network, however, did not appear in Router E's broadcast.

A similar analysis was then made of Router A's RIP broadcasts (Trace 4.10.8c). A total of 17 Routing data frames were included in the broadcast. Routing data Frame 17 correctly identified the Ethernet segment [Q.Q.110.0] as being one hop away. Unfortunately, a number of other networks that could not be reached via Router A were being advertised as reachable. In addition, the target network was not listed in this RIP message either.

The network manager concluded that both Router A and Router E had corrupted routing tables. To correct the problem, he took both routers out of service, reconfigured them, and brought them back up. No further problems were noted – the RIP routing loop had been corrected.

TRACE 4.10.8A. ROUTING LOOP SUMMARY

Sniffer Network Analyzer data 15-May at 14:31:02, ATEST.ENC, Pg 1

SUMMARY	Delta T	Destination	Source	Summary
13	1.1843	Broadcast	Danny	ARP C PA=[XXX.YYY.110.146] PRO=IP
14	0.0009	Danny	Router E	ARP R PA=[XXX.YYY.110.146] HA=0000A200226C PRO=IP
15	0.0019	Router E	Danny	TCP D=23 S=14663 SYN SEQ=170068605 LEN=0 WIN=1024
16	0.0008	Danny	Router E	ICMP Redirect (Redirect datagrams for the host)
17	0.0002	Router A	Router E	TCP D=23 S=14663 SYN SEQ=170068605 LEN=0 WIN=1024

18	0.0120	Danny	Router A	ICMP Redirect (Redirect for the network)
19	0.0033	Router E	Router A	TCP D=23 S=14663 SYN SEQ=170068605 LEN=0 WIN=1024
20	0.0008	Router A	Router E	ICMP Redirect (Redirect datagrams for the host)
21	0.0001	Router A	Router E	TCP D=23 S=14663 SYN SEQ=170068605 LEN=0 WIN=1024
22	0.0098	Router E	Router A	ICMP Redirect (Redirect datagrams for the network)
23	0.0024	Danny	Router A	ICMP Redirect (Redirect datagrams for the host)
24	0.0098	Danny	Router A	ICMP Redirect (Redirect datagrams for the network)
25	0.0028	Router E	Router A	TCP D=23 S=14663 SYN SEQ=170068605 LEN=0 WIN=1024
26	0.0015	Router A	Router E	ICMP Redirect (Redirect datagrams for the host)
27	0.0001	Router A	Router E	TCP D=23 S=14663 SYN SEQ=170068605 LEN=0 WIN=1024
28	0.0108	Router E	Router A	ICMP Redirect (Redirect datagrams for the network)
29	0.0037	Danny	Router A	ICMP Redirect (Redirect datagrams for the host)
30	0.0084	Danny	Router A	ICMP Redirect (Redirect datagrams for the network)
31	0.0032	Router E	Router A	TCP D=23 S=14663 SYN SEQ=170068605 LEN=0 WIN=1024
32	0.0008	Router A	Router E	ICMP Redirect (Redirect datagrams for the host)
33	0.0001	Router A	Router E	TCP D=23 S=14663 SYN SEQ=170068605 LEN=0 WIN=1024
34	0.0089	Router E	Router A	ICMP Redirect (Redirect datagrams for the network)
35	0.0049	Danny	Router A	ICMP Redirect (Redirect datagrams for the host)

TRACE 4.10.8B. ROUTER E RIP BROADCAST MESSAGE

```
Sniffer Network Analyzer data 15-May at 14:31:02, ERIP.ENC, Pg 1

- - - - - - - - - - - - - - - - Frame 1 - - - - - - - - - - - - - - - - -

DLC:  —— DLC Header ——
DLC:
DLC:  Frame 1 arrived at 14:31:17.3235; frame size is 386 (0182 hex) bytes.
DLC:  Destination = BROADCAST FFFFFFFFFFFF, Broadcast
DLC:  Source      = Station 0000A200226C, Router E
DLC:  Ethertype   = 0800 (IP)
DLC:
IP:   —— IP Header ——
IP:
IP:   Version = 4, header length = 20 bytes
IP:   Type of service = 00
IP:         000. .... = routine
IP:         ...0 .... = normal delay
IP:         .... 0... = normal throughput
IP:         .... .0.. = normal reliability
IP:   Total length = 372 bytes
IP:   Identification = 35481
IP:   Flags = 0X
IP:   .0.. .... = may fragment
IP:   ..0. .... = last fragment
IP:   Fragment offset = 0 bytes
IP:   Time to live = 30 seconds/hops
IP:   Protocol = 17 (UDP)
IP:   Header checksum = B3E4 (correct)
IP:   Source address = [XXX.YYY.110.146]
IP:   Destination address = [XXX.YYY.110.0]
IP:   No options
IP:
UDP:  —— UDP Header ——
UDP:
UDP:  Source port = 520 (Route)
UDP:  Destination port = 520
UDP:  Length = 352
UDP:  Checksum = 157F (correct)
UDP:
RIP:  —— RIP Header ——
RIP:
RIP:  Command = 2 (Response)
RIP:  Version = 1
```

```
RIP:  Unused  = 0
RIP:
RIP:  Routing data frame 1
RIP:    Address family identifier = 2 (IP)
RIP:    IP Address = [A.A.0.0]
RIP:    Metric     = 2
RIP:
RIP:  Routing data frame 2
RIP:    Address family identifier = 2 (IP)
RIP:    IP Address = [B.B.0.0]
RIP:    Metric     = 3
RIP:
RIP:  Routing data frame 3
RIP:    Address family identifier = 2 (IP)
RIP:    IP Address = [C.C.0.0]
RIP:    Metric     = 2
RIP:
RIP:  Routing data frame 4
RIP:    Address family identifier = 2 (IP)
RIP:    IP Address = [D.D.0.0]
RIP:    Metric     = 2
RIP:
RIP:  Routing data frame 5
RIP:    Address family identifier = 2 (IP)
RIP:    IP Address = [E.E.0.0]
RIP:    Metric     = 1
RIP:
RIP:  Routing data frame 6
RIP:    Address family identifier = 2 (IP)
RIP:    IP Address = [F.F.0.0]
RIP:    Metric     = 2
RIP:
RIP:  Routing data frame 7
RIP:    Address family identifier = 2 (IP)
RIP:    IP Address = [G.G.0.0]
RIP:    Metric     = 2
RIP:
RIP:  Routing data frame 8
RIP:    Address family identifier = 2 (IP)
RIP:    IP Address = [H.H.0.0]
RIP:    Metric     = 2
RIP:
RIP:  Routing data frame 9
RIP:    Address family identifier = 2 (IP)
```

```
RIP:     IP Address = [I.I.0.0]
RIP:     Metric     = 2
RIP:
RIP:   Routing data frame 10
RIP:     Address family identifier = 2 (IP)
RIP:     IP Address = [J.J.0.0]
RIP:     Metric     = 4
RIP:
RIP:   Routing data frame 11
RIP:     Address family identifier = 2 (IP)
RIP:     IP Address = [K.K.0.0]
RIP:     Metric     = 3
RIP:
RIP:   Routing data frame 12
RIP:     Address family identifier = 2 (IP)
RIP:     IP Address = [L.L.0.0]
RIP:     Metric     = 3
RIP:
RIP:   Routing data frame 13
RIP:     Address family identifier = 2 (IP)
RIP:     IP Address = [M.M.0.0]
RIP:     Metric     = 1
RIP:
RIP:   Routing data frame 14
RIP:     Address family identifier = 2 (IP)
RIP:     IP Address = [N.N.0.0]
RIP:     Metric     = 3
RIP:
RIP:   Routing data frame 15
RIP:     Address family identifier = 2 (IP)
RIP:     IP Address = [O.O.0.0]
RIP:     Metric     = 3
RIP:
RIP:   Routing data frame 16
RIP:     Address family identifier = 2 (IP)
RIP:     IP Address = [P.P.9.0]
RIP:     Metric     = 16 (Unreachable)
RIP:
RIP:   Routing data frame 17
RIP:     Address family identifier = 2 (IP)
RIP:     IP Address = [Q.Q.0.0]
RIP:     Metric     = 3
RIP:
```

TRACE 4.10.8C. ROUTER A RIP BROADCAST MESSAGE

```
Sniffer Network Analyzer data 15-May at 14:22:04, ARIP.ENC, Pg 1

- - - - - - - - - - - - - - - - Frame 1 - - - - - - - - - - - - - - - - -

DLC:  —— DLC Header ——
DLC:
DLC:  Frame 1 arrived at 14:22:30.9929; frame size is 386 (0182 hex) bytes.
DLC:  Destination = BROADCAST FFFFFFFFFFFF, Broadcast
DLC:  Source      = Station 0207010024FB, Router A
DLC:  Ethertype  = 0800 (IP)
DLC:
IP:   —— IP Header ——
IP:
IP:   Version = 4, header length = 20 bytes
IP:   Type of service = 08
IP:         000. .... = routine
IP:         ...0 .... = normal delay
IP:         .... 1... = high throughput
IP:         .... .0.. = normal reliability
IP:   Total length = 372 bytes
IP:   Identification = 47689
IP:   Flags = 0X
IP:   .0.. .... = may fragment
IP:   ..0. .... = last fragment
IP:   Fragment offset = 0 bytes
IP:   Time to live = 10 seconds/hops
IP:   Protocol = 17 (UDP)
IP:   Header checksum = 98A9 (correct)
IP:   Source address = [XXX.YYY.110.21]
IP:   Destination address = [XXX.YYY.110.0]
IP:   No options
IP:
UDP:  —— UDP Header ——
UDP:
UDP:  Source port = 520 (Route)
UDP:  Destination port = 520
UDP:  Length = 352
UDP:  Checksum = 14FC (correct)
UDP:
RIP:  —— RIP Header ——
RIP:
RIP:  Command = 2 (Response)
RIP:  Version = 1
```

```
RIP:  Unused  = 0
RIP:
RIP:  Routing data frame 1
RIP:    Address family identifier = 2 (IP)
RIP:    IP Address = [A.A.111.0]
RIP:    Metric    = 4
RIP:
RIP:  Routing data frame 2
RIP:    Address family identifier = 2 (IP)
RIP:    IP Address = [B.B.112.0]
RIP:    Metric    = 4
RIP:
RIP:  Routing data frame 3
RIP:    Address family identifier = 2 (IP)
RIP:    IP Address = [C.C.0.0]
RIP:    Metric    = 3
RIP:
RIP:  Routing data frame 4
RIP:    Address family identifier = 2 (IP)
RIP:    IP Address = [D.D.113.0]
RIP:    Metric    = 4
RIP:
RIP:  Routing data frame 5
RIP:    Address family identifier = 2 (IP)
RIP:    IP Address = [E.E.9.0]
RIP:    Metric    = 1
RIP:
RIP:  Routing data frame 6
RIP:    Address family identifier = 2 (IP)
RIP:    IP Address = [F.F.0.0]
RIP:    Metric    = 2
RIP:
RIP:  Routing data frame 7
RIP:    Address family identifier = 2 (IP)
RIP:    IP Address = [G.G.90.0]
RIP:    Metric    = 4
RIP:
RIP:  Routing data frame 8
RIP:    Address family identifier = 2 (IP)
RIP:    IP Address = [H.H.0.0]
RIP:    Metric    = 3
RIP:
RIP:  Routing data frame 9
RIP:    Address family identifier = 2 (IP)
```

```
RIP:     IP Address = [I.I.0.0]
RIP:     Metric     = 5
RIP:
RIP:   Routing data frame 10
RIP:     Address family identifier = 2 (IP)
RIP:     IP Address = [J.J.0.0]
RIP:     Metric     = 4
RIP:
RIP:   Routing data frame 11
RIP:     Address family identifier = 2 (IP)
RIP:     IP Address = [K.K.0.0]
RIP:     Metric     = 3
RIP:
RIP:   Routing data frame 12
RIP:     Address family identifier = 2 (IP)
RIP:     IP Address = [L.L.0.0]
RIP:     Metric     = 3
RIP:
RIP:   Routing data frame 13
RIP:     Address family identifier = 2 (IP)
RIP:     IP Address = [M.M.0.0]
RIP:     Metric     = 3
RIP:
RIP:   Routing data frame 14
RIP:     Address family identifier = 2 (IP)
RIP:     IP Address = [N.N.0.0]
RIP:     Metric     = 3
RIP:
RIP:   Routing data frame 15
RIP:     Address family identifier = 2 (IP)
RIP:     IP Address = [O.O.0.0]
RIP:     Metric     = 3
RIP:
RIP:   Routing data frame 16
RIP:     Address family identifier = 2 (IP)
RIP:     IP Address = [P.P.0.0]
RIP:     Metric     = 4
RIP:
RIP:   Routing data frame 17
RIP:     Address family identifier = 2 (IP)
RIP:     IP Address = [Q.Q.110.0]
RIP:     Metric     = 1
RIP:
```

4.10.9 Using OSPF and BGP

In our final case study, we will look at how OSPF and BGP are used within an internetwork to communicate reachability information between the various routers. The internetwork in question is based on an Ethernet backbone [140.XXX.6.Y], with three routers extending from that backbone that connect to various Ethernet and WAN segments (see Figure 4-19). Three routers participate in this communication: the Broadway Lab router [140.XXX.6.253], which runs BGP and OSPF; the Aeronautics Lab router [140.XXX.6.248], which runs OSPF; and the Science Lab router [140.XXX.6.250], which runs BGP. For the purposes of BGP communication, the Broadway Lab router connects to UUnet (autonomous system number 701), and the Science Lab connects to the Science Network (autonomous system number 297), plus other autonomous systems beyond the Science Network (which are not illustrated in Figure 4-19).

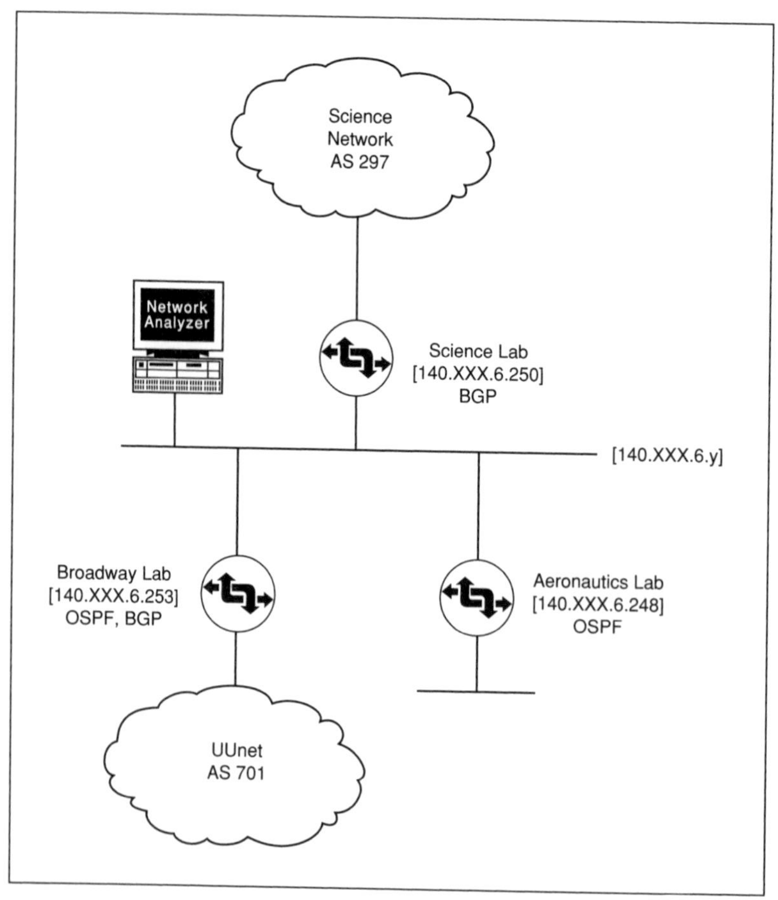

Figure 4-19 Router Communication Using OSPF and BGP

A summary of the router communication, filtered to only show the BGP and OSPF traffic, is shown in Trace 4.10.9a. Note that four frames carry OSPF information, and one frame carries BGP information. The Destination address for the OSPF messages uses the All Routers multicast address: [224.0.0.5]. The Destination address for the BGP messages uses the BGP peer of interest.

TRACE 4.10.9A. OSPF AND BGP MESSAGE SUMMARY

Sniffer Network Analyzer data from 23-Apr at 10:23:56, file NIS5.ENC, Pg 1

SUMMARY	Delta T	Destination	Source	Summary
2693	0.8539	[224.0.0.5]	Broadway	OSPF Link State Update ID=[140.XXX.1.1]
3652	1.6463	[224.0.0.5]	Aeronautics	OSPF Link State Acknowledgment ID=[140.XXX.241.100]
3862	0.4159	[224.0.0.5]	Aeronautics	OSPF Hello ID=[140.XXX.241.100]
4608	2.1827	[224.0.0.5]	Broadway	OSPF Hello ID=[140.XXX.1.1]
5841	3.2997		Broadway	Science BGP Update

The details of an OSPF Link State Update message from Frame 2693 are shown in Trace 4.10.9b. Note that the Destination address at the Data Link layer is also a multicast address (01005E000005), which is then converted into the multicast IP address of [224.0.0.5], according to the procedure outlined in RFC 1112, section 6.4. The Ethertype specifies IP as the next highest layer, and the IP header follows. Within the IP header, note that the next highest protocol specified is OSPF (Protocol = 89), the Source IP address is the address of the Broadway router [140.XXX.6.253], and the Destination IP address is the multicast address discussed above [224.0.0.5].

The first portion of the OSPF message is the OSPF header that indicates a Link State Update message (review Figure 4-8a). The Link State Update header follows next, beginning with the Number of Advertisements field (review Figure 4-8e). The Link State Advertisement Header follows next, beginning with the Link State Age field (review Figure 4-8f). This particular advertisement is an AS External Link Advertisement (Link State = 5, as shown in Figure 4-8j), which advertises destinations that are external to that autonomous system. Finally, there are seven link state advertisements, each noting a different destination network's IP address:

Link State Advertisement	Link State ID
1	[140.XXX.172.0]
2	[140.XXX.173.0]
3	[140.XXX.174.0]

Continued

Continued

4	[140.XXX.187.0]
5	[140.XXX.253.0]
6	[140.XXX.254.0]
7	[140.XXX.148.0]

TRACE 4.10.9B. OSPF LINK STATE UPDATE MESSAGE DETAILS

```
Sniffer Network Analyzer data from 23-Apr at 10:23:56, file NIS5.ENC, Pg 1

- - - - - - - - - - - - - - - - Frame 2693 - - - - - - - - - - - - - - - - -

DLC:  —— DLC Header ——
DLC:
DLC:  Frame 2693 arrived at  10:24:00.9119; frame size is 314 (013A hex) bytes.
DLC:  Destination = Multicast 01005E000005
DLC:  Source      = Station 00E0F92F20A0
DLC:  Ethertype   = 0800 (IP)
DLC:
IP:  —— IP Header ——
IP:
IP:  Version = 4, header length = 20 bytes
IP:  Type of service = C0
IP:        110. .... = internetwork control
IP:        ...0 .... = normal delay
IP:        .... 0... = normal throughput
IP:        .... .0.. = normal reliability
IP:  Total length    = 300 bytes
IP:  Identification  = 12462
IP:  Flags           = 0X
IP:        .0.. .... = may fragment
IP:        ..0. .... = last fragment
IP:  Fragment offset = 0 bytes
IP:  Time to live    = 1 seconds/hops
IP:  Protocol        = 89 (OSPFIGP)
IP:  Header checksum = 135D (correct)
IP:  Source address      = [140.XXX.6.253], Broadway
IP:  Destination address = [224.0.0.5]
IP:  No options
IP:
OSPF: —— OSPF Header ——
```

```
OSPF:
OSPF: Version = 2,  Type = 4 (Link State Update),  Length = 280
OSPF: Router ID      = [140.XXX.1.1]
OSPF: Area ID        = [0.0.0.0]
OSPF: Header checksum = 1D65 (correct)
OSPF: Authentication: Type = 0 (No Authentication),  Value = 00 00 00 00 00 00 00 00
OSPF:
OSPF: Number of Advertisements = 7
OSPF: Link State Advertisement # 1
OSPF: Link state age        = 4 (seconds)
OSPF: Optional capabilities = 00
OSPF:          .0.. .... = Opaque-LSAs not forwarded
OSPF:          ..0. .... = Demand Circuit bit
OSPF:          ...0 .... = External Attributes bit
OSPF:          .... 0... = no NSSA capability
OSPF:          .... .0.. = no multicast capability
OSPF:          .... ..0. = no external routing capability
OSPF:          .... ...0 = no Type of Service routing capability
OSPF: Link state type       = 5 (AS external link)
OSPF: Link state ID         = [140.XXX.172.0]
OSPF: Advertising Router    = [140.XXX.172.254]
OSPF: Sequence number       = 2147484307,  Checksum = 3FB3
OSPF: Length                = 36
OSPF: Network mask          = [255.255.255.0]
OSPF: Type of service       = 80
OSPF:         1... .... = Type 2 external metric
OSPF:          .... .000 = routine
OSPF: Metric                = 130
OSPF: Forwarding Address = [0.0.0.0]
OSPF: External Route Tag = 0x00000000
OSPF:    Local Info       = 0x00000000
OSPF:
OSPF: Link State Advertisement # 2
OSPF: Link state age        = 4 (seconds)
OSPF: Optional capabilities = 00
OSPF:          .0.. .... = Opaque-LSAs not forwarded
OSPF:          ..0. .... = Demand Circuit bit
OSPF:          ...0 .... = External Attributes bit
OSPF:          .... 0... = no NSSA capability
OSPF:          .... .0.. = no multicast capability
OSPF:          .... ..0. = no external routing capability
OSPF:          .... ...0 = no Type of Service routing capability
OSPF: Link state type       = 5 (AS external link)
OSPF: Link state ID         = [140.XXX.173.0]
```

```
OSPF: Advertising Router   = [140.XXX.172.254]
OSPF: Sequence number      = 2147484307,  Checksum = 34BD
OSPF: Length               = 36
OSPF: Network mask         = [255.255.255.0]
OSPF: Type of service      = 80
OSPF:         1... .... = Type 2 external metric
OSPF:         .... .000 = routine
OSPF: Metric               = 130
OSPF: Forwarding Address = [0.0.0.0]
OSPF: External Route Tag = 0x00000000
OSPF:    Local Info        = 0x00000000
OSPF:
OSPF: Link State Advertisement # 3
OSPF: Link state age       = 4 (seconds)
OSPF: Optional capabilities = 00
OSPF:         .0.. .... = Opaque-LSAs not forwarded
OSPF:         ..0. .... = Demand Circuit bit
OSPF:         ...0 .... = External Attributes bit
OSPF:         .... 0... = no NSSA capability
OSPF:         .... .0.. = no multicast capability
OSPF:         .... ..0. = no external routing capability
OSPF:         .... ...0 = no Type of Service routing capability
OSPF: Link state type      = 5 (AS external link)
OSPF: Link state ID        = [140.XXX.174.0]
OSPF: Advertising Router   = [140.XXX.172.254]
OSPF: Sequence number      = 2147484307,  Checksum = 29C7
OSPF: Length               = 36
OSPF: Network mask         = [255.255.255.0]
OSPF: Type of service      = 80
OSPF:         1... .... = Type 2 external metric
OSPF:         .... .000 = routine
OSPF: Metric               = 130
OSPF: Forwarding Address = [0.0.0.0]
OSPF: External Route Tag = 0x00000000
OSPF:    Local Info        = 0x00000000
OSPF:
OSPF: Link State Advertisement # 4
OSPF: Link state age       = 4 (seconds)
OSPF: Optional capabilities = 00
OSPF:         .0.. .... = Opaque-LSAs not forwarded
OSPF:         ..0. .... = Demand Circuit bit
OSPF:         ...0 .... = External Attributes bit
OSPF:         .... 0... = no NSSA capability
OSPF:         .... .0.. = no multicast capability
```

```
OSPF:         .... ..0. = no external routing capability
OSPF:         .... ...0 = no Type of Service routing capability
OSPF: Link state type     = 5 (AS external link)
OSPF: Link state ID       = [140.XXX.187.0]
OSPF: Advertising Router  = [140.XXX.172.254]
OSPF: Sequence number     = 2147484307,  Checksum = 994A
OSPF: Length              = 36
OSPF: Network mask        = [255.255.255.0]
OSPF: Type of service     = 80
OSPF:         1... .... = Type 2 external metric
OSPF:         .... .000 = routine
OSPF: Metric              = 130
OSPF: Forwarding Address = [0.0.0.0]
OSPF: External Route Tag = 0x00000000
OSPF:   Local Info        = 0x00000000
OSPF:
OSPF: Link State Advertisement # 5
OSPF: Link state age      = 4 (seconds)
OSPF: Optional capabilities = 00
OSPF:         .0.. .... = Opaque-LSAs not forwarded
OSPF:         ..0. .... = Demand Circuit bit
OSPF:         ...0 .... = External Attributes bit
OSPF:         .... 0... = no NSSA capability
OSPF:         .... .0.. = no multicast capability
OSPF:         .... ..0. = no external routing capability
OSPF:         .... ...0 = no Type of Service routing capability
OSPF: Link state type     = 5 (AS external link)
OSPF: Link state ID       = [140.XXX.253.0]
OSPF: Advertising Router  = [140.XXX.172.254]
OSPF: Sequence number     = 2147484317,  Checksum = ACEA
OSPF: Length              = 36
OSPF: Network mask        = [255.255.255.0]
OSPF: Type of service     = 80
OSPF:         1... .... = Type 2 external metric
OSPF:         .... .000 = routine
OSPF: Metric              = 130
OSPF: Forwarding Address = [0.0.0.0]
OSPF: External Route Tag = 0x00000000
OSPF:   Local Info        = 0x00000000
OSPF:
OSPF: Link State Advertisement # 6
OSPF: Link state age      = 4 (seconds)
OSPF: Optional capabilities = 00
OSPF:         .0.. .... = Opaque-LSAs not forwarded
```

```
OSPF:           ..0. .... = Demand Circuit bit
OSPF:           ...0 .... = External Attributes bit
OSPF:           .... 0... = no NSSA capability
OSPF:           .... .0.. = no multicast capability
OSPF:           .... ..0. = no external routing capability
OSPF:           .... ...0 = no Type of Service routing capability
OSPF: Link state type      = 5 (AS external link)
OSPF: Link state ID        = [140.XXX.254.0]
OSPF: Advertising Router   = [140.XXX.172.254]
OSPF: Sequence number      = 2147484307,  Checksum = B5EA
OSPF: Length               = 36
OSPF: Network mask         = [255.255.255.0]
OSPF: Type of service      = 80
OSPF:        1... .... = Type 2 external metric
OSPF:        .... .000 = routine
OSPF: Metric               = 130
OSPF: Forwarding Address = [0.0.0.0]
OSPF: External Route Tag = 0x00000000
OSPF:   Local Info         = 0x00000000
OSPF:
OSPF: Link State Advertisement # 7
OSPF: Link state age       = 4 (seconds)
OSPF: Optional capabilities = 00
OSPF:           .0.. .... = Opaque-LSAs not forwarded
OSPF:           ..0. .... = Demand Circuit bit
OSPF:           ...0 .... = External Attributes bit
OSPF:           .... 0... = no NSSA capability
OSPF:           .... .0.. = no multicast capability
OSPF:           .... ..0. = no external routing capability
OSPF:           .... ...0 = no Type of Service routing capability
OSPF: Link state type      = 5 (AS external link)
OSPF: Link state ID        = [192.XXX.148.0]
OSPF: Advertising Router   = [140.XXX.172.254]
OSPF: Sequence number      = 2147484307,  Checksum = B637
OSPF: Length               = 36
OSPF: Network mask         = [255.255.255.0]
OSPF: Type of service      = 80
OSPF:        1... .... = Type 2 external metric
OSPF:        .... .000 = routine
OSPF: Metric               = 130
OSPF: Forwarding Address = [0.0.0.0]
OSPF: External Route Tag = 0x00000000
OSPF:   Local Info         = 0x00000000
OSPF:
```

The details of an OSPF Link State Acknowledgment message from Frame 3652 are shown in Trace 4.10.9c. This packet is multicast from a different router, the Aeronautical Lab router, and acknowledges some previously received Link State Acknowledgments. In Frame 3652, we see the OSPF header, which specifies the Link State Acknowledgment (Type = 5). A Link State Advertisement header (review Figure 4-8f) is next, followed by a Router Links Advertisement message, with Link State Type = 1 (review Figure 4-8g). A total of eight Link State Advertisements are included in this message. Advertisements 2–8 in this Link State Acknowledgment correspond with Advertisements 1–7 in Frame 2693, above.

Link State Advertisement	Link State Type	Link State ID
1	Router links	[140.XXX.172.254]
2	AS external links	[140.XXX.172.0]
3	AS external links	[140.XXX.173.0]
4	AS external links	[140.XXX.174.0]
5	AS external links	[140.XXX.187.0]
6	AS external links	[140.XXX.253.0]
7	AS external links	[140.XXX.254.0]
8	AS external links	[140.XXX.148.0]

TRACE 4.10.9C. OSPF LINK STATE ACKNOWLEDGMENT MESSAGE DETAILS

```
Sniffer Network Analyzer data from 23-Apr at 10:23:56, file NIS5.ENC, Pg 1

---------------- Frame 3652 -----------------

DLC:  — DLC Header —
DLC:
DLC:  Frame 3652 arrived at  10:24:02.5582; frame size is 218 (00DA hex) bytes.
DLC:  Destination = Multicast 01005E000005
DLC:  Source      = Station Cisco 599718
DLC:  Ethertype   = 0800 (IP)
DLC:
IP:  — IP Header —
IP:
IP:  Version = 4, header length = 20 bytes
IP:  Type of service = C0
IP:        110. .... = internetwork control
```

```
IP:       ...0 .... = normal delay
IP:       .... 0... = normal throughput
IP:       .... .0.. = normal reliability
IP:  Total length   = 204 bytes
IP:  Identification  = 33912
IP:  Flags          = 0X
IP:       .0.. .... = may fragment
IP:       ..0. .... = last fragment
IP:  Fragment offset = 0 bytes
IP:  Time to live    = 1 seconds/hops
IP:  Protocol        = 89 (OSPFIGP)
IP:  Header checksum = BFF7 (correct)
IP:  Source address      = [140.XXX.6.248], Aeronautics
IP:  Destination address = [224.0.0.5]
IP:  No options
IP:
OSPF: —— OSPF Header ——
OSPF:
OSPF: Version = 2,  Type = 5 (Link State Acknowledgment),  Length = 184
OSPF: Router ID       = [140.XXX.241.100]
OSPF: Area ID         = [0.0.0.0]
OSPF: Header checksum = 176E (correct)
OSPF: Authentication: Type = 0 (No Authentication),  Value = 00 00 00 00 00 00 00 00
OSPF:
OSPF: Link State Advertisement Header # 1
OSPF: Link state age        = 4 (seconds)
OSPF: Optional capabilities = 02
OSPF:          .0.. .... = Opaque-LSAs not forwarded
OSPF:          ..0. .... = Demand Circuit bit
OSPF:          ...0 .... = External Attributes bit
OSPF:          .... 0... = no NSSA capability
OSPF:          .... .0.. = no multicast capability
OSPF:          .... ..1. = external routing capability
OSPF:          .... ...0 = no Type of Service routing capability
OSPF: Link state type       = 1 (Router links)
OSPF: Link state ID         = [140.XXX.172.254]
OSPF: Advertising Router    = [140.XXX.172.254]
OSPF: Sequence number       = 2147484346,  Checksum = 9A4B
OSPF: Length                = 48
OSPF:
OSPF: Link State Advertisement Header # 2
OSPF: Link state age        = 4 (seconds)
OSPF: Optional capabilities = 00
OSPF:          .0.. .... = Opaque-LSAs not forwarded
```

```
OSPF:          ..0. .... = Demand Circuit bit
OSPF:          ...0 .... = External Attributes bit
OSPF:          .... 0... = no NSSA capability
OSPF:          .... .0.. = no multicast capability
OSPF:          .... ..0. = no external routing capability
OSPF:          .... ...0 = no Type of Service routing capability
OSPF: Link state type     = 5 (AS external link)
OSPF: Link state ID       = [140.XXX.172.0]
OSPF: Advertising Router  = [140.XXX.172.254]
OSPF: Sequence number     = 2147484307,  Checksum = 3FB3
OSPF: Length              = 36
OSPF:
OSPF: Link State Advertisement Header # 3
OSPF: Link state age      = 4 (seconds)
OSPF: Optional capabilities = 00
OSPF:          .0.. .... = Opaque-LSAs not forwarded
OSPF:          ..0. .... = Demand Circuit bit
OSPF:          ...0 .... = External Attributes bit
OSPF:          .... 0... = no NSSA capability
OSPF:          .... .0.. = no multicast capability
OSPF:          .... ..0. = no external routing capability
OSPF:          .... ...0 = no Type of Service routing capability
OSPF: Link state type     = 5 (AS external link)
OSPF: Link state ID       = [140.XXX.173.0]
OSPF: Advertising Router  = [140.XXX.172.254]
OSPF: Sequence number     = 2147484307,  Checksum = 34BD
OSPF: Length              = 36
OSPF:
OSPF: Link State Advertisement Header # 4
OSPF: Link state age      = 4 (seconds)
OSPF: Optional capabilities = 00
OSPF:          .0.. .... = Opaque-LSAs not forwarded
OSPF:          ..0. .... = Demand Circuit bit
OSPF:          ...0 .... = External Attributes bit
OSPF:          .... 0... = no NSSA capability
OSPF:          .... .0.. = no multicast capability
OSPF:          .... ..0. = no external routing capability
OSPF:          .... ...0 = no Type of Service routing capability
OSPF: Link state type     = 5 (AS external link)
OSPF: Link state ID       = [140.XXX.174.0]
OSPF: Advertising Router  = [140.XXX.172.254]
OSPF: Sequence number     = 2147484307,  Checksum = 29C7
OSPF: Length              = 36
OSPF:
```

```
OSPF: Link State Advertisement Header # 5
OSPF: Link state age       = 4 (seconds)
OSPF: Optional capabilities = 00
OSPF:          .0.. .... = Opaque-LSAs not forwarded
OSPF:          ..0. .... = Demand Circuit bit
OSPF:          ...0 .... = External Attributes bit
OSPF:          .... 0... = no NSSA capability
OSPF:          .... .0.. = no multicast capability
OSPF:          .... ..0. = no external routing capability
OSPF:          .... ...0 = no Type of Service routing capability
OSPF: Link state type      = 5 (AS external link)
OSPF: Link state ID        = [140.XXX.187.0]
OSPF: Advertising Router   = [140.XXX.172.254]
OSPF: Sequence number      = 2147484307,  Checksum = 994A
OSPF: Length               = 36
OSPF:
OSPF: Link State Advertisement Header # 6
OSPF: Link state age       = 4 (seconds)
OSPF: Optional capabilities = 00
OSPF:          .0.. .... = Opaque-LSAs not forwarded
OSPF:          ..0. .... = Demand Circuit bit
OSPF:          ...0 .... = External Attributes bit
OSPF:          .... 0... = no NSSA capability
OSPF:          .... .0.. = no multicast capability
OSPF:          .... ..0. = no external routing capability
OSPF:          .... ...0 = no Type of Service routing capability
OSPF: Link state type      = 5 (AS external link)
OSPF: Link state ID        = [140.XXX.253.0]
OSPF: Advertising Router   = [140.XXX.172.254]
OSPF: Sequence number      = 2147484317,  Checksum = ACEA
OSPF: Length               = 36
OSPF:
OSPF: Link State Advertisement Header # 7
OSPF: Link state age       = 4 (seconds)
OSPF: Optional capabilities = 00
OSPF:          .0.. .... = Opaque-LSAs not forwarded
OSPF:          ..0. .... = Demand Circuit bit
OSPF:          ...0 .... = External Attributes bit
OSPF:          .... 0... = no NSSA capability
OSPF:          .... .0.. = no multicast capability
OSPF:          .... ..0. = no external routing capability
OSPF:          .... ...0 = no Type of Service routing capability
OSPF: Link state type      = 5 (AS external link)
OSPF: Link state ID        = [140.XXX.254.0]
OSPF: Advertising Router   = [140.XXX.172.254]
```

```
OSPF: Sequence number      = 2147484307,  Checksum = B5EA
OSPF: Length               = 36
OSPF:
OSPF: Link State Advertisement Header # 8
OSPF: Link state age       = 4 (seconds)
OSPF: Optional capabilities = 00
OSPF:           .0.. .... = Opaque-LSAs not forwarded
OSPF:           ..0. .... = Demand Circuit bit
OSPF:           ...0 .... = External Attributes bit
OSPF:           .... 0... = no NSSA capability
OSPF:           .... .0.. = no multicast capability
OSPF:           .... ..0. = no external routing capability
OSPF:           .... ...0 = no Type of Service routing capability
OSPF: Link state type      = 5 (AS external link)
OSPF: Link state ID        = [192.149.148.0]
OSPF: Advertising Router   = [140.XXX.172.254]
OSPF: Sequence number      = 2147484307,  Checksum = B637
OSPF: Length               = 36
OSPF:
```

Frames 3862 and 4608 in Trace 4.10.9d contain OSPF Hello messages, sent from the Aeronautics and Broadway routers, respectively. Within the OSPF header, the Type = 1 field indicates a Hello message and the Router ID indicates that this message came from network [140.XXX.241.100]. That network's Designated router is [140.XXX.6.253], the Broadway router, and its Backup Designated router is [140.XXX.6.248], the Aeronautics Lab router. In Frame 4608, the Router ID indicates that it came from network [140.XXX.1.1]. That network's Designated router is [140.XXX.6.253], the Broadway router, and its Backup Designated router is [140.XXX.6.248], the Aeronautics Lab router.

TRACE 4.10.9D. OSPF HELLO MESSAGE DETAILS

```
Sniffer Network Analyzer data from 23-Apr at 10:23:56, file NIS5.ENC, Pg 1

- - - - - - - - - - - - - - - - Frame 3862 - - - - - - - - - - - - - - - - -

DLC:  —— DLC Header ——
DLC:
DLC:  Frame 3862 arrived at  10:24:02.9741; frame size is 82 (0052 hex) bytes.
DLC:  Destination = Multicast 01005E000005
DLC:  Source      = Station Cisco 599718
DLC:  Ethertype   = 0800 (IP)
DLC:
IP:  —— IP Header ——
IP:
```

```
IP: Version = 4, header length = 20 bytes
IP: Type of service = C0
IP:     110. .... = internetwork control
IP:     ...0 .... = normal delay
IP:     .... 0... = normal throughput
IP:     .... .0.. = normal reliability
IP: Total length   = 68 bytes
IP: Identification  = 33913
IP: Flags          = 0X
IP:     .0.. .... = may fragment
IP:     ..0. .... = last fragment
IP: Fragment offset = 0 bytes
IP: Time to live   = 1 seconds/hops
IP: Protocol       = 89 (OSPFIGP)
IP: Header checksum = C07E (correct)
IP: Source address     = [140.XXX.6.248], Aeronautics
IP: Destination address = [224.0.0.5]
IP: No options
IP:
OSPF: —— OSPF Header ——
OSPF:
OSPF: Version = 2,  Type = 1 (Hello),  Length = 48
OSPF: Router ID      = [140.XXX.241.100]
OSPF: Area ID        = [0.0.0.0]
OSPF: Header checksum = C98D (correct)
OSPF: Authentication: Type = 0 (No Authentication),  Value = 00 00 00 00 00 00 00 00
OSPF:
OSPF: Network mask            = [255.255.255.0]
OSPF: Hello interval          = 10 (seconds)
OSPF: Optional capabilities   = 02
OSPF:           .0.. .... = Opaque-LSAs not forwarded
OSPF:           ..0. .... = Demand Circuit bit
OSPF:           ...0 .... = External Attributes bit
OSPF:           .... 0... = no NSSA capability
OSPF:           .... .0.. = no multicast capability
OSPF:           .... ..1. = external routing capability
OSPF:           .... ...0 = no Type of Service routing capability
OSPF: Router priority         = 1
OSPF: Router dead interval    = 40 (seconds)
OSPF: Designated router       = [140.XXX.6.253]
OSPF: Backup designated router = [140.XXX.6.248]
OSPF: Neighbor (1)            = [140.XXX.1.1]
OSPF:
```

```
- - - - - - - - - - - - - - - - Frame 4608 - - - - - - - - - - - - - - - - -

DLC:   —— DLC Header ——
DLC:
DLC:   Frame 4608 arrived at  10:24:05.1568; frame size is 82 (0052 hex) bytes.
DLC:   Destination = Multicast 01005E000005
DLC:   Source      = Station 00E0F92F20A0
DLC:   Ethertype   = 0800 (IP)
DLC:
IP:  —— IP Header ——
IP:
IP:  Version = 4, header length = 20 bytes
IP:  Type of service = C0
IP:        110. .... = internetwork control
IP:        ...0 .... = normal delay
IP:        .... 0... = normal throughput
IP:        .... .0.. = normal reliability
IP:  Total length    = 68 bytes
IP:    = 12492
IP:  Flags           = 0X
IP:        .0.. .... = may fragment
IP:        ..0. .... = last fragment
IP:  Fragment offset = 0 bytes
IP:  Time to live    = 1 seconds/hops
IP:  Protocol        = 89 (OSPFIGP)
IP:  Header checksum = 1427 (correct)
IP:  Source address      = [140.XXX.6.253], Broadway
IP:  Destination address = [224.0.0.5]
IP:  No options
IP:
OSPF: —— OSPF Header ——
OSPF:
OSPF: Version = 2,  Type = 1 (Hello),  Length = 48
OSPF: Router ID      = [140.XXX.1.1]
OSPF: Area ID        = [0.0.0.0]
OSPF: Header checksum = C98D (correct)
OSPF: Authentication: Type = 0 (No Authentication),  Value = 00 00 00 00 00 00 00 00
OSPF:
OSPF: Network mask           = [255.255.255.0]
OSPF: Hello interval         = 10 (seconds)
OSPF: Optional capabilities   = 02
OSPF:            .0.. .... = Opaque-LSAs not forwarded
OSPF:            ..0. .... = Demand Circuit bit
OSPF:            ...0 .... = External Attributes bit
```

```
OSPF:          .... 0... = no NSSA capability
OSPF:          .... .0.. = no multicast capability
OSPF:          .... ..1. = external routing capability
OSPF:          .... ...0 = no Type of Service routing capability
OSPF: Router priority       = 1
OSPF: Router dead interval   = 40 (seconds)
OSPF: Designated router      = [140.XXX.6.253]
OSPF: Backup designated router = [140.XXX.6.248]
OSPF: Neighbor (1)          = [140.XXX.241.100]
OSPF:
```

Our last example, Trace 4.10.9e, illustrates a BGP Update message sent from the Science Lab router to the Broadway router. Note that BGP messages are sent over TCP, using TCP Port 179. Within the BGP header (review Figure 4-10a), note that the Message Type field indicates an Update message (Type = 2), as shown in Figure 4-10c. The Unfeasible Routes length is zero, indicating that no routes are being withdrawn from service. Three Path Attributes follow: an Origin, indicating that the Network Layer Reachability information is interior to the originating AS; an AS path, which is followed by a sequence of AS path segments (513 and 297); and a Next Hop, which defines the IP address of the border router that should be used as the next hop to the Network Layer Reachability field. Finally, the Network Layer Reachability field contains the IP address of interest: [204.XXX.66.0].

Trace 4.10.9e. BGP Update Message Details

```
- - - - - - - - - - - - - - - - Frame 5841 - - - - - - - - - - - - - - - - -

DLC:  — DLC Header —
DLC:
DLC:  Frame 5841 arrived at  10:24:08.4565; frame size is 99 (0063 hex) bytes.
DLC:  Destination = Station 00E0F92F20A0
DLC:  Source      = Station Cisco 389872
DLC:  Ethertype   = 0800 (IP)
DLC:
IP:  — IP Header —
IP:
IP:  Version = 4, header length = 20 bytes
IP:  Type of service = C0
IP:       110. .... = internetwork control
IP:       ...0 .... = normal delay
IP:       .... 0... = normal throughput
IP:       .... .0.. = normal reliability
IP:  Total length    = 85 bytes
IP:  Identification  = 1738
```

```
IP:  Flags           = 0X
IP:        .0.. .... = may fragment
IP:        ..0. .... = last fragment
IP:  Fragment offset = 0 bytes
IP:  Time to live    = 1 seconds/hops
IP:  Protocol        = 6 (TCP)
IP:  Header checksum = 8ACA (correct)
IP:  Source address      = [140.XXX.6.250], Science
IP:  Destination address = [140.XXX.6.253], Broadway
IP:  No options
IP:
TCP:  —— TCP header ——
TCP:
TCP:  Source port             = 179 (BGP)
TCP:  Destination port        = 37590
TCP:  Sequence number         = 3540261264
TCP:  Acknowledgment number   = 641647944
TCP:  Data offset             = 20 bytes
TCP:  Flags                   = 18
TCP:              ..0. .... = (No urgent pointer)
TCP:              ...1 .... = Acknowledgment
TCP:              .... 1... = Push
TCP:              .... .0.. = (No reset)
TCP:              .... ..0. = (No SYN)
TCP:              .... ...0 = (No FIN)
TCP:  Window                  = 15852
TCP:  Checksum                = CAEE (correct)
TCP:  No TCP options
TCP:  [45 byte(s) of data]
TCP:
BGP:  ——BGP Message ——
BGP:
BGP:  16 byte Marker  (all 1's)
BGP:  Length      = 45
BGP:  BGP type    = 2 (Update)
BGP:
BGP:  Unfeasible Routes Length   = 0
BGP:     No Withdrawn Routes in this Update
BGP:  Path Attribute Length    = 18 bytes
BGP:  Attribute Flags = 4X
BGP:       0... .... = Well-known
BGP:       .1.. .... = Transitive
BGP:       ..0. .... = Complete
BGP:       ...0 .... = 1 byte Length
```

```
BGP: Attribute type code      = 1 (Origin)
BGP: Attribute Data Length    = 1
BGP: Origin type              = 0 (IGP)
BGP: Attribute Flags = 4X
BGP:      0... .... = Well-known
BGP:      .1.. .... = Transitive
BGP:      ..0. .... = Complete
BGP:      ...0 .... = 1 byte Length
BGP: Attribute type code      = 2 (AS Path)
BGP: Attribute Data Length    = 4
BGP: AS Identifier            = 513
BGP: AS Identifier            = 297
BGP: Attribute Flags = 4X
BGP:      0... .... = Well-known
BGP:      .1.. .... = Transitive
BGP:      ..0. .... = Complete
BGP:      ...0 .... = 1 byte Length
BGP: Attribute type code      = 3 (Next Hop)
BGP: Attribute Data Length    = 4
BGP: Next Hop                 = [140.XXX.6.250], Science
BGP:
BGP: Network Layer Reachability Information:
BGP:  IP Prefix Length = 24 bits, IP subnet mask [255.255.255.0]
BGP:    IP address [204.XXX.66.0]
DLC: —Frame too short —
```

Reference [4-61] is an excellent article describing OSPF multicast routing and the interaction between OSPF and other protocols, such as IGMP.

4.11 Looking Ahead

In this chapter we have covered a number of protocols that work together to deliver datagrams within the internet from one host to another. Since this transmission is based on the Internet Protocol's connectionless service, guaranteed delivery of those datagrams must be ensured by another process, the Host-to-Host Layer. We will study the two protocols that operate at the Host-to-Host Layer, UDP and TCP, in the next chapter.

4.12 References

[4-1] Roman, Bob. "Making the Big Connection." *3TECH, The 3Com Technical Journal* (Summer 1990): 14–25.

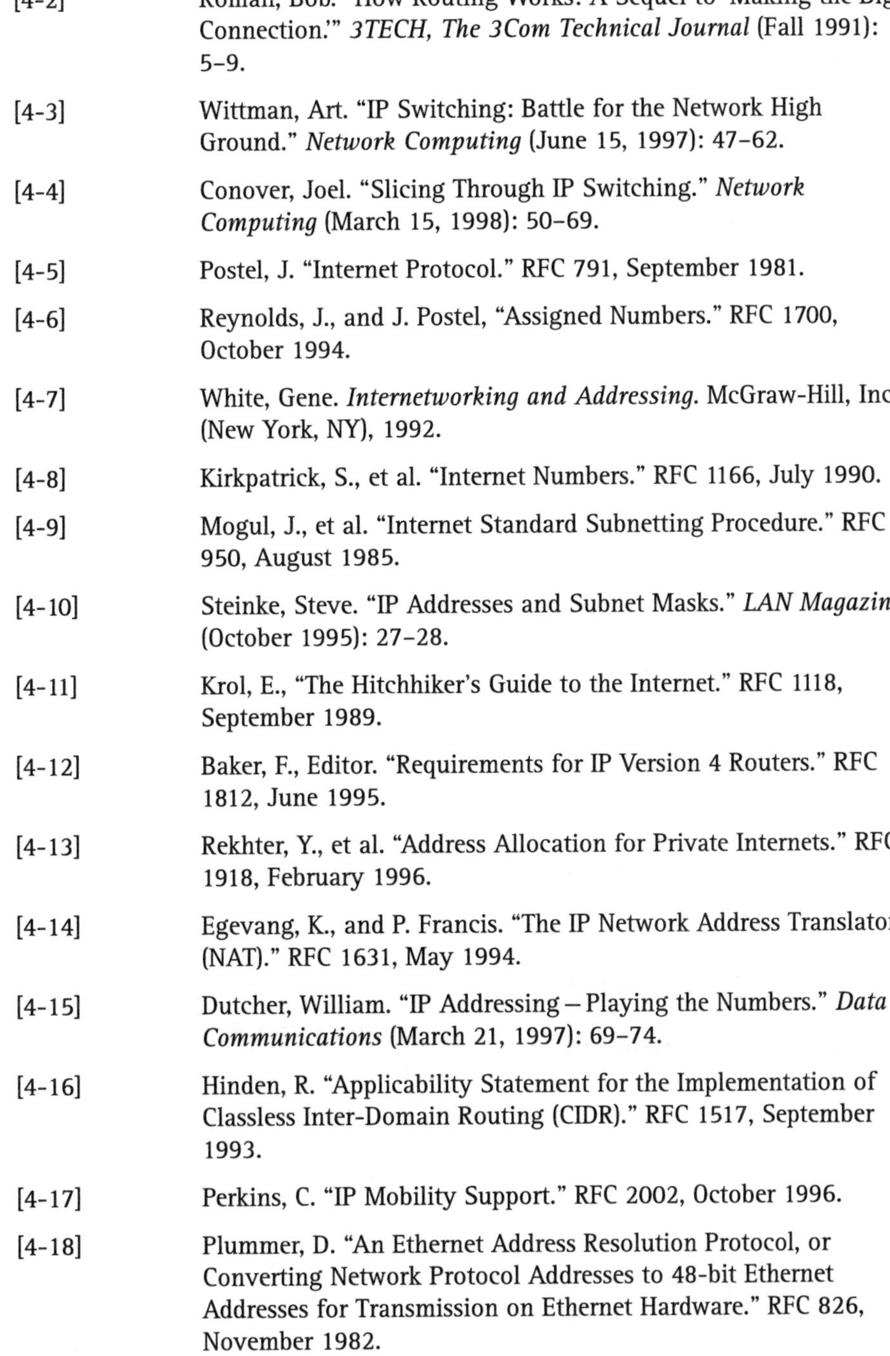

[4-2] Roman, Bob. "How Routing Works: A Sequel to 'Making the Big Connection.'" *3TECH, The 3Com Technical Journal* (Fall 1991): 5–9.

[4-3] Wittman, Art. "IP Switching: Battle for the Network High Ground." *Network Computing* (June 15, 1997): 47–62.

[4-4] Conover, Joel. "Slicing Through IP Switching." *Network Computing* (March 15, 1998): 50–69.

[4-5] Postel, J. "Internet Protocol." RFC 791, September 1981.

[4-6] Reynolds, J., and J. Postel, "Assigned Numbers." RFC 1700, October 1994.

[4-7] White, Gene. *Internetworking and Addressing.* McGraw-Hill, Inc. (New York, NY), 1992.

[4-8] Kirkpatrick, S., et al. "Internet Numbers." RFC 1166, July 1990.

[4-9] Mogul, J., et al. "Internet Standard Subnetting Procedure." RFC 950, August 1985.

[4-10] Steinke, Steve. "IP Addresses and Subnet Masks." *LAN Magazine* (October 1995): 27–28.

[4-11] Krol, E., "The Hitchhiker's Guide to the Internet." RFC 1118, September 1989.

[4-12] Baker, F., Editor. "Requirements for IP Version 4 Routers." RFC 1812, June 1995.

[4-13] Rekhter, Y., et al. "Address Allocation for Private Internets." RFC 1918, February 1996.

[4-14] Egevang, K., and P. Francis. "The IP Network Address Translator (NAT)." RFC 1631, May 1994.

[4-15] Dutcher, William. "IP Addressing – Playing the Numbers." *Data Communications* (March 21, 1997): 69–74.

[4-16] Hinden, R. "Applicability Statement for the Implementation of Classless Inter-Domain Routing (CIDR)." RFC 1517, September 1993.

[4-17] Perkins, C. "IP Mobility Support." RFC 2002, October 1996.

[4-18] Plummer, D. "An Ethernet Address Resolution Protocol, or Converting Network Protocol Addresses to 48-bit Ethernet Addresses for Transmission on Ethernet Hardware." RFC 826, November 1982.

[4-19] Finlayson, R., et al. "A Reverse Address Resolution Protocol." RFC 903, June 1984.

[4-20] Bradley, T., and C. Brown. "Inverse Address Resolution Protocol." RFC 1293, January 1992.

[4-21] Laubach, M. "Classical IP and ARP over ATM." RFC 1577, January 1994.

[4-22] Postel, J. "Multi-LAN Address Resolution." RFC 925, October 1984.

[4-23] Black, Uyless. *TCP/IP and Related Protocols,* second edition. McGraw-Hill, Inc. (New York, NY), 1995.

[4-24] Comer, Douglas E. *Internetworking with TCP/IP,* third edition. Prentice Hall, Inc. (Englewood Cliffs, NJ), 1995.

[4-25] Gilmore, John. "Bootstrap Protocol (BOOTP)." RFC 951, September 1985.

[4-26] Wimer, W. "Clarifications and Extensions for the Bootstrap Protocol." RFC 1542, October 1993.

[4-27] Alexander, S., and R. Droms. "DHCP Options and BOOTP Vendor Extensions." RFC 2132, March 1997.

[4-28] Mogul, Jeffrey. "Booting Diskless Hosts: The BOOTP Protocol." *ConneXions* (October 1988): 14–18.

[4-29] Droms, R. "Dynamic Host Configuration Protocol." RFC 2131, March 1997.

[4-30] Droms, R. "Interoperation Between DHCP and BOOTP." RFC 1534, October 1993.

[4-31] Allard, J. "DHCP – TCP/IP Network Configuration Made Easy." *ConneXions* (August 1993): 16–24.

[4-32] Demaree, Kirk. "DHCP and DNS: A Dynamic Duo." *Network Magazine* (August 1997): 65–69.

[4-33] A good resource for DHCP information is: `http://web.syr.edu/~jmwobus/comfaqs.dhcp.faq.html`.

[4-34] Hedrick, C. "Routing Information Protocol." RFC 1058, June 1988.

[4-35] Meyer, G., and S. Sherry. "Triggered Extensions to RIP to Support Demand Circuits." RFC 2091, January 1997.

[4-36] Malkin, G. "RIP Version 2 – Carrying Additional Information." RFC 1723, November 1994.

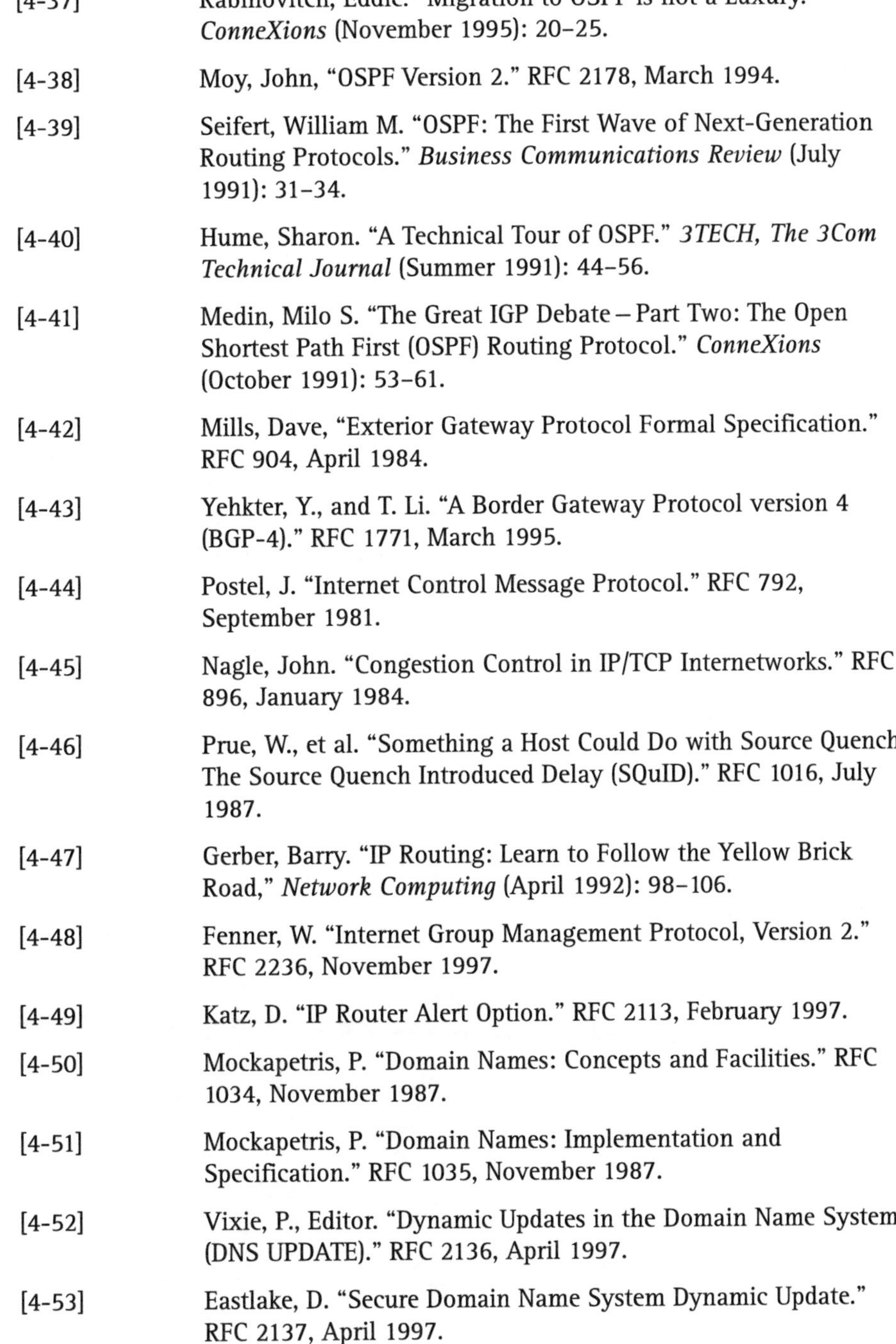

[4-37] Rabinovitch, Eddie. "Migration to OSPF is not a Luxury." *ConneXions* (November 1995): 20–25.

[4-38] Moy, John, "OSPF Version 2." RFC 2178, March 1994.

[4-39] Seifert, William M. "OSPF: The First Wave of Next-Generation Routing Protocols." *Business Communications Review* (July 1991): 31–34.

[4-40] Hume, Sharon. "A Technical Tour of OSPF." *3TECH, The 3Com Technical Journal* (Summer 1991): 44–56.

[4-41] Medin, Milo S. "The Great IGP Debate – Part Two: The Open Shortest Path First (OSPF) Routing Protocol." *ConneXions* (October 1991): 53–61.

[4-42] Mills, Dave, "Exterior Gateway Protocol Formal Specification." RFC 904, April 1984.

[4-43] Yehkter, Y., and T. Li. "A Border Gateway Protocol version 4 (BGP-4)." RFC 1771, March 1995.

[4-44] Postel, J. "Internet Control Message Protocol." RFC 792, September 1981.

[4-45] Nagle, John. "Congestion Control in IP/TCP Internetworks." RFC 896, January 1984.

[4-46] Prue, W., et al. "Something a Host Could Do with Source Quench: The Source Quench Introduced Delay (SQuID)." RFC 1016, July 1987.

[4-47] Gerber, Barry. "IP Routing: Learn to Follow the Yellow Brick Road," *Network Computing* (April 1992): 98–106.

[4-48] Fenner, W. "Internet Group Management Protocol, Version 2." RFC 2236, November 1997.

[4-49] Katz, D. "IP Router Alert Option." RFC 2113, February 1997.

[4-50] Mockapetris, P. "Domain Names: Concepts and Facilities." RFC 1034, November 1987.

[4-51] Mockapetris, P. "Domain Names: Implementation and Specification." RFC 1035, November 1987.

[4-52] Vixie, P., Editor. "Dynamic Updates in the Domain Name System (DNS UPDATE)." RFC 2136, April 1997.

[4-53] Eastlake, D. "Secure Domain Name System Dynamic Update." RFC 2137, April 1997.

[4-54] Rekhter, Yokov. "Interaction Between DHCP and DNS." Work in progress, March 1998.

[4-55] Demaree, Kirk. "DNS Gets an Update." *Network Magazine* (January 1998): 74–77.

[4-56] A good resource for DNS information is: `http://www.dns.net/dnsrd`.

[4-57] Braden, R., Editor. "Resource Reservation Protocol (RSVP) Version 1 Functional Specification." RFC 2205, September 1997.

[4-58] Roberts, Erica. "RSVP: A Priority Problem?" *Data Communications* (May 21, 1997): 58–64.

[4-59] Riggs, Brian. "RSVP Comes on Strong." *LAN Times* (November 24, 1997): 41–42.

[4-60] Auerbach, Carl. "Trouble-Busters." *LAN Magazine* (March 1995): 85–90.

[4-61] Semeria, Chuck. "IP Multicast Routing." *3TECH, The 3Com Technical Journal* (January 1996):20–27.

Chapter 5

Troubleshooting the Host-to-Host Connection

Datagrams and virtual circuits both convey information on an end-to-end basis, but each is associated with different benefits and costs. The datagram provides low overhead but foregoes rigorous reliability; the virtual circuit offers high reliability at the cost of high overhead. The choice depends on the amount of reliability that is required for the application in question, and the data that is related to that application. For example, an electronic message, which can be easily retransmitted if lost, could be sent as a datagram. File transfers, on the other hand, demand a high degree of reliability and should employ the connection-oriented virtual circuit.

In this chapter, we will study the two protocols that implement datagrams and virtual circuits: the User Datagram Protocol (UDP) and the Transmission Control Protocol (TCP). Other host-related issues are discussed in RFC 1123, "Requirements for Internet Hosts: Application and Support." The first issue to consider is how UDP and TCP fit into the ARPA architectural model.

5.1 The Host-to-Host Connection

In Chapter 3, we learned that the Network Interface Layer handles the physical connection for the LAN or WAN. In Chapter 4, we explored the Internet Layer, which routes IP datagrams from one device to another on the same network or on a different network via the internetwork. The Internet Layer also administers the 32-bit Internet addresses (used with IP) and takes care of intra-network communication (with ICMP).

Figure 5-1a shows the ARPA architectural model; as you can see, the Host-to-Host Layer is the first layer that operates exclusively within the hosts, not in the routers. Assuming that the IP datagram has arrived at the Destination host, what issues must the host (and the architect designing the internetwork) deal with in order to establish and use the communication link between the two end points?

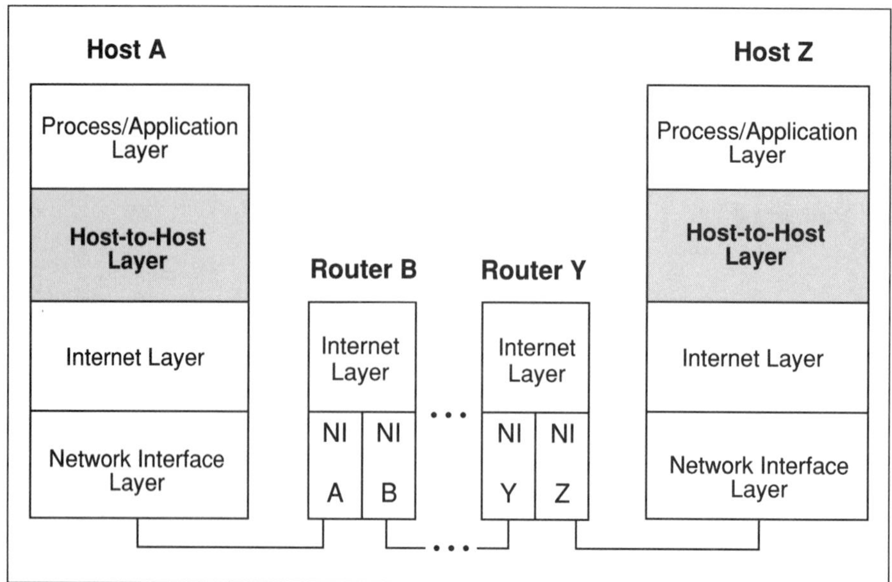

Figure 5-1a The Host-to-Host Connection

First, we must assume that the host has more than one process at its disposal. Therefore, the datagram will require additional addressing to identify the host process to which it will apply. This additional address is carried within the UDP or TCP header and is known as a Port address (we'll discuss ports in Section 5.2). Another issue to consider is reliability of the datagram; the hosts will want assurance that the datagram arrived correctly. Both the UDP and TCP headers address this concern. A third consideration is the overhead associated with the host-to-host transmission. The overhead directly relates to the type of connection – TCP or UDP – employed. It is the requirements of the Process/Application Layer that determine the choice between TCP and UDP. As shown in Figure 5-1b, the Hypertext Transfer Protocol (HTTP), File Transfer Protocol (FTP), Telecommunications Network (TELNET) protocol, and Simple Mail Transfer Protocol (SMTP) run over TCP transport. The Trivial File Transfer Protocol (TFTP), Simple Network Management Protocol (SNMP), and Sun Microsystems Inc.'s Network File System (NFS) protocols work with UDP. The Domain Name System (DNS) may employ either UDP or TCP, depending on the function being performed. We will study these Process/Application Layer protocols in depth in Chapter 6.

ARPA Layer	Protocol Implementation								OSI Layer
Process / Application	Hypertext Transfer	File Transfer	Electronic Mail	Terminal Emulation	Domain Names	File Transfer	Client / Server	Network Management	Application
	Hypertext Transfer Protocol (HTTP) RFC 2068	File Transfer Protocol (FTP) MIL-STD-1780 RFC 959	Simple Mail Transfer Protocol (SMTP) MIL-STD-1781 RFC 821	TELNET Protocol MIL-STD-1782 RFC 854	Domain Name System (DNS) RFC 1034, 1035	Trivial File Transfer Protocol (TFTP) RFC 783	Sun Microsystems Network File System Protocols (NFS) RFCs 1014, 1057, and 1094	Simple Network Management Protocol (SNMP) v1: RFC 1157 v2: RFC 1901-10 v3: RFC 2271-75	Presentation Session
Host-to-Host	Transmission Control Protocol (TCP) MIL-STD-1778 RFC 793					User Datagram Protocol (UDP) RFC 768			Transport
Internet	Address Resolution ARP RFC 826 RARP RFC 903			Internet Protocol (IP) MIL-STD-1777 RFC 791			Internet Control Message Protocol (ICMP) RFC 792		Network
Network Interface	Network Interface Cards: Ethernet, Token Ring, ARCNET, MAN and WAN RFC 894, RFC 1042, RFC 1201 and others								Data Link
	Transmission Media: Twisted Pair, Coax, Fiber Optics, Wireless Media, etc.								Physical

Figure 5-1b ARPA Host-to-Host Layer Protocols

Figure 5-1c shows where the overhead occurs. The Local Network header and trailer delimit the transmission frame and treat the higher layer information as data inside the frame. The IP header is the first component of overhead, followed by either a UDP or TCP header. If UDP is used, it requires eight octets of header overhead. If TCP is used, it requires a minimum of 20 octets of overhead, plus options and padding. As we will see in the following sections, the header overhead relates directly to the rigor of the protocols.

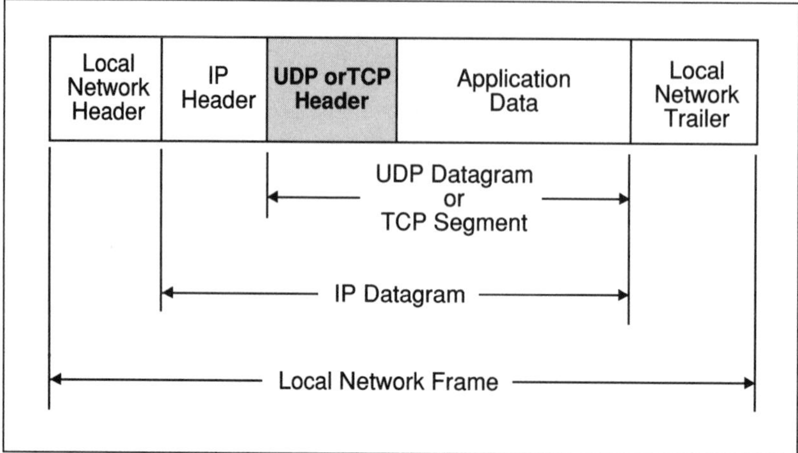

Figure 5-1c The Internet Transmission Frame and UDP/TCP Header Position

As noted above, both UDP and TCP use Port addresses to identify the incoming data stream and to multiplex it to the appropriate Host process. We'll look at the functions of the Port addresses next.

5.2 Port Addresses

In our tour of the ARPA architectural model, we've encountered addresses for each layer. Let's review these briefly. The Network Interface (or OSI Physical and Data Link) Layer requires a Hardware address. The Hardware address is assigned to the network interface card and is typically a 48-bit number that resides in a ROM on the board itself. The Hardware address gives a unique identity to each workstation on the LAN or WAN. Because that address resides in hardware, it remains constant as the device is moved from one network to another.

The Internet (or OSI Network) Layer requires a Logical address, which identifies the network to which a host is attached. As we discussed in Section 4.2, this Internet (or IP) address may be further subdivided into Subnetwork and Host IDs. This address is a 32-bit number that the network administrator assigns to the device. If the device were to be moved from one network to another, a different Internet address would be necessary. The ARP and RARP protocols that we studied in Section 4.3 correlate the Internet Layer and Network Interface Layer addresses.

The third layer of addressing is used at the Host-to-Host (or OSI Transport) Layer and completes the ARPA addressing scheme. This address is known as a *Port address*, and it identifies the user process or application within the host. Each host is presumed to have multiple applications available, such as electronic mail, databases, and so on. An identifier, known as a Port number, specifies the process the user wishes to access. These Port numbers are 16 bits long and are standardized according to their use. Internet administrators assign Port numbers 0–255; other numbers are available for local administration. A complete listing of the assigned ports is available in the Assigned Numbers document (currently RFC 1700). Some examples are given in Tables 5-1a and 5-1b.

In summary, a message sent from one host to another requires three addresses at the source and the destination to complete the communication path. The Port address (16 bits) identifies the user process (or application) and is contained within the UDP or TCP header. The Internet address (32 bits) identifies the network and host that the process is running on and is located inside the IP header. On some hosts, the combination of the Port address and the IP address is referred to as a *socket*. The Hardware address (usually 48 bits) identifies the particular host or workstation on the local network. The Hardware address, which is in the Data Link Layer header, is physically configured on the network interface card.

With that background, let's see how UDP and TCP use the Port address to complete the host-to-host connection.

TABLE 5-1A. PORT ASSIGNMENTS

Decimal	Keyword	Description
1	tcpmux	TCP Port Service Multiplexer
5	rje	Remote Job Entry
7	echo	Echo
11	systat	Active Users
13	daytime	Daytime
17	qotd	Quote of the Day
18	msp	Message Send Protocol
19	chargen	Character Generator
20	ftp-data	File Transfer Protocol [Default Data]
21	ftp	File Transfer Protocol [Control]
23	telnet	TELNET
25	smtp	Simple Mail Transfer Protocol
33	dsp	Display Support Protocol
37	time	Time
38	rap	Route Access Protocol
42	nameserver	Host Name Server
43	nicname	Who Is
49	login	Login Host Protocol
53	domain	Domain Name Server
67	bootps	Bootstrap Protocol [Server]
68	bootpc	Bootstrap Protocol [Client]
69	tftp	Trivial File Transfer Protocol
70	gopher	Gopher
79	finger	Finger
80	www-http	World Wide Web HTTP
88	kerberos	Kerberos
92	npp	Network Printing Protocol
93	dcp	Device Control Protocol
101	hostname	NIC Host Name Server
102	iso-tsap	ISO-TSAP
107	rtelnet	Remote TELNET Service
109	pop2	Post Office Protocol – v. 2
110	pop3	Post Office Protocol – v. 3
111	sunrpc	SUN Remote Procedure Call

TABLE 5-1B. PORT ASSIGNMENTS *(CONTINUED)*

Decimal	Keyword	Description
115	sftp	Simple File Transfer Protocol
129	pwdgen	Password Generator Protocol
137	netbios-ns	NetBIOS Name Service
138	netbios-dgm	NetBIOS Datagram Service
139	netbios-ssn	NetBIOS Session Service
143	imap2	Interim Mail Access Protocol v.2
144	news	News
146	iso-tp0	ISO-TP0
147	iso-ip	ISO-IP
152	bftp	Background File Transfer Program
153	sgmp	Simple Gateway Monitoring Protocol
160	sgmp-traps	SGMP-TRAPS
161	snmp	Simple Network Management Protocol
162	snmptrap	SNMPTRAP
163	cmip-manage	CMIP/TCP Manager
164	cmip-agent	CMIP/TCP Agent
165	xns-courier	Xerox
179	bgp	Border Gateway Protocol
190	gacp	Gateway Access Control Protocol
193	srmp	Spider Remote Monitoring Protocol
194	irc	Internet Relay Chat Protocol
199	smux	SNMP Multiplexing
201	at-rmtp	AppleTalk Routing Maintenance Protocol
202	at-nbp	AppleTalk Name Binding Protocol
203	at-3	AppleTalk Unused
204	at-echo	AppleTalk Echo Protocol
205	at-5	AppleTalk Unused
206	at-zis	AppleTalk Zone Information
207	at-7	AppleTalk Unused
208	at-8	AppleTalk Unused
209	tam	Trivial Authenticated Mail Protocol
220	imap3	Interactive Mail Access Protocol-v.3
246	dsp3270	Display Systems Protocol

5.3 User Datagram Protocol

As its name implies, the User Datagram Protocol, described in RFC 768 [5-1], provides a connectionless host-to-host communication path. UDP assumes that IP, which is also connectionless, is the underlying (Internet Layer) protocol. Because this service has minimal overhead, UDP has a relatively small header, as shown in Figure 5-2. The resulting message, consisting of the IP header, UDP header, and user data, is called a UDP datagram.

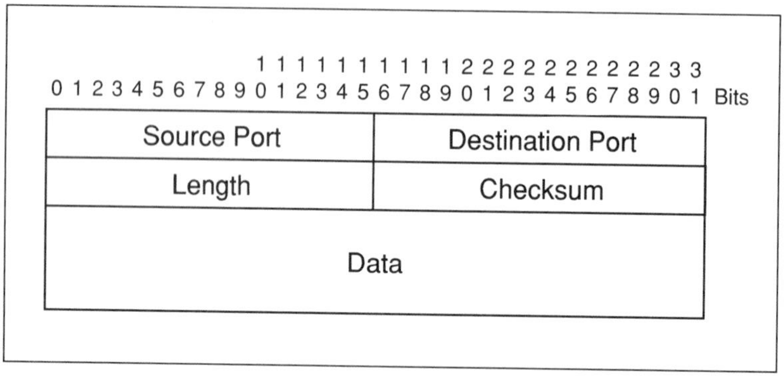

```
                    1 1 1 1 1 1 1 1 1 1 2 2 2 2 2 2 2 2 2 2 3 3
0 1 2 3 4 5 6 7 8 9 0 1 2 3 4 5 6 7 8 9 0 1 2 3 4 5 6 7 8 9 0 1  Bits
```

Source Port	Destination Port
Length	Checksum
Data	

Figure 5-2 User Datagram Protocol (UDP) Header

The first two fields are the Source and Destination Port numbers (each 2 octets long), discussed in Section 5.2. The Source Port field is optional, and when not in use is filled with zeros. The Length field (2 octets) is the length of the UDP datagram, which has a minimum value of 8 octets. The Checksum field (2 octets) is also optional and may be filled with zeros if the Upper Layer Protocol (ULP) process does not require a checksum. When the checksum is used, it is calculated from the so-called Pseudo header, which includes the Source and Destination addresses and the Protocol field from the IP header (see Figure 5-3). By including the IP address in its calculations for the checksum, the Pseudo header ensures that the UDP datagram is delivered to the correct Destination network and host. The IP Protocol field within the Pseudo header would equal 17 for UDP.

In summary, the IP Destination address routes the datagram to the correct host on the specified network, then the UDP Port address routes the datagram to the correct host process. Thus, the UDP adds Port addressing capabilities to IP's datagram service. Examples of host processes that use UDP as the host-to-host protocol include: the Time protocol, Port number 37; the Domain Name Server (DNS), Port number 53; the Bootstrap Protocol (BOOTP) server and client, Port numbers 67 and 68, respectively; the Trivial File Transfer Protocol (TFTP), Port number 69; and the Sun Microsystems Remote Procedure Call (SunRPC), Port number 111. All of these applications assume that if the host-to-host connection were to fail, a higher layer function, such as DNS, would recover. Applications that require more reliability in their end-to-end data transmissions use the more rigorous TCP, which we will discuss next.

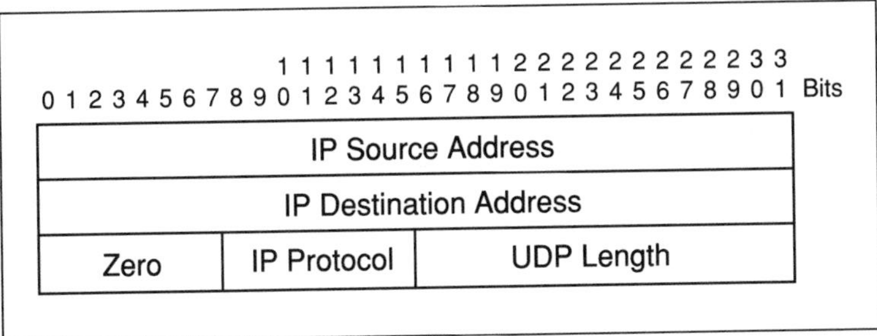

Figure 5-3 UDP Pseudo Header

5.4 Transmission Control Protocol

In Chapter 1, we learned that the Internet protocols were designed to meet U.S. government and military requirements. These requirements dictated that the data communication system be able to endure battlefield conditions. The Internet protocol designed specifically to meet the rigors of the battlefield was the Transmission Control Protocol, described in RFC 793 [5-2]. Unlike UDP, TCP is a connection-oriented protocol that is responsible for reliable communication between two end processes. The unit of data transferred is called a *stream*, which is simply a sequence of octets. The stream originates at the upper layer protocol process and is subsequently divided into TCP segments, IP datagrams, and Local Network frames. RFC 1180, "A TCP/IP Tutorial" [5-3], offers a useful summary of the way the TCP information fits into the related protocols, such as IP, and the Local Network connection, such as Ethernet. RFC 879, "The TCP Maximum Segment Size and Related Topics" [5-4], describes the relationships between TCP segments and IP datagrams.

TCP handles six functions: basic data transfer, reliability, flow control, multiplexing, connections, and precedence/ security. We will discuss these functions in detail in Section 5.5.

The TCP header (see Figure 5-4) has a minimum length of 20 octets. This header contains a number of fields – relating to connection management, data flow control, and reliability – which UDP did not require. The TCP header starts with two Port addresses (2 octets each) to identify the logical host processes at each end of the connection.

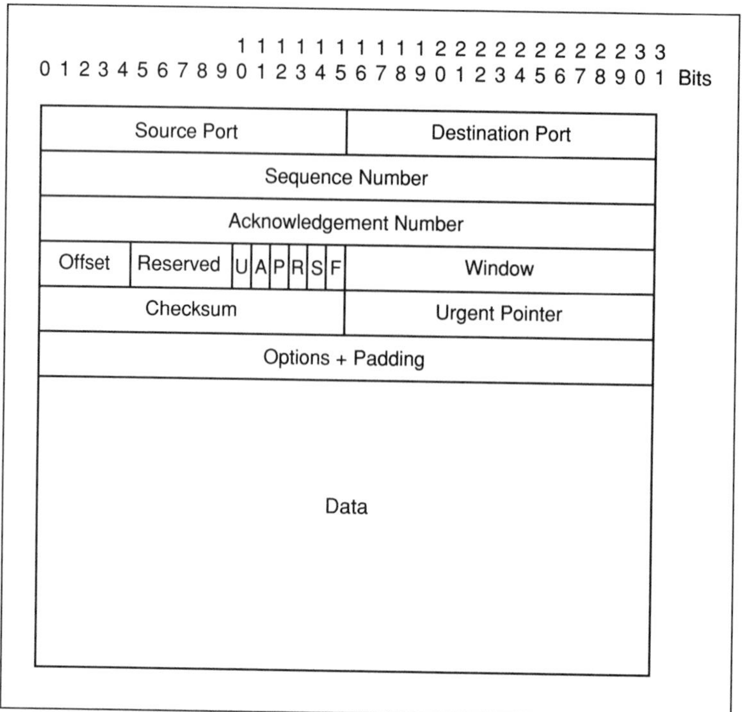

Figure 5-4 Transmission Control Protocol (TCP) Header

The Sequence Number field (4 octets) is the Sequence number given to the first octet of data. When the SYN flag bit is set, the Sequence number indicates the Initial Sequence Number (ISN) selected. The first data octet sent would then use the next Sequence number [ISN+1]. (For example, if ISN = 100, then the data would begin with SEQ = 101. If the Sequence number was not advanced by one, the process would end up in an endless loop of transmissions and acknowledgments. More on this in Section 5.5.5.) The Sequence number ensures the sequentiality of the data stream, which is a fundamental component of reliability.

The Acknowledgment Number field (4 octets) verifies the receipt of data. This protocol process is called Positive Acknowledgment or Retransmission (PAR). The process requires that each unit of data (the octet in the case of TCP) be explicitly acknowledged. If it is not, the sender will time-out and retransmit. The value in the acknowledgment is the next octet (i.e., the next Sequence number) expected from the other end of the connection. When the Acknowledgment field is in use (i.e., during a connection), the ACK flag bit is set.

The next 32-bit word (octets 13–16 in the header) contains a number of fields used for control purposes. The Data Offset field (4 bits) measures the number of 32-bit words in the TCP header. Its value indicates where the TCP header ends and the upper layer protocol (ULP) data begins. The Offset field is necessary because the TCP header has a variable, not fixed, length; therefore, the position of the first octet of ULP data may vary. Since the minimum length of the TCP header is 20 octets, the minimum value of the Data Offset field would be five 32-bit words. The next 6 bits are reserved for future use and are set equal to zero.

Six flags that control the connection and data transfer are transmitted next. Each flag has its own 1-bit field. These flags include:

- URG: Urgent Pointer field significant
- ACK: Acknowledgment field significant
- PSH: Push function
- RST: Reset the connection
- SYN: Synchronize Sequence numbers
- FIN: No more data from sender

We will study the use of these flags in greater detail in Section 5.5.

The Window field (2 octets) provides end-to-end flow control. The number in the Window field indicates the quantity of octets, beginning with the one in the Acknowledgment field, that the sender of the segment can accept. Note that the Window field, like the Acknowledgment field, is bidirectional. Since TCP provides a full-duplex communication path, both ends send control information to their peer process at the other end of the connection. In other words, my host provides both an acknowledgment and a window advertisement to your host, and your host does the same for mine. In this manner, both ends provide control information to their remote partner.

The Checksum field (2 octets) is used for error control. The checksum calculation includes a 12-octet Pseudo header, the TCP header, and ULP data. The TCP Pseudo header (shown in Figure 5-5) is similar to the UDP Pseudo header shown in Figure 5-3. Its purpose is to provide error control on the IP header, the TCP header, and the data. The fields included in the TCP Pseudo header include the Source and Destination addresses, the Protocol, and the TCP Length. The TCP Length field includes the TCP header and ULP data, but not the 12-octet Pseudo header.

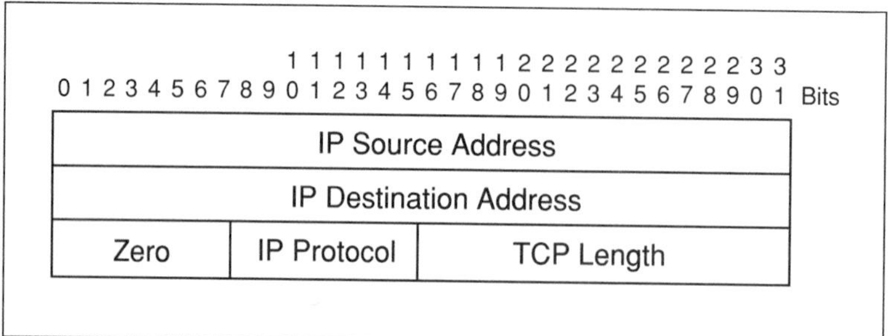

Figure 5-5 TCP Pseudo Header

The Urgent Pointer field (2 octets) allows the position of urgent data within the TCP segment to be identified. This field is used in conjunction with the Urgent (URG) control flag and points to the Sequence number of the octet that follows the urgent data. In other words, the Urgent pointer indicates the beginning of the routine (nonurgent) data.

Options and Padding fields (both variable in length) complete the TCP header. The Options field is an even multiple of octets in length and specifies options required by the TCP process within the host. One option is the maximum TCP segment size, which mandates the amount of data that the sender of the option is willing to accept. We saw this option used by the AppleTalk workstation in Trace 3.13.5. The Padding field contains a variable number of zeros that ensure that the TCP header ends on a 32-bit boundary.

Now that we've explored the fields within the TCP header, we'll see how they provide the six TCP functions: basic data transfer, reliability, flow control, multiplexing, connections, and precedence/security.

5.5 TCP Functions

TCP is a rigorous protocol, rich with the functionality demanded by its government-backed designers. In this section, we'll explore each of the six areas of TCP operation separately, and we'll conclude with a summary of the TCP state diagram. References [5-5] and [5-6] discuss the concepts of the User/TCP interface in greater detail; however, for our troubleshooting purposes, we'll focus on understanding the protocol interactions, not the internal protocol operations.

5.5.1 Basic Data Transfer

A TCP module transfers a series of octets, known as a *segment,* from one host to another. Data flows in both directions, making for a full-duplex connection. The TCP modules at each end determine the length of the segment and indicate this length in the Options field of the TCP header.

Occasionally, a TCP module requires immediate data delivery and can't wait for the segment to fill completely. In that case, an upper layer process would trigger the Push (PSH) flag within the TCP header and tell the TCP module to immediately forward all of the queued data to the receiver.

5.5.2 Reliability

So far, we've assumed that Host B has received all the data sent from Host A. Unfortunately, there's no such network utopia in the real world. The transmitted data could be lost, inadvertently duplicated, delivered out of order, or damaged. If damage occurs, the checksum will fail, alerting the receiver to the problem. The other conditions are more complex, and TCP must have mechanisms to handle them.

The cornerstones of TCP's reliability are its Sequence and Acknowledgment numbers. The Sequence number is logically attached to each outgoing octet. The receiver uses the Sequence numbers to determine whether any octets are missing or have been received out of order. TCP is a Positive Acknowledgment with Retransmission (PAR) protocol. This means that if data is received correctly, the receiving TCP module generates an Acknowledgment (ACK) number. If the transmitting TCP module does not receive an acknowledgment within the specified time, it will retransmit. No Negative Acknowledgments (NAKs) are allowed.

One of the design issues for a TCP/IP-based internetwork is optimizing the waiting time before allowing a retransmission to occur. Internetworks, by definition, contain multiple communication paths. Each of these may have a different propagation delay. In addition, the underlying infrastructure is connectionless (using IP); it is possible that a datagram could merely be delayed via a path with a longer propagation time, but not truly lost. In that case, retransmitting too quickly would consume precious bandwidth and cause confusion at the receiver if two identical messages are (eventually) received. On the other hand, if the datagram *is* truly lost, then delaying the retransmission also delays the receiver's ability to reassemble the entire message. An obvious compromise is in order. RFC 793, page 41, discusses the Retransmission Timer, and Comer [5-6] presents an excellent summary of the retransmission and timer issues. Partridge [5-7] discusses how TCP timers affect the protocol's performance, and Karn [5-8] discusses an algorithm – known as Karn's Algorithm – used to calculate the network Round Trip Time (RTT), which impacts the retransmission timers.

Figure 5-6 illustrates the TCP reliability services. (For simplicity, we'll assume that a large data file is being sent from Host A to Host B.) The first segment (SEQ 101–116) is acknowledged without error. The second segment (SEQ 117–132) is not so fortunate and experiences a transmission error. Since that segment never arrives at Host B, no acknowledgment (ACK = 133) is issued by Host B. The Retransmission Timer in Host A expires and retransmits the second segment (SEQ 117–132). When this segment is received, Host B then issues the acknowledgment.

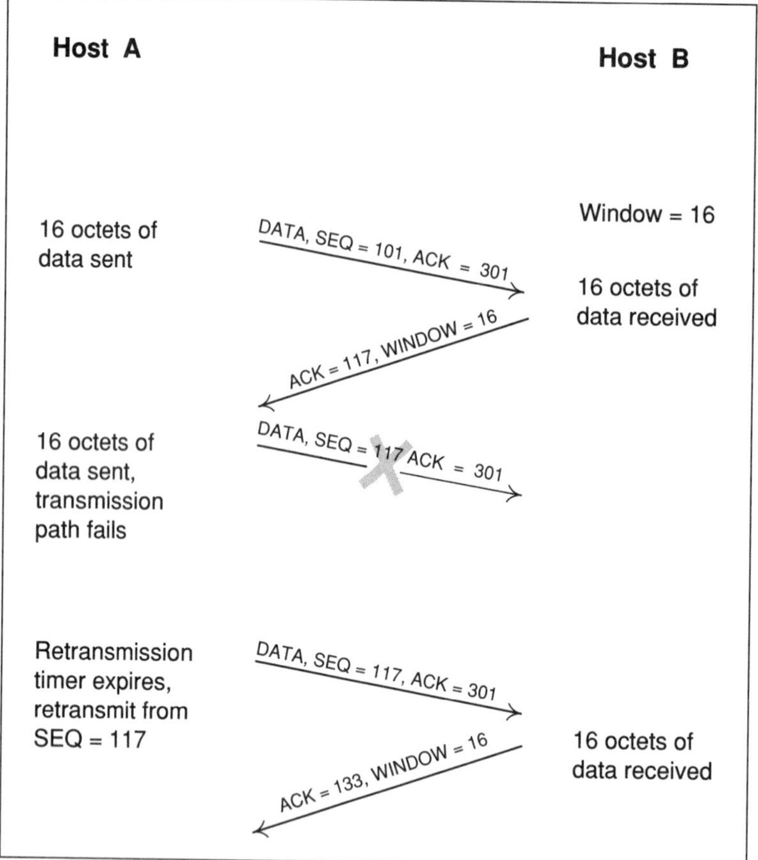

Figure 5-6 TCP Data Retransmissions

5.5.3 Flow Control

Let's begin by reviewing some terms and concepts; then we'll discuss how they relate to the Flow Control mechanism. Recall from the previous section that the Sequence number is attached by the sending device to the TCP segment and counts each octet transmitted. The Acknowledgment number indicates the next expected Sequence number, that is, the next octet of data expected from the other end of the connection. A third metric, also included within the TCP header, is the Window number. The Window indicates how many more Sequence numbers the sender of the Window is prepared to accept, and is described in RFC 813 [5-9]. The Window controls the flow of data from sender to receiver. Thus, if Host A sends Window = 1024 to Host B, it has much more available buffer space than if Host A sends Window = 10. In the first case, Host A grants Host B permission to transmit 1,024 octets of data past the current Sequence number; in the second case, only 10.

Window = 0 and Window = 1 are two special cases of *sliding window* operations. If a host returns Window = 0, it has shut down communication and will accept no more octets from the other end of the connection. Window = 1 is sometimes known as *stop-and-wait* transmission. The top portion of Figure 5-7 illustrates what happens when Window = 1. (For simplicity, we'll assume that the data is transmitted from Host A to Host B and that acknowledgments go in the opposite direction. In reality, TCP allows full-duplex operation. Therefore, data could also flow from Host B to Host A, with corresponding acknowledgments from Host A to Host B.) Host A has a large, 523K-octet file to send. Host B has set Window = 1, thereby limiting data transmissions to one octet before each acknowledgment. Thus, Host A must wait for Host B's acknowledgment before it can transmit each octet of data. Not very efficient, you might say, and few analysts would disagree.

Now suppose that Host B obtains additional buffer space and increases the value to Window = 8. Host A can now send 8 octets of data (SEQ 103–110, inclusive) before requiring an acknowledgment. When the acknowledgment arrives, it indicates the next expected Sequence number (e.g., ACK = 111 would indicate that octets numbered 103–110 arrived correctly and that it is permissible to send 16 more, beginning with SEQ = 111). Similarly, an increase to Window = 32 would allow a corresponding increase in the quantity of data transmitted. We use the term *flow control* to describe the effect of the sliding window operation because you can control the flow of data by adjusting the window value.

The window size is a parameter that requires some optimization. Too many small segments generate needless ACKs, but large segments utilize more buffers. The case study given in Section 5.7.8 provides an example of a window-related problem.

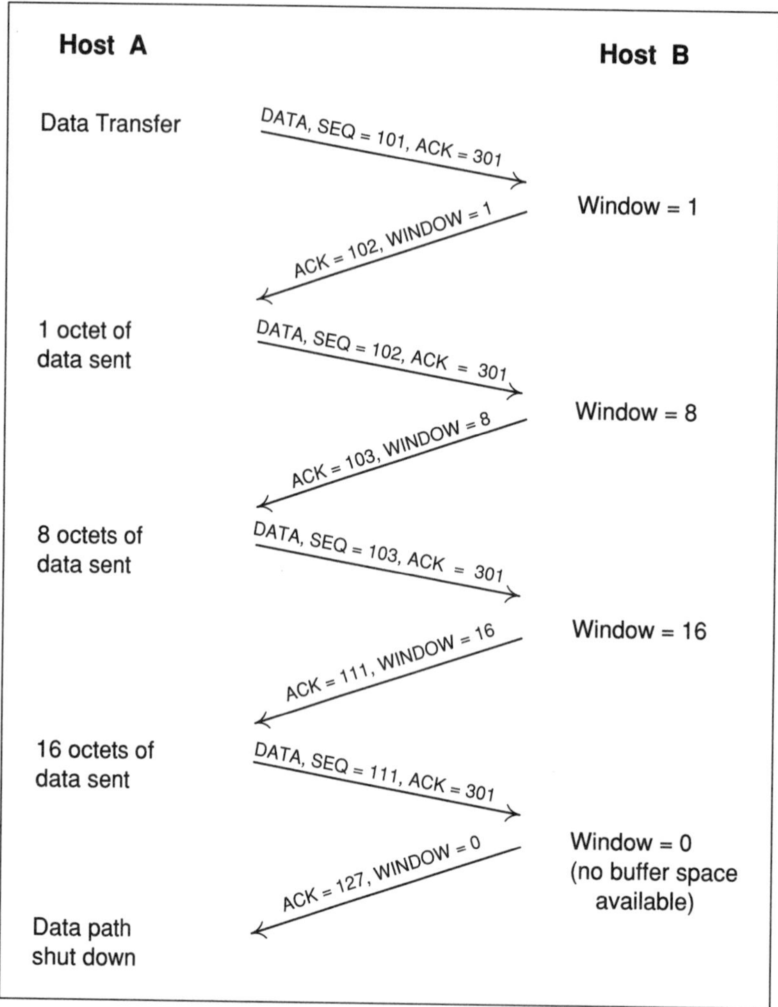

Figure 5-7 TCP Data Transfer (Window Size Varying)

5.5.4 Multiplexing

The TCP module assumes that its associated host may be a multi-function system. Indeed, the host may offer the user an entire menu of applications, and the user may want to use several of them simultaneously. TCP provides a multiplexing function to accommodate these diverse needs. In Section 5.2, we learned that the Port address (16 bits) uniquely identifies an end-user process. The host binds, or associates, a particular port with a process. Some processes, such as the major application protocols FTP, TELNET, and SMTP, have assigned Port numbers. Others may be dynamically assigned as the need arises.

A *socket* is the concatenation of the Internet address and the Port address. A *connection* is the association of a pair of sockets, although a socket is not restricted to one connection. For example, if a host has a port assigned to the TELNET protocol – say, Port 23 – there's nothing to preclude connections from multiple terminals (i.e., remote sockets) to that port. The host can also have other processes, such as the File Transfer Protocol, operating on another port, such as Port 21. Thus, we can say that TCP provides true multiplexing (the term stems from the Greek noun meaning "many paths") of the data connections into and out of a particular host.

5.5.5 Connections

Because TCP is a connection-oriented protocol, a *logical connection* (known as a virtual circuit) must be established between the two end users before any ULP data can be transmitted. The logical connection is a concatenation of many physical connections, such as Host A to LAN A, connecting to Router 1, connecting via a WAN link to Router 2, and so on. Managing this end-to-end system is much easier if you use a single identifier – the logical connection.

The logical connection is established when the ULP process recognizes the need to communicate with a distant peer and passes an OPEN command across the user/TCP interface to the TCP module in the host. The OPEN command is one of a number of primitives described in the TCP standard, RFC 793. A *primitive* is an event that requests or responds to an action from the other side of the user/TCP interface. The primary TCP primitives include OPEN, SEND, RECEIVE, CLOSE, STATUS, and ABORT. Many parameters traverse the user/TCP interface with the primitive, and therefore more descriptive names such as PASSIVE OPEN or ACTIVE OPEN are often used. Each host operating system may modify these primitives for its particular use.

The OPEN command triggers what is referred to as a *three-way handshake.* The three-way handshake ensures that both ends are prepared to transfer data, reducing the likelihood of data being sent before the distant host can accept it. (If either host becomes confused from an attempted three-way handshake, the confused host sets the Reset (RST) flag, indicating that the segment that arrived was not intended for this connection.) In most cases, one TCP module initiates the connection and another responds. However, it is possible for two TCP modules to request a connection simultaneously; RFC 793 elaborates on this condition.

RFC 793 describes the steps in the three-way handshake as follows:

- Host A to Host B: SYN, my Sequence number is X
- Host B to Host A: ACK, your Sequence number is X
- Host B to Host A: SYN, my Sequence number is Y
- Host A to Host B: ACK, your Sequence number is Y

In other words, each side of the connection sends it own Sequence number to the other end, and receives a confirmation of it in an acknowledgment from the other side. Both sides are then aware of the other's initial Sequence number, and reliable communication can proceed. It is possible (and in most cases preferred) for the second and third steps above (from Host B to Host A) to be combined into a single transmission. This combination then yields a total of three transmissions, illustrating the name "three-way handshake."

In Figure 5-8, the initiating module (Host A) generates a TCP segment with the Synchronize (SYN) flag set (SYN = 1) and an initial Sequence number chosen by the module (e.g., ISN = 100). If the connection request was acceptable, the remote TCP module (Host B) would return a TCP segment containing both an acknowledgment for Host A's ISN [ACK = 101], plus its own ISN [SEQ = 300]. Both the Synchronize and Acknowledgment (ACK) flag bits would be set (SYN = 1, ACK = 1) in that response from Host B. Note that the two TCP modules are not required to have the same ISN since these numbers are administered locally. An acknowledgment from the initiating module, Host A, is the third step of the three-way handshake. This TCP segment includes the Sequence number [SEQ = 101] plus an acknowledgment for Host B's desired ISN (ACK = 301).

Note that by convention, the ACK in the second TCP segment increments (i.e. ACK = 101) even though no data transfer occurred. Similarly, the ACK in the third segment increments (i.e. ACK = 301) even though no data transfer occurred there either. These exceptions to the normal acknowledgment process occur in order to verify receipt of the other host's ISN segment (which may not contain any data). When data transfer does begin (in the fourth and fifth segments), the same Sequence numbers as the previously corresponding ACKs are used (i.e. SEQ = 101 seen in both segments 3 and 4). Another way of saying this is that a segment containing just an ACK (and no data) would not use up a Sequence number; the three-way handshake (with the FIN flag set) *does* use a Sequence number.

To manage connection-related issues, the TCP module maintains a record known as a *Transmission Control Block* (TCB). The TCB stores a number of variables, including the Local and Remote Socket numbers, the security/precedence of the connection, and pointers to identify incoming and outgoing data streams. Two other TCP functions already discussed, reliability and flow control, manage the data transfer process. The Sequence numbers, acknowledgments, and Window numbers are the mechanisms that the reliability, flow control, and data transfer functions use to ensure their proper operation.

Let's assume the data transfer is complete and the connection is no longer required. Because TCP provides a full-duplex connection, either side may initiate the disconnect. The other end, however, must continue to receive data until the remote module has finished sending it. The TCP connection can be terminated in one of three ways: the local host can initiate the termination, the remote host can initiate it, or both can close the connection simultaneously. The shut-down procedure is the same in all three cases. For example, if the local host has completed its business, it can generate a TCP segment with the Finish (FIN) flag set (FIN = 1). The local host will continue to receive data from the remote end until it receives a TCP segment with FIN = 1 from the remote end. When the second Finish segment is acknowledged, the connection is closed.

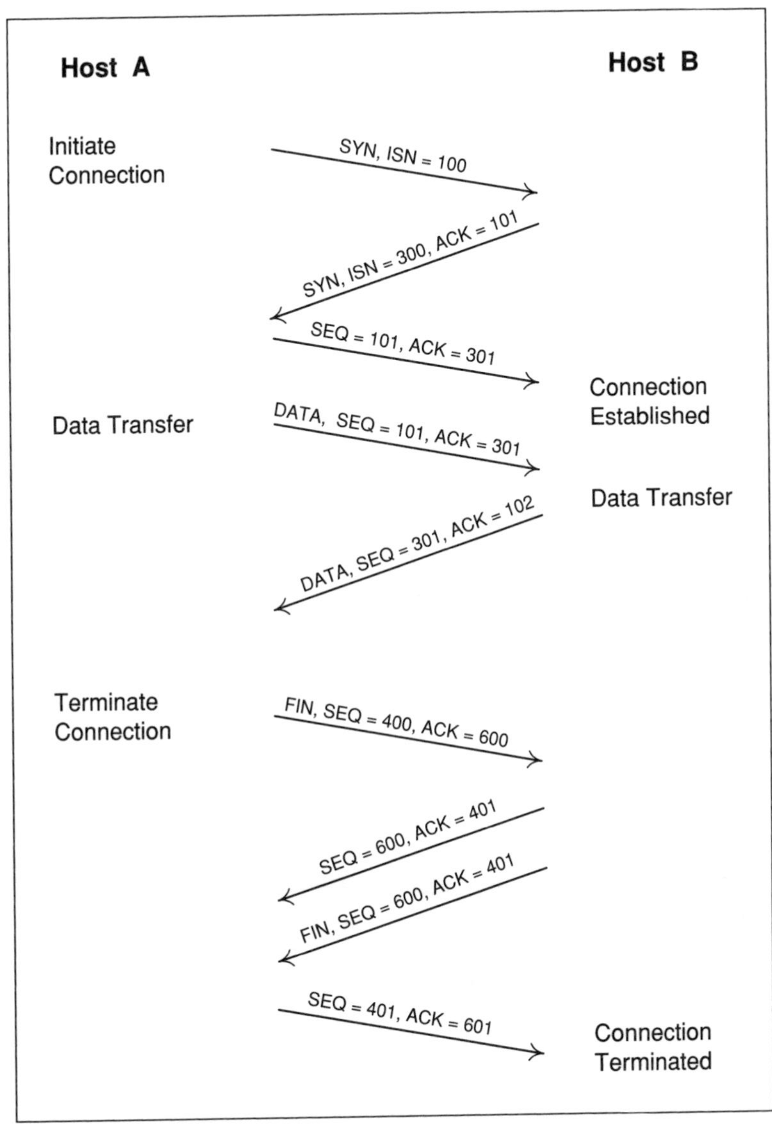

Figure 5-8 TCP Connection Establishment, Data Transfer, and Termination Events

The bottom of Figure 5-8 illustrates this scenario. Host A has finished transferring its last data segment and terminates the connection by sending [FIN, SEQ = 400, ACK = 600]. Host B acknowledges receipt of Host A's FIN by sending [SEQ =

600, ACK = 401], and then sends its own FIN [FIN, SEQ = 600, ACK = 401]. Host A acknowledges Host B's FIN with [SEQ = 401, ACK = 601], and the connection is closed.

Make a special note of the Sequence and Acknowledgment number progression in these last four segments. The first closing segment [FIN, SEQ = 400, ACK = 600] uses the Sequence and Acknowledgment numbers that were next in line. The second segment is just an acknowledgment for the first [SEQ = 600, ACK = 401], and therefore does not use up a Sequence number. The third segment contains a FIN, and again, by convention, uses the same Sequence number [SEQ = 600] as was found in the previous ACK. The fourth segment (again, operating by convention) increments the Sequence number even though it contains no data ([SEQ = 401], which corresponds with the previous ACK), and also increments the Acknowledgment number [ACK = 601]. This verifies receipt of the FIN contained in the third segment. Once again, the connection termination sequence, also called the modified three-way handshake, causes a special condition for the Sequence and Acknowledgment numbers. This FIN segment (without data) uses a Sequence number, much like the case of the SYN flag illustrated previously.

5.5.6 Precedence/Security

As a military application, TCP required precedence and security. Therefore, these two attributes may be assigned for each connection. The IP Type of Service field and security option may be used to define the requirements associated with that connection. Higher layer protocols, such as TELNET, may specify the attribute required, and the TCP module will then comply on behalf of that ULP.

5.5.7 The TCP Connection State Diagram

Like many computer processes, TCP operation is best summarized with a state diagram, shown in Figure 5-9a and discussed in detail in "TCP Connection Initiation: An Inside Look" [5-10]. TCP operation progresses from one state to another in response to events, including user calls, incoming TCP segments, and timeouts. The *user calls* are commands that cross the User/TCP interface, that is, the functions that support the communication between user processes. These include OPEN, SEND, RECEIVE, CLOSE, ABORT, and STATUS. When a TCP segment arrives, it must be examined to determine if any of the flags are set, particularly the SYN, ACK, RST, or FIN. The timeouts include the USER TIMEOUT, RETRANSMISSION TIMEOUT, and the TIME-WAIT TIMEOUT.

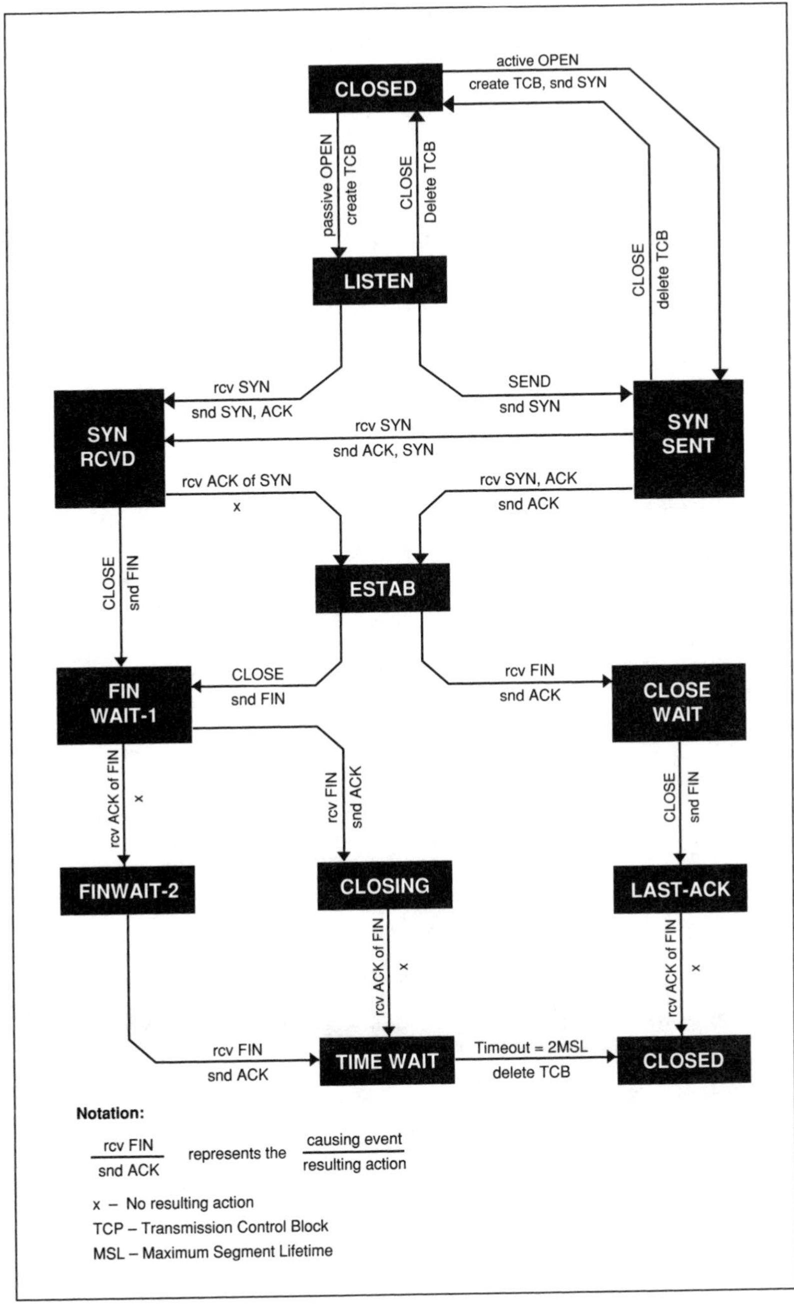

Figure 5-9a TCP Connection State Diagram

The first state entered by the TCP process is CLOSED, indicating no connection state at all. A passive OPEN creates a Transmission Control Block (TCB), which moves the process to the LISTEN state. It then waits for a connection from a remote TCP and port. If a SYN is received, a SYN, ACK is sent in response. Should another ACK be received, the connection reaches the ESTABLISHED state. When the data transfer is complete at the near end, a CLOSE is issued and a FIN sent, moving to the state FIN-WAIT-1 and subsequently FIN-WAIT-2 or CLOSING. After waiting to confirm that the remote TCP has received the ACK of its FIN, the TCB is deleted and the connection reaches the CLOSED state. In a similar manner, a FIN received from the other end of the connection moves the process to state CLOSE-WAIT, pending the completion of the local user's requirements for that connection. When the ACK of the FIN has been received, the connection once again reaches the CLOSED state. Further explanations of the various states are given in Figure 5-9b.

The meanings of the states are:

LISTEN – represents waiting for a connection request from any remote TCP and port.

SYN-SENT – represents waiting for a matching connection request after having sent a connection request.

SYN-RECEIVED – represents waiting for a confirming connection request acknowledgment after having both received and sent a connection request.

ESTABLISHED – represents an open connection, data received can be delivered to the user. The normal state for the data transfer phase of the connection.

FIN-WAIT-1 – represents waiting for a connection termination request from the remote TCP, or an acknowledgement of the connection termination request previously sent.

FIN-WAIT-2 – represents waiting for a connection termination request from the remote TCP.

CLOSE-WAIT – represents waiting for a connection termination request from the local user.

CLOSING – represents waiting for a connection termination request acknowledgment from the remote TCP.

LAST-ACK – represents waiting for an acknowledgment of the connection termination request previously sent to the remote TCP (which includes an acknowledgment of its connection termination request).

TIME-WAIT – represents waiting for enough time to pass to be sure the remote TCP received the acknowledgment of its connection termination request.

CLOSED – represents no connection state at all.

Figure 5-9b TCP Connection States

5.5.8 TCP Algorithms

Many TCP implementations include algorithms that perform specific functions. These are documented in RFC 2001 [5-11], and include:

- Slow Start: If too many segments are sent to a distant host, and a slower link, such as a WAN route via an intermediate router, is in the path to that host, congestion at that WAN route may occur. To avoid this, the Slow Start algorithm limits the amount of data that can be transmitted, as controlled by the ACKs received from the distant end.
- Congestion Avoidance: The loss of packets is a typical result of congestion between sender and receiver, and this congestion is indicated by the occurrence of a timeout or the receipt of duplicate ACKs. The Congestion Avoidance algorithm, which may operate in conjunction with Slow Start, increases the congestion window variable in linear amounts, thus limiting the data sent into the network.
- Fast Retransmit: The receipt of multiple, duplicate ACKs may indicate a lost TCP segment. The sending TCP module will then retransmit the segment that appears to be lost, without waiting for a retransmission timer to expire, thus speeding receipt of the data.
- Fast Recovery: After the Fast Retransmit algorithm resends an apparently missing segment, Congestion Avoidance, but not Slow Start, is invoked. This process is called the Fast Recovery algorithm, which avoids the Slow Start process to keep the sender from reducing the data flow abruptly. The Fast Recovery and Fast Retransmit algorithms may operate in conjunction with each other.

5.6 Troubleshooting the Host-to-Host Connection

In this chapter, we've studied the two protocols that provide end-to-end (or host-to-host) connectivity. We've seen that UDP provides connectionless service and is typically used for applications that need Port identification (or multiplexing) and basic error control. TCP offers connection-oriented service and rigorously maintains Sequence and Acknowledgment numbers to guarantee data delivery. The price for TCP's extensive error control is its additional header overhead (20 vs. 8 octets), plus the additional processing overhead required to keep track of the Sequence and Acknowledgment numbers and other connection-oriented functions.

What should you do when the host-to-host connection fails? First, you need to determine the underlying transport protocol – UDP or TCP. If the protocol is UDP, verify that connectionless service is adequate for the application. If it is, then a problem such as multiple retransmissions may result from the upper layer protocol's assumptions regarding the transport mechanism. For instance, because it has experienced overhead savings all along, the ULP may tolerate an occasional overhead-producing glitch in communications.

TCP is much more complex. In addition to verifying the Port number, look for significant events in the TCP connection. These include the three-way handshake (using the SYN and ACK flags) and the connection termination (using the RST and FIN flags). During the data transfer phase, verify that the Sequence numbers, Acknowledgments, and Window sizes are appropriate for the application, and remember that Window = 0 will close the communication path in the opposite direction.

In short, determine whether the transmitted data is reaching its destination. If it's not, study the Internet Layer for problems, as discussed in Chapter 4. If it is, examine the UDP and TCP headers to determine the source of the delivery problem. RFC 816, "Fault Isolation and Recovery" [5-12], contains interesting thoughts on internet vs. host analysis.

Now that we're steeped in the theory behind UDP and TCP operation, let's examine some case studies that demonstrate how these protocols operate (and where they might fail).

5.7 Case Studies

The case studies in this section concentrate on issues that demonstrate the host-to-host connection. We'll start with examples that use the datagram-based UDP, then we'll move to more complex examples that require the connection-oriented TCP.

5.7.1 Using BOOTP with UDP Transport

The Bootstrap Protocol (BOOTP), described in RFC 951 [5-13] and RFC 2132 [5-14], allows a client device to obtain its bootup parameters from a server. BOOTP runs over the UDP transport and uses two defined ports: Port 67 (BOOTP Server) and Port 68 (BOOTP Client). Because it uses the connectionless UDP as the transport, the connection depends on the end-user processes for reliability. The BOOTP message has a standard format (review Figure 4-6a) for both client requests and server replies, which adds to the protocol's simplicity.

Once the client locates its server and boot file, it uses the Trivial File Transfer Protocol (TFTP) to obtain the actual file, as described in References [5-15] and [5-16]. Let's look at what happens when the client can't find its server.

In this example, a Retix bridge is configured to obtain its SNMP parameters from a Sun workstation located on another segment (see Figure 5-10). Upon power-up, the bridge broadcasts a BOOTP request, looking for the BOOTP server (see Trace 5.7.1a). Unfortunately, the administrator of the Sun workstation has not loaded the

BOOTP daemon on the Sun workstation, so the BOOTP requests go unanswered. Note that the BOOTP request packets are staggered in time and transmitted at relatively long intervals (2 to 17 seconds apart).

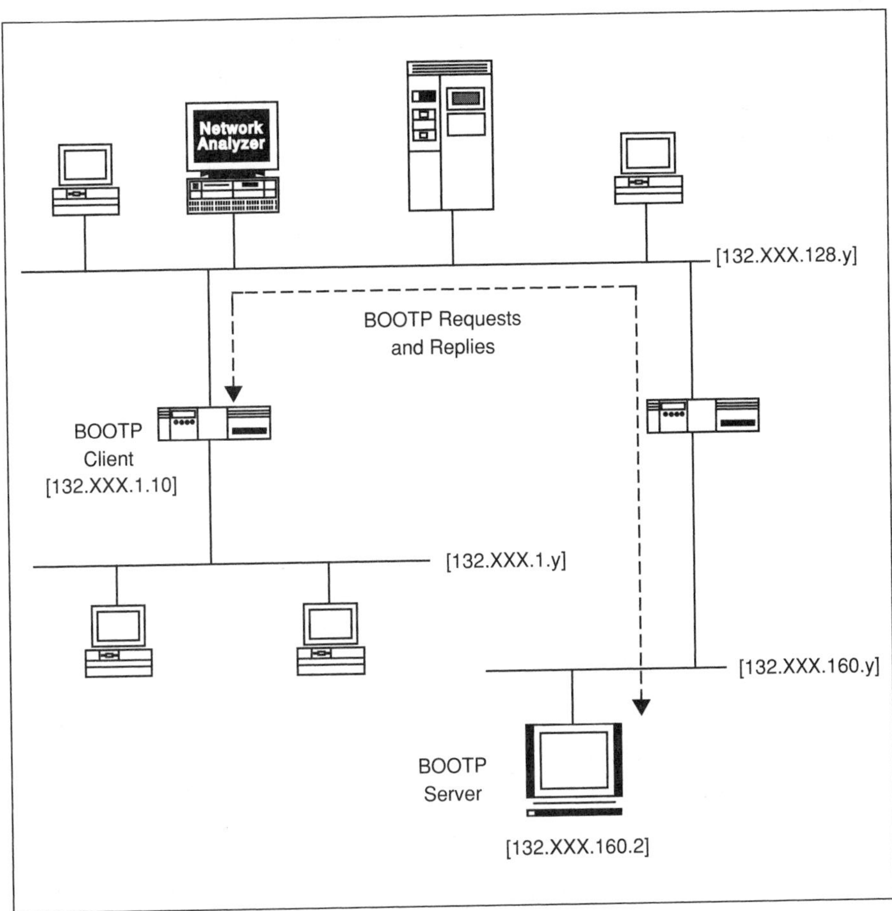

Figure 5-10 Booting Remote Bridge Using BOOTP

When the bridge administrator realizes that his device is not operating properly, he studies the repeated BOOTP requests, theorizing that the BOOTP server is not listening and therefore not responding. His assumption is correct. After the BOOTP daemon is loaded on the Sun workstation, the bridge receives a response (Frame 4 of Trace 5.7.1b). The bridge then requests its boot file from the Sun workstation and receives its information in Frame 6. An acknowledgment from the bridge (Frame 7) completes the transaction.

Details of the scenario (Trace 5.7.1c) show how the BOOTP and TFTP protocols work together. The BOOTP request (Frame 3) contains the boot file name (90034CF1) that the bridge requires. The BOOTP reply (Frame 4) contains a server-assigned IP address for the client [132.XXX.1.10] and the address of the BOOTP server [132.XXX.160.2]. The location of the boot file name (/tftpboot/90034CF1) is also included. Next, the bridge sends a TFTP Read request in Frame 5. The BOOTP server responds with a data packet containing the configuration parameters the bridge requires. A TFTP ACK from the bridge completes the transaction. With the BOOTP daemon properly installed on the Sun workstation, the bridge can receive its configuration parameters and begin initialization.

TRACE 5.7.1A. BRIDGE BOOTP UNANSWERED REQUEST SUMMARY

Sniffer Network Analyzer data 5-Sep at 14:02:52, RETXBOOT.ENC, Pg 1

SUMMARY	Delta T	Destination	Source	Summary
M 1		090077000001	Retix 034CF1	DSAP=80, I frame
2	10.8868	Broadcast	Retix 034CF1	BOOTP Request
3	2.2928	Broadcast	Retix 034CF1	BOOTP Request
4	9.8320	Broadcast	Retix 034CF1	BOOTP Request
5	2.0745	Broadcast	Retix 034CF1	BOOTP Request
6	11.0334	Broadcast	Retix 034CF1	BOOTP Request
7	2.1841	Broadcast	Retix 034CF1	BOOTP Request
8	6.1166	CMC 614107	Retix 034CF1	ARP R PA=[0.0.0.0] HA=080090034CF1 PRO=IP
9	7.2104	Broadcast	Retix 034CF	BOOTP Request
10	2.0746	Broadcast	Retix 034CF1	BOOTP Request
11	8.1893	090077000001	Retix 034CF1	DSAP=80, I frame
12	7.2135	Broadcast	Retix 034CF1	BOOTP Request
13	2.2931	Broadcast	Retix 034CF1	BOOTP Request
14	15.4028	Broadcast	Retix 034CF1	BOOTP Request
15	2.0747	Broadcast	Retix 034CF1	BOOTP Request
16	13.2180	Broadcast	Retix 034CF1	BOOTP Request
17	2.2931	Broadcast	Retix 034CF1	BOOTP Request
18	8.7395	Broadcast	Retix 034CF1	BOOTP Request
19	2.0746	Broadcast	Retix 034CF1	BOOTP Request
20	17.6970	Broadcast	Retix 034CF1	BOOTP Request
21	2.1838	Broadcast	Retix 034CF1	BOOTP Request
22	7.7562	Broadcast	Retix 034CF1	BOOTP Request
23	2.0747	Broadcast	Retix 034CF1	BOOTP Request
24	12.1260	Broadcast	Retix 034CF1	BOOTP Request
25	2.1836	Broadcast	Retix 034CF1	BOOTP Request
26	5.4624	Broadcast	Retix 034CF1	BOOTP Request
27	2.0746	Broadcast	Retix 034CF1	BOOTP Request

28	5.4625	Broadcast	Retix 034CF1	BOOTP Request
29	2.2931	Broadcast	Retix 034CF1	BOOTP Request
30	16.4951	Broadcast	Retix 034CF1	BOOTP Request
31	2.0746	Broadcast	Retix 034CF1	BOOTP Request

TRACE 5.7.1B. BRIDGE BOOTP REQUEST/REPLY SUMMARY

Sniffer Network Analyzer data 16-Mar at 09:48:26, BOOTP.ENC, Pg 1

SUMMARY	Delta T	Destination	Source	Summary
M 1		090077000001	Retix 034CF1	DSAP=80, I frame
2	6.6956	090077000001	Retix 034CF1	DSAP=80, I frame
3	4.1908	Broadcast	Retix 034CF1	BOOTP Request
4	0.5307	Retix 034CF1	Sun 0AB646	BOOTP Reply
5	0.0053	Sun 0AB646	Retix 034CF1	TFTP Read request File=/tftpboot/90034CF1
6	0.2037	Retix 034CF1	Sun 0AB646	TFTP Data packet NS=1 (Last)
7	0.0033	Sun 0AB646	Retix 034CF1	TFTP Ack NR=1
8	50.2652	090077000001	Retix 034CF1	DSAP=80, I frame

TRACE 5.7.1C. BRIDGE BOOTP REQUEST/REPLY DETAILS

Sniffer Network Analyzer data 16-Mar at 09:48:26, BOOTP.ENC, Pg 1

```
- - - - - - - - - - - - - - - Frame 3 - - - - - - - - - - - - - - - -

BOOTP: —— BOOTP Header ——
BOOTP:
BOOTP: Boot record type        = 1 (Request)
BOOTP: Hardware address type   = 1 10Mb Ethernet
BOOTP: Hardware address length = 6 bytes
BOOTP:
BOOTP: Hops = 0
BOOTP: Transaction id = 0000063F
BOOTP: Elapsed boot time = 0 seconds
BOOTP:
BOOTP: Client self-assigned IP address   = [0.0.0.0] (Unknown)
BOOTP: Client hardware address           = Retix 034CF1
BOOTP:
BOOTP: Host name      = "
```

```
BOOTP: Boot file name = "90034CF1"
BOOTP:
BOOTP: [Vendor specific information]
BOOTP:

- - - - - - - - - - - - - - Frame 4 - - - - - - - - - - - - - - - -

BOOTP: —— BOOTP Header ——
BOOTP:
BOOTP: Boot record type        = 2 (Reply)
BOOTP: Hardware address type   = 1 10Mb Ethernet
BOOTP: Hardware address length = 6 bytes
BOOTP:
BOOTP: Hops = 0
BOOTP: Transaction id = 0000063F
BOOTP: Elapsed boot time = 0 seconds
BOOTP:
BOOTP: Client self-assigned IP address   = [0.0.0.0] (Unknown)
BOOTP: Client server-assigned IP address = [132.XXX.1.10]
BOOTP: Server IP address                 = [132.XXX.160.2]
BOOTP: Gateway IP address                = [132.XXX.160.2]
BOOTP: Client hardware address           = Retix 034CF1
BOOTP:
BOOTP: Host name      = "
BOOTP: Boot file name = "i/tftpboot/90034CF1"
BOOTP:
BOOTP: [Vendor specific information]
BOOTP:

- - - - - - - - - - - - - - - Frame 5 - - - - - - - - - - - - - - - -

TFTP:   ——Trivial file transfer ——
TFTP:
TFTP:   Opcode = 1 (Read request)
TFTP:   File name = "/tftpboot/90034CF1"
TFTP:   Mode = "octet"
TFTP:
TFTP:   [Normal end of "Trivial file transfer".]
TFTP:

- - - - - - - - - - - - - - - Frame 6 - - - - - - - - - - - - - - - -

TFTP:   —— Trivial file transfer ——
TFTP:
```

```
TFTP:   Opcode = 3 (Data packet)
TFTP:   Block number = 1
TFTP:   [160 bytes of data] (Last frame)
TFTP:
TFTP:   [Normal end of "Trivial file transfer".]
TFTP:
--------------- Frame 7 -----------------
TFTP:   ——Trivial file transfer ——
TFTP:
TFTP:   Opcode = 4 (Ack)
TFTP:   Block number = 1
TFTP:
TFTP:   [Normal end of "Trivial file transfer".]
TFTP:
```

5.7.2 Clock Synchronization with UDP

As we've discussed, applications for UDP are ones in which all parties to the communication recognize and accept that the datagram may get lost and have to be retransmitted. In other words, non-mission-critical applications are more likely to utilize UDP. One example of such an application is the synchronization of the clocks on all the hosts on the internetwork. The synchronization information is included in a single datagram. Should one of the synchronization datagrams get lost, a retransmission can easily be requested. Besides, it makes little sense to establish a connection using a TCP three-way handshake (which uses three TCP segments), then to send one segment of data, then to use several more segments to close the connection. UDP seems ideal for this application. Let's see how it works.

The protocol selected is the Time protocol, described in RFC 868 [5-17]. Time is a relatively simple protocol that can be used with either UDP or TCP. It uses Port 37 and operates as shown in Figure 5-11. The Time server listens on Port 37 for a Time Request datagram. The user transmits an empty datagram to Port 37, which prompts the server to return a 32-bit number representing the current time. The user receives the Time datagram and uses that information to synchronize its clock with that of the server. The timestamp itself (the 32-bit number) counts the number of seconds that have expired since midnight on January 1, 1900, Greenwich Mean Time (GMT). RFC 868 states that this measurement will be usable until the year 2036. (The network engineer figures he'll be enjoying his retirement in Hawaii by 2036, so he decides to use the Time protocol for his internetwork.)

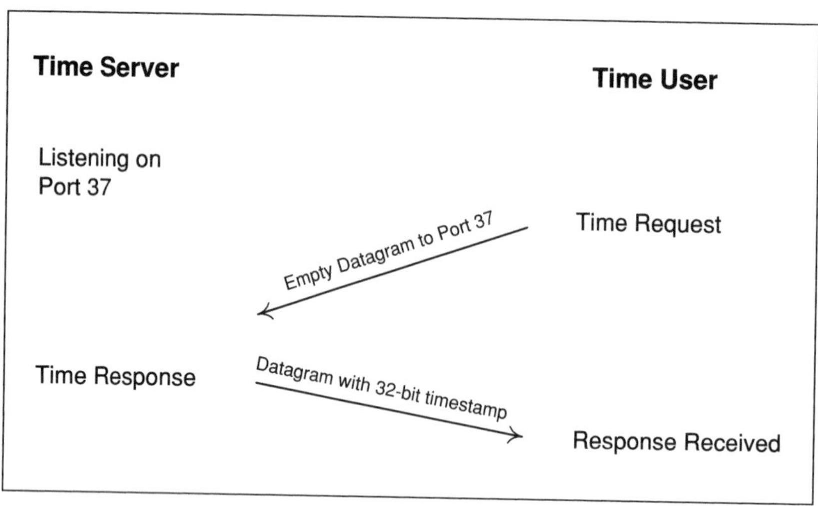

Figure 5-11 Time Protocol Implemented with UDP Transport

The internetwork in question is a series of bridged token ring networks, shown in Figure 5-12. The Time server is a Sun SPARCstation 2 running BSD UNIX 4.3 and attached to network [142.56.20.0]. The user in question is a Sun SPARCstation IPX, also running BSD UNIX 4.3 but attached to network [142.56.17.0].

Although the Time protocol is extremely simple, some confusion occurs. As the network manager discovers, the programmer who wrote the code for the user system (the Sun IPX) used an incorrect Destination Port number. We see the problem in Trace 5.7.2a. In Frame 175, the user sends an empty UDP packet to Port 2057. We know that this packet is empty because its length is only 8 octets, the length of the UDP header (review Figure 5-2). In Frame 176, the Time server (via Bridge 17.3) returns an ICMP Destination Unreachable message, specifying that the selected port is unreachable. A check of the originating message shows a total length of 28 octets, which comprise the IP header (20 octets) and the UDP header (8 octets). Both the Source and Destination addresses are correct and the checksum passes. Clearly, the Destination port (2057) causes the problem; the Time server is listening at Port 37 and does not hear the request for a timestamp.

Once the systems programmer rewrites his code, the time service request succeeds (see Trace 5.7.2b). The Sun IPX transmits an empty UDP packet in Frame 157, and the Sun SPARCstation 2 Time server [142.56.20.16] sends a correct response via the bridge. Both the request and the response are correctly addressed to and from Port 37. In the Time response (Frame 158), note that the message returned is four octets (shown as "4 byte(s) of data" in the decode of the UDP header). This data is shown as the last eight hexadecimal characters in the printout, AD 67 8E FD, which correspond to the appropriate time from the Time server.

This example illustrates two important points: UDP is clearly adequate for many host-to-host applications, but the correct addressing of the host port is vital to the success of the transmission.

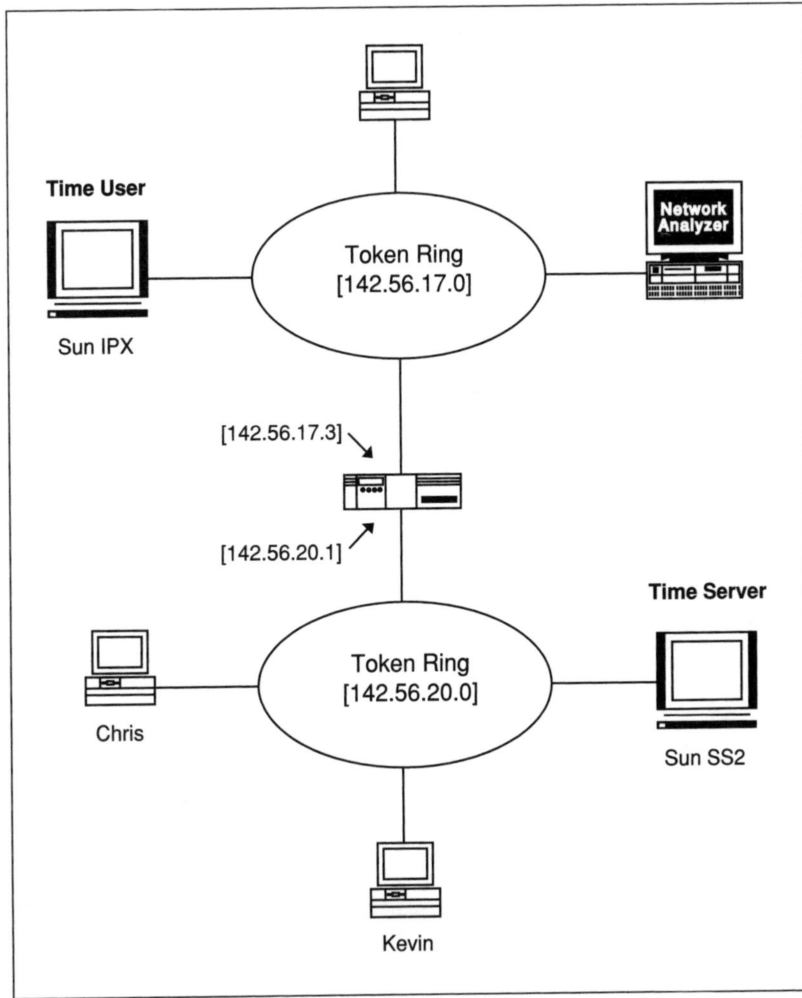

Figure 5-12 Time Service

TRACE 5.7.2A. TIME REQUEST TO INCORRECT PORT NUMBER

```
Sniffer Network Analyzer data 10-Mar at 12:52:50, TIME_BAD.TRC, Pg 1

- - - - - - - - - - - - - - - Frame 175 - - - - - - - - - - - - - - - - -

UDP:  —— UDP Header ——
UDP:
UDP:  Source port = 1157
UDP:  Destination port = 2057
UDP:  Length = 8
UDP:  No checksum
UDP:
- - - - - - - - - - - - - - - Frame 176 - - - - - - - - - - - - - - - - -
ICMP:  —— ICMP header ——
ICMP:
ICMP:  Type = 3 (Destination unreachable)
ICMP:  Code = 3 (Port unreachable)
ICMP:  Checksum = F066 (correct)
ICMP:  IP header of originating message (description follows)
ICMP:
IP:    —— IP Header ——
IP:
IP:    Version = 4, header length = 20 bytes
IP:    Type of service = 00
IP:          000. .... = routine
IP:          ...0 .... = normal delay
IP:          .... 0... = normal throughput
IP:          .... .0.. = normal reliability
IP:    Total length = 28 bytes
IP:    Identification = 60919
IP:    Flags = 0X
IP:    .0.. .... = may fragment
IP:    ..0. .... = last fragment
IP:    Fragment offset = 0 bytes
IP:    Time to live = 59 seconds/hops
IP:    Protocol = 17 (UDP)
IP:    Header checksum = 5055 (correct)
IP:    Source address = [142.56.17.4]
IP:    Destination address = [142.56.20.16]
IP:    No options
ICMP:
ICMP:  [First 8 byte(s) of data of originating message]
ICMP:
ICMP:  [Normal end of "ICMP header".]
ICMP:
```

TRACE 5.7.2B. UDP TIME SERVICE DETAILS

```
Sniffer Network Analyzer data 10-Mar at 12:40:00, TIME_WRK.TRC, Pg 1

- - - - - - - - - - - - - - - Frame 157 - - - - - - - - - - - - - - - - -

IP:   —— IP Header ——
IP:
IP:   Version = 4, header length = 20 bytes
IP:   Type of service = 00
IP:         000. .... = routine
IP:         ...0 .... = normal delay
IP:         .... 0... = normal throughput
IP:         .... .0.. = normal reliability
IP:   Total length = 28 bytes
IP:   Identification = 49402
IP:   Flags = 0X
IP:   .0.. .... = may fragment
IP:   ..0. .... = last fragment
IP:   Fragment offset = 0 bytes
IP:   Time to live = 60 seconds/hops
IP:   Protocol = 17 (UDP)
IP:   Header checksum = 7C52 (correct)
IP:   Source address = [142.56.17.4]
IP:   Destination address = [142.56.20.16]
IP:   No options
IP:
UDP:  —— UDP Header ——
UDP:
UDP:  Source port = 1141 (Time)
UDP:  Destination port = 37
UDP:  Length = 8
UDP:  No checksum
UDP:

ADDR    HEX                                                ASCII
0000    10 40 00 00 C9 09 23 4C   08 00 20 0B 8A A7 AA AA  .@....#L.. .....
0010    03 00 00 00 08 00 45 00   00 1C C0 FA 00 00 3C 11  ......E.......<.
0020    7C 52 8E 38 11 04 8E 38   14 10 04 75 00 25 00 08  |R.8...8...u.%..
0030    00 00
```

```
--------------- Frame 158 -----------------

IP: ----- IP Header -----
IP:
IP: Version = 4, header length = 20 bytes
IP: Type of service = 00
IP:      000. .... = routine
IP:      ...0 .... = normal delay
IP:      .... 0... = normal throughput
IP:      .... .0.. = normal reliability
IP: Total length = 32 bytes
IP: Identification = 27066
IP: Flags = 0X
IP: .0.. .... = may fragment
IP: ..0. .... = last fragment
IP: Fragment offset = 0 bytes
IP: Time to live = 59 seconds/hops
IP: Protocol = 17 (UDP)
IP: Header checksum = D48E (correct)
IP: Source address = [142.56.20.16]
IP: Destination address = [142.56.17.4]
IP: No options
IP:
UDP: ----- UDP Header -----
UDP:
UDP: Source port = 37 (Time)
UDP: Destination port = 1141
UDP: Length = 12
UDP: No checksum
UDP:
UDP: [4 byte(s) of data]
UDP:

ADDR    HEX                                                 ASCII
0000    18 40 08 00 20 0B 8A A7   00 00 C9 09 23 4C AA AA   .@.. .......#L..
0010    03 00 00 00 08 00 45 00   00 20 69 BA 00 00 3B 11   ......E.. i...;.
0020    D4 8E 8E 38 14 10 8E 38   11 04 00 25 04 75 00 0C   ...8...8...%.u..
0030    00 00 AD 67 8E FD                                   ...g..
```

5.7.3 Establishing and Terminating TCP Connections

In Section 5.5.5, we learned that the TCP connection must be established with a three-way handshake prior to any transmission of data. Once the data has been transferred, a modified three-way handshake terminates the connection. Let's study how these operations function, using a PC and its server as examples.

In this case study, a PC wishes to establish several logical connections to a Sun server via a single Ethernet physical connection (Figure 5-13). Different Port numbers identify the different logical connections (created using TCP's multiplexing capabilities). Let's follow the steps of one of these logical connections from establishment to data transfer to termination (see Trace 5.7.3a).

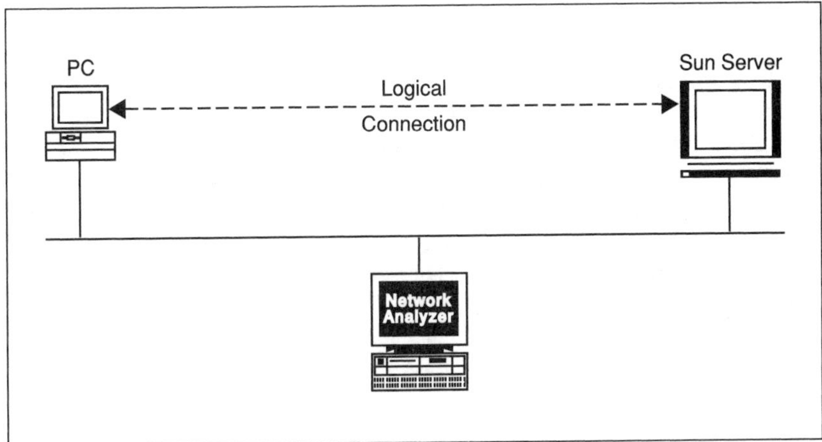

Figure 5-13 TCP Connection Establishment/Termination

A TCP segment identifies the connection establishment with the Synchronize bit set (SYN = 1) and no data in the segment (LEN = 0). We can see this in Frame 706, along with an initial Sequence number, ISN = 1988352000. Also note that the Sun server is initiating this connection and that it is advertising a rather large window size (WIN = 24576). The Source port (S = 20) identifies the File Transfer Protocol (FTP), and the Destination port (D = 1227) is assigned by the Sun server. The PC responds with a similar synchronize segment in Frame 707; the receipt of the server's segment is acknowledged (ACK = 1988352001), the PC's ISN is sent (SEQ = 201331252), but a smaller window size is allowed (WIN = 1024). Note that the Source and Destination Port numbers are now reversed, since the original source (the Sun server) has now become the PC's destination. Frame 708 completes the connection establishment, with the server acknowledging the PC's ISN (ACK = 201331253).

The details of the connection establishment are shown in Trace 5.7.3b. Note that one TCP option (the maximum segment size) is used. Maximum segment size = 1460 suggests transmission over an Ethernet/IEEE 802.3 LAN. The Ethernet/IEEE 802.3 can accommodate 1,500 octets of data within the frame. Of these, 20 octets are used for the TCP header and another 20 octets for the IP header, leaving 1,460 octets for the TCP segment. Data transfer may now proceed.

Data transfer begins in Frame 710 with a TCP segment of 1,024 octets (LEN = 1024). (Note that Frame 709 belongs to a previously established FTP connection destined for another port (D = 1219) on the same PC. While Frame 709 illustrates TCP's port multiplexing capabilities, it has nothing to do with the current discussion since it belongs to another logical connection.) The PC acknowledges receipt of the data in Frame 713 by sending ACK = 1988353025 (1988352001 + 1024 = 1988353025). The PC will not permit any more data at this time, and it indicates this by shutting its window (WIN = 0). In Frame 715, the PC's processor has caught up with its backlog (note that it was servicing Port 1219 in Frame 714) and restores data flow by sending WIN = 1024. The server responds with another 1,024 octets in Frame 716. This process proceeds normally until the server completes its business.

In Frame 779, the server finishes its business and sends the Finish flag (FIN = 1) along with its last 114 octets of data. The PC responds with an acknowledgment in Frame 780 (ACK = 1988384884), then sends a second segment (Frame 781) containing both an ACK and a FIN. Note that the details in Trace 5.7.3c indicate that the PC does not shut down the connection, but permits up to 910 more octets of data from the other end (Window = 910). The server has said its piece, however; it acknowledges the FIN and closes its end of the connection in Frame 782. Both ends of the logical connection are now closed. In the following example, we'll see what happens when both ends are unable to maintain the connection and the Reset (RST) flag is required.

TRACE 5.7.3A. TCP CONNECTION ESTABLISHMENT AND TERMINATION SUMMARY

Sniffer Network Analyzer data 27-Mar at 09:04:54, TCPMEDLY.ENC, Pg 1

SUMMARY	Delta T	Destination	Source	Summary
706	0.0027	PC	Sun Server	TCP D=1227 S=20 SYN SEQ=1988352000 LEN=0 WIN=24576
707	0.0139	Sun Server	PC	TCP D=20 S=1227 SYN ACK=1988352001 SEQ=201331252 LEN=0 WIN=1024
708	0.0006	PC	Sun Server	TCP D=1227 S=20 ACK=201331253 WIN=24576
709	0.0007	PC	Sun Server	FTP R PORT=1219

				150 ASCII data connection
710	0.0993	PC	Sun Server	TCP D=1227 S=20 ACK=201331253 SEQ=1988352001 LEN=1024 WIN=24576
711	0.0733	Sun Server	PC	TCP D=21 S=1219 ACK=1972865105 WIN=951
712	0.0008	PC	Sun Server	FTP R PORT=1219 226 ASCII Transfer complete <0D><0A>
713	0.0529	Sun Server	PC	TCP D=20 S=1227 ACK=1988353025 WIN=0
714	0.0535	Sun Server	PC	TCP D=21 S=1219 ACK=1972865135 WIN=956
715	0.0790	Sun Server	PC	TCP D=20 S=1227 ACK=1988353025 WIN=1024
716	0.0015	PC	Sun Server	TCP D=1227 S=20 ACK=201331253 SEQ=1988353025 LEN=1024 WIN=24576
717	0.1379	Sun Server	PC	TCP D=20 S=1227 ACK=1988354049 WIN=0
718	0.0644	Sun Server	PC	TCP D=20 S=1227 ACK=1988354049 WIN=1024
719	0.0015	PC	Sun Server	TCP D=1227 S=20 ACK=201331253 SEQ=1988354049 LEN=1024 WIN=24576
720	0.0553	Sun Server	PC	TCP D=20 S=1227 ACK=1988355073 WIN=1024
721	0.0015	PC	Sun Server	TCP D=1227 S=20 ACK=201331253 SEQ=1988355073 LEN=1024 WIN=24576
722	0.0575	Sun Server	PC	TCP D=20 S=1227 ACK=1988356097 WIN=1024
.				
.				
.				
779	0.0008	PC	Sun Server	TCP D=1227 S=20 FIN ACK=201331253 SEQ=1988384769 LEN=114 WIN=24576

780	0.0204	Sun Server	PC	TCP D=20 S=1227 ACK=1988384884 WIN=910
781	0.0616	Sun Server	PC	TCP D=20 S=1227 FIN ACK=1988384884 SEQ=201331253 LEN=0 WIN=910
782	0.0006	PC	Sun Server	TCP D=1227 S=20 ACK=201331254 WIN=24576

TRACE 5.7.3B. TCP CONNECTION SYNCHRONIZATION (SYN) DETAILS

```
Sniffer Network Analyzer data 27-Mar at 09:04:54, TCPMEDLY.ENC, Pg 1

- - - - - - - - - - - - - - - Frame 706 - - - - - - - - - - - - - - - - -

TCP:  ——TCP header ——
TCP:
TCP:  Source port = 20 (FTP data)
TCP:  Destination port = 1227
TCP:  Initial sequence number = 1988352000
TCP:  Data offset = 24 bytes
TCP:  Flags = 02
TCP:  ..0. .... = (No urgent pointer)
TCP:  ...0 .... = (No acknowledgment)
TCP:  .... 0... = (No push)
TCP:  .... .0.. = (No reset)
TCP:  .... ..1. = SYN
TCP:  .... ...0 = (No FIN)
TCP:  Window = 24576
TCP:  Checksum = D02F (correct)
TCP:
TCP:  Options follow
TCP:  Maximum segment size = 1460
TCP:

- - - - - - - - - - - - - - - Frame 707 - - - - - - - - - - - - - - - - -

TCP:  ——TCP header ——
TCP:
TCP:  Source port = 1227
TCP:  Destination port = 20 (FTP data)
TCP:  Initial sequence number = 201331252
TCP:  Acknowledgment number = 1988352001
TCP:  Data offset = 24 bytes
```

```
TCP:  Flags = 12
TCP:  ..0. .... = (No urgent pointer)
TCP:  ...1 .... = Acknowledgment
TCP:  .... 0... = (No push)
TCP:  .... .0.. = (No reset)
TCP:  .... ..1. = SYN
TCP:  .... ...0 = (No FIN)
TCP:  Window = 1024
TCP:  Checksum = 0DEB (correct)
TCP:
TCP:  Options follow
TCP:  Maximum segment size = 1460
TCP:

- - - - - - - - - - - - - - - Frame 708 - - - - - - - - - - - - - - - - -

TCP:  —— TCP header ——
TCP:
TCP:  Source port = 20 (FTP data)
TCP:  Destination port = 1227
TCP:  Sequence number = 1988352001
TCP:  Acknowledgment number = 201331253
TCP:  Data offset = 20 bytes
TCP:  Flags = 10
TCP:  ..0. .... = (No urgent pointer)
TCP:  ...1 .... = Acknowledgment
TCP:  .... 0... = (No push)
TCP:  .... .0.. = (No reset)
TCP:  .... ..0. = (No SYN)
TCP:  .... ...0 = (No FIN)
TCP:  Window = 24576
TCP:  Checksum = C9A7 (correct)
TCP:  No TCP options
TCP:
```

TRACE 5.7.3C. TCP CONNECTION TERMINATION (FIN) DETAILS

```
Sniffer Network Analyzer data 27-Mar at 09:04:54, TCPMEDLY.ENC, Pg 1

- - - - - - - - - - - - - - - Frame 779 - - - - - - - - - - - - - - - - -

TCP:  —— TCP header ——
TCP:
TCP:  Source port = 20 (FTP data)
```

```
TCP:  Destination port = 1227
TCP:  Sequence number = 1988384769
TCP:  Acknowledgment number = 201331253
TCP:  Data offset = 20 bytes
TCP:  Flags = 19
TCP:  ..0. .... = (No urgent pointer)
TCP:  ...1 .... = Acknowledgment
TCP:  .... 1... = Push
TCP:  .... .0.. = (No reset)
TCP:  .... ..0. = (No SYN)
TCP:  .... ...1 = FIN
TCP:  Window = 24576
TCP:  Checksum = 492C (correct)
TCP:  No TCP options
TCP:  [114 byte(s) of data]
TCP:

- - - - - - - - - - - - - - - Frame 780 - - - - - - - - - - - - - - - - -

TCP:  —— TCP header ——
TCP:
TCP:  Source port = 1227
TCP:  Destination port = 20 (FTP data)
TCP:  Sequence number = 201331253
TCP:  Acknowledgment number = 1988384884
TCP:  Data offset = 20 bytes
TCP:  Flags = 10
TCP:  ..0. .... = (No urgent pointer)
TCP:  ...1 .... = Acknowledgment
TCP:  .... 0... = (No push)
TCP:  .... .0.. = (No reset)
TCP:  .... ..0. = (No SYN)
TCP:  .... ...0 = (No FIN)
TCP:  Window = 910
TCP:  Checksum = A5A6 (correct)
TCP:  No TCP options
TCP:

- - - - - - - - - - - - - - - Frame 781 - - - - - - - - - - - - - - - - -

TCP:  ——TCP header ——
TCP:
TCP:  Source port = 1227
TCP:  Destination port = 20 (FTP data)
```

```
TCP: Sequence number = 201331253
TCP: Acknowledgment number = 1988384884
TCP: Data offset = 20 bytes
TCP: Flags = 11
TCP: ..0. .... = (No urgent pointer)
TCP: ...1 .... = Acknowledgment
TCP: .... 0... = (No push)
TCP: .... .0.. = (No reset)
TCP: .... ..0. = (No SYN)
TCP: .... ...1 = FIN
TCP: Window = 910
TCP: Checksum = A5A5 (correct)
TCP: No TCP options
TCP:

- - - - - - - - - - - - - - - Frame 782 - - - - - - - - - - - - - - - -

TCP: ——TCP header ——
TCP:
TCP: Source port = 20 (FTP data)
TCP: Destination port = 1227
TCP: Sequence number = 1988384884
TCP: Acknowledgment number = 201331254
TCP: Data offset = 20 bytes
TCP: Flags = 10
TCP: ..0. .... = (No urgent pointer)
TCP: ...1 .... = Acknowledgment
TCP: .... 0... = (No push)
TCP: .... .0.. = (No reset)
TCP: .... ..0. = (No SYN)
TCP: .... ...0 = (No FIN)
TCP: Window = 24576
TCP: Checksum = 4933 (correct)
TCP: No TCP options
TCP:
```

5.7.4 Reset TCP Connection

The TCP header contains six flags that manage the virtual circuit. In Section 5.7.3, we saw how the Acknowledgment (ACK), Synchronize (SYN), and Finish (FIN) flags are used for connection management and data transfer under normal conditions. One of the remaining flags, known as the Reset (RST) flag, is used when a TCP segment arrives that is not intended for the current connection. The RST flag is also used if a TCP module detects a fatal error or if the application process unilaterally decides to close the connection. One possible scenario is when one TCP module crashes during a session. The term used to describe this condition is a *half-open connection* because one end is maintaining its Sequence numbers and other transmission-related parameters while the other is not. When the crashed host returns to life, its Sequence numbers are unlikely to be the same as those it was using prior to the crash. As a result, it sends unexpected (and thus unacknowledged) Sequence numbers to the host at the other end of the link.

When the crashed host realizes that it has caused this confusion, it sends a Reset to its distant partner, which triggers a three-way handshake to re-establish the connection. Let's see how the Reset flag is used in a failure scenario.

In this case, a Sun workstation is communicating with a remote host located in another part of the country. A TELNET session is in progress over the internet, with the workstation emulating a host terminal. Two routers connect the local and remote Ethernet networks (see Figure 5-14). Without warning, the user loses his response from the host and starts hitting the Return key, hoping for a miracle (sound familiar?). We can see his frustration in Trace 5.7.4a. In Frame 3 all appears to be fine, but after almost two minutes of waiting (119.8658 seconds) the Sun sends a carriage return. (Note the <0D> <00> output pattern, indicating that an ASCII Carriage Return <0D> has been transmitted.) The Sun sends these characters (<0D> <00> <0D> <00>...) at increments of 2 seconds apart, then 4 seconds, 8, 16, and so on, attempting to wake up the remote host.

Unfortunately, the efforts are in vain. The remote host gets confused, sends a TCP Reset (RST = 1) in Frame 13, and disables future receptions by setting Window = 0 (Trace 5.7.4b). The Sun resets the connection, but also acknowledges the last data octet that it received in Frame 3 (ACK = 20881447). Clearly, the Sun does not want to end the conversation since it keeps Window = 4096.

The problem is traced to a bad Ethernet card connecting the remote host to its local network. The card's operation is intermittent, working part of the time – such as when the TELNET session was initialized – then failing for no apparent reason. When the failure occurred, it caused a half-open TCP connection, and ultimately the mysterious TCP Reset. When the faulty Ethernet card was replaced, no further problems occurred.

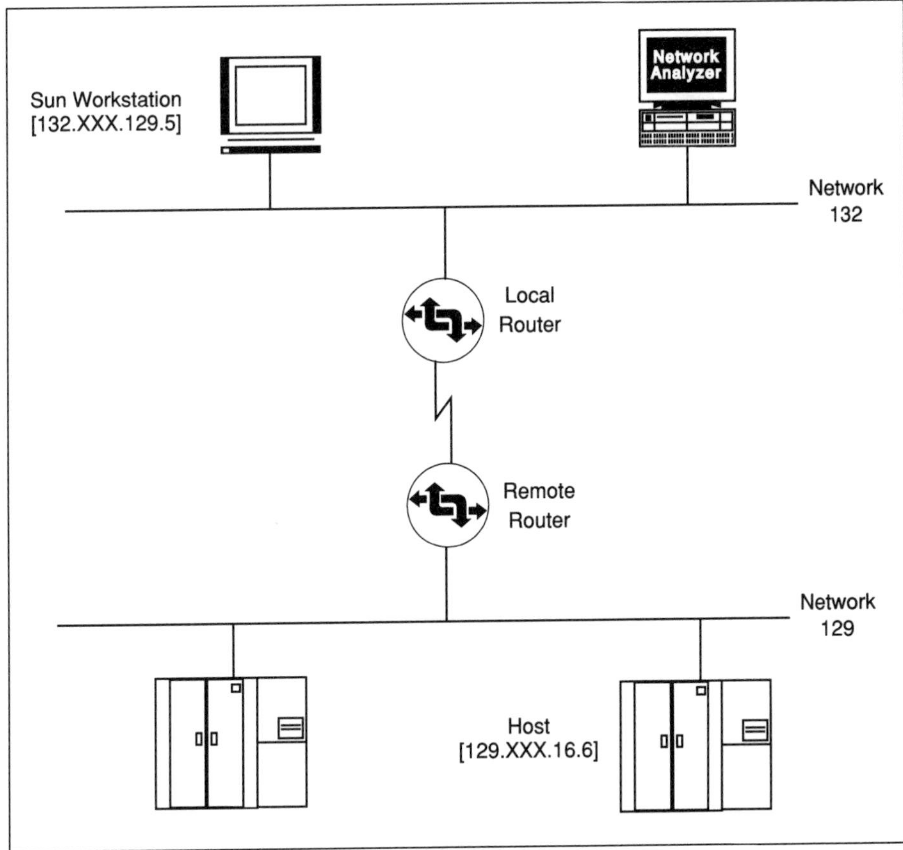

Figure 5-14 TCP Connection Reset

TRACE 5.7.4A. TCP CONNECTION RESET (RST) SUMMARY

Sniffer Network Analyzer data 14-Sep at 11:43:30, TCPRST.ENC, Pg 1

SUMMARY	Delta T	Destination	Source	Summary
M 1		Router	Sun 01DF5E	TCP D=23 S=1169 ACK=20881319 WIN=4096
2	5.0808	Sun 01DF5E	Router	Telnet R PORT=1169 FILE: ROUT (NO CHANGES)
3	0.1189	Router	Sun 01DF5E	TCP D=23 S=1169 ACK=20881447 WIN=4096
4	119.8658	Router	Sun 01DF5E	Telnet C PORT=1169 <0D><00>...

5	0.8820	Router	Sun 01DF5E	Telnet C PORT=1169 <0D><00>...
6	2.0002	Router	Sun 01DF5E	Telnet C PORT=1169 <0D><00>...
7	4.0001	Router	Sun 01DF5E	Telnet C PORT=1169 <0D><00>...
8	8.0006	Router	Sun 01DF5E	Telnet C PORT=1169 <0D><00>...
9	16.0010	Router	Sun 01DF5E	Telnet C PORT=1169 <0D><00>...
10	32.0020	Router	Sun 01DF5E	Telnet C PORT=1169 <0D><00>...
11	64.0039	Router	Sun 01DF5E	Telnet C PORT=1169 <0D><00>...
12	64.0040	Router	Sun 01DF5E	Telnet C PORT=1169 <0D><00>...
13	0.2722	Sun 01DF5E	Router	TCP D=1169 S=23 RST WIN=0
14	0.0021	Router	Sun 01DF5E	TCP D=23 S=1169 RST ACK=20881447 WIN=4096

TRACE 5.7.4B. TCP CONNECTION RESET (RST) DETAILS

Sniffer Network Analyzer data 14-Sep at 11:43:30, TCPRST.ENC, Pg 1

- - - - - - - - - - - - - - - Frame 13 - - - - - - - - - - - - - - - - -

DLC: —— DLC Header ——

DLC:

DLC: Frame 13 arrived at 12:24:26.1927; frame size is 60 (003C hex) bytes.

DLC: Destination = Station Sun 01DF5E

DLC: Source = Station PrteonE0807B, Router

DLC: Ethertype = 0800 (IP)

DLC:

IP: —— IP Header ——

IP:

IP: Version = 4, header length = 20 bytes

IP: Type of service = 00

IP: 000. .... = routine

IP: ...0 .... = normal delay

IP: .... 0... = normal throughput

IP: .... .0.. = normal reliability

IP: Total length = 40 bytes

IP: Identification = 25254

IP: Flags = 0X

IP: .0.. .... = may fragment

IP: ..0. .... = last fragment

IP: Fragment offset = 0 bytes

IP: Time to live = 19 seconds/hops

IP: Protocol = 6 (TCP)

IP: Header checksum = AE75 (correct)

IP: Source address = [129.XXX.16.6]

IP: Destination address = [132.XXX.129.5]

```
IP:  No options
IP:
TCP:  —— TCP header ——
TCP:
TCP:  Source port = 23 (Telnet)
TCP:  Destination port = 1169
TCP:  Sequence number = 20881447
TCP:  Data offset = 20 bytes
TCP:  Flags = 04
TCP:  ..0. .... = (No urgent pointer)
TCP:  ...0 .... = (No acknowledgment)
TCP:  .... 0... = (No push)
TCP:  .... .1.. = Reset
TCP:  .... ..0. = (No SYN)
TCP:  .... ...0 = (No FIN)
TCP:  Window = 0
TCP:  Checksum = 25EE (correct)
TCP:  No TCP options
TCP:

- - - - - - - - - - - - - - - Frame 14 - - - - - - - - - - - - - - - - -

DLC:  ——DLC Header ——
DLC:
DLC:  Frame 14 arrived at  12:24:26.1948; frame size is 60 (003C hex) bytes.
DLC:  Destination = Station PrteonE0807B, Router
DLC:  Source      = Station Sun   01DF5E
DLC:  Ethertype  = 0800 (IP)
DLC:
IP:  ——IP Header ——
IP:
IP:  Version = 4, header length = 20 bytes
IP:  Type of service = 00
IP:        000. .... = routine
IP:        ...0 .... = normal delay
IP:        .... 0... = normal throughput
IP:        .... .0.. = normal reliability
IP:  Total length = 40 bytes
IP:  Identification = 25255
IP:  Flags = 0X
IP:  .0.. .... = may fragment
IP:    ..0. .... = last fragment
IP:    Fragment offset = 0 bytes
IP:    Time to live = 30 seconds/hops
```

```
IP:   Protocol = 6 (TCP)
IP:   Header checksum = A374 (correct)
IP:   Source address = [132.XXX.129.5]
IP:   Destination address = [129.XXX.16.6]
IP:   No options
IP:
TCP:  —— TCP header ——
TCP:
TCP:  Source port = 1169
TCP:  Destination port = 23 (Telnet)
TCP:  Sequence number = 398210404
TCP:  Acknowledgment number = 20881447
TCP:  Data offset = 20 bytes
TCP:  Flags = 14
TCP:  ..0. .... = (No urgent pointer)
TCP:  ...1 .... = Acknowledgment
TCP:  .... 0... = (No push)
TCP:  .... .1.. = Reset
TCP:  .... ..0. = (No SYN)
TCP:  .... ...0 = (No FIN)
TCP:  Window = 4096
TCP:  Checksum = 15EE (correct)
TCP:  No TCP options
TCP:
```

5.7.5 Repeated Host Acknowledgments

TCP belongs to the class of protocols (sometimes referred to as PAR protocols) that requires a positive acknowledgment within a specified time period, or it will retransmit the data. The acknowledgment mechanism uses the 32-bit Acknowledgment number and sets the Acknowledgment (ACK) flag. The ACK flag tells the recipient TCP module to process the Acknowledgment field. The Acknowledgment field counts each octet of information received and indicates which octet is expected next. What happens when the receiver does not properly acknowledge incoming data?

In this case, an X-Windows terminal is communicating with a minicomputer. The terminal sends some information, but then seemingly locks up. At first the administrator suspects the terminal, but closer analysis reveals a defect in the host. Let's find out why.

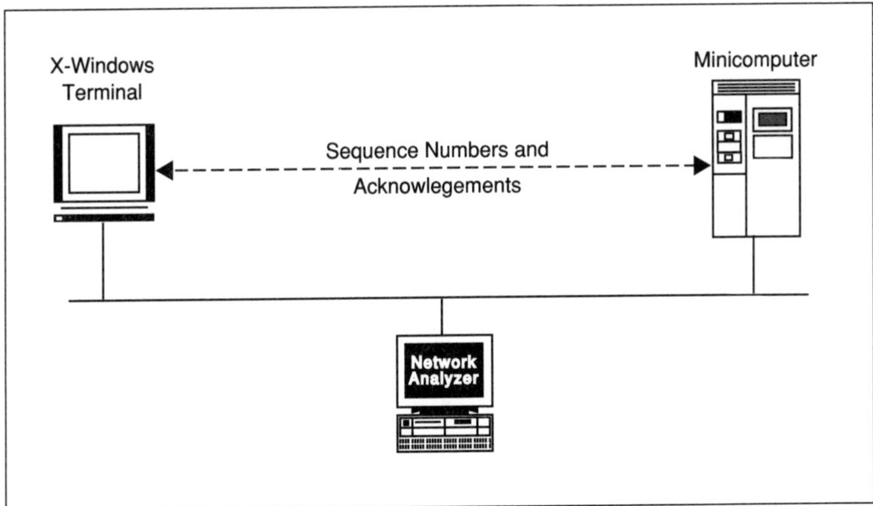

Figure 5-15 TCP Data Acknowledgments

Both the terminal and the host are attached to the same Ethernet, and the protocol analyzer is set to capture all traffic between the two devices (Figure 5-15). The initial trace reveals a TCP connection between Port 3319 and Port 6000 (the X-Windows port), as seen in Trace 5.7.5a. It is unusual, however, that all communication between host and terminal consists of TCP acknowledgments and that they all flow in one direction – host to terminal. These acknowledgments repeat roughly every millisecond (0.0008 second).

A detailed study of one of the frames reveals how the Sequence and Acknowledgment numbers are operating (see Trace 5.7.5b). The host's TCP module is stuck in a loop in which it is unable to increment the Acknowledgment number, so each TCP segment contains the same information. The IP datagram contains a total of 40 octets: 20 for the IP header and 20 for the TCP header. No higher layer data is ever transmitted. The window size is large (WIN = 4096), but the Acknowledgment number never changes (ACK = 28122874). When the terminal receives this segment, it is unable to transmit additional information because the host always asks for the same segment: 4,096 octets beginning at Sequence number 28122874. Since the host prevents the terminal from proceeding, the terminal appears to lock up.

To find the solution, the network administrator contacts the developer of the host software. The developer finds a bug in the TCP module that prevents the Acknowledgment number from incrementing. When the administrator installs a software patch, the terminal-to-host communication works as expected.

TRACE 5.7.5A. REPEATED HOST TCP ACKNOWLEDGMENTS (SUMMARY)

Sniffer Network Analyzer data 1-Oct at 11:14:40, HOSTACK.ENC, Pg 1

SUMMARY	Delta T	Destination	Source	Summary
M 1		Terminal	Host	TCP D=6000 S=3319 ACK=28122874 WIN=4096
2	0.0008	Terminal	Host	TCP D=6000 S=3319 ACK=28122874 WIN=4096
3	0.0008	Terminal	Host	TCP D=6000 S=3319 ACK=28122874 WIN=4096
4	0.0008	Terminal	Host	TCP D=6000 S=3319 ACK=28122874 WIN=4096
5	0.0008	Terminal	Host	TCP D=6000 S=3319 ACK=28122874 WIN=4096
6	0.0008	Terminal	Host	TCP D=6000 S=3319 ACK=28122874 WIN=4096
7	0.0008	Terminal	Host	TCP D=6000 S=3319 ACK=28122874 WIN=4096
8	0.0008	Terminal	Host	TCP D=6000 S=3319 ACK=28122874 WIN=4096
9	0.0008	Terminal	Host	TCP D=6000 S=3319 ACK=28122874 WIN=4096
10	0.0008	Terminal	Host	TCP D=6000 S=3319 ACK=28122874 WIN=4096
11	0.0008	Terminal	Host	TCP D=6000 S=3319 ACK=28122874 WIN=4096
12	0.0008	Terminal	Host	TCP D=6000 S=3319 ACK=28122874 WIN=4096
13	0.0008	Terminal	Host	TCP D=6000 S=3319 ACK=28122874 WIN=4096
14	0.0008	Terminal	Host	TCP D=6000 S=3319 ACK=28122874 WIN=4096
15	0.0008	Terminal	Host	TCP D=6000 S=3319 ACK=28122874 WIN=4096
16	0.0008	Terminal	Host	TCP D=6000 S=3319 ACK=28122874 WIN=4096
17	0.0008	Terminal	Host	TCP D=6000 S=3319 ACK=28122874 WIN=4096
18	0.0008	Terminal	Host	TCP D=6000 S=3319 ACK=28122874 WIN=4096
19	0.0008	Terminal	Host	TCP D=6000 S=3319 ACK=28122874 WIN=4096
20	0.0008	Terminal	Host	TCP D=6000 S=3319 ACK=28122874 WIN=4096

TRACE 5.7.5B. REPEATED HOST TCP ACKNOWLEDGMENTS (DETAILS)

```
Sniffer Network Analyzer data 1-Oct at 11:14:40, HOSTACK.ENC, Pg 1

- - - - - - - - - - - - - - - Frame 14 - - - - - - - - - - - - - - - - -

DLC:  ——DLC Header ——
DLC:
DLC:  Frame 1 arrived at  11:14:41.7541; frame size is 60 (003C hex) bytes.
DLC:  Destination = Station XXXXXX 101C43, Terminal
DLC:  Source      = Station XXXXXX 032608, Host
DLC:  Ethertype  = 0800 (IP)
DLC:
IP:  ——IP Header ——
IP:
IP:   Version = 4, header length = 20 bytes
IP:   Type of service = 00
IP:         000. .... = routine
IP:         ...0 .... = normal delay
IP:         .... 0... = normal throughput
IP:         .... .0.. = normal reliability
IP:   Total length = 40 bytes
IP:   Identification = 17411
IP:   Flags = 0X
IP:   .0.. .... = may fragment
IP:   ..0. .... = last fragment
IP:   Fragment offset = 0 bytes
IP:   Time to live = 30 seconds/hops
IP:   Protocol = 6 (TCP)
IP:   Header checksum = F380 (correct)
IP:   Source address = [XXX.YYY.1.235]
IP:   Destination address = [XXX.YYY.4.98]
IP:   No options
IP:
TCP:  ——TCP header ——
TCP:
TCP:  Source port = 3319
TCP:  Destination port = 6000 (X Windows)
TCP:  Sequence number = 3524369
TCP:  Acknowledgment number = 28122874
TCP:  Data offset = 20 bytes
TCP:  Flags = 10
TCP:  ..0. .... = (No urgent pointer)
TCP:  ...1 .... = Acknowledgment
TCP:  .... 0... = (No push)
```

```
TCP:  .... .0.. = (No reset)
TCP:  .... ..0. = (No SYN)
TCP:  .... ...0 = (No FIN)
TCP:  Window = 4096
TCP:  Checksum = 2E33 (correct)
TCP:  No TCP options
TCP:
```

5.7.6 Using the Finger User Information Protocol

In Chapter 4, we discovered that the ICMP Echo (PING) command can test the transmission path between two devices on an internetwork. Another utility, known as the Finger User Information Protocol (Finger), described in RFC 1288 [5-18], also provides some end-to-end testing. Finger provides an interface to a database of users attached to a particular host, called the Remote User Information Program (RUIP).

Finger consists of a query/response interaction based on TCP transport (Figure 5-16). To initiate Finger, a TCP connection is established with Port 79 (the Finger port) on the remote host. Then the local host's Finger utility sends a query to RUIP at the remote host. The remote host responds with the information requested. When used in an internet environment, the Finger utility not only checks the end-to-end communication path (like the ICMP Echo), but it also verifies that the remote host knows of the remote user's existence. Let's find out how to use the Finger protocol.

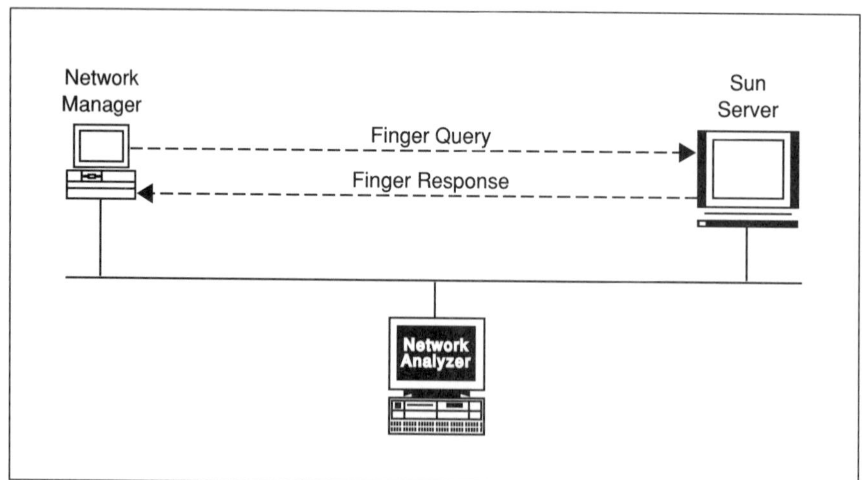

Figure 5-16 Finger User Information Protocol Operation

The network manager wishes to check on one of his users, Kevin Anderson. From his PC, he establishes a TCP connection with the Sun server to which Kevin is attached (see Trace 5.7.6a). Note that the Destination port requested in the initial TCP connection segment, Frame 801, is the Finger port, 79. The three-way handshake is completed in Frame 803, and the network manager's RUIP sends a query to the server requesting information for the user. The details of the query are shown in Trace 5.7.6b, indicating that the user name or user id (kpa) is sent with the query. Note that the Push (PSH) flag is used to send data on its way immediately.

The Sun server responds with an acknowledgment (Frame 805) followed by the RUIP response (Frame 806). The response contains 174 octets of data that pertain to user kpa. We learn the following about the user:

```
Login name: kpa        In real life: Kevin P. Anderson
Directory: /home/h0008/kpa   Shell: /bin/csh
Last login Wed Mar 27 09:22 on ttyp0 from h0009z
No unread mail
No plan
```

With the answer transmitted, the server's RUIP closes the connection in Frame 807 by setting the Finish (FIN) flag. The PC acknowledges the server's FIN (Frame 808) and sends a FIN of its own (Frame 809). The server acknowledges the final transaction in Frame 810.

In all, it took only 10 frames to learn about user kpa, his directory, shell, last login, and so on. Some of this information may be considered sensitive for security reasons, and network administrators are advised to read the security issues detailed in the Finger standard, RFC 1288. However, if you can surmount these concerns, the Finger protocol can be a valuable addition to your bag of troubleshooting techniques.

TRACE 5.7.6A. FINGER USER INFORMATION SUMMARY

Sniffer Network Analyzer data 27-Mar at 09:04:54, TCPMEDLY.ENC, Pg 1

SUMMARY	Delta T	Destination	Source	Summary
801	57.9373	Sun Server	PC	TCP D=79 S=1228 SYN SEQ=134222388 LEN=0 WIN=1024
802	0.0009	PC	Sun Server	TCP D=1228 S=79 SYN ACK=134222389 SEQ=2009792000 LEN=0 WIN=4096
803	0.0130	Sun Server	PC	TCP D=79 S=1228 ACK=2009792001 WIN=1024
804	0.0441	Sun Server	PC	TCP D=79 S=1228

				ACK=2009792001 SEQ=134222389 LEN=5 WIN=1024
805	0.1348	PC	Sun Server	TCP D=1228 S=79 ACK=134222394 WIN=4096
806	0.0433	PC	Sun Server	TCP D=1228 S=79 ACK=134222394 SEQ=2009792001 LEN=174 WIN=4096
807	0.0002	PC	Sun Server	TCP D=1228 S=79 FIN ACK=134222394 SEQ=2009792175 LEN=0 WIN=4096
808	0.0225	Sun Server	PC	TCP D=79 S=1228 ACK=2009792176 WIN=850
809	0.4897	Sun Server	PC	TCP D=79 S=1228 FIN ACK=2009792176 SEQ=134222394 LEN=0 WIN=850
810	0.0006	PC	Sun Server	TCP D=1228 S=79 ACK=134222395 WIN=4096

TRACE 5.7.6B. FINGER USER INFORMATION DETAILS

Sniffer Network Analyzer data 27-Mar at 09:04:54, TCPMEDLY.ENC, Pg 1

```
- - - - - - - - - - - - - - - Frame 804 - - - - - - - - - - - - - - - - -

TCP: ——TCP header ——
TCP:
TCP: Source port = 1228
TCP: Destination port = 79 (Finger)
TCP: Sequence number = 134222389
TCP: Acknowledgment number = 2009792001
TCP: Data offset = 20 bytes
TCP: Flags = 18
TCP: ..0. .... = (No urgent pointer)
TCP: ...1 .... = Acknowledgment
TCP: .... 1... = Push
TCP: .... .0.. = (No reset)
TCP: .... ..0. = (No SYN)
TCP: .... ...0 = (No FIN)
TCP: Window = 1024
TCP: Checksum = 2B9A (correct)
```

```
TCP:   No TCP options
TCP:   [5 byte(s) of data]
TCP:

ADDR    HEX                                                ASCII
0000    08 00 20 09 42 A4 00 00    C0 3C 55 17 08 00 45 00    .. .B....<U...E.
0010    00 2D 02 C3 00 00 40 06    63 75 8B B1 FE 5F 8B B1    .-....@.cu..._..
0020    FE D0 04 CC 00 4F 08 00    12 35 77 CA FE 01 50 18    .....O...5w...P.
0030    04 00 2B 9A 00 00 6B 70    61 0D 0A 00                ..+...kpa...

- - - - - - - - - - - - - - - Frame 805 - - - - - - - - - - - - - - - - -

TCP:   ——TCP header ——
TCP:
TCP:   Source port = 79 (Finger)
TCP:   Destination port = 1228
TCP:   Sequence number = 2009792001
TCP:   Acknowledgment number = 134222394
TCP:   Data offset = 20 bytes
TCP:   Flags = 10
TCP:   ..0. .... = (No urgent pointer)
TCP:   ...1 .... = Acknowledgment
TCP:   .... 0... = (No push)
TCP:   .... .0.. = (No reset)
TCP:   .... ..0. = (No SYN)
TCP:   .... ...0 = (No FIN)
TCP:   Window = 4096
TCP:   Checksum = F61F (correct)
TCP:   No TCP options
TCP:

ADDR    HEX                                                ASCII
0000    00 00 C0 3C 55 17 08 00    20 09 42 A4 08 00 45 00    ...<U... .B...E.
0010    00 28 D6 EE 00 00 3C 06    93 4E 8B B1 FE D0 8B B1    .(....<..N......
0020    FE 5F 00 4F 04 CC 77 CA    FE 01 08 00 12 3A 50 10    ._.O..w......:P.
0030    10 00 F6 1F 00 00 64 2E    62 79 6E 61                ......d.byna

- - - - - - - - - - - - - - - Frame 806 - - - - - - - - - - - - - - - - -

TCP:   ——TCP header ——
TCP:
TCP:   Source port = 79 (Finger)
TCP:   Destination port = 1228
```

```
TCP:  Sequence number = 2009792001
TCP:  Acknowledgment number = 134222394
TCP:  Data offset = 20 bytes
TCP:  Flags = 18
TCP:  ..0. .... = (No urgent pointer)
TCP:  ...1 .... = Acknowledgment
TCP:  .... 1... = Push
TCP:  .... .0.. = (No reset)
TCP:  .... ..0. = (No SYN)
TCP:  .... ...0 = (No FIN)
TCP:  Window = 4096
TCP:  Checksum = CAA6 (correct)
TCP:  No TCP options
TCP:  [174 byte(s) of data]
TCP:
```

```
ADDR    HEX                                                ASCII
0000    00 00 C0 3C 55 17 08 00   20 09 42 A4 08 00 45 00   ...<U... .B...E.
0010    00 D6 D6 F3 00 00 3C 06   92 9B 8B B1 FE D0 8B B1   ......<.........
0020    FE 5F 00 4F 04 CC 77 CA   FE 01 08 00 12 3A 50 18   ._.O..w......:P.
0030    10 00 CA A6 00 00 4C 6F   67 69 6E 20 6E 61 6D 65   ......Login name
0040    3A 20 6B 70 61 20 20 20   20 20 20 20 09 09 09 49   : kpa       ...I
0050    6E 20 72 65 61 6C 20 6C   69 66 65 3A 20 48 42 4F   n real life:....
0060    0D 0A 44 69 72 65 63 74   6F 72 79 3A 20 2F 68 6F   ..Directory: /ho
0070    6D 65 2F 68 30 30 30 38   2F 6B 70 61 20 20 20 20   me/h0008/kpa
0080    20 20 20 20 20 20 09 53   68 65 6C 6C 3A 20 2F 62   .Shell: /b
0090    69 6E 2F 63 73 68 0D 0A   4C 61 73 74 20 6C 6F 67   in/csh..Last log
00A0    69 6E 20 57 65 64 20 4D   61 72 20 32 37 20 30 39   in Wed Mar 27 09
00B0    3A 32 32 20 6F 6E 20 74   74 79 70 30 20 66 72 6F   :22 on ttyp0 fro
00C0    6D 20 68 30 30 30 39 7A   0D 0A 4E 6F 20 75 6E 72   m h0009z..No unr
00D0    65 61 64 20 6D 61 69 6C   0D 0A 4E 6F 20 50 6C 61   ead mail..No Plan...
00E0    6E 2E 0D 0A
```

5.7.7 Tape Backups via an Internetwork

In the last few years, the price of hard disk storage on PCs has dropped to the point where it's not uncommon to have many gigabytes of storage per workstation. But with this increasing storage comes increasing risk: the failure of a large hard disk can have disastrous consequences. To minimize this risk, many users routinely back up their hard disk onto either high-capacity cartridges or a tape drive.

In this case, the network engineer wants to back up his hard disk to a Sun SPARCstation server with an attached tape drive. Software in both the PC and the server use TCP as the transport mechanism for the backup via an internetwork (see Figure 5-17). But when the engineer begins the backup procedure on the PC side, the process suddenly fails. Initially he suspects a faulty tape drive, but further analysis reveals another problem.

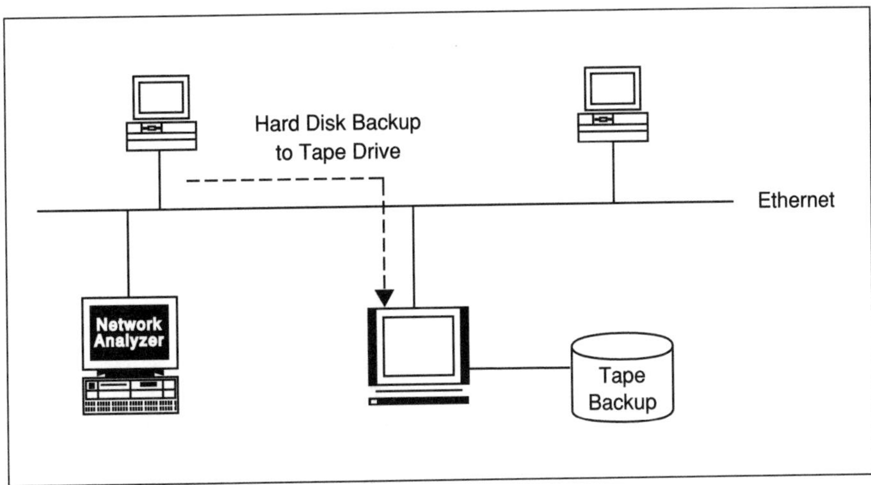

Figure 5-17 PC-to-Server Backup via Ethernet

The analysis begins with the server (shown as SPARCstn in Trace 5.7.7) sending a Window = 4096 in Frame 32 to the PC, then waiting for the data to transfer. The PC begins downloading the backup in Frame 33 and gives the server a Window = 905. The server acknowledges this data with a TCP segment of 35 octets in length (Frame 34). In response, the PC reduces its window size to 870 octets (905 - 35 = 870). Clearly, the PC's window size is more limiting than that of the server. The server, however, abruptly sends a Window = 0 in Frame 37. This segment is repeated in Frames 39 and 41. The server shuts down the communication link from the PC to the tape drive. The engineer theorizes that the server does this so it can process the incoming TCP segment and transfer the data to the tape drive. Unfortunately, the PC software does not know that this delay is necessary. The PC interprets the Window = 0 as a termination command and issues a TCP Reset (RST) command in Frame 42. This is followed by a Finish (FIN) command in Frame 44. The tape backup is aborted, but the hard disk has not been backed up completely.

The solution is to insert some delay into the PC's TCP module. When the tape drive is busy, the Sun workstation instructs its TCP module (on the server) to send Window = 0, preventing the transfer of additional data. As long as the tape drive is busy, it continues to send Window = 0. The TCP module in the PC is rewritten to accept the TCP segment with Window = 0 and then wait 10 seconds for the tape drive to catch up. If it receives two more segments with Window = 0, then the PC resets the connection. Now the backups proceed without a hitch via the internetwork.

TRACE 5.7.7. TAPE BACKUP WITH WINDOW = 0

Sniffer Network Analyzer data 27-Mar at 09:04:54, TAPEBACK.ENC, Pg 1

SUMMARY	Destination	Source	Summary
32	PC	SPARCstn	TCP D=1022 S=1023 ACK=694630 SEQ=1839168103 LEN=17 WIN=4096
33	SPARCstn	PC	TCP D=1023 S=1022 ACK=1839168120 WIN=905
34	PC	SPARCstn	TCP D=1022 S=1023 ACK=694630 SEQ=1839168120 LEN=35 WIN=4096
35	SPARCstn	PC	TCP D=1023 S=1022 ACK=1839168155 WIN=870
36	SPARCstn	PC	RSHELL C PORT=1023 <00>
37	PC	SPARCstn	TCP D=1023 S=514 ACK=698772 WIN=0
38	SPARCstn	PC	RSHELL C PORT=1023 <00>
39	PC	SPARCstn	TCP D=1023 S=514 ACK=698772 WIN=0
40	SPARCstn	PC	RSHELL C PORT=1023 <00>
41	PC	SPARCstn	TCP D=1023 S=514 ACK=698772 WIN=0
42	SPARCstn	PC	TCP D=514 S=1023 RST ACK=1839040002 WIN=1024
43	SPARCstn	PC	TCP D=1023 S=1022 ACK=1839168155 WIN=1024
44	SPARCstn	PC	TCP D=1023 S=1022 FIN ACK=1839168155 SEQ=694630 LEN=0 WIN=1024
45	PC	SPARCstn	TCP D=1022 S=1023 ACK=694631 WIN=4096
46	PC	SPARCstn	TCP D=1023 S=514 ACK=698772 WIN=1536
47	PC	SPARCstn	TCP D=1023 S=514 ACK=698772 WIN=3072
48	SPARCstn	PC	TCP D=1023 S=1022 RST ACK=1839168155 WIN=1024

5.7.8 Optimizing the TCP Window Size

The previous case study shows what the receiver's window can do. We see that when the distant host sends a value of Window = 0, the transmission path to the host effectively shuts down. If you receive a large window (say, Window = 8192), you can transmit a reasonable amount of data. Depending on the application, there should be an optimum window size that won't cause the transmitter to wait for unnecessary acknowledgments (i.e., the window is too small), yet won't overwhelm the receiver with more data than it can handle (i.e., the window is too large). As in "Goldilocks and the Three Bears," you need to find the window size that is "just right."

Two documents provide useful information about optimizing the window size: RFC 879, "The TCP Maximum Segment Size and Related Topics" [5-4], and RFC 813, "Window and Acknowledgement Strategy in TCP" [5-9]. Let's study an internetwork that needs some help in this area.

In the following case study, the internetwork consists of a headquarters location connected to three remote Ethernet segments (see Figure 5-18). Each remote segment contains a UNIX host plus a number of workstations. The remote segments are connected via bridges and 64-Kbps leased lines. The remote hosts contact these peers on a periodic basis to transfer files using a File Transfer Protocol (FTP) facility. In addition, the PC users use TELNET for remote host access. The problem is that while two hosts on the same segment can communicate without a problem, the hosts can't contact other hosts at a remote location without excessive delays and interrupts of the FTP session. Let's see why these problems occur.

To study the problem, the network engineer captures the data between one host on the headquarters segment (Hdqtr Host) and another host on a remote segment. He places the analyzer on the headquarters segment to capture the information coming to and from the remote host via the bridge (see Trace 5.7.8a). The initial analysis does not reveal any frames with errors. The remote host initiates a TCP connection in Frames 2 through 4, then starts an FTP session. The user identifies himself (Buster, in Frame 9), a password is transmitted (Frame 11), and an account is sent (Frame 15). The login completes in Frame 17, and the user can proceed. The only indication that a problem exists is the delays between frames, shown in Frames 9, 15, 17, and 19. These delays range from 6 to 18 seconds and indicate a transmission problem between the two communicating hosts.

The headquarters host initiates a second TCP data connection beginning in Frame 26. Note that the Destination Ports are different—the first connection (Frames 2 through 4) uses Destination Port = 21 (FTP Control) and Source Port = 4979. The second connection uses Source Port = 20 (FTP data) and Destination Port = 4980. By all appearances, the two hosts should have established a full-duplex connection. Note also that both hosts return Window = 0 in Frames 26 and 27, but subsequently revise that number in Frames 28, 29, and 30.

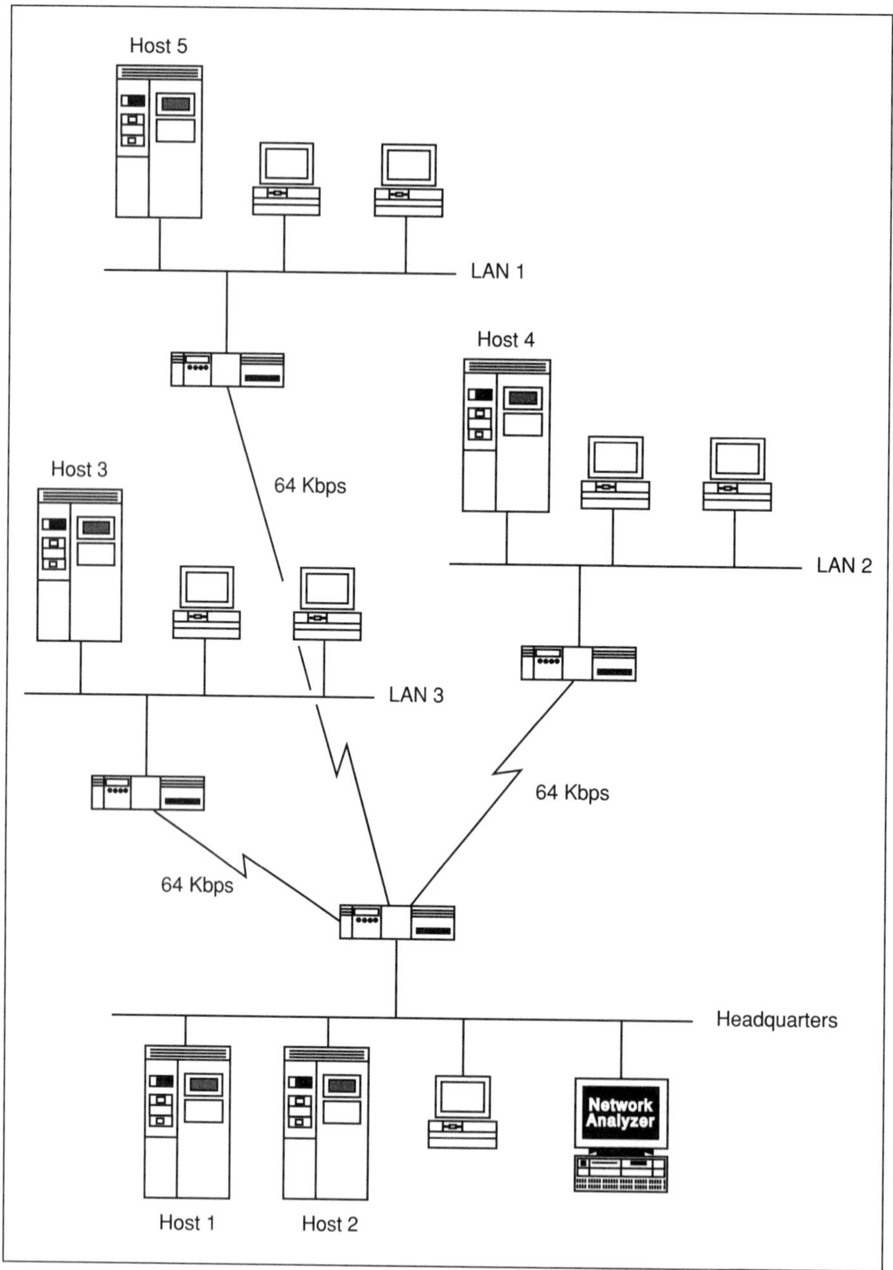

Figure 5-18 Host-to-Host Connections via WAN Bridges

Data transfer begins in Frame 31 with 512 octets of information. Successive frames convey 512 and 256 octets of data, respectively. An unexpected association of Sequence and Acknowledgment numbers occurs, however, in Trace 5.7.8b:

Frame	Data (octets)	Beginning Sequence	Ending Sequence	Acknowledgment
31	512	55278459	55278970	53214721
32	512	55278971	5279482	53214721
33	256	55279483	5279738	53214721
34	0	53214721	53214721	55278971

Frames 31 through 33 contain data from the headquarters host to the remote host. During this time no data is received in the other direction, since the Acknowledgment number remains constant (ACK = 53214721). Frame 34 contains an acknowledgment from the remote host, but note that it is the acknowledgment for the third previous segment (Frame 31). In other words, Frames 32 and 33 are still en route to the remote host, somewhere in the link between the two bridges.

The data transfer continues for a number of segments until the headquarters host abruptly terminates the connection in Frame 149 via the RST flag (see Trace 5.7.8c). The FTP connection is then closed and no additional data can be transferred. The immediately preceding frames provide the answer:

Frame	Sequence	Acknowledgment	Outstanding Data (octets)
144	55310931		
145		55306995	3,936
146	55311373		
147		55306995	4,378

The headquarters host transmits 442 octets of data in Frame 144; the remote host acknowledges a lesser amount (ACK = 55306995), leaving 3,936 octets of data unacknowledged (55310931 - 55306995 = 3,936). The problem worsens in Frames 146 and 147, with 4,378 unacknowledged octets (55311373 - 55306995 = 4,378).

Somewhere between the processing of Frames 144 and 146 a threshold within the host that counts the maximum allowable outstanding octets is crossed, causing the headquarters host to reset the connection. This threshold is half the allowable window size. The host has Window = 8,192, half of which is 4,096. In Frame 145,

3,936 octets are outstanding; in Frame 146 that number increases to 4,378, exceeding the threshold of 4,096.

The reason for the large amount of outstanding data is traced to inadequate I/O buffers on the WAN side of the bridges. Adding I/O buffers improves transmission. A second parameter, the discard threshold, is also increased inside the bridges. The discard threshold determines the maximum number of MAC-level frames that can be queued within the bridge. Setting this parameter to a higher value also improves the internetwork response. With these two bridge parameters adjusted, no further problems occur.

TRACE 5.7.8A. TCP WINDOW MANAGEMENT SUMMARY

Sniffer Network Analyzer data 23-Jan at 03:10:38, TRACE.ENC, Pg 1

SUMMARY	Delta T	Destination	Source	Summary
M 1		Bridge	Hdqtr Host	ARP R PA=[143.130.1.5] HA=08000B001180 PRO=IP
2	0.0248	Hdqtr Host	Bridge	TCP D=21 S=4979 SYN SEQ=44830720 LEN=0 WIN=4096
3	0.5002	Bridge	Hdqtr Host	TCP D=4979 S=21 SYN ACK=44830721 SEQ=55214045 LEN=0 WIN=8192
4	0.0258	Hdqtr Host	Bridge	TCP D=21 S=4979 ACK=55214046 WIN=4096
5	0.2294	Bridge	Hdqtr Host	TCP D=4979 S=21 ACK=44830721 WIN=8192
6	1.1449	Bridge	Hdqtr Host	TCP D=4979 S=21 ACK=44830721 WIN=8192
7	2.7069	Bridge	Hdqtr Host	FTP R PORT=4979 220 1100JD1100 Service ready for new user <0D><0A>
8	0.0635	Hdqtr Host	Bridge	TCP D=21 S=4979 ACK=55214090 WIN=4096
9	14.7769	Hdqtr Host	Bridge	FTP C PORT=4979 USER Buster<0D><0A>
10	0.1605	Bridge	Hdqtr Host	FTP R PORT=4979 331 User name okay, need password.<0D><0A>
11	0.0465	Hdqtr Host	Bridge	FTP C PORT=4979 PASS pass<0D><0A>
12	0.2198	Bridge	Hdqtr Host	TCP D=4979 S=21 ACK=44830745 WIN=8192
13	0.7356	Bridge	Hdqtr Host	FTP R PORT=4979

				332 Need account for login. <0D><0A>
14	0.0597	Hdqtr Host	Bridge	TCP++D=21 S=4979 ACK=55214155 WIN=4096
15	6.7912	Hdqtr Host	Bridge	FTP C PORT=4979 ACCT Rufus<0D><0A>
16	0.2171	Bridge	Hdqtr Host	TCP D=4979 S=21 ACK=44830761 WIN=8192
17	14.4493	Bridge	Hdqtr Host	FTP R PORT=4979 230 User logged in, proceed <0D><0A>
18	0.1431	Hdqtr Host	Bridge	TCP D=21 S=4979 ACK=55214186 WIN=4096
19	18.7942	Hdqtr Host	Bridge	FTP C PORT=4979 PORT 143,130,2,1,19,116 <0D><0A>
20	0.2157	Bridge	Hdqtr Host	TCP D=4979 S=21 ACK=44830786 WIN=8192
21	0.2449	Bridge	Hdqtr Host	FTP R PORT=4979 200 Command okay.<0D><0A>
22	0.0551	Hdqtr Host	Bridge	FTP C PORT=4979 RETR faithful.jog <0D><0A>
23	0.2195	Bridge	Hdqtr Host	TCP D=4979 S=21 ACK=44830809 WIN=8192
24	2.0346	Bridge	Hdqtr Host	FTP R PORT=4979 150 File status okay; about to open data conn...
25	0.0371	Hdqtr Host	Bridge	TCP D=21 S=4979 ACK=55214259 WIN=4096
26	1.0401	Bridge	Hdqtr Host	TCP D=4980 S=20 SYN SEQ=55278458 LEN=0 WIN=0
27	0.0275	Hdqtr Host	Bridge	TCP D=20 S=4980 SYN ACK=55278459 SEQ=53214720 LEN=0 WIN=0
28	0.2321	Bridge	Hdqtr Host	TCP D=4980 S=20 ACK=53214721 WIN=8192
29	0.0279	Hdqtr Host	Bridge	TCP D=20 S=4980 ACK=55278459 WIN=4096
30	0.0099	Hdqtr Host	Bridge	TCP D=20 S=4980 ACK=55278459 WIN=8192
31	0.9281	Bridge	Hdqtr Host	TCP D=4980 S=20 ACK=53214721 SEQ=55278459

				LEN=512 WIN=8192
32	0.0070	Bridge	Hdqtr Host	TCP D=4980 S=20 ACK=53214721 SEQ=55278971 LEN=512 WIN=8192
33	0.0025	Bridge	Hdqtr Host	TCP D=4980 S=20 ACK=53214721 SEQ=55279483 LEN=256 WIN=8192
34	0.3243	Hdqtr Host	Bridge	TCP D=20 S=4980 ACK=55278971 WIN=8192
35	0.0792	Bridge	Hdqtr Host	TCP D=4980 S=20 ACK=53214721 SEQ=55279739 LEN=512 WIN=8192
36	0.0033	Bridge	Hdqtr Host	TCP D=4980 S=20 ACK=53214721 SEQ=55280251 LEN=204 WIN=8192
37	0.0873	Hdqtr Host	Bridge	TCP D=20 S=4980 ACK=55280251 WIN=8192
38	0.0514	Bridge	Hdqtr Host	TCP D=4980 S=20 ACK=53214721 SEQ=55280455 LEN=512 WIN=8192
39	0.0040	Bridge	Hdqtr Host	TCP D=4980 S=20 ACK=53214721 SEQ=55280967 LEN=512 WIN=8192
40	0.0042	Bridge	Hdqtr Host	TCP D=4980 S=20 ACK=53214721 SEQ=55281479 LEN=432 WIN=8192
41	0.1563	Hdqtr Host	Bridge	TCP D=20 S=4980 ACK=55281479 WIN=8192
42	0.0448	Bridge	Hdqtr Host	TCP D=4980 S=20 ACK=53214721 SEQ=55281911 LEN=512 WIN=8192
43	0.0042	Bridge	Hdqtr Host	TCP D=4980 S=20 ACK=53214721 SEQ=55282423 LEN=512 WIN=8192
44	0.0045	Bridge	Hdqtr Host	TCP D=4980 S=20 ACK=53214721 SEQ=55282935 LEN=361 WIN=8192
45	0.1611	Hdqtr Host	Bridge	TCP D=20 S=4980 ACK=55281911 WIN=8192

.

.

.

128	0.0018	Bridge	Hdqtr Host	TCP D=4980 S=20 ACK=53214721 SEQ=55306733 LEN=37 WIN=8192
129	0.2577	Hdqtr Host	Bridge	TCP D=20 S=4980 ACK=55303791 WIN=8192
130	0.0573	Bridge	Hdqtr Host	TCP D=4980 S=20 ACK=53214721 SEQ=55306770 LEN=225 WIN=8192
131	0.0051	Bridge	Hdqtr Host	TCP D=4980 S=20 ACK=53214721 SEQ=55306995 LEN=512 WIN=8192
132	0.0037	Bridge	Hdqtr Host	TCP D=4980 S=20 ACK=53214721 SEQ=55307507 LEN=352 WIN=8192
133	0.0416	Hdqtr Host	Bridge	TCP D=20 S=4980 ACK=55304243 WIN=8192
134	0.0378	Bridge	Hdqtr Host	TCP D=4980 S=20 ACK=53214721 SEQ=55307859 LEN=512 WIN=8192
135	0.0628	Hdqtr Host	Bridge	TCP D=20 S=4980 ACK=55305267 WIN=8192
136	0.0429	Bridge	Hdqtr Host	TCP D=4980 S=20 ACK=53214721 SEQ=55308371 LEN=512 WIN=8192
137	0.0044	Bridge	Hdqtr Host	TCP D=4980 S=20 ACK=53214721 SEQ=55308883 LEN=512 WIN=8192
138	0.0521	Hdqtr Host	Bridge	TCP D=20 S=4980 ACK=55305709 WIN=8192
139	0.0285	Bridge	Hdqtr Host	TCP D=4980 S=20 ACK=53214721 SEQ=55309395 LEN=512 WIN=8192
140	0.1706	Hdqtr Host	Bridge	TCP D=20 S=4980 ACK=55306221 WIN=8192
141	0.0368	Bridge	Hdqtr Host	TCP D=4980 S=20 ACK=53214721 SEQ=55309907 LEN=512 WIN=8192
142	0.1640	Hdqtr Host	Bridge	TCP D=20 S=4980 ACK=55306995 WIN=8192
143	0.0393	Bridge	Hdqtr Host	TCP D=4980 S=20 ACK=53214721 SEQ=55310419 LEN=512 WIN=8192

144	0.0048	Bridge	Hdqtr Host	TCP D=4980 S=20 ACK=53214721 SEQ=55310931 LEN=442 WIN=8192
145	0.1554	Hdqtr Host	Bridge	TCP D=20 S=4980 ACK=55306995 WIN=8192
146	0.0211	Bridge	Hdqtr Host	TCP D=4980 S=20 ACK=53214721 SEQ=55311373 LEN=59 WIN=8192
147	0.1795	Hdqtr Host	Bridge	TCP D=20 S=4980 ACK=55306995 WIN=8192
148	0.1987	Hdqtr Host	Bridge	TCP D=20 S=4980 ACK=55306995 WIN=8192
149	1.4094	Bridge	Hdqtr Host	TCP D=4980 S=20 RST WIN=0
150	0.5261	Bridge	Hdqtr Host	FTP R PORT=4979 426 Connection is closed: A DDP ABORT WAS EXECUTED...
151	0.0648	Hdqtr Host	Bridge	TCP D=21 S=4979 ACK=55214312 WIN=4096

TRACE 5.7.8B. TCP WINDOW MANAGEMENT ACKNOWLEDGMENTS

Sniffer Network Analyzer data 23-Jan at 03:10:38, TRACE.ENC, Pg 1

```
- - - - - - - - - - - - - - - Frame 31 - - - - - - - - - - - - - - - - -

TCP: —— TCP header ——
TCP:
TCP: Source port = 20 (FTP data)
TCP: Destination port = 4980
TCP: Sequence number = 55278459
TCP: Acknowledgment number = 53214721
TCP: Data offset = 20 bytes
TCP: Flags = 10
TCP: ..0. .... = (No urgent pointer)
TCP: ...1 .... = Acknowledgment
TCP: .... 0... = (No push)
TCP: .... .0.. = (No reset)
TCP: .... ..0. = (No SYN)
TCP: .... ...0 = (No FIN)
TCP: Window = 8192
TCP: Checksum = 27AC (correct)
TCP: No TCP options
TCP: [512 byte(s) of data]
TCP:
```

```
--------------- Frame 32 ----------------

TCP:  ——TCP header ——
TCP:
TCP:  Source port = 20 (FTP data)
TCP:  Destination port = 4980
TCP:  Sequence number = 55278971
TCP:  Acknowledgment number = 53214721
TCP:  Data offset = 20 bytes
TCP:  Flags = 10
TCP:  ..0. .... = (No urgent pointer)
TCP:  ...1 .... = Acknowledgment
TCP:  .... 0... = (No push)
TCP:  .... .0.. = (No reset)
TCP:  .... ..0. = (No SYN)
TCP:  .... ...0 = (No FIN)
TCP:  Window = 8192
TCP:  Checksum = 16E8 (correct)
TCP:  No TCP options
TCP:  [512 byte(s) of data]
TCP:

--------------- Frame 33 ----------------

TCP:  ——TCP header ——
TCP:
TCP:  Source port = 20 (FTP data)
TCP:  Destination port = 4980
TCP:  Sequence number = 55279483
TCP:  Acknowledgment number = 53214721
TCP:  Data offset = 20 bytes
TCP:  Flags = 10
TCP:  ..0. .... = (No urgent pointer)
TCP:  ...1 .... = Acknowledgment
TCP:  .... 0... = (No push)
TCP:  .... .0.. = (No reset)
TCP:  .... ..0. = (No SYN)
TCP:  .... ...0 = (No FIN)
TCP:  Window = 8192
TCP:  Checksum = 0C2D (correct)
TCP:  No TCP options
TCP:  [256 byte(s) of data]
TCP:
```

```
--------------- Frame 34 -----------------

TCP:  ——TCP header ——
TCP:
TCP:  Source port = 4980
TCP:  Destination port = 20 (FTP data)
TCP:  Sequence number = 53214721
TCP:  Acknowledgment number = 55278971
TCP:  Data offset = 20 bytes
TCP:  Flags = 10
TCP:  ..0. .... = (No urgent pointer)
TCP:  ...1 .... = Acknowledgment
TCP:  .... 0... = (No push)
TCP:  .... .0.. = (No reset)
TCP:  .... ..0. = (No SYN)
TCP:  .... ...0 = (No FIN)
TCP:  Window = 8192
TCP:  Checksum = D84E (correct)
TCP:  No TCP options
TCP:
```

TRACE 5.7.8C. TCP WINDOW MANAGEMENT RESET CONDITION

```
Sniffer Network Analyzer data 23-Jan at 03:10:38, TRACE.ENC, Pg 1

--------------- Frame 144 -----------------

TCP:  ——TCP header ——
TCP:
TCP:  Source port = 20 (FTP data)
TCP:  Destination port = 4980
TCP:  Sequence number = 55310931
TCP:  Acknowledgment number = 53214721
TCP:  Data offset = 20 bytes
TCP:  Flags = 10
TCP:  ..0. .... = (No urgent pointer)
TCP:  ...1 .... = Acknowledgment
TCP:  .... 0... = (No push)
TCP:  .... .0.. = (No reset)
TCP:  .... ..0. = (No SYN)
TCP:  .... ...0 = (No FIN)
TCP:  Window = 8192
TCP:  Checksum = 1AD5 (correct)
TCP:  No TCP options
TCP:  [442 byte(s) of data]
TCP:
```

```
--------------- Frame 145 ----------------

TCP:  ——TCP header ——
TCP:
TCP:  Source port = 4980
TCP:  Destination port = 20 (FTP data)
TCP:  Sequence number = 53214721
TCP:  Acknowledgment number = 55306995
TCP:  Data offset = 20 bytes
TCP:  Flags = 10
TCP:  ..0. .... = (No urgent pointer)
TCP:  ...1 .... = Acknowledgment
TCP:  .... 0... = (No push)
TCP:  .... .0.. = (No reset)
TCP:  .... ..0. = (No SYN)
TCP:  .... ...0 = (No FIN)
TCP:  Window = 8192
TCP:  Checksum = 6AD6 (correct)
TCP:  No TCP options
TCP:

--------------- Frame 146 ----------------

TCP:  ——TCP header ——
TCP:
TCP:  Source port = 20 (FTP data)
TCP:  Destination port = 4980
TCP:  Sequence number = 55311373
TCP:  Acknowledgment number = 53214721
TCP:  Data offset = 20 bytes
TCP:  Flags = 10
TCP:  ..0. .... = (No urgent pointer)
TCP:  ...1 .... = Acknowledgment
TCP:  .... 0... = (No push)
TCP:  .... .0.. = (No reset)
TCP:  .... ..0. = (No SYN)
TCP:  .... ...0 = (No FIN)
TCP:  Window = 8192
TCP:  Checksum = E735 (correct)
TCP:  No TCP options
TCP:  [59 byte(s) of data]
TCP:
```

```
--------------- Frame 147 -----------------

TCP:  ——TCP header ——
TCP:
TCP:  Source port = 4980
TCP:  Destination port = 20 (FTP data)
TCP:  Sequence number = 53214721
TCP:  Acknowledgment number = 55306995
TCP:  Data offset = 20 bytes
TCP:  Flags = 10
TCP:  ..0. .... = (No urgent pointer)
TCP:  ...1 .... = Acknowledgment
TCP:  .... 0... = (No push)
TCP:  .... .0.. = (No reset)
TCP:  .... ..0. = (No SYN)
TCP:  .... ...0 = (No FIN)
TCP:  Window = 8192
TCP:  Checksum = 6AD6 (correct)
TCP:  No TCP options
TCP:

--------------- Frame 148 -----------------

TCP:  ——TCP header ——
TCP:
TCP:  Source port = 4980
TCP:  Destination port = 20 (FTP data)
TCP:  Sequence number = 53214721
TCP:  Acknowledgment number = 55306995
TCP:  Data offset = 20 bytes
TCP:  Flags = 10
TCP:  ..0. .... = (No urgent pointer)
TCP:  ...1 .... = Acknowledgment
TCP:  .... 0... = (No push)
TCP:  .... .0.. = (No reset)
TCP:  .... ..0. = (No SYN)
TCP:  .... ...0 = (No FIN)
TCP:  Window = 8192
TCP:  Checksum = 6AD6 (correct)
TCP:  No TCP options
TCP:
```

```
--------------- Frame 149 -----------------

TCP: ——TCP header ——
TCP:
TCP: Source port = 20 (FTP data)
TCP: Destination port = 4980
TCP: Sequence number = 55311432
TCP: Data offset = 20 bytes
TCP: Flags = 04
TCP: ..0. .... = (No urgent pointer)
TCP: ...0 .... = (No acknowledgment)
TCP: .... 0... = (No push)
TCP: .... .1.. = Reset
TCP: .... ..0. = (No SYN)
TCP: .... ...0 = (No FIN)
TCP: Window = 0
TCP: Checksum = 7ABA (correct)
TCP: No TCP options
TCP:

--------------- Frame 150 -----------------

FTP: ——FTP data ——
FTP:
FTP: 426 Connection is closed: A DDP ABORT WAS EXECUTED...
FTP:

--------------- Frame 151 -----------------

TCP: ——TCP header ——
TCP:
TCP: Source port = 4979
TCP: Destination port = 21 (FTP)
TCP: Sequence number = 44830809
TCP: Acknowledgment number = 55214312
TCP: Data offset = 20 bytes
TCP: Flags = 10
TCP: ..0. .... = (No urgent pointer)
TCP: ...1 .... = Acknowledgment
TCP: .... 0... = (No push)
TCP: .... .0.. = (No reset)
TCP: .... ..0. = (No SYN)
TCP: .... ...0 = (No FIN)
TCP: Window = 4096
TCP:             Checksum = D30A (correct)
TCP:             No TCP options
TCP:
```

5.8 Looking Ahead

This chapter marks the three-quarter point in our journey from the bottom to the top of the ARPA protocol stack. We have now made the LAN, MAN, or WAN hardware connection at the Network Interface Layer, transmitted the datagrams at the Internet Layer, and ensured the reliability of those datagrams at the Host-to-Host Layer. References [5-19] and [5-20] provide additional insight into the operation of the Host-to-Host layer and TCP. Reference [5-21] discusses why TCP has been more successful than its OSI counterparts.

Now we need some application data to send! We'll discuss these applications in the next chapter by studying protocols for file transfer, electronic mail, and remote host access.

5.9 References

[5-1] Postel, J. "User Datagram Protocol." RFC 768, August 1980.

[5-2] Postel, J., Editor. "Transmission Control Protocol." RFC 793, September 1981.

[5-3] Socolofsky, T., et al. "A TCP/IP Tutorial." RFC 1180, January 1991.

[5-4] Postel, J. "The TCP Maximum Segment Size and Related Topics." RFC 879, November 1983.

[5-5] Black, Uyless. *TCP/IP and Related Protocols,* second edition. McGraw-Hill, Inc. (New York, NY), 1995.

[5-6] Comer, Douglas E. *Internetworking with TCP/IP,* third edition. Prentice Hall, Inc. (Englewood Cliffs, NJ), 1995.

[5-7] Partridge, Craig. "Improving Your TCP: Look at the Timers." *ConneXions* (July 1987): 13–14.

[5-8] Karn, Phil. "Improving Your TCP: Karn's Algorithm." *ConneXions* (October 1988): 23.

[5-9] Clark, David D. "Window and Acknowledgement Strategy in TCP." RFC 813, July 1982.

[5-10] Minshall, Greg. "TCP Connection Initiation: An Inside Look." *ConneXions* (July 1988): 2–11.

[5-11] Stevens, W. "TCP Slow Start, Congestion Avoidance, Fast Retransmit, and Fast Recovery Algorithms." RFC 2001, January 1997.

[5-12] Clark, David D. "Fault Isolation and Recovery." RFC 816, July 1982.

[5-13] Croft, W., et al. "Bootstrap Protocol (BOOTP)." RFC 951, September 1985.

[5-14] Alexander, S., and R. Droms. "DHCP Options and BOOTP Vendor Extensions." RFC 2132, March 1997.

[5-15] Finlayson, Ross. "Bootstrap Loading Using TFTP." RFC 906, June 1984.

[5-16] Mogul, Jeffrey. "Booting Diskless Hosts: The BOOTP Protocol." *ConneXions* (October 1988): 14–18.

[5-17] Postel, J., et al. "Time Protocol." RFC 868, May 1983.

[5-18] Zimmerman, D. "The Finger User Information Protocol." RFC 1288, December 1991.

[5-19] Stevens, W. Richard. "TCP Keepalives." *ConneXions* (February 1994): 2–7.

[5-20] McCloghrie, Keith, and Marshall T. Rose. "The Internet Transport Layer." *ConneXions* (June 1994): 2–9.

[5-21] Salus, Peter H. "Protocol Wars: Is OSI Finally Dead?" *ConneXions* (August 1995): 16–19.

Chapter 6

Troubleshooting the Process/Application Connection

In this chapter, we'll study the Process/Application Layer functions. At this layer, the user interacts with the host to perform user functions. These functions may include: file transfer using the Trivial File Transfer Protocol (TFTP) or the more complex File Transfer Protocol (FTP); client/server file operations via Sun Microsystems Inc.'s Network File System (NFS); remote host access with the Telecommunications Network (TELNET) protocol; or electronic mail using the Simple Mail Transfer Protocol (SMTP). All of these protocols exhibit their own characteristics and challenges. We'll begin by exploring how they fit into the ARPA architectural model.

6.1 The Process/Application Connection

The Process/Application Layer sits at the very top of the ARPA architectural model. Unlike the Host-to-Host, Internet, and Network Interface Layers, which are transparent to end users, the Process/Application Layer is accessed by users directly via the host's operating system. (Network analysts, of course, must be prepared to troubleshoot problems at any layer!) End users use this layer's functions to perform computer operations such as file transfer, electronic mail, and so on (see Figure 6-1a).

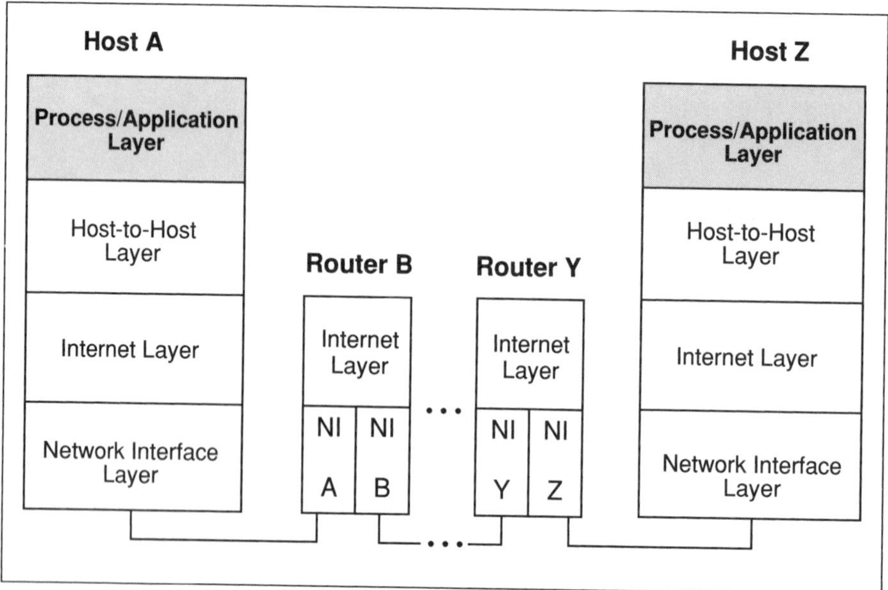

Figure 6-1a Process/Application Connection

Figure 6-1b shows examples of the significant Process/Application protocols and the standards that describe them. Since these protocols provide functions that relate to the OSI Session, Presentation, and Application Layers, they are sometimes referred to as Upper Layer Protocols (ULPs). Figure 6-1c shows the position of the Application (ULP) data within the transmission frame. The lower layer headers and trailers all serve to reliably transfer the ULP information from one host to another via the internetwork.

ARPA Layer	Protocol Implementation								OSI Layer
Process / Application	Hypertext Transfer	File Transfer	Electronic Mail	Terminal Emulation	Domain Names	File Transfer	Client / Server	Network Management	Application
	Hypertext Transfer Protocol (HTTP) RFC 2068	File Transfer Protocol (FTP) MIL-STD-1780 RFC 959	Simple Mail Transfer Protocol (SMTP) MIL-STD-1781 RFC 821	TELNET Protocol MIL-STD-1782 RFC 854	Domain Name System (DNS) RFC 1034, 1035	Trivial File Transfer Protocol (TFTP) RFC 783	Sun Microsystems Network File System Protocols (NFS) RFCs 1014, 1057, and 1094	Simple Network Management Protocol (SNMP) v1: RFC 1157 v2: RFC 1901-10 v3: RFC 2271-75	Presentation / Session
Host-to-Host	Transmission Control Protocol (TCP) MIL-STD-1778 RFC 793					User Datagram Protocol (UDP) RFC 768			Transport
Internet	Address Resolution ARP RFC 826 RARP RFC 903			Internet Protocol (IP) MIL-STD-1777 RFC 791			Internet Control Message Protocol (ICMP) RFC 792		Network
Network Interface	Network Interface Cards: Ethernet, Token Ring, ARCNET, MAN and WAN RFC 894, RFC 1042, RFC 1201 and others								Data Link
	Transmission Media: Twisted Pair, Coax, Fiber Optics, Wireless Media, etc.								Physical

Figure 6-1b ARPA Process/Application Layer Protocols

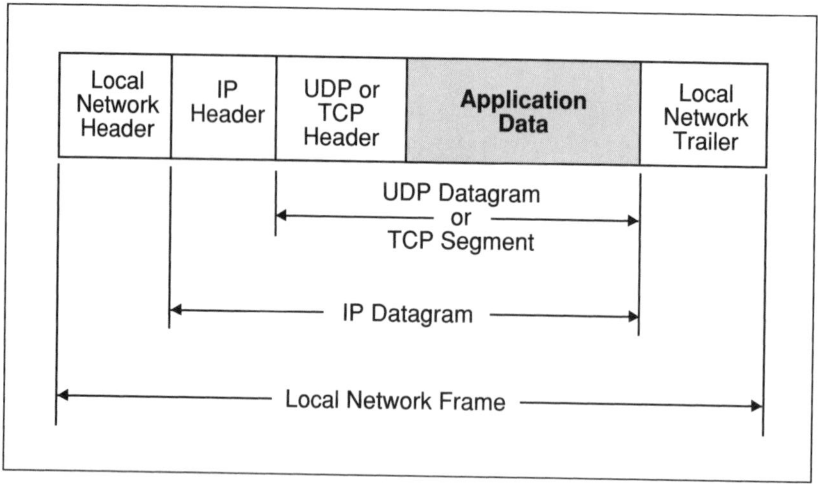

Figure 6-1c The Internet Transmission Frame and Application Data Position

To complete our tour of the ARPA architectural model, we will study the significant Process/Application protocols, beginning with TFTP. Several references provide details on the protocols discussed in this chapter. Stallings' *Handbook of Computer-Communications Standards, Volume 3, The TCP/IP Protocol Suite* [6-1] contains individual chapters on the common application protocols such as FTP, TELNET, and SMTP. RFC 1123, "Requirements for Internet Hosts: Application and Support" [6-2], details requirements that hosts must provide to properly support file transfer, remote host access, and electronic mail. Specific details and parameters for these protocols are provided in RFC 1700, the "Assigned Numbers" document [6-3]. An excerpt of RFC 1700 is provided in Appendix D for reference.

6.2 Trivial File Transfer Protocol (TFTP)

The Trivial File Transfer Protocol, described in RFC 1350 [6-4], reads and writes files or mail messages from one host to another. It offers no other functions. TFTP's strength is its simplicity. It transfers 512-octet blocks of data without excessive overhead. Because it is implemented on UDP transport, TFTP is one of the easiest ULPs to implement, but it does not guarantee data reliability.

TFTP defines five packet types, which are distinguished by an Opcode (operation code) field (see Figure 6-2):

Opcode	Operation
1	Read Request (RRQ)
2	Write Request (WRQ)
3	Data (DATA)
4	Acknowledgment (ACK)
5	Error (ERROR)

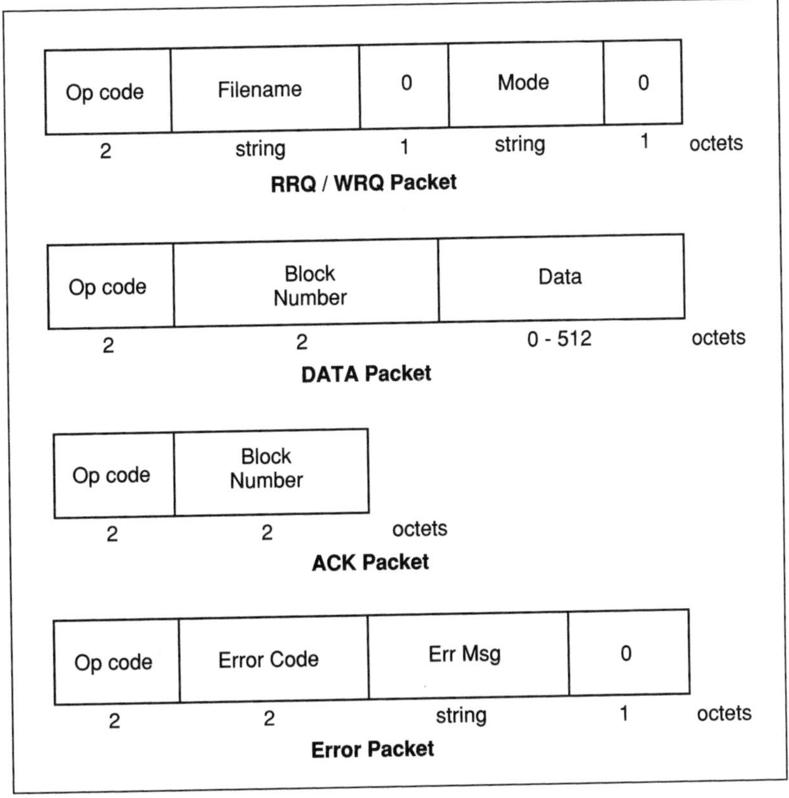

Figure 6-2 Trivial File Transfer Protocol (TFTP) Packet Formats

The Read Request (RRQ, Opcode = 1) and Write Request (WRQ, Opcode = 2) packets have the same structure. Following the Opcode (2 octets), a string of netascii characters specifies the filename. (The netascii code is an 8-bit code defined by the ANSI standard X3.4-1968.) An octet containing zero terminates the filename. The Mode field (also a string) specifies which of three data transfer modes are to be used. The choices are netascii, octet (raw 8-bit bytes), and mail. The mail mode is defined as netascii characters destined for a user instead of a host. The Mode field is terminated by an octet containing zero.

The Data packet (Opcode = 3) transfers information. A Block number (2 octets) follows the Opcode and identifies the particular 512-octet block of data being sent. The Data field (0–512 octets in length) carries the actual information. Blocks less than 512 octets in length (i.e., 0–511 octets) indicate the end of an atomic unit of transmission.

The ACK packet (Opcode = 4) is used for acknowledgment. It contains a Block Number field (2 octets) that corresponds to the similar number in the Data packet being acknowledged. For simplicity, TFTP incorporates the lock-step acknowledgment, which requires each data packet to be acknowledged prior to the transmission of another. In other words, because TFTP operates over UDP, not TCP, it has no provisions for a window mechanism, and all packets (except ERROR packets) must be acknowledged. ACK or ERROR packets acknowledge DATA and WRQ packets; DATA or ERROR packets acknowledge RRQ or ACK packets. ERROR packets require no acknowledgment.

The ERROR packet (Opcode = 5) may be used to acknowledge any of the other four packet types. It contains a 2-octet error code that describes the problem:

Value	Meaning
0	Not defined, see error message (if any)
1	File not found
2	Access violation
3	Disk full or allocation exceeded
4	Illegal TFTP operation
5	Unknown transfer ID
6	File already exists
7	No such user

An error message (ErrMsg) consisting of a netascii string followed by a zero completes the packet. When errors occur, an ERROR packet is transmitted and the connection is terminated. Hosts generate ERROR packets for three types of events: when the host cannot satisfy a request such as locating a file; when the host receives a delayed or duplicate packet; or when the host loses access to a resource such as a disk during the transfer.

Figure 6-3 shows TFTP's operation. Host A issues an RRQ or WRQ and receives a response of either DATA (for RRQ) or ACK (for WRQ). Each host initiating a connection chooses a random number between 0 and 65,535 for use as a Transfer Identifier (TID). The TID passes to UDP, which uses it as a Port address. When the RRQ or WRQ is initially transmitted from Host A, it selects a TID to identify its end of the connection and designates Destination = 69, the TFTP Port number. If the connection is accepted, the remote host, Host B, returns its TID B subscript as the source with the TID A subscript as the destination. If a WRQ was the initial transmission, an ACK with Block number = 0 is returned. If the transmission was RRQ, a DATA packet with Block number = 1 is returned. Data transfer then proceeds in 512-octet blocks, with each host identifying the appropriate Source and Destination TIDs with each DATA or ACK packet. The receipt of a DATA packet with less than 512 octets signals the termination of the connection. If errors occur during transmission, they generate an ERROR packet containing the appropriate Error Code. An example of this is provided in Section 6.10.1.

In addition to RFC 1350, several other documents provide details on TFTP operation. These include: RFC 1785, "TFTP Option Negotiation Analysis"; RFC 2347, "TFTP Option Extension"; RFC 2348, "TFTP Blocksize Option"; and RFC 2349, "TFTP Timeout Interval and Transfer Size Options."

6.3 File Transfer Protocol

One of the most popular Process/Application protocols is the File Transfer Protocol (FTP), described in RFC 959 [6-5]. RFC 2228 discusses FTP Security Extensions, and updates RFC 959. As its name implies, FTP allows local or remote client and server machines to share files and data using TCP's reliable transport.

The complete FTP service includes a User-FTP and a Server-FTP, as shown in Figure 6-4. The User-FTP includes a User Interface (UI), a User Protocol Interpreter (PI), and a User Data Transfer Process (DTP). The Server-FTP includes a Server-PI and a Server-DTP, but excludes the user interface. The User-PI initiates the logical control connection, which uses the TELNET protocol. The user (or client) uses an internally assigned Port number to connect to Server Port number 21, designated for FTP control. The data to be transferred passes from another self-assigned port on the User-DTP to Port number 20 (designated FTP data) on the Server-DTP. Thus, two Port numbers are used for the two logical communication paths: control and data.

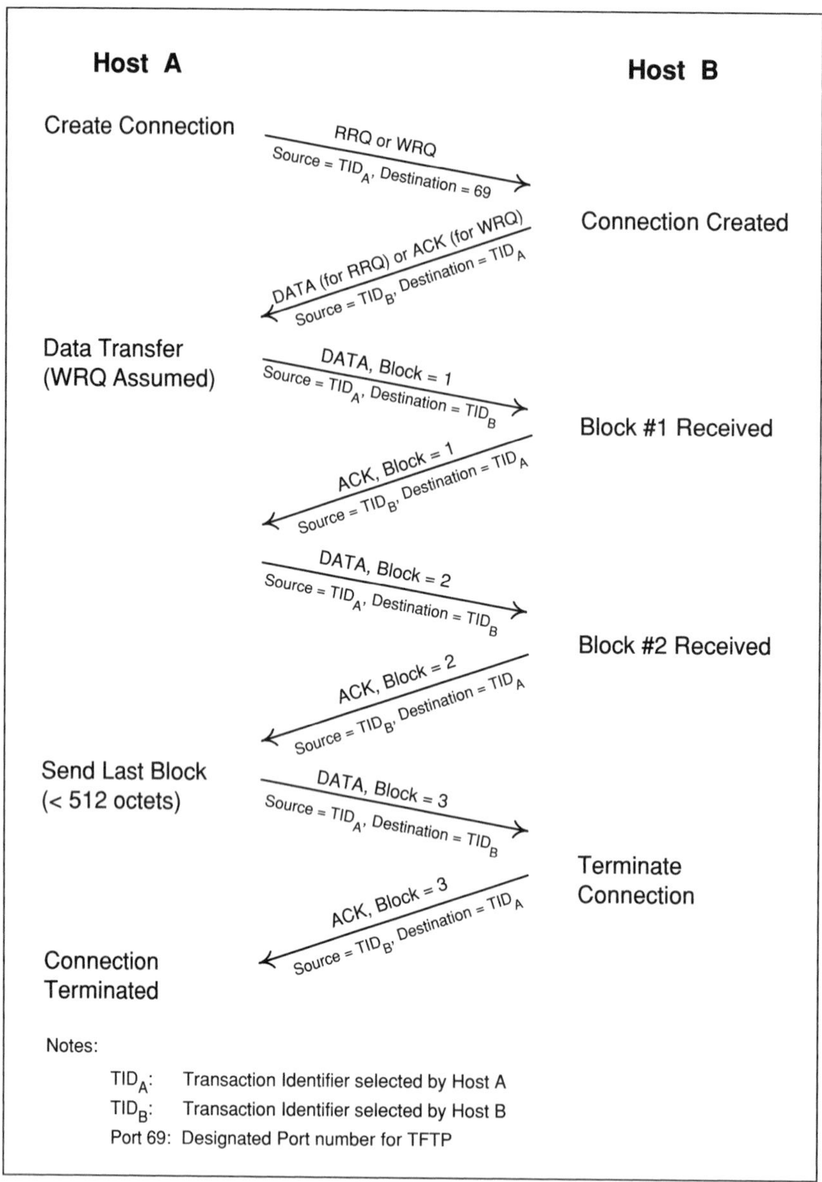

Figure 6-3 TFTP Connection, Data Transfer, and Termination

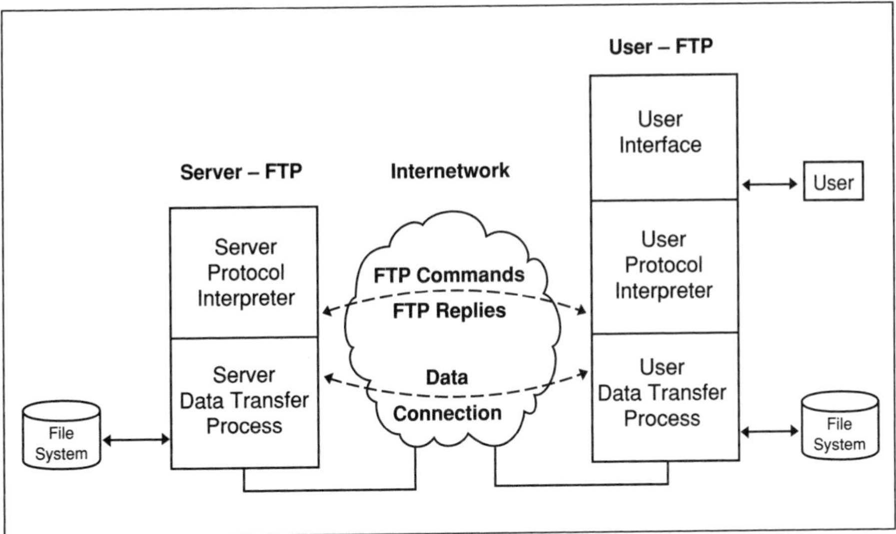

Figure 6-4 File Transfer Protocol (FTP) Model

6.3.1 Data Representation, Data Structures, and Transmission Modes

Three parameters are required to completely specify the data or file to be transferred: the Data Representation, the Data Structure, and the Transmission Mode. The data may be represented in one of four ways: ASCII (the default is 8-bit characters); EBCDIC (8-bit characters); Image (8-bit contiguous bytes), which transfers binary data; and Local, which uses a byte size defined by the local host. Similarly, there are three types of data structures: the File Structure (the default), which is a continuous sequence of data bytes; the Record Structure, which consists of continuous records; and the Page Structure, which is comprised of independent, indexed pages. Three transmission modes are available, including Stream Mode (a transmitted stream of bytes), Block Mode (a header plus a series of data blocks), and Compressed Mode (used for maximizing bandwidth). The proper operation of the data transfer between the User and Server Data Transfer Processes depends on the control commands that go between the User and Server Protocol Interpreters. We'll look at these commands next.

6.3.2 FTP Commands

FTP commands and replies are communicated between the Server and User Protocol Interpreters (review Figure 6-4). These commands are defined in three categories: Access Control, Transfer Parameter, and Service.

6.3.2.1 ACCESS CONTROL COMMANDS

The Access Control commands determine which users may access a particular file; these commands are invoked by the Server-FTP.

Command Code and Argument	Usage
USER <SP> <username> <CRLF>	Identifies the user
PASS <SP> <password> <CRLF>	User's password
ACCT <SP> <account-information> <CRLF>	User's account
CWD <SP> <pathname> <CRLF>	Change working directory
CDUP <CRLF>	Change to Parent directory
SMNT <SP> <pathname> <CRLF>	Structure Mount
REIN <CRLF>	Reinitialize, terminating the user
QUIT <CRLF>	Logout
<SP>	Represents a Space character
<CRLF>	Carriage Return, Line Feed characters

6.3.2.2 TRANSFER PARAMETER COMMANDS

The Transfer Parameter commands are used to alter the default parameters used to transfer data on an FTP connection:

Command Code and Argument	Usage
PORT <SP> <host-port> <CRLF>	Specifies the data port to be used
PASV <CRLF>	Requests the Server DTP to listen on a data port
TYPE <SP> <type-code> <CRLF>	Representation type: ASCII, EBCDIC, Image, or Local
STRU <SP> <structure-code> <CRLF>	File structure: File, Record, or Page
MODE <SP> <mode-code> <CRLF>	Transmission mode: Stream, Block, or Compressed

6.3.2.3 SERVICE COMMANDS

Service commands define the file operation requested by the user. The convention for the pathname argument is determined by the FTP Server's local conventions:

Command Code and Argument	Usage
RETR <SP> <pathname> <CRLF>	Retrieve a copy of the file from the other end
STOR <SP> <pathname> <CRLF>	Store data at the Server
STOU <CRLF>	Store Unique
APPE <SP> <pathname> <CRLF>	Append
ALLO <SP> <decimal-integer>	Allocate storage
[<SP> R <SP> <decimal-integer>] <CRLF>	
REST <SP> <marker> <CRLF>	Restart transfer at checkpoint
RNFR <SP> <pathname> <CRLF>	Rename from
RNTO <SP> <pathname> <CRLF>	Rename to
ABOR <CRLF>	Abort previous service command
DELE <SP> <pathname> <CRLF>	Delete file at Server
RMD <SP> <pathname> <CRLF>	Remove directory
MKD <SP> <pathname> <CRLF>	Make directory
PWD <CRLF>	Print working directory
LIST [<SP> <pathname>] <CRLF>	List files or text
NLST [<SP> <pathname>] <CRLF>	Name list
SITE <SP> <string> <CRLF>	Site parameters
SYST <CRLF>	Determine operating system
STAT [<SP> <pathname>] <CRLF>	Status
HELP [<SP> <string>] <CRLF>	Help information
NOOP <CRLF>	No operation

6.3.3 FTP Replies

An FTP reply consists of a three-digit number and a space, and is followed by one line of text. Each digit of the reply is significant. The first digit (value 1–5) determines whether the response is good, bad, or incomplete. The second and third digits are encoded to provide additional details regarding the reply. The values for the first digit are:

1yz	Positive Preliminary reply
2yz	Positive Completion reply
3yz	Positive Intermediate reply
4yz	Transient Negative Completion reply
5yz	Permanent Negative Completion reply

The values for the second digit are:

x0z	Syntax
x1z	Information
x2z	Connections
x3z	Authentication and accounting
x4z	Unspecified as yet
x5z	File system

The third digit gives a finer definition for each function category specified by the second digit. An example would be:

211: System status

212: Directory status

213: File status

214: Help message

The FTP specification, RFC 959, elaborates in great detail on the states and conditions that trigger these reply messages. Another useful reference is Romkey's "FTP's Tiresome Problems" [6-6], which describes some of the shortcomings of the protocol's implementation under different operating systems.

6.3.4 FTP Operation

A typical scenario in which FTP is used to retrieve a file from a remote host begins when the user initiates a connection to the remote host by entering **FTP [host address]**. For example, to retrieve an RFC, the user would enter *ftp ds.internic.net* to access the Internic's server that contains Internet documentation such as RFCs. The host responds by asking for the username and password. If the desired file is not in the root directory, the user must change to the proper subdirectory. For example, the user would enter **cd rfc** to change to the subdirectory that contains the RFCs. (Note that some host systems abbreviate certain commands. For example, the CWD command to change the current directory becomes CD. Most systems support the HELP command, which lists the commands or abbreviations accepted by the system.) The third step is for the user to tell the host the action required, such as file transfer. For example, to retrieve an RFC, the command would be **get rfcnnnn.txt**, where nnnn represents the number of the desired RFC. If the file transfer requires a different mode (such as binary), the user must specify that mode before invoking the get command. The file transfer would then begin, and the user would terminate the FTP connection (using the FTP **quit** command) when all business was completed. Another example of an FTP session is given in the case study in Section 6.10.2.

6.4 Sun Microsystems Network File System

No discussion about the Application/Process Layer would be complete without mentioning Sun Microsystems Inc.'s Network File System, commonly known as NFS. Sun released NFS in 1985 as part of the Sun Operating System (SunOS) included with Sun workstations. Since then, the NFS protocols have been adopted for a wide variety of computing platforms, including PCs, minicomputers, and large hosts.

NFS is based on a client/server paradigm where the *client* is the local computer that runs the application and the *server* is the computer that manages the file or application program. A LAN or WAN may run between the client and the server. In other words, NFS does not restrict the location of the client or server, and it provides transparent access to files regardless of their location. Any one machine can operate as both a client and a server.

Another advantage of NFS is that it allows the user to access files regardless of the operating system under which they are stored. Therefore, NFS allows directories and files to be shared between, say, an MS-DOS machine and other machines running UNIX, Digitals's VMS, IBM's MVS, or Apple Computer's Macintosh operating system. Of course, if all machines are running NFS, NFS ensures access to those files.

The foundation for the Sun protocols is the UDP and IP transport protocols, which may operate on a number of LAN/WAN interfaces. As we know, UDP provides a connectionless transport, which is not error free. The NFS client/server paradigm therefore uses a stateless protocol in which one operation (or state) must complete before another initiates. Thus, after the client makes a request, it must wait for the server's response. If the server does not respond or delays its response, the client repeats its request. A server crash therefore will not impact the client. If the client has received the application file then the client/server interaction is complete; if the client has not received the file, it will continue to resend the file request until the server is reinitialized. This aspect of the stateless protocol is particularly useful when you add the complexity of an internetwork between client and server.

The protocols that, in aggregate, make up the Sun suite are comprised of three separate modules: the Remote Procedure Call (RPC), the External Data Representation (XDR), and NFS. These three sit on top of UDP and IP (see Figure 6-5). Sun has developed RFCs for each module. The first layer of the Sun protocol stack is the RPC, defined in RFC 1057 [6-7]. The RPC establishes a logical connection between client and server. As with the establishment of a telephone call, the client sends a message to the server and waits for the server's reply. The server's reply includes the results of the requested procedure. The next layer is the XDR, specified in RFC 1014 [6-8]. XDR provides OSI Presentation Layer functions; it describes and encodes the data that is transferred to and from the client and server. The NFS protocol, version 2, described in RFC 1094 [6-9], or version 3, described in RFC 1813 [6-10], sits at the top of the Sun protocol stack. The NFS protocol defines the file and directory structures and procedures for the client and server. References [6-11] through [6-13] provide excellent background on the Sun protocols and how they compare with other distributed file systems.

The importance of the Sun protocols lies in their strong ties to the UNIX environment, coupled with the historical tie between UNIX and the Internet protocols. In other words, if you use UNIX, you are likely to also use the TCP/IP and Sun protocols. An in-depth study of these protocols is beyond the scope of this text; refer to Malamud's *Analyzing Sun Networks* [6-14] for further information.

6.5 TELNET

TELNET, which stands for Telecommunications Network, is a protocol that allows a user (or client) at a terminal to access a remote host (or server). TELNET operates with TCP transport using Port number 23 and allows the terminal and host to exchange 8-bit characters of information in a half-duplex manner. The primary standard for TELNET, RFC 854 [6-15], discusses the three objectives of the protocol; RFC 855 [6-16] considers the various TELNET options.

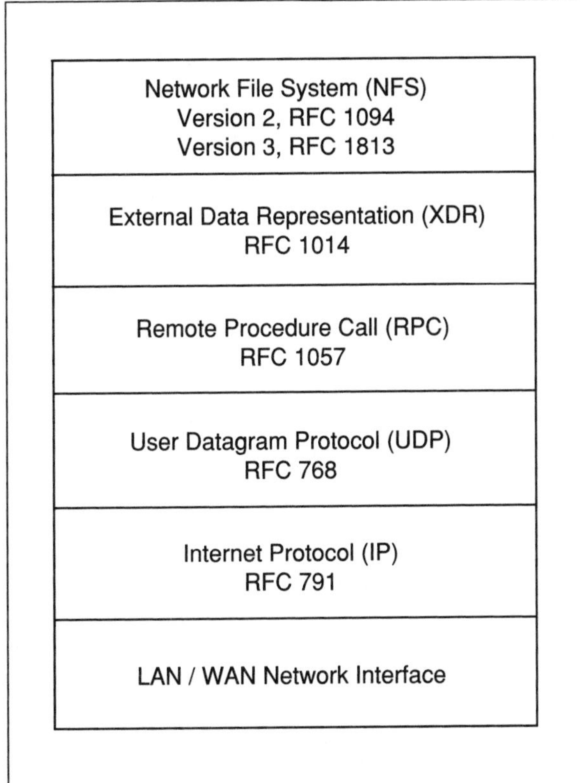

Figure 6-5 Sun Microsystems NFS Protocols

TELNET's first objective is to define the Network Virtual Terminal (NVT). The NVT is a hypothetical representation of a network-standard terminal, also called a *canonical* (or standard) form. When both ends of the connection convert their data representations into the canonical form, they can communicate regardless of whether one end is, say, a DEC VT-100 and the other an SNA Host. The defined NVT format is the 7-bit USASCII code, transmitted in 8-bit octets. Figure 6-6 illustrates the conversion process from the local terminal/host format to the NVT format. The conversion typically occurs inside the devices, although an ancillary device such as a terminal server may perform the conversion for a number of similar devices.

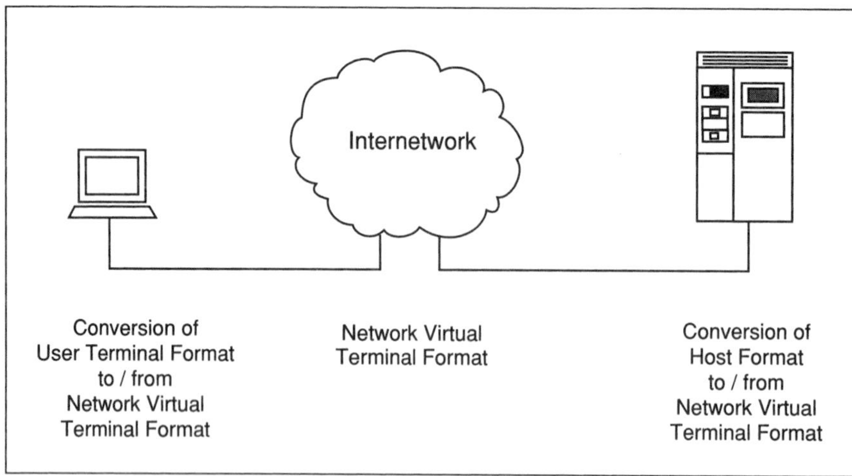

Figure 6-6 TELNET Network Virtual Terminal Operation

The second objective of TELNET is to allow clients and servers to negotiate various options. This feature allows you to use a number of different terminals (some intelligent and some not so intelligent) with equal facility. To begin the negotiation, either of the ends of the connection state their desire to negotiate a particular option. The other end of the connection can accept or reject the proposal. TELNET defines four negotiation options: WILL, WON'T, DO, and DON'T. WILL *XXX* indicates that party's desire (or offer) to begin performing option *XXX*. DO *XXX* or DON'T *XXX* are the returned positive or negative acknowledgments, respectively. DO *XXX* indicates that party's desire (or request) that the other party begin performing option *XXX*. WILL *XXX* and WON'T *XXX* are the returned positive and negative acknowledgments, respectively. For example, suppose the terminal wanted to use binary transmission. It would send a DO Binary Transmission to the remote host. The host could then respond with either a WILL Binary Transmission (a positive acknowledgment) or a WON'T Binary Transmission (a negative acknowledgment). If that terminal does not want its characters echoed across the TELNET connection it would send WON'T Echo; if the remote host agrees that no characters will be echoed it would return DON'T Echo.

The third concept of TELNET is one of symmetry in the negotiation syntax. This symmetry allows either the client or the server end of the connection to request a particular option as required, thus optimizing the service provided by the other party.

TELNET commands consist of a mandatory two-octet sequence and an optional third octet. The first octet is always the Interpret as Command (IAC) character, Code 255. The second octet is the code for one of the commands listed below. The third octet is used when options are to be negotiated, and contains the option number of interest. For example, the command "IAC DO Terminal Type" would be represented by FF FD 18 (hexadecimal), corresponding to the Codes 255 253 24 (which are represented in decimal). RFC 854 defines the following TELNET commands:

Command	Code	Meaning
SE	240	End of subnegotiation parameters
NOP	241	No operation
Data Mark	242	The data stream portion of a Synch. This should always be accompanied by a TCP Urgent notification.
Break	243	NVT character BRK
Interrupt Process	244	The function IP
Abort output	245	The function AO
Are You There	246	The function AYT
Erase character	247	The function EC
Erase Line	248	The function EL
Go ahead	249	The GA signal
SB	250	Indicates that what follows is subnegotiation of the indicated option.
WILL (option code)	251	Indicates the desire to begin performing, or confirmation that you are now performing, the indicated option.
WON'T (option code)	252	Indicates the refusal to perform, or to continue performing, the indicated option.
DO (option code)	253	Indicates the request that the other party perform, or confirmation that you are expecting the other party to perform, the indicated option.
DON'T (option code)	254	Indicates the demand that the other party stop performing, or confirmation that you are no longer expecting the other party to perform, the indicated option.
IAC	255	Data Byte 255

RFC 1700 lists the following TELNET options, along with the reference documents that provide further information:

Option	Name	Reference
0	Binary Transmission	RFC 856
1	Echo	RFC 856
2	Reconnection	NIC 50005
3	Suppress Go Ahead	RFC 858
4	Approx Message Size Negotiation	*See Reference [3-5]*
5	Status	RFC 859
6	Timing Mark	RFC 860
7	Remote Controlled Trans and Echo	RFC 726
8	Output Line Width	NIC 50005
9	Output Page Size	NIC 50005
10	Output Carriage-Return Disposition	RFC 652
11	Output Horizontal Tab Stops	RFC 653
12	Output Horizontal Tab Disposition	RFC 654
13	Output Formfeed Disposition	RFC 655
14	Output Vertical Tabstops	RFC 656
15	Output Vertical Tab Disposition	RFC 657
16	Output Linefeed Disposition	RFC 658
17	Extended ASCII	RFC 698
18	Logout	RFC 727
19	Byte Macro	RFC 735
20	Data Entry Terminal	RFC 1043
21	SUPDUP	RFC 736
22	SUPDUP Output	RFC 749
23	Send Location	RFC 779
24	Terminal Type	RFC 109
25	End of Record	RFC 885
26	TACACS User Identification	RFC 927
27	Output Marking	RFC 933

28	Terminal Location Number	RFC 946
29	Telnet 3270 Regime	RFC 1041
30	X.3 PAD	RFC 1053
31	Negotiate About Window Size	RFC 1073
32	Terminal Speed	RFC 1079
33	Remote Flow Control	RFC 1372
34	Linemode	RFC 1184
35	X Display Location	RFC 1096
36	Environment	RFC 1408
37	Authentication	RFC 1409
38	Encryption	N/A
39	New Environment	RFC 1572
255	Extended-Options-List	RFC 861

Note the large number of documents available to describe individual options. Shein's "The TELNET Protocol" [6-17] provides an excellent description of the negotiation processes. The case study in Section 6.10.3 will consider the operation of the Terminal Type option.

6.6 Simple Mail Transfer Protocol

The Simple Mail Transfer Protocol (SMTP) is based on a straightforward model of client/server computing. The model includes a sender and a receiver, both of which have access to a file system for message storage. Some type of communication channel links sender and receiver, completing the model. SMTP is intended to be a dependable message delivery system, although it does not provide absolute end-to-end reliability. It is based on TCP transport, however, which increases its effectiveness. The standard governing the SMTP system is specified in RFC 821 [6-18], while the message format is contained in "Standard for the Format of ARPA Internet Text Messages," RFC 822 [6-19]. In addition, RFC 2157 discusses mapping between X.400 and RFC 822/MIME message bodies. Reference [6-20] discusses the use of electronic mail over the Internet, while Reference [6-21] describes electronic messaging on LANs.

6.6.1 Message Transfer

The transfer of an electronic message can be divided into several distinct stages, all supported by the SMTP model (see Figure 6-7). First, the user provides input to an interface system, known as the user agent, which facilitates the entry of the mail message. Then the message is sent to the Sender-SMTP, which assigns an arbitrary Port number to the process and establishes a TCP connection with Port number 25 on its peer (Receiver-SMTP). While establishing that connection, the receiver identifies itself to the sender. Next, the mail message is transferred using the RFC 822 format (discussed in the following section). Finally, the sender signals its desire to terminate the connection, which is acknowledged by the receiver. After that acknowledgment, the TCP connection is closed.

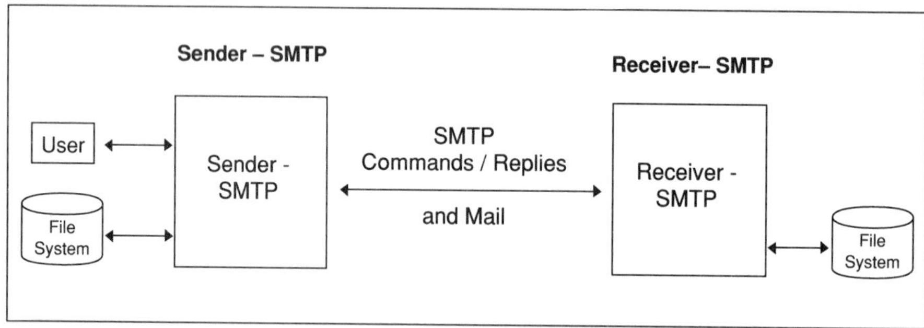

Figure 6-7 Mail Transfer Protocol (SMTP) Model

6.6.2 Message Format

RFC 822 [6-19] defines the message format used with SMTP. The message consists of a header, which contains a number of fields, and the message text. A blank line separates the header from the text. Many of the header fields are optional and depend on local implementation; however, some variation of the example below will be present in most systems. The following example of a mail format is taken from Appendix A of RFC 822 and is described as "about as complex as you're going to get."

```
Date     :    27 Aug 76 0932 PDT
From     :    Ken Davis <KDavis@This-Host.This-net>
Subject  :    Re: The Syntax in the RFC
Sender   :    KSecy@Other-Host
Reply-To :    Sam.Irving@Reg.Organization
To       :    George Jones <Group@Some-Reg.An-Org>,
              Al.Neuman@MAD.Publisher
```

```
  cc        :    Important folk:
                   Tom Softwood <Balsa@Tree.Root>,
                   "Sam Irving'@Other-Host;,
                 Standard Distribution:
                   /main/davis/people/standard@Other-Host,
                  "<Jones>standard.dist.3"@Tops-20-Host>;
  Comment   :    Sam is away on business. He asked me to handle
                 his mail for him.  Heκll be able to provide a
                 more  accurate  explanation  when  he  returns
                 next week.
  In-Reply-To:    <some.string@DBM.Group>, Georgeκs message
  X-Special-action:  This is a sample of user-defined field-
                 names.  There could also be a field-name
                 "Special-action", but its name might later be
                 preempted

Message-ID: 4231.629.XYzi-What@Other-Host
```

Note that the header fields are separated from the field contents by a colon. This example shows 11 fields in use, which is certainly more than most host mail systems use.

6.6.3 SMTP Commands

SMTP commands are comprised of a command code and an argument. The command codes are four alphabetic characters in either upper or lower case. The command code is separated from the argument by one or more space characters. Reverse path and forward path arguments are case-sensitive since each host may have a particular convention for mail addresses. The character sequence carriage return-line feed (<CRLF>) ends the argument field. Optional arguments are enclosed within square brackets.

Command Code and Argument	Usage
HELO <SP> <domain> <CRLF>	Identifies Sender-SMTP to Receiver-SMTP
MAIL <SP> FROM:<reverse-path> <CRLF>	Deliver mail data to mailbox(es)
RCPT <SP> TO:<forward-path> <CRLF>	Identify mail data recipient
DATA <CRLF>	The mail data
RSET <CRLF>	Abort current mail transaction
SEND <SP> FROM:<reverse-path> <CRLF>	Deliver mail data to terminal(s)
SOML <SP> FROM:<reverse-path> <CRLF>	Send or Mail
SAML <SP> FROM:<reverse-path> <CRLF>	Send and Mail

Command Code and Argument	Usage
VRFY <SP> <string> <CRLF>	Verify that the argument identifies a user
EXPN <SP> <string> <CRLF>	Verify that the argument identifies a mailing list
HELP [<SP> <string>] <CRLF>	Send information
NOOP <CRLF>	No operation
QUIT <CRLF>	Send OK reply, then close channel
TURN <CRLF>	Exchange Sender/Receiver roles

Note: *<SP> represents a Space character*
<CRLF> represents Carriage Return, Line Feed characters

6.6.4 SMTP Replies

The SMTP Reply messages are three digits long, and each digit has special significance. These replies are similar to the FTP codes in that the first digit is more general, whereas the third digit is more specific. The values for the first digit are:

1yz	Positive Preliminary reply
2yz	Positive Completion reply
3yz	Positive Intermediate reply
4yz	Transient Negative Completion reply
5yz	Permanent Negative Completion reply

The values for the second digit are:

x0z	Syntax
x1z	Information
x2z	Connection
x3z	Unspecified as yet
x4z	Unspecified as yet
x5z	Mail system

The third digit gives a finer definition for each of the function categories specified by the second digit. An example would be:

500:	Syntax error, command unrecognized
501:	Syntax error in parameters or arguments
502:	Command not implemented
503:	Bad sequence of commands
504:	Command parameter not implemented

If you require more information, turn to RFC 821 for specifics on command usage, state diagrams that detail the command implementation, and command/reply sequences. We will study an example of SMTP in Section 6.10.5.

6.6.5 Multipurpose Internet Mail Extensions

SMTP defined the format for the message headers; however, it made the assumption that the *contents* of that message were ASCII text. In many cases, however, email users wish to transmit other types of messages, such as a graphic or an audio or video clip. The Multipurpose Internet Mail Extensions, or MIME, provides for encoding techniques to allow these other types of messages to be transmitted after the RFC 822 (or SMTP) headers. MIME is specified in five parts, RFCs 2045–2049 (References [6-22] through [6-26]). Part One (RFC 2045) discusses the format of Internet message bodies; Part Two (RFC 2046) discusses the general structure of the MIME media typing system; Part Three (RFC 2047) describes extensions to RFC 822 to allow non-US-ASCII text data in mail fields; Part Four (RFC 2048) discusses IANA registration procedures for MIME-related facilities; and Part Five (RFC 2049) provides MIME conformance criteria, examples, and a bibliography. Other useful articles on the subject include References [6-27] through [6-29].

RFC 2045 defines additional headers that further specify the contents of the electronic message. These headers include:

- **MIME-Version header:** Specifies the MIME version for this message.
- **Content-Type header:** Specifies the type and subtype of data in the body of the message. Seven data types have been defined:
  - **Text:** Textual information in a number of different character sets.
  - **Image:** For transmitting still image (or picture) data; includes subtypes for .jpeg and .gif files.
  - **Audio:** For transmitting audio or voice data, which requires an output device such as a speaker or a telephone.

- **Video**: For transmitting video or moving image data; includes a subtype for .mpeg files.
- **Application**: Used to transmit application or binary data; includes subtypes for octet-stream and PostScript files.
- **Multipart**: Used to combine different types of data into a single message.
- **Message**: Used for encapsulating another mail message.

◆ **Content-Transfer Encoding header**: Used to specify an auxiliary encoding that was applied to the data in order to allow it to pass through mail transport mechanisms.

◆ **Content ID and Content Description headers**: Further describe the data in the message body.

Below is an example, taken from Appendix A of RFC 2049, which illustrates the use of the above headers.

> What follows is the outline of a complex multipart message. This message has five parts to be displayed serially: two introductory plain text parts, an embedded multipart message, a text/enriched object, and a closing encapsulated text message in a non-ASCII character set. The embedded multipart message has two parts to be displayed in parallel, a picture and an audio fragment.

```
MIME-Version: 1.0
From: Nathaniel Borenstein <nsb@nsb.fv.com>
To: Ned Freed <ned@innosoft.com>
Date:  Fri,07 Oct 1994 16:15:05 00700 (PDT)
Subject: A multipart example
Content-Type: multipart/mixed;
              boundary=unique-boundary-1

This is the preamble area of a multipart message.
Mail readers that understand multipart format
should ignore this preamble.
If you are reading this text, you might want to
consider changing to a mail reader that understands
how to properly display multipart messages.
—unique-boundary-1

... Some text appears here...
[Note that the blank between the boundary and the start
of the text in this part means no header fields were
given and this is text in the US-ASCII character set.
It could have been done with explicit typing as in the
next part.]
```

```
—unique-boundary-1
Content-type: text/plain; charset=US-ASCII

This could have been part of the previous part,
but illustrates explicit versus implicit typing of body
parts.

—unique-boundary-1
Content-Type: multipart/parallel;
boundary=unique-boundary-2

—unique-boundary-2
Content-Type: audio/basic
Content-Transfer-Encoding: base64

 ... base64-encoded 8000 Hz single-channel
  mu-law-format audio data goes here....

—unique-boundary-2
Content-Type: image/jpeg
Content-Transfer-Encoding: base64

... base64-encoded image data goes here....

—unique-boundary-2%

—unique-boundary-1
Content-type: text/enriched

This is <bold><italic>enriched.</italic></bold>
<smaller>as defined in RFC 1896</smaller>
<nl><nl>Isn't it
<bigger><bigger>cool?</bigger></bigger>

—unique-boundary-1
Content-Type: message/rfc822

From: (mailbox in US-ASCII)
To: (address in US-ASCII)
Subject: (subject in US-ASCII)
Content-Type: Text/plain; charset=ISO-8859-1
Content-Transfer-Encoding: Quoted-printable

 ... Additional text in ISO-8859-1 goes here ...

—unique-boundary-1—
```

As the above example illustrates, MIME provides for a great deal of flexibility for message content specification. Readers needing further technical details should consult RFCs 2045–2049.

6.7 NetBIOS

NetBIOS, the Network Basic Input Output System, was developed by IBM and Sytek, Inc. (later known as Hughes LAN Systems, Inc.) for use with the IBM PC Network program. Just as ROMBIOS enables a PC's operating system and application programs to access its local I/O devices, NetBIOS provides applications access to network devices. NetBIOS is considered an OSI Session Layer interface and has become a de facto standard. The expansion of LANs into internetworks and the popularity of TCP/IP as the primary internetworking protocol suite have created a need for the NetBIOS interface to operate over the Internet protocols. From an architectural perspective, combining NetBIOS support at the OSI Session Layer with the TCP or UDP protocols at the Transport Layer is a natural way to support the numerous existing LAN applications in a distributed internetwork environment.

Just as different vendors have written ROMBIOS routines specific to their PCs, LAN operating system vendors have also come up with their own implementations of NetBIOS. Haugdahl's *Inside NetBIOS* [6-30] describes some of these variants. RFC 1001 [6-31] and RFC 1002 [6-32] define a standard for NetBIOS support within the Internet community; hopefully, the rigorous detail contained in these RFCs will eliminate the multiple-implementation (semi-proprietary) issue that has crept into LAN environments.

Before delving into the specifics of NetBIOS use within the context of the Internet protocols, you need some background in the operation of NetBIOS. NetBIOS provides four types of primitives: Name Service, Session Service, Datagram Service, and Miscellaneous functions. Application programs use these services to locate network resources, establish and terminate connections, and transfer data.

The Name Service permits you to refer to an application, representing a resource, by a name on the internetwork. The name consists of 16 alphanumeric characters, which may be either exclusive (unique to an application) or shared (used by a group). The application registers the name to ensure that no other applications raise any objections to its use. The Name Service primitives are Add Name, Add Group Name, and Delete Name.

The Session Service is used for the reliable exchange of data between two NetBIOS applications. Each data message may be from 0 to 131,071 octets in length. The Session Service primitives are somewhat analogous to the TCP primitives discussed in Chapter 5 and include: Call, Listen, Hang Up, Send, Receive, and Session Status.

The Datagram Service provides unreliable, nonsequenced, and connectionless data transfer. The data may be transferred in two ways. In one technique, the datagram sender registers a name under which the data will be sent and specifies the name to which it will be sent. The second technique broadcasts the datagram. The Datagram Service primitives are Send Datagram, Send Broadcast Datagram, Receive Datagram, and Receive Broadcast Datagram.

Miscellaneous functions generally control the operation of the network interface and are implementation-dependent. These functions include Reset, Cancel, Adapter Status, Unlink, and Remote Program Load. IBM's token ring implementation added the Find Name primitive, which determines whether a particular name is registered on the network. (Four of the NetBIOS primitives listed above – Reset, Session Status, Unlink, and Remote Program Load – are considered local implementation issues that do not impact interoperability, and are therefore considered outside the scope of the Internet specification.)

RFC 1001 defines three types of NetBIOS end nodes and two NetBIOS support servers. The end nodes include the Broadcast (B), Point-to-Point (P), and Mixed Mode (M) types. Each of these types is specified by the operations it is allowed to perform. The NetBIOS support servers include the NetBIOS Name Server nodes (NBNS) and the NetBIOS Datagram Distribution nodes (NBDD). The NBNS manages and validates names used within the internetwork. NBNS formats the NetBIOS names to be valid Domain Name System (DNS) names and allows the NBNS to function in a fashion similar to the DNS Query service. The NBDD extends the NetBIOS datagram functions to the internet, which does not support multicast or broadcast transmissions. All of the nodes and servers are combined in various topologies of local and interconnected networks; RFC 1001 defines these details.

6.7.1 NetBIOS Name Service

NetBIOS's operation over UDP or TCP transport begins with the NetBIOS Name Service registering the name of the application to be used. The Name Query is the process by which the IP address associated with a NetBIOS name is discovered. Depending on the type of node in use (B, P, or M), the queries are either broadcast or directed to the NBNS. The exact procedures are described in RFC 1001.

NetBIOS Name Service messages use Port number 137 and are compatible with the DNS header format shown in Figure 6-8a. The structure includes a header followed by four entries – the Question section, Answer section, Authority section, and Additional Information section. A typical Name Query message would include the NetBIOS name in the Question section, followed by a Response message that provides details about the name, including its IP address. When an IP address has been found for the target name, either the Session Service (using TCP) or the Datagram Service (using UDP) may be implemented.

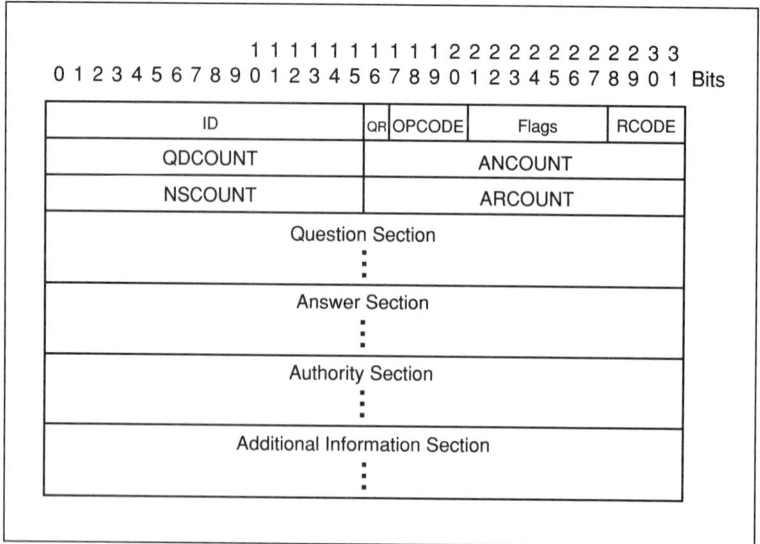

Figure 6-8a NetBIOS Name Service Header

6.7.2 NetBIOS Session Service

The NetBIOS Session Service uses Port number 139 and is implemented in three phases: session establishment, steady state, and session close. Session establishment determines the IP address and the TCP port of the called name and establishes a TCP connection with the remote device. Steady state provides data transfer and keep-alive functions. Session close terminates the session and triggers the close of the TCP session. Figure 6-9 illustrates these conditions; note the differences between the TCP and NetBIOS functions.

Figure 6-8b shows the format of the NetBIOS Session Service header. The Session Service header consists of a 4-octet header and a trailer that depends on the type of packet being transmitted. Three fields comprise the header: a Session Type field (1 octet), a Flags field (1 octet), and a Length field (2 octets). Values for the Session Type field are:

Value (hexadecimal)	Packet Type
00	Session message
81	Session request
82	Positive Session response
83	Negative Session response

Value (hexadecimal)	Packet Type
	Retarget Session response
85	Session Keep Alive

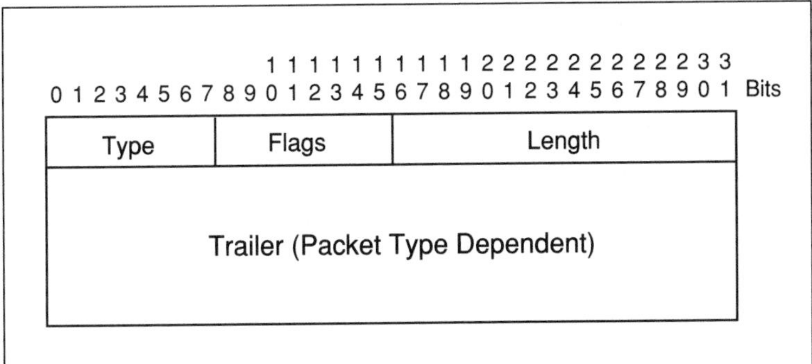

Figure 6-8b NetBIOS Session Service Header

The Flags field (1 octet) uses only Bit 7; all others are set to zero. Bit 7 is used as an extension to the Length field (also 1 octet), which specifies the number of octets contained in the trailer (i.e., nonheader) fields. When used in combination with the Flag Extension Bit, the cumulative length of the Trailer field(s) has a maximum value of 128K octets.

6.7.3 NetBIOS Datagram Service

NetBIOS datagrams use UDP transport with Port number 138. The complete NetBIOS datagram includes the IP header (20 octets), UDP header (8 octets), NetBIOS datagram header (14 octets), and the NetBIOS data. The NetBIOS data consists of the Source and Destination NetBIOS names (255 octets each) and up to 512 octets of NetBIOS user data. The complete NetBIOS datagram can be up to 1,064 octets in length, but it may need fragmentation if the maximum IP datagram length is 576 octets.

NetBIOS datagrams require a Name Query operation to determine the IP address of the destination name. The NetBIOS datagram can then be transmitted within a UDP datagram or multiple UDP datagrams, as required. Three transmission modes are available: unicast, which transmits to a unique NetBIOS name; multicast, which transmits to a group NetBIOS name; and broadcast, which uses the Send Broadcast Datagram primitive.

Figure 6-8c illustrates the NetBIOS Datagram header. The Msg Type field (1 octet) defines the datagram function:

Value (hexadecimal)	Msg_Type
10	Direct_Unique_Datagram
11	Direct_Group Datagram
12	Broadcast datagram
13	Datagram error
14	Datagram Query request
15	Datagram Positive Query response
16	Datagram Negative Query response

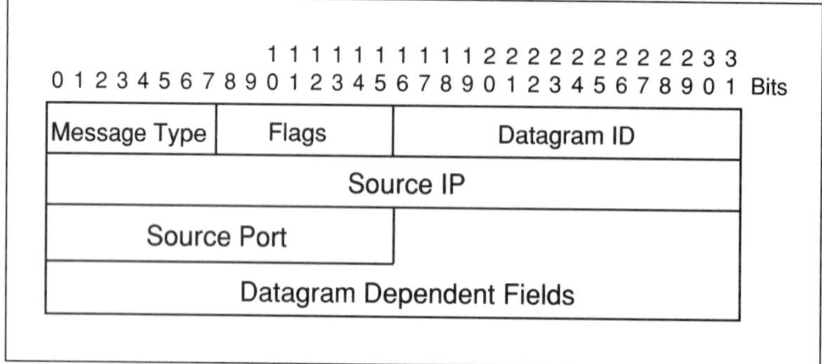

Figure 6-8c NetBIOS Datagram Header

The Flags (1 octet) define the first datagram fragment, whether more fragments will follow, and the type of source node (B, P, or M). The remaining fields support datagram service, with a Datagram ID (2 octets), the Source IP address (4 octets), Source Port (2 octets), Datagram Length (2 octets), and a Packet Offset (2 octets). Datagram-specific user data fields complete each message. We'll see an example of NetBIOS packet operation in Section 6.10.6.

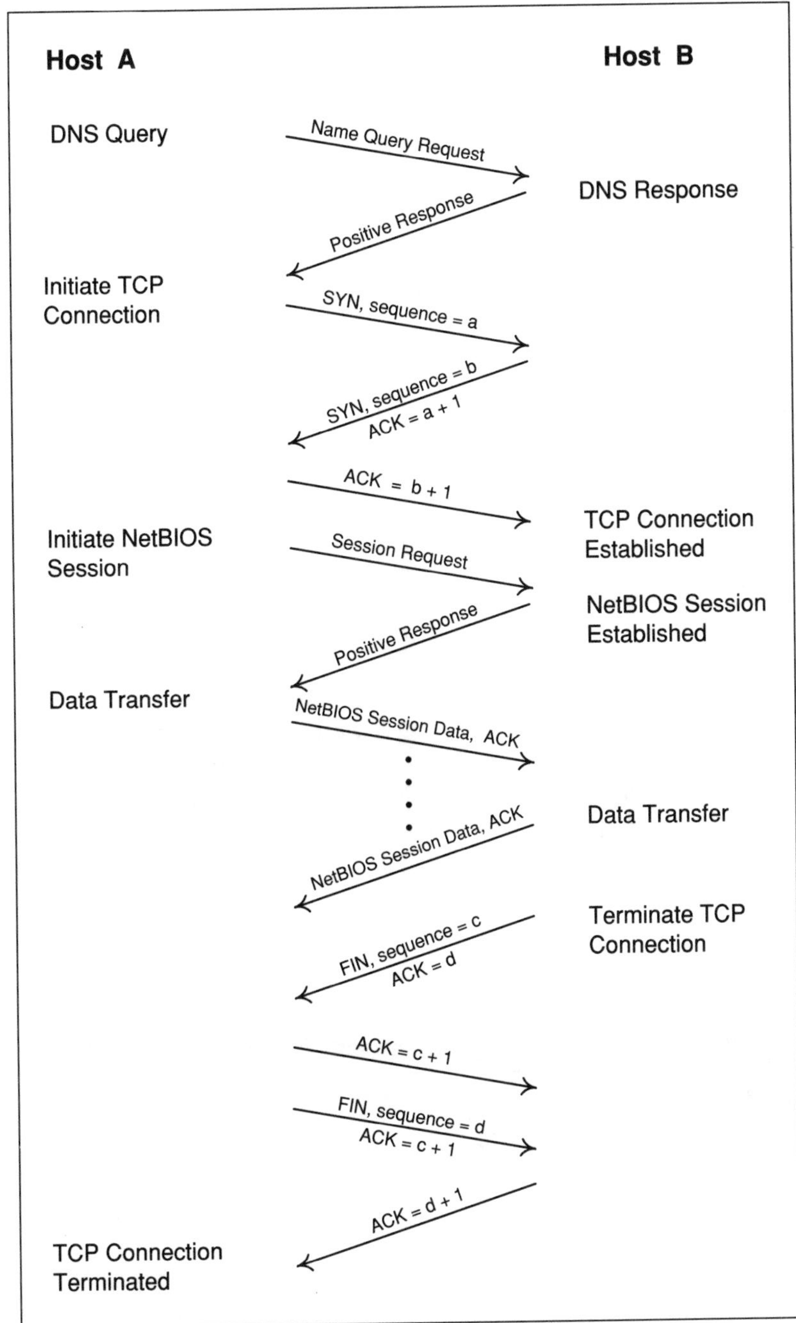

Figure 6-9 TCP and NetBIOS Connection Establishment/Disconnect Events

6.8 Hypertext Transfer Protocol

The Hypertext Transfer Protocol (HTTP), defined in RFC 2068 [6-33], is a protocol used for communication with multimedia systems and is the key mechanism used for communication within the World Wide Web (WWW). HTTP is built on a client/server paradigm, and uses TCP for transport. According to RFC 2068, HTTP can also be used for communication between user agents and proxies or gateways into other Internet-based protocol systems, including SMTP, the Network News Transfer Protocol (NNTP, defined in RFC 977), FTP, the Internet Gopher Protocol (defined in RFC 1436), and the Wide Area Information Service (WAIS, defined in RFC 1625).

The client/server interaction can be implemented using one of three topologies (Figure 6-10). In the simplest case, the User Agent sends a request chain for a particular resource to the Origin Server (Figure 6-10a). The Origin Server replies with a response chain containing the resource of interest. Note that a single connection links the User Agent and the Origin Server.

If a single link is not sufficient, various intermediaries may be inserted in the connection (Figure 6-10b). These intermediaries may be: a *proxy*, which may reformat the request; a *gateway*, which may translate the request to a protocol understandable by the Server; or a *tunnel*, which is a relay point between two connections, such as a firewall.

In some cases, communication to the distant Origin Server may not be necessary, because an intermediate point may have cached the requested information as the result of a previous (and possibly unrelated) request chain (Figure 6-10c). For example, an intermediary in the path to a popular Web server (such as *www.usatoday.com*) may cache some of the more frequently requested Web pages, such that the request chain need not travel the entire length of the connection to complete the transaction.

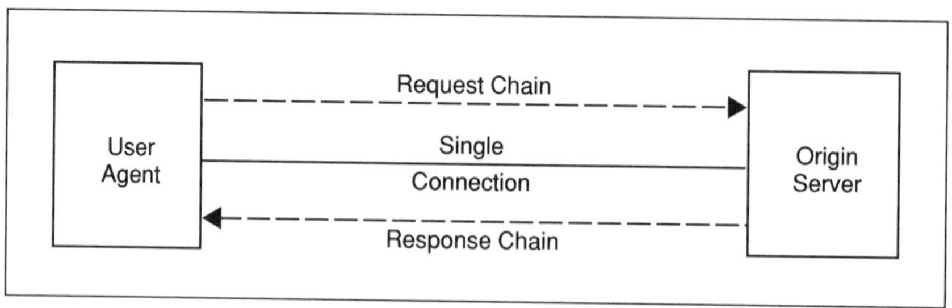

Figure 6-10a HTTP Communication with Single Connection

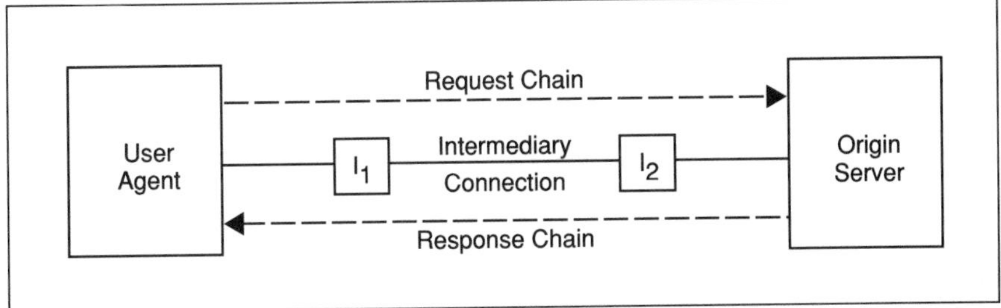

Figure 6-10b HTTP Communication with Intermediary Connection

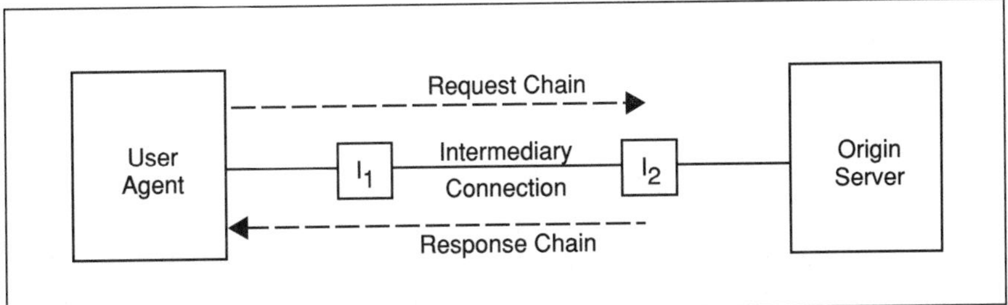

Figure 6-10c HTTP Communication with Shortened Request/Response Chain (Cache at I_2)

6.8.1 Uniform Resource Identifiers

One element of the request chain identifies the information that is being requested. The client identifies that resource using a Uniform Resource Identifier (URI), defined in RFC 1630 [6-34]. The URI may be represented as a Uniform Resource Name (URN), defined in RFC 1737 [6-35], or a Uniform Resource Locator (URL), defined in RFC 1738 [6-36]. URLs are written as follows:

```
<scheme>:<scheme-specific-part>
```

For example:

```
ftp://ftp.isi.edu/in-notes/rfc1738.txt
```

In this case, *ftp* specifies the protocol in use (the File Transfer Protocol), *ftp.isi.edu* specifies the host name, *in-notes* specifies the path within that host, and *rfc1738.txt* specifies the filename of interest.

A second example:

```
http://www.ietf.org/mailinglists.html
```

In this case, *http* specifies the Hypertext Transfer Protocol, *www.ietf.org* specifies the host name, and *mailinglists.html* specifies an HTML filename of interest.

6.8.2 HTTP Request Messages

HTTP is a request/response protocol. The client sends a Request message to the server, and the server then replies with a Response message. Request messages have the following format:

```
Request Line
Headers (general-headers, request-headers, entity-headers)
CRLF
Message Body
```

The Request-Line includes a Method Token, a Request-URI, and a protocol version, and ends with a carriage return and line feed. The Method Token indicates the operation to be performed on the resource, and could include: OPTIONS, GET, HEAD, POST, PUT, DELETE, or TRACE. The Request-URI identifies the resource upon which to apply the request. RFC 2068 gives the following example of a Request-Line:

```
GET http://www.w3.org/pub/WWW/TheProject.html HTTP/1.1
```

The Headers may include General Headers, Request Headers, and Entity Headers. General Headers are applicable to both Request and Response messages, and include:

- Cache-Control: Specifies directives that must be obeyed.
- Connection: Allows sender to specify options for that connection.
- Date: Date and time message was originated.
- Pragma: Used to include implementation-specific directives.
- Transfer-Encoding: Indicates what transformation has been applied to the message body.
- Upgrade: Specifies additional communication protocols supported.
- Via: Used by gateways and proxies to indicate intermediate protocols and recipients.

Request Headers allow the client to pass additional information about the request, and about the client itself, to the server. The Request Headers include:

- Accept: Specifies media types acceptable for the response.
- Accept-Charset: Indicates character sets acceptable for the response.
- Accept-Encoding: Restricts the content-encoding values.
- Accept-Language: Restricts the set of natural languages.
- Authorization: Contains credentials for the user agent.
- From: The email address of the human controlling the requesting user agent.
- Host: The Internet host and Port number of the requested resource.
- If-Modified-Since: Used with the GET method to make it conditional.
- If-Match: Used with a method to make it conditional.
- If-None-Match: Used with a method to make it conditional.
- If-Range: Used to request all or part of an entity.
- If-Unmodified-Since: Used with a method to make it conditional.
- Max-Forwards: Limits the number of proxies or gateways that can forward the request.
- Proxy-Authorization: Allows the client to identify itself to a proxy.
- Range: Specifies a portion of a resource.
- Referer: The address URI from which the Request-RI was obtained.
- User-Agent: Contains information about the user agent originating the request.

Entity Headers define optional metainformation about the entity-body, or if no body is present, about the resource identified by the request. The Entity Headers include:

- Allow: Lists the methods supported by the resource.
- Content-Base: Specifies the base URI.
- Content-Encoding: Modifies the media-type.
- Content-Language: Describes the natural language(s).
- Content-Length: The size of the message body, in octets.
- Content-Location: Supplies the resource location for the entity.

- Content-MD5: Provides an end-to-end message integrity check.
- Content-Range: Specifies where the partial body should be inserted.
- Content-Type: Indicates the media type of the entity-body.
- ETag: Defines the entity tag for the associated entity.
- Expires: Gives the date/time after which the response is stale.
- Last-Modified: The date/time the origin was last modified.

The CRLF includes a carriage return and line feed, which inserts a blank line in the Request Header.

The Message Body (if included in the HTTP message) is used to carry the entity-body that is associated with the request or response. (The message-body and the entity-body differ only when a transfer encoding has been applied, as discussed in RFC 2068, sections 4.3 and 14.40.) Information that is contained in the Message Body may be formatted using the Hypertext Markup Language (HTML), defined in RFC 1866 [6-37].

6.8.3 HTTP Response Messages

HTTP servers issue a Response message in reply to a Request message. Response messages have the following format:

```
Status Line
Headers (general-headers, response-headers, entity-headers)
CRLF
Message Body
```

The Status-Line consists of a protocol version followed by a numeric Status Code and its associated textual phrase. The Status Code is a three-digit integer result code that indicates the disposition of the request. RFC 2068 defines the Status Codes. The first digit of the Status Code defines the class of response. The last two digits do not have any categorization role. There are five values for the first digit:

- 1xx: Informational – Request received, continuing process.
- 2xx: Success – The action was successfully received, understood, and accepted.
- 3xx: Redirection – Further action must be taken in order to complete the request.
- 4xx: Client Error – The request contains bad syntax or cannot be fulfilled.
- 5xx: Server Error – The server failed to fulfill an apparently valid request.

The individual values of the numeric Status Codes defined for HTTP/1.1, with their associated meanings, are:

Status Code	Meaning
100	Continue
101	Switching Protocols
200	OK
201	Created
202	Accepted
203	Nonauthoritative Information
204	No Content
205	Reset Content
206	Partial Content
300	Multiple Choices
301	Moved Permanently
302	Moved Temporarily
303	See Other
304	Not Modified
305	Use Proxy
400	Bad Request
401	Unauthorized
402	Payment Required
403	Forbidden
404	Not Found
405	Method Not Allowed
406	Not Acceptable
407	Proxy Authentication Required
408	Request Time-out
409	Conflict
410	Gone

Status Code	Meaning
411	Length Required
412	Precondition Failed
413	Request Entity Too Large
414	Request-URI Too Large
415	Unsupported Media Type
500	Internal Server Error
501	Not Implemented
502	Bad Gateway
503	Service Unavailable
504	Gateway Time-out
505	HTTP Version not supported

The Response Headers allow the server to pass additional information to the client which cannot be placed in the Status-Line. The Response Headers include:

- Age: Time since response was generated at the server.
- Location: Redirects the recipient to another URI location.
- Proxy-Authenticate: Included with Proxy Authentication Required response.
- Public: Lists the methods supported by the server.
- Retry-After: Indicates how long the resource will be unavailable.
- Server: Identifies the software at the origin server.
- Vary: Indicates that the server has selected a representation of the response.
- Warning: Carries additional information about the response status.
- WWW-Authenticate: Contains the challenge indicating the authentication scheme and parameters.

The other fields in the HTTP Response message are similar to their counterparts in the Request message as described above.

6.9 Troubleshooting the Process/Application Connection

Upper layer protocol problems can be challenging to diagnose for several reasons. First, the Application/Process Layer interfaces with the end user. As we know, humans can cause well-ordered computer systems much consternation. Second, the Process/Application Layer must offer numerous options to meet the needs of its diverse clientele (humans). These options may use different file types (options for FTP) or data communication parameters (required to support a particular TELNET connection).

To diagnose these problems, you should begin by determining whether the end-to-end connectivity functions are getting the data to the required destination. If they're not, use the techniques discussed in earlier chapters to determine where in the Network Interface, Internet, or Host-to-Host Layers the problem resides, and troubleshoot the failure. If data is getting through, then an upper layer problem may exist.

Keep in mind that just because data is being received doesn't mean that it is being interpreted properly – if my terminal is transmitting ASCII characters and your host is expecting EBCDIC, we'll exchange bits, but we won't communicate. A logical question to ask, then, is whether the application is being used properly. We've all experienced problems on our PCs that have turned out to be configuration errors. The Process/Application Layer applications are no exception. As long as there's a human element, the probability of error exists. Unfortunately, that probability is higher than any of us cares to admit.

A second possibility is that the two application processes are unable to communicate with each other because of internal implementation differences. Even in this day of "open systems" (and the Internet protocols are about as open as you can get), interoperability difficulties should not be eliminated from consideration.

In addition to the protocol analyzer, a number of host-based utilities are available to monitor and diagnose Process/Application Layer problems. An excellent source of information on these utilities is RFC 1470, "FYI on a Network Management Tool Catalog: Tools for Monitoring and Debugging TCP/IP Internets and Interconnected Devices" [6-38]. Many of these tools are devised for UNIX platforms. Examples include:

- *etherfind* – A traffic monitor that runs under the Sun Operating System.
- *Internet Rover* – A network monitor for 4.x BSD UNIX systems that includes modules to test TELNET, FTP, and SMTP.
- *mconnect* – A utility available with 4.x BSD UNIX systems to test SMTP connections.

- *netstat* – A utility available with 4.x BSD UNIX that will report routing table, TCP connections, and traffic statistics.
- *snmpwatch* – A network monitoring utility, compatible with a number of UNIX versions, that reports SNMP variables that have changed in value.

In summary, consult the management utilities included with your operating system and the tools listed in RFC 1470 for assistance with diagnosing upper layer protocol problems.

6.10 Case Studies

Each of the case studies that follows illustrates the operation of a particular Process/Application Layer protocol. Admittedly, we could write volumes on each of the protocols that we've studied, but space does not permit full elaboration. Keep in mind, however, that the best references are the protocol-specific RFCs themselves, along with several supplements. These include RFC 1700, "Assigned Numbers", RFC 1122, "Requirements for Internet Hosts: Communication Layers", and RFC 1123, "Requirements for Internet Hosts – Application and Support," all of which provide details on specific parameters. Given these caveats, let's look at the operation of the upper layer protocols.

6.10.1 Using TFTP

In our first case study, a Sun workstation (shown as Sun IPX in Trace 6.10.1a) and a PC running TCP/IP workstation software attempt to use TFTP to read and write small source files.

In Frame 1, the Sun IPX initiates a connection to Station XT with a Read Request (RRQ) for file "TFTP_test" in netascii mode (Figure 6-11). Details of that frame (Trace 6.10.1b) indicate that the Sun IPX has selected Source Transaction ID 1167 (Source port = 1167) with Destination port = 69, which is defined as the TFTP port. The connection is accepted in Frame 2. Station XT selects TID 1183 (Source port = 1183) and returns the Sun IPX TID as the destination (Destination port = 1167). The TFTP header indicates a DATA packet, Block number = 1, with 128 octets of data. Frame 3 acknowledges receipt of the data and terminates that connection.

Given that success, Sun IPX next attempts to write the same file using the Write Request (WRQ) from TID = 1167 in Frame 6. Station XT sends an ACK, selecting TID 1184 (Source port = 1184) and designating Block number = 0. The 128 octets of data is successfully written from Port 1167 (Sun IPX) to Port 1184 in Frame 8. An ACK from Station XT is sent in Frame 9, terminating the connection.

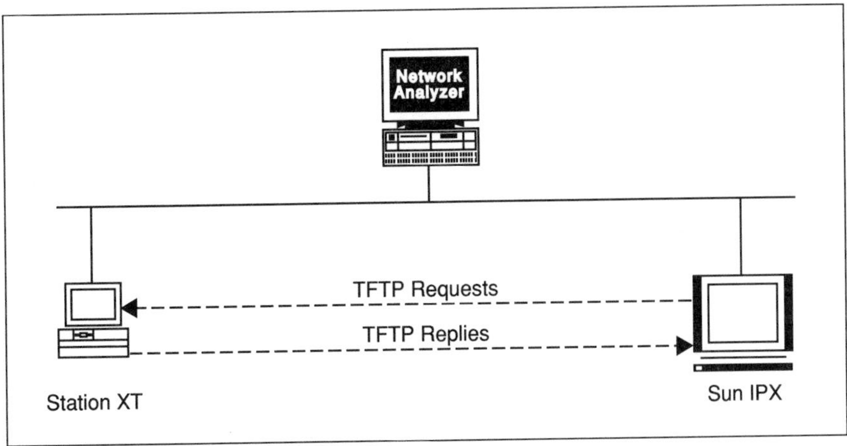

Figure 6-11 TFTP File Transfers

The next two operations are not so successful. In Frame 10, the Sun IPX sends an RRQ for file "\test" in netascii mode. Unfortunately, this file does not exist on Station XT. An ERROR packet, indicating an access violation, is returned in Frame 11. The Sun acknowledges its mistake and terminates the connection in Frame 12.

The Sun IPX makes one more attempt in Frame 16, this time a WRQ of the same file ("\test"), which still does not exist. The Sun IPX selects TID = 1167 again, while Station XT assigns TID = 1186 in Frame 17. Note that the ACK sent in response to the WRQ uses Block number = 0 (Frame 17). The Sun IPX then attempts to write the file. But it is empty (nonexistent) and no data is transferred. Station XT acknowledges the previous frame and terminates the connection.

TFTP thus performs as advertised – it transfers files with simplicity. It cannot overcome the faulty memory of the user, however, who can't seem to remember which files do and do not exist!

TRACE 6.10.1A. TFTP OPERATION SUMMARY

Sniffer Network Analyzer data 10-Mar at 13:08:44, TFTPTEST.TRC, Pg 1

SUMMARY	Delta T	Destination	Source	Summary
M 1		Station XT	Sun IPX	TFTP Read request File=TFTP_test
2	0.108	Sun IPX	Station XT	TFTP Data packet NS=1 (Last)
3	0.001	Station XT	Sun IPX	TFTP Ack NR=1
6	1.236	Station XT	Sun IPX	TFTP Write request File=TFTP_test
7	0.109	Sun IPX	Station XT	TFTP Ack NR=0
8	0.002	Station XT	Sun IPX	TFTP Data packet NS=1 (Last)

9	0.021	Sun IPX	Station XT	TFTP Ack NR=1
10	4.024	Station XT	Sun IPX	TFTP Read request File=\test
11	0.432	Sun IPX	Station XT	TFTP Error response (Access violation)
12	0.014	Station XT	Sun IPX	TFTP Ack NR=1
16	5.124	Station XT	Sun IPX	TFTP Write request File=\test
17	0.141	Sun IPX	Station XT	TFTP Ack NR=0
18	0.001	Station XT	Sun IPX	TFTP Data packet NS=1 (Last)
19	0.020	Sun IPX	Station XT	TFTP Ack NR=1

TRACE 6.10.1B. TFTP OPERATION DETAILS

```
Sniffer Network Analyzer data 10-Mar at 13:08:44, TFTPTEST.TRC, Pg 1

- - - - - - - - - - - - - - - Frame 1 - - - - - - - - - - - - - - - - -

UDP:  —— UDP Header ——
UDP:
UDP:  Source port = 1167 (TFTP)
UDP:  Destination port = 69
UDP:  Length = 29
UDP:  No checksum
UDP:
TFTP:  ——Trivial file transfer ——
TFTP:
TFTP:  Opcode = 1 (Read request)
TFTP:  File name = "TFTP_test"
TFTP:  Mode = "netascii"
TFTP:
TFTP:  [Normal end of "Trivial file transfer".]
TFTP:

- - - - - - - - - - - - - - - Frame 2 - - - - - - - - - - - - - - - - -

UDP:  ——UDP Header ——
UDP:
UDP:  Source port = 1183 (TFTP)
UDP:  Destination port = 1167
UDP:  Length = 140
UDP:  Checksum = F0DC (correct)
UDP:
TFTP:  ——Trivial file transfer ——
TFTP:
TFTP:  Opcode = 3 (Data packet)
```

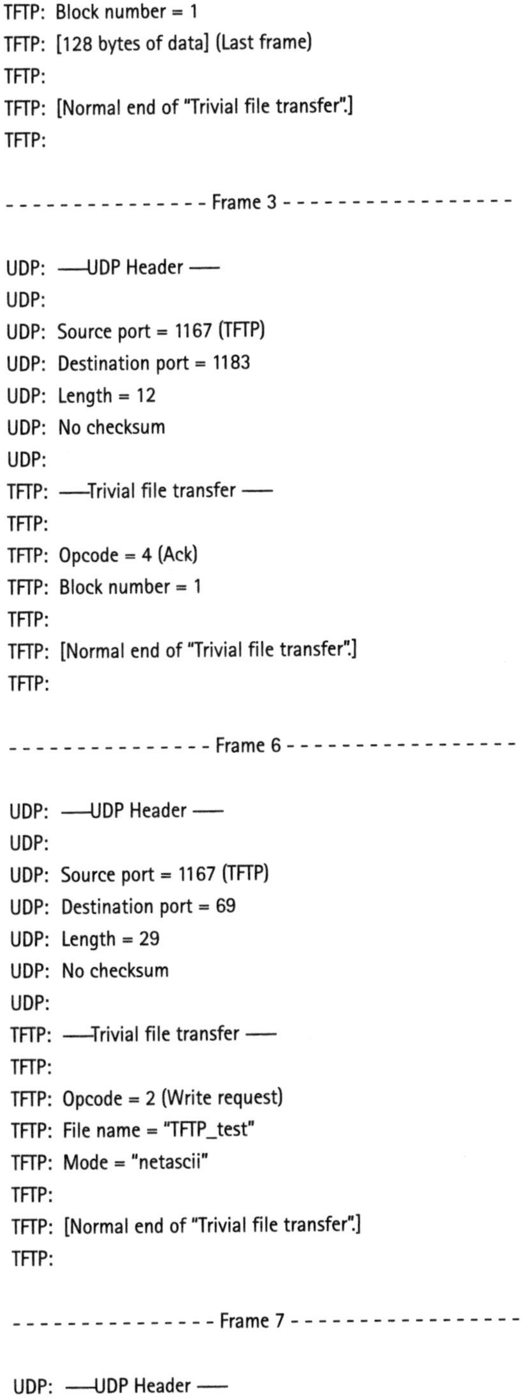

```
TFTP: Block number = 1
TFTP: [128 bytes of data] (Last frame)
TFTP:
TFTP: [Normal end of "Trivial file transfer".]
TFTP:

- - - - - - - - - - - - - - - Frame 3 - - - - - - - - - - - - - - - - -

UDP: ——UDP Header ——
UDP:
UDP: Source port = 1167 (TFTP)
UDP: Destination port = 1183
UDP: Length = 12
UDP: No checksum
UDP:
TFTP: ——Trivial file transfer ——
TFTP:
TFTP: Opcode = 4 (Ack)
TFTP: Block number = 1
TFTP:
TFTP: [Normal end of "Trivial file transfer".]
TFTP:

- - - - - - - - - - - - - - - Frame 6 - - - - - - - - - - - - - - - - -

UDP: ——UDP Header ——
UDP:
UDP: Source port = 1167 (TFTP)
UDP: Destination port = 69
UDP: Length = 29
UDP: No checksum
UDP:
TFTP: ——Trivial file transfer ——
TFTP:
TFTP: Opcode = 2 (Write request)
TFTP: File name = "TFTP_test"
TFTP: Mode = "netascii"
TFTP:
TFTP: [Normal end of "Trivial file transfer".]
TFTP:

- - - - - - - - - - - - - - - Frame 7 - - - - - - - - - - - - - - - - -

UDP: ——UDP Header ——
```

```
UDP:
UDP:  Source port = 1184 (TFTP)
UDP:  Destination port = 1167
UDP:  Length = 12
UDP:  Checksum = B7CB (correct)
UDP:
TFTP: ——Trivial file transfer ——
TFTP:
TFTP: Opcode = 4 (Ack)
TFTP: Block number = 0
TFTP:
TFTP: [Normal end of "Trivial file transfer".]
TFTP:

- - - - - - - - - - - - - - - Frame 8 - - - - - - - - - - - - - - - -

UDP:  ——UDP Header ——
UDP:
UDP:  Source port = 1167 (TFTP)
UDP:  Destination port = 1184
UDP:  Length = 140
UDP:  No checksum
UDP:
TFTP: ——Trivial file transfer ——
TFTP:
TFTP: Opcode = 3 (Data packet)
TFTP: Block number = 1
TFTP: [128 bytes of data] (Last frame)
TFTP:
TFTP: [Normal end of "Trivial file transfer".]
TFTP:

- - - - - - - - - - - - - - - Frame 9 - - - - - - - - - - - - - - - -

UDP:  ——UDP Header ——
UDP:
UDP:  Source port = 1184 (TFTP)
UDP:  Destination port = 1167
UDP:  Length = 12
UDP:  Checksum = B7CA (correct)
UDP:
TFTP: ——Trivial file transfer ——
TFTP:
TFTP: Opcode = 4 (Ack)
```

```
TFTP: Block number = 1
TFTP:
TFTP: [Normal end of "Trivial file transfer".]
TFTP:

- - - - - - - - - - - - - - - Frame 10 - - - - - - - - - - - - - - - - -

UDP: ——UDP Header ——
UDP:
UDP: Source port = 1167 (TFTP)
UDP: Destination port = 69
UDP: Length = 25
UDP: No checksum
UDP:
TFTP: ——Trivial file transfer ——
TFTP:
TFTP: Opcode = 1 (Read request)
TFTP: File name = "\test"
TFTP: Mode = "netascii"
TFTP:
TFTP: [Normal end of "Trivial file transfer".]
TFTP:

- - - - - - - - - - - - - - - Frame 11 - - - - - - - - - - - - - - - - -

UDP: ——UDP Header ——
UDP:
UDP: Source port = 1185 (TFTP)
UDP: Destination port = 1167
UDP: Length = 41
UDP: Checksum = 7497 (correct)
UDP:
TFTP: ——Trivial file transfer ——
TFTP:
TFTP: Opcode = 5 (Error response)
TFTP: Error code = 2 (Access violation)
TFTP: Error message = "unable to open file for read"
TFTP:
TFTP: [Normal end of "Trivial file transfer".]
TFTP:

- - - - - - - - - - - - - - - Frame 12 - - - - - - - - - - - - - - - - -

UDP: ——UDP Header ——
```

```
UDP:
UDP: Source port = 1167 (TFTP)
UDP: Destination port = 1185
UDP: Length = 12
UDP: No checksum
UDP:
TFTP: ——Trivial file transfer ——
TFTP:
TFTP: Opcode = 4 (Ack)
TFTP: Block number = 1
TFTP:
TFTP: [Normal end of "Trivial file transfer".]
TFTP:

- - - - - - - - - - - - - - - Frame 16 - - - - - - - - - - - - - - - - -

UDP: ——UDP Header ——
UDP:
UDP: Source port = 1167 (TFTP)
UDP: Destination port = 69
UDP: Length = 25
UDP: No checksum
UDP:
TFTP: ——Trivial file transfer ——
TFTP:
TFTP: Opcode = 2 (Write request)
TFTP: File name = "\test"
TFTP: Mode = "netascii"
TFTP:
TFTP: [Normal end of "Trivial file transfer".]
TFTP:

- - - - - - - - - - - - - - - Frame 17 - - - - - - - - - - - - - - - - -

UDP: ——UDP Header ——
UDP:
UDP: Source port = 1186 (TFTP)
UDP: Destination port = 1167
UDP: Length = 12
UDP: Checksum = B7C9 (correct)
UDP:
TFTP: ——Trivial file transfer ——
TFTP:
TFTP: Opcode = 4 (Ack)
```

```
TFTP: Block number = 0
TFTP:
TFTP: [Normal end of "Trivial file transfer".]
TFTP:

- - - - - - - - - - - - - - - Frame 18 - - - - - - - - - - - - - - - - -

UDP: —UDP Header —
UDP:
UDP: Source port = 1167 (TFTP)
UDP: Destination port = 1186
UDP: Length = 12
UDP: No checksum
UDP:
TFTP: —Trivial file transfer —
TFTP:
TFTP: Opcode = 3 (Data packet)
TFTP: Block number = 1
TFTP: [0 bytes of data] (Last frame)
TFTP:
TFTP: [Normal end of "Trivial file transfer".]
TFTP:

- - - - - - - - - - - - - - - Frame 19 - - - - - - - - - - - - - - - - -

UDP: —UDP Header —
UDP:
UDP: Source port = 1186 (TFTP)
UDP: Destination port = 1167
UDP: Length = 12
UDP: Checksum = B7C8 (correct)
UDP:
TFTP: —Trivial file transfer —
TFTP:
TFTP: Opcode = 4 (Ack)
TFTP: Block number = 1
TFTP:
TFTP: [Normal end of "Trivial file transfer".]
TFTP:
```

6.10.2 Collaborative Efforts of FTP, ARP, and TFTP

In the case study in Section 5.7.1, we examined the process by which a device can obtain its boot and configuration files (known as load and parameter images) from the internetwork. The following case study shows a similar process, using the ARP and TFTP protocols. ARP determines the device's (in this case, a bridge's) Internet (IP) address, and TFTP transfers the load and parameter files to the bridge. We'll also use FTP to transfer a new version of the bridge's load image to the TFTP server prior to the start of the ARP/TFTP sequence. Let's see what happens when these three processes must interact.

The topology of this internetwork consists of local and remote Ethernet segments connected via bridges (see Figure 6-12). The network manager, Ross, has received a new version of the bridge software from the manufacturer on an MS-DOS formatted floppy. Ross uses FTP Software's PC/TCP to transfer the new bridge software from a PC (known as Snoopy) to the TFTP Server, which is a Sun SPARCstation (known as Maestro). Ross establishes a TCP control connection to Port number 21 on Maestro (Frames 2 through 4 of Trace 6.10.2a) and logs in (Frames 5 through 12). Next, Ross stores the new bridge boot image (filename rb1w1.sys) on Maestro in subdirectory /home/tftpboot (Frame 13). Maestro initiates an FTP data connection to Snoopy's Port number 20 in Frames 15 through 17, and the ASCII file transfer begins in Frame 19. Since the file is rather large, it does not complete until Frame 305, at which time both the FTP and TCP connections are terminated (Frames 306 through 314 of Trace 6.10.2b).

Next, Ross resets the local bridge (known as MX-3510) so that it can obtain and boot from the new load image. The bridges Ross uses are designed to get their boot and configuration files from a number of different servers that might exist on a network. In Frame 315, the bridge broadcasts for a proprietary boot server; in Frame 316, the bridge broadcasts for a BOOTP server; in Frame 317, the bridge broadcasts for a DEC file server using DEC's Maintenance Operations Protocol (MOP); finally, in Frame 318, the bridge broadcasts a RARP Request looking for its Internet address. This operation is successful and the bridge uses its IP address to broadcast a TFTP Read request (Frame 320). The SPARCstation (Maestro) responds, triggering the bridge to request a file transfer of the boot image using TFTP (Frame 327). Unfortunately, the file transfer is not successful (see Frame 1393). Details of the error response (Trace 6.10.2c) indicate a Transfer Size Error, with "22 bytes of additional data present." This error message prompts Ross to speculate that the boot image file should have been transferred in FTP Binary mode instead of ASCII mode.

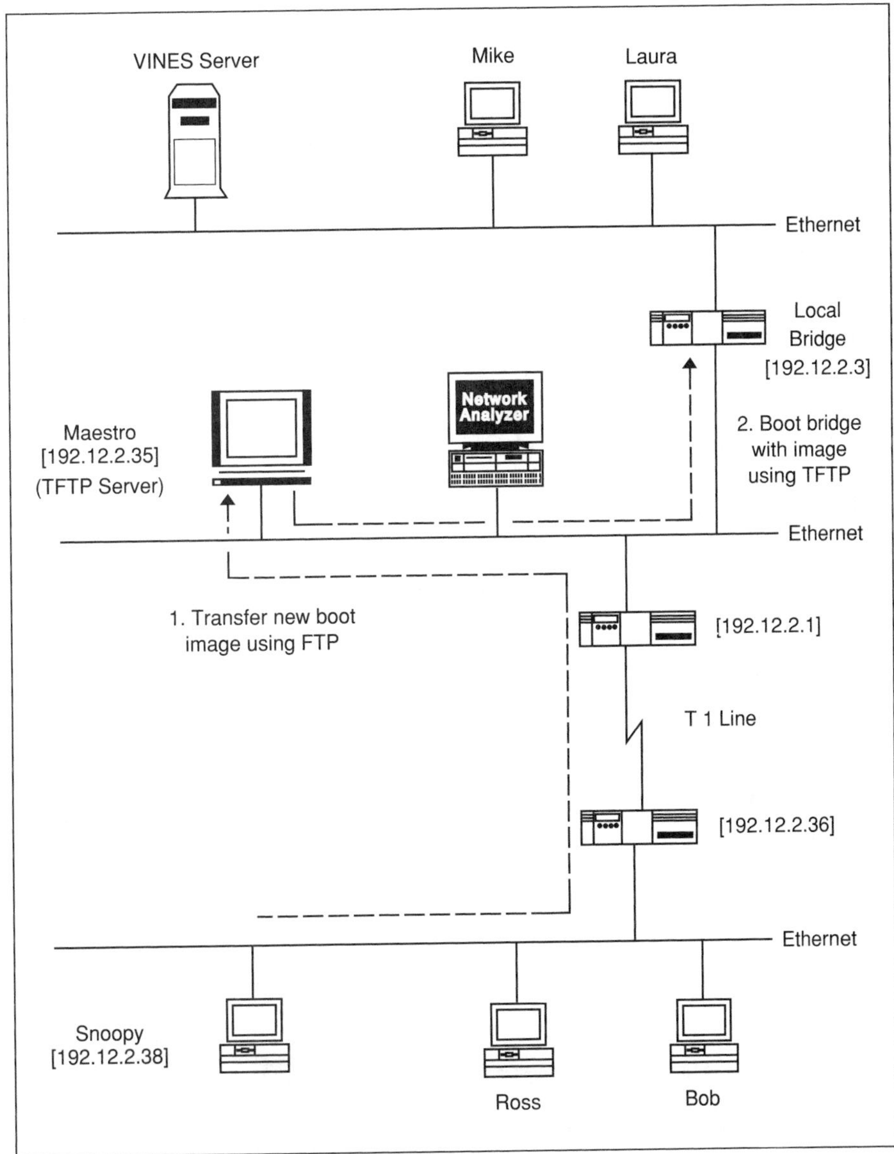

Figure 6-12 File Transfer of Bridge Boot Image

Ross begins again, this time setting the FTP transfer mode to Binary when he loads the file from Snoopy to Maestro. A TCP connection between Snoopy and Maestro is established (Frames 1408 through 1410 of Trace 6.10.2d), and the FTP file transfer begins. But this time the File Type is set for Image (Type I in Frame 1417). The Binary (or Image) data connection is opened in Frame 1426 and completes in Frame 1692 (Trace 6.10.2e). The local bridge is again reset and its boot sequence started (Frames 1696 through 1707). The boot image (filename x004db3.img) is transferred from Maestro to the local bridge, using TFTP in Frames 1708 through 2774. A second file (x004db3.prm) is transferred in Frames 2787 through 2819. The bridge boot sequence is now complete. The lesson learned: check the data representation parameter, or file type, to avoid corrupting the transferred file.

TRACE 6.10.2A. BOOT IMAGE TRANSFER USING FTP ASCII CONNECTION

Sniffer Network Analyzer data 30-Aug at 14:07:42, BINARY.ENC, Pg 1

SUMMARY	Delta T	Destination	Source	Summary
M 1	AB0000020000	Local Bridge	MOP	RC System ID Receipt=0
2	1.2376	Maestro	Snoopy	TCP D=21 S=20294 SYN SEQ=19468734 LEN=0 WIN=2048
3	0.0009	Snoopy	Maestro	TCP D=20294 S=21 SYN ACK=19468735 SEQ=716544001 LEN=0 WIN=4096
4	0.0016	Maestro	Snoopy	TCP D=21 S=20294 ACK=716544002 WIN=2048
5	0.1115	Snoopy	Maestro	FTP R PORT=20294 220 maestro FTP server (SunOS 4.1) ready.<0D><0A>
6	0.0374	Maestro	Snoopy	FTP C PORT=20294 USER root<0D><0A>
7	0.0073	Snoopy	Maestro	FTP R PORT=20294 331 Password required 230 User root logged in.<0D><0A>
10	0.1621	Maestro	Snoopy	TCP D=21 S=20294 ACK=716544104 WIN=1946
11	21.4760	Maestro	Snoopy	FTP C PORT=20294 PORT 192,12,2, 38,79,71<0D><0A>
12	0.0127	Snoopy	Maestro	FTP R PORT=20294 200 PORT command successful <0D><0A>

13	0.0105	Maestro	Snoopy	FTP C PORT=20294 STOR /home/tftpboot /rb1w1.sys_v2.0<0D><0A>
14	0.0169	Snoopy	Maestro	TCP D=20294 S=21 ACK=19468819 WIN=4096
15	0.0601	Snoopy	Maestro	TCP D=20295 S=20 SYN SEQ=719936001 LEN=0 WIN=24576
16	0.0020	Maestro	Snoopy	TCP D=20 S=20295 SYN ACK=719936002 SEQ=19468825 LEN=0 WIN=2048
17	0.0006	Snoopy	Maestro	TCP D=20295 S=20 ACK=19468826 WIN=24576
18	0.0018	Snoopy	Maestro	FTP R PORT=20294 150 ASCII data connection for /home/tftpboot/rb1w1...
19	0.1108	Maestro	Snoopy	TCP D=20 S=20295 ACK=719936002 SEQ=19468826
	0.0065	Maestro	Snoopy	TCP D=20 S=20295 ACK=719936002 SEQ=19470015 LEN=1460 WIN=2048
21	0.0058	Maestro	Snoopy	TCP D=20 S=20295 ACK=719936002 SEQ=19471475 LEN=1460 WIN=2048
22	0.0024	Snoopy	Maestro	TCP D=20295 S=20 ACK=19472935 WIN=24576

TRACE 6.10.2B. ASCII FILE TRANSFER COMPLETION AND UNSUCCESSFUL BRIDGE BOOT

Sniffer Network Analyzer data 30-Aug at 14:07:42, BINARY.ENC, Pg 1

SUMMARY	Delta T	Destination	Source	Summary
.				
.				
.				
301	0.0059	Maestro	Snoopy	TCP D=20 S=20295 ACK=719936002 SEQ=19739400 LEN=1123 WIN=2048
302	0.0053	Maestro	Snoopy	TCP D=20 S=20295 ACK=719936002 SEQ=19740523 LEN=1460 WIN=2048
303	0.0039	Maestro	Snoopy	TCP D=20 S=20295 FIN

				ACK=719936002 SEQ=19741983 LEN=627 WIN=2048
304	0.0007	Snoopy	Maestro	TCP D=20295 S=20 ACK=19742611 WIN=23949
305	0.0098	Snoopy	Maestro	FTP R PORT=20294 226 ASCII Transfer complete.<0D><0A>
306	0.0003	Snoopy	Maestro	TCP D=20295 S=20 FIN ACK=19742611 SEQ=719936002 LEN=0 WIN=24576
307	0.0020	Maestro	Snoopy	TCP D=21 S=20294 ACK=716544246 WIN=1804
308	0.0015	Maestro	Snoopy	TCP D=20 S=20295 ACK=719936003 WIN=2048
309	45.9027	Maestro	Snoopy	FTP C PORT=20294 QUIT<0D><0A>
310	0.0091	Snoopy	Maestro	FTP R PORT=20294 221 Goodbye.<0D><0A>
311	0.0060	Maestro	Snoopy	TCP D=21 S=20294 FIN ACK=716544260 SEQ=19468825 LEN=0 WIN=1790
312	0.0006	Snoopy	Maestro	TCP D=20294 S=21 ACK=19468826 WIN=4096
313	0.0009	Snoopy	Maestro	TCP D=20294 S=21 FIN ACK=19468826 SEQ=716544260 LEN=0 WIN=4096
314	0.0020	Maestro	Snoopy	TCP D=21 S=20294 ACK=716544261 WIN=1790
315	9.3205	09008780FFFF	Local Bridge	Ethertype=0889 (Unknown)
316	4.0209	Broadcast	Local Bridge	BOOTP Request
317	4.0194	AB0000010000	Local Bridge	MOP DL Request Program Device Type=UNA Program Type=System
318	8.0203	Broadcast	Local Bridge	ARP C HA=080087004DB3 PRO=IP
319	3.0660	Local Bridge	Maestro	ARP R PA=[192.12.2.3] HA=080087004DB3 PRO=IP
320	0.9553	Broadcast	Local Bridge	TFTP Read request File=x004db3.img
321	0.0168	Local Bridge	Maestro	UDP D=2001 S=1416 LEN=524
322	0.0037	Maestro	Local Bridge	UDP D=1416 S=2001 LEN=70
323	3.9820	Broadcast	Local Bridge	ARP C PA=[192.12.2.35] PRO=IP
324	0.0004	Local Bridge	Maestro	ARP R PA=[192.12.2.35] HA=080020103553 PRO=IP

325	7.9964	Maestro	Local Bridge	ARP C PA=[192.12.2.35] PRO=IP
326	0.0004	Local Bridge	Maestro	ARP R PA=[192.12.2.35] HA=080020103553 PRO=IP
327	0.0010	Maestro	Local Bridge	TFTP Read request File=x004db3.img
328	0.0167	Local Bridge	Maestro	TFTP Data packet NS=1
329	0.1344	Maestro	Local Bridge	TFTP Ack NR=1
330	0.0015	Local Bridge	Maestro	TFTP Data packet NS=2
331	0.0021	Maestro	Local Bridge	TFTP Ack NR=2
.				
.				
.				
1390	0.0013	Local Bridge	Maestro	TFTP Data packet NS=532
1391	0.0022	Maestro	Local Bridge	TFTP Ack NR=532
1392	0.0012	Local Bridge	Maestro	TFTP Data packet NS=533
1393	0.0012	Maestro	Local Bridge	TFTP Error response (Not defined)
1394	0.0018	Maestro	Local Bridge	TFTP Write request File=loaderr.dmp
1395	3.0193	Local Bridge	Maestro	TFTP Error response (File not found)
1396	0.0047	Broadcast	Local Bridge	TFTP Read request File=type57.img
1397	3.0045	Local Bridge	Maestro	UDP D=2002 S=1421 LEN=27
1398	0.9889	09008780FFFF	Local Bridge	Ethertype=0889 (Unknown)

TRACE 6.10.2C. TFTP ERROR RESPONSE DETAILS

Sniffer Network Analyzer data 30-Aug at 14:07:42, BINARY.ENC, Pg 1

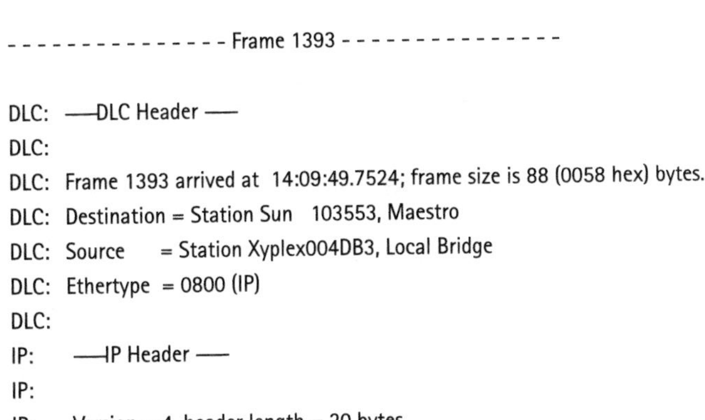

```
- - - - - - - - - - - - - - - Frame 1393 - - - - - - - - - - - - - - -

DLC:  ——DLC Header ——
DLC:
DLC:  Frame 1393 arrived at  14:09:49.7524; frame size is 88 (0058 hex) bytes.
DLC:  Destination = Station Sun   103553, Maestro
DLC:  Source      = Station Xyplex004DB3, Local Bridge
DLC:  Ethertype  = 0800 (IP)
DLC:
IP:    ——IP Header ——
IP:
IP:    Version = 4, header length = 20 bytes
IP:    Type of service = 00
```

```
IP:         000. .... = routine
IP:         ...0 .... = normal delay
IP:         .... 0... = normal throughput
IP:         .... .0.. = normal reliability
IP:     Total length = 74 bytes
IP:     Identification = 539
IP:     Flags = 0X
IP:     .0.. .... = may fragment
IP:     ..0. .... = last fragment
IP:     Fragment offset = 0 bytes
IP:     Time to live = 100 seconds/hops
IP:     Protocol = 17 (UDP)
IP:     Header checksum = D049 (correct)
IP:     Source address = [192.12.2.3]
IP:     Destination address = [192.12.2.35]
IP:     No options
IP:
UDP: ——UDP Header ——
UDP:
UDP: Source port = 2003 (TFTP)
UDP: Destination port = 1417
UDP: Length = 54
UDP: No checksum
UDP:
TFTP: ——Trivial file transfer ——
TFTP:
TFTP: Opcode = 5 (Error response)
TFTP: Error code = 0 (Not defined)
TFTP: Error message = "Transfer size error"
TFTP:
TFTP: *** 22 byte(s) of additional data present ***
TFTP:
TFTP: [Abnormal end of "Trivial file transfer".]
TFTP:
```

TRACE 6.10.2D. BOOT IMAGE TRANSFER USING FTP BINARY CONNECTION

```
Sniffer Network Analyzer data 30-Aug at 14:07:42, BINARY.ENC, Pg 1

SUMMARY  Delta T     Destination   Source        Summary
.
.
.
.
1399     4.0200      Broadcast     Local Bridge  BOOTP Request
1400     4.0185      AB0000010000  Local Bridge  MOP DL Request Program
                                                    Device Type=UNA
                                                    Program Type=System
1401     8.0202      Broadcast     Local Bridge  ARP C HA=080087004DB3 PRO=IP
1402     3.0631      Local Bridge  Maestro       ARP R PA=[192.12.2.3]
                                                    HA=080087004DB3 PRO=IP
1403     0.9579      Broadcast     Local Bridge  TFTP Read request
                                                    File=x004db3.img
1404     0.0180      Local Bridge  Maestro       UDP D=2001 S=1423 LEN=524
1405     0.0037      Maestro       Local Bridge  UDP D=1423 S=2001 LEN=70
1406     3.9809      Broadcast     Local Bridge  ARP C PA=[192.12.2.35] PRO=IP
1407     0.0004      Local Bridge  Maestro       ARP R PA=[192.12.2.35]
                                                    HA=080020103553 PRO=IP
1408     25.2853     Maestro       Snoopy        TCP D=21 S=20296 SYN
                                                    SEQ=19468830 LEN=0
                                                    WIN=2048
1409     0.0010      Snoopy        Maestro       TCP D=20296 S=21 SYN
                                                    ACK=19468831
                                                    SEQ=739648001
                                                    LEN=0 WIN=4096
1410     0.0016      Maestro       Snoopy        TCP D=21 S=20296
                                                    ACK=739648002 WIN=2048
1411     0.1149      Snoopy        Maestro       FTP R PORT=20296
                                                    220 maestro FTP server
                                                    (SunOS 4.1) ready.<0D><0A>
1412     0.0377      Maestro       Snoopy        FTP C PORT=20296
                                                    USER root<0D><0A>
1413     0.0075      Snoopy        Maestro       FTP R PORT=20296
                                                    331 Password required for
                                                    root.<0D><0A>
1414     0.0249      Maestro       Snoopy        FTP C PORT=20296
                                                    PASS bugoff<0D><0A>
1415     0.0480      Snoopy        Maestro       FTP R PORT=20296
                                                    230 User root logged
                                                    in.<0D><0A>
```

```
1416   0.1375    Maestro   Snoopy    TCP D=21 S=20296
                                          ACK=739648104 WIN=1946
1417   6.2568    Maestro   Snoopy    FTP C PORT=20296
                                          TYPE I<0D><0A>
1418   0.0015    Snoopy    Maestro   FTP R PORT=20296
                                          200 Type set to I.<0D><0A>
1419   0.1605    Maestro   Snoopy    TCP D=21 S=20296
                                          ACK=739648124 WIN=1926
1420   23.3762   Maestro   Snoopy    FTP C PORT=20296
                                          PORT 192,12,2,38,
                                          79,73<0D><0A>
1421   0.0126    Snoopy    Maestro   FTP R PORT=20296
                                          200 PORT command success-
ful
                                          <0D><0A>
1422   0.0118    Maestro   Snoopy    FTP C PORT=20296
                                          STOR /home/tftpboot
                                          /rb1w1.sys_v2.0<0D><0A>
1423   0.0919    Snoopy    Maestro   TCP D=20297 S=20 SYN
                                          SEQ=744128001
                                          LEN=0 WIN=24576
1424   0.0015    Maestro   Snoopy    TCP D=20 S=20297 SYN
                                          ACK=744128002
                                          SEQ=19468841
                                          LEN=0 WIN=2048
1425   0.0006    Snoopy    Maestro   TCP D=20297 S=20
                                          ACK=19468842 WIN=24576
1426   0.0018    Snoopy    Maestro   FTP R PORT=20296
                                          150 Binary data connection
                                          for /home/tftpboot/rb1w...
1427   0.1065    Maestro   Snoopy    TCP D=20 S=20297
                                          ACK=744128002
                                          SEQ=19468842
                                          LEN=1460 WIN=2048
1428   0.0031    Maestro   Snoopy    TCP D=20 S=20297
                                          ACK=744128002
                                          SEQ=19470302
                                          LEN=1460 WIN=2048
1429   0.0013    Snoopy    Maestro   TCP D=20297 S=20
                                          ACK=19471762 WIN=24576
.
.
```

TRACE 6.10.2E. BINARY FILE TRANSFER COMPLETION AND SUCCESSFUL BRIDGE BOOT

Sniffer Network Analyzer data 30-Aug at 14:07:42, BINARY.ENC, Pg 1

SUMMARY	Delta T	Destination	Source	Summary
.				
.				
.				
1687	0.0087	Maestro	Snoopy	TCP D=20 S=20297 ACK=744128002 SEQ=19738450 LEN=1460 WIN=2048
1688	0.0031	Maestro	Snoopy	TCP D=20 S=20297 ACK=744128002 SEQ=19739910 LEN=1460 WIN=2048
1689	0.0002	Snoopy	Maestro	TCP D=20297 S=20 ACK=19739910 WIN=24576
1690	0.0026	Maestro	Snoopy	TCP D=20 S=20297 FIN ACK=744128002 SEQ=19741370 LEN=240 WIN=2048
1691	0.0005	Snoopy	Maestro	TCP D=20297 S=20 ACK=19741611 WIN=22876
1692	0.0092	Snoopy	Maestro	FTP R PORT=20296 226 Binary Transfer complete.<0D><0A>
1693	0.0003	Snoopy	Maestro	TCP D=20297 S=20 FIN ACK=19741611 SEQ=744128002 LEN=0 WIN=24576
1694	0.0020	Maestro	Snoopy	TCP D=21 S=20296 ACK=739648268 WIN=1782
1695	0.0008	Maestro	Snoopy	TCP D=20 S=20297 ACK=744128003 WIN=2048
1696	31.6613	09008780FFFF	Local Bridge	Ethertype=0889 (Unknown)
1697	4.0209	Broadcast	Local Bridge	BOOTP Request
1698	4.0194	AB0000010000	Local Bridge	MOP DL Request Program Device Type=UNA Program Type=System
1699	8.0204	Broadcast	Local Bridge	ARP C HA=080087004DB3 PRO=IP
1700	3.0628	Local Bridge	Maestro	ARP R PA=[192.12.2.3] HA=080087004DB3 PRO=IP

1701	0.9584	Broadcast	Local Bridge	TFTP Read request File=x004db3.img
1702	0.0168	Local Bridge	Maestro	UDP D=2001 S=1426 LEN=524
1703	0.0037	Maestro	Local Bridge	UDP D=1426 S=2001 LEN=70
1704	3.9820	Broadcast	Local Bridge	ARP C PA=[192.12.2.35] PRO=IP
1705	0.0004	Local Bridge	Maestro	ARP R PA=[192.12.2.35] HA=080020103553 PRO=IP
1706	7.9964	Maestro	Local Bridge	ARP C PA=[192.12.2.35] PRO=IP
1707	0.0004	Local Bridge	Maestro	ARP R PA=[192.12.2.35] HA=080020103553 PRO=IP
1708	0.0010	Maestro	Local Bridge	TFTP Read request File=x004db3.img
1709	0.0168	Local Bridge	Maestro	TFTP Data packet NS=1
1710	0.1344	Maestro	Local Bridge	TFTP Ack NR=1
1711	0.0015	Local Bridge	Maestro	TFTP Data packet NS=2
1712	0.0021	Maestro	Local Bridge	TFTP Ack NR=2
.				
.				
.				
2771	0.0012	Local Bridge	Maestro	TFTP Data packet NS=532
2772	0.0022	Maestro	Local Bridge	TFTP Ack NR=532
2773	0.0011	Local Bridge	Maestro	TFTP Data packet NS=533 (Last)
2774	0.0019	Maestro	Local Bridge	TFTP Ack NR=533
2775	11.3936	09008780FFFF	Local Bridge	Ethertype=0889 (Unknown)
2776	4.0129	Broadcast	Local Bridge	BOOTP Request
2777	4.0195	AB0000010000	Local Bridge	MOP DL Request Program Device Type=UNA Program Type=System
2778	8.0205	Broadcast	Local Bridge	ARP C HA=080087004DB3 PRO=IP
2779	3.0610	Local Bridge	Maestro	ARP R PA=[192.12.2.3] HA=080087004DB3 PRO=IP
2780	0.9599	Broadcast	Local Bridge	TFTP Read request File=x004db3.prm
2781	0.0159	Local Bridge	Maestro	UDP D=2001 S=1440 LEN=524
2782	0.0016	Maestro	Local Bridge	UDP D=1440 S=2001 LEN=70
2783	3.9846	Broadcast	Local Bridge	ARP C PA=[192.12.2.35] PRO=IP
2784	0.0004	Local Bridge	Maestro	ARP R PA=[192.12.2.35] HA=080020103553 PRO=IP
2785	7.9971	Maestro	Local Bridge	ARP C PA=[192.12.2.35] PRO=IP
2786	0.0004	Local Bridge	Maestro	ARP R PA=[192.12.2.35] HA=080020103553 PRO=IP

2787	0.0010	Maestro	Local Bridge	TFTP Read request
			File=x004db3.prm	
2788	0.0163	Local Bridge	Maestro	TFTP Data packet NS=1
2789	0.0147	Maestro	Local Bridge	TFTP Ack NR=1
2790	0.0015	Local Bridge	Maestro	TFTP Data packet NS=2
2791	0.0021	Maestro	Local Bridge	TFTP Ack NR=2
.				
.				
.				
2814	0.0012	Local Bridge	Maestro	TFTP Data packet NS=14
2815	0.0021	Maestro	Local Bridge	TFTP Ack NR=14
2816	0.0013	Local Bridge	Maestro	TFTP Data packet NS=15
2817	0.0022	Maestro	Local Bridge	TFTP Ack NR=15
2818	0.0012	Local Bridge	Maestro	TFTP Data packet NS=16 (Last)
2819	0.0021	Maestro	Local Bridge	TFTP Ack NR=16

6.10.3 Selecting the Proper Terminal Option for TELNET

In Section 6.5 we studied TELNET and discussed a number of options for converting the local terminal/host format into the Network Virtual Terminal format. These options are a common source of TELNET incompatibilities.

In this example, users attached to an Ethernet have two options for communicating with an SNA host (see Figure 6-13). The first option is to use DEC VT-100 terminals through a terminal server connected to the Ethernet. The second option is to use FTP Software Inc.'s PC/TCP application suite on a workstation to connect directly to the Ethernet. The users discover, however, that the terminal server option does not work while the PC/TCP option does. Let's explore why.

The first attempt to access the SNA host is via the terminal server, shown in Trace 6.10.3a. The terminal session begins with a TCP connection in Frames 32 through 34 and continues with the TELNET option negotiations. These include the Terminal Type (Frames 36 through 41), End of Record (Frames 42 through 44), Binary Transmission (Frames 45 through 47), and so on. Data transfer from the SNA host begins in Frame 53, but has little success. The terminal server is allowing a rather small window size, ranging from 0 to 256 octets. In Frame 112, the terminal server resets the TCP connection, terminating communication. At this point, the user sees the terminal server prompt on his VT-100 terminal and realizes that the host connection has failed.

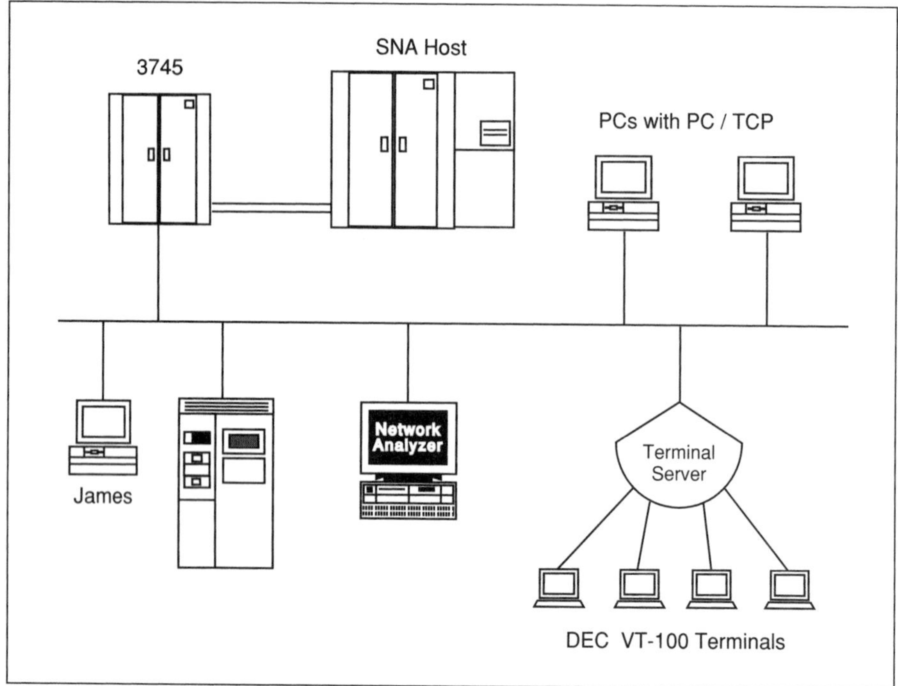

Figure 6-13 TELNET Access to IBM Using TN3270

To test the process, the network administrator, James, goes to a workstation that has the PC/TCP software package and attempts the same session with the SNA host (see Trace 6.10.3b). Frames 94 through 96 show the TCP connection being established, followed by the same TELNET option negotiation sequence. A significant difference is the window size that the workstation allows (1707–2048 octets) and the orderly termination of the TCP connection in Frames 256 through 259. This time, James is able to log into the host, conduct his business, and properly terminate the connection. Since this session was successful but the one via the terminal server was not, James decides to check the options negotiated in each case.

Returning to Trace 6.10.3a, the only option open for negotiation is the Terminal Type, beginning in Frame 39, which we know from the Interpret as Command (IAC) Subnegotiation (SB). Trace 6.10.3c shows the details of that negotiation. The SNA host sends FF FA 18 H, meaning "Interpret as Command, Subnegotiation of option 18H (Terminal Type)." The terminal server responds in Frame 41 with FF FA 18...H, indicating that its terminal type is an IBM-3278-2 (shown in the ASCII decode of Frame 41).

James performs a similar analysis of the trace derived from the workstation's successful connection to the host. Reviewing Trace 6.10.3b, the Terminal Type negotiation is requested in Frame 97 and occurs in Frames 99 and 100. In Frame 99 of

Trace 6.10.3d, the SNA host indicates the negotiation of the terminal type (FF FA 18H), but this time the response is different. The workstation responds with IBM-3278-2-E instead of the IBM-3278-2 which the terminal server sent. This difference suggests to James that the terminal server was not supporting the Extended (E) Attribute set, causing the connection to fail. A check of the defined TELNET terminal types in RFC 1700 and RFC 1091 [6-39] confirms that the two were indeed different. The workstation software supported the IBM-3278-2-E type, allowing the host connection to succeed. The terminal server did not provide support, so that connection failed. What appeared to be a small problem inhibited communication. Readers needing additional details on TN3270 should consult References [6-40] and [6-41].

TRACE 6.10.3A. HOST ACCESS VIA TERMINAL SERVER (SUMMARY)

Sniffer Network Analyzer data 22-Nov at 15:04:36, JK1.ENC, Pg 1

SUMMARY	Delta T	Destination	Source	Summary
32	38.6694	SNA Host	Term Server	TCP D=23 S=5029 SYN SEQ=159638 LEN=0 WIN=256
33	0.0016	Term Server	SNA Host	TCP D=5029 S=23 SYN ACK=159639 SEQ=849951745 LEN=0 WIN=4096
34	0.0021	SNA Host	Term Server	TCP D=23 S=5029 ACK=849951746 WIN=256
35	0.0020	SNA Host	Term Server	Telnet C PORT=5029 IAC Do Echo
36	0.0273	Term Server	SNA Host	Telnet R PORT=5029 IAC Do Terminal type
37	0.0032	SNA Host	Term Server	TCP D=23 S=5029 ACK=849951749 WIN=253
38	0.0022	SNA Host	Term Server	Telnet C PORT=5029 IAC Will Terminal type
39	0.0033	Term Server	SNA Host	Telnet R PORT=5029 IAC SB ...
40	0.0023	SNA Host	Term Server	TCP D=23 S=5029 ACK=849951755 WIN=250
41	0.0027	SNA Host	Term Server	Telnet C PORT=5029 IAC SB ...
42	0.0258	Term Server	SNA Host	Telnet R PORT=5029 IAC Do End of record
43	0.0023	SNA Host	Term Server	TCP D=23 S=5029 ACK=849951761 WIN=250

44	0.0033	SNA Host	Term Server	Telnet C PORT=5029 IAC Will End of record
45	0.0034	Term Server	SNA Host	Telnet R PORT=5029 IAC Do Binary transmission
46	0.0022	SNA Host	Term Server	TCP D=23 S=5029 ACK=849951767 WIN=250
47	0.0499	SNA Host	Term Server	Telnet C PORT=5029 IAC Will Binary transmission
48	0.0041	Term Sun	SNA Host	Telnet R PORT=5029 IAC Do Echo
49	0.0027	SNA Host	Term Sun	TCP D=23 S=5029 ACK=849951770 WIN=253
50	0.0014	Term Sun	SNA Host	Telnet R PORT=5029 IAC Won't Echo
51	0.0017	SNA Host	Term Sun	Telnet C PORT=5029 IAC Wonít Echo
52	0.0024	SNA Host	Term Sun	TCP D=23 S=5029 ACK=849951773 WIN=256
53	0.0029	Term Sun	SNA Host	Telnet R PORT=5029 <05>...
54	0.0022	SNA Host	Term Sun	TCP D=23 S=5029 ACK=849951783 WIN=246
55	0.0602	Term Sun	SNA Host	Telnet R PORT=5029 <05>...
56	0.0031	SNA Host	Term Sun	TCP D=23 S=5029 ACK=849952029 WIN=10
57	0.0018	Term Sun	SNA Host	Telnet R PORT=5029 <11>...
58	0.0482	SNA Host	Term Sun	TCP D=23 S=5029 ACK=849952029 WIN=256
59	0.0146	SNA Host	Term Sun	TCP D=23 S=5029 ACK=849952037 WIN=256
60	3.5586	SNA Host	Term Sun	Telnet C PORT=5029 }...
61	0.0662	Term Sun	SNA Host	Telnet R PORT=5029 <05>...
62	0.0024	SNA Host	Term Sun	TCP D=23 S=5029 ACK=849952083 WIN=210
63	0.0348	SNA Host	Term Sun	TCP D=23 S=5029 ACK=849952083 WIN=256
64	0.0482	Term Sun	SNA Host	Telnet R PORT=5029 <05>...
65	0.0025	SNA Host	Term Sun	TCP D=23 S=5029 ACK=849952093 WIN=246
66	0.0573	Term Sun	SNA Host	Telnet R PORT=5029 <05>...
67	0.0031	SNA Host	Term Sun	TCP D=23 S=5029 ACK=849952339 WIN=10
68	0.0490	SNA Host	Term Sun	TCP D=23 S=5029 ACK=849952339 WIN=256

69	0.0016	Term Sun	SNA Host	Telnet R PORT=5029 ...
70	0.0031	SNA Host	Term Sun	TCPD=23 S=5029 ACK=849952595 WIN=0
71	0.0275	SNA Host	Term Sun	TCP D=23 S=5029 ACK=849952595 WIN=256
72	0.0017	Term Sun	SNA Host	Telnet R PORT=5029 ...
73	0.0031	SNA Host	Term Sun	TCP D=23 S=5029 ACK=849952851 WIN=0
74	0.0252	SNA Host	Term Sun	TCP D=23 S=5029 ACK=849952851 WIN=256
75	0.0019	Term Sun	SNA Host	Telnet R PORT=5029 ...
76	0.0032	SNA Host	Term Sun	TCP D=23 S=5029 ACK=849953107 WIN=0
77	0.0240	SNA Host	Term Sun	TCP D=23 S=5029 ACK=849953107 WIN=255
78	0.0017	Term Sun	SNA Host	Telnet R PORT=5029 ...
79	0.0044	SNA Host	Term Sun	TCP D=23 S=5029 ACK=849953362 WIN=0
80	0.0244	SNA Host	Term Sun	TCP D=23 S=5029 ACK=849953362 WIN=256
81	0.0014	Term Sun	SNA Host	Telnet R PORT=5029 <00><00><11>[a<\...
82	0.0021	SNA Host	Term Sun	TCP D=23 S=5029 ACK=849953377 WIN=241
83	8.5150	SNA Host	Term Sun	Telnet C PORT=5029 }\}<11>...
84	0.0670	Term Sun	SNA Host	TCP D=5029 S=23 ACK=159718 WIN=4096
85	1.0446	Term Sun	SNA Host	Telnet R PORT=5029 <05>...
86	0.0031	SNA Host	Term Sun	TCP D=23 S=5029 ACK=849953633 WIN=0
87	0.0505	SNA Host	Term Sun	TCP D=23 S=5029 ACK=849953633 WIN=255
88	0.0020	Term Sun	SNA Host	Telnet R PORT=5029 ...
89	0.0038	SNA Host	Term Sun	TCP D=23 S=5029 ACK=849953888 WIN=0
90	0.0250	SNA Host	Term Sun	TCP D=23 S=5029 ACK=849953888 WIN=256
91	0.0016	Term Sun	SNA Host	Telnet R PORT=5029 ...
92	0.0031	SNA Host	Term Sun	TCP D=23 S=5029 ACK=849954144 WIN=0
93	0.0260	SNA Host	Term Sun	TCP D=23 S=5029 ACK=849954144 WIN=256
94	0.0016	Term Sun	SNA Host	Telnet R PORT=5029 ...

95	0.0031	SNA Host	Term Sun	TCP D=23 S=5029 ACK=849954400 WIN=0
96	0.0259	SNA Host	Term Sun	TCP D=23 S=5029 ACK=849954400 WIN=256
97	0.0016	Term Sun	SNA Host	Telnet R PORT=5029 @...
98	0.0031	SNA Host	Term Sun	TCP D=23 S=5029 ACK=849954656 WIN=0
99	0.0258	SNA Host	Term Sun	TCP D=23 S=5029 ACK=849954656 WIN=256
100	0.0015	Term Sun	SNA Host	Telnet R PORT=5029 <1D>...
101	0.0025	SNA Host	Term Sun	TCP D=23 S=5029 ACK=849954776 WIN=136
102	0.0384	SNA Host	Term Sun	TCP D=23 S=5029 ACK=849954776 WIN=256
103	2.7735	SNA Host	Term Sun	Telnet C PORT=5029 }\~<11>\}...
104	0.0239	Term Sun	SNA Host	Telnet R PORT=5029 <05>...
105	0.0022	SNA Host	Term Sun	TCP D=23 S=5029 ACK=849954780 WIN=252
106	1.9587	Term Sun	SNA Host	Telnet R PORT=5029 <05>...
107	0.0022	SNA Host	Term Sun	TCP D=23 S=5029 ACK=849954790 WIN=246
108	2.2797	Term Sun	SNA Host	Telnet R PORT=5029 <05>...
109	0.0021	SNA Host	Term Sun	TCP D=23 S=5029 ACK=849954800 WIN=246
110	3.2919	Term Sun	SNA Host	Telnet R PORT=5029 <11><00><06>@<00>...
111	0.0025	SNA Host	Term Sun	TCPD=23 S=5029 ACK=849954815 WIN=241
112	0.0116	SNA Host	Term Sun	TCP D=23 S=5029 RST WIN=0

TRACE 6.10.3B. HOST ACCESS VIA PC (SUMMARY)

Sniffer Network Analyzer data 22-Nov at 17:01:38, JK2.ENC, Page 1

SUMMARY	Delta T	Destination	Source	Summary
94	0.0003	SNA Host	Workstation	TCP D=23 S=28207 SYN SEQ=112068096 LEN=0 WIN=2048
95	0.0015	Workstation	SNA Host	TCP D=28207 S=23 SYN ACK=112068097 SEQ=1722719745

				LEN=0 WIN=4096
96	0.0006	SNA Host	Workstation	TCP D=23 S=28207 ACK=1722719746 WIN=2048
97	0.0283	Workstation	SNA Host	Telnet R PORT=28207 IAC Do Terminal type
98	0.0126	SNA Host	Workstation	Telnet C PORT=28207 IAC Will Terminal type
99	0.0045	Workstation	SNA Host	Telnet R PORT=28207 IAC SB ...
100	0.0013	SNA Host	Workstation	Telnet C PORT=28207 IAC SB ...
101	0.0262	Workstation	SNA Host	Telnet R PORT=28207 IAC Do End of record
102	0.0015	SNA Host	Workstation	Telnet C PORT=28207 IAC Will End of record
103	0.0034	Workstation	SNA Host	Telnet R PORT=28207 IAC Do Binary transmission
104	0.0014	SNA Host	Workstation	Telnet C PORT=28207 IAC Do End of record
105	0.0754	Workstation	SNA Host	TCP D=28207 S=23 ACK=112068124 WIN=4096
106	0.0007	SNA Host	Workstation	Telnet C PORT=28207 IAC Will Binary transmission
107	0.0100	Workstation	SNA Host	Telnet R PORT=28207 <05>...
108	0.2144	SNA Host	Workstation	TCP D=23 S=28207 ACK=1722719777 WIN=2017
109	0.0017	Workstation	SNA Host	Telnet R PORT=28207 <05>...
110	0.2181	SNA Host	Workstation	TCP D=23 S=28207 ACK=1722720031 WIN=1763
140	4.0319	SNA Host	Workstation	Telnet C PORT=28207 }...
141	0.0862	Workstation	SNA Host	Telnet R PORT=28207 <05>...
142	0.1659	SNA Host	Workstation	TCP D=23 S=28207 ACK=1722720077 WIN=1717
143	0.6708	Workstation	SNA Host	Telnet R PORT=28207 <05>...
144	0.0008	SNA Host	Workstation	TCP D=23 S=28207 ACK=1722720087 WIN=1707
145	0.0506	Workstation	SNA Host	Telnet R PORT=28207 <05>...
146	0.0016	SNA Host	Workstation	TCP D=23 S=28207 ACK=1722721371 WIN=2048
202	17.0982	SNA Host	Workstation	Telnet C PORT=28207 }...
203	0.0559	Workstation	SNA Host	TCP D=28207 S=23 ACK=112068172 WIN=4096
206	1.7954	Workstation	SNA Host	Telnet R PORT=28207 <05>...
207	0.0016	SNA Host	Workstation	TCP D=23 S=28207 ACK=1722722830 WIN=2048

216	5.9596	SNA Host	Workstation	Telnet C PORT=28207 }\~<11>\}...
217	0.0457	Workstation	SNA Host	TCP D=28207 S=23 ACK=112068181 WIN=4096
218	0.5606	Workstation	SNA Host	Telnet R PORT=28207 <05>...
219	0.0008	SNA Host	Workstation	TCP D=23 S=28207 ACK=1722722834 WIN=2044
220	1.5828	Workstation	SNA Host	Telnet R PORT=28207 <05>...
221	0.0008	SNA Host	Workstation	TCP D=23 S=28207 ACK=1722722844 WIN=2034
222	1.3582	Workstation	SNA Host	Telnet R PORT=28207 <05>...
223	0.0007	SNA Host	Workstation	TCP D=23 S=28207 ACK=1722722854 WIN=2024
224	1.3963	Workstation	SNA Host	Telnet R PORT=28207 <11><00><06>@<00>...
225	0.0007	SNA Host	Workstation	TCP D=23 S=28207 ACK=1722722869 WIN=2009
256	16.3941	SNA Host	Workstation	TCP D=23 S=28207 FIN ACK=1722722869 SEQ=112068181 LEN=0 WIN=2009
257	0.0014	Workstation	SNA Host	TCP D=28207 S=23 ACK=112068182 WIN=4096
258	0.0058	Workstation	SNA Host	TCP D=28207 S=23 FIN ACK=112068182 SEQ=1722722869 LEN=0 WIN=4096
259	0.0007	SNA Host	Workstation	TCP D=23 S=28207 ACK=1722722870 WIN=2009

TRACE 6.10.3C. TELNET PARAMETERS FROM TERMINAL SERVER

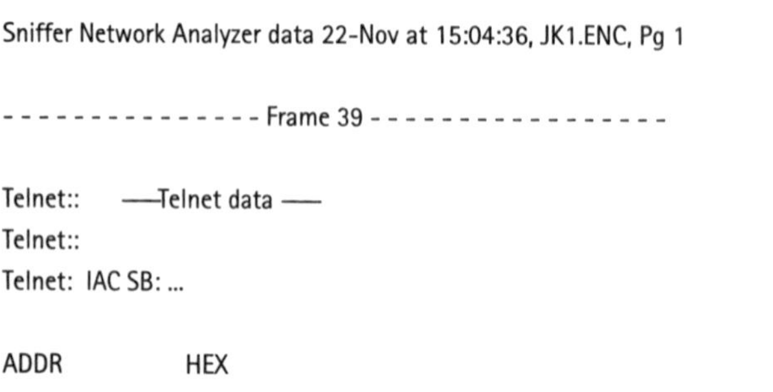

Sniffer Network Analyzer data 22-Nov at 15:04:36, JK1.ENC, Pg 1

- - - - - - - - - - - - - - - Frame 39 - - - - - - - - - - - - - - - - -

Telnet:: —Telnet data —

Telnet::

Telnet: IAC SB: ...

ADDR	HEX		ASCII
0000	08 00 87 00 AA 61 02 60	8C 2E 21 56 08 00 45 00	.....a.`..!V..E.
0010	00 2E F9 11 00 00 1E 06	FE EA 90 48 04 0F 90 48	...........H...H

0020	80 2E 00 17 13 A5 32 A9	3C 05 00 02 6F 9D 50 18	......2.<...o.P.
0030	10 00 F1 01 00 00 FF FA	18 01 FF F0	....

- - - - - - - - - - - - - - - Frame 40 - - - - - - - - - - - - - - - - -

TCP: —TCP header —
TCP:
TCP: Source port = 5029
TCP: Destination port = 23 (Telnet)
TCP: Sequence number = 159645
TCP: Acknowledgment number = 849951755
TCP: Data offset = 20 bytes
TCP: Flags = 10
TCP: ..0. .... = (No urgent pointer)
TCP: ...1 .... = Acknowledgment
TCP: .... 0... = (No push)
TCP: .... .0.. = (No reset)
TCP: .... ..0. = (No SYN)
TCP: ....0 = (No FIN)
TCP: Window = 250
TCP: Checksum = 17FD (correct)
TCP: No TCP options
TCP:

ADDR	HEX		ASCII
0000	02 60 8C 2E 21 56 08 00	87 00 AA 61 08 00 45 00	.`..!V.....a..E.
0010	00 28 00 5D 00 00 40 06	D5 A5 90 48 80 2E 90 48	.(.]..@....H...H
0020	04 0F 13 A5 00 17 00 02	6F 9D 32 A9 3C 0B 50 10	........o.2.<.P.
0030	00 FA 17 FD 00 00 00 00	00 00 00 00	....

- - - - - - - - - - - - - - - Frame 41 - - - - - - - - - - - - - - - - -

Telnet:: —Telnet data —
Telnet::
Telnet:IAC SB:

ADDR	HEX		ASCII
0000	02 60 8C 2E 21 56 08 00	87 00 AA 61 08 00 45 00	.`..!V.....a..E.
0010	00 38 00 5E 00 00 40 06	D5 94 90 48 80 2E 90 48	.8.^..@....H...H
0020	04 0F 13 A5 00 17 00 02	6F 9D 32 A9 3C 0B 50 18	........o.2.<.P.
0030	01 00 D1 E6 00 00 FF FA	18 00 49 42 4D 2D 33 32	..........IBM-32
0040	37 38 2D 32 FF F0		78-2..

TRACE 6.10.3D. Telnet PARAMETERS FROM PC

```
Sniffer Network Analyzer data 22-Nov at 17:01:38, JK2.ENC, Pg

- - - - - - - - - - - - - - - Frame 99 - - - - - - - - - - - - - - - - -

Telnet::      —Telnet data —
Telnet::
Telnet:IAC SB:

ADDR     HEX                                                         ASCII
0000     00 00 C0 A6 99 27 02 60      8C 2E 21 56 08 00 45 00      .....í.`..!V..E.
0010     00 2E FE 8B 00 00 1E 06      F9 89 90 48 04 0F 90 48      ...........H...H
0020     80 15 00 17 6E 2F 66 AE      9E 05 06 AE 06 04 50 18      ....n/f.......P.
0030     10 00 63 78 00 00 FF FA      18 01 FF F0                  ..cx........

- - - - - - - - - - - - - - - Frame 100 - - - - - - - - - - - - - - - - -

Telnet:  —Telnet data —
Telnet::
Telnet:IAC SB

ADDR     HEX                                                         ASCII
0000     02 60 8C 2E 21 56 00 00      C0 A6 99 27 08 00 45 10      .`..!V.....í..E.
0010     00 3A 00 05 00 00 40 06      D5 F4 90 48 80 15 90 48      .:....@....H...H
0020     04 0F 6E 2F 00 17 06 AE      06 04 66 AE 9E 0B 50 18      ..n/......f...P.
0030     07 F7 10 1F 00 00 FF FA      18 00 49 42 4D 2D 33 32      ..........IBM-32
0040     37 38 2D 32 2D 45 FF F0                                   78-2-E..
```

6.10.4 TELNET over ATM

As a second example of TELNET operation, consider the network shown in Figure 6-14, which includes a TELNET client PC attached to a local network, a router, an ATM switch, and a Sun workstation, which is the TELNET server. The client wishes to connect to the Sun server, but must traverse the router and switch to get there. To accomplish this requires that three connections be established: an ATM connection, a TCP connection, and a TELNET connection. Trace 6.10.4a shows the details of these protocol operations. The ATM connection is established in Frames 1–6, the TCP connection is established in Frames 7–9, and the TELNET session begins in Frame 13 with the parameter negotiations, login, password, and so on.

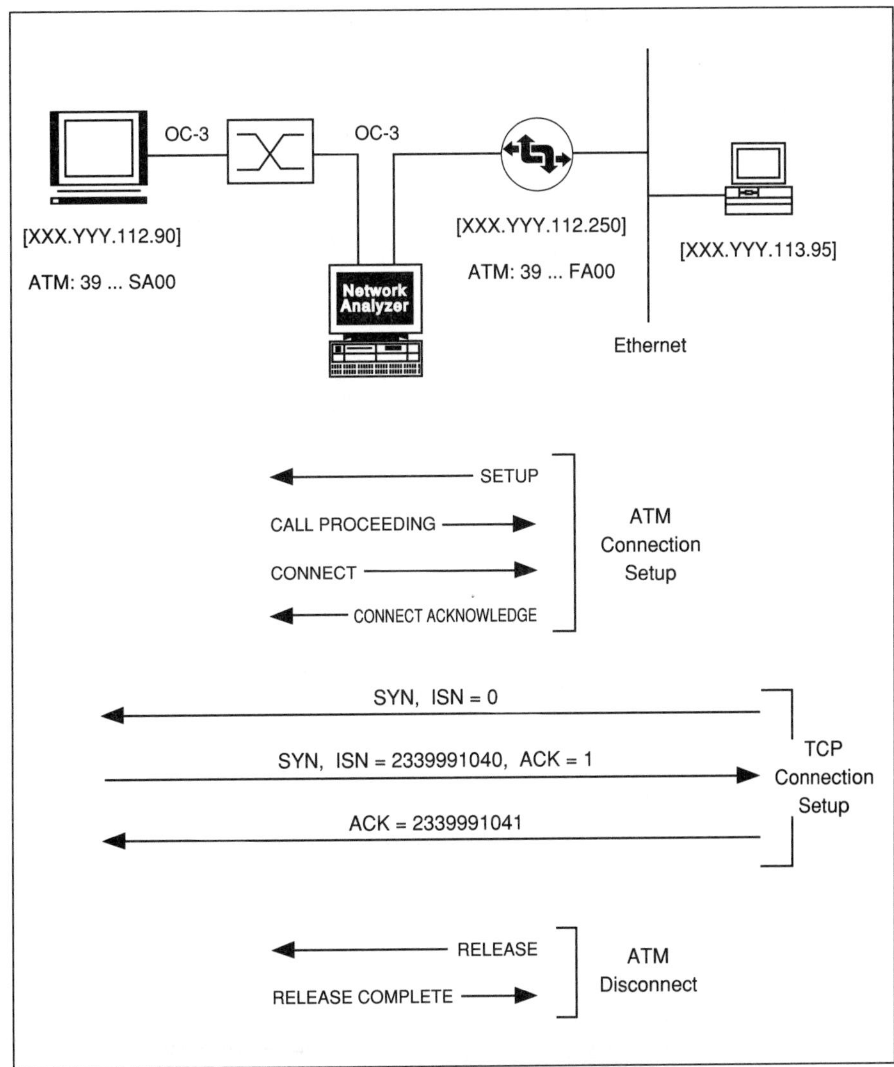

Figure 6-14 TELNET Connection via ATM

TRACE 6.10.4A. TELNET OVER ATM SUMMARY

Sniffer Network Analyzer data from 23-Jan at 14:46:34, file JIM02.ATC, Pg 1

SUMMARY	Delta T	Destination	Source	Summary
1		ATM Switch	Router	Q2931 Setup
2	0.02720	Router	ATM Switch	Q2931 Call proceeding
3	0.06651	Router	ATM Switch	Q2931 Connect
4	0.00221	[0.0.0.0]	Router	ARP
5	0.00081	ATM Switch	Router	Q2931 Connect acknowledge
6	0.00024	Sun	Router	ARP PRO=IP
7	0.47088	Sun	Client	TCP D=23 S=1405 SYN SEQ=0 LEN=0 WIN=512
8	0.00200	Client	Sun	TCP D=1405 S=23 SYN ACK=1 SEQ=2339991040 LEN=0 WIN=64240
9	0.00273	Sun	Client	TCP D=23 S=1405 ACK=2339991041 WIN=512
10	0.23528	Client	Sun	Telnet R PORT=1405 IAC Do Terminal type
11	0.39640	ATM Switch	Router	SSCOP POLL PDU(Trans Stat Info)
12	0.00393	Router	ATM Switch	SSCOP STAT PDU(Receiver State Info)
13	0.16819	Client	Sun	Telnet R PORT=1405 IAC Do Terminal type
14	0.44008	Sun	Client	TCP D=2S=1405 ACK=2339991044 WIN=509
15	0.00280	Sun	Client	TCPD=23S=1405 ACK=2339991044 WIN=512
16	0.00166	Sun	Client	Telnet C PORT=1405 AC Will Terminal type
17	0.00178	Client	Sun	Telnet R PORT=1405 IAC SB ...
18	0.00543	Sun	Client	TCPD=23S=1405 ACK=2339991050 WIN=512
19		Sun	Client	Telnet C PORT=1405 IAC SB ...
20	0.05405	Client	Sun	TelnetRPORT=1405IAC Will Echo
21	0.05856	Sun	Client	TCPD=23S=1405ACK=2339991108 WIN=512
22	0.00154	Sun	Client	Telnet C PORT=1405 IAC Do Echo
23	0.00153	Sun	Client	Telnet C PORT=1405 IAC Do Suppress go-ahead

24	0.00128	Client	Sun	TCPD=1405S=23ACK=21 WIN=64240
25	0.00020	Sun	Client	TelnetCPORT=1405IACWonít Echo
26	0.00197	Client	Sun	Telnet R PORT=1405IACDonítEcho
27	0.04013	Sun	Client	TCPD=23S=1405ACK=2339991111 WIN=512
28	0.00123	Client	Sun	Telnet R PORT=1405 login:
29	0.01264	Sun	Client	TCPD=23S=1405ACK=2339991118 WIN=512
30	3.57176	Sun	Client	Telnet C PORT=1405 t
31	0.00254	Client	Sun	Telnet R PORT=1405 t
32	0.01943	Sun	Client	TCPD=23S=1405ACK=2339991119 WIN=512
33	0.21528	Sun	Client	Telnet C PORT=1405 e
34	0.00258	Client	Sun	Telnet R PORT=1405 e
35	0.02181	Sun	Client	TCPD=23S=1405ACK=2339991120 WIN=512
36	0.06454	Sun	Client	Telnet C PORT=1405 s
37	0.00249	Client	Sun	Telnet R PORT=1405 s
38	0.11268	Sun	Client	TCPD=23S=1405ACK=2339991121 WIN=512
39	0.08181	Sun	Client	Telnet C PORT=1405 t
40	0.00245	Client	Sun	Telnet R PORT=1405 t
41	0.03649	Sun	Client	TCPD=23S=1405ACK=2339991122 WIN=512
42	0.98535	Sun	Client	Telnet C PORT=1405 <0D>
43	0.00265	Client	Sun	Telnet R PORT=1405 <0D0A>
44	0.02949	Sun	Client	TCPD=23S=1405ACK=2339991124 WIN=512
45	0.00125	Client	Sun	Telnet R PORT=1405 Password:
46	0.01018	Sun	Client	TCPD=23S=1405ACK=2339991134 WIN=512
47	1.37244	Sun	Client	Telnet C PORT=1405 t
48	0.05069	Client	Sun	TCPD=1405S=23ACK=30 WIN=64240
49	0.13462	Sun	Client	Telnet C PORT=1405 e
50	0.05406	Client	Sun	TCPD=1405S=23ACK=31 WIN=64240
51	0.02487	Sun	Client	Telnet C PORT=1405 s
52	0.05280	Client	Sun	TCPD=1405S=23ACK=32 WIN=64240
53	0.14366	Sun	Client	Telnet C PORT=1405 t
54	0.05610	Client	Sun	TCPD=1405S=23ACK=33 WIN=64240

55	0.35760	Sun	Client	Telnet C PORT=1405 <0D>
56	0.04223	Client	Sun	Telnet R PORT=1405 <0D0A>
57	0.09575	Sun	Client	TCPD=23S=1405ACK=2339991136 WIN=512
58	0.00124	Client	Sun	Telnet R PORT=1405 Last login: Fri Jan 19 15:41:37 on console<0D0A>
59	0.01039	Sun	Client	TCPD=23S=1405ACK=2339991180 WIN=512
60	0.31170	Client	Sun	Telnet R PORT=1405 Sun Microsystems Inc. SunOS 5.4 Generi.
61	0.03638	Sun	Client	TCPD=23S=1405ACK=2339991239 WIN=512
62	0.20412	Client	Sun	Telnet R PORT=1405 Arches%
63	0.03536	Sun	Client	TCP D=23 S=1405ACK=233999124 WIN=512

The details of the ATM connection setup are shown in Trace 6.10.4b. Recall that ATM is a connection-oriented network and requires that the communication path be established prior to sending any data. This process is somewhat similar to placing a telephone call, in which the initiator (or sender) enters the address (or telephone number) of the desired receiver and then relies on the network to establish a data path to the distant point. The messages that are used to establish, maintain, and terminate the connection are called signalling messages; in the case of ATM, they are defined by an ITU-T standard known as Q.2931. These signalling messages are sent on a preassigned virtual connection, VPCI = 0 and VCI = 5.

The connection establishment process begins with a SETUP message transmitted from the router to the ATM switch. Note from Figure 6-14 that the network analyzer is on the right-hand side of the ATM switch, capturing the traffic between the switch and the router. As a result, it cannot capture the traffic on the left-hand side of the switch. This entire call connection process was initiated by communication from the client PC, via the Ethernet LAN, to the router, which in turn sent the SETUP message to the ATM switch. As a result of the analyzer position, we are not able to see this initial client-to-router communication. In response to the client's actions, the router sent the SETUP to the ATM switch, which the Sniffer captured this, and we can see it in this trace.

Returning to Trace 6.10.4b, the ATM Cell Header is shown first, specifying the signaling channel (VPI = 0, VCI = 5) for communication. Next comes the Service Specific Connection Oriented Protocol (SSCOP) header, which provides for the reliable exchange of signaling information across an ATM interface. The Q.2931 signaling message is transmitted next; it includes the message type (SETUP) plus a number of parameters, which are carried within data units called Information Elements, or IEs. These IEs include: an ATM Traffic Descriptor, Broadband Bearer

Capability, Called Party Number, Calling Party Number, Quality of Service, ATM Adaptation Layer Parameters, and Broadband Low Layer Information. Frame 2 shows the CALL PROCEEDING message (from the ATM switch to the router) with a Connection Identifier IE, which identifies the virtual path (VPCI = 0) and virtual channel (VCI = 34) assigned to this call. A CONNECT message from the ATM switch to the router is seen in Frame 3; it also contains a Connection Identifier IE (VPCI = 0, VCI = 34) confirming the channel assignment. A CONNECT ACKNOWLEDGE message is sent from the router in Frame 5, completing the connection establishment process.

Frames 4 and 6 contain address resolution information. In Frame 4, the router sends an Inverse ARP Request (a broadcast) looking for the IP address of the TELNET server. Frame 6 contains the TELNET server's response:

```
ATM: 39000000000000000000000000000A145705A00,
     corresponds with IP: [XXX.YYY.112.90]
ATM: 39000000000000000000000000000A14570FA00,
     corresponds with IP: [XXX.YYY.112.250]
```

TRACE 6.10.4B TELNET OVER ATM CONNECTION SETUP

```
Sniffer Network Analyzer data from 23-Jan at 14:46:34, file JIM02.ATC, Pg 1

--------------- Frame 1 -----------------

ATM:   ——ATM Cell Header ——
ATM:
ATM:   Frame 1 arrived at  14:48:45.35599; frame size is 112 (0070 hex) bytes.
ATM:   Link = DTE
ATM:   Virtual path id = 0
ATM:   Virtual channel id = 5
ATM:
SSCOP: ——SSCOP trailer ——
SSCOP:
SSCOP: Sequenced Data PDU
SSCOP: SD send seq num N(S) = 94
SSCOP:
Q2931: ——UNI 3.x Signaling v
Q2931:
Q2931: Protocol discriminator   = 09
Q2931: Length of call reference = 3 bytes
Q2931: Call reference value     = 0003D8
Q2931: Message type             = 05 (Setup)
Q2931: Message type Flag/Action = 80
```

```
Q2931:              ...0 .... = flag
Q2931:              .... ..00 = action (Clear call)
Q2931: Message Length          = 97
Q2931:
Q2931: Info element id       = 59 (ATM traffic descriptor)
Q2931: Coding Standard/Action = 80
Q2931:              1... .... =       ext
Q2931:              .00. .... =       code stand (ITU-T standardized)
Q2931:              ...0 0000 =       IE field (not significant)
Q2931: Length of info element = 9 byte(s)
Q2931: Forward peak cell rate (CLP = 0+1)
Q2931:            id      = 132
Q2931:            rate     = 1 cells/sec
Q2931:                     424 bps
Q2931: Backward peak cell rate (CLP = 0+1)
Q2931:            id      = 133
Q2931:            rate     = 1 cells/sec
Q2931:                     424 bps
Q2931: Best effort indicator = 190
Q2931:
Q2931: Info element id       = 5E (Broadband bearer capability)
Q2931: Coding Standard/Action = 80
Q2931:              1... .... =       ext
Q2931:              .00. .... =       code stand (ITU-T standardized)
Q2931:              ...0 0000 =       IE field (not significant)
Q2931: Length of info element = 3 byte(s)
Q2931: Bearer class          = BCOB-X
Q2931: Traffic type          = No indication
Q2931: Timing requirements    = No indication
Q2931: Susceptibility to clipping = Not susceptible to clipping
Q2931: User plane conn config    = Point-to-point
Q2931:
Q2931: Info element id       = 70 (Called party number)
Q2931: Coding Standard/Action = 80
Q2931:              1... .... =       ext
Q2931:              .00. .... =       code stand (ITU-T standardized)
Q2931:              ...0 0000 =       IE field (not significant)
Q2931: Length of info element = 21 byte(s)
Q2931:              1... .... =       ext
Q2931:              .000 .... =       type of num (Unknown)
Q2931:              .... 0010 =       addressing/num plan id (ATM Endsystem Address)
Q2931: Authority and format id = DCC ATM Format
Q2931: Data country code  = 0
Q2931: HO_DSP          = 00000000000000000000
```

```
Q2931: End system id     = 0000A145705A
Q2931: selector          = 0
Q2931:
Q2931: Info element id       = 6C (Calling party number)
Q2931: Coding Standard/Action = 80
Q2931:             1... .... =     ext
Q2931:             .00. .... =     code stand (ITU-T standardized)
Q2931:             ...0 0000 =     IE field (not significant)
Q2931: Length of info element = 22 byte(s)
Q2931:             0... .... =     ext
Q2931:             .000 .... =     type of num (Unknown)
Q2931:             .... 0010 =     addressing/num plan id (ATM Endsystem Address)
Q2931:             1... .... =     ext
Q2931:             .00. .... =     Presentation indicator (Presentation allowed)
Q2931:             .... ..00 =     Screening indicator (User-provided, not screened)
Q2931: Authority and format id = DCC ATM Format
Q2931: Data country code  = 0
Q2931: HO_DSP          = 00000000000000000000
Q2931: End system id     = 0000A14570FA
Q2931: selector          = 0
Q2931:
Q2931: Info element id       = 5C (Quality of service)
Q2931: Coding Standard/Action = E0
Q2931:             1... .... =     ext
Q2931:             .11. .... =     code stand (Standard defined for network)
Q2931:             ...0 0000 =     IE field (not significant)
Q2931: Length of info element = 2 byte(s)
Q2931: QoS class
Q2931:    forward   = QoS class 0 - Unspecified QoS class
Q2931:    backward  = QoS class 0 - Unspecified QoS class
Q2931:
Q2931: Info element id       = 58 (ATM adaptation layer parameters)
Q2931: Coding Standard/Action = 80
Q2931:             1... .... =     ext
Q2931:             .00. .... =     code stand (ITU-T standardized)
Q2931:             ...0 0000 =     IE field (not significant)
Q2931: Length of info element = 11 byte(s)
Q2931: AAL type           = AAL type 5
Q2931: Forward max CPCS-SDU
Q2931:               id   = 140
Q2931:               size = 4478
Q2931: Backward max CPCS-SDU
Q2931:               id   = 129
Q2931:               size = 4478
```

```
Q2931: Mode
Q2931:                 id  = 131
Q2931:               mode  = Message mode
Q2931: UNI 3.0 signaling
Q2931: SSCS type
Q2931:    id   = 132
Q2931:    type = Null
Q2931:
Q2931: Info element id        = 5F (Broadband low layer information)
Q2931: Coding Standard/Action = 80
Q2931:              1... .... =        ext
Q2931:              .00. .... =        code stand (ITU-T standardized)
Q2931:              ...0 0000 =        IE field (not significant)
Q2931: Length of info element = 1 byte(s)
Q2931: Layer 2 protocol
Q2931:              1... .... = ext
Q2931:              .10. .... = layer 2 id
Q2931:              ...0 1100 = User info layer 2 protocol (LAN logical link control (ISO 8802/2))
Q2931:

- - - - - - - - - - - - - - - Frame 2 - - - - - - - - - - - - - - - - -

ATM:   —ATM Cell Header —
ATM:
ATM:   Frame 2 arrived at  14:48:45.38319; frame size is 24 (0018 hex) bytes.
ATM:   Link = DCE
ATM:   Virtual path id = 0
ATM:   Virtual channel id = 5
ATM:
SSCOP: —SSCOP trailer —
SSCOP:
SSCOP: Sequenced Data PDU
SSCOP: SD send seq num N(S) = 94
SSCOP:
Q2931: —UNI 3.x Signaling —
Q2931:
Q2931: Protocol discriminator   = 09
Q2931: Length of call reference = 3 bytes
Q2931: Call reference value     = 8003D8
Q2931: Message type             = 02 (Call proceeding)
Q2931: Message type Flag/Action = 80
Q2931:              ...0 .... = flag
Q2931:              .... ..00 = action (Clear call)
Q2931: Message Length           = 9
```

```
Q2931:
Q2931: Info element id      = 5A (Connection identifier)
Q2931: Coding Standard/Action = 80
Q2931:            1... .... =      ext
Q2931:            .00. .... =      code stand (ITU-T standardized)
Q2931:            ...0 0000 =      IE field (not significant)
Q2931: Length of info element = 5 byte(s)
Q2931:    1... .... = ext
Q2931:    .00. .... = spare
Q2931:    ...0 1... = VP assoc signaling
Q2931:    .... .000 = Preferred/exclusive
Q2931:       VPCI = 0
Q2931:       VCI  = 34
Q2931

- - - - - - - - - - - - - - - Frame 3 - - - - - - - - - - - - - - - - -

ATM:    ——ATM Cell Header ——
ATM:
ATM:    Frame 3 arrived at  14:48:45.44969; frame size is 24 (0018 hex) bytes.
ATM:    Link = DCE
ATM:    Virtual path id = 0
ATM:    Virtual channel id = 5
ATM:
SSCOP:  ——SSCOP trailer ——
SSCOP:
SSCOP:  Sequenced Data PDU
SSCOP:  SD send seq num N(S) = 95
SSCOP:
Q2931:  ——UNI 3.x Signaling ——
Q2931:
Q2931:  Protocol discriminator  = 09
Q2931:  Length of call reference = 3 bytes
Q2931:  Call reference value    = 8003D8
Q2931:  Message type            = 07 (Connect)
Q2931:  Message type Flag/Action = 80
Q2931:            ...0 .... = flag
Q2931:            .... ..00 = action (Clear call)
Q2931:  Message Length          = 9
Q2931:
Q2931:  Info element id      = 5A (Connection identifier)
Q2931:  Coding Standard/Action = 80
Q2931:            1... .... =      ext
Q2931:            .00. .... =      code stand (ITU-T standardized)
```

```
Q2931:          ...0 0000 =       IE field (not significant)
Q2931:  Length of info element = 5 byte(s)
Q2931:     1... .... = ext
Q2931:     .00. .... = spare
Q2931:     ...0 1... = VP assoc signaling
Q2931:     .... .000 = Preferred/exclusive
Q2931:        VPCI = 0
Q2931:        VCI  = 34
Q2931

- - - - - - - - - - - - - - - Frame 4 - - - - - - - - - - - - - - - - -

ATM:  ——ATM Cell Header ——
ATM:
ATM:  Frame 4 arrived at  14:48:45.45191; frame size is 48 (0030 hex) bytes.
ATM:  Link = DTE
ATM:  Virtual path id = 0
ATM:  Virtual channel id = 34
ATM:
LLC:  ——LLC Header ——
LLC:
LLC:  DSAP Address = AA, DSAP IG Bit = 00 (Individual Address)
LLC:  SSAP Address = AA, SSAP CR Bit = 00 (Command)
LLC:  Unnumbered frame: UI
LLC:
SNAP:  ——SNAP Header ——
SNAP:
SNAP:  Type = 0806 (ARP)
SNAP:
ARP:  ——ARP/RARP frame ——
ARP:
ARP:  Hardware type = 19 (ATM)
ARP:  Protocol type = 0800 (IP)
ARP:  Source ATM num
ARP:        type = ATM Forum NSAPA format
ARP:      length = 20
ARP:  Target ATM subaddr
ARP:        type = ATM Forum NSAPA format
ARP:      length = 0
ARP:  Opcode 8 (InARP_REQUEST)
ARP:  Length of source prot addr      = 4
ARP:  Target ATM num
ARP:        type = ATM Forum NSAPA format
ARP:      length = 0
```

```
ARP:    Target ATM num
ARP:         type = ATM Forum NSAPA format
ARP:       length = 0
ARP:    Length of target prot addr     = 4
ARP:    source ATM num  = 39000000000000000000000000000A14570FA00
ARP:    source prot addr  = [XXX.YYY.112.250]
ARP:    target prot addr  = [0.0.0.0]
ARP:

- - - - - - - - - - - - - - - Frame 5 - - - - - - - - - - - - - - - - -

ATM:    —ATM Cell Header —
ATM:
ATM:    Frame 5 arrived at  14:48:45.45272; frame size is 16 (0010 hex) bytes.
ATM:    Link = DTE
ATM:    Virtual path id = 0
ATM:    Virtual channel id = 5
ATM:
SSCOP:  —SSCOP trailer —
SSCOP:
SSCOP:  Sequenced Data PDU
SSCOP:  SD send seq num N(S) = 95
SSCOP:
Q2931:  —UNI 3.x Signaling —
Q2931:
Q2931:  Protocol discriminator   = 09
Q2931:  Length of call reference = 3 bytes
Q2931:  Call reference value     = 0003D8
Q2931:  Message type             = 0F (Connect acknowledge)
Q2931:  Message type Flag/Action = 80
Q2931:               ...0 .... = flag
Q2931:               .... ..00 = action (Clear call)
Q2931:  Message Length           = 0

- - - - - - - - - - - - - - - Frame 6 - - - - - - - - - - - - - - - - -

ATM:    —ATM Cell Header —
ATM:
ATM:    Frame 6 arrived at  14:48:45.45296; frame size is 68 (0044 hex) bytes.
ATM:    Link = DCE
ATM:    Virtual path id = 0
ATM:    Virtual channel id = 34
ATM:
LLC:    —LLC Header —
```

```
LLC:
LLC:  DSAP Address = AA, DSAP IG Bit = 00 (Individual Address)
LLC:  SSAP Address = AA, SSAP CR Bit = 00 (Command)
LLC:  Unnumbered frame: UI
LLC:
SNAP:  ---SNAP Header óó
SNAP:
SNAP:  Type = 0806 (ARP)
SNAP:
ARP:  —ARP/RARP frame —
ARP:
ARP:  Hardware type = 19 (ATM)
ARP:  Protocol type = 0800 (IP)
ARP:  Source ATM num
ARP:        type = ATM Forum NSAPA format
ARP:      length = 20
ARP:  Target ATM subaddr
ARP:        type = ATM Forum NSAPA format
ARP:      length = 0
ARP:  Opcode 9 (InARP_REPLY)
ARP:  Length of source prot addr     = 4
ARP:  Target ATM num
ARP:        type = ATM Forum NSAPA format
ARP:      length = 20
ARP:  Target ATM num
ARP:        type = ATM Forum NSAPA format
ARP:      length = 0
ARP:  Length of target prot addr     = 4
ARP:  source ATM num  = 3900000000000000000000000000A145705A00
ARP:  source prot addr  = [XXX.YYY.112.90]
ARP:  target ATM num  = 3900000000000000000000000000A14570FA00
ARP:  target prot addr  = [XXX.YYY.112.250]
ARP:
```

Now that the ATM connection is established between the router and the ATM switch, the TCP connection between the TELNET client (the PC) and the TELNET server (the Sun) may proceed. This communication is illustrated in Frames 7–9 (Trace 6.10.4c). In Frame 7, the client initiates the three-way handshake with SYN, ISN = 0. The Sun responds in Frame 8 with SYN, ISN = 2339991040, ACK = 1. The client then confirms the connection in Frame 9 with ACK, SEQ = 1, ACK = 2339991041. The workstation and server are now logically configured for a connection to Port 23 (TELNET). As a final note, look at the ATM Cell Header and observe that the virtual circuit that was established between the ATM switch and the router is now in use (VPI = 0, VCI = 34).

TRACE 6.10.4C. TELNET OVER ATM TCP THREE-WAY HANDSHAKE

```
Sniffer Network Analyzer data from 23-Jan at 14:46:34, JIM02.ATC, Pg 1

- - - - - - - - - - - - - - - Frame 7 - - - - - - - - - - - - - - - - -

ATM:  —ATM Cell Header —
ATM:
ATM:  Frame 7 arrived at  14:48:45.92383; frame size is 52 (0034 hex) bytes.
ATM:  Link = DTE
ATM:  Virtual path id = 0
ATM:  Virtual channel id = 34
ATM:
LLC:  ---LLC Header óó
LLC:
LLC:  DSAP Address = AA, DSAP IG Bit = 00 (Individual Address)
LLC:  SSAP Address = AA, SSAP CR Bit = 00 (Command)
LLC:  Unnumbered frame: UI
LLC:
SNAP:  —SNAP Header —
SNAP:
SNAP:  Type = 0800 (IP)
SNAP:
IP:   ---IP Header óó
IP:
IP:   Version = 4, header length = 20 bytes
IP:   Type of service = 00
IP:        000. .... = routine
IP:        ...0 .... = normal delay
IP:        .... 0... = normal throughput
IP:        .... .0.. = normal reliability
IP:   Total length    = 44 bytes
IP:   Identification  = 60067
IP:   Flags           = 0X
IP:        .0.. .... = may fragment
IP:        ..0. .... = last fragment
IP:   Fragment offset = 0 bytes
IP:   Time to live    = 31 seconds/hops
IP:   Protocol        = 6 (TCP)
IP:   Header checksum = 8CE4 (correct)
IP:   Source address      = [XXX.YYY.113.95]
IP:   Destination address = [XXX.YYY.112.90]
IP:   No options
IP:
TCP:  —TCP header —
```

```
TCP:
TCP:  Source port          = 1405
TCP:  Destination port     = 23 (Telnet)
TCP:  Initial sequence number = 0
TCP:  Data offset          = 24 bytes
TCP:  Flags                = 02
TCP:              ..0. .... = (No urgent pointer)
TCP:              ...0 .... = (No acknowledgment)
TCP:              .... 0... = (No push)
TCP:              .... .0.. = (No reset)
TCP:              .... ..1. = SYN
TCP:              .... ...0 = (No FIN)
TCP:  Window               = 512
TCP:  Checksum             = 6C4E (correct)
TCP:
TCP:  Options follow
TCP:  Maximum segment size   = 1460
TCP:

- - - - - - - - - - - - - - - Frame 8 - - - - - - - - - - - - - - - -

ATM: ——ATM Cell Header ——
ATM:
ATM: Frame 8 arrived at  14:48:45.92584; frame size is 52 (0034 hex) bytes.
ATM: Link = DCE
ATM: Virtual path id = 0
ATM: Virtual channel id = 34
ATM:
LLC:  ——LLC Header ——
LLC:
LLC:  DSAP Address = AA, DSAP IG Bit = 00 (Individual Address)
LLC:  SSAP Address = AA, SSAP CR Bit = 00 (Command)
LLC:  Unnumbered frame: UI
LLC:
SNAP:  ——SNAP Header ——
SNAP:
SNAP:  Type = 0800 (IP)
SNAP:
IP:   ——IP Header ——
IP:
IP:   Version = 4, header length = 20 bytes
IP:   Type of service = 00
IP:        000. .... = routine
IP:        ...0 .... = normal delay
```

```
IP:        .... 0... = normal throughput
IP:        .... .0.. = normal reliability
IP:    Total length    = 44 bytes
IP:    Identification  = 22919
IP:    Flags           = 4X
IP:        .1.. .... = donít fragment
IP:        ..0. .... = last fragment
IP:    Fragment offset = 0 bytes
IP:    Time to live    = 255 seconds/hops
IP:    Protocol        = 6 (TCP)
IP:    Header checksum = FDFF (correct)
IP:    Source address       = [XXX.YYY.112.90]
IP:    Destination address = [XXX.YYY.113.95]
IP:    No options
IP:
TCP:  ——TCP header ——
TCP:
TCP:  Source port            = 23 (Telnet)
TCP:  Destination port       = 1405
TCP:  Initial sequence number = 2339991040
TCP:  Acknowledgment number   = 1
TCP:  Data offset            = 24 bytes
TCP:  Flags                  = 12
TCP:              ..0. .... = (No urgent pointer)
TCP:              ...1 .... = Acknowledgment
TCP:              .... 0... = (No push)
TCP:              .... .0.. = (No reset)
TCP:              .... ..1. = SYN
TCP:              .... ...0 = (No FIN)
TCP:  Window                 = 64240
TCP:  Checksum               = 79D2 (correct)
TCP:
TCP:  Options follow
TCP:  Maximum segment size   = 1460
TCP:

- - - - - - - - - - - - - - - Frame 9 - - - - - - - - - - - - - - - -

ATM:  ——ATM Cell Header ——
ATM:
ATM:  Frame 9 arrived at  14:48:45.92857; frame size is 54 (0036 hex) bytes.
ATM:  Link = DTE
ATM:  Virtual path id = 0
ATM:  Virtual channel id = 34
```

```
ATM:
LLC: ——LLC Header ——
LLC:
LLC: DSAP Address = AA, DSAP IG Bit = 00 (Individual Address)
LLC: SSAP Address = AA, SSAP CR Bit = 00 (Command)
LLC: Unnumbered frame: UI
LLC:
SNAP: ——SNAP Header ——
SNAP:
SNAP: Type = 0800 (IP)
SNAP:
IP: ——IP Header ——
IP:
IP: Version = 4, header length = 20 bytes
IP: Type of service = 00
IP:      000. .... = routine
IP:      ...0 .... = normal delay
IP:      .... 0... = normal throughput
IP:      .... .0.. = normal reliability
IP: Total length    = 40 bytes
IP: Identification  = 60068
IP: Flags           = 0X
IP:      .0.. .... = may fragment
IP:      ..0. .... = last fragment
IP: Fragment offset = 0 bytes
IP: Time to live    = 31 seconds/hops
IP: Protocol        = 6 (TCP)
IP: Header checksum = 8CE7 (correct)
IP: Source address      = [XXX.YYY.113.95]
IP: Destination address = [XXX.YYY.112.90]
IP: No options
IP:
TCP: ——TCP header ——
TCP:
TCP: Source port            = 1405
TCP: Destination port       = 23 (Telnet)
TCP: Sequence number        = 1
TCP: Acknowledgment number  = 2339991041
TCP: Data offset            = 20 bytes
TCP: Flags                  = 18
TCP:            ..0. .... = (No urgent pointer)
TCP:            ...1 .... = Acknowledgment
TCP:            .... 1... = Push
TCP:            .... .0.. = (No reset)
```

```
TCP:            .... ..0. = (No SYN)
TCP:            .... ...0 = (No FIN)
TCP:  Window              = 512
TCP:  Checksum            = 8A78 (correct)
TCP:  No TCP options
TCP:
```

The TELNET session then continues until the end users have completed their business. At that time, the TELNET session is terminated, the TCP connection is also terminated, and the ATM connection is then ready to be taken down. The ATM disconnect sequence is shown in Frames 132 and 135 (Trace 6.10.4d). Note that in Frame 132, the call reference (0003D8) matches the call reference of the initial connection in Frame 1, and that the Q.2931 message type is a RELEASE. A single IE specifies the cause of the release (normal). Frame 135 confirms the release with a RELEASE COMPLETE message. As with the previous frame, this message is sent over the signaling channel (VPI = 0 and VCI = 5.)

In summary, TCP/IP communication over a connection-oriented network such as ATM requires steps for call setup and disconnect that a connectionless network such as an Ethernet does not require. In our next case study, we return to a token ring network example and see how electronic mail communication can present a challenge.

TRACE 6.10.4D. TELNET OVER ATM CONNECTION RELEASE

```
Sniffer Network Analyzer data from 23-Jan at 14:46:34, file JIM02.ATC, Pg 1

- - - - - - - - - - - - - - - Frame 132 - - - - - - - - - - - - - - - - -

ATM: —ATM Cell Header —
ATM:
ATM: Frame 132 arrived at  14:49:11.93324; frame size is 20 (0014 hex) bytes.
ATM: Link = DTE
ATM: Virtual path id = 0
ATM: Virtual channel id = 5
ATM:
SSCOP: —SSCOP trailer —
SSCOP:
SSCOP: Sequenced Data PDU
SSCOP: SD send seq num N(S) = 98
SSCOP:
Q2931: —UNI 3.x Signaling —
Q2931:
Q2931: Protocol discriminator  = 09
Q2931: Length of call reference = 3 bytes
```

```
Q2931: Call reference value    = 0003D8
Q2931: Message type            = 4D (Release)
Q2931: Message type Flag/Action = 80
Q2931:             ...0 .... = flag
Q2931:             .... ..00 = action (Clear call)
Q2931: Message Length          = 6
Q2931:
Q2931: Info element id         = 08 (Cause)
Q2931: Coding Standard/Action = 80
Q2931: 1... .... =        ext
Q2931: .00. .... =        code stand(ITU-T standardized)
Q2931: ...0 0000 =        IE field(not significant)
Q2931: Length of info element = 2 byte(s)
Q2931: Octet 5
Q2931: 1... .... = ext
Q2931: .000 .... = spare
Q2931: .... 0000 = location(User)
Q2931: cause value = normal, unspecified
Q2931
- - - - - - - - - - - - - - - Frame 135 - - - - - - - - - - - - - - - - -
ATM: —ATM Cell Header —
ATM:
ATM: Frame 135 arrived at  14:49:11.94152; frame size is 20 (0014 hex) bytes.
ATM: Link = DCE
ATM: Virtual path id = 0
ATM: Virtual channel id = 5
ATM:
SSCOP: —SSCOP trailer —
SSCOP:
SSCOP: Sequenced Data PDU
SSCOP: SD send seq num N(S) = 98
SSCOP:
Q2931: —UNI 3.x Signaling —
Q2931:
Q2931: Protocol discriminator  = 09
Q2931: Length of call reference = 3 bytes
Q2931: Call reference value    = 8003D8
Q2931: Message type            = 5A (Release complete)
Q2931: Message type Flag/Action = 80
Q2931:             ...0 .... = flag
Q2931:             .... ..00 = action (Clear call)
Q2931: Message Length          = 6
Q2931:
Q2931: Info element id         = 08 (Cause)
```

```
Q2931: Coding Standard/Action = 80
Q2931: 1... .... =          ext
Q2931: .00. .... =          code stand(ITU-T standardized)
Q2931: ...0 0000 =          IE field(not significant)
Q2931: Length of info element = 2 byte(s)
Q2931: Octet 5
Q2931: 1... .... = ext
Q2931: .000 .... = spare
Q2931: .... 0000 = location(User)
Q2931: cause value = normal, unspecified
Q2931:
```

6.10.5 SMTP Interoperability Problems

One of the premises of any mail system – be it the postal service, voice messaging, or an electronic text system – is that it must be a duplex, not a simplex, operation. Duplex means that if I send you a message, you should be able to reply to me. Let's see what happens when this assumption is invalid.

The network in this case study is a single token ring to which a number of dissimilar workstations are attached (see Figure 6-15). The underlying operating systems are all variants of UNIX running on IBM RS/6000 and Sun SPARCstation II workstations. All of these workstations are implementing an SMTP package and theoretically should be interoperable. Unfortunately, this theory proves incorrect. When the RS/6000 sends a message to the Sun SPARCstation II (SS2), the message is delivered properly. But when the SS2 replies to the message, the delivery fails. The process for each workstation is as follows:

1. The user invokes the workstation's native mail program (Sendmail) to send a message.
2. The Sendmail program invokes SMTP for delivery via the network.
3. The recipient workstation obtains the SMTP message from the network and sends it to its native mail program (also Sendmail in this case).
4. The Sendmail program deposits the message in the recipient user's mailbox.

The process thus involves two significant operations. One – Steps 1 and 4 – is visible to the workstation but invisible to the network, while the other – Steps 2 and 3 – is visible to the network but invisible to the workstation.

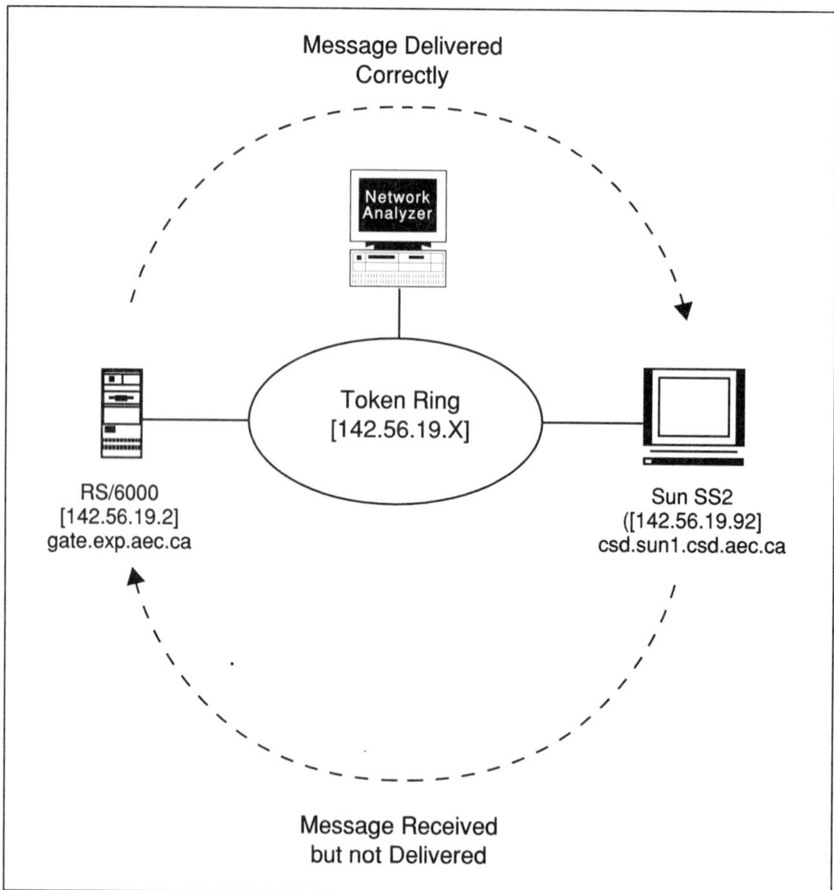

Figure 6-15 Mail Delivery Incompatibilities

In Trace 6.10.5, we see the portion that is visible to the network and thus available for capture by the network analyzer (note that this trace was filtered to remove non-SMTP frames, so all frames are not necessarily in sequential order). The first scenario involves the RS/6000 sending a message to the SS2. The following steps are involved:

1. Establishing the SMTP connection:
   HELO <SP> <source mailbox> <CRLF>
   shown in Frames 535–537

2. Identifying the message originator:
   MAIL <SP> FROM: <source mailbox> <CRLF>
   shown in Frames 538–539

3. Identifying the message recipient:
   RCPT <SP> TO: <receiving mailbox> <CRLF>
   shown in Frames 540–541
4. Transferring the text of the message:
   DATA <CRLF>
   shown in Frames 542–548
5. Closing the SMTP connection:
   QUIT <CRLF>
   shown in Frames 549–550

To verify that the message was delivered, the recipient host (SS2) transmits a "delivering mail..." message in Frame 550. The host process (invisible to the network) then takes over, delivering the mail to the recipient's mailbox. The message appears at the SS2, and all is well.

To verify the connectivity, the SS2 then attempts to reply to the message from the RS/6000. Unfortunately, this operation is unsuccessful and the failure is not readily apparent from the network's point of view. Reviewing Trace 6.10.5, we see a similar mail scenario:

1. Establishing connection: Frames 580–582
2. Identifying originator: Frames 583–594
3. Identifying recipient: Frames 595–597
4. Transferring text: Frames 598–603
5. Closing connection: Frames 604–605

This message was never delivered from the SS2 to the RS/6000, although that isn't readily apparent from the trace file. The clue that a problem existed was found by comparing the acknowledgment messages from the recipients. Recall that the message from the RS/6000 to the SS2 was received and delivered to the end user. The SS2 returned the following message in Frame 548:

```
250 Mail accepted <0D><0A>
```

The message from the SS2 to the RS/6000 was received but not delivered to the end user. The RS/6000 returned the following message in Frame 603:

```
250 Ok <0D><0A>
```

The differences in the two host acknowledgments prompted the network manager, Chris, to check the error log on the RS/6000 host. This is what he found:

```
  ----Transcript of session follows ----
>> HELO gate.exp.aec.ca
<<< 553 Local configuration error, hostname not recognized as local
554 <cdutchyn@gate.exp.aec.ca.>... Service unavailable: Bad file
number
  ----Unsent message follows ----
Received: from csd_sun1.csd.aec.ca by gate.exp.aec.ca (AIX 3.1/UCB
5.61/4.03)
       id AA28142; Thu, 16 Apr 92 11:30:44 -0600
Received: by csd_sun1.csd.aec.ca.csd.aec.ca
       id AA00372; Thu, 16 Apr 92 11:37:42 MDT
Date: Thu, 16 Apr 92 11:37:42 MDT
From: cdutchyn@csd.aec.ca (Christopher J. Dutchyn)
Message-Id: <9204161737.AA00372@csd_sun1.csd.aec.ca.csd.aec.ca>
To: cdutchyn@gate.exp.aec.ca.
Subject: This is a test.

This is a test response.  If it were a real response, it would
contain more information about what you should know.

Chris
```

The message indicates that the SS2 placed an extra period (.) at the end of the intended recipient's address. Therefore, the recipient was noted as <cdutchyn@gate.exp.aec.ca.> instead of <cdutchyn@gate.exp.aec.ca>. When the address was delivered to the RS/6000 (gate.exp.aec.ca), the RS/6000 was unable to recognize its own address because of the additional period. As a result, the connection failed at the HELO message and the following message was returned:

```
553 Local Configuration error,
       hostname not recognized as local
```

Since this error message occurred in the SMTP process within the RS/6000 host and was never transmitted via the network to the SS2, the message transfer appeared fine from a protocol point of view. Only when the error log of the RS/6000 host was examined did the actual source of the problem (the extraneous period after "ca") surface. Chris then studied the configuration of the SS2 host in greater detail, discovered a configuration error in the name server, and corrected the problem.

TRACE 6.10.5. SMTP MAIL SERVICE SUMMARY

Sniffer Network Analyzer data 16-Apr at 10:35:48, file SMTP.TRC, Pg 1

SUMMARY	Delta T	Destination	Source	Summary
535		RS/6000	SUN SS2	SMTP R PORT=2047 220 csd_sun1.csd.aec.ca. csd.aec.ca
536	0.004	SUN SS2	RS/6000	SMTP C PORT=2047 HELO gate.exp.aec.ca <0D><0A>
537	0.007	RS/6000	SUN SS2	SMTP R PORT=2047 250 csd_sun1.csd.aec.ca. csd.aec.ca Hello gate.exp....
538	0.003	SUN SS2	RS/6000	SMTP C PORT=2047 MAIL From:<cdutchyn @gate.exp.aec.ca> <0D><0A>
539	0.143	RS/6000	SUN SS2	SMTP R PORT=2047 250 postmaster Sender ok<0D><0A>
540	0.012	SUN SS2	RS/6000	SMTP C PORT=2047 RCPT To:<cdutchyn @csd_sun1.csd.aec.ca> <0D><0A>
541	0.111	RS/6000	SUN SS2	SMTP R PORT=2047 250 <cdutchyn @csd_sun1.csd.aec.ca> ... Recipient ok...
542	0.004	SUN SS2	RS/6000	SMTP C PORT=2047 DATA<0D><0A>
543	0.055	RS/6000	SUN SS2	SMTP R PORT=2047 354 Enter mail, end with "." on a line by itself<0D>...
545	0.026	SUN SS2	RS/6000	SMTP C PORT=2047 Received: by gate.exp.aec.ca
547	0.200	SUN SS2	RS/6000	SMTP C PORT=2047 .<0D><0A>
548	0.008	RS/6000	SUN SS2	SMTP R PORT=2047 250 Mail accepted <0D><0A>
549	0.004	SUN SS2	RS/6000	SMTP C PORT=2047 QUIT<0D><0A>

550	0.003	RS/6000	SUN SS2	SMTP R PORT=2047 221 csd_sun1.csd.aec.ca. csd.aec.ca delivering mail...
580	63.636	SUN SS2	RS/6000	SMTP R PORT=1041 220 gate.exp.aec.ca
581	0.006	RS/6000	SUN SS2	SMTP C PORT=1041 HELO csd_sun1.csd.aec.ca. csd.aec.ca<0D><0A>
582	0.007	SUN SS2	RS/6000	SMTP R PORT=1041 250 gate.exp.aec.ca Hello csd_sun1.csd.aec.ca. csd....
583	0.004	RS/6000	SUN SS2	SMTP C PORT=1041 MAIL From:<cdutchyn @csd.aec.ca><0D><0A>
594	1.229	SUN SS2	RS/6000	SMTP R PORT=1041 250 <cdutchyn @csd.aec.ca>... Sender ok<0D><0A>
595	0.006	RS/6000	SUN SS2	SMTP C PORT=1041 RCPT To:<cdutchyn @gate.exp.aec.ca.> <0D><0A>
597	1.029	SUN SS2	RS/6000	SMTP R PORT=1041 250 <cdutchyn @gate.exp.aec.ca.> Recipient ok<0D>...
598	0.004	RS/6000	SUN SS2	SMTP C PORT=1041 DATA<0D><0A>
599	0.018	SUN SS2	RS/6000	SMTP R PORT=1041 354 Enter mail, end with "." on a line by itself<0D>...
600	0.016	RS/6000	SUN SS2	SMTP C PORT=1041 Received: by csd_sun1.csd.aec.ca. csd.aec.ca.
602	0.035	RS/6000	SUN SS2	SMTP C PORT=1041 .<0D><0A>
603	0.117	SUN SS2	RS/6000	SMTP R PORT=1041 250 Ok<0D><0A>
604	0.006	RS/6000	SUN SS2	SMTP C PORT=1041 QUIT<0D><0A>
605	0.022	SUN SS2	RS/6000	SMTP R PORT=1041 221 gate.exp.aec.ca closing connection <0D><0A>

6.10.6 NetBIOS and TCP Interactions

The following example of NetBIOS service illustrates how all of the ARPA layers must cooperate in order to ensure proper protocol operation. The objective in this case study is for one workstation (shown as Art in Trace 6.10.6a) to use the resources on another workstation, known as Robert (Figure 6-16). The trace begins with Art broadcasting a NetBIOS Name Service (DNS) Query looking for Robert. Details of the query in Frame 1 of Trace 6.10.6b show a Source port of 275 assigned to NetBIOS service within the UDP header. The query consists of a single question providing the name, type, and class of the object. The response returned in Frame 2 provides necessary details about Robert. These details include the uniqueness of the name and that Robert is a B-type (broadcast) node with an IP address of [XXX.YYY.200.85]. Now that Art knows more about Robert, he can use Robert's resources.

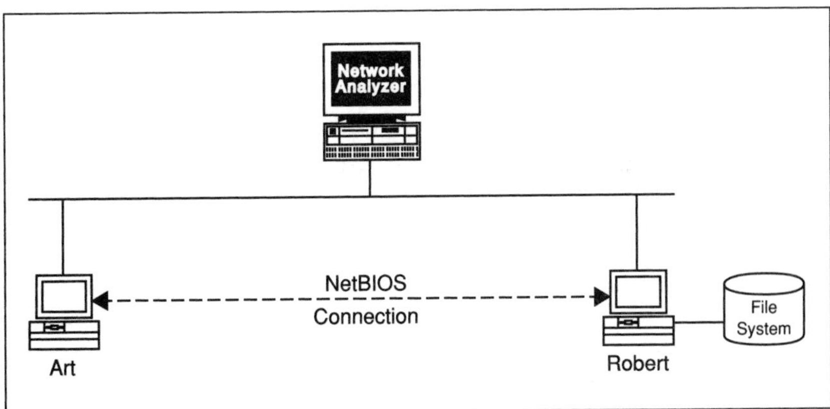

Figure 6-16 Workstation Communication Using NetBIOS

Frames 3–5 show a TCP connection initiated by Art and accepted by Robert. The NetBIOS Session Service begins in Frame 6 and is shown in detail in Trace 6.10.6c. Art begins with a NetBIOS Session Request message (Type = 81) having a length of 74 octets. The data consists of the called and calling names, ROBERT and ARTL, respectively. Robert then responds with a Positive Response (or Session Confirm) message, Type = 82. The logical session is now established.

Art must now negotiate the language he will use to communicate with Robert. To do so, he uses the Server Message Block (SMB) protocol. SMB was developed by Microsoft Corp. to enable a DOS-based client workstation to communicate with its server. SMB information is carried as data inside a NetBIOS message. Speaking in OSI terms, NetBIOS is providing the Session Layer (i.e., logical) connection while SMB information defines the format of the data to be transmitted and thus provides

Presentation Layer functions. We see the protocol being negotiated in Frames 9 and 11.

The connection that Art is really after – access to Robert's disk drive – is shown in Frames 13 and 15 (see Trace 6.10.6d). This process is completed in Frame 19. Art may then search the specified directory on Robert's disk (Frame 22), finding one file in Frame 24. A subsequent search (Frame 26) returns ten additional filenames (Frame 28). No more files are noted in Frame 33, prompting Art to his next task: finding the disk attributes (Frames 35 and 38). Finished with his work, Art issues an SMB Disconnection message (Frame 40), which is acknowledged in Frame 42. The TCP connection is then torn down, using the FIN messages from both Art and Robert in Frames 44 and 45, respectively.

Notice the pattern of protocol operation: TCP establishes the end-to-end connection before NetBIOS and SMB undertake the logical session. When there is no longer a need for communication, the higher layer protocol (SMB) terminates the logical connection and TCP then terminates the end-to-end connection. We will use this process of multi-layer protocol interaction in our next case study, which investigates the operation of a Windows-based workstation.

TRACE 6.10.6A. NETBIOS OVER UDP AND TCP (SUMMARY)

```
Sniffer Network Analyzer data 6-Nov at 11:04:32, TCPNETB.ENC, Pg 1

SUMMARY  Delta T   Destination  Source   Summary
M   1              Broadcast    Art      DNS C ID=41128
                                          OP=QUERY
                                          NAME=ROBERT
    2   0.0018     Art          Robert   DNS R ID=41128 STAT=OK
    3   0.0243     Robert       Art      TCP D=139 S=257 SYN
                                          SEQ=172249 LEN=0
                                          WIN=1024
    4   0.0028     Art          Robert   TCP D=257 S=139 SYN
                                          ACK=172250 SEQ=257461
                                          LEN=0 WIN=2152
    5   0.0160     Robert       Art      TCP D=139 S=257
                                          ACK=257462 WIN=1024
    6   0.0046     Robert       Art      NETB D=ROBERT S=ARTL<00>
                                          Session request
    7   0.0041     Art          Robert   NETB Session confirm
    8   0.0204     Robert       Art      TCP D=139 S=257
                                          ACK=257466 WIN=1020
    9   0.0106     Robert       Art      SMB C PC NETWORK PROGRAM  1.0
   10   0.0043     Art          Robert   TCP D=257 S=139
                                          ACK=172391 WIN=2011
   11   0.0036     Art          Robert   SMB R Negotiated Protocol 0
```

12	0.0191	Robert	Art	TCP D=139 S=257 ACK=257507 WIN=979
13	0.0096	Robert	Art	SMB C Connect A:\\ROBERT\DISK
14	0.0048	Art	Robert	TCP D=257 S=139 ACK=172451 WIN=1951
15	0.0077	Art	Robert	SMB R T=8F15 Connected
16	0.0138	Robert	Art	TCP D=139 S=257 ACK=257550 WIN=936
17	0.0347	Robert	Art	SMB C End of Process
18	0.0057	Art	Robert	TCP D=257 S=139 ACK=172490 WIN=1912
19	0.0057	Art	Robert	SMB R OK
20	0.0163	Robert	Art	TCP D=139 S=257 ACK=257589 WIN=897
21	0.1437	Art	Robert	TCP D=257 S=139 ACK=172490 WIN=2152
22	19.4487	Robert	Art	SMB C Search \????????.???
23	0.0054	Art	Robert	TCP D=257 S=139 ACK=172551 WIN=2091
24	0.0157	Art	Robert	SMB R 1 entry found (done)
25	0.0157	Robert	Art	TCP D=139 S=257 ACK=257676 WIN=810
26	0.0676	Robert	Art	SMB C Search \????????.???
27	0.0054	Art	Robert	TCP D=257 S=139 ACK=172612 WIN=2030
28	0.0276	Art	Robert	SMB R 10 entries found (done)
29	0.0188	Robert	Art	TCP D=139 S=257 ACK=258150 WIN=1024
30	0.1490	Art	Robert	TCP D=257 S=139 ACK=172612 WIN=2152
31	0.0852	Robert	Art	SMB C Continue Search
32	0.0052	Art	Robert	TCP D=257 S=139 ACK=172681 WIN=2083
33	0.0098	Art	Robert	SMB R No more files
34	0.0135	Robert	Art	TCP D=139 S=257 ACK=258194 WIN=980
35	0.0127	Robert	Art	SMB C Get Disk Attributes
36	0.0051	Art	Robert	TCP D=257 S=139 ACK=172720 WIN=2044
37	0.2589	Art	Robert	TCP D=257 S=139 ACK=172720 WIN=2152
38	0.9522	Art	Robert	SMB R Got Disk Attributes

39	0.0144	Robert	Art	TCP D=139 S=257 ACK=258243 WIN=931
40	4.5501	Robert	Art	SMB C T=8F15 Disconnect
41	0.0059	Art	Robert	TCP D=257 S=139 ACK=172759 WIN=2113
42	0.0057	Art	Robert	SMB R OK
43	0.0173	Robert	Art	TCP D=139 S=257 ACK=258282 WIN=892
44	0.0146	Robert	Art	TCP D=139 S=257 FIN ACK=258282 SEQ=172759 LEN=0 WIN=892
45	0.0029	Art	Robert	TCP D=257 S=139 FIN ACK=172760 SEQ=258282 LEN=0 WIN=2113
46	0.0116	Robert	Art	TCP D=139 S=257 ACK=258283 WIN=892
47	2.5477	Robert	Art	TCP D=139 S=257 ACK=258283 WIN=892
48	0.0018	Art	Robert	TCP D=257 S=139 RST WIN=892

TRACE 6.10.6B. NETBIOS NAME SERVICE QUERY/RESPONSE

Sniffer Network Analyzer data 6-Nov at 11:04:32, TCPNETB.ENC, Pg 1

```
- - - - - - - - - - - - - - - Frame 1 - - - - - - - - - - - - - - - - -

DLC:  ——DLC Header ——
DLC:
DLC:  Frame 1 arrived at  11:04:51.3527; frame size is 92 (005C hex) bytes.
DLC:  Destination = BROADCAST FFFFFFFFFFFF, Broadcast
DLC:  Source      = Station Bridge011084, Art
DLC:  Ethertype  = 0800 (IP)
DLC:
IP:    ——IP Header ——
IP:
IP:    Version = 4, header length = 20 bytes
IP:    Type of service = 00
IP:          000. .... = routine
IP:          ...0 .... = normal delay
IP:          .... 0... = normal throughput
IP:          .... .0.. = normal reliability
IP:    Total length = 78 bytes
IP:    Identification = 19
```

```
IP:   Flags = 0X
IP:   .0.. .... = may fragment
IP:   ..0. .... = last fragment
IP:   Fragment offset = 0 bytes
IP:   Time to live = 30 seconds/hops
IP:   Protocol = 17 (UDP)
IP:   Header checksum = 1420 (correct)
IP:   Source address = [XXX.YYY.200.99]
IP:   Destination address = [255.255.255.255]
IP:   No options
IP:
UDP:  ——UDP Header ——
UDP:
UDP:  Source port = 275 (NetBIOS)
UDP:  Destination port = 137
UDP:  Length = 58
UDP:  Checksum = 8153 (correct)
UDP:
DNS:  ---Internet Domain Name Service header óó
DNS:
DNS:  ID = 41128
DNS:  Flags = 01
DNS:  0... .... = Command
DNS:  .000 0... = Query
DNS:  .... ..0. = Not truncated
DNS:  .... ...1 = Recursion desired
DNS:  Flags = 1X
DNS:  ...1 .... = Broadcast packet
DNS:  Question count = 1, Answer count = 0
DNS:  Authority count = 0, Additional record count = 0
DNS:
DNS:  Question section:
DNS:     Name = ROBERT
DNS:     Type = NetBIOS name service (NetBIOS name,32)
DNS:     Class = Internet (IN,1)
DNS:
DNS:  [Normal end of "Internet Domain Name Service header".]
DNS:

- - - - - - - - - - - - - - - Frame 2 - - - - - - - - - - - - - - - - -

DLC:  ——DLC Header ——
DLC:
DLC:  Frame 2 arrived at  11:04:51.3545; frame size is 104 (0068 hex) bytes.
```

```
DLC:  Destination = Station Bridge011084, Art
DLC:  Source      = Station U-B   F5D800, Robert
DLC:  Ethertype   = 0800 (IP)
DLC:
IP:   —IP Header —
IP:
IP:   Version = 4, header length = 20 bytes
IP:   Type of service = 00
IP:        000. .... = routine
IP:        ...0 .... = normal delay
IP:        .... 0... = normal throughput
IP:        .... .0.. = normal reliability
IP:   Total length = 90 bytes
IP:   Identification = 18756
IP:   Flags = 0X
IP:   .0.. .... = may fragment
IP:   ..0. .... = last fragment
IP:   Fragment offset = 0 bytes
IP:   Time to live = 60 seconds/hops
IP:   Protocol = 17 (UDP)
IP:   Header checksum = 2483 (correct)
IP:   Source address = [XXX.YYY.200.85]
IP:   Destination address = [XXX.YYY.200.99]
IP:   No options
IP:
UDP:  —UDP Header —
UDP:
UDP:  Source port = 137 (NetBIOS)
UDP:  Destination port = 275
UDP:  Length = 70
UDP:  Checksum = EC85 (correct)
UDP:
DNS:  —Internet Domain Name Service header—
DNS:
DNS:  ID = 41128
DNS:  Flags = 85
DNS:  1... .... = Response
DNS:  .... .1.. = Authoritative answer
DNS:  .000 0... = Query
DNS:  .... ..0. = Not truncated
DNS:  Flags = 0X
DNS:  ...0 .... = Unicast packet
DNS:  0... .... = Recursion not available
DNS:  Response code = OK (0)
```

```
DNS: Question count = 0, Answer count = 1
DNS: Authority count = 0, Additional record count = 0
DNS: Answer section:
DNS:    Name = ROBERT
DNS:    Type = NetBIOS name service (NetBIOS name,32)
DNS:    Class = Internet (IN,1)
DNS:    Time-to-live = 0 (seconds)
DNS: Node flags = 00
DNS:  0... .... = Unique NetBIOS name
DNS:  .00. .... = B-type node
DNS: Node address = [XXX.YYY.200.85]
DNS:
DNS: [Normal end of "Internet Domain Name Service header".]
DNS:
```

TRACE 6.10.6C. NETBIOS SESSION REQUEST/CONFIRM

```
Sniffer Network Analyzer data 6-Nov at 11:04:32, TCPNETB.ENC, Pg 1

- - - - - - - - - - - - - - - Frame 6 - - - - - - - - - - - - - - - - -

DLC:  ——DLC Header——
DLC:
DLC:  Frame 6 arrived at  11:04:51.4023; frame size is 132 (0084 hex) bytes.
DLC:  Destination = Station U-B   F5D800, Robert
DLC:  Source      = Station Bridge011084, Art
DLC:  Ethertype  = 0800 (IP)
DLC:
IP:    ——IP Header ——
IP:
IP:    Version = 4, header length = 20 bytes
IP:    Type of service = 00
IP:         000. .... = routine
IP:         ...0 .... = normal delay
IP:         .... 0... = normal throughput
IP:         .... .0.. = normal reliability
IP:    Total length = 118 bytes
IP:    Identification = 281
IP:    Flags = 0X
IP:    .0.. .... = may fragment
IP:    ..0. .... = last fragment
IP:    Fragment offset = 0 bytes
IP:    Time to live = 30 seconds/hops
IP:    Protocol = 6 (TCP)
```

```
IP:    Header checksum = 8A9D (correct)
IP:    Source address = [XXX.YYY.200.99]
IP:    Destination address = [XXX.YYY.200.85]
IP:    No options
IP:
TCP:  ----TCP header ----
TCP:
TCP:  Source port = 257
TCP:  Destination port = 139
TCP:  Sequence number = 172250
TCP:  Acknowledgment number = 257462
TCP:  Data offset = 20 bytes
TCP:  Flags = 10
TCP:  ..0. .... = (No urgent pointer)
TCP:  ...1 .... = Acknowledgment
TCP:  .... 0... = (No push)
TCP:  .... .0.. = (No reset)
TCP:  .... ..0. = (No SYN)
TCP:  .... ...0 = (No FIN)
TCP:  Window = 1024
TCP:  Checksum = EFCD (correct)
TCP:  No TCP options
TCP:  [78 byte(s) of data]
TCP:
NETB: ----NetBIOS Session protocol ----
NETB:
NETB: Type = 81 (Session request)
NETB: Flags = 00
NETB: Total session packet length = 74
NETB: Called NetBIOS name = ROBERT
NETB: Calling NetBIOS name = ARTL<00>
NETB:

- - - - - - - - - - - - - - - Frame 7 - - - - - - - - - - - - - - - - -

DLC:  ----DLC Header ----
DLC:
DLC:  Frame 7 arrived at  11:04:51.4065; frame size is 60 (003C hex) bytes.
DLC:  Destination = Station Bridge011084, Art
DLC:  Source      = Station U-B   F5D800, Robert
DLC:  Ethertype  = 0800 (IP)
DLC:
IP:    ----IP Header ----
IP:
```

```
IP:    Version = 4, header length = 20 bytes
IP:    Type of service = 00
IP:        000. .... = routine
IP:        ...0 .... = normal delay
IP:        .... 0... = normal throughput
IP:        .... .0.. = normal reliability
IP:    Total length = 44 bytes
IP:    Identification = 2
IP:    Flags = 0X
IP:    .0.. .... = may fragment
IP:    ..0. .... = last fragment
IP:    Fragment offset = 0 bytes
IP:    Time to live = 60 seconds/hops
IP:    Protocol = 6 (TCP)
IP:    Header checksum = 6DFE (correct)
IP:    Source address = [XXX.YYY.200.85]
IP:    Destination address = [XXX.YYY.200.99]
IP:    No options
IP:
TCP:   ----TCP header ----
TCP:
TCP:   Source port = 139
TCP:   Destination port = 257
TCP:   Sequence number = 257462
TCP:   Acknowledgment number = 172328
TCP:   Data offset = 20 bytes
TCP:   Flags = 18
TCP:   ..0. .... = (No urgent pointer)
TCP:   ...1 .... = Acknowledgment
TCP:   .... 1... = Push
TCP:   .... .0.. = (No reset)
TCP:   .... ..0. = (No SYN)
TCP:   .... ...0 = (No FIN)
TCP:   Window = 2074
TCP:   Checksum = 8471 (correct)
TCP:   No TCP options
TCP:   [4 byte(s) of data]
TCP:
NETB: ----NetBIOS Session protocol ----
NETB:
NETB: Type = 82 (Positive response)
NETB: Flags = 00
NETB: Total session packet length = 0
NETB:
```

TRACE 6.10.6D. NETBIOS WITH SERVER MESSAGE BLOCK INFORMATION

```
Sniffer Network Analyzer data 6-Nov at 11:04:32, TCPNETB.ENC, Pg 1

- - - - - - - - - - - - - - - Frame 13 - - - - - - - - - - - - - - - - -

DLC:  ——DLC Header ——
DLC:
DLC:  Frame 13 arrived at  11:04:51.4744; frame size is 114 (0072 hex) bytes.
DLC:  Destination = Station U-B   F5D800, Robert
DLC:  Source      = Station Bridge011084, Art
DLC:  Ethertype  = 0800 (IP)
DLC:
IP:   ——IP Header ——
IP:
IP:   Version = 4, header length = 20 bytes
IP:   Type of service = 00
IP:        000. .... = routine
IP:        ...0 .... = normal delay
IP:        .... 0... = normal throughput
IP:        .... .0.. = normal reliability
IP:   Total length = 100 bytes
IP:   Identification = 285
IP:   Flags = 0X
IP:   .0.. .... = may fragment
IP:   ..0. .... = last fragment
IP:   Fragment offset = 0 bytes
IP:   Time to live = 30 seconds/hops
IP:   Protocol = 6 (TCP)
IP:   Header checksum = 8AAB (correct)
IP:   Source address = [XXX.YYY.200.99]
IP:   Destination address = [XXX.YYY.200.85]
IP:   No options
IP:
TCP:  ——TCP header ——
TCP:
TCP:  Source port = 257
TCP:  Destination port = 139
TCP:  Sequence number = 172391
TCP:  Acknowledgment number = 257507
TCP:  Data offset = 20 bytes
TCP:  Flags = 10
TCP:  ..0. .... = (No urgent pointer)
TCP:  ...1 .... = Acknowledgment
TCP:  .... 0... = (No push)
```

```
TCP:  .... .0.. = (No reset)
TCP:  .... ..0. = (No SYN)
TCP:  .... ...0 = (No FIN)
TCP:  Window = 979
TCP:  Checksum = D716 (correct)
TCP:  No TCP options
TCP:  [60 byte(s) of data]
TCP:
NETB: ——NetBIOS Session protocol ——
NETB:
NETB: Type = 00 (Session data)
NETB: Flags = 00
NETB: Total session packet length = 56
NETB:
SMB:  ——SMB Tree Connect Command ——
SMB:
SMB:  Function = 70 (Tree Connect)
SMB:  Tree id      (TID) = 0000
SMB:  Process id   (PID) = 0000
SMB:  File pathname = "\\ROBERT\DISK"
SMB:  Password = ""
SMB:  Device name = "A:"
SMB:

- - - - - - - - - - - - - - - Frame 15 - - - - - - - - - - - - - - - - -

DLC:  ——DLC Header ——
DLC:
DLC:  Frame 15 arrived at  11:04:51.4870; frame size is 97 (0061 hex) bytes.
DLC:  Destination = Station Bridge011084, Art
DLC:  Source      = Station U-B   F5D800, Robert
DLC:  Ethertype  = 0800 (IP)
DLC:
IP:   ——IP Header ——
IP:
IP:   Version = 4, header length = 20 bytes
IP:   Type of service = 00
IP:         000. .... = routine
IP:         ...0 .... = normal delay
IP:         .... 0... = normal throughput
IP:         .... .0.. = normal reliability
IP:   Total length = 83 bytes
IP:   Identification = 4
IP:   Flags = 0X
```

```
IP:    .0.. .... = may fragment
IP:    ..0. .... = last fragment
IP:    Fragment offset = 0 bytes
IP:    Time to live = 60 seconds/hops
IP:    Protocol = 6 (TCP)
IP:    Header checksum = 6DD5 (correct)
IP:    Source address = [XXX.YYY.200.85]
IP:    Destination address = [XXX.YYY.200.99]
IP:    No options
IP:
TCP:   ----TCP header ----
TCP:
TCP:   Source port = 139
TCP:   Destination port = 257
TCP:   Sequence number = 257507
TCP:   Acknowledgment number = 172451
TCP:   Data offset = 20 bytes
TCP:   Flags = 10
TCP:   ..0. .... = (No urgent pointer)
TCP:   ...1 .... = Acknowledgment
TCP:   .... 0... = (No push)
TCP:   .... .0.. = (No reset)
TCP:   .... ..0. = (No SYN)
TCP:   .... ...0 = (No FIN)
TCP:   Window = 1951
TCP:   Checksum = 97A2 (correct)
TCP:   No TCP options
TCP:   [43 byte(s) of data]
TCP:
NETB:  ----NetBIOS Session protocol ----
NETB:
NETB:  Type = 00 (Session data)
NETB:  Flags = 00
NETB:  Total session packet length = 39
NETB:
SMB:   ----SMB Tree Connect Response ----
SMB:
SMB:   Function = 70 (Tree Connect)
SMB:   Tree id     (TID) = 0000
SMB:   Process id  (PID) = 0000
SMB:   Return code = 0,0 (OK)
SMB:   Maximum transmit size = 8240
SMB:   TID = 8F15
SMB:
```

6.10.7 Implementing Multiple Protocol Stacks

Much has been said about workstation environments that allow the user to perform multiple operations simultaneously, such as printing while working on a spreadsheet. Such environments include IBM's OS/2 and Microsoft's Windows and LAN Manager. In any operating system, the user must be sure that the application is compatible with the environment. When multiple applications are involved, the scenario gets more complex. Let's look at what can happen in an environment that mixes DOS, OS/2, Windows, and a TCP/IP workstation package.

The internetwork in question contains two token rings in two separate locations. One ring contains an OS/2 Server and a number of workstations, and the other ring contains an SNA host. Routers connect the two rings (see Figure 6-17). The network administrator decides to experiment and combine multiple protocol stacks and operating systems on his workstation. For his experiment, he plans to use a TCP/IP workstation package to access the SNA host via the router. His workstation is running Windows, and the DOS-based TCP/IP workstation package resides on an OS/2 Server.

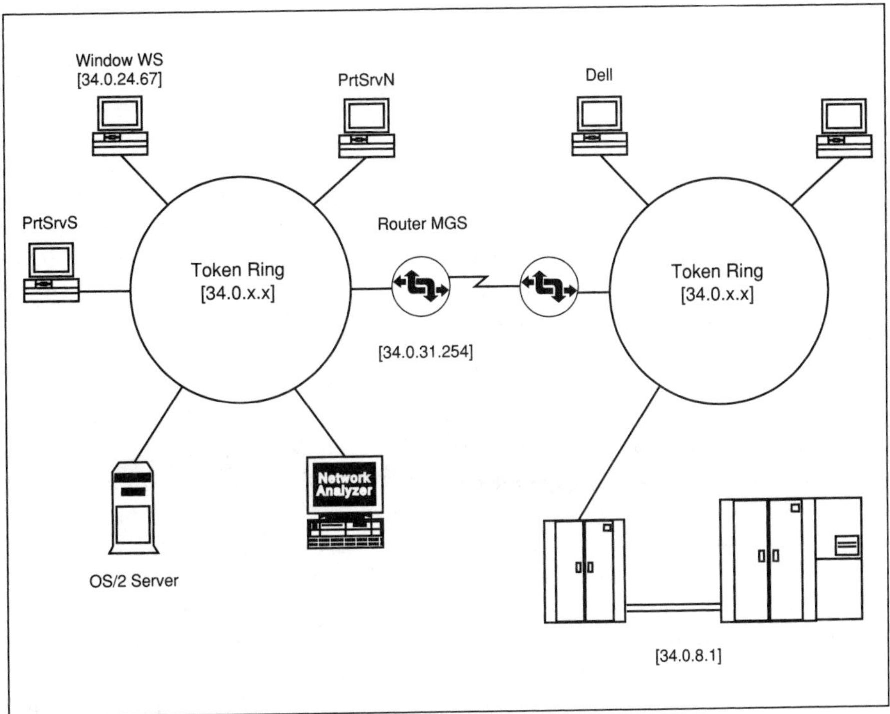

Figure 6-17 Multiprotocol Environment

Trace 6.10.7a begins with the Windows workstation (shown as Windows WS) entering the token ring. Frames 1 through 7 show the workstation transmitting two MAC Duplicate Address Test frames, reporting a change in its Stored Upstream Address (SUA) to the Configuration Report Server (CRS), and obtaining its initialization parameters from the Ring Parameter Server (RPS). Beginning in Frame 8, the Windows workstation begins to log into the OS/2 Server, known as ISCSWEST. NetBIOS Name Service messages verify the various names that Windows WS requires. A NetBIOS session is initialized in Frame 35 and confirmed in Frame 37. The protocol is then negotiated (Frames 39 and 43) and the SMB connection established (Frames 47 and 51). Subsequent Frames 52 through 470 (not shown) complete the login and establish a session with a print server, PrtSrv S. Beginning in Frame 471, a connection is made to a second print server, PrtSrv N. This connection follows a similar sequence of events: find the name (Frame 471), initialize the session (Frame 477), negotiate the protocol (Frame 481), and establish the connection (Frame 489). The workstation is then idle for a few seconds while the administrator ponders his next move.

The administrator starts Windows, shown in Frame 519. The TCP/IP workstation program that is required to access the remote SNA host is resident on the OS/2 Server. Since that program is DOS-based, the administrator opens a DOS Window and begins to load the file (shown as PFTP in Frame 582). The file opens properly (Frame 586), is read from the OS/2 Server (Frames 597 through 864, not shown in the trace), and closes (Frames 865 through 868). The Windows workstation is now ready to connect to the remote host using FTP. The workstation [34.0.24.67] broadcasts an ARP looking for the router that can connect it to the host [34.0.31.254]. It finds the router (Frame 874) and establishes a TCP connection (Frames 875 through 877) to Port = 5044. A second TCP connection to Port = 5054 is established (Frames 913 through 917), but is terminated shortly thereafter (Frames 922 through 924). The last indication of TCP-related protocol activity is in Frame 926; subsequent frames are NetBIOS Keep Alives (Frame 927), LLC Polls (Frames 928 through 934), and MAC-layer transmissions (Frame 935). It appears that the TCP/IP application is no longer active.

An indication that a problem exists comes in Frame 1001, a Report Soft Error frame (see Trace 6.10.7b). This frame is sent from the Windows workstation to the Ring Error Monitor (REM), indicating receiver congestion. In other words, the receiver of Windows workstation does not have sufficient buffer space for all the data that it is receiving. These MAC Report Soft Error frames continue to be transmitted, with no higher layer processes active. Note that the remainder of the trace (Frames 1072 through 1093) shows no NetBIOS Session Alive messages and that the Windows workstation does not answer the polls from the OS/2 Server. The workstation has been reduced to its MAC-layer operation.

The problem was traced to an incompatibility between the DOS application, the DOS Window (under Microsoft Windows), and the OS/2 LAN Server. The problem was resolved by operating the TCP/IP workstation program from a DOS-based, rather than a Windows-based, workstation. Multilayer incompatibilities can produce unusual behaviors!

TRACE 6.10.7A. TCP/IP PROTOCOLS UNDER WINDOWS (SUMMARY)

Sniffer Network Analyzer data 30-May at 10:53:14, TCPWIN.TRC, Pg 1

SUMMARY	Delta T	Destination	Source	Summary
M 1		Windows WS	Windows WS	MAC Duplicate Address Test
2	0.002	Windows WS	Windows WS	MAC Duplicate Address Test
3	0.490	Config Srv	Windows WS	MAC Report SUA Change
4	0.012	Broadcast	Windows WS	MAC StandbyMonitorPresent
5	0.000	Param Server	Windows WS	MAC Request Initialization
6	0.005	Windows WS	Station RPS.	MAC Initialize Ring Station
7	0.000	Station RPS.	Windows WS	MAC Response
8	0.010	NetBIOS	Windows WS	NETB Check name ISCW7166<00>
9	0.990	NetBIOS	Windows WS	NETBCheckname ISCW7166<00>
10	0.499	NetBIOS	Windows WS	NETB Check name ISCW7166<00>
11	0.500	NetBIOS	Windows WS	NETBCheck name ISCW7166<00>
12	0.499	NetBIOS	Windows WS	NETB Check name ISCW7166<00>
13	0.499	NetBIOS	Windows WS	NETB Check name ISCW7166<00>
14	0.500	NetBIOS	Windows WS	NETB Check group ISCDWEST<00>
15	0.999	NetBIOS	Windows WS	NETB Check group ISCDWEST<00>
16	0.499	NetBIOS	Windows WS	NETB Check group ISCDWEST<00>
17	0.499	NetBIOS	Windows WS	NETB Check group ISCDWEST<00>
18	0.499	NetBIOS	Windows WS	NETB Check group ISCDWEST<00>
19	0.499	NetBIOS	Windows WS	NETB Check group ISCDWEST<00>
20	0.486	Broadcast	Windows WS	MAC Standby Monitor Present
21	6.373	NetBIOS	Windows WS	NETB Check name DATZ343
22	0.624	Broadcast	Windows WS	MAC Standby Monitor Present
23	0.013	NetBIOS	Windows WS	NETB Check name DATZ343 ISCDWES

24	0.499	NetBIOS	Windows WS	NETB Check name DATZ343 ISCDWES
25	0.500	NetBIOS	Windows WS	NETB Check name DATZ343 ISCDWES
26	0.499	NetBIOS	Windows WS	NETB Check name DATZ343 ISCDWES
27	0.499	NetBIOS	Windows WS	NETB Check name DATZ343 ISCDWES
28	0.529	NetBIOS	Windows WS	SMB C Transaction \MAILSLOT\NET\ NETLOGON
29	0.144	NetBIOS	Windows WS	NETB Find name ISCSWEST
30	0.002	Windows WS	OS/2 Server	NETB Name ISCSWEST recognized
31	0.001	OS/2 Server	Windows WS	LLC C D=F0 S=F0 SABME P
32	0.001	Windows WS	OS/2 Server	LLC R D=F0 S=F0 UA F
33	0.000	OS/2 Server	Windows WS	LLC C D=F0 S=F0 RR NR=0 P
34	0.000	Windows WS	OS/2 Server	LLC R D=F0 S=F0 RR NR=0 F
35	0.000	OS/2 Server	Windows WS	NETB D=21 S=01 Session init
36	0.001	Windows WS	OS/2 Server	LLC R D=F0 S=F0 RR NR=1
37	0.000	Windows WS	OS/2 Server	NETB D=01 S=21 Session conf
38	0.000	OS/2 Server	Windows WS	LLC R D=F0 S=F0 RR NR=1
39	0.002	OS/2 Server	Windows WS	SMB C PC NET PGM 1.0 (more)
40	0.001	Windows WS	OS/2 Server	LLC R D=F0 S=F0 RR NR=2
41	0.000	Windows WS	OS/2 Server	NETB D=01 S=21 Data ACK
42	0.000	OS/2 Server	Windows WS	LLC R D=F0 S=F0 RR NR=2
43	0.009	Windows WS	OS/2 Server	SMB R Negotiated Protocol 4
44	0.000	OS/2 Server	Windows WS	LLC R D=F0 S=F0 RR NR=3
45	0.001	OS/2 Server	Windows WS	NETB D=21 S=01 Data ACK

46	0.001	Windows WS	OS/2 Server	LLC R D=F0 S=F0 RR NR=3
47	0.002	OS/2 Server	Windows WS	SMB C Setup account DATZ343 SMB C Connect ?????\\ISCSWEST\IPC$
48	0.001	Windows WS	OS/2 Server	LLC R D=F0 S=F0 RR NR=4
49	0.000	Windows WS	OS/2 Server	NETB D=01 S=21 Data ACK
50	0.000	OS/2 Server	Windows WS	LLC R D=F0 S=F0 RR NR=4
51	0.056	Windows WS	OS/2 Server	SMB R Setup SMB R IPC Connected
.				
.				
.				
471	0.004	NetBIOS	Windows WS	NETB Find name PRTSRVN
472	0.003	Windows WS	PrtSvrN	NETB Name PRTSRVN recognized
473	0.001	PrtSvrN	Windows WS	LLC C D=F0 S=F0 SABME P
474	0.001	Windows WS	PrtSvrN	LLC R D=F0 S=F0 UA F
475	0.000	PrtSvrN	Windows WS	LLC C D=F0 S=F0 RR NR=0 P
476	0.000	Windows WS	PrtSvrN	LLC R D=F0 S=F0 RR NR=0 F
477	0.000	PrtSvrN	Windows WS	NETB D=F6 S=04 Session init
478	0.001	Windows WS	PrtSvrN	LLC R D=F0 S=F0 RR NR=1
479	0.001	Windows WS	PrtSvrN	NETB D=04 S=F6 Session conf
480	0.000	PrtSvrN	Windows WS	LLC R D=F0 S=F0 RR NR=1
481	0.002	PrtSvrN	Windows WS	SMB C PC NET PGM 1.0 (more)
482	0.001	Windows WS	PrtSvrN	LLC R D=F0 S=F0 RR NR=2
483	0.001	Windows WS	PrtSvrN	NETB D=04 S=F6 Data ACK
484	0.000	PrtSvrN	Windows WS	LLC R D=F0 S=F0 RR NR=2
485	0.004	Windows WS	PrtSvrN	SMB R Negotiated Protocol 0

486	0.000	PrtSvrN	Windows WS	LLC R D=F0 S=F0 RR NR=3
487	0.001	PrtSvrN	Windows WS	NETB D=F6 S=04 Data ACK
488	0.001	Windows WS	PrtSvrN	LLC R D=F0 S=F0 RR NR=3
489	0.001	PrtSvrN	Windows WS	SMB C Connect LPT1:\\PRTSRVN\LASER3N
490	0.001	Windows WS	PrtSvrN	LLC R D=F0 S=F0 RR NR=4
491	0.001	Windows WS	PrtSvrN	NETB D=04 S=F6 Data ACK
492	0.000	PrtSvrN	Windows WS	LLC R D=F0 S=F0 RR NR=4
493	0.008	Windows WS	PrtSvrN	SMB R T=11D1 Connected
494	0.000	PrtSvrN	Windows WS	LLC R D=F0 S=F0 RR NR=5
495	0.001	PrtSvrN	Windows WS	NETB D=F6 S=04 Data ACK
.				
.				
.				
519	0.727	OS/2 Server	Windows WS	SMB C Open \BIN\WINSTART.BAT
520	0.001	Windows WS	OS/2 Server	LLC R D=F0 S=F0 RR NR=87
521	0.000	Windows WS	OS/2 Server	NETB D=02 S=22 Data ACK
522	0.001	OS/2 Server	Windows WS	LLC R D=F0 S=F0 RR NR=92
.				
.				
.				
582	1.248	OS/2 Server	Windows WS	SMB C Open \BIN\PFTP.EXE
583	0.001	Windows WS	OS/2 Server	LLC R D=F0 S=F0 RR NR=90
584	0.000	Windows WS	OS/2 Server	NETB D=02 S=22 Data ACK
585	0.002	OS/2 Server	Windows WS	LLC R D=F0 S=F0 RR NR=95
586	0.043	Windows WS	OS/2 Server	SMB R F=0016 Opened
587	0.001	OS/2 Server	Windows WS	LLC R D=F0 S=F0 RR

				NR=96
588	0.004	OS/2 Server	Windows WS	NETB D=22 S=02 Data ACK
589	0.000	Windows WS	OS/2 Server	LLC R D=F0 S=F0 RR NR=91
590	0.014	OS/2 Server	Windows WS	SMB C F=0016 Rd Bk Raw 64 at 0
591	0.002	Windows WS	OS/2 Server	NETB D=02 S=22 Data ACK
592	0.000	Windows WS	OS/2 Server	LLC R D=F0 S=F0 RR NR=92
593	0.001	Windows WS	OS/2 Server	NETB D=02 S=22 Data, 64 bytes
594	0.000	OS/2 Server	Windows WS	LLC R D=F0 S=F0 RR NR=97
595	0.001	OS/2 Server	Windows WS	LLC R D=F0 S=F0 RR NR=98
596	0.003	OS/2 Server	Windows WS	NETB D=22 S=02 Data ACK
.				
.				
.				
865	0.007	OS/2 Server	Windows WS	SMB C F=0016 Close
866	0.001	Windows WS	OS/2 Server	LLC R D=F0 S=F0 RR NR=118
867	0.000	Windows WS	OS/2 Server	NETB D=02 S=22 Data ACK
868	0.003	Windows WS	OS/2 Server	SMB R Closed
869	0.000	OS/2 Server	Windows WS	LLC R D=F0 S=F0 RR NR=77
870	0.002	OS/2 Server	Windows WS	LLC R D=F0 S=F0 RR NR=78
871	0.004	OS/2 Server	Windows WS	NETB D=22 S=02 Data ACK
872	0.001	Windows WS	OS/2 Server	LLC R D=F0 S=F0 RR NR=119
873	0.124	Broadcast	Windows WS	ARP C PA=[34.0.31.254] PRO=IP
874	0.001	Windows WS	Router MGS	ARP R PA=[34.0.31.254] HA=00003000EF30 PRO=IP
875	0.014	Router MGS	Windows WS	TCP D=21 S=5044 SYN SEQ=0 LEN=0 WIN=512

876	0.071	Windows WS	Router MGS	TCP D=5044 S=21 SYN ACK=1 SEQ=76544276 LEN=0 WIN=8192
877	0.009	Router MGS	Windows WS	TCP D=21 S=5044 ACK=76544277 WIN=512
878	0.066	Windows WS	Router MGS	FTP R PORT=5044 220-FTPSERVE at ISCHOOARNA, 11:01:08 on 05/30/91<0D>...
879	0.010	Router MGS	Windows WS	TCP D=21 S=5044 ACK=76544387 WIN=511
880	0.585	PrtSvrS	Windows WS	LLC C D=F0 S=F0 RR NR=5 P
881	0.000	Windows WS	PrtSvrS	LLC R D=F0 S=F0 RR NR=6 F
882	2.006	Broadcast	Windows WS	MAC Standby Monitor Present
883	0.689	Broadcast	Windows WS	MAC Standby Monitor Present
884	0.301	OS/2 Server	Windows WS	LLC C D=F0 S=F0 RR NR=78 P
885	0.000	PrtSvrN	Windows WS	LLC C D=F0 S=F0 RR NR=6 P
886	0.000	Windows WS	OS/2 Server	LLC R D=F0 S=F0 RR NR=119 F
887	0.000	Windows WS	PrtSvrN	LLC R D=F0 S=F0 RR NR=6 F
888	0.106	Router MGS	Windows WS	FTP C PORT=5044 USER datz343<0D><0A>
889	0.080	Windows WS	Router MGS	TCP D=5044 S=21 ACK=15 WIN=8178
890	0.015	Windows WS	Router MGS	FTP R PORT=5044 331 Send password please. <0D><0A>
891	0.008	Router MGS	Windows WS	TCP D=21 S=5044 ACK=76544414 WIN=511
892	0.520	Windows WS	PrtSvrS	LLC C D=F0 S=F0 RR NR=6 P
893	0.000	PrtSvrS	Windows WS	LLC R D=F0 S=F0 RR NR=5 F
894	2.305	Router MGS	Windows WS	FTP C PORT=5044 PASS puffer<0D><0A>

895	0.036	Windows WS	Router MGS	TCP D=5044 S=21 ACK=28 WIN=8165
896	0.377	Windows WS	Router MGS	FTP R PORT=5044 230 DATZ343 is logged on<0D><0A>
897	0.007	Router MGS	Windows WS	TCP D=21 S=5044 ACK=76544441 WIN=511
898	0.538	PrtSvrS	Windows WS	LLC C D=F0 S=F0 RR NR=5 P
899	0.000	PrtSvrN	Windows WS	LLC C D=F0 S=F0 RR NR=6 P
900	0.000	OS/2 Server	Windows WS	LLC C D=F0 S=F0 RR NR=78 P
901	0.000	Windows WS	PrtSvrS	LLC R D=F0 S=F0 RR NR=6 F
902	0.000	Windows WS	PrtSvrN	LLC R D=F0 S=F0 RR NR=6 F
903	0.000	Windows WS	OS/2 Server	LLC R D=F0 S=F0 RR NR=119 F
904	2.554	Router MGS	Windows WS	FTP C PORT=5044 port 34,0,24,67, 19,190<0D><0A>
905	0.093	Windows WS	Router MGS	TCP D=5044 S=21 ACK=52 WIN=8141
906	0.012	Windows WS	Router MGS	FTP R PORT=5044 200 Port request OK.<0D><0A>
907	0.004	Broadcast	Windows WS	MAC Standby Monitor Present
908	0.004	Router MGS	Windows WS	TCP D=21 S=5044 ACK=76544463 WIN=511
909	0.039	Router MGS	Windows WS	FTP C PORT=5044 LIST<0D><0A>
910	0.048	Windows WS	Router MGS	TCP D=5044 S=21 ACK=58 WIN=8135
911	0.971	Windows WS	PrtSvrS	LLC C D=F0 S=F0 RR NR=6 P
912	0.000	PrtSvrS	Windows WS	LLC R D=F0 S=F0 RR NR=5 F
913	0.217	Windows WS	Router MGS	TCP D=5054 S=20 SYN SEQ=167535876 LEN=0 WIN=8192
914	0.007	Router MGS	Windows WS	TCP D=20 S=5054 SYN ACK=167535877 SEQ=0 LEN=0 WIN=512

915	0.004	Windows WS	Router MGS	FTP R PORT=5044 125 List started OK.<0D><0A>
916	0.008	Router MGS	Windows WS	TCP D=21 S=5044 ACK=76544485 WIN=511
917	0.025	Windows WS	Router MGS	TCP D=5054 S=20 ACK=1 WIN=8192
918	0.004	OS/2 Server	Windows WS	LLC C D=F0 S=F0 RR NR=78 P
919	0.000	PrtSvrN	Windows WS	LLC C D=F0 S=F0 RR NR=6 P
920	0.000	Windows WS	OS/2 Server	LLC R D=F0 S=F0 RR NR=119 F
921	0.000	Windows WS	PrtSvrN	LLC R D=F0 S=F0 RR NR=6 F
922	0.055	Windows WS	Router MGS	TCP D=5054 S=20 FIN ACK=1 SEQ=167535877 LEN=187 WIN=8192
923	0.008	Router MGS	Windows WS	TCP D=20 S=5054 FIN ACK=167536065 SEQ=1 LEN=0 WIN=511
924	0.044	Windows WS	Router MGS	TCP D=5054 S=20 ACK=2 WIN=8191
925	0.014	Windows WS	Router MGS	FTP R PORT=5044 250 List completed successfully.<0D><0A>
926	0.166	Router MGS	Windows WS	TCP D=21 S=5044 ACK=76544519 WIN=511
927	1.447	Windows WS	PrtSvrS	NETB Session alive
928	0.001	PrtSvrS	Windows WS	LLC R D=F0 S=F0 RR NR=6
929	2.259	PrtSvrN	Windows WS	LLC C D=F0 S=F0 RR NR=6 P
930	0.000	OS/2 Server	Windows WS	LLC C D=F0 S=F0 RR NR=78 P
931	0.000	Windows WS	PrtSvrN	LLC R D=F0 S=F0 RR NR=6 F
932	0.000	Windows WS	OS/2 Server	LLC R D=F0 S=F0 RR NR=119 F
933	0.998	PrtSvrS	Windows WS	LLC C D=F0 S=F0 RR NR=6 P
934	0.000	Windows WS	PrtSvrS	LLC R D=F0 S=F0 RR NR=6 F
935	0.667	Broadcast	Windows WS	MAC Standby Monitor

				Present
.				
.				
.				
996	0.215	Broadcast	Windows WS	MAC Standby Monitor Present
997	0.567	Windows WS	PrtSvrN	NETB Session alive
998	0.414	PrtSvrN	Windows WS	LLC C D=F0 S=F0 RR NR=6 P
999	0.000	Windows WS	PrtSvrN	LLC R D=F0 S=F0 RR NR=6 F
1000	0.670	Windows WS	PrtSvrN	LLC C D=F0 S=F0 RR NR=6 P
1001	0.328	Error Mon.	Windows WS	MAC Report Soft Error
.				
.				
.				
1071	0.678	Error Mon.	Windows WS	MAC Report Soft Error
1072	0.046	Windows WS	PrtSvrS	LLC C D=F0 S=F0 RR NR=6 P
1073	0.273	PrtSvrS	Windows WS	LLC C D=F0 S=F0 RR NR=6 P
1074	0.000	OS/2 Server	Windows WS	LLC C D=F0 S=F0 RR NR=78 P
1075	0.000	Windows WS	PrtSvrS	LLC R D=F0 S=F0 RR NR=6 F
1076	0.000	Windows WS	OS/2 Server	LLC R D=F0 S=F0 RR NR=119 F
1077	0.053	Windows WS	OS/2 Server	LLC C D=F0 S=F0 RR NR=119 P
1078	0.675	Windows WS	PrtSvrS	LLC R D=F0 S=F0 DM
1079	1.189	Error Mon.	Windows WS	MAC Report Soft Error
1080	0.087	Broadcast	Windows WS	MAC Standby Monitor Present
1081	1.047	Windows WS	OS/2 Server	LLC C D=F0 S=F0 RR NR=119 P
1082	1.904	Error Mon.	Windows WS	MAC Report Soft Error
1083	1.095	Windows WS	OS/2 Server	LLC C D=F0 S=F0 RR NR=119 P
1084	2.184	Error Mon.	Windows WS	MAC Report Soft Error
1085	0.777	Broadcast	Windows WS	MAC Standby Monitor Present
1086	0.037	Windows WS	OS/2 Server	LLC C D=F0 S=F0 RR NR=119 P

1087	2.183	Error Mon.	Windows WS	MAC Report Soft Error
1088	0.815	Windows WS	OS/2 Server	LLC C D=F0 S=F0 RR NR=119 P
1089	2.183	Error Mon.	Windows WS	MAC Report Soft Error
1090	0.815	Windows WS	OS/2 Server	LLC C D=F0 S=F0 RR NR=119 P
1091	0.961	Broadcast	Windows WS	MAC Standby Monitor Present
1092	1.221	Error Mon.	Windows WS	MAC Report Soft Error
1093	0.815	Windows WS	OS/2 Server	LLC C D=F0 S=F0 RR NR=119 P

TRACE 6.10.7B. WINDOWS WORKSTATION REPORT SOFT ERROR DETAILS

```
Sniffer Network Analyzer data 30-May at 10:53:14, TCPWIN.TRC, Pg 1

- - - - - - - - - - - - - Frame 1001 - - - - - - - - - - - - - - - - -

DLC:  ——DLC Header ——
DLC:
DLC:  Frame 1001 arrived at  10:56:07.766; frame size is 48 (0030 hex) bytes.
DLC:  AC: Frame priority 0,  Reservation priority 0,  Monitor count 1
DLC:  FC: MAC frame,  PCF attention code: None
DLC:  FS: Addr recognized indicators: 00, Frame copied indicators: 00
DLC:  Destination = Functional address C00000000008, Error Mon.
DLC:  Source      = Station IBM   6B95E7, Windows WS
DLC:
MAC: ——MAC data ——
MAC:
MAC: MAC Command: Report Soft Error
MAC: Source: Ring station, Destination: Ring Error Monitor
MAC: Subvector type: Isolating Error Counts
MAC:      0 line errors,      0 internal errors,      0 burst errors
MAC:         0 AC errors,          0 abort delimiters transmitted
MAC: Subvector type: Non-Isolating Error Counts
MAC:      0 lost frame errors,   3 receiver congestion,   0 FC errors
MAC:         0 frequency errors,    0 token errors
MAC: Subvector type: Physical Drop Number 00000000
MAC: Subvector type: Upstream Neighbor Address 400006020014
MAC:
```

6.10.8 Web Page Access Using HTTP

In the final case study in this chapter, we will study how HTTP is used to access a Web page. For this example, we will access our company Web server, `www.diginet.com`, from a remote workstation via the Internet (Figure 6-18). We will first access the home page, second access a listing of the networking tutorials, and third access information about the *Troubleshooting TCP/IP* tutorial.

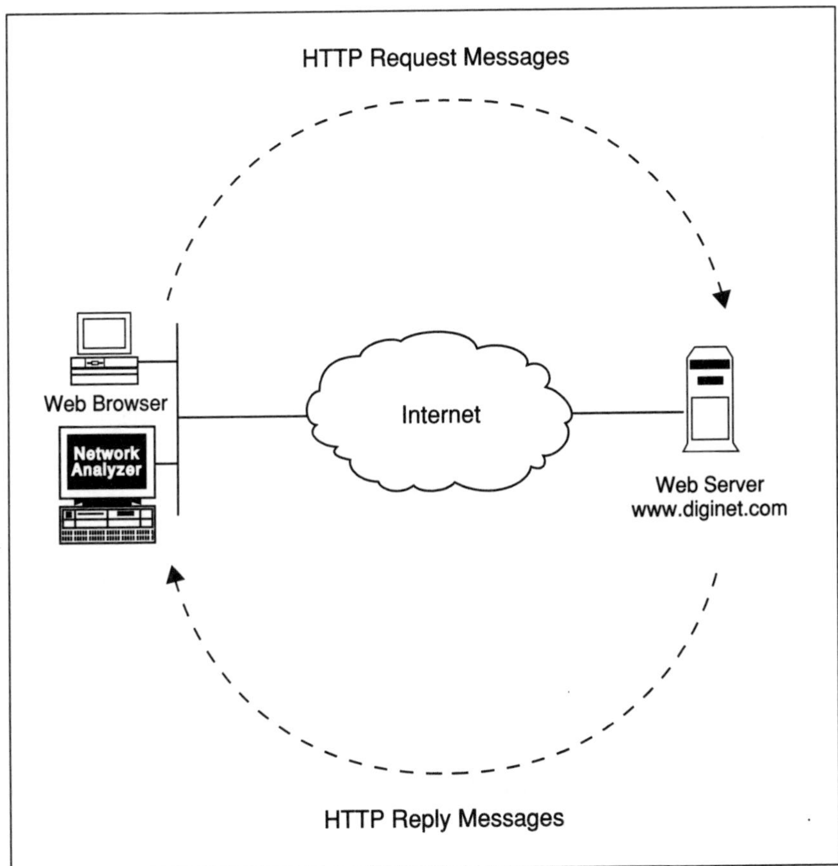

Figure 6-18 Web Page Access Using HTTP

A summary of the Remote Client's activities is shown in Trace 6.10.8a. There are several significant events that occur in this trace. First, the Remote Client establishes TCP connections with the `www.diginet.com` Web server. Note that the Client opens multiple logical connections, using different Source Port numbers, over the same physical link. All of the Destination Port numbers are Port = 80, the HTTP port. These connections are:

Frames	Port Number
9–11	34438
17–19	34439
21–23	34440

(Note that this trace has been filtered to only show the most relevant information, and that even with filtering, some additional communication, which does not pertain to this case, is included.)

Also throughout this communication session, the Client is sending Request messages to the `www.diginet.com` Web server and receiving Response messages in return. These messages are:

Frames	Port Number	File Requested	Information Requested
12–13	34438	*www.diginet.com*	Home Page
95–96	34440	*tutorial.html*	Tutorial page
121–122	34438	*troubletcp.html*	TCP/IP tutorial outline

The responses from the Web server include HTML and graphics files (such as Skidsblue.gif in Frame 24, Homepage1.gif in Frame 25, tutorial.html in Frame 95, and image54.gif in Frame 98) that eventually appear on the Client's workstation. After the requested information has been obtained, the user closes the HTTP application, which in turn initiates a closing of the TCP logical connections, signaled by the TCP FIN command:

Frame	Port Number Connection Closed
238	34440
240	34439
263	34438

TRACE 6.10.8A. DIGINET CORPORATION WEB SITE ACCESS SUMMARY

Sniffer Network Analyzer data from 30-Apr-98 at 09:58:22, file DNC.ENC, Pg 1

SUMMARY	Delta T	Destination	Source	Summary
9	0.0088	www.diginet.com	Remote Client	TCP D=80 S=34438 SYN

				SEQ=3089805603 LEN=0 WIN=8760
10	0.0083	Remote Client	www.diginet.com	TCP D=34438 S=80 SYN ACK=3089805604 SEQ=1037380740 LEN=0 WIN=61320
11	0.0004	www.diginet.com	Remote Client	TCP D=80 S=34438 ACK=1037380741 WIN=8760
12	0.0018	www.diginet.com	Remote Client	HTTP C Port=34438 GET / HTTP/1.0
13	0.0311	Remote Client	www.diginet.com	HTTP R Port=34438 OK
14	0.0020	www.diginet.com	Remote Client	TCP D=80 S=34438 ACK=1037381875 WIN=8760
15	0.0156	Remote Client	[XXX.YYY.73.73]	TCP D=34437 S=80 ACK=3074884629 WIN=8760
16	0.2158	[XXX.YYY.73.73]	Remote Client	TCP D=80 S=34435 FIN ACK=587129866 SEQ=3074501490 LEN=0 WIN=8760
17	0.0062	www.diginet.com	Remote Client	TCP D=80 S=34439 SYN SEQ=3089845435 LEN=0 WIN=8760
18	0.0034	Remote Client	www.diginet.com	TCP D=34439 S=80 SYN ACK=3089845436 SEQ=1037450141 LEN=0 WIN=61320
19	0.0004	www.diginet.com	Remote Client	TCP D=80 S=34439 ACK=1037450142 WIN=8760
20	0.0028	[XXX.YYY.73.73]	Remote Client	TCP D=80 S=34434 FIN ACK=587055032 SEQ=3074419387 LEN=0 WIN=8760
21	0.0014	www.diginet.com	Remote Client	TCP D=80 S=34440 SYN SEQ=3089875978 LEN=0 WIN=8760
22	0.0049	Remote Client	www.diginet.com	TCP D=34440 S=80 SYN ACK=3089875979 SEQ=1037577189 LEN=0 WIN=61320

23	0.0005	www.diginet.com	Remote Client	TCP D=80 S=34440 ACK=1037577190 WIN=8760
24	0.0397	www.diginet.com	Remote Client	HTTP C Port=34439 GET /Skidsblue.gif HTTP/1.0
25	0.0067	www.diginet.com	Remote Client	HTTP C Port=34440 GET /Homepage1.gif HTTP/1.0
26	0.0115	Remote Client	[XXX.YYY.73.73]	TCP D=34435 S=80 ACK=3074501491 WIN=8760
27	0.0067	Remote Client	www.diginet.com	HTTP R Port=34439 OK
28	0.0012	Remote Client	www.diginet.com	HTTP R Port=34440 OK
32	0.0091	Remote Client	www.diginet.com	HTTP R Port=34440 Graphics Data
33	0.0072	Remote Client	www.diginet.com	HTTP R Port=34439 Graphics Data
34	0.0096	Remote Client	www.diginet.com	HTTP R Port=34439 Graphics Data
35	0.0112	www.diginet.com	Remote Client	TCP D=80 S=34439 ACK=1037453062 WIN=8760
36	0.0099	www.diginet.com	Remote Client	TCP D=80 S=34440 ACK=1037578650 WIN=8760
37	0.0001	www.diginet.com	Remote Client	TCP D=80 S=34440 ACK=1037580110 WIN=8760
38	0.0071	Remote Client	www.diginet.com	HTTP R Port=34439 Graphics Data
39	0.0123	Remote Client	www.diginet.com	HTTP R Port=34440 Graphics Data
.				
.				
.				
91	0.0083	Remote Client	www.diginet.com	HTTP R Port=34440 Graphics Data
92	0.0046	Remote Client	www.diginet.com	HTTP R Port=34440 Graphics Data
93	0.0172	www.diginet.com	Remote Client	TCP D=80 S=34440 ACK=1037628290 WIN=8760

94	0.0714	www.diginet.com	Remote Client	TCP D=80 S=34440 ACK=1037630466 WIN=8760
95	2.7206	www.diginet.com	Remote Client	HTTP C Port=34440 GET /tutorial.html HTTP/1.0
96	0.0208	Remote Client	www.diginet.com	HTTP R Port=34440 OK
97	0.0485	www.diginet.com	Remote Client	TCP D=80 S=34440 ACK=1037631432 WIN=8760
98	0.1167	www.diginet.com	Remote Client	HTTP C Port=34439 GET /image54.gif HTTP/1.0
99	0.0267	Remote Client	www.diginet.com	HTTP R Port=34439 OK
100	0.0097	Remote Client	www.diginet.com	HTTP R Port=34439 Graphics Data
101	0.0067	Remote Client	www.diginet.com	HTTP R Port=34439 Graphics Data
102	0.0097	Remote Client	www.diginet.com	HTTP R Port=34439 Graphics Data
103	0.0050	www.diginet.com	Remote Client	TCP D=80 S=34439 ACK=1037458151 WIN=8760
104	0.0046	Remote Client	www.diginet.com	HTTP R Port=34439 Graphics Data
105	0.0088	Remote Client	www.diginet.com	HTTP R Port=34439 Graphics Data
106	0.0097	Remote Client	www.diginet.com	HTTP R Port=34439 Graphics Data
107	0.0245	www.diginet.com	Remote Client	TCP D=80 S=34439 ACK=1037462247 WIN=8760
108	0.0001	www.diginet.com	Remote Client	TCP D=80 S=34439 ACK=1037466623 WIN=8760
109	0.0208	Remote Client	www.diginet.com	HTTP R Port=34439 Graphics Data
114	0.0085	Remote Client	www.diginet.com	HTTP R Port=34439 Graphics Data
115	0.0014	www.diginet.com	Remote Client	TCP D=80 S=34439 ACK=1037469543 WIN=8760
116	0.0001	www.diginet.com	Remote Client	TCP D=80 S=34439 ACK=1037472463 WIN=8760

117	0.0001	www.diginet.com	Remote Client	TCP D=80 S=34439 ACK=1037475383 WIN=8760
118	0.0231	Remote Client	www.diginet.com	HTTP R Port=34439 Graphics Data
119	0.0066	Remote Client	www.diginet.com	HTTP R Port=34439 Graphics Data
120	0.0900	www.diginet.com	Remote Client	TCP D=80 S=34439 ACK=1037477863 WIN=6280
121	2.0799	www.diginet.com	Remote Client	HTTP C Port=34438 GET /troubletcp.html HTTP/1.0
122	0.0357	Remote Client	www.diginet.com	HTTP R Port=34438 OK
123	0.0445	www.diginet.com	Remote Client	TCP D=80 S=34438 ACK=1037382456 WIN=8760
124	0.1261	www.diginet.com	Remote Client	HTTP C Port=34440 GET /image9.gif HTTP/1.0
125	0.0405	Remote Client	www.diginet.com	HTTP R Port=34440 OK
126	0.0101	Remote Client	www.diginet.com	HTTP R Port=34440 Graphics Data
127	0.0069	Remote Client	www.diginet.com	HTTP R Port=34440 Graphics Data
128	0.0012	www.diginet.com	Remote Client	TCP D=80 S=34440 ACK=1037632892 WIN=8760
129	0.0102	Remote Client	www.diginet.com	HTTP R Port=34440 Graphics Data
130	0.0082	Remote Client	www.diginet.com	HTTP R Port=34440 Graphics Data
131	0.0095	Remote Client	www.diginet.com	HTTP R Port=34440 Graphics Data
.				
.				
.				
232	7.1343	Remote Client	www.diginet.com	TCP D=34438 S=80 FIN ACK=3089806269 SEQ=1037407993 LEN=0 WIN=61320
233	0.0004	www.diginet.com	Remote Client	TCP D=80 S=34438 ACK=1037407994 WIN=8760

234	3.0438	Remote Client	[XXX.YYY.1.4]	DNS C ID=65073 OP=QUERY NAME=117.37.172.140 .in-addr.arpa
235	0.0022	[XXX.YYY.1.4]	Remote Client	DNS R ID=65073 STAT=OK NAME=117.37.172.140 in-addr.arpa
236	0.9173	Remote Client	[XXX.YYY.30.2]	NTP/SNTP Version 3
237	0.0012	[XXX.YYY.30.2]	Remote Client	NTP/SNTP Version 3
238	1.8867	Remote Client	www.diginet.com	TCP D=34440 S=80 FIN ACK=3089876905 SEQ=1037659772 LEN=0 WIN=61320
239	0.0004	www.diginet.com	Remote Client	TCP D=80 S=34440 ACK=1037659773 WIN=8760
240	0.1867	Remote Client	www.diginet.com	TCP D=34439 S=80 FIN ACK=3089846382 SEQ=1037500743 LEN=0 WIN=61320
241	0.0001	www.diginet.com	Remote Client	TCP D=80 S=34439 ACK=1037500744 WIN=8760
242	0.2287	Remote Client	[XXX.YYY.35.1..	NTP/SNTP Version 3
243	0.0011	[XXX.YYY.35.1..	Remote Client	NTP/SNTP Version 3
244	0.9355	[XXX.YYY.105...	Remote Client	TCP D=1090 S=80 FIN ACK=13563200 SEQ=3092005668 LEN=0 WIN=8760
245	0.0925	Remote Client	[XXX.YYY.105...	TCP D=80 S=1090 ACK=3092005669 WIN=7878
246	3.5564	[XXX.YYY.0.1]	Remote Client	IGMP Version 1, Unknown
247	0.3732	[XXX.YYY.73.73]	Remote Client	TCP D=80 S=34436 FIN ACK=587147383 SEQ=3074601632 LEN=0 WIN=8760
248	0.0644	Remote Client	[XXX.YYY.73.73]	TCP D=34436 S=80 ACK=3074601633 WIN=8760
249	0.0326	[XXX.YYY.130.17]	Remote Client	TCP D=80 S=34441 SYN SEQ=3094428755 LEN=0 WIN=8760

```
250      0.0688    Remote Client     [XXX.YYY.130.17]    TCP D=34441 S=80 SYN
                                                           ACK=3094428756
                                                           SEQ=27046812 LEN=0
                                                           WIN=8760
```

Looking at the details of the home page request (Trace 6.10.8b), note that the HTTP Request message specifies the type of request (GET), protocol version (HTTP/1.0), host name (www.diginet.com), and the acceptable types of the response (image/gif, etc.). Note that Line 6 in Frame 12 is the blank line (CRLF), and that there is no message body in the Response.

In the Reply message given in Frame 13, note the status line, which contains the protocol (HTTP/1.1) and numeric status code (200 OK), plus various headers that indicate information about the server, file, date, and so on. Line 11 in Frame 13 is the blank line (CRLF); this is followed by the message body, which contains the HTML file describing the DigiNet Corporation home page, other hyperlinks, and so on.

TRACE 6.10.8B. HTTP DIGINET CORPORATION HOME PAGE DETAILS

```
Sniffer Network Analyzer data from 30-Apr at 09:58:22, file DNC.ENC, Pg 1

- - - - - - - - - - - - - - - - Frame 12 - - - - - - - - - - - - - - - - -

HTTP: —— Hypertext Transfer Protocol ——
HTTP:
HTTP: Line  1:  GET / HTTP/1.0
HTTP: Line  2:  Connection: Keep-Alive
HTTP: Line  3:  User-Agent: Mozilla/3.01 (X11; I; SunOS 5.6 sun4m)
HTTP: Line  4:  Host: www.diginet.com
HTTP: Line  5:  Accept: image/gif, image/x-xbitmap, image/jpeg, image/pjpeg,
HTTP:           */*
HTTP: Line  6:
HTTP:

- - - - - - - - - - - - - - - - Frame 13 - - - - - - - - - - - - - - - - -

HTTP: —— Hypertext Transfer Protocol ——
HTTP:
HTTP: Line  1:  HTTP/1.1 200 OK
HTTP: Line  2:  Date: Thu, 30 Apr 1998 17:02:15 GMT
HTTP: Line  3:  Server: Apache/1.2.4
HTTP: Line  4:  Last-Modified: Wed, 03 Dec 1997 22:35:23 GMT
HTTP: Line  5:  ETag: "901390-358-3485deab"
HTTP: Line  6:  Content-Length: 856
HTTP: Line  7:  Accept-Ranges: bytes
```

```
HTTP: Line  8: Keep-Alive: timeout=15, max=100
HTTP: Line  9: Connection: Keep-Alive
HTTP: Line 10: Content-Type: text/html
HTTP: Line 11:
HTTP: Line 12: <HTML>
HTTP: Line 13: <HEAD>
HTTP: Line 14:   <META NAME="GENERATOR" CONTENT="Adobe PageMill 2.0 Mac">
HTTP: Line 15:   <TITLE>DigiNet Home Page</TITLE>
HTTP: Line 16: </HEAD>
HTTP: Line 17: <BODY BGCOLOR="#f8faff" LINK="#f720ff" ALINK="#ff0af1" BACKG
HTTP:                 ROUND="Skidsblue.gif">
HTTP: Line 18:
HTTP: Line 19: <P ALIGN=CENTER><MAP NAME="Homepage1">
HTTP: Line 20:     <AREA SHAPE="circle" COORDS="276,104,12" HREF="brutus.html">
HTTP: Line 21:     <AREA SHAPE="circle" COORDS="320,126,13" HREF="boomer.html">
HTTP: Line 22:     <AREA SHAPE="circle" COORDS="371,136,13" HREF="publications.html">
HTTP: Line 23:     <AREA SHAPE="circle" COORDS="454,115,12" HREF="tutorial.html">
HTTP: Line 24:     <AREA SHAPE="circle" COORDS="427,70,13" HREF="principal.html">
HTTP: Line 25:     <AREA SHAPE="circle" COORDS="353,44,12" HREF="previousas
HTTP:                 signments.html">
HTTP: Line 26:     <AREA SHAPE="circle" COORDS="284,44,12" HREF="capabilities.html">
HTTP: Line 27: </MAP><IMG SRC="Homepage1.gif" WIDTH="493" HEIGHT="360" ALIG
HTTP:                 N="BOTTOM"
HTTP: Line 28: NATURALSIZEFLAG="3" USEMAP="#Homepage1" ISMAP>
HTTP: Line 29: </BODY>
HTTP: Line 30: </HTML>
HTTP:
```

After perusing the DigiNet Corporation home page, the user clicks on a hyperlink that points to the various tutorials. This issues an HTTP GET message, sent in Frame 95, and the resulting data transfer that begins in Frame 96 (Trace 6.10.8c). In Frame 95 you see the URI (tutorial.html), the host (www.diginet.com), and other information required to accurately communicate the request to the Web server. The Response begins in Frame 96 with the HTML coding of the tutorials page.

TRACE 6.10.8C. HTTP DIGINET CORPORATION TUTORIAL PAGE DETAILS

```
Sniffer Network Analyzer data from 30-Apr at 09:58:22, file DNC.ENC, Pg 1

- - - - - - - - - - - - - - - - Frame 95 - - - - - - - - - - - - - - - - -

HTTP: —— Hypertext Transfer Protocol ——
HTTP:
HTTP: Line  1:  GET /tutorial.html HTTP/1.0
HTTP: Line  2:  Referer: http://www.diginet.com/
HTTP: Line  3:  Connection: Keep-Alive
HTTP: Line  4:  User-Agent: Mozilla/3.01 (X11; I; SunOS 5.6 sun4m)
HTTP: Line  5:  Host: www.diginet.com
HTTP: Line  6:  Accept: image/gif, image/x-xbitmap, image/jpeg, image/pjpeg, */*
HTTP: Line  7:
HTTP:

- - - - - - - - - - - - - - - - Frame 96 - - - - - - - - - - - - - - - - -

HTTP: —— Hypertext Transfer Protocol ——
HTTP:
HTTP: Line  1:  HTTP/1.1 200 OK
HTTP: Line  2:  Date: Thu, 30 Apr 1998 17:02:19 GMT
HTTP: Line  3:  Server: Apache/1.2.4
HTTP: Line  4:  Last-Modified: Tue, 02 Dec 1997 20:39:30 GMT
HTTP: Line  5:  ETag: "80f432-2b1-34847202"
HTTP: Line  6:  Content-Length: 689
HTTP: Line  7:  Accept-Ranges: bytes
HTTP: Line  8:  Keep-Alive: timeout=15, max=99
HTTP: Line  9:  Connection: Keep-Alive
HTTP: Line 10:  Content-Type: text/html
HTTP: Line 11:
HTTP: Line 12:  <HTML>
HTTP: Line 13:  <HEAD>
HTTP: Line 14:    <META NAME="GENERATOR" CONTENT="Adobe PageMill 2.0 Mac">
HTTP: Line 15:    <TITLE>Tutorials</TITLE>
HTTP: Line 16:  </HEAD>
HTTP: Line 17:  <BODY BGCOLOR="#fffdfd" LINK="#ff17f7" BACKGROUND="Skidsblue.gif">
HTTP: Line 18:
HTTP: Line 19:  <P ALIGN=CENTER><MAP NAME="image54">
HTTP: Line 20:      <AREA SHAPE="circle" COORDS="373,135,14" HREF="managinter.html">
HTTP: Line 21:      <AREA SHAPE="circle" COORDS="456,114,14" HREF="implemipv6.html">
HTTP: Line 22:      <AREA SHAPE="circle" COORDS="429,70,14" HREF="troubletcp.html">
HTTP: Line 23:      <AREA SHAPE="circle" COORDS="355,44,14" HREF="analizbroad.html">
HTTP: Line 24:      <AREA SHAPE="circle" COORDS="285,44,15" HREF="intnetdesign.html">
```

```
HTTP: Line 25: </MAP><IMG SRC="image54.gif" WIDTH="530" HEIGHT="339" ALIGN=
HTTP:                "BOTTOM" NATURALSIZEFLAG=
HTTP: Line 26: "3" USEMAP="#image54" ISMAP>
HTTP: Line 27: </BODY>
HTTP: Line 28: </HTML>
HTTP:
```

The user next clicks on the hyperlink that points to the *Troubleshooting TCP/IP* tutorial. This action generates the HTTP Request message shown in Frame 121, and the subsequent Response message and the file transfer that begins in Frame 122 (Trace 6.10.8d). These messages are similar to the two that were described above, except that the Port number used for this transmission (34438) is different from the Port number of the previous transmission (34440). Recall from our discussion above that the Client's Web browser application opened multiple logical connections when it first accessed the Web server, and that we are now seeing the use of those various connections.

TRACE 6.10.8D. HTTP DIGINET CORPORATION TROUBLESHOOTING TCP/IP TUTORIAL PAGE DETAILS

```
Sniffer Network Analyzer data from 30-Apr at 09:58:22, file DNC.ENC, Pg 1

---------------- Frame 121 ----------------

HTTP: —— Hypertext Transfer Protocol ——
HTTP:
HTTP: Line  1: GET /troubletcp.html HTTP/1.0
HTTP: Line  2: Referer: http://www.diginet.com/tutorial.html
HTTP: Line  3: Connection: Keep-Alive
HTTP: Line  4: User-Agent: Mozilla/3.01 (X11; I; SunOS 5.6 sun4m)
HTTP: Line  5: Host: www.diginet.com
HTTP: Line  6: Accept: image/gif, image/x-xbitmap, image/jpeg, image/pjpeg,*/*
HTTP: Line  7:
HTTP:

---------------- Frame 122 ----------------

HTTP: —— Hypertext Transfer Protocol ——
HTTP:
HTTP: Line  1: HTTP/1.1 200 OK
HTTP: Line  2: Date: Thu, 30 Apr 1998 17:02:22 GMT
HTTP: Line  3: Server: Apache/1.2.4
HTTP: Line  4: Last-Modified: Tue, 02 Dec 1997 20:38:38 GMT
HTTP: Line  5: ETag: "80f430-130-348471ce"
```

```
HTTP: Line  6: Content-Length: 304
HTTP: Line  7: Accept-Ranges: bytes
HTTP: Line  8: Keep-Alive: timeout=15, max=99
HTTP: Line  9: Connection: Keep-Alive
HTTP: Line 10: Content-Type: text/html
HTTP: Line 11:
HTTP: Line 12: <HTML>
HTTP: Line 13: <HEAD>
HTTP: Line 14:   <META NAME="GENERATOR" CONTENT="Adobe PageMill 2.0 Mac">
HTTP: Line 15:   <TITLE>Troubleshooting TCP/IP</TITLE>
HTTP: Line 16: </HEAD>
HTTP: Line 17: <BODY BGCOLOR="#fdfffc" LINK="#ff22f2" BACKGROUND="Skidsblue.gif>
HTTP: Line 18:
HTTP: Line 19: <P ALIGN=CENTER><IMG SRC="image9.gif" WIDTH="576" HEIGHT="67
HTTP:                    0" ALIGN="BOTTOM"
HTTP: Line 20: NATURALSIZEFLAG="3">
HTTP: Line 21: </BODY>
HTTP: Line 22: </HTML>
HTTP:
```

6.11 Looking Ahead

In this chapter, we have completed our tour of the ARPA protocol stack as far as user applications are concerned. We have one more higher layer topic to consider: the management of TCP/IP-based internetworks. We will study the Simple Network Management Protocol (SNMP) in Chapter 7.

6.12 References

[6-1] Stallings, William. *Handbook of Computer-Communications Standards, Vol. 3, The TCP/IP Protocol Suite,* second edition. MacMillan Publishing Company (Carmel, Indiana), 1990.

[6-2] Braden, R. "Requirements for Internet Hosts: Application and Support." RFC 1123, October 1989.

[6-3] Reynolds, J., and J. Postel. "Assigned Numbers." RFC 1700, October 1994.

[6-4] Sollins, K. R. "The TFTP Protocol (Revision 2)." RFC 1350, July 1992.

[6-5] Postel, J. "File Transfer Protocol." RFC 959, October 1985.

[6-6] Romkey, John. “FTP’s Tiresome Problems.” *ConneXions* (September 1987): 9–11.

[6-7] Sun Microsystems, Inc. “RPC: Remote Procedure Call Protocol Specification, Version 2.” RFC 1057, June 1988.

[6-8] Sun Microsystems, Inc. “XDR: External Data Representation Standard.” RFC 1014, June 1987.

[6-9] Sun Microsystems, Inc. “NFS: Network File System Protocol Specification.” RFC 1094, March 1989.

[6-10] B. Callaghan, et al. “NFS Version 3 Protocol Specification.” RFC 1813, June 1995.

[6-11] Gerber, Barry. “Distributing Files Unix Style: An NFS Primer.” *Network Computing* (December 1991): 88–90.

[6-12] Alderson, Bill, and J. Scott Haugdahl. “NFS Woes Creating Work Nightmare.” *Network Computing* (May 15, 1995): 111–112.

[6-13] Ballard, Jeff. “NFS Gateway Products for NT: A New Spin on NFS to the Desktop.” *Network Computing* (June 1, 1998): 98–104.

[6-14] Malamud, Carl. *Analyzing Sun Networks.* Van Nostrand Reinhold (New York), 1992.

[6-15] Postel, J., and J. Reynolds. “TELNET Protocol Specification.” RFC 854, May 1983.

[6-16] Postel, J., and J. Reynolds. “TELNET Option Specifications.” RFC 855, May 1983.

[6-17] Shein, Barry. “The TELNET Protocol.” *ConneXions* (October 1989): 32–38.

[6-18] Postel, J. “Simple Mail Transfer Protocol.” RFC 821, August 1982.

[6-19] Crocker, David H. “Standard for the Format of ARPA Internet Text Messages.” RFC 822, August 1982.

[6-20] Crocker, David. “Back to Basics: Internet Electronic Mail.” *ConneXions* (January 1995): 8–17.

[6-21] Steinke, Steve. “Priority E-Mail.” *LAN Magazine* (July 1995): 46–52.

[6-22] Freed, N., and N. Borenstein. “Multipurpose Internet Mail Extensions (MIME) Part One: Format of Internet Message Bodies.” RFC 2045, November 1996.

[6-23] Freed, N., and N. Borenstein. "Multipurpose Internet Mail Extensions (MIME) Part Two: Media Types." RFC 2046, November 1996.

[6-24] Moore, K. "MIME (Multipurpose Internet Mail Extensions) Part Three: Message Header Extensions for Non-ASCII Text." RFC 2047, November 1996.

[6-25] Freed, N., et al. "Multipurpose Internet Mail Extensions (MIME) Part Four: Registration Procedures." RFC 2048, November 1996.

[6-26] Freed, N., and N. Borenstein. "Multipurpose Internet Mail Extensions (MIME) Part Five: Conformance Criteria and Examples." RFC 2049, November 1996.

[6-27] Robertson, Bruce. "MIME Speaks Volumes." *Network Computing* (November 1, 1994): 135–138.

[6-28] Backman, Dan. "Secure E-Mail Clients: Not Quite Ready For S/MIME Prime Time. Stay Tuned." *Network Computing* (February 1, 1998): 94–102.

[6-29] Jander, Mary. "One-for-All Mail Call." *Data Communications* (May 21, 1998): 78–88.

[6-30] Haugdahl, J. Scott. *Inside NetBIOS*, third edition. Architecture Technology Corporation (Minneapolis, Minn.), 1992.

[6-31] NetBIOS Working Group. "Protocol Standard for a NetBIOS Service on TCP/UDP Transport: Concepts and Methods." RFC 1001, March 1987.

[6-32] NetBIOS Working Group. "Protocol Standard for a NetBIOS Service on a TCP/UDP Transport: Detailed Specifications." RFC 1002, March 1987.

[6-33] Fielding, R., et al. "Hypertext Transfer Protocol – HTTP/1.1." RFC 2068, January 1997.

[6-34] Berners-Lee, T., et al. "Uniform Resource Identifiers in WWW, a Unifying Syntax for the Expression of Names and Addresses of Objects on the Network as used in the World-Wide Web." RFC 1630, June 1994.

[6-35] Sollins, K., and L. Masinter. "Functional Requirements for Uniform Resource Names." RFC 1737, December 1994.

[6-36] Berners-Lee, T., et al. "Uniform Resource Locators (URL)." RFC 1738, December 1994.

[6-37] Berners-Lee, T., and D. Connolly. "Hypertext Markup Language – 2.0." RFC 1866, November 1995.

[6-38] Enger, R., and J. Reynolds. "FYI on a Network Management Tool Catalog: Tools for Monitoring and Debugging TCP/IP Internets and Interconnected Devices." RFC 1470, June 1993.

[6-39] VanBokkelen, J. "TELNET Terminal-Type Option." RFC 1091, February 1989.

[6-40] Nasr, Alex. "TN3270: An Interoperability Option." *3TECH, The 3Com Technical Journal* (Winter 1992): 51–59.

[6-41] Marsh, Bob. "How Important is TN3270 to You?" *Network Computing* (May 1993): 144–148.

Chapter 7

Managing the Internet

The term *network management* means different things to different people. A corporate executive might consider the value of his or her internetwork – such as the data and time savings that come from internetworking – and the costs associated with downtime. A vendor sees potential sales opportunities; any incompatibilities between the network management system and the devices to be managed mean a potential opportunity to sell another product or service. Finally, the network manager – the person in the trenches, catching it from users, corporate managers, and vendors – sees "network management" as a dream; it's something he or she will be able to accomplish once all the fires are out and as long as no new fires erupt in the meantime.

So how can a network manager find the time to design a plan to save time? Is that manager operating in a *reactive* or a *proactive* mode? These issues have faced many managers of TCP/IP-related internetworks, and they undoubtedly gave rise to the development of the most popular protocol for internetwork management: the Simple Network Management Protocol (SNMP). In this chapter, we'll study the alternatives for managing TCP/IP-based internetworks: SNMP, plus other options from ISO and IEEE, both based on ISO's Common Management Information Protocol, or CMIP.

Over the last few years, a major skirmish has been waged within the network management community regarding Internet (SNMP) vs. ISO (CMIP) network management solutions. (This skirmish is part of a bigger battle, however – the Internet vs. OSI protocol wars. The most famous combatants were TCP/IP and GOSIP (Government Open Systems Interconnection Profile), with TCP/IP being declared the clear winner [7-1].) While the CMIP solution has made some inroads, primarily with the telephone carriers and in Europe, SNMP has gathered extremely widespread support among internetworking vendors of hardware, software, and network management platform products.

We'll begin by discussing the issue of network management in general, and then we'll look at the various protocol alternatives individually. In response to the marketplace directives, however, we will invest the majority of our discussion time on the most popular solution – SNMP.

7.1 Managing Internetworks

All major players in the computing marketplace offer some type of network management system. These vendors include Cabletron Systems, Compaq Computer Corp., (formerly Digital Equipment Corp.) Hewlett-Packard, IBM, Novell, Intel, and a host of others. The requirement for network management systems undoubtedly grew out of the need to manage numerous terminals that were initially connected to mainframes and later to LANs. Today, network or internetwork management systems assist the human manager in understanding and dealing with the complexities of the internetwork.

Network management systems have many common threads, regardless of their size, shape, or manufacturer. ISO 7498-4 [7-2], which accompanies the Open Systems Interconnection Reference Model (OSI-RM), summarizes these similarities and offers a framework for network management. The standard divides the functions of network management into five Specific Management Functional Areas (SMFAs), shown in Figure 7-1. These include fault management, accounting management, configuration management, performance management, and security management. We'll look at each of these areas individually, although in practice there is some overlap between them.

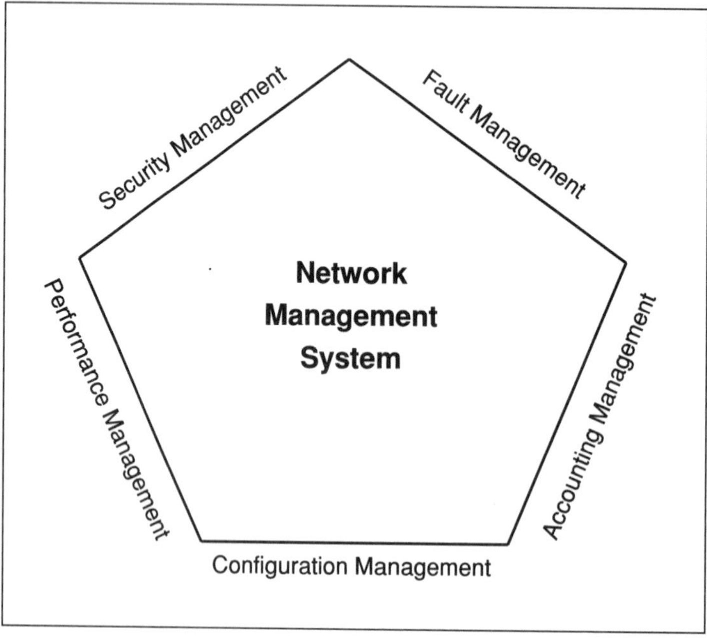

Figure 7-1 OSI Specific Management Functional Areas

7.1.1 Fault Management

A fault within open systems is defined as something that causes those systems "to fail to meet their operational objectives." Three elements are involved in managing system faults: detection of the fault, isolation of the fault to a particular component, and correction of the fault. Fault management, therefore, may include the maintenance of error logs, error detection processes, and diagnostic testing procedures. For many managers, the term network management is synonymous with fault management.

7.1.2 Accounting Management

As businesses strive to more clearly identify their sources of revenue and expense, the practice of charging individual groups or organizations for their use of network resources is becoming more common. Accounting management provides mechanisms to identify costs, to inform the users of costs incurred, and to associate tariff information with resource use.

7.1.3 Configuration Management

Configuration management involves detailing parameters of network configuration, the current topology, and operational status of the network, as well as associating user names with devices. Also included is the ability to change the configuration of the system when necessary. Medium to large networks often find that the human resource costs necessary to move, add, and change network devices such as terminals (sometimes known as the MAC costs) can be very high.

7.1.4 Performance Management

Performance and fault management are difficult to separate. High performance usually implies a low incidence of faults. Performance management, however, goes beyond minimizing faults; it is responsible for gathering statistics on the operation of the network, maintaining and analyzing logs of the state of the system, and optimizing network operation.

7.1.5 Security Management

In the past few years, with news about viruses, worms, and hackers loose on the Internet, network security has become a new subindustry. In addition, the growing interest in electronic commerce, especially over the World Wide Web, has heightened network managers' awareness of security concerns. The issue of security management includes the ability to create, delete, and control security services; to distribute security-related information; or to report security-related events. Other areas of responsibility include enforcing secure passwords for users; controlling access to subnets or hosts via switches, routers, or gateways; and providing remote access to network elements for purposes of network diagnostics.

7.1.6 Managing TCP/IP-Based Internetworks

After our discussion about managing open systems, it's logical to ask if there's any difference between managing generic open systems and TCP/IP-based internetworks. Theoretically, the answer is no, since all internetworks are based on some type of layered architecture, be it OSI, ARPA, or SNA. Practically, however, there are big differences. First, there's a difference in perspective: TCP/IP-based internetworks are designed to be multivendor systems; systems built solely upon SNA or DECnet are single-vendor systems. Managers of multivendor systems start with different assumptions than those who purchase all their equipment from one supplier. If you know it's your job (not the vendor's) to integrate all of the subsystems, you'll look at management as an integral part of the internetwork, not an ancillary element.

A second difference lies in the implementation of network management systems and the protocols available for use. Within the Internet community, the Simple Network Management Protocol (SNMP) has gathered the most support from network management system vendors and from internetworking device manufacturers. A second standard, known as the Common Management Information Protocol (CMIP), has received international support from organizations such as the ISO, CCITT, and IEEE. A TCP/IP-based version of CMIP, known as CMOT (CMIP over TCP/IP), is also available as RFC 1189, but it has not gathered the widespread support of SNMP. Both SNMP and CMIP/CMOT are based on an Agent/Manager paradigm, which bears some resemblance to the Client/Server paradigm with which we are now all familiar. We'll study this model in the next section.

In RFC 1052, the Internet Architecture Board (IAB) declared support for the use of both SNMP and CMIP/CMOT; however, industry consensus in the last few years has overwhelmingly moved in favor of the SNMP solution. Various papers in two issues of *ConneXions, The Interoperability Report* provide practical information on the management of TCP/IP-based internetworks [7-3]. Marshall Rose's [7-4] and Uyless Black's [7-5] books are also valuable references in the network management arena. A companion text, *Managing Internetworks with SNMP* [7-6], illustrates the use of SNMP with a number of protocol analyzer–based case studies.

7.2 The Agent/Manager Model

In the last few years, computing architectures have migrated from centralized, mainframe-based environments to distributed, minicomputer environments to today's popular client/server LAN environments. The architecture of network management systems has mirrored the migration path of computing architectures. They have moved from host-based systems to distributed systems to today's systems, which use a methodology called the Agent/Manager Model (shown in Figure 7-2) that resembles the Client/Server paradigm. (Agent/Manager is also called the Managed System/Managing System.)

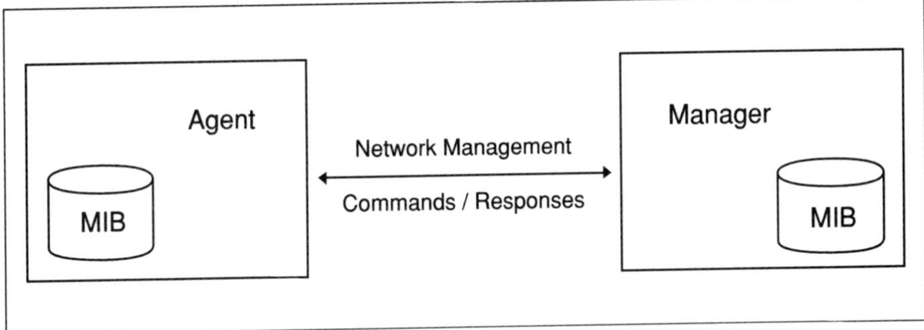

Figure 7-2 The Agent/Manager Model

To begin with, the Agent/Manager system manages devices, which are called *objects*. ISO 7498-4 [7-2] defines four characteristics for each object: its attributes, its operations, the notifications it issues, and its relationships with other objects. Thus, the term object goes beyond a physical device to encompass the device's behaviors. The definition for each object is contained in the Management Information Base (MIB), which we will discuss in the next section.

The *Agent* resides in the object and reports the object's current status to the Manager. Most internetworking products, from the simplest bridge to the most complex ATM switch, come with an embedded SNMP agent.

The *Manager* is a console that maintains global knowledge of the internetwork in question. The console includes three functions: a Graphical User Interface (GUI), a database, and communications facilities. The GUI enables the human manager to visualize the internetwork. With most systems, the GUI draws a topological map that indicates the location and status (normal, abnormal, alarm, and so on) of each managed element and the links between elements. The console's database keeps track of the internetwork elements and the parameters for those elements. The console also includes a mechanism for communicating with the managed elements using a protocol such as SNMP or CMIP. These three functions enable the Manager to see what is happening on the internetwork, to communicate with the devices being managed to query or modify parameters, and to dynamically oversee the internetwork's operation. Two excellent articles that describe the Agent/Manager paradigm are [7-7] and [7-8].

Two protocols that employ this Agent/Manager paradigm are SNMP and CMIP/CMOT. Over the past few years, a controversy has raged in the internetworking industry over whether the SNMP or the CMIP/CMOT protocol will emerge as the predominant choice for network management. Both have a number of advantages and disadvantages. For example, SNMP is a proven technology, while CMIP is not as widely deployed. SNMP is relatively inexpensive in its implementation, while CMIP is not. On the other hand, CMIP is much more powerful than SNMP, although many current internetwork applications are satisfied with SNMP. CMIP is also an international (ISO) standard; SNMP is a de facto (Internet) standard. CMIP is connection-oriented, hence more reliable, while SNMP is connectionless. References [7-9] and [7-10] provide further historical details on the underlying philosophies of these two protocols; we will look at these protocols individually in Sections 7.4 through 7.7. For a number of years, however, SNMP has been the preferred network management protocol, and for that reason we will concentrate our discussion on SNMP.

Once you've implemented the Agent/Manager paradigm and selected a way to communicate (i.e., SNMP or CMIP) between internetwork elements, you're almost ready to manage the internetwork. The final issue to consider is the type and amount of information you need to keep track of. We will discuss the nature of management information in the next section.

7.3 The SNMP Network Management Process

In the previous section, we discussed how the Agent/Manager model carries network management information between devices on a distributed, managed internetwork. The type and amount of network management information transmitted over the internet determines the amount of processing and storage the Agent and the Manager will require, and it may also impact the choice of network management protocol – simple (SNMP) or more complex (CMIP/CMOT).

The information is contained within a management system that, because of the complexity of the information being managed, consists of multiple components: the Structure of Management Information (SMI), the Management Information Base (MIB), and the protocol (such as SNMP). The SMI identifies the structures that describe the management information, the MIB details the objects to be managed, and the protocol communicates between Agent and Manager.

In the next few sections, we will look at the SMI, the MIB, and the protocol. Readers should be advised that the area of network management in general, and SNMP in particular, is a very dynamic subject, with new elements of the architectures added frequently. With SNMP, versions of the protocol have been defined:

SNMPv1 (1990); SNMPv2 (1993); a revised SNMPv2, often called SNMPv2C, for Community-based SNMP (1996); and SNMPv3 (1998). The original Internet-standard Network Management Framework (SNMPv1) is defined in three documents: the SMI, RFC 1155 [7-11]; the MIB definitions, RFC 1212 [7-12]; and the protocol, RFC 1157 [7-13]. SNMPv2C (which obsoletes the 1993 version of SNMPv2) is defined in eight documents, RFCs 1901–1908, and is known as the SNMPv2 framework. SNMPv3 is defined in RFCs 2271–2275.

As of this writing, the vast majority of the SNMP implementations within the internetworking industry have embraced SNMPv1, even though versions 2 and 3 of the protocol contain significant improvements. These enhancements notwithstanding, we will concentrate our discussion on SNMPv1, but will also describe the improvements that these other versions promise to bring to the network management process.

7.3.1 The Structure of Management Information

Since internetworks can be quite large and can maintain voluminous amounts of information about each device, network managers need a way to organize and manage that information. The SMI provides a mechanism to name and organize objects. The MIB stores the information about each managed object.

The SMI uses a conceptual tree, with various objects representing the leaves, to help users visualize the structure of the Internet. The objects are represented using the concepts from an ISO protocol known as Abstract Syntax Notation-1 (ASN.1) [7-14]. The SMI assigns each object a sequence of integers, known as an Object Identifier, or OID, to locate its position on the tree (see Figure 7-3).

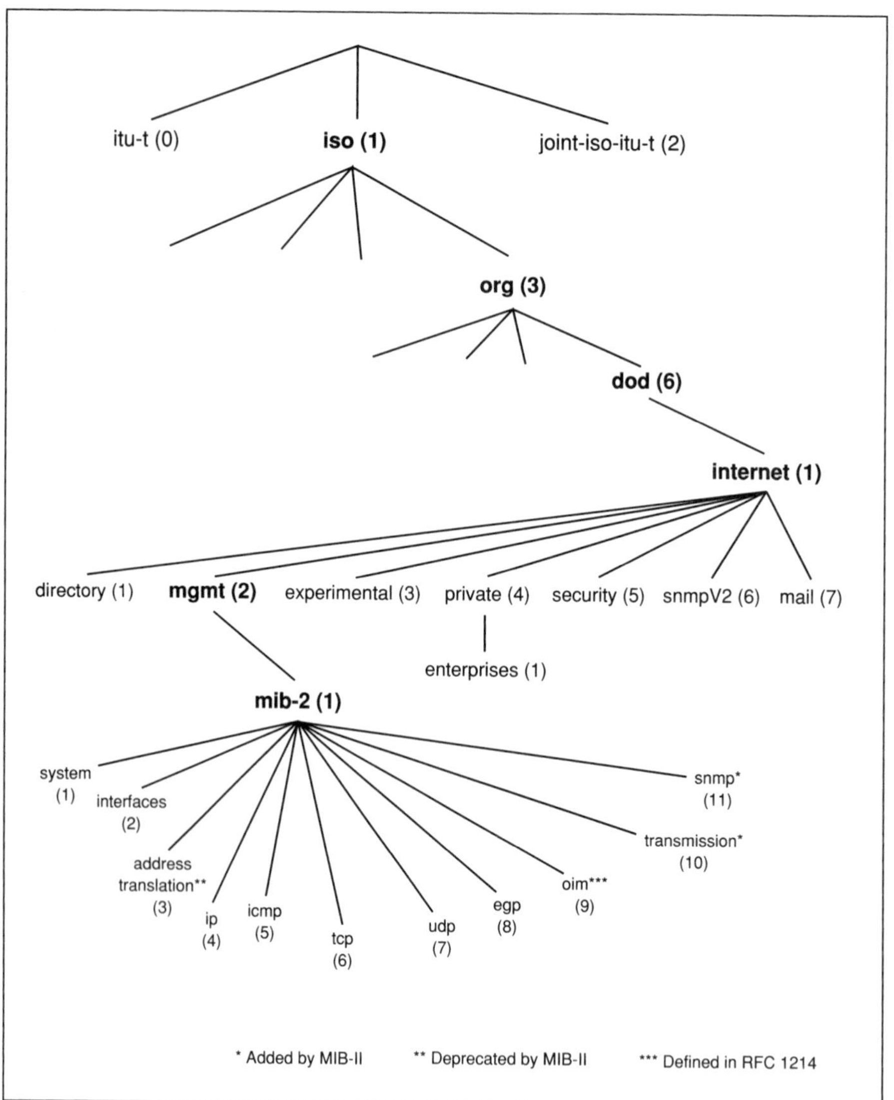

Figure 7-3 The Internet Object Identifier Tree

The root of the tree has no name, but it has three branches called children. Different standards bodies administer different branches: the ITU-T is in charge of Branch 0; ISO administers Branch 1; ITU-T and ISO jointly administer Branch 2.

ISO designates its branch for several organizations. For example, it has assigned branch 3 to other international organizations *(org)*. One of these organizations is the U.S. Department of Defense, which is assigned branch 6 (and designated *dod*). The first branch under *dod* is designated, for the Internet objects *(internet)*. Therefore, to reach the Internet branch, all Object Identifiers begin with {1.3.6.1}, which means that their path from the root is *iso, org, dod, internet*. Historically, Object Identifiers have been enclosed in curly braces, as in {1.3.6.1}.

The Internet branch has seven subbranches defined: *directory* (1), *mgmt* (2), *experimental* (3), *private* (4), *security* (5), *SNMPV2* (6), and *mail* (7). *Directory* is planned for the OSI Directory; *mgmt* is used for objects defined in the Internet Activities Board (IAB)-approved documents; *experimental* is used for Internet experiments; *private* is used to define vendor-specific (or private MIB) objects; *security* is for management security; *SNMPV2* contains SNMPv2-specific objects; and *mail* is used for mail objects.

The Internet Assigned Numbers Authority (IANA) administers the *experimental* and *private* branches and documents these administrations in the Assigned Numbers document (currently RFC 1700). IANA designates Branch 1 under the *private* branch for enterprises and assigns vendors an enterprise branch to identify their various devices. For example, an Object Identifier associated with the ABC Company would be designated {1.3.6.1.4.1.a}. The {1.3.6.1} designates the *internet* branch, 4.1 indicates a *private, enterprise* branch, and *a* is assigned to the ABC Company. The ABC Company could further assign identifiers for its switches, routers, network adapters, and so on – for example, {1.3.6.1.4.1.a.1.1}.

In addition to the Object Identifier, the SNMPv1 SMI defines six object (or data) types. These include the NetworkAddress, IpAddress, Counter, Gauge, TimeTicks, and Opaque. For example, the IpAddress type represents a 32-bit Internet address. Further explanations about the syntax and usage of the types are given in RFC 1155. SNMPv2 and SNMPv3 define additional data types, which will be discussed in Sections 7.5 and 7.6, respectively.

7.3.2 Management Information Base

While the SMI defines the tree structure for the Object Identifiers, the MIB defines information about the actual objects being managed and/or controlled. For example, the MIB might store an IP routing table and its table entries.

Two versions of the Internet MIB for SNMPv1 have been published: MIB-I, RFC 1156 [7-15], and the enhanced MIB-II, RFC 1213 [7-16]. Within each MIB, the objects are divided into various groups. Grouping the objects accomplishes two objectives: it allows a more orderly assignment of Object Identifiers, and it defines the objects that the Agents must implement. The currently defined groups include:

Group	Object ID	Description
system	mib-2 1	Description of that entity.
interfaces	mib-2 2	Number of network interfaces that can send/receive IP datagrams.
at	mib-2 3	Tables of Network Address to Physical Address translations.
ip	mib-2 4	IP routing and datagram statistics.
icmp	mib-2 5	ICMP I/O statistics.
tcp statistics.	mib-2 6	TCP connection parameters and
udp	mib-2 7	UDP traffic statistics and datagram delivery problems.
egp	mib-2 8	EGP traffic, neighbors, and states.
transmission	mib-2 10	Transmission media information.
snmp	mib-2 11	SNMP-related objects.

MIB-II has rendered the Address Translation (AT) group obsolete and has added the Transmission and SNMP groups. MIB-II has also added new values, variables, tables, columns, and so on, to other groups. For example, the standard mentions a CMOT Object Identifier (mib-2 9), which is described in RFC 1214 on OSI Internet Management (OIM). Three excellent sources of information on MIBs include David Perkins' "How to Read and Use an SNMP MIB" [7-17], David Perkins' and Evan McGinnis' book, *Understanding SNMP MIBs* [7-18], and Bob Stewart's "Development and Integration of a Management Information Base" [7-19].

A number of MIBs, both standard and vendor-specific (private), have been developed. One example is the RMON MIB, used for Remote Network Monitoring. Its functions include managing critical functions of remote networks, such as traffic thresholds, collisions on a particular segment, and alarms. Several RFCs define RMON functions: RFC 1757 [7-20] discusses RMON for Ethernet networks, and RFC 1513 [7-21] deals with RMON extensions to support token ring networks. In addition, RMON functions supporting upper layer protocol functions, known as RMON2, have been developed [7-22]. References [7-23] and [7-24] are recent journal articles that discuss RMON and RMON2 applications.

Below is a representative list of available MIBs. For current information, see the (unofficial) index listed in the *Simple Times* newsletter [7-25].

RFC	Subject
1156	Management Information Base (MIB-I)
1212	Concise MIB Definitions
1213	Management Information Base (MIB-II)
1214	OSI Internet Management MIB (Historic)
1406	DS1/E1 Interface Type MIB
1407	DS3/E3 Interface Type MIB
1493	Bridge MIB
1512	FDDI Interface Type MIB
1516	IEEE 802.3 Repeater MIB
1525	Source Routing Bridge MIB
1559	DECnet Phase IV MIB
1659	RS-232 Interface Type MIB
1660	Parallel Printer Interface Type MIB
1694	SMDS Interface Protocol (SIP) Interface Type MIB
1695	ATM MIB
1742	AppleTalk MIB
1748	IEEE 802.5 Token Ring Interface Type MIB
1757	Remote Network Monitoring (RMON) MIB
1759	Printer MIB
1850	OSPF version 2 MIB
2115	Frame Relay DTE Interface Type MIB
2021	RMON2 MIB
2358	Ethernet Interfaces MIB

7.4 Simple Network Management Protocol Version 1 (SNMPv1)

So far, we've discussed two of the three elements of a network management system: the Structure of Management Information (SMI) and the Management Information Base (MIB). These elements provide management information and the mechanism for accessing that information. The third element is the protocol used between the Agent and the Manager.

The IAB determined the need for a network management protocol and reported it in RFC 1052 [7-26]. The IAB concluded at that time that SNMP should be used in the short term, with OSI-based management strategies as the long-term solution. Network managers, however, needed solutions that could be implemented immediately. Since SNMP was available, it became the protocol of choice. Marketplace experience over the last few years has demonstrated the predominance of SNMP over OSI-based solutions, indicating that it has become more than just a short-term solution. Recent SNMP MIB developments, supporting broadband networking solutions such as frame relay, SMDS, and ATM, also testify to the firm foothold that SNMP has gathered within the network management community. Many analysts predict that it will be the favored long-term solution as well.

SNMP, which we will study in this section and in Sections 7.5 and 7.6, is used predominantly with TCP/IP-based internets. CMIP/CMOT is intended for OSI-based internetworks and IEEE 802 LANs. We will discuss the OSI and IEEE strategies in Sections 7.7 and 7.8.

7.4.1 SNMPv1 Architecture

The Simple Network Management Protocol was based on the Simple Gateway Monitoring Protocol (SGMP) described in RFC 1028. It was developed to be an efficient means of sending network management information over a UDP transport using Port numbers 161 (SNMP) and 162 (SNMPTRAP).

Although SNMP is an application, it is somewhat different from the other application protocols discussed in Chapter 6. As articulated by Case et al., "network management is an application fundamentally different in its requirements than any other application that makes use of the network" [7-27]. These differences include network management's needs for ubiquity, supporting instrumentation, and robustness that may not be necessary for other upper layer processes.

The SNMP architecture (see Figure 7-4) contains several elements that we explored earlier in this chapter. SNMP offers a management system that includes the SNMP Manager. The managed system includes an SNMP Agent, resources to be managed, and the SNMP messages (such as the Get and the GetResponse) that communicate the management information. Note that the protocol implements only five messages – a testimony to the "simple" part of SNMP's name.

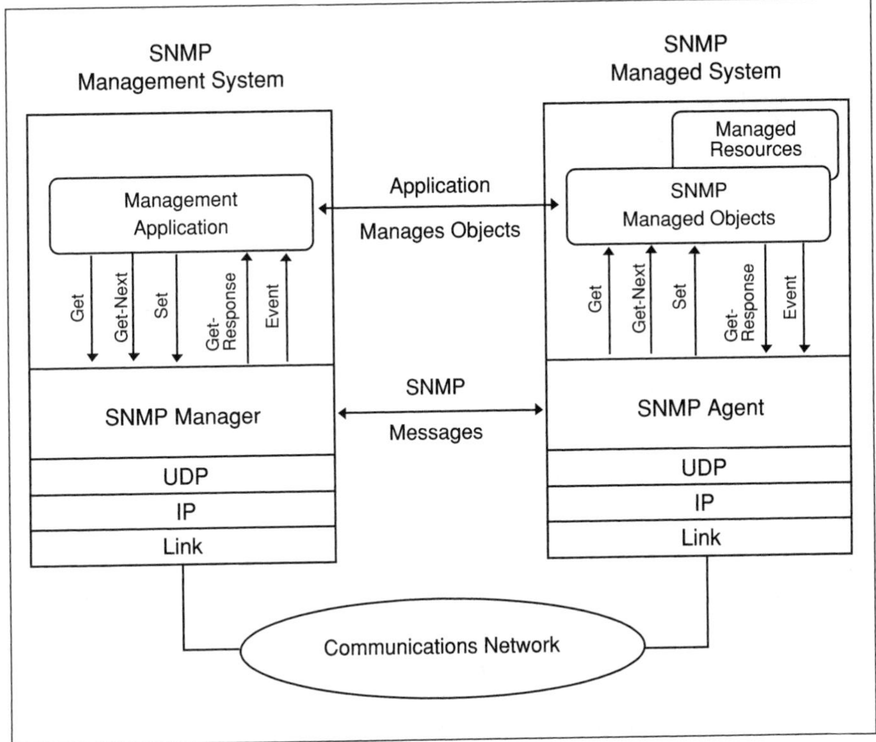

Figure 7-4 Simple Network Management Protocol Version 1 Architecture
(© 1990, IEEE)

7.4.2 SNMPv1 Messages

SNMP is a *polling* protocol in which the Manager asks a question (the poll) and the Agent responds. UDP transport transmits all SNMP messages, and all messages use Port number 161 except the Trap message, which uses Port number 162. The standard does not require SNMP implementations to accept messages that exceed 484 octets in length, although support for larger datagrams is recommended.

The SNMP message follows the UDP header and is placed within a transmission frame (see Figure 7-5). The message consists of a Version Identifier, an SNMP Community name, and the SNMP Protocol Data Units (PDUs). The Version Identifier ensures that both SNMP endpoints use the same version of the protocol. The Community name is encoded as a string of octets and is used for authentication; it ensures the proper relationship between the requesting SNMP Manager and the responding SNMP Agent. The combination of the Version Identifier and the Community name is sometimes called the Authentication header. This header is found in all SNMP messages.

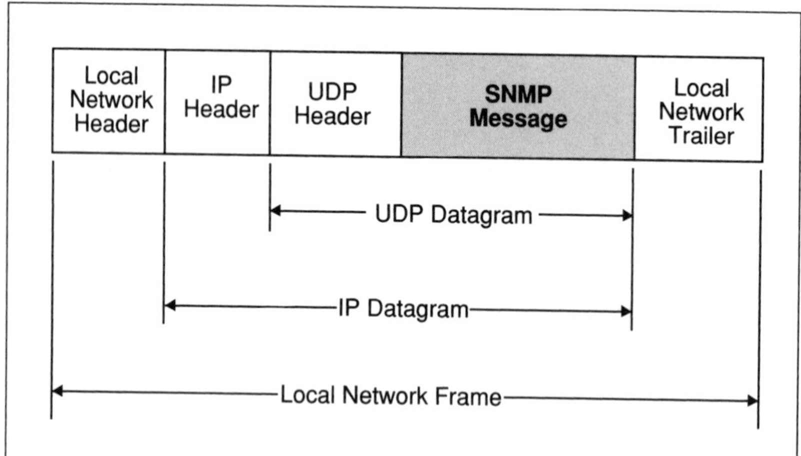

Figure 7-5 SNMP Message within a Transmission Frame

Five PDUs are defined for SNMP. These include GetRequest, GetResponse, GetNextRequest, SetRequest, and Trap. The GetRequest allows the SNMP Manager to access information stored in the Agent. The GetNextRequest is similar, but allows the Manager to obtain multiple values in the tree. SetRequest is used to change the value of a variable. GetResponse is a response to the GetRequest, GetNextRequest, or SetRequest, and also contains error and status information. Finally, the Trap PDU reports on an event that has occurred.

PDUs have two general structures, one for the Request/Response PDUs and another for the Trap (see Figures 7-6a and 7-6b, respectively). The Request/Response PDUs contain five fields that identify and transfer the management information in question. The first subfield is a PDU Type, which specifies which of the five PDUs is in use. The values are:

Value	PDU Type
0	GetRequest
1	GetNextRequest
2	GetResponse
3	SetRequest
4	Trap

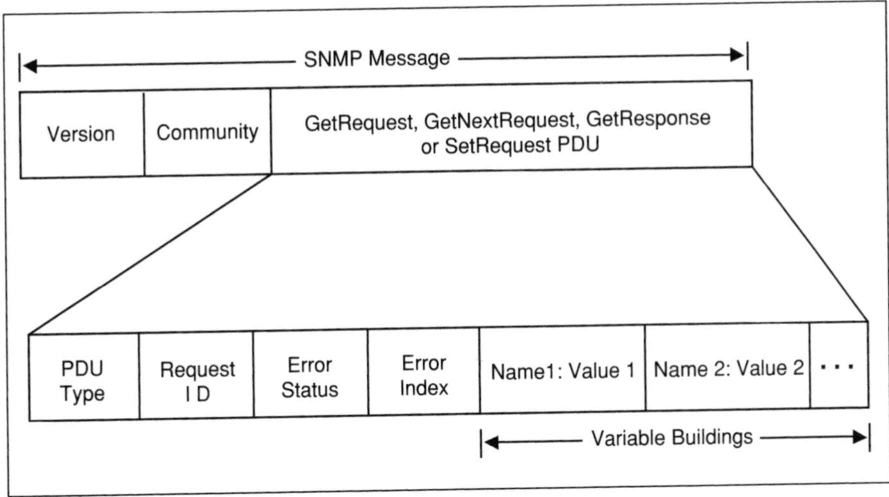

Figure 7-6a SNMPv1 Get Request, GetNextRequest, GetResponse, and SetRequest PDU Structures

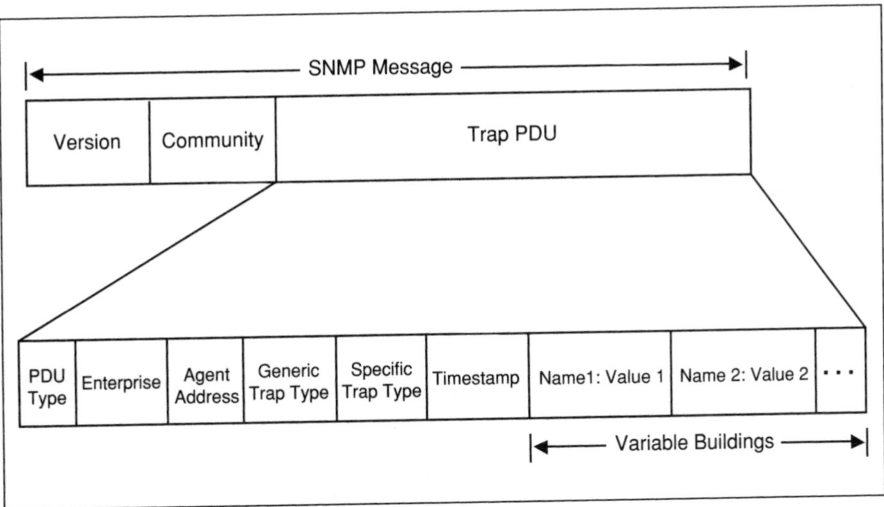

Figure 7-6b SNMPv1 Trap PDU Structure

The Request ID field correlates the request from the SNMP Manager with the response from the SNMP Agent. The Error Status field indicates that some exception occurred while processing the request. Values for that field are:

Value	Error	Description
0	noError	No error
1	tooBig	Operation results are too big for a single SNMP message
2	noSuchName	Unknown variable name
3	badValue	Incorrect value or variable when using SetRequest
4	readOnly	SetRequest not allowed for read-only variable
5	genErr	Other error

The Error Index field points to the variable in the Variable Bindings field that caused the error. The first variable is given variable number 1, the second variable number 2, and so on. The last field is the Variable Bindings (VarBind) field, which contains the management information being requested. A VarBind pairs an object name with its value. An example of a VarBind would be a sysDescr (System Description) for object {1.3.6.1.2.1.1.1}, paired with a value that indicates the vendor-specified name for that system.

Because the Trap PDU reports on events rather than responding to the Manager's query, it requires a different message structure. Seven fields follow the Trap PDU's Version and Community fields (review Figure 7-6b). The first field is the PDU Type, with the Trap assigned Type = 4. The second field is called Enterprise and contains the SNMP Agent's sysObjectID, which indicates the type of network management system located in that Agent. Next, the Agent Address field contains the IP address of the SNMP Agent that generated this trap. The Generic Trap Type specifies the exact type of message. There are seven possible values for this field:

Value	Trap	Description
0	coldStart	The sending protocol entity is reinitializing; the Agent configuration or protocol entity implementation may be altered.
1	warmStart	The sending protocol entity is reinitializing; however, no alterations have been made.
2	linkDown	Communication link in the Agent has failed.
3	linkUp	Communication link in the Agent is now up.
4	Authentication Failure	The sending protocol entity has received an improperly authenticated message.

Value	Trap	Description
5	egpNeighborLoss	An EGP peer is down.
6	enterpriseSpecific	An enterprise-specific event has occurred, as defined in the Enterprise field that follows.

The Specific Trap Type elaborates on the type of trap indicated. The Timestamp field transmits the current value of the Agent's sysUpTime object, specifying when the indicated event occurred. As with the Request/Response PDUs, the Variable Bindings contain pairs of object names and values. Examples of the various SNMP PDUs will be explored in Section 7.11.

7.5 Simple Network Management Protocol Version 2 (SNMPv2)

Despite its popularity, SNMP has some disadvantages. One obvious limitation is SNMP's use of a connectionless architecture based on UDP transport. As discussed in Chapter 5, connectionless systems lack the reliability many applications may require. Second, it is cumbersome to retrieve SNMP information because the protocol offers no way to filter information. Thus, the SNMP Manager must obtain all the value(s) of the object(s), then determine whether they're of interest. (In contrast, CMIP allows conditional commands that query the value first, then determine whether the value should be transmitted.) Third, and associated with the information retrieval issue, polling of SNMP information (the GetRequest/GetResponse sequences) may consume precious internetwork bandwidth, especially if that polling is done over a WAN connection. Finally, the limited amount of security originally designed into the protocol (via the Community string) is not adequate for many internetwork applications.

As SNMP implementations became more widespread, the inadequacies of this "simple" protocol became more apparent. In 1992, the IETF began the process of formally addressing these issues, which fell into two major categories: protocol enhancements and security enhancements. The results from these two efforts were combined into what became known as SNMPv2, and were published as RFCs 1441–1452 in May 1993. References [7-28] and [7-29] detail the capabilities of SNMPv2.

Unfortunately, these enhancements, particularly in the area of security, were relatively complex. As a result, the marketplace, from both the perspective of the network management platform vendors (with their Managers) and the internetworking hardware/software vendors (with their Agents), did not readily embrace these enhancements [7-30].

As a result, the IETF went back to the drawing board and modified SNMPv2 to reflect more workable solutions. The results, published in January 1996 in RFCs 1901–1908 [7-31], document that work. The new version has been called SNMPv2C, where the "C" represents a *community-based* administrative framework. An SNMP community is defined in SNMPv1 (RFC 1157) as "a pairing of an SNMP agent with some arbitrary set of SNMP application entities." Further, each of these SNMP communities is named by a string of octets, called the Community string. The Community string occupies a field within the SNMPv1 that acts like a password, ensuring a simple form of security between Manager and Agent.

In areas not relating to security, the revised version kept many of the original SNMPv2 enhancements. These include the availability of additional data types, the ability to retrieve large amounts of data with a single command (the GETBULK message), and the use of other transport protocols, such as AppleTalk, Novell's IPX, and the OSI Connectionless-mode Network Service (CLNS) and Connection-oriented Network Service (CONS) protocols. In essence, the complex security provisions from SNMPv2 were relaxed, while the other protocol enhancements were left largely in place. Two security frameworks were proposed: SNMPv2u, defined in RFC 1910; and SNMPv2*, defined in IETF draft documents. This work formed the basis for SNMPv3.

7.6 Simple Network Management Protocol Version 3 (SNMPv3)

The requirement to enhance SNMP management frameworks, with an eye toward larger, enterprise-wide internetworks, was one of the driving factors behind the development of SNMPv3, which is documented in RFCs 2271 [7-32] through 2275. The SNMPv3 development efforts were built on the SNMPv2C, SNMPv2u, and SNMPv2* research projects, and incorporated many of the protocol enhancements from that previous work.

The focus of the SNMPv3 development efforts has been in the areas of security, administration, and remote configuration. The security aspects include authentication and privacy, plus authorization and access control. The Message Digest version 5 (MD5) and Data Encryption Standard (DES) protocols are used for these security features. The administrative framework describes the relationship between an Agent and the devices that the Agent is managing. This framework deals with the naming of entities, policies, usernames, management of security keys, proxy relationships, and so on.

In addition, interoperability with existing SNMPv1 and SNMPv2 products was also a prime development consideration, as it is well understood that the large installed base of SNMPv1 Agents will not be upgraded overnight to SNMPv3. Mechanisms for coexistence are thus required and are included as part of the

SNMPv3 development. Many of these issues are explored in the *Simple Times* newsletter [7-25].

7.7 Common Management Information Protocol (CMIP/CMOT)

The ISO defined a framework for network management, ISO 7498-4 (discussed in Section 7.1), and the five Specific Management Functional Areas (SMFAs) shown in Figure 7-1. CMIP/CMOT does not have the market acceptance of SNMP. However, for certain applications, such as those that require more rigorous error control, CMIP/CMOT has been used. To allow for a complete discussion on network management alternatives, this section briefly describes the attributes of these protocols. Readers should keep in mind that this discussion is primarily for academic, not implementation, purposes.

ISO defines a Management Service interface that allows management applications to communicate within the OSI environment. This interface is the Common Management Information Service (CMIS), described in ISO/IEC 9595 [7-33]. The CMIS services provide for management operation, retrieval of information, and notification of network events. These services, along with the type of service, confirmed (C) or nonconfirmed (NC), are listed below:

Service	Type	Description
M-GET	C	Information retrieval.
M-CANCEL-GET	C	Cancel outstanding M-GET.
M-SET	C/NC	Modify management information.
M-ACTION	C/NC	Perform an action.
M-CREATE	C	Create an instance of a managed object.
M-DELETE	C	Delete an instance of a managed object.
M-EVENT-REPORT	C/NC	Report of managed object event.

Mark Klerer's "The OSI Management Architecture: An Overview" [7-34] and Ian Sugarbroad's "An OSI-Based Interoperability Architecture for Managing Hybrid Networks" [7-35] put the OSI network management architectural issues into perspective.

The second half of ISO's network management protocol story is the Common Management Information Protocol (CMIP), defined in ISO/IEC 9596-1 [7-36]. CMIP communicates network management information between systems. This protocol is much more rigorous than SNMP for several reasons. First, CMIP was designed for open systems rather than for a single implementation such as the Internet, which necessarily increases the complexity of the operation. Second, CMIP is an association-oriented protocol, which means that the two CMIP processes must establish an association before sending any management messages. (Recall that SNMP is connectionless.) This association is governed by two ISO Application Layer standards: the Remote Operation Service Element (ROSE) and the Association Control Service Element (ACSE).

The benefits of CMIP's rigor are seen in the services it can perform beyond those available with SNMP. One example is *filtering,* which allows you to make an operation (such as an M-SET) conditional upon the value of an object's attribute. A second example is *scoping,* which allows you to apply the management operation to a portion of the object class. These enhancements come with a price, however. The CMIP Agent consumes up to 400 Kbytes of memory, while its SNMPv1 counterpart requires only 10 Kbytes [7-37].

As discussed earlier, the IAB, as reported in RFC 1109, intended to provide a migration path from SNMP to CMIP, allowing TCP/IP-based internetworks to migrate to OSI protocols. RFC 1189 [7-38] defined the protocol portion of this migration – the CMOT (CMIP over TCP/IP) protocol suite. (At the time of this writing, however, RFC 1189 has been classified as "historic," further substantiating the discussion at the beginning of this chapter about the strength of SNMP over CMIP solutions.)

The CMOT protocol suite (see Figure 7-7) uses the Internet protocols at the lower layers while incorporating the OSI management-related protocols, such as CMIP, at the higher layers. Either TCP or UDP may be used at the Transport Layer. Port numbers 163 (CMIP-Manager) and 164 (CMIP-Agent) are used for addressing at those layers. Lightweight Presentation Protocol (LPP), described in RFC 1085 [7-39], is defined for the Presentation Layer. LPP maps the ISO Management Service calls to or from TCP or UDP. Reference [7-40] provides further details on the design of CMOT.

In addition to using the CMIP protocol, the OSI-based network management scheme required modifications to the MIB. In Section 7.3.2, we discussed the Internet standards and private MIBs that support the SNMP and/or CMIP protocols. At one time, the developers attempted to devise an SMI/MIB for use with both SNMP and CMIP. But as the development process got underway, the developers discovered that independent standards would best serve the industry. As a result, they wrote a MIB specifically for OSI Internetwork Management, or OIM: RFC 1214 [7-41]. This MIB was designed as a companion to the Internet MIB-II (RFC 1213) to make the additions necessary to support CMIP. Like CMOT, the OIM MIB has been designated as "historic."

One of the additions to MIB-II is a branch for OSI Internet Management (OIM). Reviewing Figure 7-3, note that under MIB (1), group number 9 is defined for OIM. This group number is reserved for OIM and has a branch of its own, defined in RFC 1214. The structure of that branch is:

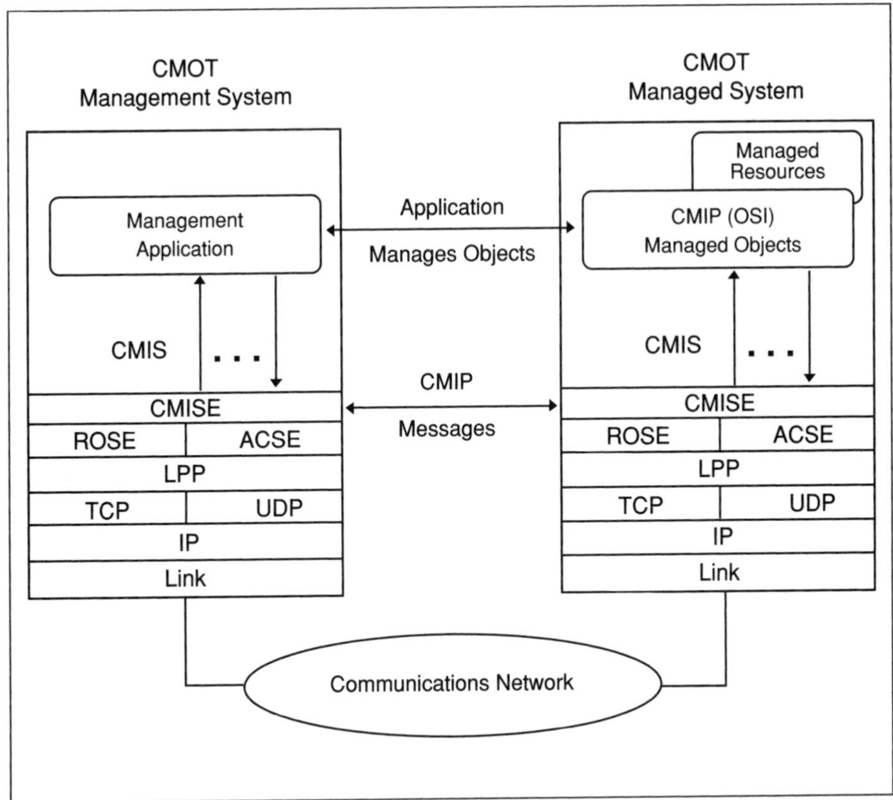

Figure 7-7 Common Management Information Protocol (CMOT) over TCP/IP Architecture (© 1990, IEEE)

Object	Identifier
cmotVersion:	oim 1
cmotACSEInfo:	oim 2
cmotSystemId:	oim 3
misc:	oim 4
objects:	oim 5
attributes:	oim 6
events:	oim 7
nameforms:	oim 8
actions:	oim 9

Other additions support ISO definitions, names, events, and name hierarchies as required by the OSI Structure of Management Information, designated ISO/IEC DIS 10165-1, 2, and 3. The OSI MIB itself is rather lengthy; readers contemplating a transition to OSI protocol stacks should study that document in its entirety.

Those network managers who plan a transition from TCP/IP and the Internet protocols to an OSI-based architecture may find themselves rather lonely, as the overwhelming choice of the industry has been to support SNMP, not CMIP/CMOT. To further amplify this point, the IETF has declared RFC 1214 "historic," meaning that few, if any, implementations are expected in the future.

7.8 IEEE LAN/MAN Management

The IEEE Project 802 LAN standards, such as 802.3 and 802.5, have been stable since the mid-1980s. With this basic architecture in place, the IEEE has been able to concentrate on the management of existing LANs and on emerging Metropolitan Area Network (MAN) architectures. The IEEE 802.1 standards, specifically 802.1B [7-42], are an outgrowth of those efforts.

The IEEE management structure is based on two other standards: the IEEE 802.2 Logical Link Control (LLC) and the ISO CMIP. It is sometimes referred to as CMOL (CMIP over LLC). The defined protocol uses the LLC connectionless service (called LLC Type 1), with the management information formatted according to the CMIP standard, ISO/IEC 9596-1 [7-36].

As a standards body, the IEEE has focused primarily on the Physical and Data Link Layers, with only a secondary interest in the rest of the OSI protocol stack. This focus extends to the functions it provides for LAN management. These functions are layered above the IEEE LAN/MAN Physical, Medium Access Control, and Logical Link Control Layers (see Figure 7-8).

Three elements are necessary to communicate management information between hosts: the Convergence Protocol Entity (CPE), the LAN/MAN Management Protocol Entity (LMMPE), and the LAN/MAN Management Service (LMMS). The CPE, which uses the Convergence Protocol, is the lowest layer element. The convergence function allows the two CPEs to be aware of the existence of their peers (detecting reboots, etc.) and to determine whether the information coming from their peers is in sequence and without loss or duplication. The LMMPE uses the LAN/MAN management protocol, derived from CMIP. The LMMS is the management service available to the LAN/MAN Management User (LMMU). LMMS uses the ISO CMIS to define its service offerings. The LMMUs are the Manager and Agent processes.

Like their ISO relatives, the IEEE LAN/MAN management standards have not received wide acceptance in the marketplace, deferring, again, to the strength of SNMP.

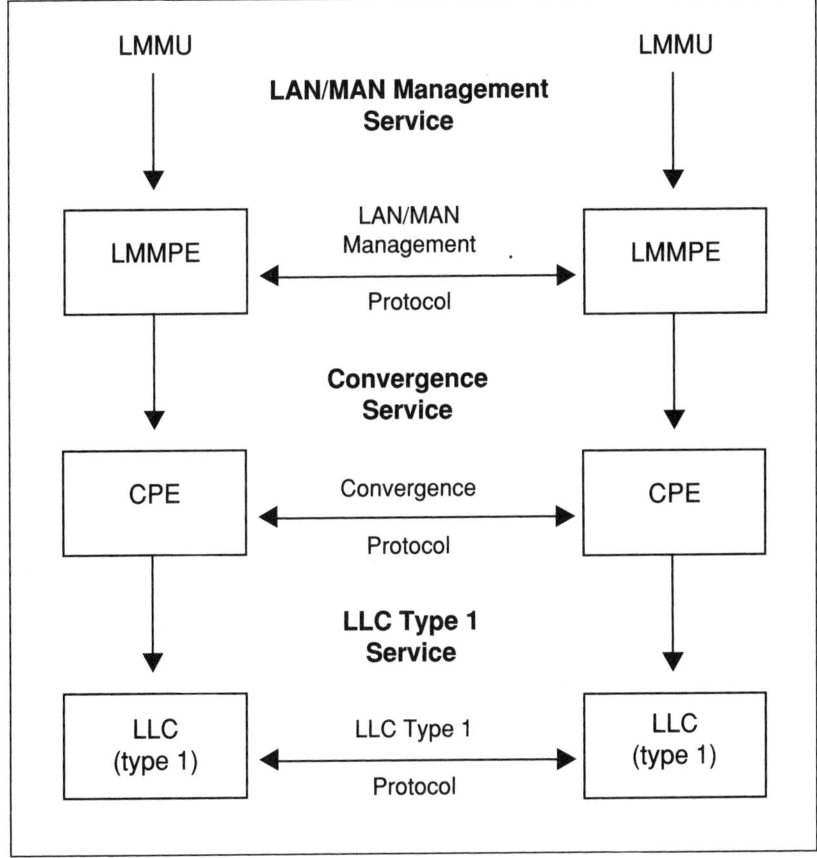

Figure 7-8 LAN/MAN Management Communication Architecture (© 1992, IEEE)

7.9 Desktop Management Task Force

The Desktop Management Task Force (DMTF) was founded in 1992 by Digital Equipment Corp. (now part of Compaq Computer Corp.), Hewlett-Packard, IBM, Intel, Microsoft, Novell, SunConnect (now known as SunSoft), and SynOptics Communications (now known as Nortel Networks). The purpose of the DMTF is to develop a standard set of Application Programming Interfaces (APIs) that access and manage desktop systems, components, and related peripherals. At the present time, more than 300 organizations are members of the DMTF.

The Desktop Management Interface (DMI) technology is the management architecture developed by the DMTF (see Figure 7-9). The focus of the DMI is on desktop and LAN management, independent of the hardware system, software operating system, or network operating system in use. DMI is designed to be integrated with all network management protocols and consoles, such as SNMP and CMIP.

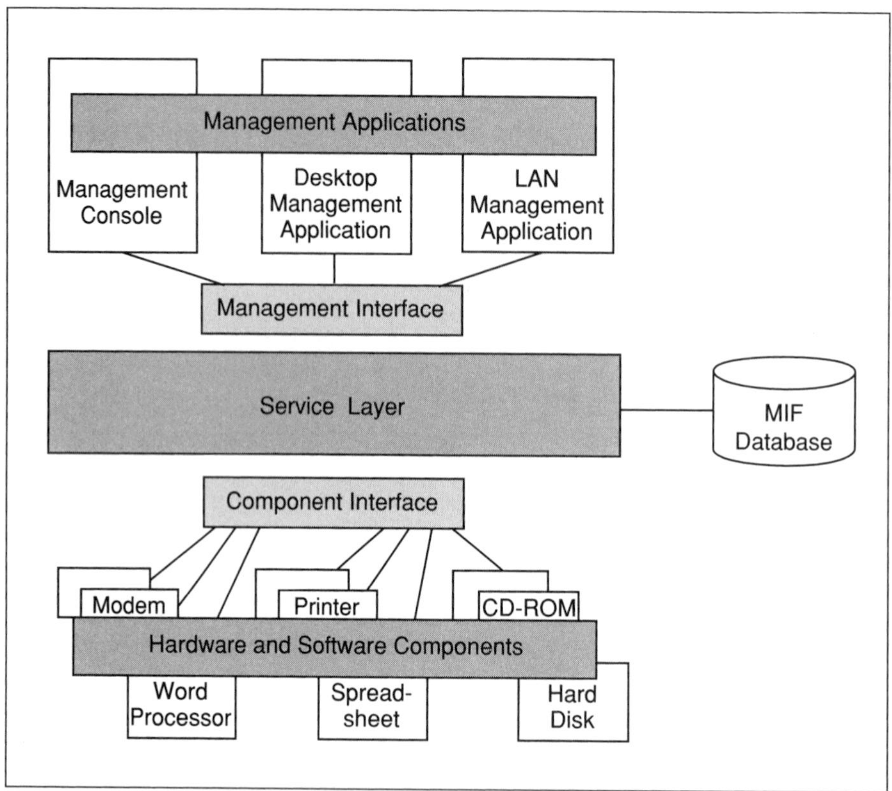

Figure 7-9 Management Interface
(Courtesy of the Desktop Management Task Force)

The DMI architecture is divided into three layers: the Management Applications Layer, which interfaces with various agents; the Service Layer, which includes the Management Information File (MIF) database; and the Hardware/Software Component Layer, which interfaces with the actual components being managed.

A second network management initiative, which is also spearheaded by the DMTF, is called the Web-Based Enterprise Management, or WBEM. This project focuses on the development of Web technology to access management information. Reference [7-43] provides contact information for the DMTF, and Reference [7-44] provides information on WBEM.

7.10 Network Management Systems

At the beginning of this chapter, we mentioned that the network management marketplace is a rapidly growing industry, comprised of a virtual "who's who" of internetworking vendors. The players in this market fall into two general categories:

minicomputer and/or mainframe manufacturers, and internetworking device manufacturers. These two types of vendors come to internetwork management from two different perspectives.

The minicomputer/mainframe manufacturers such as IBM, Hewlett-Packard, and SunSoft, use a host-centric approach to their internetwork management systems. Systems such as these may incorporate system-proprietary information along with SNMP for communication with other systems.

The second group of players in the network management market are vendors of internetworking devices such as bridges and routers, network operating systems, workstations, protocol analyzers, and other hardware devices. These companies develop SNMP agents for their specific products, such as a LAN switch, but may also develop an application program or suite of programs that integrates with one of the network management platforms. These add-on applications enhance the manageability of the internetworking devices, going beyond the capabilities of SNMP to provide enhanced graphics and topological maps of the internetwork, advanced configuration tools, documentation aides, and other tools.

Survey articles and buyer's guides appear frequently in the journals to assist the network manager in finding the best product for their application. References [7-45] through [7-51] are recent examples of these articles.

7.11 Case Study

Our final case study will consider the IEEE 802.3 network shown in Figure 7-10. The SNMP Manager is a PC-based network management application running on a PC. The SNMP Agent is a Xyplex, Inc. 10BASE-T hub card. In their respective specifications, both products claim to be compatible with MIB-I and MIB-II. Let's see if they are compatible with each other.

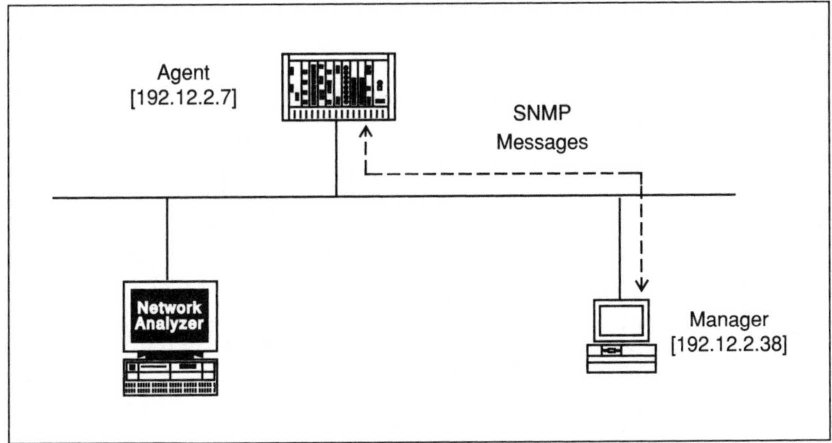

Figure 7-10 SNMP over Ethernet

To confirm compatibility, the network manager, Ross, instructs the SNMP Manager to query the System Group Objects (branch {1.3.6.1.2.1.1} in Figure 7-11). There are seven objects to be queried. The Manager issues requests for these objects in the order in which they appear in the subtree (see Trace 7.11a). The first request (Frame 31) asks for the sysDescr, the next for the sysObjectID and sysUpTime, and so on. Replies from the Agent begin in Frame 37. These identify the Xyplex 10BASE-T Hub, the system up time, the system contact, and so on.

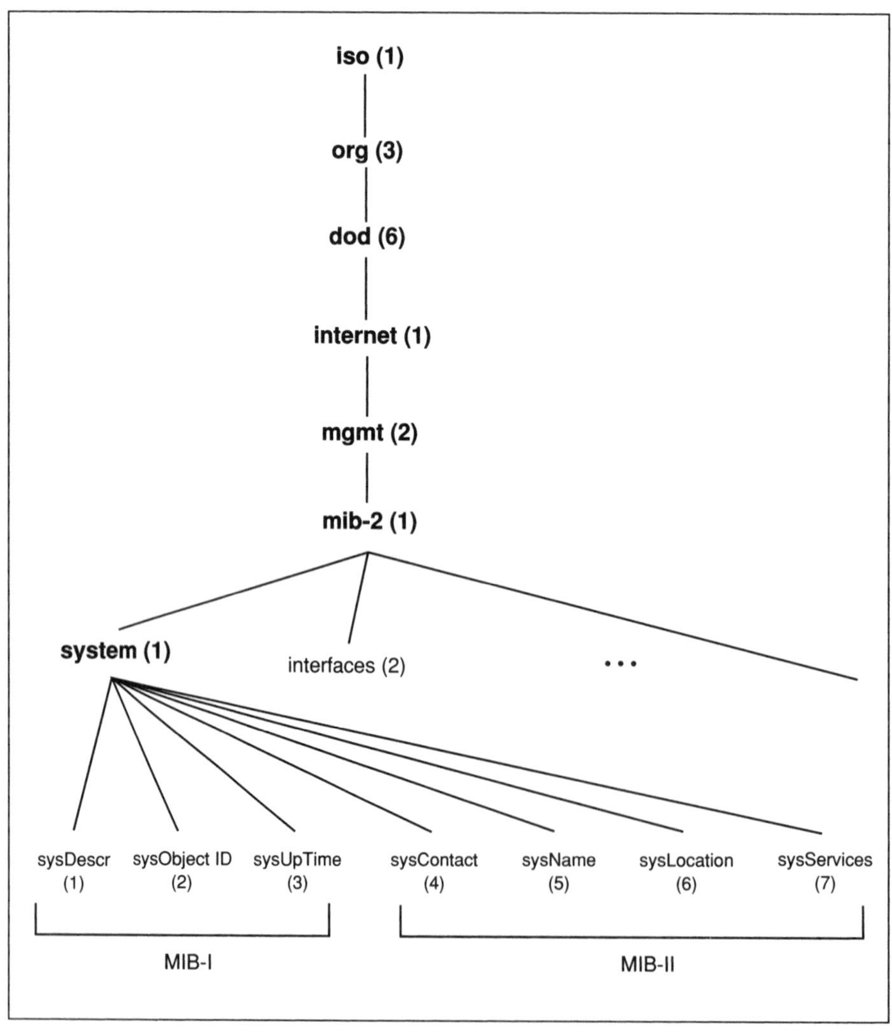

Figure 7-11 Internet MIB Tree for the System Group

Trace 7.11b shows the details of these Request/Response pairs. Note that for every GetRequest from the SNMP Manager, a corresponding GetResponse is returned. Frames 31 and 37 show the details of all protocol layers, which include the IP and UDP headers. Within the UDP header, the Destination port = 161 specifies the SNMP protocol. Also note that the GetNextRequest in Frame 31 uses a Request ID of 227475461. The corresponding response (Frame 37) uses the same number for identification. The next GetNextRequest (Frame 32) uses a different Request ID (227541001), which is repeated in the corresponding GetResponse (Frame 38). This pattern of Request/Response correlation continues through Frame 42.

Satisfied with these results, Ross decides to test the SetRequest PDU in Frame 43. The object that he elects to change is the sysContact, object {1.3.6.1.2.1.1.4.0}. The value of this object contains the name of the person responsible for the local network administration. Ross quickly realizes that he can accomplish two things with this one command: he can verify the compatibility of the two vendors' SNMP message sets, and he can change his own personal job responsibilities by putting someone else's name in this field. To do this, Ross enters the Community name for security purposes, the Object ID {1.3.6.1.2.1.1.4.0}, and the new value of that object (Bob Pjontek). The SNMP Agent on the hub responds in Frame 44 with the expected results. The SetRequest works, and Bob Pjontek is now the new network administrator. Ross wishes Bob well in his new responsibilities and moves on to the next test.

For his last compatibility check, Ross wishes to change the sysLocation object {1.3.6.1.2.1.1.6.0} using the SetRequest command in Frame 45. To Ross's surprise, the GetResponse returned by the hub in Frame 46 contains an Error Status = 3, indicating that a bad value was included in the SetRequest command. The Error index shows that the bad value is the second variable (Ottawa Demo Lab). Ross is perplexed as to why this SetRequest failed, while the previous command (Frames 43 and 44) succeeded. The only clue is an error code on the console that reads Object: Unknown.

A close examination of the two vendors' product manuals reveals the incompatibility. The hub manual shows that it does not allow a SetRequest for the sysLocation object for reasons of security. Since SNMP offers limited security (via the Authentication header), the hub vendor elected to allow a GetRequest to all objects, but a SetRequest to only some objects. This action does not violate the SNMP standard, but merely demonstrates the vendor's concern for internetwork security.

This experiment demonstrates another valuable lesson in today's "open systems" environments. The Internet protocols, being public domain standards, are about as open as you can get. Nevertheless, vendor-specific implementations must still be considered. This is another good example of why it's important to understand the vendor's implementation of the protocol as well as the protocol itself.

TRACE 7.11A. SNMP MESSAGE SUMMARY

Sniffer Network Analyzer data 8-Sep at 00:07:34, file SNMPTEST.ENC, Pg 1

SUMMARY	Delta T	Destination	Source	Summary
31	22.2384	Agent	Manager	SNMP Next sysDescr =
32	0.0031	Agent	Manager	SNMP Next sysObjectID, sysUpTime
33	0.0023	Agent	Manager	SNMP Next system.4 =
34	0.0019	Agent	Manager	SNMP Next system.5 =
35	0.0020	Agent	Manager	SNMP Next system.6 =
36	0.0020	Agent	Manager	SNMP Next system.7 = 0
37	0.0094	Manager	Agent	SNMP Got sysDescr = MX-3610 Xyplex 10BASE-T Hub<0A> Xyplex hardware MX-3610 00.00.00 Rom 440000<0A>Xypl...
38	0.0110	Manager	Agent	SNMP Got sysObjectID, sysUpTime
39	0.0086	Manager	Agent	SNMP Got system.4.0 = Ross Dunthorne, LAA Inc., Ottawa, Ontario.
40	0.0085	Manager	Agent	SNMP Got system.5.0 = MX-3610
41	0.0084	Manager	Agent	SNMP Got system.6.0 =
42	0.0085	Manager	Agent	SNMP Got system.7.0 = 78
43	16.3451	Agent	Manager	SNMP Set system.4.0 = Bob Pjontek, LAA Inc., Ottawa, Ontario.
44	0.0118	Manager	Agent	SNMP Got system.4.0 = Bob Pjontek, LAA Inc., Ottawa, Ontario.
45	49.9424	Agent	Manager	SNMP Set system.6.0 = Ottawa Demo Lab
46	0.0105	Manager	Agent	SNMP Got Bad value system.6.0 = Ottawa Demo Lab

TRACE 7.11B. SNMP MESSAGE DETAILS

```
Sniffer Network Analyzer data 8-Sep at 00:07:34, file SNMPTEST.ENC, Pg 1

- - - - - - - - - - - - - - - Frame 31 - - - - - - - - - - - - - - - - -

DLC:  ——DLC Header——
DLC:
DLC:  Frame 31 arrived at  00:08:24.5855; frame size is 84 (0054 hex) bytes.
DLC:  Destination = Station Xyplex004DB7, Agent
DLC:  Source      = Station NwkGnl0813FE, Manager
DLC:  Ethertype  = 0800 (IP)
DLC:
IP:  ——IP Header——
IP:
IP:  Version = 4, header length = 20 bytes
IP:  Type of service = 00
IP:        000. .... = routine
IP:        ...0 .... = normal delay
IP:        .... 0... = normal throughput
IP:        .... .0.. = normal reliability
IP:  Total length = 70 bytes
IP:  Identification = 3658
IP:  Flags = 0X
IP:  .0.. .... = may fragment
IP:  ..0. .... = last fragment
IP:  Fragment offset = 0 bytes
IP:  Time to live = 255 seconds/hops
IP:  Protocol = 17 (UDP)
IP:  Header checksum = 2917 (correct)
IP:  Source address = [192.12.2.38]
IP:  Destination address = [192.12.2.7]
IP:  No options
IP:
UDP:  ——UDP Header——
UDP:
UDP:  Source port = 9669 (SNMP)
UDP:  Destination port = 161
UDP:  Length = 50
UDP:  Checksum = F42C (correct)
UDP:
SNMP:  ——Simple Network Management Protocol——
SNMP:
SNMP: Version = 0
SNMP: Community = public
```

```
SNMP: Command = Get next request
SNMP: Request ID = 227475461
SNMP: Error status = 0 (No error)
SNMP: Error index = 0
SNMP:
SNMP: Object = {1.3.6.1.2.1.1.1} (sysDescr)
SNMP: Value =
SNMP:

- - - - - - - - - - - - - - - Frame 32 - - - - - - - - - - - - - - - -

UDP: ——UDP Header ——
UDP:
UDP: Source port = 9669 (SNMP)
UDP: Destination port = 161
UDP: Length = 64
UDP: Checksum = 69A2 (correct)
UDP:
SNMP: ——Simple Network Management Protocol ——
SNMP:
SNMP: Version = 0
SNMP: Community = public
SNMP: Command = Get next request
SNMP: Request ID = 227541001
SNMP: Error status = 0 (No error)
SNMP: Error index = 0
SNMP:
SNMP: Object = {1.3.6.1.2.1.1.2} (sysObjectID)
SNMP: Value = }
SNMP:
SNMP: Object = {1.3.6.1.2.1.1.3} (sysUpTime)
SNMP: Value = 0 hundredths of a second
SNMP:

- - - - - - - - - - - - - - - Frame 33 - - - - - - - - - - - - - - - -

UDP: ——UDP Header ——
UDP:
UDP: Source port = 9669 (SNMP)
UDP: Destination port = 161
UDP: Length = 50
UDP: Checksum = DE29 (correct)
UDP:
SNMP: ——Simple Network Management Protocol ——
```

```
SNMP:
SNMP: Version = 0
SNMP: Community = public
SNMP: Command = Get next request
SNMP: Request ID = 227606553
SNMP: Error status = 0 (No error)
SNMP: Error index = 0
SNMP:
SNMP: Object = {1.3.6.1.2.1.1.4} (system.4)
SNMP: Value =
SNMP:

- - - - - - - - - - - - - - - Frame 34 - - - - - - - - - - - - - - - -

UDP: ----UDP Header ----
UDP:
UDP: Source port = 9669 (SNMP)
UDP: Destination port = 161
UDP: Length = 50
UDP: Checksum = D928 (correct)
UDP:
SNMP: ----Simple Network Management Protocol ----
SNMP:
SNMP: Version = 0
SNMP: Community = public
SNMP: Command = Get next request
SNMP: Request ID = 227672093
SNMP: Error status = 0 (No error)
SNMP: Error index = 0
SNMP:
SNMP: Object = {1.3.6.1.2.1.1.5} (system.5)
SNMP: Value =
SNMP:

- - - - - - - - - - - - - - - Frame 35 - - - - - - - - - - - - - - - -

UDP: ----UDP Header ----
UDP:
UDP: Source port = 9669 (SNMP)
UDP: Destination port = 161
UDP: Length = 50
UDP: Checksum = D427 (correct)
UDP:
SNMP: ----Simple Network Management Protocol ----
```

```
SNMP:
SNMP: Version = 0
SNMP: Community = public
SNMP: Command = Get next request
SNMP: Request ID = 227737633
SNMP: Error status = 0 (No error)
SNMP: Error index = 0
SNMP:
SNMP: Object = {1.3.6.1.2.1.1.6} (system.6)
SNMP: Value  =
SNMP:

- - - - - - - - - - - - - - - Frame 36 - - - - - - - - - - - - - - - - -

UDP:  —— UDP Header ——
UDP:
UDP:  Source port = 9669 (SNMP)
UDP:  Destination port = 161
UDP:  Length = 51
UDP:  Checksum = CE22 (correct)
UDP:
SNMP: —— Simple Network Management Protocol ——
SNMP:
SNMP: Version = 0
SNMP: Community = public
SNMP: Command = Get next request
SNMP: Request ID = 227803173
SNMP: Error status = 0 (No error)
SNMP: Error index = 0
SNMP:
SNMP: Object = {1.3.6.1.2.1.1.7} (system.7)
SNMP: Value  = 0
SNMP:

- - - - - - - - - - - - - - - Frame 37 - - - - - - - - - - - - - - - - -

DLC:  —— DLC Header ——
DLC:
DLC:  Frame 37 arrived at  00:08:24.6065; frame size is 186 (00BA hex) bytes.
DLC:  Destination = Station NwkGnl0813FE, Manager
DLC:  Source      = Station Xyplex004DB7, Agent
DLC:  Ethertype  = 0800 (IP)
DLC:
IP:   —— IP Header ——
```

```
IP:
IP:  Version = 4, header length = 20 bytes
IP:  Type of service = 00
IP:       000. .... = routine
IP:       ...0 .... = normal delay
IP:       .... 0... = normal throughput
IP:       .... .0.. = normal reliability
IP:  Total length = 172 bytes
IP:  Identification = 82
IP:  Flags = 0X
IP:  .0.. .... = may fragment
IP:  ..0. .... = last fragment
IP:  Fragment offset = 0 bytes
IP:  Time to live = 64 seconds/hops
IP:  Protocol = 17 (UDP)
IP:  Header checksum = F5A9 (correct)
IP:  Source address = [192.12.2.7]
IP:  Destination address = [192.12.2.38]
IP:  No options
IP:
UDP:  ——UDP Header ——
UDP:
UDP:  Source port = 161 (SNMP)
UDP:  Destination port = 9669
UDP:  Length = 152
UDP:  No checksum
UDP:
SNMP:  ——Simple Network Management Protocol ——
SNMP:
SNMP:  Version = 0
SNMP:  Community = public
SNMP:  Command = Get response
SNMP:  Request ID = 227475461
SNMP:  Error status = 0 (No error)
SNMP:  Error index = 0
SNMP:
SNMP:  Object = {1.3.6.1.2.1.1.1.0} (sysDescr.0)
SNMP:  Value  = MX-3610 - Xyplex 10BASE-T Hub<0A>Xyplex hardware MX-3610 00.00.00 Rom
440000<0A> ...
SNMP:

- - - - - - - - - - - - - - - Frame 38 - - - - - - - - - - - - - - - - -

UDP:   ——UDP Header ——
```

```
UDP:
UDP:  Source port = 161 (SNMP)
UDP:  Destination port = 9669
UDP:  Length = 76
UDP:  No checksum
UDP:
SNMP: ——Simple Network Management Protocol ——
SNMP:
SNMP: Version = 0
SNMP: Community = public
SNMP: Command = Get response
SNMP: Request ID = 227541001
SNMP: Error status = 0 (No error)
SNMP: Error index = 0
SNMP:
SNMP: Object = {1.3.6.1.2.1.1.2.0} (sysObjectID.0)
SNMP: Value  = {1.3.6.1.4.1.33.1.4}
SNMP:
SNMP: Object = {1.3.6.1.2.1.1.3.0} (sysUpTime.0)
SNMP: Value  = 1058882 hundredths of a second
SNMP:

- - - - - - - - - - - - - - - Frame 39 - - - - - - - - - - - - - - - - -

UDP:  ——UDP Header ——
UDP:
UDP:  Source port = 161 (SNMP)
UDP:  Destination port = 9669
UDP:  Length = 93
UDP:  No checksum
UDP:
SNMP: ——Simple Network Management Protocol ——
SNMP:
SNMP: Version = 0
SNMP: Community = public
SNMP: Command = Get response
SNMP: Request ID = 227606553
SNMP: Error status = 0 (No error)
SNMP: Error index = 0
SNMP:
SNMP: Object = {1.3.6.1.2.1.1.4.0} (system.4.0)
SNMP: Value  = Ross Dunthorne, LAA Inc., Ottawa, Ontario.
SNMP:
```

```
--------------- Frame 40 ----------------

UDP:  —— UDP Header ——
UDP:
UDP:  Source port = 161 (SNMP)
UDP:  Destination port = 9669
UDP:  Length = 58
UDP:  No checksum
UDP:
SNMP: ——Simple Network Management Protocol ——
SNMP:
SNMP: Version = 0
SNMP: Community = public
SNMP: Command = Get response
SNMP: Request ID = 227672093
SNMP: Error status = 0 (No error)
SNMP: Error index = 0
SNMP:
SNMP: Object = {1.3.6.1.2.1.1.5.0} (system.5.0)
SNMP: Value  = MX-3610
SNMP:

--------------- Frame 41 ----------------

UDP:  ——UDP Header ——
UDP:
UDP:  Source port = 161 (SNMP)
UDP:  Destination port = 9669
UDP:  Length = 51
UDP:  No checksum
UDP:
SNMP: ——Simple Network Management Protocol ——
SNMP:
SNMP: Version = 0
SNMP: Community = public
SNMP: Command = Get response
SNMP: Request ID = 227737633
SNMP: Error status = 0 (No error)
SNMP: Error index = 0
SNMP:
SNMP: Object = {1.3.6.1.2.1.1.6.0} (system.6.0)
SNMP: Value  =
SNMP:
```

```
---------------- Frame 42 ----------------

UDP: ——UDP Header ——
UDP:
UDP: Source port = 161 (SNMP)
UDP: Destination port = 9669
UDP: Length = 52
UDP: No checksum
UDP:
SNMP: ——Simple Network Management Protocol ——
SNMP:
SNMP: Version = 0
SNMP: Community = public
SNMP: Command = Get response
SNMP: Request ID = 227803173
SNMP: Error status = 0 (No error)
SNMP: Error index = 0
SNMP:
SNMP: Object = {1.3.6.1.2.1.1.7.0} (system.7.0)
SNMP: Value  = 78
SNMP:

---------------- Frame 43 ----------------

UDP: ——UDP Header ——
UDP:
UDP: Source port = 9669 (SNMP)
UDP: Destination port = 161
UDP: Length = 68
UDP: Checksum = 1198 (correct)
UDP:
SNMP: ——Simple Network Management Protocol ——
SNMP:
SNMP: Version = 0
SNMP: Community = xyplex
SNMP: Command = Set request
SNMP: Request ID = 227868677
SNMP: Error status = 0 (No error)
SNMP: Error index = 0
SNMP:
SNMP: Object = {1.3.6.1.2.1.1.4.0} (system.4.0)
SNMP: Value  = Bob Pjontek, LAA Inc., Ottawa, Ontario.
SNMP:
```

```
--------------- Frame 44 -----------------

UDP:  —UDP Header —
UDP:
UDP:  Source port = 161 (SNMP)
UDP:  Destination port = 9669
UDP:  Length = 68
UDP:  No checksum
UDP:
SNMP: —Simple Network Management Protocol —
SNMP:
SNMP: Version = 0
SNMP: Community = xyplex
SNMP: Command = Get response
SNMP: Request ID = 227868677
SNMP: Error status = 0 (No error)
SNMP: Error index = 0
SNMP:
SNMP: Object = {1.3.6.1.2.1.1.4.0} (system.4.0)
SNMP: Value  = Bob Pjontek, LAA Inc., Ottawa, Ontario.
SNMP:

--------------- Frame 45 -----------------

UDP:  —UDP Header —
UDP:
UDP:  Source port = 9669 (SNMP)
UDP:  Destination port = 161
UDP:  Length = 66
UDP:  Checksum = 2C01 (correct)
UDP:
SNMP: —Simple Network Management Protocol —
SNMP:
SNMP: Version = 0
SNMP: Community = xyplex
SNMP: Command = Set request
SNMP: Request ID = 227999749
SNMP: Error status = 0 (No error)
SNMP: Error index = 0
SNMP:
SNMP: Object = {1.3.6.1.2.1.1.6.0} (system.6.0)
SNMP: Value  = Ottawa Demo Lab
SNMP:
```

```
---------------- Frame 46 -----------------

UDP: —— UDP Header v
UDP:
UDP: Source port = 161 (SNMP)
UDP: Destination port = 9669
UDP: Length = 66
UDP: No checksum
UDP:
SNMP: —— Simple Network Management Protocol ——
SNMP:
SNMP: Version = 0
SNMP: Community = xyplex
SNMP: Command = Get response
SNMP: Request ID = 227999749
SNMP: Error status = 3 (Bad value)
SNMP: Error index = 2
SNMP:
SNMP: Object = {1.3.6.1.2.1.1.6.0} (system.6.0)
SNMP: Value  = Ottawa Demo Lab
SNMP:
```

7.12 Looking Ahead

In the first seven chapters, we have concentrated on internetwork architectures that are based on IP version 4. In our concluding chapter, Chapter 8, we will study the next generation Internet Protocol, designated IPng or IP version 6 (IPv6).

7.13 References

[7-1] Salus, Peter H. "Protocol Wars: Is OSI Finally Dead?" *ConneXions* (August 1995): 16–19.

[7-2] International Organization for Standardization, *Information Processing Systems – Open Systems Interconnection – Basic Reference Model – Part 4: Management Framework*, ISO 7498-4-1989.

[7-3] Special Issues: Network Management (March 1989); Network Management and Network Security (August 1990). *ConneXions*.

[7-4] Rose, Marshall T. *The Simple Book: An Introduction to Management of TCP/IP-Based Internets*, second edition. Prentice-Hall (Englewood Cliffs, NJ), 1996.

[7-5] Black, Uyless. *Network Management Standards*, second edition. McGraw-Hill (New York, NY), 1995.

[7-6] Miller, Mark A. *Managing Internetworks with SNMP*, third edition. IDG Books Worldwide, Inc. (Foster City, CA), 1999.

[7-7] White, David W. "Internet Management – SNMP and CMOT: Two Ways to Do the Same Thing." *LAN Magazine* (July 1989): 147–150.

[7-8] Thomas, Larry J. "The Distributed Management Choice." *LAN Technology* (April 1992): 53–70.

[7-9] Ben-Artzi, Amatzia, et al. "Network Management of TCP/IP Networks: Present and Future." *IEEE Network Magazine* (July 1990): 35–43.

[7-10] McCloghrie, K., and Marshall T. Rose. "Network Management of TCP/IP-Based Internets." *ConneXions* (March 1989): 3–9.

[7-11] Rose, M., and K. McCloghrie. "Structure and Identification of Management Information for TCP/IP-Based Internets." RFC 1155, May 1990.

[7-12] Rose, M., et al. "Concise MIB Definitions." RFC 1212, March 1991.

[7-13] Case, J., et al. "A Simple Network Management Protocol (SNMP)." RFC 1157, May 1990.

[7-14] Organization for Standardization, Information Technology: Abstract Syntax Notation One (ASN.1): Specification of Basic Notation, ISO/IEC 8824-1: 1995.

[7-15] McCloghrie, K., et al. "Management Information Base for Network Management of TCP/IP-based Internets." RFC 1156, May 1990.

[7-16] McCloghrie, K., and M. Rose. "Management Information Base for Network Management of TCP/IP-Based Internets: MIB-II." RFC 1213, March 1991.

[7-17] Perkins, David. "How to Read and Use an SNMP MIB." *3TECH, The 3Com Technical Journal* (Spring 1991): 31–55.

[7-18] Perkins, David, and Evan McGinnis. *Understanding SNMP MIBs*. Prentice-Hall, Inc. (Upper Saddle River, NJ), 1997.

[7-19] Stewart, Bob. "Development and Integration of a Management Information Base." *ConneXions* (June 1991): 2–11.

[7-20] Waldbusser, S. "Remote Network Monitoring Management Information Base." RFC 1757, February 1995.

[7-21] Waldbusser, S. "Token Ring Extensions to the Remote Network Monitoring MIB." RFC 1513, September 1993.

[7-22] Waldbusser, S. "Remote Network Monitoring Management Information Base." RFC 2021, January 1997.

[7-23] Soref, Jeremy. "RMON The Enterprise Management Standard." *Data Communications* (March 21, 1996): 67–72.

[7-24] Peter. "RMON: To the Network Layer And Beyond!" *Network Computing* (February 15, 1998): 62–84.

[7-25] The *Simple Times* is an openly available newsletter devoted to SNMP Technology. For subscription information, send a message to: st-subscriptions@simple-times.org, with a subject line of *help*. Back issues are available at:
`http://www.simple-times.org`

[7-26] Cerf, V. "IAB Recommendations for the Development of Internet Network Management Standards." RFC 1052, April 1988.

[7-27] Case, Jeffrey D., et al. "Network Management and the Design of SNMP." *ConneXions* (March 1989): 22–26.

[7-28] Jander, Mary. "SNMP2: Coming Soon to a Network Near You." *Data Communications* (November 1992): 66–76.

[7-29] Stallings, William. "SNMPv2: The New Direction in Network Management." *Network Computing* (July 1993): 140–143.

[7-30] Huntington-Lee, Jill. "SNMP Version 2 Update." ComNet 1996 Conference Session Notes, January 1996.

[7-31] Case, J., et al. "Introduction to Community-Based SNMPv2." RFC 1901, January 1996.

[7-32] Harrington, D., et al. "An Architecture for Describing SNMP Management Frameworks." RFC 2271, January 1998.

[7-33] International Organization for Standardization. *Information Processing Systems – Open Systems Interconnection – Common management information service definition*, ISO/IEC 9595, CCITT Recommendation X.710, IEEE 802.1-91/20, November 1990.

[7-34] Klerer, Mark. "The OSI Management Architecture: An Overview." *IEEE Network Magazine* (March 1988): 20–29.

[7-35] Sugarbroad, Ian. "An OSI-Based Interoperability Architecture for Managing Hybrid Networks." *IEEE Communications Magazine* (March 1990): 61–69.

[7-36] International Organization for Standardization. *Information Processing Systems – Open Systems Interconnection – Common management information protocol specification*, ISO/IEC 9596-1, CCITT X.711, IEEE 802.1-91/21, November 1990.

[7-37] Jander, Mary. "CMIP Gets a New Chance." *Data Communications* (September 1991): 51–56.

[7-38] Warrier, U., et al. "The Common Management Information Services and Protocols for the Internet (CMOT and CMIP)." RFC 1189, October 1990.

[7-39] Rose, M. T. "ISO Presentation Services on Top of TCP/IP-Based Internets." RFC 1085, December 1988.

[7-40] Ben-Artzi, Amatzia. "The CMOT Network Management Architecture." *ConneXions* (March 1989): 14–19.

[7-41] Labarre, L., Editor. "OSI Internet Management: Management Information Base." RFC 1214, April 1991.

[7-42] Institute of Electrical and Electronics Engineers. "LAN/MAN Management." ANSI/IEEE Std 802.1B, 1995.

[7-43] The Desktop Management Task Force may be contacted at:
Desktop Management Task Force
C/O MacKenzie Kesselring, Inc.
200 SW Market Street, Suite 450
Portland, OR 97201
Tel: (503) 294-0739
Fax: (503) 225-0765
Email: dmtf-info@dmtf.org
`www.dmtf.org`

[7-44] Information on Web-Base Enterprise Management (WBEM) is available at `www.dmtf.org`.

[7-45] Backman, Dan. "Web-based Management – 9 Products to Help Simplify Your Network." *Network Computing* (July 15, 1997): 50–59.

[7-46] Newman, David, Tadesse Giorgis, and Brent Melson. "Probing RMON2." *Data Communications* (May 21, 1998): 67–75.

[7-47] Backman, Dan. "Basking in Glory." *Network Computing* (August 15, 1998): 41–47.

[7-48] Boardman, Bruce. "Network Management Solutions Lack Clear Leader." *Network Computing* (August 15, 1998): 45–48.

[7-49] Herman, James. "The Challenge of Managing Broadband Networks." *Business Communications Review* (October 1995): 54–67.

[7-50] Gibbs, Mark. "No Pain, No Gain." *Network World* (August 17. 1998): 33–36.

[7-51] Connolly, P. J. "Master of Your Domain." *LAN Times* (October 12, 1998): 51–59.

Chapter 8

The Next Generation

In the late 1980s and the early 1990s, networks in particular, and networking in general experienced phenomenal growth. About that same time, the funding and usage policies that governed Internet traffic changed, moving the Internet from a government-sponsored network primarily focused on education and research to a widely available network that included commercial ventures as part of its modus operandi. The end result became more host connections, more users, and more traffic on the Internet.

Possibly more importantly, a shortage of IP addresses was anticipated, with the "Date of Doom" forecast for March 1994 – the predicted time at which part of the current IP address space would be exhausted [8-1]. In response to these concerns, in July 1991, the Internet Engineering Task Force (IETF) began the process of researching the problem, soliciting proposals for solutions, and narrowing in on a conclusion, describing this preliminary process in RFC 1380 [8-2], published in November 1992. In addition, a new research area, called the IPng Area, was commissioned by the IETF to formally study these issues.

8.1 IPng Development

In December 1993, RFC 1550 was distributed, titled "IP: Next Generπation (IPng) White Paper Solicitation" [8-3]. This RFC invited any interested party to submit their comments regarding any specific requirements for the IPng or any key factors that should be considered during the IPng selection process. Twenty-one responses were submitted that addressed a variety of topics, including: security (RFC 1675), a large corporate user's view (RFC 1687), a cellular industry view (RFC 1674), and a cable television industry view (RFC 1686). Many of these papers, plus a complete listing of the white paper responses are given in Scott Bradner and Allison Mankin's book *IPng – Internet Protocol Next Generation* [8-4].

The IPng Area commissioned RFC 1726, "Technical Criteria for Choosing IP The Next Generation (IPng)" [8-5], to define a set of criteria that would be used in the IPng evaluation process. Seventeen criteria were noted:

- Scale – the IPng Protocol must scale to allow the identification and addressing of at least 1012 end systems and 109 individual networks.
- Topological Flexibility – the routing architecture and protocols of IPng must allow for many different network topologies.

- Performance – a state-of-the-art, commercial-grade router must be able to process and forward IPng traffic at speeds capable of fully utilizing common, commercially available, high-speed media at the time.
- Robust Service – the network service and its associated routing and control protocols must be robust.
- Transition – the protocol must have a straightforward transition plan from the current IPv4.
- Media Independence – the protocol must work across an internetwork of many different LAN, MAN, and WAN media, with individual link speeds ranging from a ones-of-bits per second to hundreds of gigabits per second.
- Unreliable Datagram Service – the protocol must support an unreliable datagram delivery service.
- Configuration, Administration and Operation – the protocol must permit easy and largely distributed configuration and operation. The automatic configuration of hosts and routers is required.
- Secure Operation – IPng must provide a secure network layer.
- Unique Naming – IPng must assign all IP-Layer objects global, ubiquitous, Internet unique names.
- Access and Documentation – the protocols that define IPng, its associated protocols, and the routing protocols, must be published in the standards track RFCs, be freely available, and be without licensing fees for implementation.
- Multicast – the protocol must support both unicast and multicast packet transmission.
- Extensibility – the protocol must be extensible; it must be able to evolve to meet the future service needs of the Internet.
- Network Service – the protocol must allow the network to associate packets with particular service classes, and must provide them with the services specified by those classes.
- Mobility – the protocol must support mobile hosts, networks, and internetworks.
- Control Protocol – the protocol must include elementary support for testing and debugging networks.
- Private Networks – IPng must allow users to build private internetworks on top of the basic Internet infrastructure.

Several proposals were evaluated vis-a-vis the above criteria. In January 1995, RFC 1752, "The Recommendation for the IP Next Generation Protocol," was issued [8-6]. This paper summarized the evaluations of three IPng proposals: Common Architecture for the Internet (CATNIP) [8-7] and [8-8], Simple Internet Protocol Plus (SIPP) [8-9] and [8-10], and the TCP/UDP Over CLNP-Addressed Networks (TUBA) [8-11] and [8-12].

8.1.1 Common Architecture for the Internet (CATNIP)

The objective of the CATNIP proposal is to provide some commonality between Internet, OSI, and Novell protocols. To accomplish this, CATNIP integrates a number of Network layer protocols, including the ISO Connectionless Network Protocol (CLNP), IP, and Novell's Internetwork Packet Exchange (IPX) protocol. In addition, the CATNIP design allows a number of Transport protocols, including the ISO Transport Protocol, class 4 (TP4), Connectionless Transport Protocol (CLTP), TCP, UDP, and Novell's Sequenced Packet Exchange (SPX), to run over any of the above Network layer protocols. According to the proposal, it would be possible for a single Transport layer protocol such as TCP, to operate over one Network layer protocol (such as IPv4) at one end of the connection, and over another Network layer protocol, (such as CLNP) at the other. As documented in RFC 1752, the reviewers felt that CATNIP met five of the key criteria, did not meet two of the criteria, and had mixed reviews or an unknown conclusion on the remaining criteria.

8.1.2 Simple Internet Protocol Plus (SIPP)

The objective of SIPP is to provide a new, evolutionary step from IPv4. As such, the IPv4 functions which worked were retained, and functions which did not were removed. In addition, SIPP installation is planned as a software upgrade and SIPP is interoperable with the existing IPv4. SIPP revises the IP header for more efficient processing and also increases the size of the IP addresses from 32 to 64 bits in length. As documented in RFC 1752, the reviewers felt that SIPP met ten of the key criteria, did not meet two of the criteria, and had mixed reviews or an unknown conclusion on the remaining criteria.

8.1.3 TCP/UDP over CLNP-Addressed Networks (TUBA)

The key strategy behind TUBA is to replace the existing IPv4 Network layer with the ISO CLNP. There are two benefits to this: providing for increased address space, while allowing for TCP or UDP and related upper-layer applications to operate unchanged. The addresses defined for CLNP (and therefore in TUBA) are called Network Service Access Points, or NSAPs, which are variable length addresses. The use of CLNP at the Network layer would be supported by existing ISO routing protocols, including the Inter Domain Routing Protocol (IDRP), the Intermediate

System-to-Intermediate System (IS-IS) protocol, and the End System-to-Intermediate System (ES-IS) protocol. As documented in RFC 1752, the reviewers felt that TUBA met five of the key criteria, did not meet one of the criteria, and had mixed reviews or an unknown conclusion on the remaining criteria.

As reported in RFC 1752, all three proposals exhibited significant problems, and CATNIP in particular was determined to be "too incomplete to be considered." As a result of these discussions, the SIPP proposal was revised, incorporating 128-bit addresses and dealing with other concerns. The final recommendation incorporated this revised SIPP proposal, coupled with the autoreconfiguration and transition elements of TUBA, the addressing work based upon the Classless Inter-Domain Routing, or CIDR (an intermediate solution to the address depletion problem [8-13] and [8-14]), plus routing header enhancements.

8.2 IPv6 Capabilities

Declaring a winner in athletic or political contests is a straightforward process; however, with protocol designs the process is not always as clear. As such there was no single "winner" of the IPv6 design contest, but instead combined several proposals, drawing on the individual strengths of each. To quote from RFC 1752:

> This proposal represents a synthesis of multiple IETF efforts with much of the basic protocol coming from the SIPP effort, the autoconfiguration and transition portions influenced by TUBA, the addressing structure based on CIDR work and the routing header evolving out of the SDRP [Source Demand Routing Protocol] deliberations.

RFC 1752 goes on to describe the important features of IPng, formally designated IPv6. These capabilities include:

- Expanded addressing and routing – increasing the IP address field from 32 to 128 bits in length allows for a much greater number of addressable nodes, more levels of addressing hierarchy, defining new types of addresses, etc.
- Simplified header format – eliminating or making optional some of the IPv4 header fields to reduce the packet handling overhead, thus providing some compensation for the larger addresses. Even with the addresses, which are four times as long, the IPv6 header is only 40 octets in length, compared with 20 octets for IPv4.
- Extension headers and options – IPv6 options are placed in separate headers located after the core IPv6 header information, such that processing at every intermediate stop between source and destination may not be required.
- Authentication and privacy – required support in all implementations of IPv6 to authenticate the sender of a packet and to encrypt the contents of that packet, as required.

- Autoreconfiguration – support from node address assignments up to the use of the Dynamic Host Reconfiguration Protocol (DHCP).
- Source routes – support for a header that supports the Source Demand Routing Protocol (SDRP), such that a source-selected route may complement the route determined by the existing routing protocols.
- Simple and flexible transition – a transition plan with four basic requirements:
- Incremental upgrade – allowing existing IPv4 hosts to be upgraded at any time without a dependency on other hosts or routers being upgraded.
- Incremental deployment – new IPv6 hosts and routers can be installed at any time without any prerequisites.
- Easy addressing – when existing installed IPv4 hosts or routers are upgraded to IPv6, they may continue to use their existing address, without needing a new assigned address.
- Low start-up costs – little or no preparation work is needed in order to upgrade existing IPv4 systems to IPv6, or to deploy new IPv6 systems.
- Quality of service capabilities – a new capability is added to enable the labeling of packets belonging to particular traffic "flows" for which the sender has requested special handling, such as non-default quality of service or "real-time" service.

8.3 IPv6 Documentation

The Internet Protocol – of any version – is the fundamental platform upon which the entire Internet Protocol suite is based. A revision to this protocol has a number of far-reaching effects, as illustrated by the following list of RFCs that have been published on the subject as of this writing:

RFC	Subject
1550	IPng White Paper Solicitation
1726	Technical Criteria for IPng
1752	Recommendation for IPng
1809	Using the Flow Label Field in IPv6
1810	Reports on MD5 Performance
1881	IPv6 Address Allocation Management

Continued

Continued

RFC	Subject
1887	An Architecture for IPv6 Unicast Address Allocation
1888	OSI NSAPs and IPv6
1897	IPv6 Testing Address Allocation
1924	A Compact Representation of IPv6 Addresses
1933	Transition Mechanisms for IPv6 Hosts and Routers
1981	Path MTU Discovery for IPv6
2030	Simple Network Time Protocol (SNTP) Version 4 for IPv4, IPv6 and OSI
2073	An IPv6 Provider-Based Unicast Address Format
2080	RIPng for IPv6
2133	Basic Socket Interface Extensions for IPv6
2147	TCP and UDP over IPv6 Jumbograms
2185	Routing Aspects of IPv6 Transition
2283	Multiprotocol Extensions for BGP-4
2292	Advanced Sockets API for IPv6
2365	Administratively Scoped IP Multicast
2373	IPv6 Addressing Architecture
2374	An IPv6 Aggregatable Global Unicast Address Format
2401	Security Architecture for the Internet Protocol
2402	IP Authentication Header
2406	IP Encapsulating Security Payload (ESP)
2375	IPv6 Multicast Address Assignments
2460	Internet Protocol, Version 6 (IPv6)
2461	Neighbor Discovery for IPv6
2462	IPv6 Stateless Address Autoconfiguration
2463	Internet Control Message Protocol (ICMPv6) for the Internet Protocol Version 6
2464	A Method for the Transmission of IPv6 Packets over Ethernet Networks
2467	Transmission of IPv6 Packets Over FDDI Networks

RFC	Subject
2470	IPv6 over Token Ring Networks
2472	IPv6 over PPP
2491	IPv6 over NBNA Networks
2492	IPv6 over ATM Networks
2497	IPv6 over ARCnet Networks

To keep abreast of these IPv6 developments, subscribe to the Internet's IPng mailing list by sending email to:

```
ipng-request@sunroof.eng.sun.com
```

8.4 IPv6 Specification

RFC 2460 [8-15], the IPv6 specification, summarizes the following changes from IPv4 to IPv6:

- Expanded Addressing Capabilities – increasing the address size from 32 bits to 128 bits, supporting more levels of address hierarchy, many more addressable nodes, scalable multicast addresses, plus the anycast address, which is used to send a packet to any one of a group of nodes.
- Header Format Simplification – eliminating or making optional some of the header fields, thus reducing the protocol processing overhead of the IPv6 header.
- Improved Support for Extensions and Options – including more efficient forwarding, less stringent limits on the length of options, and greater flexibility for future options.
- Flow Labeling Capability – a new function which enables packets which belong to a particular traffic "flow" to be labeled for special handling.
- Authentication and Privacy – extensions to support authentication, data integrity, and optional data confidentiality.

8.5 The IPv6 Header

The IPv6 header is 40 octets in length, with eight fields (see Figure 8-1).

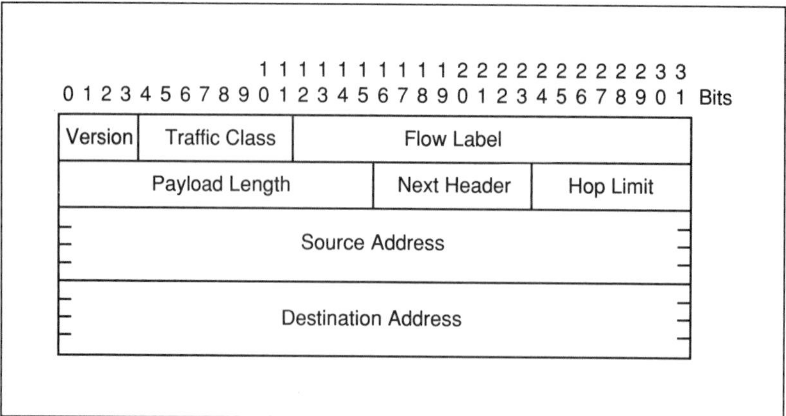

Figure 8-1 IPv6 Header Format

The Version field is four bits in length and identifies the version of the protocol. For IPv6, Version = 6.

The Traffic Class field is eight bits in length and is intended to enable a source to identify the desired delivery of its packets.

The Flow Label field is 20 bits in length and may be used by a host to request special handling for certain packets, such as those with a non-default quality of service.

The Payload Length field is a 16-bit unsigned integer which measures the length, given in octets, of the payload (i.e. the balance of the IPv6 packet). Payloads greater than 65,535 are allowed, and are called jumbo payloads. To indicate a jumbo payload, the value of the Payload Length is set to zero, and the actual payload length is carried in a Jumbo Payload hop-by-hop option.

The Next Header field is eight bits in length and identifies the header immediately following the IPv6 header. This field uses the same values as the IPv4 Protocol field. Examples are:

Value	Header
0	Hop-by-Hop Options
1	ICMPv4
4	IP in IP (encapsulation)
6	TCP
17	UDP
43	Routing
44	Fragment

50	Encapsulating Security Payload
51	Authentication
58	ICMPv6
59	None (no next header)
60	Destination Options

The Hop Limit field is eight bits in length and is decremented by one by each node that forwards the packet. When the Hop Limit equals zero, the packet is discarded and an error message is returned.

The Source Address is a 128-bit field that identifies the originator of the packet.

The Destination Address field is a 128-bit field that identifies the intended recipient of the packet, although possibly not the ultimate recipient of the packet, if a Routing header is present.

8.5.1 Extension Headers

The IPv6 design simplified the existing IPv4 header by placing many of the existing fields in optional headers. In this way, the processing of ordinary packets is not complicated by undue overhead, while the more complex conditions are still provided for. An IPv6 packet, which consists of an IPv6 packet plus its payload, may consist of zero, one, or more extension headers, as shown in Figure 8-2. Note the values of the Next Header fields in each example shown in the Figure. In the first case, no extension headers are required, the Next Header = TCP; and the TCP header and any upper layer protocol data follows. In the second case, a Routing header is required, therefore the IPv6 Next Header = Routing; in the Routing header, Next Header = TCP, and the TCP header and any upper layer protocol data follows. In the third case, both the Routing and Fragment headers are required, with the Next Header fields identified accordingly.

The Hop-by-Hop Options header carries information that must be examined and processed by every node along a packet's delivery path, including the destination node. As a result, the Hop-by-Hop Options header, when present, must immediately follow the IPv6 header. The other extension headers are not examined or processed by any node along a packet's delivery path, until the packet reaches its intended destination(s). When processed, the operation is performed in the order in which the headers appear in the packet.

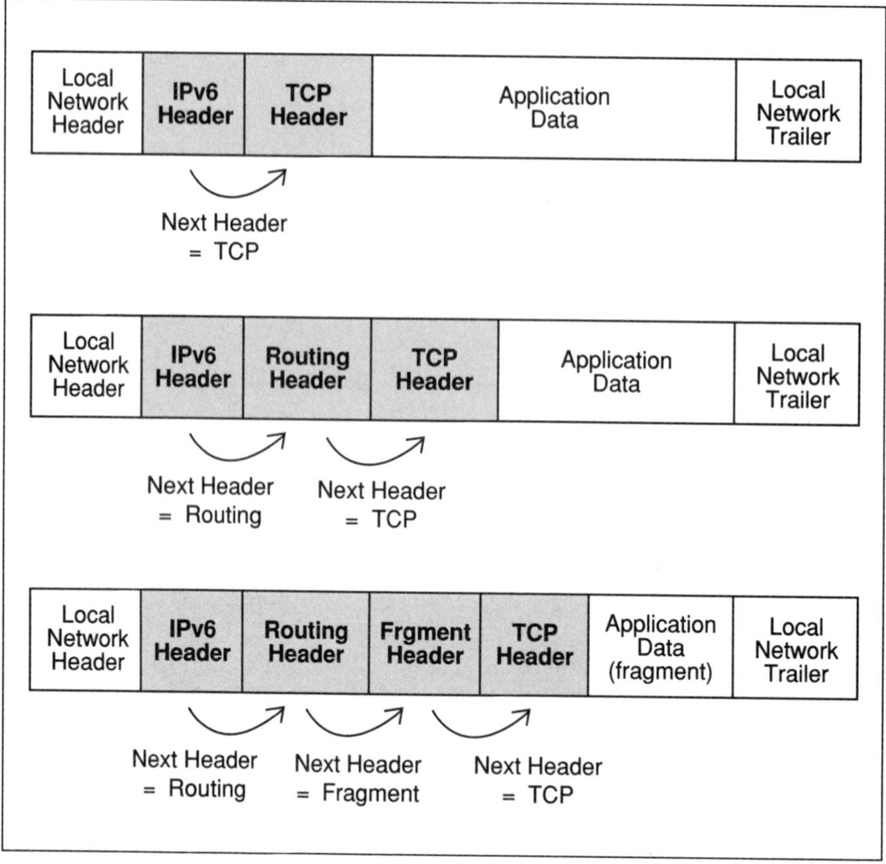

Figure 8-2 IPv6 Next Header Field Operation

8.5.2 Extension Header Order

RFC 2460 recommends that the extension headers be placed in the IPv6 packet in a particular order:

- IPv6 header
- Hop-by-Hop Options header
- Destination Options header (for options to be processed by the first destination that appears in the IPv6 Destination Address field, plus any subsequent destinations listed in the Routing header)
- Routing header
- Fragment header
- Authentication header (as detailed in RFC 2402)

- Encapsulating Security Payload header (as detailed in RFC 2406)
- Destination Options header (for options to be processed by the final destination only)
- Upper Layer Protocol header (TCP, and so on)

Figure 8-3 illustrates the IPv6 and optional headers, with their suggested order.

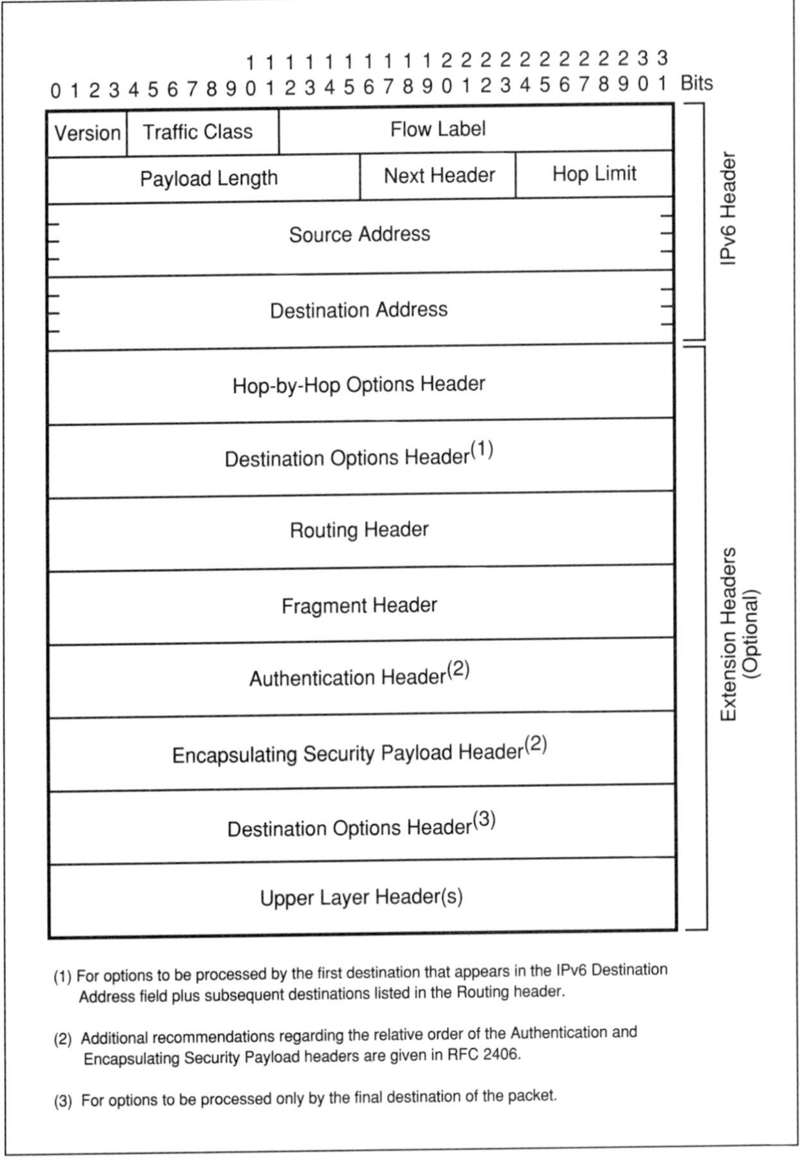

Figure 8-3 IPv6 Packet Format

8.5.3 Hop-by-Hop Options Header

The Hop-by-Hop Options header carries optional information that must be examined by every node along a packet's delivery path (see Figure 8-4). The presence of the Hop-by-Hop Options header is identified by a value of 0 in the Next Header field of the IPv6 header. This header contains two fields, plus options.

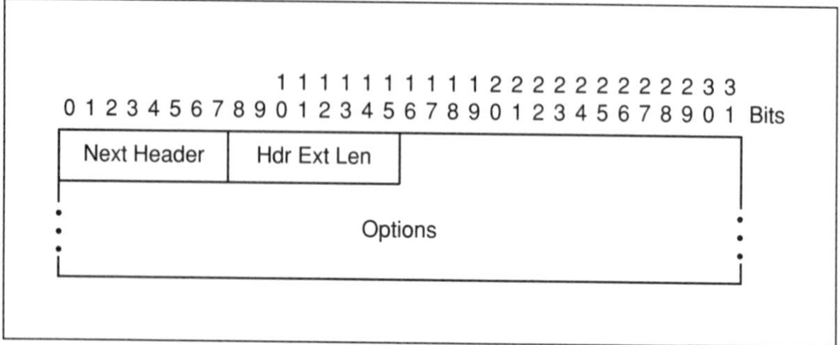

Figure 8-4 IPv6 Hop-by-Hop Options Header

The Next Header field is eight bits in length and identifies the header immediately following the Hop-by-Hop Options header. This field uses the same values as the IPv4 Protocol field.

The Header Extension Length (Hdr Ext Len) field is eight bits in length and measures the length of the Hop-by-Hop Options header in 8-octet units, not counting the first 8 octets.

The Options field is variable in length, as long as the complete Hop-by-Hop Options header is an integer multiple of eight octets in length. The options themselves are defined using a type-length-value (TLV) encoding format that is described in detail in the IPv6 Specification document. One option that is defined in that document is the Jumbo Payload option, which is used to send IPv6 packets that are longer than 65,535 octets.

8.5.4 Destination Options Header

The Destination Options header carries optional information that needs to be examined only by a packet's destination node(s), as shown in Figure 8-5. The presence of the Destination Options header is identified by a value of 60 in the preceding header's Next Header field. This header contains two fields, plus options.

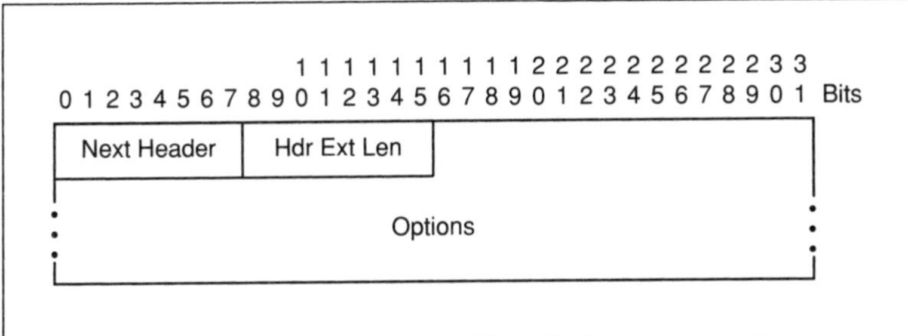

Figure 8-5 IPv6 Destination Options Header

The Next Header field is eight bits in length and identifies the header immediately following the Destination Options header. This field uses the same values as the IPv4 Protocol field.

The Header Extension Length (Hdr Ext Len) field is eight bits in length and measures the length of the Destination Options header in 8-octet units, not counting the first 8 octets.

The Options field is variable in length, such that the complete Destination Options header is an integer multiple of eight octets in length. The options themselves are defined using a type-length-value (TLV) encoding format that is described in detail in the IPv6 specification document. Two options are defined: the Pad1 option, used to insert one octet of padding into the Options area of a header; and PadN, used to insert two or more octets of padding into the Options area of a header.

8.5.5 Routing Header

The Routing Header lists one or more intermediate nodes that are "visited" on the path from the source to the destination (see Figure 8-6). The presence of the Routing header is identified by a value of 43 in the preceding header's Next Header field. This header contains four fields, plus type-specific data.

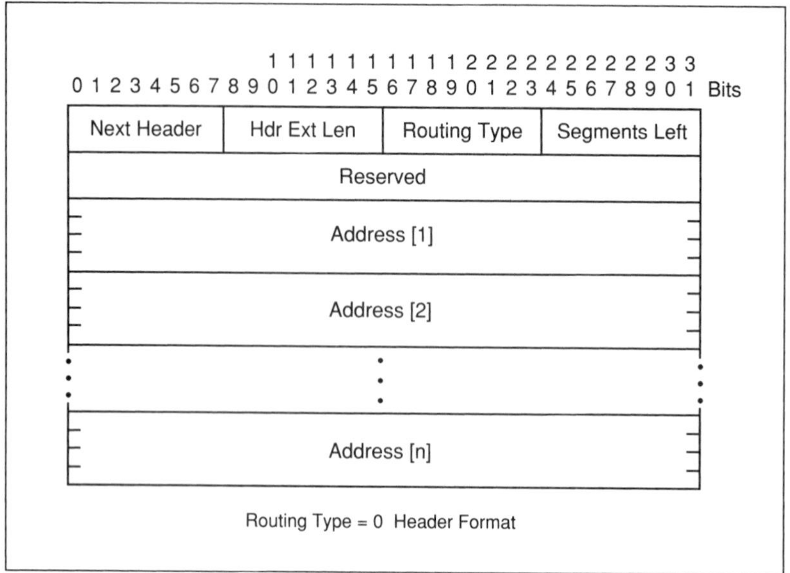

Figure 8-6 IPv6 Routing Header (Type = 0)

The Next Header field is eight bits in length and identifies the header immediately following the Routing header. This field uses the same values as the IPv4 Protocol field.

The Header Extension Length (Hdr Ext Len) field is eight bits in length and measures the length of the Routing header in 8-octet units, not counting the first 8 octets.

The Routing Type field is eight bits in length and identifies a particular Routing header variant. The IPv6 specification document defines one variant, Routing Type 0.

The Segments Left field is eight bits in length and indicates the number of route segments remaining, or in other words, the number of explicitly listed intermediate nodes still to be visited before reaching the final destination.

A Reserved field (32 bits) and the 128-bit addresses would complete the Routing Header.

8.5.6 Fragment Header

The Fragment header is used by an IPv6 source to send packets that are larger than would fit in the path maximum transmission unit (MTU) to their destinations (see Figure 8-7). The presence of the Fragment header is identified by a value of 44 in the preceding header's Next Header field. Note that fragmentation for IPv6 is only done at the source node, not at intermediate routers along the packet's delivery path.

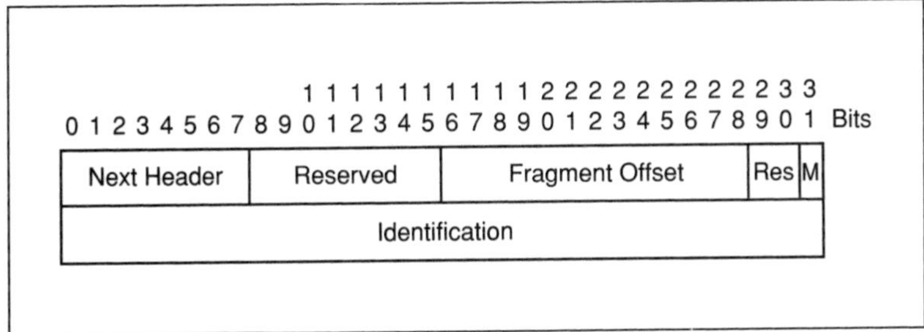

Figure 8-7 IPv6 Fragment Header

The Fragment header contains six fields. The Next Header field is eight bits in length and identifies the header immediately following the Fragment header. This field uses the same values as the IPv4 Protocol field.

The Reserved field is eight bits in length and is reserved for future use. This field is initialized to zero for transmission and is ignored on reception.

The Fragment Offset field is a 13-bit unsigned integer which measures the offset, in 8-octet units, of the data following this header, relative to the start of the fragmentable part of the original packet.

A second Reserved field is two bits in length and is reserved for future use. This field is initialized to zero for transmission and is ignored on reception.

The M flag is one bit in length and determines if more fragments are coming (M = 1) or if this is the last fragment (M = 0).

The Identification field is 32 bits in length; it uniquely identifies the fragmented packet(s) during the reassembly process.

8.5.7 Authentication Header

Assuring secure data transmissions has become an increasingly important issue for network managers. The Internet community has addressed these issues in RFC 2401, "Security Architecture for the Internet Protocol" [8-16]. RFC 2401 contains several definitions which are important to the implementation of the accompanying protocols:

- Authentication: the property of knowing that the data received is the same as the data that was sent, and that the claimed sender is in fact the actual sender.
- Integrity: the property of ensuring that data is transmitted from source to destination without undetected alteration.
- Confidentiality: the property of communicating such that the intended recipients know what was being sent, but unintended parties cannot determine what was sent.
- Encryption: a mechanism commonly used to provide confidentiality.

Two headers are discussed in RFC 2401 to provide the IP security mechanisms. The Authentication header is defined in RFC 2402 [8-17], and the IP Encapsulating Security Payload (ESP) is defined in RFC 2406 [8-18].

The IP Authentication header provides integrity and authentication without confidentiality, and is illustrated in Figure 8-8. The presence of the Authentication header is identified by a value of 51 in the preceding header's Next Header field. This header contains five fields.

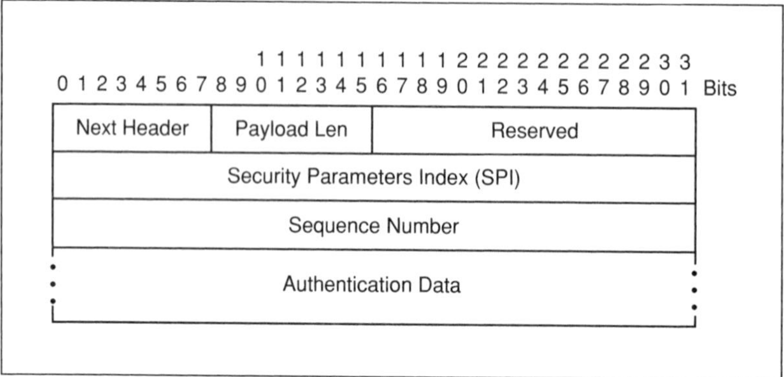

Figure 8-8 IPv6 Authentication Header

The Next Header field is eight bits in length and identifies the header immediately following the Authentication header. This field uses the same values as the IPv4 Protocol field.

The Payload Len (length) field is eight bits in length and provides the length of the Authentication field in 32-bit words. The minimum value is 0 words, which is only used in the case of a "null" authentication algorithm.

The Reserved field is sixteen bits in length and is reserved for future use. This field is initialized to zero for transmission. It is included in the Authentication Data calculation, but is otherwise ignored on reception.

The Sequence Number field is 32 bits in length, and is initialized to zero by both sender and receiver when the logical security relationship between the two parties (known as the security association, and further defined below) is established.

The Security Parameters Index (SPI) field is a 32-bit pseudo-random value that identifies the security association for this datagram. The security association, as defined in RFC 2401, may include the Authentication algorithm, algorithm mode band key(s) being used with the IP Authentication header, the Encryption algorithm, algorithm mode and transform being used with the IP Encapsulating Security Payload, plus other security-related parameters. The value of SPI = 0 is reserved to indicate that "no security association exists." Other values, in the range of 1-255, are reserved for future use by the Internet Assigned Numbers Authority (IANA).

The Authentication Data is a variable-length field, containing an integral number of 32-bit words.

For additional details, refer to RFCs 2401 and 2402.

8.5.8 Encapsulating Security Payload Header

The Encapsulating Security Payload (ESP) Header is designed to provide integrity and confidentiality to IP datagrams; it may also provide authentication, depending on the algorithm used. The ESP header may also be used in conjunction with the Authentication header described above. The ESP process operates by encrypting the data to be protected and then placing that encrypted information in the data portion of the ESP payload. Depending upon the specific requirements, the mechanism may be used either to encrypt a Transport Layer segment, such as TCP or UDP data, or it may encrypt an entire IP datagram. The presence of the ESP header is identified by a value of 50 in the preceding header's Next Header field. This header is illustrated in Figure 8-9 and contains seven fields.

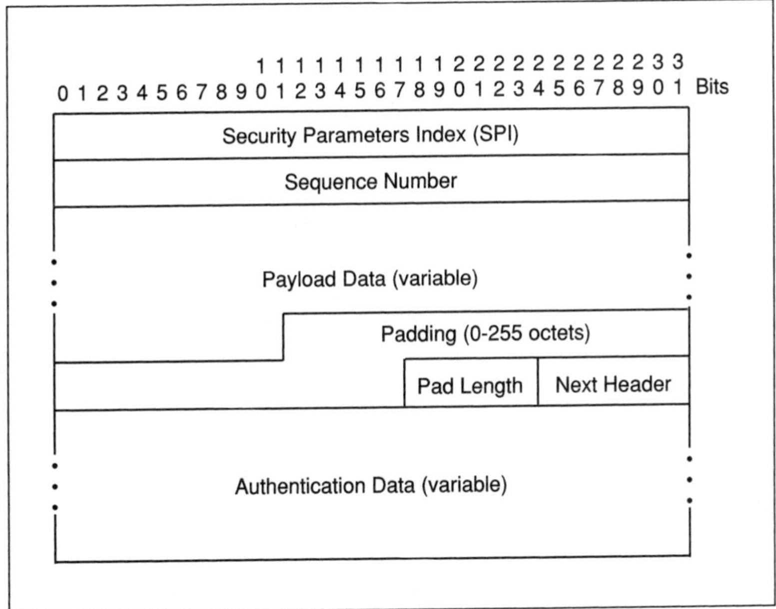

Figure 8-9 IPv6 Encapsulating Security Payload Header

The Security Parameter Association is a 32-bit pseudo-random value identifying the security association (as described above) for this datagram. If no security association exists, this field contains a value of zero. In addition, SPI values from 00000001 - 000000FFH are reserved by the IANA for future use.

The Sequence Number field is 32 its in length, and is initialized to zero by both sender and receiver when the security association is established.

The Payload Data field is a variable length field containing data described by the Next Header field.

The Padding field may optionally contain 0-255 octets of pad information, thus making the ESP header longer than actually required (and thus providing an additional element of security). The Pad Length field, which is one octet in length, indicates the number of Pad octets that have been sent.

The Next Header field is eight bits in length and identifies the header immediately following the ESP header. This field uses the same values as the IPv4 Protocol field.

The Authentication Data is a variable-length field which contains the authentication information.

For additional details, refer to RFC 2406 [8-18].

8.5.9 No Next Header

The value of 59 in the Next Header field of an IPv6 packet or any of the extension headers indicates that nothing follows that header. As such, this is called a No Next Header.

8.6 IPv6 Addressing

As we discussed previously, one of the incentives behind the IPng effort which resulted in IPv6 was the limitations of the 32-bit IPv4 address structure. These new address formats are defined in RFC 2373, "IPv6 Addressing Architecture" [8-19], and RFC 1924, "Compact Representation of IPv6 Addresses."

8.6.1 IPv6 Address Types

RFC 2373 defines three different types of IPv6 addresses:

- Unicast – an identifier to a single interface. A packet sent to a unicast address is delivered to the interface identified by that address (see Figure 8-10a).
- Anycast – an identifier for a set of interfaces (typically belonging to different nodes). A packet sent to an anycast address is delivered to one of the interfaces identified by that address (the "nearest" one, according to the routing protocol's measure of distance), shown in Figure 8-10b.
- Multicast – an identifier for a set of interfaces (typically belonging to different nodes). A packet sent to a multicast address is delivered to all interfaces identified by that address (see Figure 8-10c).

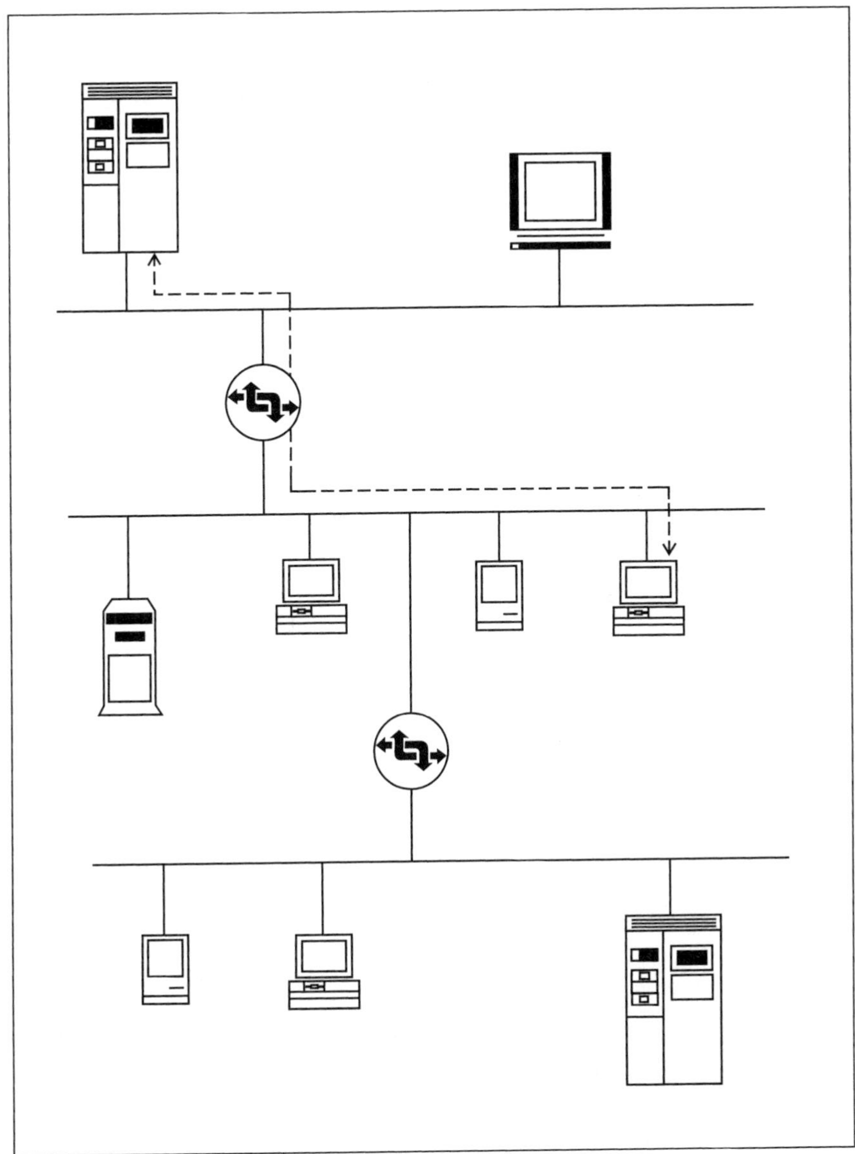

Figure 8-10a Unicast Addressing

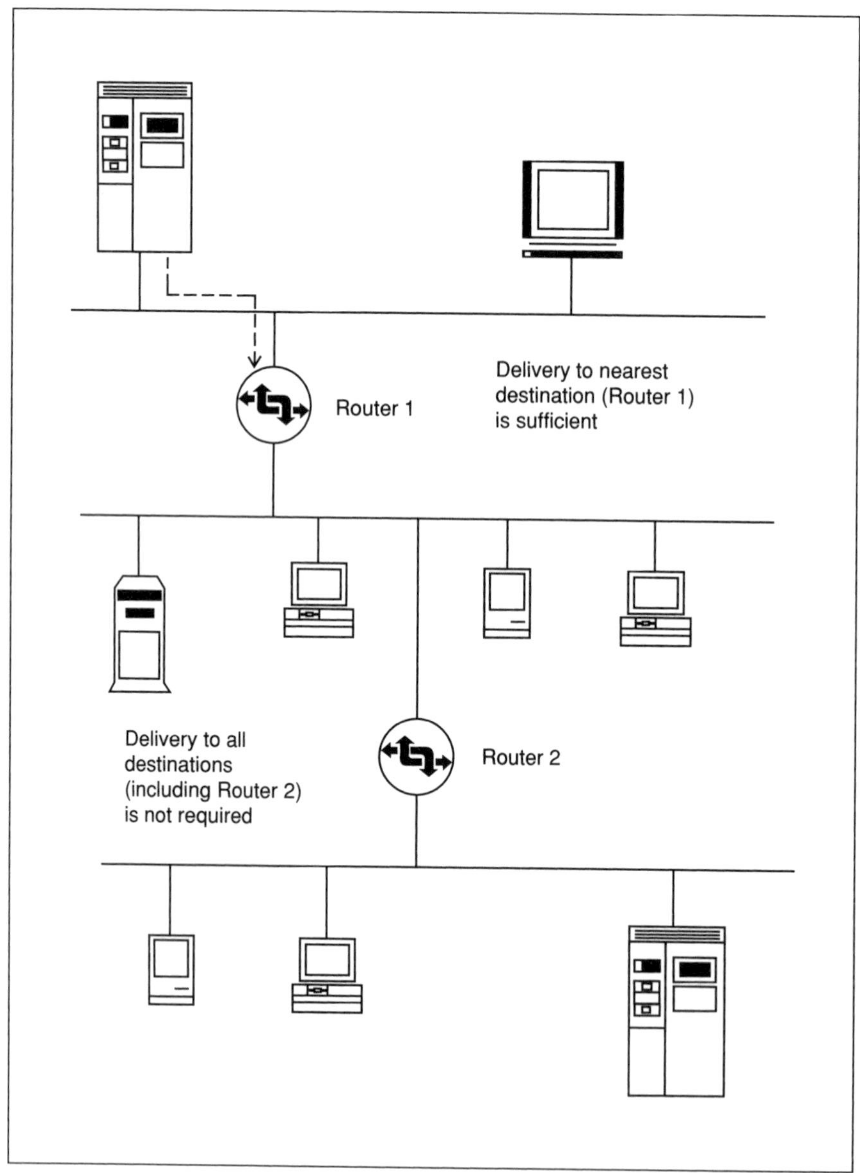

Figure 8-10b Anycast Addressing

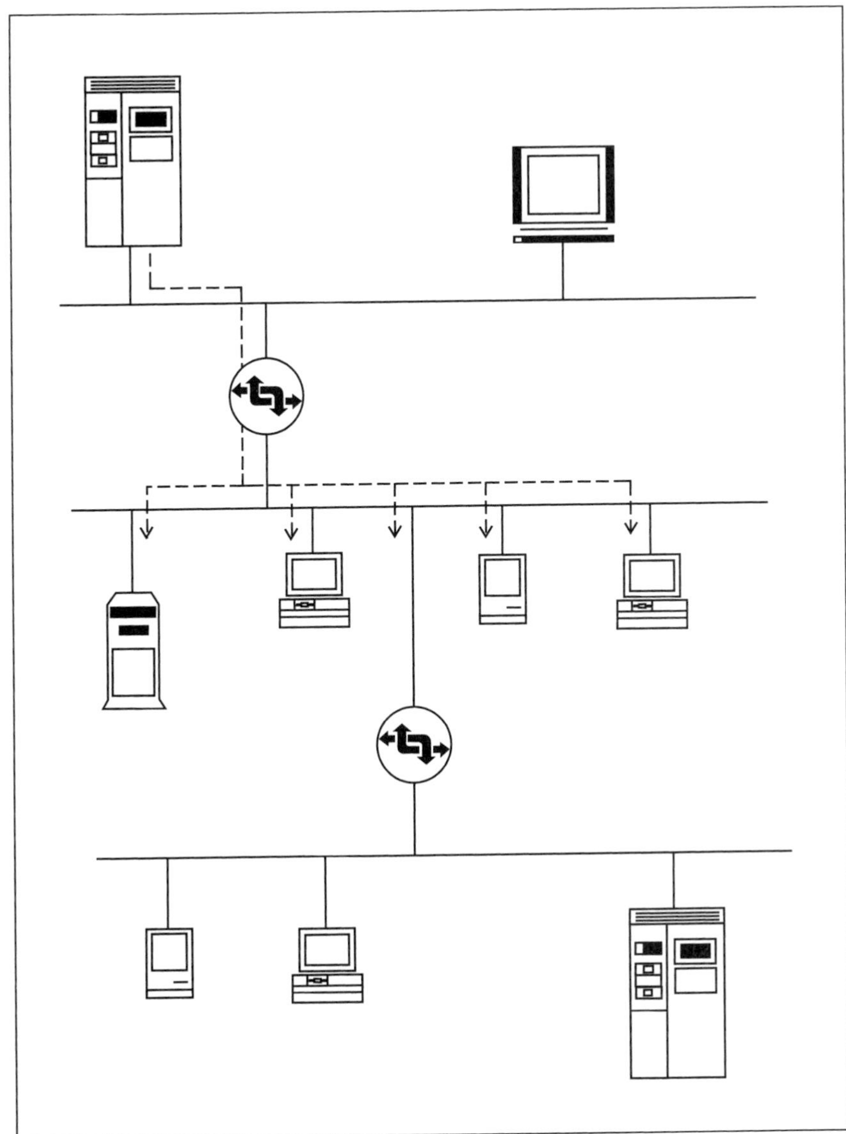

Figure 8-10c Multicast Addressing

Note that the term broadcast does not appear, because the broadcast function is replaced by the multicast definition. In addition, IPv6 addresses of all types are assigned to interfaces, not nodes, such that one node (such as a router) may have multiple interfaces, and therefore multiple unicast addresses. In addition, a single interface may be assigned multiple addresses.

8.6.2 IPv6 Address Representation

IPv4 addresses are typically represented in dotted decimal notation. As such, a 32-bit address is divided into four 8-bit sections, and then each section is represented by a decimal number between 0 and 255, for example [129.144.52.38].

Since IPv6 addresses are 128 bits long, a different method of representation is required. As specified in the Addressing Architecture document, RFC 2373, the preferred representation is:

```
x:x:x:x:x:x:x:x
```

where each "x" represents 16 bits, and each of those 16-bit sections is defined in hexadecimal. For example, an IPv6 address could be of the form:

```
FEDC:BA98:7654:3210:FEDC:BA98:7654:3210
```

Note that each of the 16-bit sections is separated by colons, and that four hexadecimal numbers are used to represent each 16-bit section. Should any one of the 16-bit sections contain leading zeros, those zeros are not required. For example:

```
1080:0000:0000:0000:0008:0800:200C:417A
```

may be simplified to:

```
1080:0:0:0:8:800:200C:417A
```

If long strings of zeros appear in an address, a double colon "::" may be used to indicate multiple groups of 16-bits of zeros, which further simplifies the example shown above:

```
1080::8:800:200C:417A
```

The use of the double colon is restricted to appear only once in an address, although it may be used to compress either the leading or trailing zeros in an address. For example, a loopback address of:

```
0:0:0:0:0:0:0:1
```

could be simplified as:

```
::1
```

For additional details, see RFCs 2373 and 1924.

8.6.3 IPv6 Address Prefixes

The 128-bit IPv6 address may be divided into a number of subfields to provide maximum flexibility for both current and future address representations. The leading bits, called the format prefix, define the specific type of IPv6 address. RFC 2373 defines a number of these prefixes, as shown in Figure 8-11. Note that address space has been allocated for NSAP, IPX, aggregatable global, site local, and other addresses. Also note that multicast addresses begin with the binary value 11111111; any other prefix identifies a unicast address. Anycast addresses are part of the allocation for unicast addresses, and are not given a unique identifier.

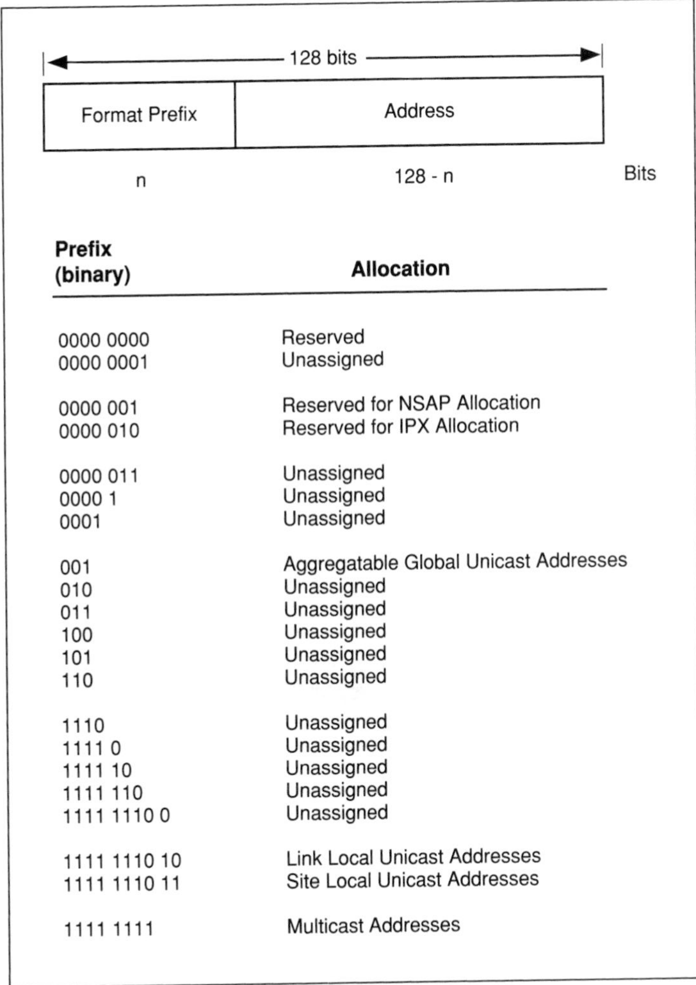

Prefix (binary)	Allocation
0000 0000	Reserved
0000 0001	Unassigned
0000 001	Reserved for NSAP Allocation
0000 010	Reserved for IPX Allocation
0000 011	Unassigned
0000 1	Unassigned
0001	Unassigned
001	Aggregatable Global Unicast Addresses
010	Unassigned
011	Unassigned
100	Unassigned
101	Unassigned
110	Unassigned
1110	Unassigned
1111 0	Unassigned
1111 10	Unassigned
1111 110	Unassigned
1111 1110 0	Unassigned
1111 1110 10	Link Local Unicast Addresses
1111 1110 11	Site Local Unicast Addresses
1111 1111	Multicast Addresses

Figure 8-11 IPv6 Addressing Architecture

8.6.3.1 UNICAST ADDRESSES

A number of forms for unicast addresses have been defined for IPv6, some with more complex structures that provide for hierarchical address assignments. The simplest form would be a unicast address with no internal structure, in other words, with no address-defined hierarchy. The next possibility would be to specify a subnet prefix within the 128-bit address, thus dividing the address into a subnet prefix (with n bits) and an interface ID (with 128 - n bits). For applications where more hierarchy is required, a specific type of address, called the Aggregatable Global Unicast Address is defined. This address type allows multiple levels of hierarchy, starting with network providers of IPv6 service, and graduating down to the networks, sub-networks, and then finally to the end user devices. In summary, with a 128-bit address space available, a number of addressing structures are possible. RFC 2373 illustrates many of these.

8.6.3.2 SPECIAL ADDRESSES

Two addresses have special meanings. The address 0:0:0:0:0:0:0:0 (also represented as 0::0) is defined as the unspecified address and indicates the absence of an address. This address might be used upon startup when a node has not yet had an address assigned. The unspecified address may never be assigned to any node.

The address 0:0:0:0:0:0:0:1 (also represented as 0::1) is defined as the loopback address. This address is used by a node to send a packet to itself. The loopback address may never be assigned to any interface.

8.6.3.3 TRANSITION ADDRESSES

Two special addresses have been defined for IPv4/IPv6 transition networks. The first such address is called an IPv4-Compatible IPv6 address. It is used when two IPv6 devices (such as hosts or routers) need to communicate via an IPv4 routing infrastructure. The devices at the edge of the IPv4 would use this special unicast address that carries an IPv4 address in the low order 32 bits. Note that the prefix is 96 bits of all zeros (see Figure 8-12).

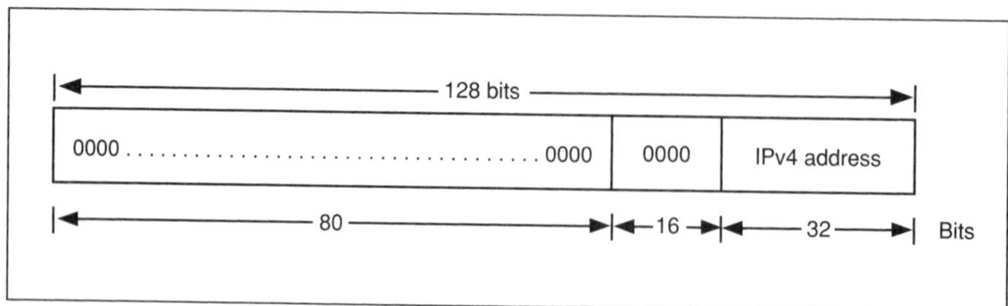

Figure 8-12 IPv4-Compatible IPv6 Address

The second type of transition address is called an IPv4-Mapped IPv6 address (see Figure 8-13). This address is used by IPv4-only nodes which do not support IPv6.

For example, an IPv6 host would use an IPv4-Mapped IPv6 address to communicate with another host which only supported IPv4. Note that the prefix is 80 bits of zeros, followed by 16 bits of ones.

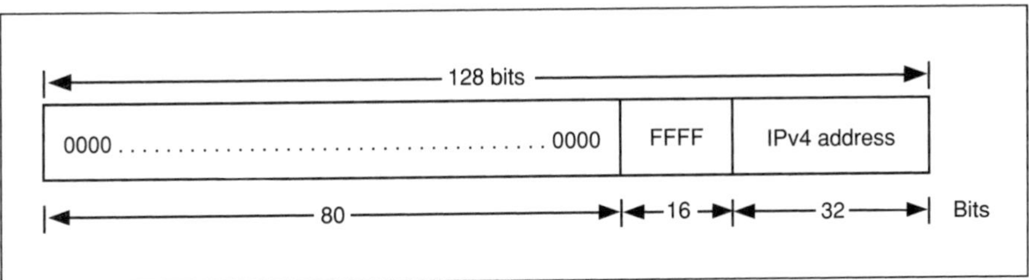

Figure 8-13 IPv4-Mapped IPv6 Address

8.7 ICMPv6 for IPv6

The Internet Control Message Protocol, version 6 (ICMPv6) [8-20], is a revised version of the ICMP defined in RFC 792, which incorporates a number of changes required to support IPv6. In addition, functions from the Internet Group Membership Protocol (IGMP), specified in RFC 1112 [8-21], have been incorporated into ICMPv6. Note that like ICMP for IPv4, ICMPv6 is considered to be an integral part of IPv6, and must be implemented by every IPv6 node. The presence of the ICMPv6 header is identified by a value of 58 in the preceding header's Next Header field.

The ICMPv6 message format is very similar to its IPv4 counterpart. This message format is illustrated in Figure 8-14 and contains four fields:

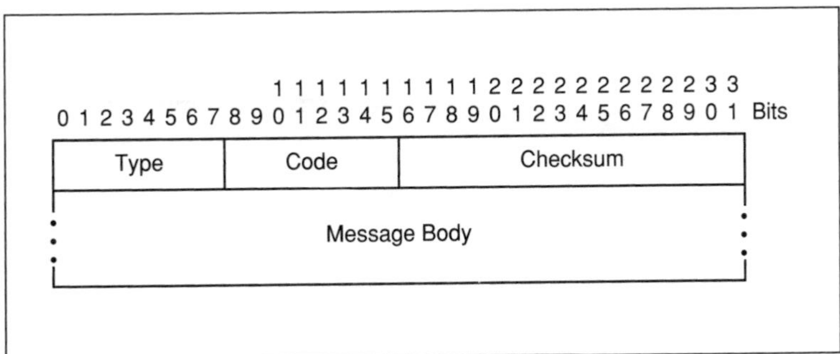

Figure 8-14 ICMPv6 Message Format

The Type field is eight bits in length and indicates the type of the message. The Type field values are divided into two groups: Error messages (Types 0-127) and Informational messages (Types 128-255). The Error messages include:

Type	Message
1	Destination unreachable
2	Packet too big
3	Time exceeded
4	Parameter problem

The Informational messages include:

Type	Message
128	Echo request
129	Echo reply
130	Multicast listener query
131	Multicast listener report
132	Multicast listener done
133	Router solicitation
134	Router advertisement
135	Neighbor solicitation
136	Neighbor advertisement
137	Redirect

The Code field is eight bits in length and is used to create additional message information. For example, for the Destination Unreachable message, the following code values are defined:

Code	Meaning
0	No route to destination
1	Communication with destination administratively prohibited
2	Not a neighbor

3	Address unreachable
4	Port unreachable

Definitions for other message codes are contained in RFC 1885.

The Checksum is a 16-bit field that is used to detect data corruption in the ICMPv6 message and parts of the IPv6 header.

Specifics of the ICMPv6 message formats and their parameters can be found in RFC 1885.

8.8 The Great Transition: IPv4 to IPv6

The benefits derived from a new protocol must also be balanced by the costs associated with making a transition from the existing systems. These logistical and technical issues have been addressed in RFC1933 "Transition Mechanisms for IPv6 Hosts and Routers," [8-22].

The developers of IPv6 recognized that not all systems would upgrade from IPv4 to IPv6 in the immediate future, and that for some systems, that upgrade may not be for years. To complicate matters, most internetworks are heterogeneous systems, with various routers, hosts, etc. manufactured by different vendors. If such a multivendor system were to be upgraded at one time, IPv6 capabilities would be required on all of the individual elements before the larger project could be attempted. Another (much larger) issue becomes the worldwide Internet, which operates across 24 different time zones. Upgrading this system in a single process would be even more difficult.

Given the above constraints, it therefore becomes necessary to develop strategies for IPv4 and IPv6 to coexist, until such time as IPv6 becomes the preferred option. At the time of this writing, two mechanisms for this coexistence have been proposed: a dual IP layer and IPv6 over IPv4 tunneling. These two alternatives will be discussed in the following sections.

8.8.1 Dual IP Layers

The simplest mechanism for IPv4 and IPv6 coexistence is for both of the protocol stacks to be implemented on the same device. That device, which could be either a host or a router, is then referred to as an IPv6/IPv4 node. The IPv6/IPv4 node has the capability to send and receive both IPv4 and IPv6 packets, and can therefore interoperate with an IPv4 device using IPv4 packets and with an IPv6 device using IPv6 packets (see Figure 8-15). The IPv6/IPv4 node would be configured with addresses that support both protocols, and those addresses might or might not be related to each other. Other address-related functions, such as the Dynamic Host

Configuration Protocol (DHCP), the Bootstrap Protocol (BOOTP), and the Domain Name System (DNS), may also be involved in this process.

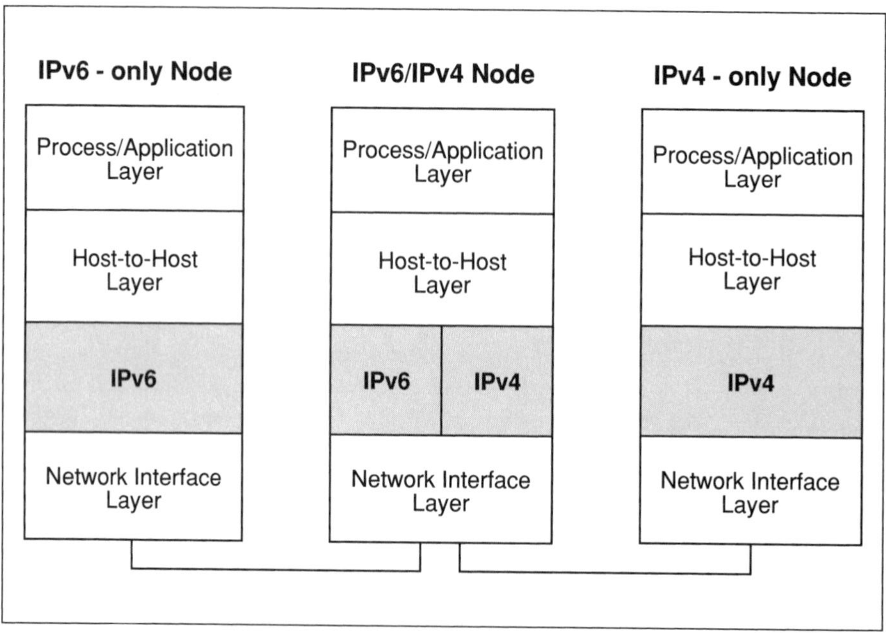

Figure 8-15 Dual IP Layer Architecutre

8.8.2 Tunneling

Tunneling is a process whereby information from one protocol is encapsulated inside the frame or packet of another architecture, thus enabling the original data to be carried over that second architecture. The tunneling scenarios for IPv6/IPv4 are designed to enable an existing IPv4 infrastructure to carry IPv6 packets by encapsulating the IPv6 information inside IPv4 packets.

The encapsulation process is illustrated in Figure 8-16. Note that the resulting IPv4 packet contains both an IPv4 header and an IPv6 header, plus all of the upper-layer information, such as the TCP header, application data, and so on. The tunneling process involves three distinct steps: encapsulation, decapsulation, and tunnel management. At the encapsulating node (or tunnel entry point), the IPv4 header is created, and the encapsulated packet is transmitted. At the decapsulating node (or tunnel exit point), the IPv4 header is removed and the IPv6 packet is processed. In addition, the encapsulating node may maintain configuration information regarding the tunnels that are established, such as the maximum transfer unit (MTU) size that is supported in that tunnel.

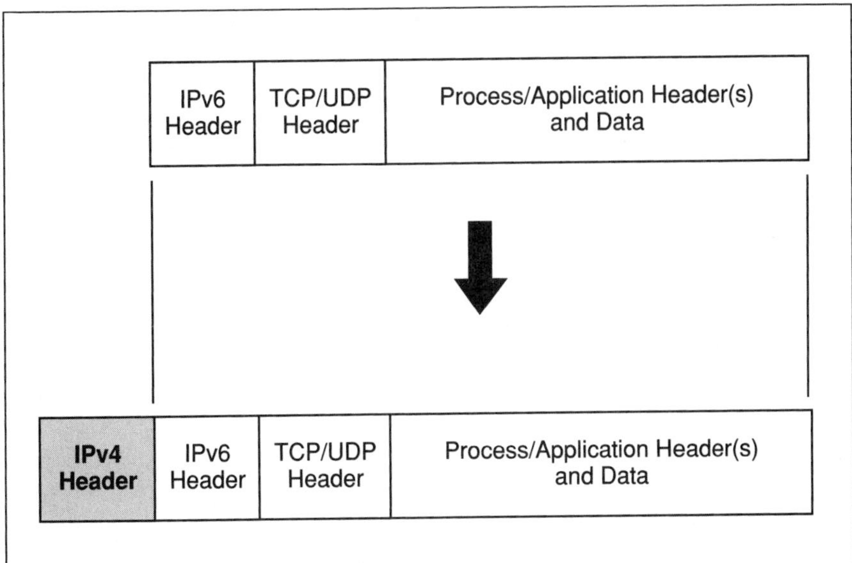

Figure 8-16 Encapsulating IPv6 in IPv4

RFC 1933 defines four possible tunnel configurations that could be established between routers and hosts:

- Router-to-Router: IPv6/IPv4 routers that are separated by an IPv4 infrastructure tunnel IPv6 packets between themselves. In this case, the tunnel would span one segment of the packet's end-to-end path.
- Host-to-Router: an IPv6/IPv4 host tunnels IPv6 packets to an IPv6/IPv4 router that is reachable via an IPv4 infrastructure. In this case, the tunnel would span the first segment of the packet's end-to-end path.
- Host-to-Host: IPv6/IPv4 hosts that are interconnected by an IPv4 infrastructure can tunnel IPv6 packets across the IPv4 infrastructure. In this case, the tunnel spans the packet's entire end-to-end path.
- Router-to-Host: IPv6/IPv4 routers can tunnel IPv6 packets to an IPv6/IPv4 host which is the final destination. In this case, the tunnel would span only the final segment of the packet's end-to-end path.

For a tunnel to operate, addresses of both the tunnel endpoint and the packet's destination must be known, and these two addresses are not necessarily the same. The manner in which the tunnel endpoint address is determined defines one of two types of tunnels: an automatic tunnel or a configured tunnel. These alternatives will be explored below.

From the above four tunneling scenarios, the first two terminate on a router, which then decapsulates the information and forwards the IPv6 packet to its final destination. Note that the tunnel endpoint address is different from the final destination endpoint address. This requires the node performing the tunneling to determine the tunnel endpoint from some configuration information. For this reason, this type of tunneling is called configured tunneling.

In the last two tunneling scenarios, the termination point of the tunnel and the final destination of the IPv6 packet are the same – both end at a host. In this case, the tunnel endpoint address and the IPv6 packet endpoint address both identify the same device. But note that the tunnel endpoint address is an IPv4 address, while the host address is an IPv6 address. If the IPv4 and IPv6 addresses can be correlated, the tunneling process is considerably simplified. For this reason, this type of tunneling is called automatic tunneling. This is, in fact, the purpose of the IPv4-compatible IPv6 address (review Figure 8-12). Note from the figure that the 32-bit IPv4 address occupies the lower 32 bits of the IPv6 address, and that the balance of the address is filled with all zeros.

For further details on tunneling and associated functions, see RFC 1933.

As expected, IPv6 has generated a great deal of interest among users, vendors, and network managers. References [8-23] through [8-38] are examples of recent journal articles that discuss various aspects of the protocol, and References [8-39] through [8-41] are recent books that discuss the new protocol and implementation strategies. The IPv6 industry web site [8-42] provides current information on various IPv6 vendor implementations.

8.9 References

[8-1] Mankin, Allison. "The Trillion Node Internet: An Update on IPv6." *ComNet 1996 Conference Proceedings*, January 1996.

[8-2] Gross, P., and P. Almquist. "IESG Deliberations on Routing and Addressing." RFC 1380, November 1992.

[8-3] Bradner, S., and A. Mankin. "IP: Next Generation (IPng) White Paper Solicitation." RFC 1550, December 1993.

[8-4] Bradner, Scott O., and Allison Mankin, Editors. *IPng – Internet Protocol Next Generation.* Addison-Wesley Publishing Company, (Reading, MA), 1996.

[8-5] Partridge, C., and F. Kastenholz. "Technical Criteria for Choosing IP The Next Generation (IPng)." RFC 1726, December 1994.

[8-6] Bradner, S., and A. Mankin. "The Recommendation for the IP Next Generation Protocol." RFC 1752, January 1995.

[8-7] McGovern, M., and R. Ullman. "CATNIP: Common Architecture for the Internet." RFC 1707, October 1994.

[8-8] McGovern, Michael, and Robert Ullmann. "The CATNIP: Purrposed Common Architecture for the Internet." *ConneXions* (May 1994): 18-27.

[8-9] Hinden, R. "Simple Internet Protocol Plus White Paper." RFC 1710, October 1994.

[8-10] Hinden, Robert M. "Simple Internet Protocol Plus (SIPP) Overview." *ConneXions* (May 1994): 34-48.

[8-11] Callon, R. "TCP and UDP with Bigger Addresses (TUBA)." RFC 1347, June 1992.

[8-12] Ford, Peter S., et al. "TUBA: CLNP as IPng." *ConneXions* (May 1994): 28-33.

[8-13] Fuller, V., et al. "Classless Inter-Domain Routing (CIDR): An Address Assignment and Aggregation Strategy." RFC 1519, 1993.

[8-14] Solensky, Frank. "CIDR Effects: Getting More Out of IPv4." *ConneXions* (May 1994): 14-17.

[8-15] Deering, S., and R. Hinden. "Internet Protocol, Version 6 (IPv6) Specification." RFC 2460, December 1998.

[8-16] Kent, S. and Atkinson, R. "Security Architecture for the Internet Protocol." RFC 2401, November 1998.

[8-17] Kent, S. and Atkinson, R. "IP Authentication Header." RFC 2402, November 1998.

[8-18] Kent, S. and Atkinson, R. "IP Encapsulating Security Payload (ESP)." RFC 2406, November 1998.

[8-19] Hinden, R., and S. Deering, Editors. "IP Version 6 Addressing Architecture." RFC 2373, July 1998.

[8-20] Conta, A., and S. Deering. "Internet Control Message Protocol (ICMPv6) for the Internet Protocol Version 6 (IPv6) Specification." RFC 2463, December 1998.

[8-21] Deering, S. "Host Extensions for IP Multicasting." RFC 1112, August 1989.

[8-22] Gilligan, Robert E. and Erik Nordmark. RFC 1933, "Transition Mechanisms for IPv6 Hosts and Routers." April 1996.

[8-23] Special Issue: IP – The Next Generation. *ConneXions* (May 1994).

[8-24] Britton, E. G., et al. "TCP/IP: The Next Generation." *IBM Systems Journal* (Volume 34, number 3, 1995): 452-471.

[8-25] Dixon, Tim. "IPng – What it Means for OSI." *ConneXions* (March 1995): 19-23.

[8-26] Hinden, Robert M. "IP Next Generation Overview." *ConneXions* (March 1995): 2-18.

[8-27] Moskowitz, Robert G. "Plan Now for the New Internet Protocol." *Network Computing* (May 1, 1995): 144-150.

[8-28] Callon, Ross. "Migrate to IPng or Retrofit IP?" *Network World* (June 5, 1995): 41.

[8-29] Cooney, Michael. "Is IP at a Fork In the Road?" *Network World* (October 23, 1995): 24.

[8-30] Gilligan , Robert E., and Ross Callon. "IPv6 Transitions Mechanisms Overview." *ConneXions* (October 1995): 2-17.

[8-31] Miller, Mark. "Finding your way through the new IP." *Network World* (December 16, 1996): 43-45.

[8-32] Miller, Mark. "Making the move – the path for an orderly transition from IPv4 to IPv6." *Network World* (January 20, 1997): 37-42.

[8-33] Kessler, Gary. "IPv6: The Next Generation Internet Protocol" *Network Magazine* (February 1997): 32-39.

[8-34] Salamone, Salvatore. "Upgrading IP: Awash in a Sea of Protocol Options." InternetWeek (December 8, 1997): 52-53.

[8-35] Fink, Robert. "Boning Up on IPv6" *Byte* (March 1998): 3-8.

[8-36] Spangler, Todd. "Providing the Net IP Addresses to Spare." *Internet World* (March 23, 1998): 24-25

[8-37] Talley, Brooks. "IPv6 Cuts Address Chaos." *InfoWorld* (August 24, 1998): 61-62.

[8-38] Tadjer, Rivka "'Six' Appeal" *Network Computing* (September 1, 1998): 45-55.

[8-39] Huitema, Christian. IPv6: *The New Internet Protocol*, second edition. Prentice-Hall, Inc., (Upper Saddle River, NJ) 1996.

[8-40] Murphy, Eamon, et. al. *TCP/IP Tutorial and Technical Overview.* Prentice Hall PTR (Upper Saddle River, NJ), 1998.

[8-41] Miller, Mark A. *Implementing IPv6,* IDG Books Worldwide, Inc., (Foster City, CA) 1998.

[8-42] The IPv6 Industry Home Page is located at: `http://playground.sun.com/pub/ipng/html`.

Appendix A

About the CD-ROM

The CD contains a collection of public domain Internet documents, from the Internet Architecture Board (IAB), Internet Engineering Task Force (IETF), Internet Research Group (IRG), and other Internet-related organizations. The CD also contains names and addresses of selected manufacturers of TCP/IP-related Internetworking products and the complete listing of Internet parameters (Appendixes H and I, respectively).

Each document category is placed in a separate subdirectory identified by document type. These include:

- BCP - the Best Current Practices documents
- FYI - the For Your Information documents
- IMR - the Internet Monthly Report documents, starting with January 1994

RFC - the Request for Comments documents, starting with RFC 700, and in subdirectories by hundreds (e.g. RFC 1800 is in subdirectory RFC18XX)

- RTR - the RARE Technical Report documents
- STD - the Internet Standard documents

In addition there are two other subdirectories which include:

- INDEX - index files for the FYIs, RFCs and STDs
- RETRIEVE - retrieval instructions for the above files. Files on this CD are either in ASCII text (.txt) or PostScript (.ps) formats

Each RFC document published at the present time carries the following notice:

Copyright (C) The Internet Society (1999). All Rights Reserved.

> This document and translations of it may be copied and furnished to others, and derivative works that comment on or otherwise explain it or assist in its implementation may be prepared, copied, published and distributed, in whole or in part, without restriction of any kind, provided that the above copyright notice and this paragraph are included on all such copies and derivative works. However, this document itself may not be modified in any way, such as by removing the copyright notice

Appendix B

Broadband Technology Forums

ADSL Forum
39355 California Street, Suite 307
Fremont, CA 94538
Tel: (510) 608-5905
Fax: (510) 608-5917
E-mail: adslforum@adsl.com
www.adsl.com

ATM Forum
Worldwide Headquarters
2570 W El Camino Real, Suite 304
Mountain View, CA 94040-1313
Tel: (650) 949-6700
Fax: (650) 949-6705
E-mail: info@atmforum.com
www.atmforum.com

ATM Forum
European Office
Avenue De Tervueren #402
1150 Brussels Belgium
Tel: 32 2 761 66.77
Fax: 32 2 761 66.79
E-mail: euroinfo@atmforum.com
www.atmforum.com

ATM Forum
Asia-Pacific Office
Hamamatsucho Suzuki Building 3F
1-2-11, Hamamatsucho, Minato-ku
Tokyo 105-0013, Japan
Tel: 81.3.3438.3694
Fax: 81.3.3438.3698
E-mail: apinfo@atmforum.com
www.atmforum.com

Frame Relay Forum
North American Office
39355 California Street, Suite 307
Fremont, CA 94538
Tel: (510) 608-5920
Fax: (510) 608-5917
E-mail: frf@frforum.com
ftp://frforum.com
www.frforum.com

North American ISDN User's Forum
c/o NIST
Building 820 Room 445
Gaithersburg, MD 20899
Tel: (301) 975-2937
Fax: (301) 926 9675
E-mail: niuf@nist.gov
www.niuf.nist.gov

Appendix C

Sources of Internet Information

Many of the administrative functions for the Internet are handled by the InterNIC, which is operated by Network Solutions, Inc.:

InterNIC Registration Services
Network Solutions, Inc.
505 Huntmar Park Drive
Herndon, VA 22070
Tel: (703) 742-4777
Fax: (703) 742-8449
`www.internic.net`

Internet Organizations

A number of groups contribute to the management, operation, and proliferation of the Internet. These include (in alphabetical order):

CommerceNet
4005 Miranda Avenue, Suite 175
Palo Alto, CA 94304
Tel: (650) 858-1930
Fax: (650) 858-1936
E-mail: info@commerce.net
`www.commerce.net`

Commercial Internet Exchange Association
1041 Sterling Road, Suite 104A
Herndon, VA 20170
Tel: (703) 709-8200
Fax: (703) 709-5249
E-mail: helpdesk@cix.org
`www.cix.org`

Internet Architecture Board
E-mail: iab @isi.edu
www.iab.org

Internet Assigned Numbers Authority
P.O. Box 12607
Marina del Rey, CA 90292-3607
Tel: (310) 822-1511
Fax: (310) 823-6714
E-mail: iana@iana.org
www.iana.org

Internet Engineering Task Force
E-mail: ietf-info@ietf.org
www.ietf.org

Internet Service Providers Consortium
646A Venice Road
Venice, CA 90291
Tel: (310) 827-8466
Fax: (310) 827-8434
www.ispc.org

Internet Society
12020 Sunrise Valley Drive, Suite 210
Reston, VA 20191
Tel: (703) 648-9888
Fax: (703) 648-9887
E-mail: isoc@isoc.org
www.isoc.org

North American Network Operators Group
c/o Merit Network
5251 Plymouth Road, Suite C
Ann Arbor, MI 48105
Tel: (734) 764-9430
E-mail: nanog-support@merit.edu
www.nanog.org

World Wide Web Consortium
c/o MIT Laboratory for Computer Science
545 Technology Square
Cambridge, MA 02139
Tel: (617) 253-2613
Fax: (617) 258-5999
E-mail: admin@w3.org
`www.w3.org`

Obtaining RFCs

The following is an excerpt from the file `rfc-retrieval.txt`, which is available from many of the RFC repositories listed below. This information is subject to change. Obtain the current version of this file if problems occur. Also note that each RFC site may have instructions for file retrieval (such as a particular subdirectory) that are unique to that location.

RFCs may be obtained via EMAIL or FTP from many RFC Repositories. The Primary Repositories will have the RFC available when it is first announced, as will many Secondary Repositories. Some Secondary Repositories may take a few days to make available the most recent RFCs.

Many of these repositories also now have World Wide Web servers. Try the following URL as a starting point:

```
http://www.isi.edu/rfc-editor/
```

Primary Repositories

RFCs can be obtained via FTP from, NIS.NSF.NET, NISC.JVNC.NET, FTP.ISI.EDU, WUARCHIVE.WUSTL.EDU, SRC.DOC.IC.AC.UK, FTP.NCREN.NET, FTP.SESQUI.NET, FTP.NIC.IT, FTP.IMAG.FR or WWW.NORMOS.ORG.

NIS.NSF.NET

To obtain RFCs from NIS.NSF.NET via FTP, login with username "anonymous" and password "name@host.domain"; then connect to the directory of RFCs with cd /internet/documents/rfc. The file name is of the form rfcnnnn.txt (where nnnn refers to the RFC number).

For sites without FTP capability, electronic mail query is available from NIS.NSF.NET. Address the request to NIS-INFO@NIS.NSF.NET and leave the subject field of the message blank. The first text line of the message must be "send rfcnnnn.txt" with nnnn the RFC number.

Contact: rfc-mgr@merit.edu

NISC.JVNC.NET

RFCs can be obtained via FTP from NISC.JVNC.NET, with the pathname rfc/rfcNNNN.txt (where NNNN refers to the number of the RFC). An index can be obtained with the pathname rfc/rfc-index.txt

JvNCnet also provides a mail service for those sites which cannot use FTP. Address the request to SENDRFC@NISC.JVNC.NET and in the "Subject:" field of the message indicate the RFC number, as in "Subject: rfcNNNN" (where NNNN is the RFC number). Please note that RFCs whose numbers are less than 1000 need not place a leading "0". (For example, RFC932 is fine.) For a complete index to the RFC library, enter "rfc-index" in the "Subject:" field, as in "Subject: rfc-index". No text in the body of the message is needed.

Contact: rfc-admin@nisc.jvnc.net

FTP.ISI.EDU

RFCs can be obtained via FTP from FTP.ISI.EDU, with the pathname in-notes/rfcnnnn.txt (where "nnnn" refers to the number of the RFC). Login with FTP username "anonymous" and password "name@host.domain".

RFCs can also be obtained via electronic mail from ISI.EDU by using the RFC-INFO service. Address the request to rfc-info@isi.edu with a message body of:

```
Retrieve: RFC
Doc-ID: RFCnnnn
```

(Where "nnnn" refers to the number of the RFC (always use 4 digits - the DOC-ID of RFC 822 is "RFC0822")). The RFC-INFO@ISI.EDU server provides other ways of selecting RFCs based on keywords and such; for more information send a message to rfc-info@isi.edu with the message body "help: help".

Contact: RFC-Manager@ISI.EDU

WUARCHIVE.WUSTL.EDU

RFCs can also be obtained via FTP from WUARCHIVE.WUSTL.EDU, with the pathname info/rfc/rfcnnnn.txt.Z (where "nnnn" refers to the number of the RFC and "Z" indicates that the document is in compressed form).

At WUARCHIVE.WUSTL.EDU the RFCs are in an "archive" file system and various archives can be mounted as part of an NFS file system. Please contact Chris Myers (chris@wugate.wustl.edu) if you want to mount this file system in your NFS.

WUArchive now keeps RFC's and STD's under ftp://wuarchive.wustl.edu./doc/ or http://wuarchive.wustl.edu./doc/.

Contact: chris@wugate.wustl.edu

SRC.DOC.IC.AC.UK

RFCs can be obtained via FTP from SRC.DOC.IC.AC.UK with the pathname rfc/rfc-nnnn.txt.gz or rfc/rfcnnnn.ps.gz (where "nnnn" refers to the number of the RFC). Login with FTP username "anonymous" and password "your-email-address". To obtain the RFC Index, use the pathname rfc/rfc-index.txt.gz. (The trailing .gz indicates that the document is in compressed form.)

SRC.DOC.IC.AC.UK also provides an automatic mail service for those sites in the UK which cannot use FTP. Address the request to info-server@doc.ic.ac.uk with a Subject: line of "wanted" and a message body of:

request sources
topic path rfc/rfcnnnn.txt.gz
request end
(Where "nnnn" refers to the number of the RFC.) Multiple requests may be included in the same message by giving multiple "topic path" commands on separate lines. To request the RFC Index, the command should read: topic path rfc/rfc-index.txt.gz

They are also available by HTTP in http://sunsite.doc.ic.ac.uk/rfc/.

The archive is available using NIFTP and the ISO FTAM system.

Contact: ukuug-soft@doc.ic.ac.uk

FTP.NCREN.NET

To obtain RFCs from FTP.NCREN.NET via FTP, login with username "anonymous" and your internet e-mail address as password. The RFCs can be found in the directory /rfc, with file names of the form rfcNNNN.txt or rfcNNNN.ps where NNNN refers to the RFC number.

This repository is also accessible via WAIS and the Internet Gopher.

Contact: rfc-mgr@ncren.net

FTP.SESQUI.NET

RFCs can be obtained via FTP from FTP.SESQUI.NET, with the pathname pub/rfc/rfcnnnn.xxx (where "nnnn" refers to the number of the RFC and xxx indicates the document form, txt for ASCII and ps for Postscript).

At FTP.SESQUI.NET the RFCs are in an "archive" file system and various archives can be mounted as part of an NFS file system. Please contact RFC-maintainer (rfc-maint@sesqui.net) if you want to mount this file system in your NFS.

Contact: rfc-maint@sesqui.net

FTP.NIC.IT

RFCs can be obtained from the ftp.nic.it FTP archive with the pathname rfc/rfc-nnnn.txt (where "nnnn" refers to the number of the RFC). Login with FTP, username "anonymous" and password "name@host.domain".

The summary of ways to get RFC from the Italian Network Information Center is the following:

- Via ftp: ftp.nic.it directory rfc
- Via WWW: http://www.nic.it/mirrors/rfc
- Via e-mail: send a message to listserv@nic.it whose body contains "get RFC/rfc<number>.[txt,ps]".

For receiving a full list of the existing RFCs include in the body the command "index RFC/rfc".

Contact: D.Vannozzi@cnuce.cnr.it

FTP.IMAG.FR

RFCs can be obtained via FTP from ftp.imag.fr with the pathname /pub/archive/IETF/rfc/rfcnnnn.txt (where "nnnn" refers to the number of the RFC).

Login with FTP username "anonymous" and password "your-email-address". To obtain the RFC Index, use the pathname /pub/archive/IETF/rfc/rfc-index.txt

Internet drafts & other IETF related documents are also mirrored in the /pub/archive/IETF directory.

Contact: rfc-adm@imag.fr

WWW.NORMOS.ORG

RFCs, STD, BCP, FYI, RTR, IEN, Internet-Drafts, RIPE and other internet engineering documents can be found at http://www.normos.org and ftp://ftp.normos.org.

The rfcs are available as http://www.normos.org/ietf/rfc/rfcXXXX.txt and ftp://ftp.normos.org/ietf/rfc/rfcXXXX.txt.

STD,BCP,FYI,RTR,IEN documents are available as http://www.normos.org/ietf/[std,bcp,fyi,rtr,ien]/[std,bcp,fyi,rtr,ien]XXXX.txt and ftp://ftp.normos.org/ietf/[std,bcp,fyi,rtr,ien]/[std,bcp,fyi,rtr,ien]XXXX.txt.

Internet-drafts are available as http://www.normos.org/ietf/internet-drafts/draft-....txt and ftp://ftp.normos.org/ietf/internet-drafts/draft-....txt.

Full-text search and database queries are available from the web interface.

Please send questions, comments, suggestions to info@normos.org.

Secondary Repositories

Australia and Pacific Rim

Site: munnari
Contact: Robert Elz <kre@cs.mu.OZ.AU>
Host: munnari.oz.au
Directory: rfc (rfc's in compressed format rfcNNNN.Z; postscript rfc's rfcNNNN.ps.Z)
Site: The Programmers' Society University of Technology, Sydney
Contact: ftp@progsoc.uts.edu.au
Host: ftp.progsoc.uts.edu.au
Directory: rfc (or std).

Both are stored uncompressed.

Denmark

Site: University of Copenhagen
Host: ftp.denet.dk
Directory: rfc

Finland

Site: FUNET
Host: nic.funet.fi
Directory: index/RFC
Directory: /pub/netinfo/rfc
Notes: RFCs in compressed format. Also provides email access by sending mail to archive-server@nic.funet.fi.

France

Site: Centre d'Informatique Scientifique et Medicale (CISM)
Contact: ftpmaint@univ-lyon1.fr
Host: ftp.univ-lyon1.fr
Directories:pub/rfc/* Classified by hundreds pub/mirrors/rfc Mirror of Internic
Notes: Files compressed with gzip. Online decompression done by the FTP server
Site: Institut National de la Recherche en Informatique et Automatique (INRIA)
Address: info-server@inria.fr
Notes: RFCs are available via email to the above address. Info Server manager is Mireille Yamajako (yamajako@inria.fr).

Germany

Site: EUnet Germany
Host: ftp.Germany.EU.net
Directory: pub/documents/rfc

Netherlands
Site: Eunet
Host: mcsun.eu.net
Directory: rfc
Notes: RFCs in compressed format.

Norway
Host: ugle.unit.no
Directory: pub/rfc

Romania
Site: SunSITE Romania at the Politehnica University of Bucharest
Contact: space@sunsite.pub.ro
Host: sunsite.pub.ro/pub/rfc or via http://sunsite.pub.ro/pub/mirrors/ds.internic.net

South Africa
Site: The Internet Solution
Contact: ftp-admin@is.co.za
Host: ftp.is.co.za
Directory: internet/in-notes/rfc

Sweden
Host: sunic.sunet.se
Directory: rfc
Host: chalmers.se
Directory: rfc

United States
Site: cerfnet
Contact: help@cerf.net
Host: nic.cerf.net
Directory: netinfo/rfc

Site: NASA NAIC
Contact: rfc-updates@naic.nasa.gov
Host: naic.nasa.gov
Directory: files/rfc

Site: NIC.DDN.MIL (DOD users only)
Contact: NIC@nic.ddn.mil
Host: NIC.DDN.MIL
Directory: rfc/rfcnnnn.txt
Note: DOD users only may obtain RFC's via FTP from NIC.DDN.MIL. Internet users should *not* use this source due to inadequate connectivity.

Site: uunet
Contact: James Revell revell@uunet.uu.net
Host: ftp.uu.net
Directory: inet/rfc

UUNET Archive

UUNET archive, which includes the RFCs, various IETF documents, and other information regarding the internet, is available to the public via anonymous ftp (to ftp.uu.net) and anonymous uucp, and will be available via an anonymous kermit server soon. Get the file /archive/inet/ls-lR.Z for a listing of these documents.

Any site in the US running UUCP may call +1 900 GOT SRCS and use the login "uucp". There is no password. The phone company will bill you at $0.50 per minute for the call. The 900 number only works from within the US.

The RFC-Info Service

The following describes the RFC-Info Service, which is an Internet document and information retrieval service. The text that follows describes in detail the service, which was obtained by using "Help:Help" as discussed below.

RFC-Info is an e-mail based service to help in locating and retrieving RFCs, FYIs, STDs, and IMRs. Users can ask for "lists" of all RFCs, FYIs, STDs, and IMRs having certain attributes such as their ID number, keywords, title, author, issuing organization, and date.

To use the service send e-mail to RFC-INFO@ISI.EDU with your requests in the body of the message. Feel free to put anything in the SUBJECT, the system ignores it. The body of the message is processed with case independence.

To get started you may send a message to RFC-INFO@ISI.EDU with requests such as in the following examples (without the explanation between []):

`Help: Help`	[to get this information page]
`List: FYI`	[list the FYI notes]
`List: RFC` `    keywords: window`	[list RFCs with window as keyword or in title]
`List: FYI` `    Keywords: window`	[list FYIs about windows]

```
List: *                    [list all documents by Cooper]
    Author: Cooper
List: RFC                  [list RFCs about ARPANET, ARPA NETWORK, etc.]
    title: ARPA*NET
List: RFC                  [list RFCs issued by MITRE, dated 7+8/1991]
  Organization: MITRE
  Dated-after:  Jul-01-1991
  Dated-before: Aug-31-1991
List: RFC                  [list RFCs obsoleting a given RFC]
    Obsoletes: RFC0010
List: RFC                  [list RFCs by authors starting with "Bracken"]
    Author: Bracken*       [* is a wild card matching all endings]
List: IMR                  [list the IMRs for the first 6 months of 92]
    Dated-after: Dec-31-1991
    Dated-before: Jul-01-1992
Retrieve: RFC              [retrieve RFC 822]
    Doc-ID: RFC0822        [note, always 4 digits in RFC#]
Retrieve: FYI              [retrieve FYI 4]
    Doc-ID: FYI0004        [note, always 4 digits in FYI#]
Retrieve: STD              [retrieve STD 1]
    Doc-ID: STD0001        [note, always 4 digits in STD#]
Retrieve: IMR              [retrieve May 1992 Internet Monthly Report]
    Doc-ID: IMR9205        [note, always 4 digits = YYMM]
    Help: Manual           [to retrieve the long user manual, 30+ pages]
    Help: List             [how to use the LIST request]
    Help: Retrieve         [how to use the RETRIEVE request]
    Help: Topics           [list topics for which help is available]
List: Dates                ["Dates" is such a topic]
List: keywords             [list the keywords in use]
List: organizations        [list the organizations known to the system]
```

A useful way to test this service is to retrieve the file Where and how to get new RFCs (which is also the file rfc-retrieval.txt noted above in the section Obtaining RFCs). Place the following in the message body:

```
Help: ways_to_get_rfcs
```

Internet Mailing Lists

A number of mailing lists are maintained on the Internet for the purposes of soliciting information and discussions on specific subjects. In addition, a number of the Internet Engineering Task Force (IETF) working groups maintain a list for the exchange of information that is specific to that group.

For example, the IETF maintains two lists: the IETF General Discussion list and the IETF Announcement list. To join the IETF Announcement list, send a request to:

`ietf-announce-request@ietf.org`

To join the IETF General Discussion, send a request to:

`ietf-request@ietf.org`

A number of other mailing lists are available. To join a mailing list, send a message to the associated request list:

`listname-request@listhost (for example, snmp-request@psi.com)`

With the following as the message body:

`subscribe listname (for example, subscribe snmp)`

A complete listing of the current IETF working groups and their respective mailing lists is available at:

`http://www.ietf.org/maillist.html`

Appendix D

RFC Index

This Appendix lists RFC 1000 (August 1987) through RFC 2583 (March 1999) in numerical order. This appendix is an excerpt from the file *rfc-index.txt*, which can be obtained in its entirety from the RFC Repositories (see Appendix C, the instructions below for retrieving RFC documents, or the last line before the first RFC listing).

RFC citations appear in this format:
NUM STD "Title of RFC", Author 1, ... Author 5., Issue date. (Pages=##) (Format=.txt or .ps) (FYI ##) (STD ##) (RTR ##) (Obsoletes RFC####) (Updates RFC####)

Key to citations:

- #### is the RFC number; ## p. is the total number of pages.
- The format and byte information follows the page information in parenthesis. The format, either ASCII text (TXT) or PostScript (PS) or both, is noted, followed by an equals sign and the number of bytes for that version (PostScript is a registered trademark of Adobe Systems Incorporated). The example (Format: PS=xxx TXT=zzz bytes) shows that the PostScript version of the RFC is xxx bytes and the ASCII text version is zzz bytes.
- The (Also FYI ##) phrase gives the equivalent FYI number if the RFC was also issued as an FYI document.
- "Obsoletes xxx" refers to other RFCs that this one replaces; "Obsoleted by xxx" refers to RFCs that have replaced this one. "Updates xxx" refers to other RFCs that this one merely updates (but does not replace); "Updated by xxx" refers to RFCs that have been updated by this one (but not replaced). Only immediately succeeding and/or preceding RFCs are indicated, not the entire history of each related earlier or later RFC in a related series.

For example:

1129 "Internet time synchronization: The Network Time Protocol", D. Mills, 10/01/1989. (Pages=29) (Format=.ps)

Many RFCs are available online; if not, this is indicated by (Not online).

Online copies are available via FTP from the InterNIC Directory and Database Services server, ds.internic.net, as rfc/rfc####.txt or rfc/rfc####.ps (#### is the RFC number without leading zeroes).

RFCs may be requested through electronic mail from the InterNIC Directory and Database Services automated mail server by sending a message to mailserv@ds.internic.net. In the body of the message, include the following command:

`document-by-name rfcNNNN`

where *NNNN* is the number of the RFC. For PostScript RFCs, specify the extension, e.g. "document-by-name rfcNNNN.ps". Multiple requests can be sent in a single message by specifying each document in a comma-separated list (e.g. "document-by-name rfc*NNNN*, rfc*YYYY*"), or by including multiple "document-by-name" commands on separate lines.

The RFC Index can be requested by typing

document-by-name rfc-index

1000 Request For Comments reference guide. J.K. Reynolds, J. Postel. Aug-01-1987. (Format: TXT=323960 bytes) (Obsoletes RFC0999) (Status: UNKNOWN)

1001 Protocol standard for a NetBIOS service on a TCP/UDP transport: Concepts and methods. NetBIOS Working Group. Defense Advanced Research Projects Agency, Internet Activities Board, End-to-End Services Task Force. Mar-01-1987. (Format: TXT=158437 bytes) (Status: STANDARD)

1002 Protocol standard for a NetBIOS service on a TCP/UDP transport: Detailed specifications. NetBIOS Working Group. Defense Advanced Research Projects Agency, Internet Activities Board, End-to-End Services Task Force. Mar-01-1987. (Format: TXT=170262 bytes) (Status: STANDARD)

1003 Issues in defining an equations representation standard. A.R. Katz. Mar-01-1987. (Format: TXT=19816 bytes) (Status: UNKNOWN)

1004 Distributed-protocol authentication scheme. D.L. Mills. Apr-01-1987. (Format: TXT=21402 bytes) (Status: EXPERIMENTAL)

1005 ARPANET AHIP-E Host Access Protocol (enhanced AHIP). A. Khanna, A.G. Malis. May-01-1987. (Format: TXT=69957 bytes) (Status: UNKNOWN)

1006 ISO transport services on top of the TCP: Version 3. M.T. Rose, D.E. Cass. May-01-1987. (Format: TXT=31935 bytes) (Obsoletes RFC0983) (Status: STANDARD)

1007 Military supplement to the ISO Transport Protocol. W. McCoy. Jun-01-1987. (Format: TXT=51280 bytes) (Status: UNKNOWN)

1008 Implementation guide for the ISO Transport Protocol. W. McCoy. Jun-01-1987. (Format: TXT=204664 bytes) (Status: UNKNOWN)

1009 Requirements for Internet gateways. R.T. Braden, J. Postel. Jun-01-1987. (Format: TXT=128173 bytes) (Obsoletes RFC0985) (Obsoleted by RFC1812) (Status: HISTORIC)

1010 Assigned numbers. J.K. Reynolds, J. Postel. May-01-1987. (Format: TXT=78179 bytes) (Obsoletes RFC0990) (Obsoleted by RFC1060) (Status: HISTORIC)

1011 Official Internet protocols. J.K. Reynolds, J. Postel. May-01-1987. (Format: TXT=74593 bytes) (Obsoletes RFC0991) (Status: UNKNOWN)

1012 Bibliography of Request For Comments 1 through 999. J.K. Reynolds, J. Postel. Jun-01-1987. (Format: TXT=129194 bytes) (Status: INFORMATIONAL)

1013 X Window System Protocol, version 11: Alpha update April 1987. R.W. Scheifler. Jun-01-1987. (Format: TXT=244905 bytes) (Status: UNKNOWN)

1014 XDR: External Data Representation standard. Inc. Sun Microsystems. Jun-01-1987. (Format: TXT=39316 bytes) (Status: UNKNOWN)

1015 Implementation plan for interagency research Internet. B.M. Leiner. Jul-01-1987. (Format: TXT=63159 bytes) (Status: UNKNOWN)

1016 Something a host could do with source quench: The Source Quench Introduced Delay (SQuID). W. Prue, J. Postel. Jul-01-1987. (Format: TXT=47922 bytes) (Status: UNKNOWN)

1017 Network requirements for scientific research: Internet task force on scientific computing. B.M. Leiner. Aug-01-1987. (Format: TXT=49512 bytes) (Status: UNKNOWN)

1018 Some comments on SQuID. A.M. McKenzie. Aug-01-1987. (Format: TXT=7931 bytes) (Status: UNKNOWN)

1019 Report of the Workshop on Environments for Computational Mathematics. D. Arnon. Sep-01-1987. (Format: TXT=21151 bytes) (Status: UNKNOWN)

1020 Internet numbers. S. Romano, M.K. Stahl. Nov-01-1987. (Format: TXT=146864 bytes) (Obsoletes RFC0997) (Obsoleted by RFC1062, RFC1117, RFC1166) (Status: UNKNOWN)

1021 High-level Entity Management System (HEMS). C. Partridge, G. Trewitt. Oct-01-1987. (Format: TXT=12993 bytes) (Status: HISTORIC)

1022 High-level Entity Management Protocol (HEMP). C. Partridge, G. Trewitt. Oct-01-1987. (Format: TXT=25348 bytes) (Status: UNKNOWN)

1023 HEMS monitoring and control language. G. Trewitt, C. Partridge. Oct-01-1987. (Format: TXT=40992 bytes) (Obsoleted by RFC1076) (Status: UNKNOWN)

1024 HEMS variable definitions. C. Partridge, G. Trewitt. Oct-01-1987. (Format: TXT=126536 bytes) (Status: UNKNOWN)

1025 TCP and IP bake off. J. Postel. Sep-01-1987. (Format: TXT=11648 bytes) (Status: UNKNOWN)

1026 Addendum to RFC 987: (Mapping between X.400 and RFC-822). S.E. Kille. Sep-01-1987. (Format: TXT=7117 bytes) (Obsoleted by RFC1327, RFC1495, RFC2156) (Updates RFC0987) (Updated by RFC1138, RFC1148) Status: UNKNOWN)

1027 Using ARP to implement transparent subnet gateways. S. Carl-Mitchell, J.S. Quarterman. Oct-01-1987. (Format: TXT=21297 bytes) (Status: UNKNOWN)

1028 Simple Gateway Monitoring Protocol. J. Davin, J.D. Case, M. Fedor, M.L. Schoffstall. Nov-01-1987. (Format: TXT=82440 bytes) (Status: HISTORIC)

1029 More fault tolerant approach to address resolution for a Multi-LAN system of Ethernets. G. Parr. May-01-1988. (Format: TXT=44019 bytes) (Status: UNKNOWN)

1030 On testing the NETBLT Protocol over divers networks. M.L. Lambert. Nov-01-1987. (Format: TXT=40964 bytes) (Status: UNKNOWN)

1031 MILNET name domain transition. W.D. Lazear. Nov-01-1987. (Format: TXT=20137 bytes) (Status: UNKNOWN)

1032 Domain administrators guide. M.K. Stahl. Nov-01-1987. (Format: TXT=29454 bytes) (Status: UNKNOWN)

1033 Domain administrators operations guide. M. Lottor. Nov-01-1987. (Format: TXT=37263 bytes) (Status: UNKNOWN)

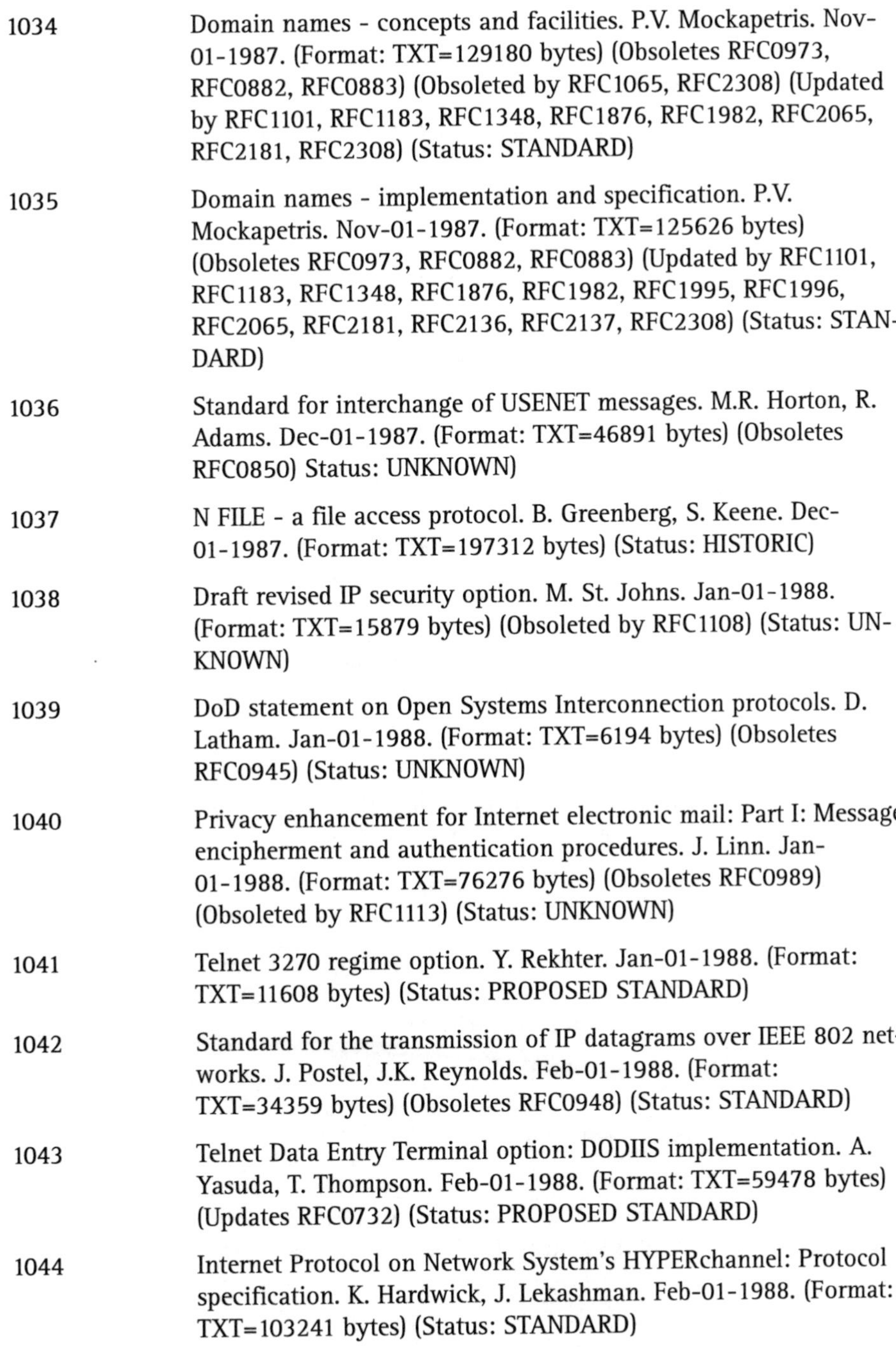

1034 Domain names - concepts and facilities. P.V. Mockapetris. Nov-01-1987. (Format: TXT=129180 bytes) (Obsoletes RFC0973, RFC0882, RFC0883) (Obsoleted by RFC1065, RFC2308) (Updated by RFC1101, RFC1183, RFC1348, RFC1876, RFC1982, RFC2065, RFC2181, RFC2308) (Status: STANDARD)

1035 Domain names - implementation and specification. P.V. Mockapetris. Nov-01-1987. (Format: TXT=125626 bytes) (Obsoletes RFC0973, RFC0882, RFC0883) (Updated by RFC1101, RFC1183, RFC1348, RFC1876, RFC1982, RFC1995, RFC1996, RFC2065, RFC2181, RFC2136, RFC2137, RFC2308) (Status: STANDARD)

1036 Standard for interchange of USENET messages. M.R. Horton, R. Adams. Dec-01-1987. (Format: TXT=46891 bytes) (Obsoletes RFC0850) Status: UNKNOWN)

1037 N FILE - a file access protocol. B. Greenberg, S. Keene. Dec-01-1987. (Format: TXT=197312 bytes) (Status: HISTORIC)

1038 Draft revised IP security option. M. St. Johns. Jan-01-1988. (Format: TXT=15879 bytes) (Obsoleted by RFC1108) (Status: UNKNOWN)

1039 DoD statement on Open Systems Interconnection protocols. D. Latham. Jan-01-1988. (Format: TXT=6194 bytes) (Obsoletes RFC0945) (Status: UNKNOWN)

1040 Privacy enhancement for Internet electronic mail: Part I: Message encipherment and authentication procedures. J. Linn. Jan-01-1988. (Format: TXT=76276 bytes) (Obsoletes RFC0989) (Obsoleted by RFC1113) (Status: UNKNOWN)

1041 Telnet 3270 regime option. Y. Rekhter. Jan-01-1988. (Format: TXT=11608 bytes) (Status: PROPOSED STANDARD)

1042 Standard for the transmission of IP datagrams over IEEE 802 networks. J. Postel, J.K. Reynolds. Feb-01-1988. (Format: TXT=34359 bytes) (Obsoletes RFC0948) (Status: STANDARD)

1043 Telnet Data Entry Terminal option: DODIIS implementation. A. Yasuda, T. Thompson. Feb-01-1988. (Format: TXT=59478 bytes) (Updates RFC0732) (Status: PROPOSED STANDARD)

1044 Internet Protocol on Network System's HYPERchannel: Protocol specification. K. Hardwick, J. Lekashman. Feb-01-1988. (Format: TXT=103241 bytes) (Status: STANDARD)

1045 VMTP: Versatile Message Transaction Protocol: Protocol specification. D.R. Cheriton. Feb-01-1988. (Format: TXT=272058 bytes) (Status: EXPERIMENTAL)

1046 Queuing algorithm to provide type-of-service for IP links. W. Prue, J. Postel. Feb-01-1988. (Format: TXT=30106 bytes) (Status: UNKNOWN)

1047 Duplicate messages and SMTP. C. Partridge. Feb-01-1988. (Format: TXT=5888 bytes) (Status: UNKNOWN)

1048 BOOTP vendor information extensions. P.A. Prindeville. Feb-01-1988. (Format: TXT=15423 bytes) (Obsoleted by RFC1084, RFC1395, RFC1497, RFC1533) (Status: UNKNOWN)

1049 Content-type header field for Internet messages. M.A. Sirbu. Mar-01-1988. (Format: TXT=18923 bytes) (Status: STANDARD)

1050 RPC: Remote Procedure Call Protocol specification. Inc. Sun Microsystems. Apr-01-1988. (Format: TXT=51540 bytes) (Obsoleted by RFC1057) (Status: HISTORIC)

1051 Standard for the transmission of IP datagrams and ARP packets over ARCNET networks. P.A. Prindeville. Mar-01-1988. (Format: TXT=7779 bytes) (Obsoleted by RFC1201, STD0046) (Status: UNKNOWN)

1052 IAB recommendations for the development of Internet network management standards. V.G. Cerf. Apr-01-1988. (Format: TXT=30569 bytes) (Status: UNKNOWN)

1053 Telnet X.3 PAD option. S. Levy, T. Jacobson. Apr-01-1988. (Format: TXT=48952 bytes) (Status: PROPOSED STANDARD)

1054 Host extensions for IP multicasting. S.E. Deering. May-01-1988. (Format: TXT=45465 bytes) (Obsoletes RFC0988) (Obsoleted by RFC1112) (Status: UNKNOWN)

1055 Nonstandard for transmission of IP datagrams over serial lines: SLIP. J.L. Romkey. Jun-01-1988. (Format: TXT=12911 bytes) (Status: STANDARD)

1056 PCMAIL: A distributed mail system for personal computers. M.L. Lambert. Jun-01-1988. (Format: TXT=85368 bytes) (Obsoletes RFC0993) (Status: INFORMATIONAL)

1057 RPC: Remote Procedure Call Protocol specification: Version 2. Inc. Sun Microsystems. Jun-01-1988. (Format: TXT=52462 bytes) (Obsoletes RFC1050) (Status: INFORMATIONAL)

1058 Routing Information Protocol. C.L. Hedrick. Jun-01-1988. (Format: TXT=93285 bytes) (Updated by RFC1388, RFC1723) (Status: HISTORIC)

1059 Network Time Protocol (version 1) specification and implementation. D.L. Mills. Jul-01-1988. (Format: TXT=140890 bytes) (Obsoletes RFC0958) (Obsoleted by RFC1119, RFC1305) (Status: UNKNOWN)

1060 Assigned numbers. J.K. Reynolds, J. Postel. Mar-01-1990. (Format: TXT=177923 bytes) (Obsoletes RFC1010) (Obsoleted by RFC1340) (Status: HISTORIC)

1061 November 1993. (Not online) (Status: UNKNOWN)

1062 Internet numbers. S. Romano, M.K. Stahl, M. Recker. Aug-01-1988. (Format: TXT=198729 bytes) (Obsoletes RFC1020) (Obsoleted by RFC1117, RFC1166) (Status: UNKNOWN)

1063 IP MTU discovery options. J.C. Mogul, C.A. Kent, C. Partridge, K. McCloghrie. Jul-01-1988. (Format: TXT=27121 bytes) (Obsoleted by RFC1191) (Status: UNKNOWN)

1064 Interactive Mail Access Protocol: Version 2. M.R. Crispin. Jul-01-1988. (Format: TXT=57813 bytes) (Obsoleted by RFC1176, RFC1203) (Status: UNKNOWN)

1065 Structure and identification of management information for TCP/IP-based internets. K. McCloghrie, M.T. Rose. Aug-01-1988. (Format: TXT=38858 bytes) (Obsoletes RFC1034) (Obsoleted by RFC1155, STD0016) (Status: UNKNOWN)

1066 Management Information Base for network management of TCP/IP-based internets. K. McCloghrie, M.T. Rose. Aug-01-1988. (Format: TXT=135177 bytes) (Obsoleted by RFC1156) (Status: UNKNOWN)

1067 Simple Network Management Protocol. J.D. Case, M. Fedor, M.L. Schoffstall, J. Davin. Aug-01-1988. (Format: TXT=69592 bytes) (Obsoleted by RFC1098) (Status: UNKNOWN)

1068 Background File Transfer Program (BFTP). A.L. DeSchon, R.T. Braden. Aug-01-1988. (Format: TXT=51004 bytes) (Status: UNKNOWN)

1069 Guidelines for the use of Internet-IP addresses in the ISO Connectionless-Mode Network Protocol. R.W. Callon, H.W. Braun. Feb-01-1989. (Format: TXT=24268 bytes) (Obsoletes RFC0986) (Status: UNKNOWN)

1070 Use of the Internet as a subnetwork for experimentation with the OSI network layer. R.A. Hagens, N.E. Hall, M.T. Rose. Feb-01-1989. (Format: TXT=37354 bytes) (Status: UNKNOWN)

1071 Computing the Internet checksum. R.T. Braden, D.A. Borman, C. Partridge. Sep-01-1988. (Format: TXT=54941 bytes) (Updated by RFC1141) (Status: UNKNOWN)

1072 TCP extensions for long-delay paths. V. Jacobson, R.T. Braden. Oct-01-1988. (Format: TXT=36000 bytes) (Obsoleted by RFC1323) (Status: UNKNOWN)

1073 Telnet window size option. D. Waitzman. Oct-01-1988. (Format: TXT=7639 bytes) (Status: PROPOSED STANDARD)

1074 NSFNET backbone SPF based Interior Gateway Protocol. J. Rekhter. Oct-01-1988. (Format: TXT=10872 bytes) (Status: UNKNOWN)

1075 Distance Vector Multicast Routing Protocol. D. Waitzman, C. Partridge, S.E. Deering. Nov-01-1988. (Format: TXT=54731 bytes) (Status: EXPERIMENTAL)

1076 HEMS monitoring and control language. G. Trewitt, C. Partridge. Nov-01-1988. (Format: TXT=98774 bytes) (Obsoletes RFC1023) (Status: UNKNOWN)

1077 Critical issues in high bandwidth networking. B.M. Leiner. Nov-01-1988. (Format: TXT=116464 bytes) (Status: UNKNOWN)

1078 TCP port service Multiplexer (TCPMUX). M. Lottor. Nov-01-1988. (Format: TXT=3248 bytes) (Status: UNKNOWN)

1079 Telnet terminal speed option. C.L. Hedrick. Dec-01-1988. (Format: TXT=4942 bytes) (Status: PROPOSED STANDARD)

1080 Telnet remote flow control option. C.L. Hedrick. Nov-01-1988. (Format: TXT=6688 bytes) (Obsoleted by RFC1372) (Status: UNKNOWN)

1081 Post Office Protocol: Version 3. M.T. Rose. Nov-01-1988. (Format: TXT=37009 bytes) (Obsoleted by RFC1225) (Status: UNKNOWN)

1082 Post Office Protocol: Version 3: Extended service offerings. M.T. Rose. Nov-01-1988. (Format: TXT=25423 bytes) (Status: UNKNOWN)

1083 IAB official protocol standards. Defense Advanced Research Projects Agency, Internet Activities Board. Dec-01-1988. (Format: TXT=27128 bytes) (Obsoleted by RFC1100, RFC1250, RFC2200, RFC2300, STD0001, RFC2400) (Status: HISTORIC)

1084 BOOTP vendor information extensions. J.K. Reynolds. Dec-01-1988. (Format: TXT=16327 bytes) (Obsoletes RFC1048) (Obsoleted by RFC1395, RFC1497, RFC1533) (Status: UNKNOWN)

1085 ISO presentation services on top of TCP/IP based internets. M.T. Rose. Dec-01-1988. (Format: TXT=64643 bytes) (Status: UNKNOWN)

1086 ISO-TP0 bridge between TCP and X.25. J.P. Onions, M.T. Rose. Dec-01-1988. (Format: TXT=19934 bytes) (Status: UNKNOWN)

1087 Ethics and the Internet. Defense Advanced Research Projects Agency, Internet Activities Board. Jan-01-1989. (Format: TXT=4582 bytes) (Status: UNKNOWN)

1088 Standard for the transmission of IP datagrams over NetBIOS networks. L.J. McLaughlin. Feb-01-1989. (Format: TXT=5749 bytes) (Status: STANDARD)

1089 SNMP over Ethernet. M.L. Schoffstall, C. Davin, M. Fedor, J.D. Case. Feb-01-1989. (Format: TXT=4458 bytes) (Status: UNKNOWN)

1090 SMTP on X.25. R. Ullmann. Feb-01-1989. (Format: TXT=6141 bytes) (Status: UNKNOWN)

1091 Telnet terminal-type option. J. VanBokkelen. Feb-01-1989. (Format: TXT=13439 bytes) (Obsoletes RFC0930) (Status: PROPOSED STANDARD)

1092 EGP and policy based routing in the new NSFNET backbone. J. Rekhter. Feb-01-1989. (Format: TXT=11865 bytes) (Status: UNKNOWN)

1093 NSFNET routing architecture. H.W. Braun. Feb-01-1989. (Format: TXT=20629 bytes) (Status: UNKNOWN)

1094 NFS: Network File System Protocol specification. Inc. Sun Microsystems. Mar-01-1989. (Format: TXT=51454 bytes) (Also RFC1813) (Status: INFORMATIONAL)

1095 Common Management Information Services and Protocol over TCP/IP (CMOT). U.S. Warrier, L. Besaw. Apr-01-1989. (Format: TXT=157506 bytes) (Obsoleted by RFC1189) (Status: UNKNOWN)

1096 Telnet X display location option. G.A. Marcy. Mar-01-1989. (Format: TXT=4634 bytes) (Status: PROPOSED STANDARD)

1097 Telnet subliminal-message option. B. Miller. Apr-01-1989. (Format: TXT=5490 bytes) (Status: UNKNOWN)

1098 Simple Network Management Protocol (SNMP). J.D. Case, M. Fedor, M.L. Schoffstall, C. Davin. Apr-01-1989. (Format: TXT=71563 bytes) (Obsoletes RFC1067) (Obsoleted by RFC1157) (Status: UNKNOWN)

1099 Request for Comments Summary: RFC Numbers 1000-1099. J. Reynolds. December 1991. (Format: TXT=49108 bytes) (Status: INFORMATIONAL)

1100 IAB official protocol standards. Defense Advanced Research Projects Agency, Internet Activities Board. Apr-01-1989. (Format: TXT=30101 bytes) (Obsoletes RFC1083) (Obsoleted by RFC1130, RFC1250, RFC2200, RFC2300, STD0001, RFC2400) (Status: HISTORIC)

1101 DNS encoding of network names and other types. P.V. Mockapetris. Apr-01-1989. (Format: TXT=28677 bytes) (Updates RFC1034, RFC1035) (Status: UNKNOWN)

1102 Policy routing in Internet protocols. D.D. Clark. May-01-1989. (Format: TXT=59664 bytes) (Status: UNKNOWN)

1103 Proposed standard for the transmission of IP datagrams over FDDI Networks. D. Katz. Jun-01-1989. (Format: TXT=19439 bytes) (Obsoleted by RFC1188) (Status: UNKNOWN)

1104 Models of policy based routing. H.W. Braun. Jun-01-1989. (Format: TXT=25468 bytes) (Status: UNKNOWN)

1105 Border Gateway Protocol (BGP). K. Lougheed, Y. Rekhter. Jun-01-1989. (Format: TXT=37644 bytes) (Obsoleted by RFC1163) (Status: EXPERIMENTAL)

1106 TCP big window and NAK options. R. Fox. Jun-01-1989. (Format: TXT=37105 bytes) (Status: UNKNOWN)

1107 Plan for Internet directory services. K.R. Sollins. Jul-01-1989. (Format: TXT=51773 bytes) (Status: INFORMATIONAL)

1108 U.S. Department of Defense Security Options for the Internet Protocol. S. Kent. November 1991. (Format: TXT=41791 bytes) (Obsoletes RFC1038) (Status: HISTORIC)

1109 Report of the second Ad Hoc Network Management Review Group. V.G. Cerf. Aug-01-1989. (Format: TXT=20642 bytes) (Status: UNKNOWN)

1110 Problem with the TCP big window option. A.M. McKenzie. Aug-01-1989. (Format: TXT=5778 bytes) (Status: UNKNOWN)

1111 Request for comments on Request for Comments: Instructions to RFC authors. J. Postel. Aug-01-1989. (Format: TXT=11793 bytes) (Obsoletes RFC0825) (Obsoleted by RFC1543, RFC2223) (Status: INFORMATIONAL)

1112 Host extensions for IP multicasting. S.E. Deering. Aug-01-1989. (Format: TXT=39904 bytes) (Obsoletes RFC0988, RFC1054) (Updated by RFC2236) (Status: STANDARD)

1113 Privacy enhancement for Internet electronic mail: Part I - message encipherment and authentication procedures. J. Linn. Aug-01-1989. (Format: TXT=89293 bytes) (Obsoletes RFC0989, RFC1040) (Obsoleted by RFC1421) (Status: HISTORIC)

1114 Privacy enhancement for Internet electronic mail: Part II - certificate-based key management. S.T. Kent, J. Linn. Aug-01-1989. (Format: TXT=69661 bytes) (Obsoleted by RFC1422) (Status: HISTORIC)

1115 Privacy enhancement for Internet electronic mail: Part III - algorithms, modes, and identifiers. J. Linn. Aug-01-1989. (Format: TXT=18226 bytes) (Obsoleted by RFC1423) (Status: HISTORIC)

1116 Telnet Linemode option. D.A. Borman. Aug-01-1989. (Format: TXT=47473 bytes) (Obsoleted by RFC1184) (Status: PROPOSED STANDARD)

1117 Internet numbers. S. Romano, M.K. Stahl, M. Recker. Aug-01-1989. (Format: TXT=324666 bytes) (Obsoletes RFC1062, RFC1020, RFC0997) (Obsoleted by RFC1166) (Status: INFORMATIONAL)

1118 Hitchhikers guide to the Internet. E. Krol. Sep-01-1989. (Format: TXT=62757 bytes) (Status: INFORMATIONAL)

1119 Network Time Protocol (version 2) specification and implementation. D.L. Mills. Sep-01-1989. (Format: TXT=143, PS=518020 bytes) (Obsoletes RFC0958, RFC1059) (Obsoleted by RFC1305) (Status: STANDARD)

1120 Internet Activities Board. V. Cerf. Sep-01-1989. (Format: TXT=26123 bytes) (Obsoleted by RFC1160) (Status: INFORMATIONAL)

1121 Act one - the poems. J. Postel, L. Kleinrock, V.G. Cerf, B. Boehm. Sep-01-1989. (Format: TXT=10644 bytes) (Status: INFORMATIONAL)

1122 Requirements for Internet hosts - communication layers. R.T. Braden. Oct-01-1989. (Format: TXT=295992 bytes) (Status: STANDARD)

1123 Requirements for Internet hosts - application and support. R.T. Braden. Oct-01-1989. (Format: TXT=245503 bytes) (Updates RFC0822) (Updated by RFC2181) (Status: STANDARD)

1124 Policy issues in interconnecting networks. B.M. Leiner. Sep-01-1989. (Format: TXT=118, PS=315692 bytes) (Status: UNKNOWN)

1125 Policy requirements for inter Administrative Domain routing. D. Estrin. Nov-01-1989. (Format: TXT=55248, PS=282123 bytes) (Status: UNKNOWN)

1126 Goals and functional requirements for inter-autonomous system routing. M. Little. Oct-01-1989. (Format: TXT=62725 bytes) (Status: UNKNOWN)

1127 Perspective on the Host Requirements RFCs. R.T. Braden. Oct-01-1989. (Format: TXT=41267 bytes) (Status: INFORMATIONAL)

1128 Measured performance of the Network Time Protocol in the Internet system. D.L. Mills. Oct-01-1989. (Format: TXT=314, PS=633742 bytes) (Status: UNKNOWN)

1129 Internet time synchronization: The Network Time Protocol. D.L. Mills. Oct-01-1989. (Format: TXT=298, PS=551697 bytes) (Status: UNKNOWN)

1130 IAB official protocol standards. Defense Advanced Research Projects Agency, Internet Activities Board. Oct-01-1989. (Format: TXT=33858 bytes) (Obsoletes RFC1100) (Obsoleted by RFC1140, RFC1250, RFC2200, RFC2300, STD0001, RFC2400) (Status: HISTORIC)

1131 OSPF specification. J. Moy. Oct-01-1989. (Format: TXT=268, PS=857280 bytes) (Obsoleted by RFC1247) (Status: PROPOSED STANDARD)

1132 Standard for the transmission of 802.2 packets over IPX networks. L.J. McLaughlin. Nov-01-1989. (Format: TXT=8128 bytes) (Status: STANDARD)

1133 Routing between the NSFNET and the DDN. J.Y. Yu, H.W. Braun. Nov-01-1989. (Format: TXT=23169 bytes) (Status: INFORMATIONAL)

1134 Point-to-Point Protocol: A proposal for multi-protocol transmission of datagrams over Point-to-Point links. D. Perkins. Nov-01-1989. (Format: TXT=87352 bytes) (Obsoleted by RFC1171) (Status: PROPOSED STANDARD)

1135 Helminthiasis of the Internet. J.K. Reynolds. Dec-01-1989. (Format: TXT=77033 bytes) (Status: INFORMATIONAL)

1136 Administrative Domains and Routing Domains: A model for routing in the Internet. S. Hares, D. Katz. Dec-01-1989. (Format: TXT=22158 bytes) (Status: INFORMATIONAL)

1137 Mapping between full RFC 822 and RFC 822 with restricted encoding. S. Kille. Dec-01-1989. (Format: TXT=6266 bytes) (Updates RFC0976) (Status: HISTORIC)

1138 Mapping between X.400(1988) / ISO 10021 and RFC 822. S.E. Kille. Dec-01-1989. (Format: TXT=191029 bytes) (Obsoleted by RFC1327, RFC1495, RFC2156) (Updates RFC0822, RFC0987, RFC1026) (Updated by RFC1148) (Status: EXPERIMENTAL)

1139 Echo function for ISO 8473. R.A. Hagens. Jan-01-1990. (Format: TXT=14229 bytes) (Obsoleted by RFC1574, RFC1575) (Status: PROPOSED STANDARD)

1140 IAB official protocol standards. Defense Advanced Research Projects Agency, Internet Activities Board. May-01-1990. (Format: TXT=60501 bytes) (Obsoletes RFC1130) (Obsoleted by RFC1200, RFC1250, RFC2200, RFC2300, STD0001, RFC2400) (Status: HISTORIC)

1141 Incremental updating of the Internet checksum. T. Mallory, A. Kullberg. Jan-01-1990. (Format: TXT=3587 bytes) (Updates RFC1071) (Updated by RFC1624) (Status: INFORMATIONAL)

1142 OSI IS-IS Intra-domain Routing Protocol. D. Oran. Feb-01-1990. (Format: TXT=425379, PS=1204297 bytes) (Status: INFORMATIONAL)

1143 The Q Method of Implementing TELNET Option Negotiation. D.J. Bernstein. Feb-01-1990. (Format: TXT=23331 bytes) (Status: EXPERIMENTAL)

1144 Compressing TCP/IP headers for low-speed serial links. V. Jacobson. Feb-01-1990. (Format: TXT=120959, PS=534729 bytes) (Status: PROPOSED STANDARD)

1145 TCP alternate checksum options. J. Zweig, C. Partridge. Feb-01-1990. (Format: TXT=11052 bytes) (Obsoleted by RFC1146) (Status: EXPERIMENTAL)

1146 TCP alternate checksum options. J. Zweig, C. Partridge. Mar-01-1990. (Format: TXT=10955 bytes) (Obsoletes RFC1145) (Status: EXPERIMENTAL)

1147 FYI on a network management tool catalog: Tools for monitoring and debugging TCP/IP internets and interconnected devices. R.H. Stine. Apr-01-1990. (Format: TXT=336906, PS=555225 bytes) (Obsoleted by RFC1470) (Updated by FYI0002) (Also FYI0002) (Status: INFORMATIONAL)

1148 Mapping between X.400(1988) / ISO 10021 and RFC 822. S.E. Kille.

Mar-01-1990. (Format: TXT=194292 bytes) (Obsoleted by RFC1327, RFC1495, RFC2156) (Updates RFC0822, RFC0987, RFC1026, RFC1138) (Status: EXPERIMENTAL)

1149 Standard for the transmission of IP datagrams on avian carriers. D. Waitzman. Apr-01-1990. (Format: TXT=3329 bytes) (Status: EXPERIMENTAL)

1150 FYI on FYI: Introduction to the FYI Notes. G.S. Malkin, J.K. Reynolds. Mar-01-1990. (Format: TXT=7867 bytes) (Also FYI0001) (Status: INFORMATIONAL)

1151 Version 2 of the Reliable Data Protocol (RDP). C. Partridge, R.M. Hinden. Apr-01-1990. (Format: TXT=8293 bytes) (Updates RFC0908) (Status: EXPERIMENTAL)

1152 Workshop report: Internet research steering group workshop on very-high-speed networks. C. Partridge. Apr-01-1990. (Format: TXT=64003 bytes) (Status: INFORMATIONAL)

1153 Digest message format. F.J. Wancho. Apr-01-1990. (Format: TXT=6632 bytes) (Status: EXPERIMENTAL)

1154 Encoding header field for internet messages. D. Robinson, R. Ullmann. Apr-01-1990. (Format: TXT=12214 bytes) (Obsoleted by RFC1505) (Status: EXPERIMENTAL)

1155 Structure and identification of management information for TCP/IP-based internets. M.T. Rose, K. McCloghrie. May-01-1990. (Format: TXT=40927 bytes) (Obsoletes RFC1065) (Also STD0016) (Status: STANDARD)

1156 Management Information Base for network management of TCP/IP-based internets. K. McCloghrie, M.T. Rose. May-01-1990. (Format: TXT=138781 bytes) (Obsoletes RFC1066) (Status: HISTORIC)

1157 Simple Network Management Protocol (SNMP). J.D. Case, M. Fedor, M.L. Schoffstall, C. Davin. May-01-1990. (Format: TXT=74894 bytes) (Obsoletes RFC1098) (Status: STANDARD)

1158 Management Information Base for network management of TCP/IP-based internets: MIB-II. M.T. Rose. May-01-1990. (Format: TXT=212152 bytes) (Obsoleted by RFC1213, STD0017) (Status: DRAFT STANDARD)

1159 Message Send Protocol. R. Nelson. Jun-01-1990. (Format: TXT=3957 bytes) (Status: EXPERIMENTAL)

1160 Internet Activities Board. V. Cerf. May-01-1990. (Format: TXT=28182 bytes) (Obsoletes RFC1120) (Status: INFORMATIONAL)

1161 SNMP over OSI. M.T. Rose. Jun-01-1990. (Format: TXT=16036 bytes) (Obsoleted by RFC1418) (Status: EXPERIMENTAL)

1162 Connectionless Network Protocol (ISO 8473) and End System to Intermediate System (ISO 9542) Management Information Base. G. Satz. Jun-01-1990. (Format: TXT=109893 bytes) (Obsoleted by RFC1238) (Status: EXPERIMENTAL)

1163 Border Gateway Protocol (BGP). K. Lougheed, Y. Rekhter. Jun-01-1990. (Format: TXT=69404 bytes) (Obsoletes RFC1105) (Obsoleted by RFC1267) (Status: HISTORIC)

1164 Application of the Border Gateway Protocol in the Internet. J.C. Honig, D. Katz, M. Mathis, Y. Rekhter, J.Y. Yu. Jun-01-1990. (Format: TXT=56278 bytes) (Obsoleted by RFC1268) (Status: HISTORIC)

1165 Network Time Protocol (NTP) over the OSI Remote Operations Service. J. Crowcroft, J.P. Onions. Jun-01-1990. (Format: TXT=18277 bytes) (Status: EXPERIMENTAL)

1166 Internet numbers. S. Kirkpatrick, M.K. Stahl, M. Recker. Jul-01-1990. (Format: TXT=566778 bytes) (Obsoletes RFC1117, RFC1062, RFC1020) (Status: INFORMATIONAL)

1167 Thoughts on the National Research and Education Network. V.G. Cerf. Jul-01-1990. (Format: TXT=20682 bytes) (Status: INFORMATIONAL)

1168 Intermail and Commercial Mail Relay services. A. Westine, A.L. DeSchon, J. Postel, C.E. Ward. Jul-01-1990. (Format: TXT=40306, PS=149816 bytes) (Status: INFORMATIONAL)

1169 Explaining the role of GOSIP. V.G. Cerf, K.L. Mills. Aug-01-1990. (Format: TXT=30255 bytes) (Status: INFORMATIONAL)

1170 Public key standards and licenses. R.B. Fougner. Jan-01-1991. (Format: TXT=3144 bytes) (Status: INFORMATIONAL)

1171 Point-to-Point Protocol for the transmission of multi-protocol datagrams over Point-to-Point links. D. Perkins. Jul-01-1990. (Format: TXT=92321 bytes) (Obsoletes RFC1134) (Obsoleted by RFC1331) (Status: DRAFT STANDARD)

1172 Point-to-Point Protocol (PPP) initial configuration options. D. Perkins, R. Hobby. Jul-01-1990. (Format: TXT=76132 bytes) (Obsoleted by RFC1331) (Status: PROPOSED STANDARD)

1173 Responsibilities of host and network managers: A summary of the "oral tradition" of the Internet. J. VanBokkelen. Aug-01-1990. (Format: TXT=12527 bytes) (Status: INFORMATIONAL)

1174 IAB recommended policy on distributing internet identifier

assignment and IAB recommended policy change to internet "connected" status. V.G. Cerf. Aug-01-1990. (Format: TXT=21321 bytes) (Status: INFORMATIONAL)

1175 FYI on where to start: A bibliography of internetworking information. K.L. Bowers, T.L. LaQuey, J.K. Reynolds, K. Roubicek, M.K. Stahl, A. Yuan. Aug-01-1990. (Format: TXT=67330 bytes) (Also FYI0003) (Status: INFORMATIONAL)

1176 Interactive Mail Access Protocol: Version 2. M.R. Crispin. Aug-01-1990. (Format: TXT=67330 bytes) (Obsoletes RFC1064) (Status: EXPERIMENTAL)

1177 FYI on Questions and Answers: Answers to commonly asked "new internet user" questions. G.S. Malkin, A.N. Marine, J.K. Reynolds. Aug-01-1990. (Format: TXT=52852 bytes) (Obsoleted by RFC1206, FYI0004) (Also FYI0004) (Status: INFORMATIONAL)

1178 Choosing a name for your computer. D. Libes. Aug-01-1990. (Format: TXT=18472 bytes) (Also FYI0005) (Status: INFORMATIONAL)

1179 Line printer daemon protocol. L. McLaughlin. Aug-01-1990. Format: TXT=24324 bytes) (Status: INFORMATIONAL)

1180 TCP/IP tutorial. T.J. Socolofsky, C.J. Kale. Jan-01-1991. (Format: TXT=65494 bytes) (Status: INFORMATIONAL)

1181 RIPE Terms of Reference. R. Blokzijl. Sep-01-1990. (Format: TXT=2523 bytes) (Status: INFORMATIONAL)

1182 (Not online) (Status: UNKNOWN)

1183 New DNS RR Definitions. C.F. Everhart, L.A. Mamakos, R. Ullmann, P.V. Mockapetris. Oct-01-1990. (Format: TXT=23788 bytes) (Updates RFC1034, RFC1035) (Status: EXPERIMENTAL)

1184 Telnet Linemode Option. D.A. Borman. Oct-01-1990. (Format: TXT=53085 bytes) (Obsoletes RFC1116) (Status: DRAFT STANDARD)

1185 TCP Extension for High-Speed Paths. V. Jacobson, R.T. Braden, L. Zhang. Oct-01-1990. (Format: TXT=49508 bytes) (Obsoleted by RFC1323) (Status: EXPERIMENTAL)

1186 MD4 Message Digest Algorithm. R.L. Rivest. Oct-01-1990. (Format: TXT=35391 bytes) (Status: INFORMATIONAL)

1187 Bulk Table Retrieval with the SNMP. M.T. Rose, K. McCloghrie, J.R. Davin. Oct-01-1990. (Format: TXT=27220 bytes) (Status: EXPERIMENTAL)

1188 Proposed Standard for the Transmission of IP Datagrams over FDDI Networks. D. Katz. Oct-01-1990. (Format: TXT=22424 bytes) (Obsoletes RFC1103) (Status: DRAFT STANDARD)

1189 Common Management Information Services and Protocols for the Internet (CMOT and CMIP). U.S. Warrier, L. Besaw, L. LaBarre, B.D. Handspicker. Oct-01-1990. (Format: TXT=32928 bytes) (Obsoletes RFC1095) (Status: HISTORIC)

1190 Experimental Internet Stream Protocol: Version 2 (ST-II). C. Topolcic. Oct-01-1990. (Format: TXT=386909 bytes) (Obsoletes IEN 119) (Obsoleted by RFC1819) (Status: EXPERIMENTAL)

1191 Path MTU discovery. J.C. Mogul, S.E. Deering. Nov-01-1990. (Format: TXT=47936 bytes) (Obsoletes RFC1063) (Status: DRAFT STANDARD)

1192 Commercialization of the Internet summary report. B. Kahin. Nov-01-1990. (Format: TXT=35253 bytes) (Status: INFORMATIONAL)

1193 Client requirements for real-time communication services. D. Ferrari. Nov-01-1990. (Format: TXT=61540 bytes) (Status: INFORMATIONAL)

1194 Finger User Information Protocol. D.P. Zimmerman. Nov-01-1990. (Format: TXT=24626 bytes) (Obsoletes RFC0742) (Obsoleted by RFC1288, RFC1196) (Status: DRAFT STANDARD)

1195 Use of OSI IS-IS for routing in TCP/IP and dual environments. R.W. Callon. Dec-01-1990. (Format: TXT=187866, PS=362052 bytes) (Status: PROPOSED STANDARD)

1196 Finger User Information Protocol. D.P. Zimmerman. Dec-01-1990. (Format: TXT=24799 bytes) (Obsoletes RFC1194, 742) (Obsoleted by RFC1288) (Status: DRAFT STANDARD)

1197 Using ODA for translating multimedia information. M. Sherman. Dec-01-1990. (Format: TXT=3620 bytes) (Status: INFORMATIONAL)

1198 FYI on the X window system. R.W. Scheifler. Jan-01-1991. (Format: TXT=3629 bytes) (Also FYI0006) (Status: INFORMATIONAL)

1199 Request for Comments Summary Notes: 1100-1199. J. Reynolds. Dec-01-1991. (Format: TXT=46443 bytes) (Status: INFORMATIONAL)

1200 IAB official protocol standards. Defense Advanced Research Projects Agency, Internet Activities Board. Apr-01-1991. (Format: TXT=67069 bytes) (Obsoletes RFC1140) (Obsoleted by RFC1250, RFC2200, RFC2300, STD0001, RFC2400) (Status: HISTORIC)

1201 Transmitting IP traffic over ARCNET networks. D. Provan. Feb-01-1991. (Format: TXT=16959 bytes) (Obsoletes RFC1051) (Status: STANDARD)

1202 Directory Assistance service. M.T. Rose. Feb-01-1991. (Format: TXT=21645 bytes) (Status: INFORMATIONAL)

1203 Interactive Mail Access Protocol: Version 3. J. Rice. Feb-01-1991. (Format: TXT=123325 bytes) (Obsoletes RFC1064) (Status: HISTORIC)

1204 Message Posting Protocol (MPP). S. Yeh, D. Lee. Feb-01-1991. (Format: TXT=11371 bytes) (Status: EXPERIMENTAL)

1205 5250 Telnet interface. P. Chmielewski. Feb-01-1991. (Format: TXT=27179 bytes) (Status: INFORMATIONAL)

1206 FYI on Questions and Answers: Answers to commonly asked "new Internet user" questions. G.S. Malkin, A.N. Marine. Feb-01-1991. (Format: TXT=72479 bytes) (Obsoletes RFC1177) (Obsoleted by FYI0004, RFC1325) (Also FYI0004) (Status: INFORMATIONAL)

1207 FYI on Questions and Answers: Answers to commonly asked "experienced Internet user" questions. G.S. Malkin, A.N. Marine, J.K. Reynolds. Feb-01-1991. (Format: TXT=33385 bytes) (Also FYI0007) (Status: INFORMATIONAL)

1208 Glossary of networking terms. O.J. Jacobsen, D.C. Lynch. Mar-01-1991. (Format: TXT=41156 bytes) (Status: INFORMATIONAL)

1209 Transmission of IP datagrams over the SMDS Service. D.M. Piscitello, J. Lawrence. Mar-01-1991. (Format: TXT=25280 bytes) (Status: STANDARD)

1210 Network and infrastructure user requirements for transatlantic research collaboration: Brussels, July 16-18, and Washington July 24-25, 1990. V.G. Cerf, P.T. Kirstein, B. Randell. Mar-01-1991. (Format: TXT=79048 bytes) (Status: INFORMATIONAL)

1211 Problems with the maintenance of large mailing lists. A. Westine, J. Postel. Mar-01-1991. (Format: TXT=96167 bytes) (Status: INFORMATIONAL)

1212 Concise MIB definitions. M.T. Rose, K. McCloghrie. Mar-01-1991. (Format: TXT=43579 bytes) (Status: STANDARD)

1213 Management Information Base for Network Management of TCP/IP-based internets:MIB-II. K. McCloghrie, M.T. Rose. Mar-01-1991. (Format: TXT=146080 bytes) (Obsoletes RFC1158) (Updated by RFC2011, RFC2012, RFC2013) (Status: STANDARD)

1214 OSI internet management: Management Information Base. L. LaBarre. Apr-01-1991. (Format: TXT=172564 bytes) (Status: HISTORIC)

1215 Convention for defining traps for use with the SNMP. M.T. Rose. Mar-01-1991. (Format: TXT=19336 bytes) (Status: INFORMATIONAL)

1216 Gigabit network economics and paradigm shifts. P. Richard, P. Kynikos. Apr-01-1991. (Format: TXT=8130 bytes) (Status: INFORMATIONAL)

1217 Memo from the Consortium for Slow Commotion Research (CSCR). V.G. Cerf. Apr-01-1991. (Format: TXT=11079 bytes) (Status: INFORMATIONAL)

1218 Naming scheme for c=US. North American Directory Forum.. Apr-01-1991. (Format: TXT=42698 bytes) (Obsoleted by RFC1255, RFC1417) (Status: INFORMATIONAL)

1219 On the assignment of subnet numbers. P.F. Tsuchiya. Apr-01-1991. (Format: TXT=30609 bytes) (Status: INFORMATIONAL)

1220 Point-to-Point Protocol extensions for bridging. F. Baker. Apr-01-1991. (Format: TXT=38165 bytes) (Obsoleted by RFC1638) (Status: PROPOSED STANDARD)

1221 Host Access Protocol (HAP) specification: Version 2. W. Edmond. Apr-01-1991. (Format: TXT=152740 bytes) (Updates RFC0907) (Status: INFORMATIONAL)

1222 Advancing the NSFNET routing architecture. H.W. Braun, Y. Rekhter. May-01-1991. (Format: TXT=15067 bytes) (Status: INFORMATIONAL)

1223 OSI CLNS and LLC1 protocols on Network Systems HYPERchannel. J.M. Halpern. May-01-1991. (Format: TXT=29601 bytes) (Status: INFORMATIONAL)

1224 Techniques for managing asynchronously generated alerts. L. Steinberg. May-01-1991. (Format: TXT=54303 bytes) (Status: EXPERIMENTAL)

1225 Post Office Protocol: Version 3. M.T. Rose. May-01-1991. (Format: TXT=37340 bytes) (Obsoletes RFC1081) (Obsoleted by RFC1460) (Status: DRAFT STANDARD)

1226 Internet protocol encapsulation of AX.25 frames. B. Kantor. May-01-1991. (Format: TXT=2573 bytes) (Status: EXPERIMENTAL)

1227 SNMP MUX protocol and MIB. M.T. Rose. May-01-1991. (Format: TXT=25868 bytes) (Status: HISTORIC)

1228 SNMP-DPI: Simple Network Management Protocol Distributed Program Interface. G. Carpenter, B. Wijnen. May-01-1991. (Format: TXT=96972 bytes) (Obsoleted by RFC1592) (Status: EXPERIMENTAL)

1229 Extensions to the generic-interface MIB. K. McCloghrie. May-01-1991. (Format: TXT=36022 bytes) (Obsoleted by RFC1573) (Updated by RFC1239) (Status: PROPOSED STANDARD)

1230 IEEE 802.4 Token Bus MIB. K. McCloghrie, R. Fox. May-01-1991. (Format: TXT=53100 bytes) (Updated by RFC1239) (Status: HISTORIC)

1231 IEEE 802.5 Token Ring MIB. K. McCloghrie, R. Fox, E. Decker. May-01-1991. (Format: TXT=53542 bytes) (Obsoleted by RFC1743, RFC1748) (Updated by RFC1239) (Status: PROPOSED STANDARD)

1232 Definitions of managed objects for the DS1 Interface type. F. Baker, C.P. Kolb. May-01-1991. (Format: TXT=60757 bytes) (Obsoleted by RFC1406) (Updated by RFC1239) (Status: PROPOSED STANDARD)

1233 Definitions of managed objects for the DS3 Interface type. T.A. Cox, K. Tesink. May-01-1991. (Format: TXT=49559 bytes) (Obsoleted by RFC1407) (Updated by RFC1239) (Status: PROPOSED STANDARD)

1234 Tunneling IPX traffic through IP networks. D. Provan. Jun-01-1991. (Format: TXT=12333 bytes) (Status: PROPOSED STANDARD)

1235 Coherent File Distribution Protocol. J. Ioannidis, Jr. Maguire, G.Q.. Jun-01-1991. (Format: TXT=29345 bytes) (Status: EXPERIMENTAL)

1236 IP to X.121 address mapping for DDN. Jr. Morales, L.F., P.R. Hasse. Jun-01-1991. (Format: TXT=12626 bytes) (Status: INFORMATIONAL)

1237 Guidelines for OSI NSAP Allocation in the Internet. R. Collela, E.P. Gardner, R.W. Callon. Jul-01-1991. (Format: TXT=116989, PS=160478 bytes) (Obsoleted by RFC1629) (Status: PROPOSED STANDARD)

1238 CLNS MIB for use with Connectionless Network Protocol (ISO 8473) and End System to Intermediate System (ISO 9542). G. Satz. Jun-01-1991. (Format: TXT=65159 bytes) (Obsoletes RFC1162) (Status: EXPERIMENTAL)

1239 Reassignment of experimental MIBs to standard MIBs. J.K. Reynolds. Jun-01-1991. (Format: TXT=3656 bytes) (Updates RFC1229, RFC1230, RFC1231, RFC1232, RFC1233) (Status: PROPOSED STANDARD)

1240 OSI connectionless transport services on top of UDP: Version 1. C. Shue, W. Haggerty, K. Dobbins. Jun-01-1991. (Format: TXT=18140 bytes) (Status: PROPOSED STANDARD)

1241 Scheme for an internet encapsulation protocol: Version 1. R.A. Woodburn, D.L. Mills. Jul-01-1991. (Format: TXT=42468, PS=128921 bytes) (Status: EXPERIMENTAL)

1242 Benchmarking terminology for network interconnection devices. S. Bradner. Jul-01-1991. (Format: TXT=22817 bytes) (Status: INFORMATIONAL)

1243 AppleTalk Management Information Base. S. Waldbusser. Jul-01-1991. (Format: TXT=61985 bytes) (Obsoleted by RFC1742) (Status: PROPOSED STANDARD)

1244 Site Security Handbook. J.P. Holbrook, J.K. Reynolds. Jul-01-1991. (Format: TXT=259129 bytes) (Obsoleted by RFC2196, FYI0008) (Also FYI0008) (Status: INFORMATIONAL)

1245 OSPF Protocol Analysis. J. Moy. Jul-01-1991. (Format: TXT=26160, PS=33546 bytes) (Also RFC1247, RFC1246) (Status: INFORMATIONAL)

1246 Experience with the OSPF Protocol. J. Moy. Jul-01-1991. (Format: TXT=70441, PS=141924 bytes) (Also RFC1247, RFC1245) (Status: INFORMATIONAL)

1247 OSPF Version 2. J. Moy. Jul-01-1991. (Format: TXT=433332, PS=989724 bytes) (Obsoletes RFC1131) (Obsoleted by RFC1583) (Also RFC1246, RFC1245) (Status: DRAFT STANDARD)

1248 OSPF Version 2 Management Information Base. F. Baker, R. Coltun. Jul-01-1991. (Format: TXT=74347 bytes) (Obsoleted by RFC1252) (Status: PROPOSED STANDARD)

1249 DIXIE Protocol Specification. T. Howes, M. Smith, B. Beecher. Aug-01-1991. (Format: TXT=20028 bytes) (Also RFC1202) (Status: INFORMATIONAL)

1250 IAB OFFICIAL PROTOCOL STANDARDS. J. Postel. Aug-01-1991. (Format: TXT=62555 bytes) (Obsoletes RFC1200, RFC1100, RFC1083, RFC1130, RFC1140) (Obsoleted by RFC2200, RFC2300, STD0001, RFC2400) (Also RFC1060, RFC1011, RFC1160) (Status: HISTORIC)

1251 Who's Who in the Internet: Biographies of IAB, IESG and IRSG Members. G. Malkin. Aug-01-1991. (Format: TXT=70383 bytes) (Also FYI0009) (Status: INFORMATIONAL)

1252 OSPF Version 2 Management Information Base. F. Baker, R. Coltun. Aug-01-1991. (Format: TXT=74471 bytes) (Obsoletes RFC1248) (Obsoleted by RFC1253) (Also RFC1247, RFC1245) (Status: PROPOSED STANDARD)

1253 OSPF Version 2 Management Information Base. F. Baker, R. Coltun. Aug-01-1991. (Format: TXT=74453 bytes) (Obsoletes RFC1252) (Obsoleted by RFC1850) (Also RFC1247, RFC1245, RFC1246) (Status: PROPOSED STANDARD)

1254 Gateway Congestion Control Survey. A. Mankin, K. Ramakrishnan. Jul-01-1991. (Format: TXT=67609 bytes) (Status: INFORMATIONAL)

1255 A Naming Scheme for c=US. The North American Directory Forum. Sep-01-1991. (Format: TXT=51103 bytes) (Obsoletes RFC1218) (Obsoleted by RFC1417) (Status: INFORMATIONAL)

1256 ICMP Router Discovery Messages. S. Deering. Sep-01-1991. (Format: TXT=43059 bytes) (Also RFC0792) (Status: PROPOSED STANDARD)

1257 Isochronous applications do not require jitter-controlled networks. C. Partridge. Sep-01-1991. (Format: TXT=11075 bytes) (Status: INFORMATIONAL)

1258 BSD Rlogin. B. Kantor. Sep-01-1991. (Format: TXT=10763 bytes) (Status: INFORMATIONAL)

1259 Building the open road: The NREN as test-bed for the national public network. M. Kapor. Sep-01-1991. (Format: TXT=61654 bytes) (Status: INFORMATIONAL)

1260 (Not online) (Status: UNKNOWN)

1261 Transition of Nic Services. S. Williamson, L. Nobile. Sep-01-1991. (Format: TXT=4244 bytes) (Status: INFORMATIONAL)

1262 Guidelines for Internet Measurement Activities. V.G. Cerf. Oct-01-1991. (Format: TXT=6381 bytes) (Status: INFORMATIONAL)

1263 TCP Extensions Considered Harmful. S. O'Malley, L.L. Peterson. Oct-01-1991. (Format: TXT=54078 bytes) (Status: INFORMATIONAL)

1264 Internet Engineering Task Force Internet Routing Protocol Standardization Criteria. R.M. Hinden. Oct-01-1991. (Format: TXT=17016 bytes) (Status: INFORMATIONAL)

1265 BGP Protocol Analysis. Y. Rekhter. Oct-01-1991. (Format: TXT=20728 bytes) (Status: INFORMATIONAL)

1266 Experience with the BGP Protocol. Y. Rekhter. Oct-01-1991. (Format: TXT=21938 bytes) (Status: INFORMATIONAL)

1267 Border Gateway Protocol 3 (BGP-3). K. Lougheed, Y. Rekhter. Oct-01-1991. (Format: TXT=80724 bytes) (Obsoletes RFC1163) (Status: HISTORIC)

1268 Application of the Border Gateway Protocol in the Internet. Y. Rekhter, P. Gross. Oct-01-1991. (Format: TXT=31102 bytes) (Obsoletes RFC1164) (Obsoleted by RFC1655) (Status: HISTORIC)

1269 Definitions of Managed Objects for the Border Gateway Protocol: Version 3. S. Willis, J.W. Burruss. Oct-01-1991. (Format: TXT=25717 bytes) (Status: PROPOSED STANDARD)

1270 SNMP Communications Services. F. Kastenholz. Oct-01-1991. (Format: TXT=26167 bytes) (Status: INFORMATIONAL)

1271 Remote Network Monitoring Management Information Base. S. Waldbusser. Nov-01-1991. (Format: TXT=184111 bytes) (Obsoleted by RFC1757) (Status: PROPOSED STANDARD)

1272 Internet Accounting: Background. C. Mills, D. Hirsh, G.R. Ruth. Nov-01-1991. (Format: TXT=46562 bytes) (Status: INFORMATIONAL)

1273 Measurement Study of Changes in Service-Level Reachability in the Global TCP/IP Internet: Goals, Experimental Design, Implementation, and Policy Considerations. M.F. Schwartz. Nov-01-1991. (Format: TXT=19949 bytes) (Status: INFORMATIONAL)

1274 The COSINE and Internet X.500 Schema. P. Barker, S. Kille. November 1991. (Format: TXT=92827 bytes) (Status: PROPOSED STANDARD)

1275 Replication Requirements to provide an Internet Directory using X.500. S.E. Hardcastle-Kille. November 1991. (Format: TXT=4616, PS=83736 bytes) (Status: INFORMATIONAL)

1276 Replication and Distributed Operations extensions to provide an Internet Directory using X.500. S.E. Hardcastle-Kille. November 1991. (Format: TXT=33731, PS=217170 bytes) (Status: PROPOSED STANDARD)

1277 Encoding Network Addresses to Support Operation over Non-OSI Lower Layers. S.E. Hardcastle-Kille. November 1991. (Format: TXT=22254, PS=176169 bytes) (Status: PROPOSED STANDARD)

1278 A string encoding of Presentation Address. S.E. Hardcastle-Kille. November 1991. (Format: TXT=10256, PS=128696 bytes) (Status: INFORMATIONAL)

1279 X.500 and Domains. S.E. Hardcastle-Kille. November 1991. (Format: TXT=26669, PS=170029 bytes) (Status: EXPERIMENTAL)

1280 IAB OFFICIAL PROTOCOL STANDARDS. J. Postel. March 1992. (Format: TXT=70458 bytes) (Obsoleted by RFC2200, RFC2300, STD0001, RFC2400) (Status: HISTORIC)

1281 Guidelines for the Secure Operation of the Internet. R. Pethia, S. Crocker, B. Fraser. November 1991. (Format: TXT=22618 bytes) (Status: INFORMATIONAL)

1282 BSD Rlogin. B. Kantor. December 1991. (Format: TXT=10704 bytes) (Status: INFORMATIONAL)

1283 SNMP over OSI. M. Rose. December 1991. (Format: TXT=16857 bytes) (Obsoleted by RFC1418) (Status: EXPERIMENTAL)

1284 Definitions of Managed Objects for the Ethernet-like Interface Types. J. Cook. December 1991. (Format: TXT=43225 bytes) (Obsoleted by RFC1398) (Status: PROPOSED STANDARD)

1285 FDDI Management Information Base. J. Case. January 1992. (Format: TXT=99747 bytes) (Updated by RFC1512) (Status: PROPOSED STANDARD)

1286 Definitions of Managed Objects for Bridges. E. Decker, P. Langille, A. Rijsinghani, K. McCloghrie. December, 1991. (Format: TXT=79104 bytes) (Obsoleted by RFC1493, RFC1525) (Status: PROPOSED STANDARD)

1287 Towards the Future Internet Architecture. D. Clark, L. Chapin, V. Cerf, R. Braden, R. Hobby. December 1991. (Format: TXT=59812 bytes) (Status: INFORMATIONAL)

1288 The Finger User Information Protocol. D. Zimmerman. December 1991. (Format: TXT=25161 bytes) (Obsoletes RFC1196, RFC1194, RFC0742) (Status: DRAFT STANDARD)

1289 DECnet Phase IV MIB Extensions. J. Saperia. December 1991. (Format: TXT=122272 bytes) (Obsoleted by RFC1559) (Status: PROPOSED STANDARD)

1290 There's Gold in them thar Networks! or Searching for Treasure in all the Wrong Places. J. Martin. December 1991. (Format: TXT=46997 bytes) (Obsoleted by RFC1402, FYI0010) (Also FYI0010) (Status: INFORMATIONAL)

1291 Mid-Level Networks Potential Technical Services. V. Aggarwal. December 1991. (Format: TXT=24314, PS=218918 bytes) (Status: INFORMATIONAL)

1292 A Catalog of Available X.500 Implementations. R. Lang, R. Wright. January 1992. (Format: TXT=129468 bytes) (Obsoleted by RFC1632, FYI0011) (Status: INFORMATIONAL)

1293 Inverse Address Resolution Protocol. T. Bradley, C. Brown. January 1992. (Format: TXT=11368 bytes) (Obsoleted by RFC2390) (Status: PROPOSED STANDARD)

1294 Multiprotocol Interconnect over Frame Relay. T. Bradley, C. Brown, A. Malis. January 1992. (Format: TXT=54992 bytes) (Obsoleted by RFC1490, RFC2427, STD0055) (Status: PROPOSED STANDARD)

1295 User Bill of Rights for entries and listings in the Public Directory. The North American Directory Forum. January 1992. (Format: TXT=3502 bytes) (Obsoleted by RFC1417) (Status: INFORMATIONAL)

1296 Internet Growth (1981-1991). M. Lottor. January 1992. (Format: TXT=20103 bytes) (Status: INFORMATIONAL)

1297 NOC Internal Integrated Trouble Ticket System Functional Specification Wishlist ("NOC TT REQUIREMENTS"). D. Johnson. January 1992. (Format: TXT=32964 bytes) (Status: INFORMATIONAL)

1298 SNMP over IPX. R. Wormley, S. Bostock. February 1992. (Format: TXT=7878 bytes) (Obsoleted by RFC1420) (Status: INFORMATIONAL)

1299 Summary of 1200-1299. M. Kennedy. January 1997. (Format: TXT=36594 bytes) (Status: INFORMATIONAL)

1300 Remembrances of Things Past. S. Greenfield. February 1992. (Format: TXT=4963 bytes) (Status: INFORMATIONAL)

1301 Multicast Transport Protocol. S. Armstrong, A. Freier, K. Marzullo. February 1992. (Format: TXT=91976 bytes) (Status: INFORMATIONAL)

1302 Building a Network Information Services Infrastructure. D. Sitzler, P. Smith, A. Marine. February, 1992. (Format: TXT=29135 bytes) (Also FYI0012) (Status: INFORMATIONAL)

1303 A Convention for Describing SNMP-based Agents. K. McCloghrie, M. Rose. February 1992. (Format: TXT=22915 bytes) (Also RFC1155, RFC1212, RFC1213, RFC1157) (Status: INFORMATIONAL)

1304 Definitions of Managed Objects for the SIP Interface Type. T. Cox, K. Tesink, Editors. February 1992. (Format: TXT=52491 bytes) (Obsoleted by RFC1694) (Status: PROPOSED STANDARD)

1305 Network Time Protocol (Version 3) Specification, Implementation. David L. Mills. March 1992. (Format: TXT=307085 bytes) (Obsoletes RFC0958, RFC1059, RFC1119) (Status: DRAFT STANDARD)

1306 Experiences Supporting By-Request Circuit-Switched T3 Networks. A. Nicholson, J. Young. March 1992. (Format: TXT=25788 bytes) (Status: INFORMATIONAL)

1307 Dynamically Switched Link Control Protocol. J. Young, A. Nicholson. March 1992. (Format: TXT=24145 bytes) (Status: EXPERIMENTAL)

1308 Executive Introduction to Directory Services Using the X.500 Protocol. C. Weider, J. Reynolds. March 1992. (Format: TXT=9392 bytes) (Status: INFORMATIONAL)

1309 Technical Overview of Directory Services Using the X.500 Protocol. C. Weider, J. Reynolds, S. Heker. March 1992. (Format: TXT=35694 bytes) (Status: INFORMATIONAL)

1310 The Internet Standards Process. Lyman Chapin. March 1992. (Format: TXT=54738 bytes) (Obsoleted by RFC1602) (Status: INFORMATIONAL)

1311 Introduction to the STD Notes. J. Postel. March 1992. (Format: TXT=11308 bytes) (Status: INFORMATIONAL)

1312 Message Send Protocol 2. R. Nelson, G. Arnold. April 1992. (Format: TXT=18037 bytes) (Status: EXPERIMENTAL)

1313 Today's Programming for KRFC AM 1313 Internet Talk Radio. C. Partridge. 1 April 1992. (Format: TXT=5444 bytes) (Status: INFORMATIONAL)

1314 A File Format for the Exchange of Images in the Internet. A. Katz, D. Cohen. April 1992. (Format: TXT=54072 bytes) (Status: PROPOSED STANDARD)

1315 Management Information Base for Frame Relay DTEs. C. Brown, F. Baker, C. Carvalho. April 1992. (Format: TXT=33825 bytes) (Obsoleted by RFC2115) (Status: PROPOSED STANDARD)

1316 Definitions of Managed Objects for Character Stream Devices. B. Stewart. April 1992. (Format: TXT=35143 bytes) (Obsoleted by RFC1658) (Status: PROPOSED STANDARD)

1317 Definitions of Managed Objects for RS-232-like Hardware Devices. B. Stewart. April 1992. (Format: TXT=30442 bytes) (Obsoleted by RFC1659) (Status: PROPOSED STANDARD)

1318 Definitions of Managed Objects for Parallel-printer-like Hardware Devices. B. Stewart. April 1992. (Format: TXT=19570 bytes) (Obsoleted by RFC1660) (Status: PROPOSED STANDARD)

1319 The MD2 Message-Digest Algorithm. B. Kaliski. April 1992. (Format: TXT=25661 bytes) (Status: INFORMATIONAL)

1320 The MD4 Message-Digest Algorithm. R. Rivest. April 1992. (Format: TXT=32407 bytes) (Status: INFORMATIONAL)

1321 The MD5 Message-Digest Algorithm. R. Rivest. April 1992. (Format: TXT=35222 bytes) (Status: INFORMATIONAL)

1322 A Unified Approach to Inter-Domain Routing. D. Estrin, Y. Rekhter, S. Hotz. May 1992. (Format: TXT=96934 bytes) (Status: INFORMATIONAL)

1323 TCP Extensions for High Performance. V. Jacobson, R. Braden, D. Borman. May 1992. (Format: TXT=84558 bytes) (Obsoletes RFC1072, RFC1185) (Status: PROPOSED STANDARD)

1324 A Discussion on Computer Network Conferencing. D. Reed. May 1992. (Format: TXT=24988 bytes) (Status: INFORMATIONAL)

1325 FYI on Questions and Answers Answers to Commonly asked "New Internet User" Questions. G. Malkin, A. Marine. May 1992. (Format: TXT=91884 bytes) (Obsoletes RFC1206) (Obsoleted by RFC1594, FYI0004) (Also FYI0004) (Status: INFORMATIONAL)

1326 Mutual Encapsulation Considered Dangerous. P. Tsuchiya. May 1992. (Format: TXT=11277 bytes) (Status: INFORMATIONAL)

1327 Mapping between X.400(1988) / ISO 10021 and RFC 822. S. Hardcastle-Kille. May 1992. (Format: TXT=228598 bytes) (Obsoletes RFC987, RFC1026, RFC1138, RFC1148) (Obsoleted by RFC1495, RFC2156) (Updates RFC0822, RFC0822) (Status: PROPOSED STANDARD)

1328 X.400 1988 to 1984 downgrading. S. Hardcastle-Kille. May 1992. (Format: TXT=10006 bytes) (Status: PROPOSED STANDARD)

1329 Thoughts on Address Resolution for Dual MAC FDDI Networks. P. Kuehn. May 1992. (Format: TXT=58150 bytes) (Status: INFORMATIONAL)

1330 Recommendations for the Phase I Deployment of OSI Directory Services (X.500) and OSI Message Handling Services (X.400) within the ESNET Community. ESCC X.500/X.400 Task Force, ESnet Site Coordinating Committee (ESCC). May 1992. (Format: TXT=192925 bytes) (Status: INFORMATIONAL)

1331 The Point-to-Point Protocol (PPP) for the Transmission of Multi-protocol Datagrams over Point-to-Point Links. W. Simpson. May 1992. (Format: TXT=129892 bytes) (Obsoletes RFC1171, RFC1172) (Obsoleted by RFC1548) (Status: PROPOSED STANDARD)

1332 The PPP Internet Protocol Control Protocol (IPCP). G. McGregor. May 1992. (Format: TXT=17613 bytes) (Obsoletes 1172) (Status: PROPOSED STANDARD)

1333 PPP Link Quality Monitoring. W. Simpson. May 1992. (Format: TXT=29965 bytes) (Obsoleted by RFC1989) (Status: PROPOSED STANDARD)

1334 PPP Authentication Protocols. B. Lloyd, W. Simpson. October 1992. (Format: TXT=33248 bytes) (Obsoleted by RFC1994) (Status: PROPOSED STANDARD)

1335 A Two-Tier Address Structure for the Internet: A Solution to the Problem of Address Space Exhaustion. Z. Wang, J. Crowcroft. May 1992. (Format: TXT=15418 bytes) (Status: INFORMATIONAL)

1336 Who's Who in the Internet: Biographies of IAB, IESG and IRSG Members. G. MAlkin. May 1992. (Format: TXT=92119 bytes) (Status: INFORMATIONAL)

1337 TIME-WAIT Assassination Hazards in TCP. R. Braden. May 1992. (Format: TXT=22887 bytes) (Status: INFORMATIONAL)

1338 Supernetting: an Address Assignment and Aggregation Strategy. V. Fuller, T. Li, J. Yu, K. Varadhan. June 1992. (Format: TXT=47975 bytes) (Obsoleted by RFC1519) (Status: INFORMATIONAL)

1339 Remote Mail Checking Protocol. S. Dorner, P. Resnick. June 1992. (Format: TXT=13115 bytes) (Status: EXPERIMENTAL)

1340 ASSIGNED NUMBERS. J. Reynolds,J. Postel. July 1992. (Format: TXT=232974 bytes) (Obsoletes RFC1060) (Obsoleted by RFC1700) (Status: HISTORIC)

1341 MIME (Multipurpose Internet Mail Extensions): Mechanisms for Specifying and Describing the Format of Internet Message Bodies. N. Borenstein, N. Freed. June 1992. (Format: TXT=211117, PS=347082 bytes) (Obsoleted by RFC1521) (Status: PROPOSED STANDARD)

1342 Representation of Non-ASCII Text in Internet Message Headers. K. Moore. June 1992. (Format: TXT=15845 bytes) (Obsoleted by RFC1522) (Status: INFORMATIONAL)

1343 A User Agent Configuration Mechanism for Multimedia Mail Format Information. N. Borenstein. June 1992. (Format: TXT=29295, PS=59978 bytes) (Status: INFORMATIONAL)

1344 Implications of MIME for Internet Mail Gateways. N. Borenstein. June 1992. (Format: TXT=25872, PS=51812 bytes) (Status: INFORMATIONAL)

1345 Character Mnemonics and Character Sets. K. Simonsen. June 1992. (Format: TXT=249737 bytes) (Status: INFORMATIONAL)

1346 Resource Allocation, Control, and Accounting for the Use of Network Resources. P. Jones. June 1992. (Format: TXT=13084 bytes) (Status: INFORMATIONAL)

1347 TCP and UDP with Bigger Addresses (TUBA), A Simple Proposal for Internet Addressing and Routing. R. Callon. June 1992. (Format: TXT=26563, PS=42398 bytes) (Status: INFORMATIONAL)

1348 DNS NSAP RRs. B. Manning. July 1992. (Format: TXT=6871 bytes) (Obsoleted by RFC1637) (Updates RFC1034, RFC1035) (Updated by RFC1637) (Status: EXPERIMENTAL)

1349 Type of Service in the Internet Protocol Suite. P. Almquist. July 1992. (Format: TXT=68949 bytes) (Status: PROPOSED STANDARD)

1350 THE TFTP PROTOCOL (REVISION 2). K. Sollins. July 1992. (Format: TXT=24599 bytes) (Obsoletes RFC0784) (Updates RFC1350, RFC1783) (Updated by RFC1782, RFC1783, RFC1784, RFC1350, RFC1785, RFC2347, RFC2348, RFC2349) (Also STD0033) (Status: STANDARD)

1351 SNMP Administrative Model. J. Davin, J. Galvin, K. McCloghrie. July 1992. (Format: TXT=80721 bytes) (Status: PROPOSED STANDARD)

1352 SNMP Security Protocols. J. Galvin,K. McCloghrie,J. Davin. July 1992. (Format: TXT=95732 bytes) (Status: PROPOSED STANDARD)

1353 Definitions of Managed Objects for Administration of SNMP Parties. K. McCloghrie, J. Davin, J. Galvin. July 1992. (Format: TXT=59556 bytes) (Status: PROPOSED STANDARD)

1354 IP Forwarding Table MIB. F. Baker. July 1992. (Format: TXT=24905 bytes) (Obsoleted by RFC2096) (Status: PROPOSED STANDARD)

1355 Privacy and Accuracy Issues in Network Information Center Databases. J. Curran, A. Marine. August 1992. (Format: TXT=8858 bytes) (Also FYI0015) (Status: INFORMATIONAL)

1356 Multiprotocol Interconnect on X.25 and ISDN in the Packet Mode. A. Malis, D. Robinson, R. Ullmann. August 1992. (Format: TXT=32043 bytes) (Obsoletes RFC0877) (Status: DRAFT STANDARD)

1357 A Format for E-mailing Bibliographic Records. D. Cohen. July 1992. (Format: TXT=25021 bytes) (Obsoleted by RFC1807) (Status: INFORMATIONAL)

1358 Charter of the Internet Architecture Board (IAB). L. Chapin. August 1992. (Format: TXT=11328 bytes) (Obsoleted by RFC1601) (Status: INFORMATIONAL)

1359 Connecting to the Internet - What Connecting Institutions Should Anticipate. ACM SIGUCCS. August 1992. (Format: TXT=53449 bytes) (Also FYI0016) (Status: INFORMATIONAL)

1360 IAB Official Protocol Standards. J. Postel. September 1992. (Format: TXT=71860 bytes) (Obsoleted by RFC1410, RFC2200, RFC2300, STD0001, RFC2400) (Also RFC1280) (Status: HISTORIC)

1361 Simple Network Time Protocol (SNTP). D. Mills. August 1992. (Format: TXT=23812 bytes) (Obsoleted by RFC1769) (Also RFC1305) (Status: INFORMATIONAL)

1362 Novell IPX over Various WAN Media (IPXWAN). M. Allen. September 1992. (Format: TXT=30219 bytes) (Obsoleted by RFC1634) (Status: INFORMATIONAL)

1363 A Proposed Flow Specification. C. Partridge. September 1992. (Format: TXT=59214 bytes) (Status: INFORMATIONAL)

1364 BGP OSPF Interaction. K. Varadhan. September 1992. (Format: TXT=32121 bytes) (Obsoleted by RFC1403) (Also RFC1247, RFC1267) (Status: PROPOSED STANDARD)

1365 An IP Address Extension Proposal. K. Siyan. September 1992. (Format: TXT=12790 bytes) (Status: INFORMATIONAL)

1366 Guidelines for Management of IP Address Space. E. Gerich. October 1992. (Format: TXT=17793 bytes) (Obsoleted by RFC1466) (Status: INFORMATIONAL)

1367 Schedule for IP Address Space Management Guidelines. C. Topolcic. October 1992. (Format: TXT=4780 bytes) (Obsoleted by RFC1467) (Status: INFORMATIONAL)

1368 Definition of Managed Objects for IEEE 802.3 Repeater Devices. D. McMaster, K. McCloghrie. October 1992. (Format: TXT=83905 bytes) (Obsoleted by RFC1516) (Status: PROPOSED STANDARD)

1369 Implementation Notes and Experience for the Internet Ethernet MIB. F. Kastenholz. October 1992. (Format: TXT=13961 bytes) (Status: PROPOSED STANDARD)

1370 Applicability Statement for OSPF. Internet Architecture Board, L. Chapin. October 1992. (Format: TXT=4303 bytes) (Status: PROPOSED STANDARD)

1371 Choosing a Common IGP for the IP Internet. P. Gross. October 1992. (Format: TXT=18168 bytes) (Status: INFORMATIONAL)

1372 Telnet Remote Flow Control Option. C. Hedrick, D. Borman. October 1992. (Format: TXT=11098 bytes) (Obsoletes RFC1080) (Status: PROPOSED STANDARD)

1373 Portable DUAs. T. Tignor. October 1992. (Format: TXT=19931 bytes) (Status: INFORMATIONAL)

1374 IP and ARP on HIPPI. J. Renwick, A. Nicholson. October 1992. (Format: TXT=100903 bytes) (Status: PROPOSED STANDARD)

1375 Suggestion for New Classes of IP Addresses. P. Robinson. October 1992. (Format: TXT=16990 bytes) (Status: INFORMATIONAL)

1376 The PPP DECnet Phase IV Control Protocol (DNCP). S. Senum. November 1992. (Format: TXT=12448 bytes) (Obsoleted by RFC1762) (Status: PROPOSED STANDARD)

1377 The PPP OSI Network Layer Control Protocol (OSINLCP). D. Katz. November 1992. (Format: TXT=22109 bytes) (Status: PROPOSED STANDARD)

1378 The PPP AppleTalk Control Protocol (ATCP). B. Parker. November 1992. (Format: TXT=28496 bytes) (Status: PROPOSED STANDARD)

1379 Extending TCP for Transactions – Concepts. R. Braden. November 1992. (Format: TXT=91353 bytes) (Status: INFORMATIONAL)

1380 IESG Deliberations on Routing and Addressing. P. Gross, P. Almquist. November 1992. (Format: TXT=49415 bytes) (Status: INFORMATIONAL)

1381 SNMP MIB Extension for X.25 LAPB. D. Throop, F. Baker. November 1992. (Format: TXT=71253 bytes) (Status: PROPOSED STANDARD)

1382 SNMP MIB Extension for the X.25 Packet Layer. D. Throop. November 1992. (Format: TXT=153877 bytes) (Status: PROPOSED STANDARD)

1383 An Experiment in DNS Based IP Routing. C. Huitema. December 1992. (Format: TXT=32680 bytes) (Status: EXPERIMENTAL)

1384 Naming Guidelines for Directory Pilots. P. Barker & S.E. Hardcastle-Kille. February 1993. (Format: TXT=25870, PS=175044 bytes) (Obsoleted by RFC1617, RTR0011) (Status: INFORMATIONAL)

1385 EIP: The Extended Internet Protocol. Z. Wang. November 1992. (Format: TXT=39123 bytes) (Status: INFORMATIONAL)

1386 The US Domain. A. Cooper, J. Postel. December 1992. (Format: TXT=62310 bytes) (Obsoleted by RFC1480) (Status: INFORMATIONAL)

1387 RIP Version 2 Protocol Analysis. G. Malkin. January 1993. (Format: TXT=5598 bytes) (Obsoleted by RFC1721) (Status: INFORMATIONAL)

1388 RIP Version 2 Carrying Additional Information. G. Malkin. January 1993. (Format: TXT=16227 bytes) (Obsoleted by RFC1723) (Updates RFC1058) (Status: PROPOSED STANDARD)

1389 RIP Version 2 MIB Extensions. G. Malkin, F. Baker. January 1993. (Format: TXT=23569 bytes) (Obsoleted by RFC1724) (Status: PROPOSED STANDARD)

1390 Transmission of IP and ARP over FDDI Networks. D. Katz. January 1993. (Format: TXT=22077 bytes) (Status: STANDARD)

1391 The Tao of the IETF: A Guide for New Attendees of the Internet Engineering Task Force. G. Malkin. January 1993. (Format: TXT=41892 bytes) (Obsoleted by RFC1539, FYI0017) (Also FYI0017) (Status: INFORMATIONAL)

1392 Internet Users' Glossary. G. Malkin, T. LaQuey Parker. January 1993. (Format: TXT=104624 bytes) (Obsoleted by RFC1983, FYI0018) (Also FYI0018) (Status: INFORMATIONAL)

1393 Traceroute Using an IP Option. G. Malkin. January 1993. (Format: TXT=13140 bytes) (Status: EXPERIMENTAL)

1394 Relationship of Telex Answerback Codes to Internet Domains. P. Robinson. January 1993. (Format: TXT=43776 bytes) (Status: INFORMATIONAL)

1395 BOOTP Vendor Information Extensions. J. Reynolds. January 1993. (Format: TXT=16314 bytes) (Obsoletes RFC1084, RFC1048) (Obsoleted by RFC1497, RFC1533) (Updates RFC951, RFC0951) (Status: DRAFT STANDARD)

1396 The Process for Organization of Internet Standards Working Group (POISED). S. Crocker. January 1993. (Format: TXT=22096 bytes) (Status: INFORMATIONAL)

1397 Default Route Advertisement In BGP2 and BGP3 Version of The Border Gateway Protocol. D. Haskin. January 1993. (Format: TXT=4124 bytes) (Status: PROPOSED STANDARD)

1398 Definitions of Managed Objects for the Ethernet-Like Interface Types. F. Kastenholz. January 1993. (Format: TXT=36684 bytes) (Obsoletes RFC1284) (Obsoleted by RFC1643, STD0050, RFC1623) (Status: DRAFT STANDARD)

1399 Summary of 1300-1399. J. Elliott. January 1997. (Format: TXT=43662 bytes) (Status: INFORMATIONAL)

1400 Transition and Modernization of the Internet Registration Service. S. Williamson. March 1993. (Format: TXT=13008 bytes) (Status: INFORMATIONAL)

1401 Correspondence between the IAB and DISA on the use of DNS. Internet Architecture Board. January 1993. (Format: TXT=12528 bytes) (Status: INFORMATIONAL)

1402 There's Gold in them thar Networks! or Searching for Treasure in all the Wrong Places. J. Martin. January 1993. (Format: TXT=71176 bytes) (Obsoletes RFC1290) (Also FYI0010) (Status: INFORMATIONAL)

1403 BGP OSPF Interaction. K. Varadhan. January 1993. (Format: TXT=36173 bytes) (Obsoletes RFC1364) (Status: PROPOSED STANDARD)

1404 A Model for Common Operational Statistics. B. Stockman. January 1993. (Format: TXT=52814 bytes) (Obsoleted by RFC1857) (Status: INFORMATIONAL)

1405 Mapping between X.400(1984/1988) and Mail-11 (DECnet mail). C. Allocchio. January 1993. (Format: TXT=33885 bytes) (Obsoleted by RFC2162) (Status: EXPERIMENTAL)

1406 Definitions of Managed Objects for the DS1 and E1 Interface Types. F. Baker & J. Watt, Editors. January 1993. (Format: TXT=97559 bytes) (Obsoletes RFC1232) (Status: PROPOSED STANDARD)

1407 Definitions of Managed Objects for the DS3/E3 Interface Type. Tracy A. Cox AND Kaj Tesink are both with:. January 1993. (Format: TXT=90682 bytes) (Obsoletes RFC1233) (Status: PROPOSED STANDARD)

1408 Telnet Environment Option. D. Borman, Editor. January 1993. (Format: TXT=13936 bytes) (Updated by RFC1571) (Status: HISTORIC)

1409 Telnet Authentication Option. D. Borman, Editor. January 1993. (Format: TXT=13119 bytes) (Obsoleted by RFC1416) (Status: EXPERIMENTAL)

1410 IAB Official Protocol Standards. J. Postel, Editor. March 1993. (Format: TXT=76524 bytes) (Obsoletes RFC1360) (Obsoleted by RFC1500, RFC2200, RFC2300, STD0001, RFC2400) (Status: HISTORIC)

1411 Telnet Authentication: Kerberos Version 4. D. Borman, Editor. January 1993. (Format: TXT=7967 bytes) (Status: EXPERIMENTAL)

1412 Telnet Authentication: SPX. K. Alagappan. January 1993. (Format: TXT=6952 bytes) (Status: EXPERIMENTAL)

1413	Identification Protocol. M. StJohns. January 1993. (Format: TXT=16291 bytes) (Obsoletes RFC931) (Status: PROPOSED STANDARD)
1414	Identification MIB. M. StJohns & M. Rose. January 1993. (Format: TXT=14165 bytes) (Status: PROPOSED STANDARD)
1415	FTP-FTAM Gateway Specification. J. Mindel & R. Slaski. January 1993. (Format: TXT=128261 bytes) (Status: PROPOSED STANDARD)
1416	Telnet Authentication Option. D. Borman, Editor. February 1993. (Format: TXT=13270 bytes) (Obsoletes RFC1409) (Status: EXPERIMENTAL)
1417	NADF Standing Documents: A Brief Overview. The North American Directory Forum. February 1993. (Format: TXT=7270 bytes) (Obsoletes RFC1295, RFC1255, RFC1218) (Obsoleted by RFC1758) (Status: INFORMATIONAL)
1418	SNMP over OSI. M. Rose. March 1993. (Format: TXT=7721 bytes) (Obsoletes RFC1161, RFC1283) (Status: PROPOSED STANDARD)
1419	SNMP over AppleTalk. G. Minshall & M. Ritter. March 1993. (Format: TXT=16470 bytes) (Status: PROPOSED STANDARD)
1420	SNMP over IPX. S. Bostock. March 1993. (Format: TXT=6762 bytes) (Obsoletes RFC1298) (Status: PROPOSED STANDARD)
1421	Privacy Enhancement for Internet Electronic Mail: Part I: Message Encryption and Authentication Procedures. J. Linn. February 1993. (Format: TXT=103894 bytes) (Obsoletes RFC1113) (Status: PROPOSED STANDARD)
1422	Privacy Enhancement for Internet Electronic Mail: Part II: Certificate-Based Key Management. S. Kent. February 1993. (Format: TXT=86085 bytes) (Obsoletes RFC1114) (Status: PROPOSED STANDARD)
1423	Privacy Enhancement for Internet Electronic Mail: Part III: Algorithms, Modes, and Identifiers. D. Balenson. February 1993. (Format: TXT=33277 bytes) (Obsoletes RFC1115) (Status: PROPOSED STANDARD)
1424	Privacy Enhancement for Internet Electronic Mail: Part IV: Key Certification and Related Services. B. Kaliski. February 1993. (Format: TXT=17537 bytes) (Status: PROPOSED STANDARD)

1425 SMTP Service Extensions. J. Klensin, WG Chair, N. Freed, Editor, M. Rose,E. Stefferud & D. Crocker. February 1993. (Format: TXT=20932 bytes) (Obsoleted by RFC1651) (Status: PROPOSED STANDARD)

1426 SMTP Service Extension for 8bit-MIMEtransport. J. Klensin, WG Chair, N. Freed, Editor, M. Rose, E. Stefferud & D. Crocker. February 1993. (Format: TXT=11661 bytes) (Obsoleted by RFC1652) (Status: PROPOSED STANDARD)

1427 SMTP Service Extension for Message Size Declaration. J. Klensin, WG Chair, N. Freed, Editor, K. Moore. February 1993. (Format: TXT=17856 bytes) (Obsoleted by RFC1653) (Status: PROPOSED STANDARD)

1428 Transition of Internet Mail from Just-Send-8 to 8bit-SMTP/MIME. G. Vaudreuil. February 1993. (Format: TXT=12064 bytes) (Status: INFORMATIONAL)

1429 Listserv Distribute Protocol. E. Thomas. February 1993. (Format: TXT=17759 bytes) (Status: INFORMATIONAL)

1430 A Strategic Plan for Deploying an Internet X.500 Directory Service. S. Hardcastle-Kille, E. Huizer, V. Cerf, R. Hobby & S. Kent. February 1993. (Format: TXT=47587 bytes) (Status: INFORMATIONAL)

1431 DUA Metrics (OSI-DS 33 (v2)). P. Barker. February 1993. (Format: TXT=42240 bytes) (Status: INFORMATIONAL)

1432 Recent Internet Books. J. Quarterman. March 1993. (Format: TXT=27089 bytes) (Status: INFORMATIONAL)

1433 Directed ARP. J. Garrett, J. Hagan & J. Wong. March 1993. (Format: TXT=41028 bytes) (Status: EXPERIMENTAL)

1434 Data Link Switching: Switch-to-Switch Protocol. R. Dixon & D. Kushi. March 1993. (Format: TXT=80182, PS=292006 bytes) (Obsoleted by RFC1795) (Status: INFORMATIONAL)

1435 IESG Advice from Experience with Path MTU Discovery. S. Knowles. March 1993. (Format: TXT=2708 bytes) (Status: INFORMATIONAL)

1436 The Internet Gopher Protocol (a distributed document search and retrieval protocol). F. Anklesaria, M. McCahill, P. Lindner, D. Johnson, D. Torrey & B. Albert. March 1993. (Format: TXT=36493 bytes) (Status: INFORMATIONAL)

1437 The Extension of MIME Content-Types to a New Medium. N. Borenstein & M. Linimon. 1 April 1993. (Format: TXT=13356 bytes) (Status: INFORMATIONAL)

1438 Internet Engineering Task Force Statements Of Boredom (SOBs). A. Lyman Chapin & C. Huitema. 1 April 1993. (Format: TXT=3044 bytes) (Status: INFORMATIONAL)

1439 The Uniqueness of Unique Identifiers. C. Finseth. March 1993. (Format: TXT=20477 bytes) (Status: INFORMATIONAL)

1440 SIFT/UFT: Sender-Initiated/Unsolicited File Transfer. R. Troth. July 1993. (Format: TXT=17366 bytes) (Status: EXPERIMENTAL)

1441 Introduction to version 2 of the Internet-standard Network Management Framework. J. Case, K. McCloghrie, M. Rose, & S. Waldbusser. April 1993. (Format: TXT=25386 bytes) (Status: PROPOSED STANDARD)

1442 Structure of Management Information for version 2 of the Simple Network Management Protocol (SNMPv2). J. Case, K. McCloghrie, M. Rose, & S. Waldbusser. April 1993. (Format: TXT=95779 bytes) (Obsoleted by RFC1902) (Status: PROPOSED STANDARD)

1443 Textual Conventions for version 2 of the Simple Network Management Protocol (SNMPv2). J. Case, K. McCloghrie, M. Rose, & S. Waldbusser. April 1993. (Format: TXT=60947 bytes) (Obsoleted by RFC1903) (Status: PROPOSED STANDARD)

1444 Conformance Statements for version 2 of the Simple Network Management Protocol (SNMPv2). J. Case, K. McCloghrie, M. Rose, & S. Waldbusser. April 1993. (Format: TXT=57744 bytes) (Obsoleted by RFC1904) (Status: PROPOSED STANDARD)

1445 Administrative Model for version 2 of the Simple Network Management Protocol (SNMPv2). J. Galvin & K. McCloghrie. April 1993. (Format: TXT=99443 bytes) (Status: HISTORIC)

1446 Security Protocols for version 2 of the Simple Network Management Protocol (SNMPv2). J. Galvin & K. McCloghrie. April 1993. (Format: TXT=108733 bytes) (Status: HISTORIC)

1447 Party MIB for version 2 of the Simple Network Management Protocol (SNMPv2). K. McCloghrie & J. Galvin. April 1993. (Format: TXT=80762 bytes) (Status: HISTORIC)

1448 Protocol Operations for version 2 of the Simple Network Management Protocol (SNMPv2). J. Case, K. McCloghrie, M. Rose, & S. Waldbusser. April 1993. (Format: TXT=74224 bytes) (Obsoleted by RFC1905) (Status: PROPOSED STANDARD)

1449 Transport Mappings for version 2 of the Simple Network Management Protocol (SNMPv2). J. Case, K. McCloghrie, M. Rose, & S. Waldbusser. April 1993. (Format: TXT=41161 bytes) (Obsoleted by RFC1906) (Status: PROPOSED STANDARD)

1450 Management Information Base for version 2 of the Simple Network Management Protocol (SNMPv2). J. Case, K. McCloghrie, M. Rose, & S. Waldbusser. April 1993. (Format: TXT=42172 bytes) (Obsoleted by RFC1907) (Status: PROPOSED STANDARD)

1451 Manager-to-Manager Management Information Base. J. Case, K. McCloghrie, M. Rose, & S. Waldbusser. April 1993. (Format: TXT=62935 bytes) (Status: HISTORIC)

1452 Coexistence between version 1 and version 2 of the Internet-standard Network Management Framework. J. Case, K. McCloghrie, M. Rose, & S. Waldbusser. April 1993. (Format: TXT=32176 bytes) (Obsoleted by RFC1908) (Status: PROPOSED STANDARD)

1453 A Comment on Packet Video Remote Conferencing and the Transport/Network Layers. W. Chimiak. April 1993. (Format: TXT=23563 bytes) (Status: INFORMATIONAL)

1454 Comparison of Proposals for Next Version of IP. T. Dixon. May 1993. (Format: TXT=35064 bytes) (Status: INFORMATIONAL)

1455 Physical Link Security Type of Service. D. Eastlake, III. May 1993. (Format: TXT=12391 bytes) (Status: EXPERIMENTAL)

1456 Conventions for Encoding the Vietnamese Language VISCII: VIetnamese Standard Code for Information Interchange VIQR: VIetnamese Quoted-Readable Specification. Vietnamese Standardization Working Group. May 1993. (Format: TXT=14775 bytes) (Status: INFORMATIONAL)

1457 Security Label Framework for the Internet. R. Housley. May 1993. (Format: TXT=35802 bytes) (Status: INFORMATIONAL)

1458 Requirements for Multicast Protocols. R. Braudes & S. Zabele. May 1993. (Format: TXT=48106 bytes) (Status: INFORMATIONAL)

1459 Internet Relay Chat Protocol. J. Oikarinen & D. Reed. May 1993. (Format: TXT=138964 bytes) (Status: EXPERIMENTAL)

1460 Post Office Protocol - Version 3. M. Rose. June 1993. (Format: TXT=38827 bytes) (Obsoletes RFC1225) (Obsoleted by RFC1725) (Status: DRAFT STANDARD)

1461 SNMP MIB extension for Multiprotocol Interconnect over X.25. D. Throop. May 1993. (Format: TXT=47945 bytes) (Status: PROPOSED STANDARD)

1462 FYI on "What is the Internet?". E. Krol & E. Hoffman. May 1993. (Format: TXT=27811 bytes) (Also FYI0020) (Status: INFORMATIONAL)

1463 FYI on Introducing the Internet– A Short Bibliography of Introductory Internetworking Readings. E. Hoffman & L. Jackson. May 1993. (Format: TXT=7116 bytes) (Also FYI0019) (Status: INFORMATIONAL)

1464 Using the Domain Name System To Store Arbitrary String Attributes. R. Rosenbaum. May 1993. (Format: TXT=7953 bytes) (Status: EXPERIMENTAL)

1465 Routing Coordination for X.400 MHS Services Within a Multi Protocol / Multi Network Environment Table Format V3 for Static Routing. D. Eppenberger. May 1993. (Format: TXT=66833 bytes) (Status: EXPERIMENTAL)

1466 Guidelines for Management of IP Address Space. E. Gerich. May 1993. (Format: TXT=22262 bytes) (Obsoletes RFC1366) (Status: INFORMATIONAL)

1467 Status of CIDR Deployment in the Internet. C. Topolcic. August 1993. (Format: TXT=20720 bytes) (Obsoletes RFC1367) (Status: INFORMATIONAL)

1468 Japanese Character Encoding for Internet Messages. J. Murai, M. Crispin & E. van der Poel. June 1993. (Format: TXT=10970 bytes) (Status: INFORMATIONAL)

1469 IP Multicast over Token-Ring Local Area Networks. T. Pusateri. June 1993. (Format: TXT=8189 bytes) (Status: PROPOSED STANDARD)

1470 FYI on a Network Management Tool Catalog: Tools for Monitoring and Debugging TCP/IP Internets and Interconnected Devices. R. Enger & J. Reynolds. June 1993. (Format: TXT=308528 bytes) (Obsoletes RFC1147) (Also FYI0002) (Status: INFORMATIONAL)

1471 The Definitions of Managed Objects for the Link Control Protocol of the Point-to-Point Protocol. F. Kastenholz. June 1993. (Format: TXT=53558 bytes) (Status: PROPOSED STANDARD)

1472 The Definitions of Managed Objects for the Security Protocols of the Point-to-Point Protocol. F. Kastenholz. June 1993. (Format: TXT=27152 bytes) (Status: PROPOSED STANDARD)

1473 The Definitions of Managed Objects for the IP Network Control Protocol of the Point-to-Point Protocol. F. Kastenholz. June 1993. (Format: TXT=20484 bytes) (Status: PROPOSED STANDARD)

1474 The Definitions of Managed Objects for the Bridge Network Control Protocol of the Point-to-Point Protocol. F. Kastenholz. June 1993. (Format: TXT=31846 bytes) (Status: PROPOSED STANDARD)

1475 TP/IX: The Next Internet. R. Ullmann. June 1993. (Format: TXT=77854 bytes) (Status: EXPERIMENTAL)

1476 RAP: Internet Route Access Protocol. R. Ullmann. June 1993. (Format: TXT=45560 bytes) (Status: EXPERIMENTAL)

1477 IDPR as a Proposed Standard. M. Steenstrup. July 1993. (Format: TXT=32238 bytes) (Status: PROPOSED STANDARD)

1478 An Architecture for Inter-Domain Policy Routing. M. Steenstrup. July 1993. (Format: TXT=90673 bytes) (Status: PROPOSED STANDARD)

1479 Inter-Domain Policy Routing Protocol Specification: Version 1. M. Steenstrup. July 1993. (Format: TXT=275823 bytes) (Status: PROPOSED STANDARD)

1480 The US Domain. A. Cooper & J. Postel. June 1993. (Format: TXT=100556 bytes) (Obsoletes RFC1386) (Status: INFORMATIONAL)

1481 IAB Recommendation for an Intermediate Strategy to Address the Issue of Scaling. C. Huitema. July 1993. (Format: TXT=3502 bytes) (Status: INFORMATIONAL)

1482 Aggregation Support in the NSFNET Policy-Based Routing Database. Mark Knopper & Steven J. Richardson. July 1993. (Format: TXT=25330 bytes) (Status: INFORMATIONAL)

1483 Multiprotocol Encapsulation over ATM Adaptation Layer 5. Juha Heinanen. July 1993. (Format: TXT=35192 bytes) (Status: PROPOSED STANDARD)

1484 Using the OSI Directory to achieve User Friendly Naming (OSI-DS 24 (v1.2)). S. Hardcastle-Kille. July 1993. (Format: TXT=48974 bytes) (Obsoleted by RFC1781) (Updated by RFC1781) (Status: EXPERIMENTAL)

1485 A String Representation of Distinguished Names (OSI-DS 23 (v5)). S. Hardcastle-Kille. July 1993. (Format: TXT=11158 bytes) (Obsoleted by RFC1779) (Status: PROPOSED STANDARD)

1486 An Experiment in Remote Printing. M. Rose & C. Malamud. August 1993. (Format: TXT=26373 bytes) (Obsoleted by RFC1528, RFC1529) (Status: EXPERIMENTAL)

1487 X.500 Lightweight Directory Access Protocol. W. Yeong, T. Howes, & S. Kille. July 1993. (Format: TXT=44947 bytes) (Obsoleted by RFC1777) (Status: PROPOSED STANDARD)

1488 The X.500 String Representation of Standard Attribute Syntaxes. T. Howes, S. Kille, W. Yeong, & C. Robbins. July 1993. (Format: TXT=17182 bytes) (Obsoleted by RFC1778) (Status: PROPOSED STANDARD)

1489 Registration of a Cyrillic Character Set. A. Chernov. July 1993. (Format: TXT=7798 bytes) (Status: INFORMATIONAL)

1490 Multiprotocol Interconnect over Frame Relay. T. Bradley, C. Brown, & A. Malis. July 1993. (Format: TXT=75206 bytes) (Obsoletes RFC1294) (Obsoleted by RFC2427, STD0055) (Status: DRAFT STANDARD)

1491 A Survey of Advanced Usages of X.500. C. Weider & R. Wright. July 1993. (Format: TXT=34883 bytes) (Also FYI0021) (Status: INFORMATIONAL)

1492 An Access Control Protocol, Sometimes Called TACACS. C. Finseth. July 1993. (Format: TXT=41880 bytes) (Status: INFORMATIONAL)

1493 Definitions of Managed Objects for Bridges. E. Decker, P. Langille, A. Rijsinghani, & K. McCloghrie. July 1993. (Format: TXT=74493 bytes) (Obsoletes RFC1286) (Status: DRAFT STANDARD)

1494 Equivalences between 1988 X.400 and RFC-822 Message Bodies. H. Alvestrand & S. Thompson. August 1993. (Format: TXT=37273 bytes) (Status: PROPOSED STANDARD)

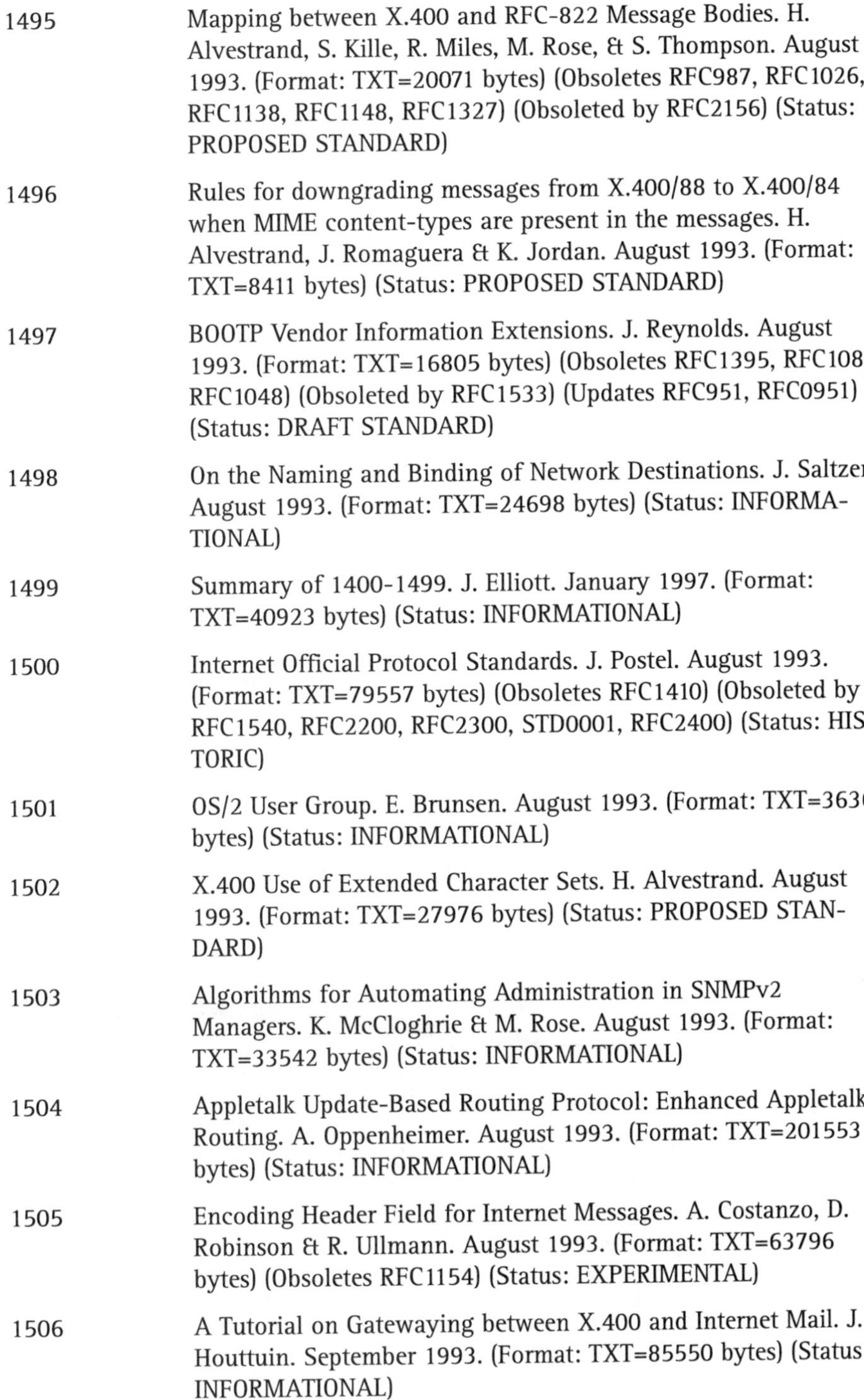

1495 Mapping between X.400 and RFC-822 Message Bodies. H. Alvestrand, S. Kille, R. Miles, M. Rose, & S. Thompson. August 1993. (Format: TXT=20071 bytes) (Obsoletes RFC987, RFC1026, RFC1138, RFC1148, RFC1327) (Obsoleted by RFC2156) (Status: PROPOSED STANDARD)

1496 Rules for downgrading messages from X.400/88 to X.400/84 when MIME content-types are present in the messages. H. Alvestrand, J. Romaguera & K. Jordan. August 1993. (Format: TXT=8411 bytes) (Status: PROPOSED STANDARD)

1497 BOOTP Vendor Information Extensions. J. Reynolds. August 1993. (Format: TXT=16805 bytes) (Obsoletes RFC1395, RFC1084, RFC1048) (Obsoleted by RFC1533) (Updates RFC951, RFC0951) (Status: DRAFT STANDARD)

1498 On the Naming and Binding of Network Destinations. J. Saltzer. August 1993. (Format: TXT=24698 bytes) (Status: INFORMATIONAL)

1499 Summary of 1400-1499. J. Elliott. January 1997. (Format: TXT=40923 bytes) (Status: INFORMATIONAL)

1500 Internet Official Protocol Standards. J. Postel. August 1993. (Format: TXT=79557 bytes) (Obsoletes RFC1410) (Obsoleted by RFC1540, RFC2200, RFC2300, STD0001, RFC2400) (Status: HISTORIC)

1501 OS/2 User Group. E. Brunsen. August 1993. (Format: TXT=3636 bytes) (Status: INFORMATIONAL)

1502 X.400 Use of Extended Character Sets. H. Alvestrand. August 1993. (Format: TXT=27976 bytes) (Status: PROPOSED STANDARD)

1503 Algorithms for Automating Administration in SNMPv2 Managers. K. McCloghrie & M. Rose. August 1993. (Format: TXT=33542 bytes) (Status: INFORMATIONAL)

1504 Appletalk Update-Based Routing Protocol: Enhanced Appletalk Routing. A. Oppenheimer. August 1993. (Format: TXT=201553 bytes) (Status: INFORMATIONAL)

1505 Encoding Header Field for Internet Messages. A. Costanzo, D. Robinson & R. Ullmann. August 1993. (Format: TXT=63796 bytes) (Obsoletes RFC1154) (Status: EXPERIMENTAL)

1506 A Tutorial on Gatewaying between X.400 and Internet Mail. J. Houttuin. September 1993. (Format: TXT=85550 bytes) (Status: INFORMATIONAL)

1507 DASS - Distributed Authentication Security Service. C. Kaufman. September 1993. (Format: TXT=287809 bytes) (Status: PROPOSED STANDARD)

1508 Generic Security Service Application Program Interface. J. Linn. September 1993. (Format: TXT=111228 bytes) (Obsoleted by RFC2078) (Status: PROPOSED STANDARD)

1509 Generic Security Service API : C-bindings. J. Wray. September 1993. (Format: TXT=99608 bytes) (Status: PROPOSED STANDARD)

1510 The Kerberos Network Authentication Service (V5). J. Kohl & C. Neuman. September 1993. (Format: TXT=275395 bytes) (Status: PROPOSED STANDARD)

1511 Common Authentication Technology Overview. J. Linn. September 1993. (Format: TXT=4185 bytes) (Status: INFORMATIONAL)

1512 FDDI Management Information Base. J. Case & A. Rijsinghani. September 1993. (Format: TXT=108589 bytes) (Updates RFC1285) (Status: PROPOSED STANDARD)

1513 Token Ring Extensions to the Remote Network Monitoring MIB. S. Waldbusser. September 1993. (Format: TXT=121974 bytes) (Updates 1271) (Status: PROPOSED STANDARD)

1514 Host Resources MIB. P. Grillo & S. Waldbusser. September 1993. (Format: TXT=63775 bytes) (Status: PROPOSED STANDARD)

1515 Definitions of Managed Objects for IEEE 802.3 Medium Attachment Units (MAUs). D. McMaster, K. McCloghrie & S. Roberts. September 1993. (Format: TXT=52828 bytes) (Status: PROPOSED STANDARD)

1516 Definitions of Managed Objects for IEEE 802.3 Repeater Devices. D. McMaster & K. McCloghrie. September 1993. (Format: TXT=82918 bytes) (Obsoletes RFC1368) (Obsoleted by RFC2108) (Status: DRAFT STANDARD)

1517 Applicability Statement for the Implementation of Classless Inter-Domain Routing (CIDR). Internet Engineering Steering Group, R. Hinden. September 1993. (Format: TXT=7357 bytes) (Status: PROPOSED STANDARD)

1518 An Architecture for IP Address Allocation with CIDR. Y. Rekhter & T. Li. September 1993. (Format: TXT=72609 bytes) (Status: PROPOSED STANDARD)

1519 Classless Inter-Domain Routing (CIDR): an Address Assignment and Aggregation Strategy. V. Fuller, T. Li, J. Yu, & K. Varadhan. September 1993. (Format: TXT=59998 bytes) (Obsoletes RFC1338) (Status: PROPOSED STANDARD)

1520 Exchanging Routing Information Across Provider Boundaries in the CIDR Environment. Y. Rekhter & C. Topolcic. September 1993. (Format: TXT=20389 bytes) (Status: INFORMATIONAL)

1521 MIME (Multipurpose Internet Mail Extensions) Part One: Mechanisms for Specifying and Describing the Format of Internet Message Bodies. N. Borenstein & N. Freed. September 1993. (Format: TXT=187424, PS=393670 bytes) (Obsoletes RFC1341) (Obsoleted by RFC2045, RFC2046, RFC2047, RFC2048, RFC2049, BCP0013) (Updated by RFC1590) (Status: DRAFT STANDARD)

1522 MIME (Multipurpose Internet Mail Extensions) Part Two: Message Header Extensions for Non-ASCII Text. K. Moore. September 1993. (Format: TXT=22502 bytes) (Obsoletes RFC1342) (Obsoleted by RFC2045, RFC2046, RFC2047, RFC2048, RFC2049, BCP0013) (Status: DRAFT STANDARD)

1523 The text/enriched MIME Content-type. N. Borenstein. September 1993. (Format: TXT=32691 bytes) (Obsoleted by RFC1563, RFC1896) (Status: INFORMATIONAL)

1524 A User Agent Configuration Mechanism For Multimedia Mail Format Information. N. Borenstein. September 1993. (Format: TXT=26464 bytes) (Status: INFORMATIONAL)

1525 Definitions of Managed Objects for Source Routing Bridges. E. Decker, K. McCloghrie, P. Langille & A. Rijsinghani. September 1993. (Format: TXT=38100 bytes) (Obsoletes RFC1286) (Status: PROPOSED STANDARD)

1526 Assignment of System Identifiers for TUBA/CLNP Hosts. D. Piscitello. September 1993. (Format: TXT=16848 bytes) (Status: INFORMATIONAL)

1527 What Should We Plan Given the Dilemma of the Network?. G. Cook. September 1993. (Format: TXT=46935 bytes) (Status: INFORMATIONAL)

1528 Principles of Operation for the TPC.INT Subdomain: Remote Printing – Technical Procedures. C. Malamud & M. Rose. October 1993. (Format: TXT=18576 bytes) (Obsoletes RFC1486) (Status: EXPERIMENTAL)

1529 Principles of Operation for the TPC.INT Subdomain: Remote Printing – Administrative Policies. C. Malamud & M. Rose. October 1993. (Format: TXT=11142 bytes) (Obsoletes RFC1486) (Status: INFORMATIONAL)

1530 Principles of Operation for the TPC.INT Subdomain: General Principles and Policy. C. Malamud & M. Rose. October 1993. (Format: TXT=15031 bytes) (Status: INFORMATIONAL)

1531 Dynamic Host Configuration Protocol. R. Droms. October 1993. (Format: TXT=96192 bytes) (Status: PROPOSED STANDARD)

1532 Clarifications and Extensions for the Bootstrap Protocol. W. Wimer. October 1993. (Format: TXT=51545 bytes) (Obsoleted by RFC1542) (Updates RFC0951) (Status: PROPOSED STANDARD)

1533 DHCP Options and BOOTP Vendor Extensions. S. Alexander & R. Droms. October 1993. (Format: TXT=50919 bytes) (Obsoletes RFC1497, RFC1395, RFC1084, RFC1048) (Obsoleted by RFC2132) (Status: PROPOSED STANDARD)

1534 Interoperation Between DHCP and BOOTP. R. Droms. October 1993. (Format: TXT=6966 bytes) (Status: DRAFT STANDARD)

1535 A Security Problem and Proposed Correction With Widely Deployed DNS Software. E. Gavron. October 1993. (Format: TXT=9722 bytes) (Status: INFORMATIONAL)

1536 Common DNS Implementation Errors and Suggested Fixes. A. Kumar, J. Postel, C. Neuman, P. Danzig & S. Miller. October 1993. (Format: TXT=25476 bytes) (Status: INFORMATIONAL)

1537 Common DNS Data File Configuration Errors. P. Beertema. October 1993. (Format: TXT=19825 bytes) (Obsoleted by RFC1912) (Status: INFORMATIONAL)

1538 Advanced SNA/IP : A Simple SNA Transport Protocol. W. Behl, B. Sterling & W. Teskey. October 1993. (Format: TXT=21217 bytes) (Status: INFORMATIONAL)

1539 The Tao of IETF - A Guide for New Attendees of the Internet Engineering Task Force. G. Malkin. October 1993. (Format: TXT=48199 bytes) (Obsoletes RFC1391) (Obsoleted by FYI0017, RFC1718) (Status: INFORMATIONAL)

1540 Internet Official Protocol Standards. J. Postel. October 1993. (Format: TXT=75496 bytes) (Obsoletes RFC1500) (Obsoleted by RFC1600, RFC2200, RFC2300, STD0001, RFC2400) (Also STD0001) (Status: HISTORIC)

1541 Dynamic Host Configuration Protocol. R. Droms. October 1993. (Format: TXT=96950 bytes) (Obsoletes RFC1531) (Obsoleted by RFC2131) (Status: PROPOSED STANDARD)

1542 Clarifications and Extensions for the Bootstrap Protocol. W. Wimer. October 1993. (Format: TXT=52948 bytes) (Obsoletes RFC1532) (Updates RFC0951) (Status: DRAFT STANDARD)

1543 Instructions to RFC Authors. J. Postel. October 1993. (Format: TXT=31383 bytes) (Obsoletes RFC1111, RFC0825) (Obsoleted by RFC2223) (Status: INFORMATIONAL)

1544 The Content-MD5 Header Field. M. Rose. November 1993. (Format: TXT=6478 bytes) (Obsoleted by RFC1864) (Status: PROPOSED STANDARD)

1545 FTP Operation Over Big Address Records (FOOBAR). D. Piscitello. November 1993. (Format: TXT=8985 bytes) (Obsoleted by RFC1639) (Status: EXPERIMENTAL)

1546 Host Anycasting Service. C. Partridge, T. Mendez, & W. Milliken. November 1993. (Format: TXT=22263 bytes) (Status: INFORMATIONAL)

1547 Requirements for an Internet Standard Point-to-Point Protocol. D. Perkins. December 1993. (Format: TXT=49810 bytes) (Status: INFORMATIONAL)

1548 The Point-to-Point Protocol (PPP). W. Simpson. December 1993. (Format: TXT=111638 bytes) (Obsoletes RFC1331) (Obsoleted by RFC1661) (Updated by RFC1570) (Status: DRAFT STANDARD)

1549 PPP in HDLC Framing. W. Simpson. December 1993. (Format: TXT=36352 bytes) (Obsoleted by RFC1662, STD0051) (Status: DRAFT STANDARD)

1550 IP: Next Generation (IPng) White Paper Solicitation. S. Bradner & A. Mankin. December 1993. (Format: TXT=12472 bytes) (Status: INFORMATIONAL)

1551 Novell IPX Over Various WAN Media (IPXWAN). M. Allen. December 1993. (Format: TXT=54210 bytes) (Obsoleted by RFC1634) (Status: INFORMATIONAL)

1552 The PPP Internetworking Packet Exchange Control Protocol (IPXCP). W. Simpson. December 1993. (Format: TXT=29173 bytes) (Status: PROPOSED STANDARD)

1553	Compressing IPX Headers Over WAN Media (CIPX). S. Mathur & M. Lewis. December 1993. (Format: TXT=47450 bytes) (Status: PROPOSED STANDARD)
1554	ISO-2022-JP-2: Multilingual Extension of ISO-2022-JP. M. Ohta & K. Handa. December 1993. (Format: TXT=11449 bytes) (Status: INFORMATIONAL)
1555	Hebrew Character Encoding for Internet Messages. H. Nussbacher & Y. Bourvine. December 1993. (Format: TXT=9273 bytes) (Status: INFORMATIONAL)
1556	Handling of Bi-directional Texts in MIME. H. Nussbacher. December 1993. (Format: TXT=5602 bytes) (Status: INFORMATIONAL)
1557	Korean Character Encoding for Internet Messages. U. Choi, K. Chon & H. Park. December 1993. (Format: TXT=8736 bytes) (Status: INFORMATIONAL)
1558	A String Representation of LDAP Search Filters. T. Howes. December 1993. (Format: TXT=5239 bytes) (Obsoleted by RFC1960) (Status: INFORMATIONAL)
1559	DECnet Phase IV MIB Extensions. J. Saperia. December 1993. (Format: TXT=125427 bytes) (Obsoletes RFC1289) (Status: DRAFT STANDARD)
1560	The MultiProtocol Internet. B. Leiner & Y. Rekhter. December 1993. (Format: TXT=16651 bytes) (Status: INFORMATIONAL)
1561	Use of ISO CLNP in TUBA Environments. D. Piscitello. December 1993. (Format: TXT=55902 bytes) (Status: EXPERIMENTAL)
1562	Naming Guidelines for the AARNet X.500 Directory Service. G. Michaelson & M. Prior. December 1993. (Format: TXT=6884 bytes) (Status: INFORMATIONAL)
1563	The text/enriched MIME Content-type. N. Borenstein. January 1994. (Format: TXT=32913, PS=73543 bytes) (Obsoletes RFC1523) (Obsoleted by RFC1896) (Status: INFORMATIONAL)
1564	DSA Metrics (OSI-DS 34 (v3)). P. Barker & R. Hedberg. January 1994. (Format: TXT=46205 bytes) (Status: INFORMATIONAL)
1565	Network Services Monitoring MIB. S. Kille & N. Freed. January 1994. (Format: TXT=29761 bytes) (Obsoleted by RFC2248) (Status: PROPOSED STANDARD)

1566 Mail Monitoring MIB. S. Kille & N. Freed. January 1994. (Format: TXT=33136 bytes) (Obsoleted by RFC2249) (Status: PROPOSED STANDARD)

1567 X.500 Directory Monitoring MIB. G. Mansfield & S. Kille. January 1994. (Format: TXT=33527 bytes) (Status: PROPOSED STANDARD)

1568 Simple Network Paging Protocol - Version 1(b). A. Gwinn. January 1994. (Format: TXT=16558 bytes) (Obsoleted by RFC1645) (Status: INFORMATIONAL)

1569 Principles of Operation for the TPC.INT Subdomain: Radio Paging – Technical Procedures. M. Rose. January 1994. (Format: TXT=12597 bytes) (Obsoleted by RFC1703) (Status: INFORMATIONAL)

1570 PPP LCP Extensions. W. Simpson. January 1994. (Format: TXT=35719 bytes) (Updates RFC1548) (Status: PROPOSED STANDARD)

1571 Telnet Environment Option Interoperability Issues. D. Borman. January 1994. (Format: TXT=8117 bytes) (Updates RFC1408) (Status: INFORMATIONAL)

1572 Telnet Environment Option. S. Alexander. January 1994. (Format: TXT=14676 bytes) (Status: PROPOSED STANDARD)

1573 Evolution of the Interfaces Group of MIB-II. K. McCloghrie, F. Kastenholz. January 1994. (Format: TXT=123057 bytes) (Obsoletes RFC1229, RFC1573) (Obsoleted by RFC1573, RFC2233) (Status: PROPOSED STANDARD)

1574 Essential Tools for the OSI Internet. S. Hares & C. Wittbrodt. February 1994. (Format: TXT=27735 bytes) (Obsoletes RFC1139) (Status: INFORMATIONAL)

1575 An Echo Function for CLNP (ISO 8473). S. Hares & C. Wittbrodt. February 1994. (Format: TXT=22479 bytes) (Obsoletes RFC1139) (Status: DRAFT STANDARD)

1576 TN3270 Current Practices. J. Penner. January 1994. (Format: TXT=24477 bytes) (Status: INFORMATIONAL)

1577 Classical IP and ARP over ATM. M. Laubach. January 1994. (Format: TXT=41239 bytes) (Obsoleted by RFC2225) (Status: PROPOSED STANDARD)

1578 FYI on Questions and Answers - Answers to Commonly Asked "Primary and Secondary School Internet User" Questions. J. Sellers. February 1994. (Format: TXT=113646 bytes) (Obsoleted by FYI0022, RFC1941) (Also FYI0022) (Status: INFORMATIONAL)

1579 Firewall-Friendly FTP. S. Bellovin. February 1994. (Format: TXT=8806 bytes) (Status: INFORMATIONAL)

1580 Guide to Network Resource Tools. EARN Staff. March 1994. (Format: TXT=235112 bytes) (Also FYI0023) (Status: INFORMATIONAL)

1581 Protocol Analysis for Extensions to RIP to Support Demand Circuits. G. Meyer. February 1994. (Format: TXT=7536 bytes) (Status: INFORMATIONAL)

1582 Extensions to RIP to Support Demand Circuits. G. Meyer. February 1994. (Format: TXT=63271 bytes) (Status: PROPOSED STANDARD)

1583 OSPF Version 2. J. Moy. March 1994. (Format: TXT=532636, PS=990794 bytes) (Obsoletes RFC1247) (Obsoleted by RFC2178) (Status: DRAFT STANDARD)

1584 Multicast Extensions to OSPF. J. Moy. March 1994. (Format: TXT=262463, PS=426358 bytes) (Status: PROPOSED STANDARD)

1585 MOSPF: Analysis and Experience. J. Moy. March 1994. (Format: TXT=29754 bytes) (Status: INFORMATIONAL)

1586 Guidelines for Running OSPF Over Frame Relay Networks. O. deSouza & M. Rodrigues. March 1994. (Format: TXT=14968 bytes) (Status: INFORMATIONAL)

1587 The OSPF NSSA Option. R. Coltun & V. Fuller. March 1994. (Format: TXT=37412 bytes) (Status: PROPOSED STANDARD)

1588 White Pages Meeting Report. J. Postel & C. Anderson. February 1994. (Format: TXT=77945 bytes) (Status: INFORMATIONAL)

1589 A Kernel Model for Precision Timekeeping. D. Mills. March 1994. (Format: TXT=88129 bytes) (Status: INFORMATIONAL)

1590 Media Type Registration Procedure. J. Postel. March 1994. (Format: TXT=13044 bytes) (Obsoleted by RFC2045, RFC2046, RFC2047, RFC2048, RFC2049, BCP0013) (Updates RFC1521) (Status: INFORMATIONAL)

1591 Domain Name System Structure and Delegation. J. Postel. March 1994. (Format: TXT=16481 bytes) (Status: INFORMATIONAL)

1592 Simple Network Management Protocol Distributed Protocol Interface Version 2.0. B. Wijnen, G. Carpenter, K. Curran, A. Sehgal, & G. Waters. March 1994. (Format: TXT=135259 bytes) (Obsoletes RFC1228) (Status: EXPERIMENTAL)

1593 SNA APPN Node MIB. W. McKenzie & J. Cheng. March 1994. (Format: TXT=207882 bytes) (Status: INFORMATIONAL)

1594 FYI on Questions and Answers - Answers to Commonly asked "New Internet User" Questions. A. Marine, J. Reynolds, & G. Malkin. March 1994. (Format: TXT=98753 bytes) (Obsoletes RFC1325) (Also FYI0004) (Status: INFORMATIONAL)

1595 Definitions of Managed Objects for the SONET/SDH Interface Type. T. Brown & K. Tesink. March 1994. (Format: TXT=121937 bytes) (Status: PROPOSED STANDARD)

1596 Definitions of Managed Objects for Frame Relay Service. T. Brown, Editor. March 1994. (Format: TXT=88795 bytes) (Obsoleted by RFC1604) (Status: PROPOSED STANDARD)

1597 Address Allocation for Private Internets. Y. Rekhter, B. Moskowitz, D. Karrenberg & G. de Groot. March 1994. (Format: TXT=17430 bytes) (Obsoleted by BCP0005, RFC1918) (Status: INFORMATIONAL)

1598 PPP in X.25. W. Simpson. March 1994. (Format: TXT=13835 bytes) (Status: PROPOSED STANDARD)

1599 Summary of 1500-1599. M. Kennedy. January 1997. (Format: TXT=43761 bytes) (Status: INFORMATIONAL)

1600 Internet Official Protocol Standards. J. Postel. March 1994. (Format: TXT=80958 bytes) (Obsoletes RFC1540) (Obsoleted by RFC1610, RFC2200, RFC2300, STD0001, RFC2400) (Status: HISTORIC)

1601 Charter of the Internet Architecture Board (IAB). C. Huitema. March 1994. (Format: TXT=12424 bytes) (Obsoletes RFC1358) (Status: INFORMATIONAL)

1602 The Internet Standards Process – Revision 2. Internet Architecture Board and Internet Engineering Steering Group. March 1994. (Format: TXT=88465 bytes) (Obsoletes RFC1310) (Obsoleted by RFC2026, BCP0009) (Updated by RFC1871, BCP0002) (Status: INFORMATIONAL)

1603 IETF Working Group Guidelines and Procedures. E. Huizer & D. Crocker. March 1994. (Format: TXT=63900 bytes) (Obsoleted by RFC2418, BCP0025) (Updated by RFC1871, BCP0002) (Status: INFORMATIONAL)

1604 Definitions of Managed Objects for Frame Relay Service. T. Brown, Editor. March 1994. (Format: TXT=88770 bytes) (Obsoletes RFC1596) (Status: PROPOSED STANDARD)

1605 SONET to Sonnet Translation. W. Shakespeare. 1 April 1994. (Format: TXT=4451 bytes) (Status: INFORMATIONAL)

1606 A Historical Perspective On The Usage Of IP Version 9. J. Onions. 1 April 1994. (Format: TXT=8398 bytes) (Status: INFORMATIONAL)

1607 A VIEW FROM THE 21ST CENTURY. V. Cerf. 1 April 1994. (Format: TXT=28165 bytes) (Status: INFORMATIONAL)

1608 Representing IP Information in the X.500 Directory. T. Johannsen, G. Mansfield, M. Kosters & S. Sataluri. March 1994. (Format: TXT=40269 bytes) (Status: EXPERIMENTAL)

1609 Charting Networks in the X.500 Directory. G. Mansfield, T. Johannsen & M. Knopper. March 1994. (Format: TXT=30044 bytes) (Status: EXPERIMENTAL)

1610 Internet Official Protocol Standards. J. Postel. July 1994. (Format: TXT=81346 bytes) (Obsoletes RFC1600) (Obsoleted by RFC1720, RFC2200, RFC2300, STD0001, RFC2400) (Also STD0001) (Status: HISTORIC)

1611 DNS Server MIB Extensions. R. Austein & J. Saperia. May 1994. (Format: TXT=58700 bytes) (Status: PROPOSED STANDARD)

1612 DNS Resolver MIB Extensions. R. Austein & J. Saperia. May 1994. (Format: TXT=61382 bytes) (Status: PROPOSED STANDARD)

1613 cisco Systems X.25 over TCP (XOT). J. Forster, G. Satz, G. Glick & R. Day. May 1994. (Format: TXT=29267 bytes) (Status: INFORMATIONAL)

1614 Network Access to Multimedia Information. C. Adie. May 1994. (Format: TXT=187253 bytes) (Status: INFORMATIONAL)

1615 Migrating from X.400(84) to X.400(88). J. Houttuin & J. Craigie. May 1994. (Format: TXT=39693 bytes) (Status: INFORMATIONAL)

1616 X.400(1988) for the Academic and Research Community in Europe. RARE WG-MSG Task Force 88, E. Huizer & J. Romaguera, Editors. May 1994. (Format: TXT=107432 bytes) (Status: INFORMATIONAL)

1617 Naming and Structuring Guidelines for X.500 Directory Pilots. P. Barker, S. Kille & T. Lenggenhager. May 1994. (Format: TXT=56739 bytes) (Obsoletes RFC1384) (Status: INFORMATIONAL)

1618 PPP over ISDN. W. Simpson. May 1994. (Format: TXT=14896 bytes) (Status: PROPOSED STANDARD)

1619 PPP over SONET/SDH. W. Simpson. May 1994. (Format: TXT=8893 bytes) (Status: PROPOSED STANDARD)

1620 Internet Architecture Extensions for Shared Media. B. Braden, J. Postel & Y. Rekhter. May 1994. (Format: TXT=44999 bytes) (Status: INFORMATIONAL)

1621 Pip Near-term Architecture. P. Francis. May 1994. (Format: TXT=128905 bytes) (Status: INFORMATIONAL)

1622 Pip Header Processing. P. Francis. May 1994. (Format: TXT=34837 bytes) (Status: INFORMATIONAL)

1623 Definitions of Managed Objects for the Ethernet-like Interface Types. F. Kastenholz. May 1994. (Format: TXT=38745 bytes) (Obsoletes RFC1398) (Obsoleted by RFC1643, STD0050) (Also STD0050) (Status: STANDARD)

1624 Computation of the Internet Checksum via Incremental Update. A. Rijsinghani, Editor. May 1994. (Format: TXT=9836 bytes) (Updates RFC1141) (Status: INFORMATIONAL)

1625 WAIS over Z39.50-1988. M. St. Pierre, J. Fullton, K. Gamiel, J. Goldman,B. Kahle, J. Kunze, H. Morris & F. Schiettecatte. June 1994. (Format: TXT=14694 bytes) (Status: INFORMATIONAL)

1626 Default IP MTU for use over ATM AAL5. R. Atkinson. May 1994. (Format: TXT=11841 bytes) (Obsoleted by RFC2225) (Status: PROPOSED STANDARD)

1627 Network 10 Considered Harmful (Some Practices Shouldn't be Codified). E. Lear, E. Fair, D. Crocker & T. Kessler. June 1994. (Format: TXT=18823 bytes) (Obsoleted by BCP0005, RFC1918) (Status: INFORMATIONAL)

1628 UPS Management Information Base. J. Case. May 1994. (Format: TXT=83439 bytes) (Status: PROPOSED STANDARD)

1629	Guidelines for OSI NSAP Allocation in the Internet. R. Colella, R. Callon, E. Gardner & Y. Rekhter. May 1994. (Format: TXT=131640 bytes) (Obsoletes RFC1237) (Status: DRAFT STANDARD)
1630	Universal Resource Identifiers in WWW: A Unifying Syntax for the Expression of Names and Addresses of Objects on the Network as used in the World-Wide Web. T. Berners-Lee. June 1994. (Format: TXT=57601 bytes) (Status: INFORMATIONAL)
1631	The IP Network Address Translator (NAT). K. Egevang & P. Francis. May 1994. (Format: TXT=22714 bytes) (Status: INFORMATIONAL)
1632	A Revised Catalog of Available X.500 Implementations. A. Getchell & S. Sataluri, Editors. May 1994. (Format: TXT=124111 bytes) (Obsoletes RFC1292) (Obsoleted by RFC2116, FYI0011) (Also FYI0011) (Status: INFORMATIONAL)
1633	Integrated Services in the Internet Architecture: an Overview. R. Braden, D. Clark & S. Shenker. June 1994. (Format: TXT=89691, PS=207016 bytes) (Status: INFORMATIONAL)
1634	Novell IPX Over Various WAN Media (IPXWAN). M. Allen. May 1994. (Format: TXT=55347 bytes) (Obsoletes RFC1551, RFC1362) (Status: INFORMATIONAL)
1635	How to Use Anonymous FTP. P. Deutsch, A. Emtage & A. Marine. May 1994. (Format: TXT=27258 bytes) (Also FYI0024) (Status: INFORMATIONAL)
1636	Report of IAB Workshop on Security in the Internet Architecture - February 8-10, 1994. R. Braden, D. Clark, S. Crocker & C. Huitema. June 1994. (Format: TXT=130761 bytes) (Status: INFORMATIONAL)
1637	DNS NSAP Resource Records. B. Manning & R. Colella. June 1994. (Format: TXT=21768 bytes) (Obsoletes RFC1348) (Obsoleted by RFC1706) (Updates RFC1348) (Status: EXPERIMENTAL)
1638	PPP Bridging Control Protocol (BCP). F. Baker & R. Bowen. June 1994. (Format: TXT=58477 bytes) (Obsoletes RFC1220) (Status: PROPOSED STANDARD)
1639	FTP Operation Over Big Address Records (FOOBAR). D. Piscitello. June 1994. (Format: TXT=10055 bytes) (Obsoletes RFC1545) (Status: EXPERIMENTAL)

1640 The Process for Organization of Internet Standards Working Group (POISED). S. Crocker. June 1994. (Format: TXT=21780 bytes) (Status: INFORMATIONAL)

1641 Using Unicode with MIME. D. Goldsmith & M. Davis. July 1994. (Format: TXT=11258, PS=20451 bytes) (Status: EXPERIMENTAL)

1642 UTF-7 - A Mail-Safe Transformation Format of Unicode. D. Goldsmith & M. Davis. July 1994. (Format: TXT=27770, PS=50907 bytes) (Obsoleted by RFC2152) (Status: EXPERIMENTAL)

1643 Definitions of Managed Objects for the Ethernet-like Interface Types. F. Kastenholz. July 1994. (Format: TXT=39008 bytes) (Obsoletes RFC1623, RFC1398) (Also STD0050) (Status: STANDARD)

1644 T/TCP – TCP Extensions for Transactions Functional Specification. R. Braden. July 1994. (Format: TXT=87362 bytes) (Status: EXPERIMENTAL)

1645 Simple Network Paging Protocol - Version 2. A. Gwinn. July 1994. (Format: TXT=31243 bytes) (Obsoletes RFC1568) (Obsoleted by RFC1861, RFC1863) (Status: INFORMATIONAL)

1646 TN3270 Extensions for LUname and Printer Selection. C. Graves, T. Butts & M. Angel. July 1994. (Format: TXT=27564 bytes) (Status: INFORMATIONAL)

1647 TN3270 Enhancements. B. Kelly. July 1994. (Format: TXT=84420 bytes) (Obsoleted by RFC2355) (Status: PROPOSED STANDARD)

1648 Postmaster Convention for X.400 Operations. A. Cargille. July 1994. (Format: TXT=8761 bytes) (Status: PROPOSED STANDARD)

1649 Operational Requirements for X.400 Management Domains in the GO-MHS Community. R. Hagens & A. Hansen. July 1994. (Format: TXT=28138 bytes) (Status: INFORMATIONAL)

1650 Definitions of Managed Objects for the Ethernet-like Interface Types using SMIv2. F. Kastenholz. August 1994. (Format: TXT=40484 bytes) (Obsoleted by RFC2357, RFC2358) (Status: PROPOSED STANDARD)

1651 SMTP Service Extensions. Klensin, N. Freed, M. Rose, E. Stefferud & D. Crocker. July 1994. (Format: TXT=22153 bytes) (Obsoletes RFC1425) (Obsoleted by RFC1869, STD0010) (Status: DRAFT STANDARD)

1652 SMTP Service Extension for 8bit-MIMEtransport. Klensin, N. Freed, M. Rose, E. Stefferud & D. Crocker. July 1994. (Format: TXT=11842 bytes) (Obsoletes RFC1426) (Status: DRAFT STANDARD)

1653 SMTP Service Extension for Message Size Declaration. J. Klensin, N. Freed & K. Moore. July 1994. (Format: TXT=17883 bytes) (Obsoletes RFC1427) (Obsoleted by RFC1870, STD0011) (Also STD0011) (Status: DRAFT STANDARD)

1654 A Border Gateway Protocol 4 (BGP-4). Y. Rekhter & T. Li, Editors. July 1994. (Format: TXT=130118 bytes) (Obsoleted by RFC1771) (Status: PROPOSED STANDARD)

1655 Application of the Border Gateway Protocol in the Internet. Y. Rekhter & P. Gross, Editors. July 1994. (Format: TXT=43664 bytes) (Obsoletes RFC1268) (Obsoleted by RFC1772) (Status: PROPOSED STANDARD)

1656 BGP-4 Protocol Document Roadmap and Implementation Experience. P. Traina. July 1994. (Format: TXT=7705 bytes) (Obsoleted by RFC1773) (Status: PROPOSED STANDARD)

1657 Definitions of Managed Objects for the Fourth Version of the Border Gateway Protocol (BGP-4) using SMIv2. S. Willis, J. Burruss, J. Chu, Editor. July 1994. (Format: TXT=45505 bytes) (Status: DRAFT STANDARD)

1658 Definitions of Managed Objects for Character Stream Devices using SMIv2. B. Stewart. July 1994. (Format: TXT=32579 bytes) (Obsoletes RFC1316) (Status: DRAFT STANDARD)

1659 Definitions of Managed Objects for RS-232-like Hardware Devices using SMIv2. B. Stewart. July 1994. (Format: TXT=36479 bytes) (Obsoletes RFC1317) (Status: DRAFT STANDARD)

1660 Definitions of Managed Objects for Parallel-printer-like Hardware Devices using SMIv2. B. Stewart. July 1994. (Format: TXT=16784 bytes) (Obsoletes RFC1318) (Status: DRAFT STANDARD)

1661 The Point-to-Point Protocol (PPP). W. Simpson, Editor. July 1994. (Format: TXT=103026 bytes) (Obsoletes RFC1548) (Updated by RFC2153) (Also STD0051) (Status: STANDARD)

1662 PPP in HDLC-like Framing. W. Simpson, Editor. July 1994. (Format: TXT=48058 bytes) (Obsoletes RFC1549) (Also STD0051) (Status: STANDARD)

1663 PPP Reliable Transmission. D. Rand. July 1994. (Format: TXT=17281 bytes) (Status: PROPOSED STANDARD)

1664 Using the Internet DNS to Distribute RFC1327 Mail Address Mapping Tables. C. Allocchio, A. Bonito, B. Cole, S. Giordano & R. Hagens. August 1994. (Format: TXT=50783 bytes) (Obsoleted by RFC2163) (Status: EXPERIMENTAL)

1665 Definitions of Managed Objects for SNA NAUs using SMIv2. Z. Kielczewski, D. Kostick & K. Shih, Editors. July 1994. (Format: TXT=133381 bytes) (Obsoleted by RFC1666) (Status: PROPOSED STANDARD)

1666 Definitions of Managed Objects for SNA NAUs using SMIv2. Z. Kielczewski, D. Kostick & Shih, Editors. August 1994. (Format: TXT=134385 bytes) (Obsoletes RFC1665) (Status: PROPOSED STANDARD)

1667 Modeling and Simulation Requirements for IPng. S. Symington, D. Wood & M. Pullen. August 1994. (Format: TXT=17291 bytes) (Status: INFORMATIONAL)

1668 Unified Routing Requirements for IPng. D. Estrin, T. Li & Y. Rekhter. August 1994. (Format: TXT=5106 bytes) (Status: INFORMATIONAL)

1669 Market Viability as a IPng Criteria. J. Curran. August 1994. (Format: TXT=8099 bytes) (Status: INFORMATIONAL)

1670 Input to IPng Engineering Considerations. D. Heagerty. August 1994. (Format: TXT=5350 bytes) (Status: INFORMATIONAL)

1671 IPng White Paper on Transition and Other Considerations. B. Carpenter. August 1994. (Format: TXT=17631 bytes) (Status: INFORMATIONAL)

1672 Accounting Requirements for IPng. N. Brownlee. August 1994. (Format: TXT=6185 bytes) (Status: INFORMATIONAL)

1673 Electric Power Research Institute Comments on IPng. R. Skelton. August 1994. (Format: TXT=7476 bytes) (Status: INFORMATIONAL)

1674 A Cellular Industry View of IPng. M. Taylor. August 1994. (Format: TXT=6157 bytes) (Status: INFORMATIONAL)

1675 Security Concerns for IPng. S. Bellovin. August 1994. (Format: TXT=8290 bytes) (Status: INFORMATIONAL)

1676 INFN Requirements for an IPng. A. Ghiselli, D. Salomoni & C. Vistoli. August 1994. (Format: TXT=8493 bytes) (Status: INFORMATIONAL)

1677 Tactical Radio Frequency Communication Requirements for IPng. B. Adamson. August 1994. (Format: TXT=24065 bytes) (Status: INFORMATIONAL)

1678 IPng Requirements of Large Corporate Networks. E. Britton & J. Tavs. August 1994. (Format: TXT=18650 bytes) (Status: INFORMATIONAL)

1679 HPN Working Group Input to the IPng Requirements Solicitation. D. Green, P. Irey, D. Marlow & K. O'Donoghue. August 1994. (Format: TXT=22974 bytes) (Status: INFORMATIONAL)

1680 IPng Support for ATM Services. C. Brazdziunas. August 1994. (Format: TXT=17846 bytes) (Status: INFORMATIONAL)

1681 On Many Addresses per Host. S. Bellovin. August 1994. (Format: TXT=11964 bytes) (Status: INFORMATIONAL)

1682 IPng BSD Host Implementation Analysis. J. Bound. August 1994. (Format: TXT=22295 bytes) (Status: INFORMATIONAL)

1683 Multiprotocol Interoperability In IPng. R. Clark, M. Ammar & K. Calvert. August 1994. (Format: TXT=28201 bytes) (Status: INFORMATIONAL)

1684 Introduction to White Pages Services based on X.500. P. Jurg. August 1994. (Format: TXT=22985 bytes) (Status: INFORMATIONAL)

1685 Writing X.400 O/R Names. H. Alvestrand. August 1994. (Format: TXT=21242 bytes) (Also RTR0012) (Status: INFORMATIONAL)

1686 IPng Requirements: A Cable Television Industry Viewpoint. M. Vecchi. August 1994. (Format: TXT=39052 bytes) (Status: INFORMATIONAL)

1687 A Large Corporate User's View of IPng. E. Fleischman. August 1994. (Format: TXT=34120 bytes) (Status: INFORMATIONAL)

1688 IPng Mobility Considerations. W. Simpson. August 1994. (Format: TXT=19151 bytes) (Status: INFORMATIONAL)

1689 A Status Report on Networked Information Retrieval: Tools and Groups. J. Foster. August 1994. (Format: TXT=375469 bytes) (Also FYI0025, RTR0013) (Status: INFORMATIONAL)

1690 Introducing the Internet Engineering and Planning Group (IEPG). G. Huston. August 1994. (Format: TXT=3013 bytes) (Status: INFORMATIONAL)

1691 The Document Architecture for the Cornell Digital Library. W. Turner. August 1994. (Format: TXT=20438 bytes) (Status: INFORMATIONAL)

1692 Transport Multiplexing Protocol (TMux). P. Cameron, D. Crocker, D. Cohen & J. Postel. August 1994. (Format: TXT=26163 bytes) (Status: PROPOSED STANDARD)

1693 An Extension to TCP : Partial Order Service. T. Connolly, P. Amer & P. Conrad. November 1994. (Format: TXT=90100 bytes) (Status: EXPERIMENTAL)

1694 Definitions of Managed Objects for SMDS Interfaces using SMIv2. T. Brown & K. Tesink, Editors. August 1994. (Format: TXT=70856 bytes) (Obsoletes RFC1304) (Status: DRAFT STANDARD)

1695 Definitions of Managed Objects for ATM Management Version 8.0 using SMIv2. M. Ahmed & K. Tesink, Editors. August 1994. (Format: TXT=175461 bytes) (Status: PROPOSED STANDARD)

1696 Modem Management Information Base (MIB) using SMIv2. J. Barnes, L. Brown, R. Royston & S. Waldbusser. August 1994. (Format: TXT=54054 bytes) (Status: PROPOSED STANDARD)

1697 Relational Database Management System (RDBMS) Management Information Base (MIB) using SMIv2. D. Brower, Editor, B. Purvy, RDBMSMIB Working Group Chair, A. Daniel, M. Sinykin & J. Smith. August 1994. (Format: TXT=76202 bytes) (Status: PROPOSED STANDARD)

1698 Octet Sequences for Upper-Layer OSI to Support Basic Communications Applications. P. Furniss. October 1994. (Format: TXT=67433 bytes) (Status: INFORMATIONAL)

1699 Summary of 1600-1699. J. Elliott. January 1997. (Format: TXT=40674 bytes) (Status: INFORMATIONAL)

1700 ASSIGNED NUMBERS. J. Reynolds,J. Postel. October 1994. (Format: TXT=458860 bytes) (Obsoletes RFC1340) (Also STD0002) (Status: STANDARD)

1701 Generic Routing Encapsulation (GRE). S. Hanks, T. Li, D. Farinacci, P. Traina. October 1994. (Format: TXT=15460 bytes) (Status: INFORMATIONAL)

1702 Generic Routing Encapsulation over IPv4 networks. S. Hanks, T. Li, D. Farinacci, P. Traina. October 1994. (Format: TXT=7288 bytes) (Status: INFORMATIONAL)

1703	Principles of Operation for the TPC.INT Subdomain: Radio Paging – Technical Procedures. M. Rose. October 1994. (Format: TXT=17985 bytes) (Obsoletes RFC1569) (Status: INFORMATIONAL)
1704	On Internet Authentication. N. Haller & R. Atkinson. October 1994. (Format: TXT=42269 bytes) (Status: INFORMATIONAL)
1705	Six Virtual Inches to the Left: The Problem with IPng. R. Carlson & D. Ficarella. October 1994. (Format: TXT=65222 bytes) (Status: INFORMATIONAL)
1706	DNS NSAP Resource Records. B. Manning & R. Colella. October 1994. (Format: TXT=19721 bytes) (Obsoletes RFC1637) (Status: INFORMATIONAL)
1707	CATNIP: Common Architecture for the Internet. M. McGovern & R. Ullmann. October 1994. (Format: TXT=37568 bytes) (Status: INFORMATIONAL)
1708	NTP PICS PROFORMA - For the Network Time Protocol Version 3. D. Gowin. October 1994. (Format: TXT=26523 bytes) (Status: INFORMATIONAL)
1709	K-12 Internetworking Guidelines. J. Gargano, D. Wasley. November 1994. (Format: TXT=66659, PS=662030 bytes) (Also FYI0026) (Status: INFORMATIONAL)
1710	Simple Internet Protocol Plus White Paper. R. Hinden. October 1994. (Format: TXT=56910 bytes) (Status: INFORMATIONAL)
1711	Classifications in E-mail Routing. J. Houttuin. October 1994. (Format: TXT=47584 bytes) (Status: INFORMATIONAL)
1712	DNS Encoding of Geographical Location. C. Farrell, M. Schulze, S. Pleitner & D. Baldoni. November 1994. (Format: TXT=13237 bytes) (Status: EXPERIMENTAL)
1713	Tools for DNS debugging. A. Romao. November 1994. (Format: TXT=33500 bytes) (Also FYI0027) (Status: INFORMATIONAL)
1714	Referral Whois Protocol (RWhois). S. Williamson & M. Kosters. November 1994. (Format: TXT=85395, PS=204207 bytes) (Obsoleted by RFC2167) (Status: INFORMATIONAL)
1715	The H Ratio for Address Assignment Efficiency. C. Huitema. November 1994. (Format: TXT=7392 bytes) (Status: INFORMATIONAL)

1716 Towards Requirements for IP Routers. P. Almquist, F. Kastenholz. November 1994. (Format: TXT=432330 bytes) (Obsoleted by RFC1812) (Status: INFORMATIONAL)

1717 The PPP Multilink Protocol (MP). K. Sklower, B. Lloyd, G. McGregor & D. Carr. November 1994. (Format: TXT=46264 bytes) (Obsoleted by RFC1990) (Status: PROPOSED STANDARD)

1718 The Tao of IETF - A Guide for New Attendees of the Internet Engineering Task Force. The IETF Secretariat & G. Malkin. November 1994. (Format: TXT=50477 bytes) (Obsoletes RFC1539) (Also FYI0017) (Status: INFORMATIONAL)

1719 A Direction for IPng. P. Gross. December 1994. (Format: TXT=11118 bytes) (Status: INFORMATIONAL)

1720 Internet Official Protocol Standards. J. Postel. November 1994. (Format: TXT=89063 bytes) (Obsoletes RFC1610) (Obsoleted by RFC1780, STD0001, RFC1880, RFC1920, RFC2200, RFC2300, RFC2400) (Also STD0001) (Status: HISTORIC)

1721 RIP Version 2 Protocol Analysis. G. Malkin. November 1994. (Format: TXT=6680 bytes) (Obsoletes RFC1387) (Status: INFORMATIONAL)

1722 RIP Version 2 Protocol Applicability Statement. G. Malkin. November 1994. (Format: TXT=10236 bytes) (Status: DRAFT STANDARD)

1723 RIP Version 2 - Carrying Additional Information. G. Malkin. November 1994. (Format: TXT=18597 bytes) (Obsoletes RFC1388) (Updates RFC1058) (Status: DRAFT STANDARD)

1724 RIP Version 2 MIB Extension. G. Malkin & F. Baker. November 1994. (Format: TXT=29645 bytes) (Obsoletes RFC1389) (Status: DRAFT STANDARD)

1725 Post Office Protocol - Version 3. J. Myers & M. Rose. November 1994. (Format: TXT=35058 bytes) (Obsoletes RFC1460) (Obsoleted by RFC1939, STD0053) (Status: DRAFT STANDARD)

1726 Technical Criteria for Choosing IP The Next Generation (IPng). C. Partridge & F. Kastenholz. December 1994. (Format: TXT=74109 bytes) (Status: INFORMATIONAL)

1727 A Vision of an Integrated Internet Information Service. C. Weider & P. Deutsch. December 1994. (Format: TXT=28468 bytes) (Status: INFORMATIONAL)

1728	Resource Transponders. C. Weider. December 1994. (Format: TXT=12092 bytes) (Status: INFORMATIONAL)
1729	Using the Z39.50 Information Retrieval Protocol. C. Lynch. December 1994. (Format: TXT=20927 bytes) (Status: INFORMATIONAL)
1730	INTERNET MESSAGE ACCESS PROTOCOL - VERSION 4. M. Crispin. December 1994. (Format: TXT=156660 bytes) (Obsoleted by RFC2060, RFC2061) (Status: PROPOSED STANDARD)
1731	IMAP4 Authentication Mechanisms. J. Myers. December 1994. (Format: TXT=11433 bytes) (Status: PROPOSED STANDARD)
1732	IMAP4 COMPATIBILITY WITH IMAP2 AND IMAP2BIS. M. Crispin. December 1994. (Format: TXT=9276 bytes) (Status: INFORMATIONAL)
1733	DISTRIBUTED ELECTRONIC MAIL MODELS IN IMAP4. M. Crispin. December 1994. (Format: TXT=6205 bytes) (Status: INFORMATIONAL)
1734	POP3 AUTHentication command. J. Myers. December 1994. (Format: TXT=8499 bytes) (Status: PROPOSED STANDARD)
1735	NBMA Address Resolution Protocol (NARP). J. Heinanen & R. Govindan. December 1994. (Format: TXT=24485 bytes) (Status: EXPERIMENTAL)
1736	Functional Recommendations for Internet Resource Locators. J. Kunze. February 1995. (Format: TXT=22415 bytes) (Status: INFORMATIONAL)
1737	Functional Requirements for Uniform Resource Names. K. Sollins & L. Masinter. December 1994. (Format: TXT=16337 bytes) (Status: INFORMATIONAL)
1738	Uniform Resource Locators (URL). T. Berners-Lee, L. Masinter & M. McCahill. December 1994. (Format: TXT=51348 bytes) (Updated by RFC1808, RFC2368) (Status: PROPOSED STANDARD)
1739	A Primer On Internet and TCP/IP Tools. G. Kessler & S. Shepard. December 1994. (Format: TXT=102676 bytes) (Obsoleted by RFC2151, FYI0030) (Status: INFORMATIONAL)
1740	MIME Encapsulation of Macintosh Files - MacMIME. P. Faltstrom, D. Crocker & E. Fair. December 1994. (Format: TXT=31297 bytes) (Status: PROPOSED STANDARD)

1741 MIME Content Type for BinHex Encoded Files. P. Faltstrom, D. Crocker & E. Fair. December 1994. (Format: TXT=10155 bytes) (Status: INFORMATIONAL)

1742 AppleTalk Management Information Base II. S. Waldbusser & K. Frisa. January 1995. (Format: TXT=168306 bytes) (Obsoletes RFC1243) (Status: PROPOSED STANDARD)

1743 IEEE 802.5 MIB using SMIv2. K. McCloghrie, E. Decker. December 1994. (Format: TXT=43224 bytes) (Obsoletes RFC1231) (Obsoleted by RFC1748) (Status: DRAFT STANDARD)

1744 Observations on the Management of the Internet Address Space. G. Huston. December 1994. (Format: TXT=32411 bytes) (Status: INFORMATIONAL)

1745 BGP4/IDRP for IP--OSPF Interaction. K. Varadhan, S. Hares, Y. Rekhter. December 1994. (Format: TXT=43675 bytes) (Status: PROPOSED STANDARD)

1746 Ways to Define User Expectations. B. Manning & D. Perkins. December 1994. (Format: TXT=46164 bytes) (Status: INFORMATIONAL)

1747 Definitions of Managed Objects for SNA Data Link Control (SDLC) using SMIv2. J. Hilgeman, Chair, S. Nix, A. Bartky, & W. Clark, Editor. January 1995. (Format: TXT=147388 bytes) (Status: PROPOSED STANDARD)

1748 IEEE 802.5 MIB using SMIv2. K. McCloghrie & E. Decker. December 1994. (Format: TXT=43224 bytes) (Obsoletes RFC1743, RFC1231) (Updated by RFC1749) (Status: DRAFT STANDARD)

1749 IEEE 802.5 Station Source Routing MIB using SMIv2. K. McCloghrie, F. Baker & E. Decker. December 1994. (Format: TXT=17563 bytes) (Updates RFC1748) (Status: PROPOSED STANDARD)

1750 Randomness Recommendations for Security. D. Eastlake, 3rd, S. Crocker & J. Schiller. December 1994. (Format: TXT=73842 bytes) (Status: INFORMATIONAL)

1751 A Convention for Human-Readable 128-bit Keys. D. McDonald. December 1994. (Format: TXT=31428 bytes) (Status: INFORMATIONAL)

1752 The Recommendation for the IP Next Generation Protocol. S. Bradner & A. Mankin. January 1995. (Format: TXT=127784 bytes) (Status: PROPOSED STANDARD)

1753 IPng Technical Requirements Of the Nimrod Routing and Addressing Architecture. N. Chiappa. December 1994. (Format: TXT=46586 bytes) (Status: INFORMATIONAL)

1754 IP over ATM Working Group's Recommendations for the ATM Forum's Multiprotocol BOF Version 1. M. Laubach. January 1995. (Format: TXT=13483 bytes) (Status: INFORMATIONAL)

1755 ATM Signaling Support for IP over ATM. M. Perez, F. Liaw, D. Grossman, A. Mankin, E. Hoffman & A. Malis. February 1995. (Format: TXT=55209 bytes) (Status: PROPOSED STANDARD)

1756 REMOTE WRITE PROTOCOL - VERSION 1.0. T. Rinne. January 1995. (Format: TXT=22078 bytes) (Status: EXPERIMENTAL)

1757 Remote Network Monitoring Management Information Base. S. Waldbusser. February 1995. (Format: TXT=208117 bytes) (Obsoletes RFC1271) (Status: DRAFT STANDARD)

1758 NADF Standing Documents: A Brief Overview. The North American Directory Forum. February 1995. (Format: TXT=7294 bytes) (Obsoletes RFC1417) (Status: INFORMATIONAL)

1759 Printer MIB. R. Smith, F. Wright, T. Hastings, S. Zilles & J. Gyllenskog. March 1995. (Format: TXT=239228 bytes) (Status: PROPOSED STANDARD)

1760 The S/KEY One-Time Password System. N. Haller. February 1995. (Format: TXT=31124 bytes) (Status: INFORMATIONAL)

1761 Snoop Version 2 Packet Capture File Format. B. Callaghan & R. Gilligan. February 1995. (Format: TXT=10761 bytes) (Status: INFORMATIONAL)

1762 The PPP DECnet Phase IV Control Protocol (DNCP). S. Senum. March 1995. (Format: TXT=12709 bytes) (Obsoletes RFC1376) (Status: DRAFT STANDARD)

1763 The PPP Banyan Vines Control Protocol (BVCP). S. Senum. March 1995. (Format: TXT=17817 bytes) (Status: PROPOSED STANDARD)

1764 The PPP XNS IDP Control Protocol (XNSCP). S. Senum. March 1995. (Format: TXT=9525 bytes) (Status: PROPOSED STANDARD)

1765 OSPF Database Overflow. J. Moy. March 1995. (Format: TXT=21613 bytes) (Status: EXPERIMENTAL)

1766 Tags for the Identification of Languages. H. Alvestrand. March 1995. (Format: TXT=16966 bytes) (Status: PROPOSED STANDARD)

1767 MIME Encapsulation of EDI Objects. D. Crocker. March 1995. (Format: TXT=15293 bytes) (Status: PROPOSED STANDARD)

1768 Host Group Extensions for CLNP Multicasting. D. Marlow. March 1995. (Format: TXT=111499 bytes) (Status: EXPERIMENTAL)

1769 Simple Network Time Protocol (SNTP). D. Mills. March 1995. (Format: TXT=34454 bytes) (Obsoletes RFC1361) (Obsoleted by RFC2030) (Status: INFORMATIONAL)

1770 IPv4 Option for Sender Directed Multi-Destination Delivery. C. Graff. March 1995. (Format: TXT=11606 bytes) (Status: INFORMATIONAL)

1771 A Border Gateway Protocol 4 (BGP-4). Y. Rekhter & T. Li. March 1995. (Format: TXT=131903 bytes) (Obsoletes RFC1654) (Status: DRAFT STANDARD)

1772 Application of the Border Gateway Protocol in the Internet. Y. Rekhter & P. Gross. March 1995. (Format: TXT=43916 bytes) (Obsoletes RFC1655) (Status: DRAFT STANDARD)

1773 Experience with the BGP-4 protocol. P. Traina. March 1995. (Format: TXT=19936 bytes) (Obsoletes RFC1656) (Status: INFORMATIONAL)

1774 BGP-4 Protocol Analysis. P. Traina, Editor. March 1995. (Format: TXT=23823 bytes) (Status: INFORMATIONAL)

1775 To Be “On” the Internet. D. Crocker. March 1995. (Format: TXT=8454 bytes) (Status: INFORMATIONAL)

1776 The Address is the Message. S. Crocker. March 1995. (Format: TXT=2051 bytes) (Status: INFORMATIONAL)

1777 Lightweight Directory Access Protocol. W. Yeong, T. Howes & S. Kille. March 1995. (Format: TXT=45459 bytes) (Obsoletes RFC1487) (Status: DRAFT STANDARD)

1778 The String Representation of Standard Attribute Syntaxes. T. Howes, S. Kille, W. Yeong & C. Robbins. March 1995. (Format: TXT=19053 bytes) (Obsoletes RFC1488) (Status: DRAFT STANDARD)

1779 A String Representation of Distinguished Names. S. Kille. March 1995. (Format: TXT=12429 bytes) (Obsoletes RFC1485) (Status: DRAFT STANDARD)

1780 INTERNET OFFICIAL PROTOCOL STANDARDS. J. Postel, Editor. March 1995. (Format: TXT=86594 bytes) (Obsoletes RFC1720) (Obsoleted by RFC1800, STD0001, RFC1880, RFC1920, RFC2200, RFC2300, RFC2400) (Also STD0001) (Status: HISTORIC)

1781 Using the OSI Directory to Achieve User Friendly Naming. S. Kille. March 1995. (Format: TXT=47129 bytes) (Obsoletes RFC1484) (Updates RFC1484) (Status: PROPOSED STANDARD)

1782 TFTP Option Extension. G. Malkin & A. Harkin. March 1995. (Format: TXT=11508 bytes) (Obsoleted by RFC2347) (Updates RFC1350) (Status: PROPOSED STANDARD)

1783 TFTP Blocksize Option. G. Malkin & A. Harkin. March 1995. (Format: TXT=7814 bytes) (Obsoleted by RFC2348) (Updates RFC1350) (Updated by RFC1350) (Status: PROPOSED STANDARD)

1784 TFTP Timeout Interval and Transfer Size Options. G. Malkin & A. Harkin. March 1995. (Format: TXT=6106 bytes) (Obsoleted by RFC2349) (Updates RFC1350) (Status: PROPOSED STANDARD)

1785 TFTP Option Negotiation Analysis. G. Malkin & A. Harkin. March 1995. (Format: TXT=3354 bytes) (Updates RFC1350) (Status: INFORMATIONAL)

1786 Representation of IP Routing Policies in a Routing Registry (ripe-81++). T. Bates, E. Gerich, L. Joncheray, J-M. Jouanigot, D. Karrenberg, M. Terpstra, & J. Yu. March 1995. (Format: TXT=133643 bytes) (Status: INFORMATIONAL)

1787 Routing in a Multi-provider Internet. Y. Rekhter. April 1995. (Format: TXT=20754 bytes) (Status: INFORMATIONAL)

1788 ICMP Domain Name Messages. W. Simpson. April 1995. (Format: TXT=11722 bytes) (Status: EXPERIMENTAL)

1789 INETPhone: Telephone Services and Servers on Internet. C. Yang. April 1995. (Format: TXT=14186 bytes) (Status: INFORMATIONAL)

1790 An Agreement between the Internet Society and Sun Microsystems, Inc. in the Matter of ONC RPC and XDR Protocols. V. Cerf. April 1995. (Format: TXT=8226 bytes) (Status: INFORMATIONAL)

1791 TCP And UDP Over IPX Networks With Fixed Path MTU. T. Sung. April 1995. (Format: TXT=22347 bytes) (Status: EXPERIMENTAL)

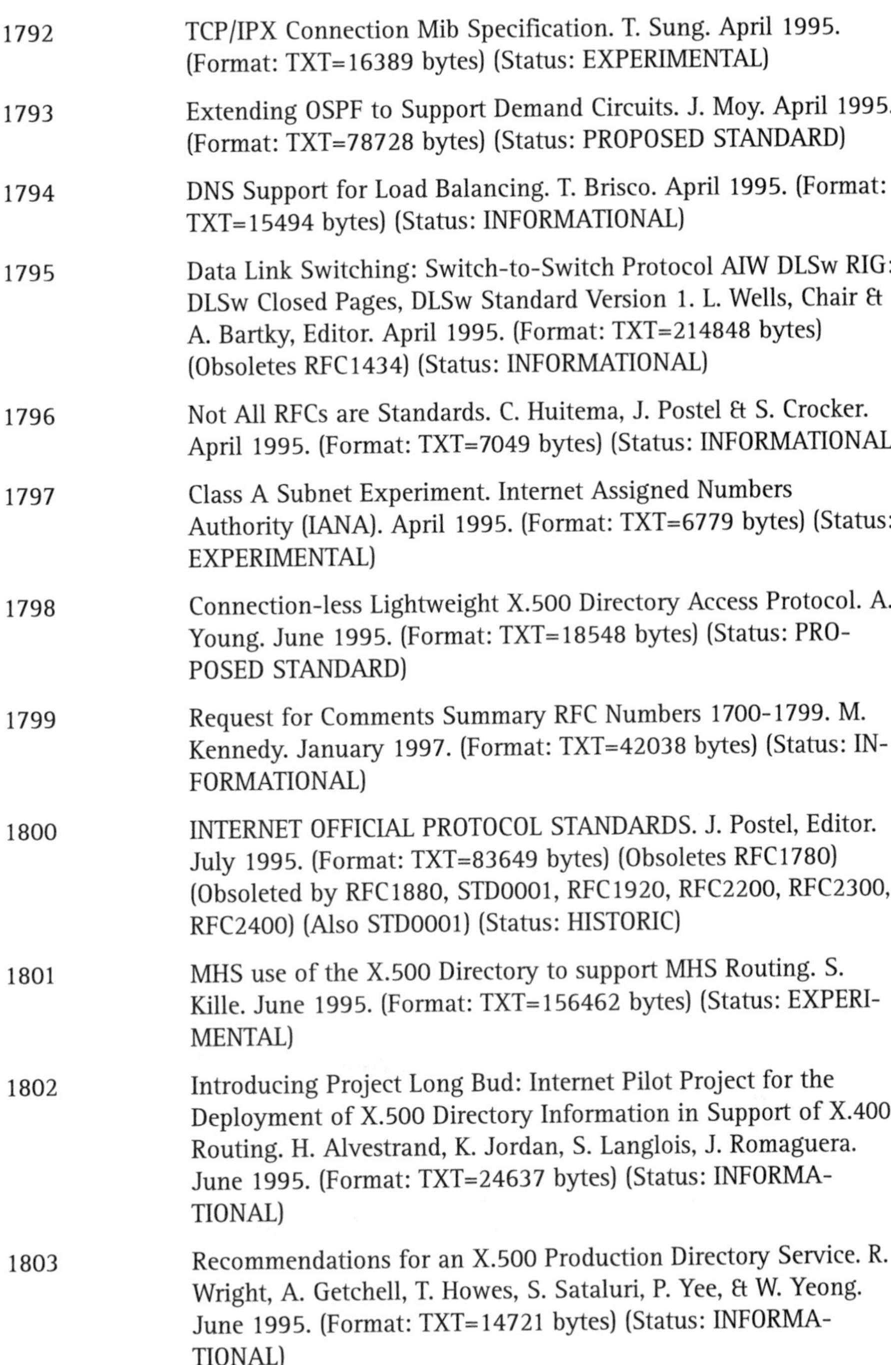

1792 TCP/IPX Connection Mib Specification. T. Sung. April 1995. (Format: TXT=16389 bytes) (Status: EXPERIMENTAL)

1793 Extending OSPF to Support Demand Circuits. J. Moy. April 1995. (Format: TXT=78728 bytes) (Status: PROPOSED STANDARD)

1794 DNS Support for Load Balancing. T. Brisco. April 1995. (Format: TXT=15494 bytes) (Status: INFORMATIONAL)

1795 Data Link Switching: Switch-to-Switch Protocol AIW DLSw RIG: DLSw Closed Pages, DLSw Standard Version 1. L. Wells, Chair & A. Bartky, Editor. April 1995. (Format: TXT=214848 bytes) (Obsoletes RFC1434) (Status: INFORMATIONAL)

1796 Not All RFCs are Standards. C. Huitema, J. Postel & S. Crocker. April 1995. (Format: TXT=7049 bytes) (Status: INFORMATIONAL)

1797 Class A Subnet Experiment. Internet Assigned Numbers Authority (IANA). April 1995. (Format: TXT=6779 bytes) (Status: EXPERIMENTAL)

1798 Connection-less Lightweight X.500 Directory Access Protocol. A. Young. June 1995. (Format: TXT=18548 bytes) (Status: PROPOSED STANDARD)

1799 Request for Comments Summary RFC Numbers 1700-1799. M. Kennedy. January 1997. (Format: TXT=42038 bytes) (Status: INFORMATIONAL)

1800 INTERNET OFFICIAL PROTOCOL STANDARDS. J. Postel, Editor. July 1995. (Format: TXT=83649 bytes) (Obsoletes RFC1780) (Obsoleted by RFC1880, STD0001, RFC1920, RFC2200, RFC2300, RFC2400) (Also STD0001) (Status: HISTORIC)

1801 MHS use of the X.500 Directory to support MHS Routing. S. Kille. June 1995. (Format: TXT=156462 bytes) (Status: EXPERIMENTAL)

1802 Introducing Project Long Bud: Internet Pilot Project for the Deployment of X.500 Directory Information in Support of X.400 Routing. H. Alvestrand, K. Jordan, S. Langlois, J. Romaguera. June 1995. (Format: TXT=24637 bytes) (Status: INFORMATIONAL)

1803 Recommendations for an X.500 Production Directory Service. R. Wright, A. Getchell, T. Howes, S. Sataluri, P. Yee, & W. Yeong. June 1995. (Format: TXT=14721 bytes) (Status: INFORMATIONAL)

1804 Schema Publishing in X.500 Directory. G. Mansfield, P. Rajeev, S. Raghavan, T. Howes. June 1995. (Format: TXT=18268 bytes) (Status: EXPERIMENTAL)

1805 Location-Independent Data/Software Integrity Protocol. A. Rubin. June 1995. (Format: TXT=13352 bytes) (Status: INFORMATIONAL)

1806 Communicating Presentation Information in Internet Messages: The Content-Disposition Header. R. Troost, S. Dorner. June 1995. (Format: TXT=15548 bytes) (Updated by RFC2183) (Status: EXPERIMENTAL)

1807 A Format for Bibliographic Records. R. Lasher & D. Cohen. June 1995. (Format: TXT=29417 bytes) (Obsoletes RFC1357) (Status: INFORMATIONAL)

1808 Relative Uniform Resource Locators. R. Fielding. June 1995. (Format: TXT=34950 bytes) (Updates RFC1738) (Updated by RFC2368) (Status: PROPOSED STANDARD)

1809 Using the Flow Label Field in IPv6. C. Partridge. June 1995. (Format: TXT=13591 bytes) (Status: INFORMATIONAL)

1810 Report on MD5 Performance. J. Touch. June 1995. (Format: TXT=16607 bytes) (Status: INFORMATIONAL)

1811 U.S. Government Internet Domain Names. Federal Networking Council. June 1995. (Format: TXT=6641 bytes) (Obsoleted by RFC1816) (Status: INFORMATIONAL)

1812 Requirements for IP Version 4 Routers. F. Baker. June 1995. (Format: TXT=415740 bytes) (Obsoletes RFC1716, RFC1009) (Status: PROPOSED STANDARD)

1813 NFS Version 3 Protocol Specification. B. Callaghan, B. Pawlowski & P. Staubach. June 1995. (Format: TXT=229793 bytes) (Also RFC1094) (Status: INFORMATIONAL)

1814 Unique Addresses are Good. E. Gerich. June 1995. (Format: TXT=5936 bytes) (Status: INFORMATIONAL)

1815 Character Sets ISO-10646 and ISO-10646-J-1. M. Ohta. July 1995. (Format: TXT=11823 bytes) (Status: INFORMATIONAL)

1816 U.S. Government Internet Domain Names. Federal Networking Council. August 1995. (Format: TXT=17979 bytes) (Obsoletes RFC1811) (Obsoleted by RFC2146) (Status: INFORMATIONAL)

1817 CIDR and Classful Routing. Y. Rekhter. August 1995. (Format: TXT=3416 bytes) (Status: INFORMATIONAL)

1818 Best Current Practices. J. Postel, T. Li & Y. Rekhter. August 1995. (Format: TXT=4114 bytes) (Also BCP0001) (Status: BEST CURRENT PRACTICE)

1819 Internet Stream Protocol Version 2 (ST2) Protocol Specification - Version ST2+. L. Delgrossi & L. Berger, Editors. August 1995. (Format: TXT=266875 bytes) (Obsoletes RFC1190, IEN119) (Status: EXPERIMENTAL)

1820 Multimedia E-mail (MIME) User Agent Checklist. E. Huizer. August 1995. (Format: TXT=14672 bytes) (Obsoleted by RFC1844) (Status: INFORMATIONAL)

1821 Integration of Real-time Services in an IP-ATM Network Architecture. Borden, Crawley, Davie & Batsell. August 1995. (Format: TXT=64466 bytes) (Status: INFORMATIONAL)

1822 A Grant of Rights to Use a Specific IBM patent with Photuris. J. Lowe. August 1995. (Format: TXT=2664 bytes) (Status: INFORMATIONAL)

1823 The LDAP Application Program Interface. T. Howes & M. Smith. August 1995. (Format: TXT=41081 bytes) (Status: INFORMATIONAL)

1824 The Exponential Security System TESS: An Identity-Based Cryptographic Protocol for Authenticated Key-Exchange (E.I.S.S.-Report 1995/4). H. Danisch. August 1995. (Format: TXT=45540 bytes) (Status: INFORMATIONAL)

1825 Security Architecture for the Internet Protocol. R. Atkinson. August 1995. (Format: TXT=56772 bytes) (Status: PROPOSED STANDARD)

1826 IP Authentication Header. R. Atkinson. August 1995. (Format: TXT=27583 bytes) (Status: PROPOSED STANDARD)

1827 IP Encapsulating Security Payload (ESP). R. Atkinson. August 1995. (Format: TXT=30278 bytes) (Status: PROPOSED STANDARD)

1828 IP Authentication using Keyed MD5. P. Metzger & W. Simpson. August 1995. (Format: TXT=9800 bytes) (Status: PROPOSED STANDARD)

1829 The ESP DES-CBC Transform. P. Karn, P. Metzger & W. Simpson. August 1995. (Format: TXT=19291 bytes) (Status: PROPOSED STANDARD)

1830 SMTP Service Extensions for Transmission of Large and Binary MIME Messages. G. Vaudreuil. August 1995. (Format: TXT=16555 bytes) (Status: EXPERIMENTAL)

1831 RPC: Remote Procedure Call Protocol Specification Version 2. R. Srinivasan. August 1995. (Format: TXT=37798 bytes) (Status: PROPOSED STANDARD)

1832 XDR: External Data Representation Standard. R. Srinivasan. August 1995. (Format: TXT=47418 bytes) (Status: DRAFT STANDARD)

1833 Binding Protocols for ONC RPC Version 2. R. Srinivasan. August 1995. (Format: TXT=24449 bytes) (Status: PROPOSED STANDARD)

1834 Whois and Network Information Lookup Service, Whois++. J. Gargano & K. Weiss. August 1995. (Format: TXT=14429 bytes) (Status: INFORMATIONAL)

1835 Architecture of the WHOIS++ service. P. Deutsch, R. Schoultz, P. Faltstrom & C. Weider. August 1995. (Format: TXT=80581 bytes) (Status: PROPOSED STANDARD)

1836 Representing the O/R Address hierarchy in the X.500 Directory Information Tree. S. Kille. August 1995. (Format: TXT=20175 bytes) (Obsoleted by RFC2294) (Status: EXPERIMENTAL)

1837 Representing Tables and Subtrees in the X.500 Directory. S. Kille. August 1995. (Format: TXT=10924 bytes) (Obsoleted by RFC2293) (Status: EXPERIMENTAL)

1838 Use of the X.500 Directory to support mapping between X.400 and RFC 822 Addresses. S. Kille. August 1995. (Format: TXT=12216 bytes) (Obsoleted by RFC2164) (Status: EXPERIMENTAL)

1841 PPP Network Control Protocol for LAN Extension. J. Chapman, D. Coli, A. Harvey, B. Jensen & K. Rowett. September 1995. (Format: TXT=146206 bytes) (Status: INFORMATIONAL)

1842 ASCII Printable Characters-Based Chinese Character Encoding for Internet Messages. Y. Wei, Y. Zhang, J. Li, J. Ding & Y. Jiang. August 1995. (Format: TXT=24143 bytes) (Status: INFORMATIONAL)

1843 HZ - A Data Format for Exchanging Files of Arbitrarily Mixed Chinese and ASCII characters. F. Lee. August 1995. (Format: TXT=8787 bytes) (Status: INFORMATIONAL)

1844 Multimedia E-mail (MIME) User Agent Checklist. E. Huizer. August 1995. (Format: TXT=15072 bytes) (Obsoletes RFC1820) (Status: INFORMATIONAL)

1845 SMTP Service Extension for Checkpoint/Restart. D. Crocker, N. Freed & A. Cargille. September 1995. (Format: TXT=15399 bytes) (Status: EXPERIMENTAL)

1846 SMTP 521 Reply Code. A. Durand & F. Dupont. September 1995. (Format: TXT=6558 bytes) (Status: EXPERIMENTAL)

1847 Security Multiparts for MIME: Multipart/Signed and Multipart/Encrypted. J. Galvin, S. Murphy, S. Crocker & N. Freed. October 1995. (Format: TXT=23679 bytes) (Status: PROPOSED STANDARD)

1848 MIME Object Security Services. S. Crocker, N. Freed, J. Galvin & S. Murphy. October 1995. (Format: TXT=95010 bytes) (Status: PROPOSED STANDARD)

1850 OSPF Version 2 Management Information Base. F. Baker & R. Coltun. November 1995. (Format: TXT=140255 bytes) (Obsoletes RFC1253) (Status: DRAFT STANDARD)

1851 The ESP Triple DES Transform. P. Karn, P. Metzger, W. Simpson. September 1995. (Format: TXT=20000 bytes) (Status: EXPERIMENTAL)

1852 IP Authentication using Keyed SHA. P. Metzger, W. Simpson. September 1995. (Format: TXT=9367 bytes) (Status: EXPERIMENTAL)

1853 IP in IP Tunneling. W. Simpson. October 1995. (Format: TXT=14803 bytes) (Status: INFORMATIONAL)

1854 SMTP Service Extension for Command Pipelining. N. Freed. October 1995. (Format: TXT=14097 bytes) (Obsoleted by RFC2197) (Status: PROPOSED STANDARD)

1855 Netiquette Guidelines. S. Hambridge. October 1995. (Format: TXT=46185 bytes) (Also FYI0028) (Status: INFORMATIONAL)

1856 The Opstat Client-Server Model for Statistics Retrieval. H. Clark. October 1995. (Format: TXT=29954 bytes) (Status: INFORMATIONAL)

1857 A Model for Common Operational Statistics. M. Lambert. October 1995. (Format: TXT=55314 bytes) (Obsoletes RFC1404) (Status: INFORMATIONAL)

1858 Security Considerations for IP Fragment Filtering. G. Ziemba, D. Reed & P. Traina. October 1995. (Format: TXT=20468 bytes) (Status: INFORMATIONAL)

1859 ISO Transport Class 2 Non-use of Explicit Flow Control over TCP RFC1006 extension. Y. Pouffary. October 1995. (Format: TXT=14572 bytes) (Status: INFORMATIONAL)

1860 Variable Length Subnet Table For IPv4. T. Pummill & B. Manning. October 1995. (Format: TXT=5694 bytes) (Obsoleted by RFC1878) (Status: INFORMATIONAL)

1861 Simple Network Paging Protocol - Version 3 -Two-Way Enhanced. A. Gwinn. October 1995. (Format: TXT=49181 bytes) (Obsoletes RFC1645) (Status: INFORMATIONAL)

1862 Report of the IAB Workshop on Internet Information Infrastructure, October 12-14, 1994. M. McCahill, J. Romkey, M. Schwartz, K. Sollins, T. Verschuren & C. Weider. November 1995. (Format: TXT=62483 bytes) (Status: INFORMATIONAL)

1863 A BGP/IDRP Route Server alternative to a full mesh routing. D. Haskin. October 1995. (Format: TXT=37426 bytes) (Obsoletes RFC1645) (Status: EXPERIMENTAL)

1864 The Content-MD5 Header Field. J. Myers & M. Rose. October 1995. (Format: TXT=7216 bytes) (Obsoletes RFC1544) (Status: DRAFT STANDARD)

1865 EDI Meets the Internet Frequently Asked Questions about Electronic Data Interchange (EDI) on the Internet. W. Houser, J. Griffin, & C. Hage. January 1996. (Format: TXT=98361 bytes) (Status: INFORMATIONAL)

1866 Hypertext Markup Language - 2.0. T. Berners-Lee & D. Connolly. November 1995. (Format: TXT=146904 bytes) (Status: PROPOSED STANDARD)

1867 Form-based File Upload in HTML. E. Nebel & L. Masinter. November 1995. (Format: TXT=26183 bytes) (Status: EXPERIMENTAL)

1868 ARP Extension - UNARP. G. Malkin. November 1995. (Format: TXT=7681 bytes) (Status: EXPERIMENTAL)

1869 SMTP Service Extensions. J. Klensin, N. Freed, M. Rose, E. Stefferud & D. Crocker. November 1995. (Format: TXT=23299 bytes) (Obsoletes RFC1651) (Also STD0010) (Status: STANDARD)

1870 SMTP Service Extension for Message Size Declaration. J. Klensin, N. Freed, & K. Moore. November 1995. (Format: TXT=18226 bytes) (Obsoletes RFC1653) (Also STD0010) (Status: STANDARD)

1871 Addendum to RFC 1602 – Variance Procedure. J. Postel. November 1995. (Format: TXT=7747 bytes) (Updates RFC1602, RFC1603) (Also BCP0002) (Status: BEST CURRENT PRACTICE)

1872 The MIME Multipart/Related Content-type. E. Levinson. December 1995. (Format: TXT=15565 bytes) (Obsoleted by RFC2112) (Status: EXPERIMENTAL)

1873 Message/External-Body Content-ID Access Type. E. Levinson. December 1995. (Format: TXT=5878 bytes) (Status: EXPERIMENTAL)

1874 SGML Media Types. E. Levinson. December 1995. (Format: TXT=12515 bytes) (Status: EXPERIMENTAL)

1875 UNINETT PCA Policy Statements. N. Berge. December 1995. (Format: TXT=19089 bytes) (Status: INFORMATIONAL)

1876 A Means for Expressing Location Information in the Domain Name System. C. Davis, P. Vixie, T. Goodwin & I. Dickinson. January 1996. (Format: TXT=29631 bytes) (Updates RFC1034, RFC1035) (Status: EXPERIMENTAL)

1877 PPP Internet Protocol Control Protocol Extensions for Name Server Addresses. S. Cobb. December 1995. (Format: TXT=10591 bytes) (Status: INFORMATIONAL)

1878 Variable Length Subnet Table For IPv4. T. Pummill & B. Manning. December 1995. (Format: TXT=19414 bytes) (Obsoletes RFC1860) (Status: INFORMATIONAL)

1879 Class A Subnet Experiment Results and Recommendations. B. Manning. January 1996. (Format: TXT=10589 bytes) (Status: INFORMATIONAL)

1880 INTERNET OFFICIAL PROTOCOL STANDARDS. J. Postel, Editor. November 1995. (Format: TXT=89153 bytes) (Obsoletes RFC1780, RFC1720, RFC1800, RFC1880) (Obsoleted by RFC1880, RFC1920, RFC2200, RFC2300, STD0001, RFC2400) (Also STD0001) (Status: HISTORIC)

1881 IPv6 Address Allocation Management. IAB & IESG. December 1995. (Format: TXT=3215 bytes) (Status: INFORMATIONAL)

1882 The 12-Days of Technology Before Christmas. B. Hancock. December 1995. (Format: TXT=9130 bytes) (Status: INFORMATIONAL)

1883 Internet Protocol, Version 6 (IPv6) Specification. S. Deering & R. Hinden. December 1995. (Format: TXT=82089 bytes) (Status: PROPOSED STANDARD)

1884 IP Version 6 Addressing Architecture. R. Hinden & S. Deering, Editors. December 1995. (Format: TXT=37860 bytes) (Obsoleted by RFC2373) (Status: PROPOSED STANDARD)

1885 Internet Control Message Protocol (ICMPv6) for the Internet Protocol Version 6 (IPv6). A. Conta, S. Deering. December 1995. (Format: TXT=32214 bytes) (Status: PROPOSED STANDARD)

1886 DNS Extensions to support IP version 6. S. Thomson & C. Huitema. December 1995. (Format: TXT=6424 bytes) (Status: PROPOSED STANDARD)

1887 An Architecture for IPv6 Unicast Address Allocation. Y. Rekhter & T. Li, Editors. December 1995. (Format: TXT=66066 bytes) (Status: INFORMATIONAL)

1888 OSI NSAPs and IPv6. J. Bound, B. Carpenter, D. Harrington, J. Houldsworth & A. Lloyd. August 1996. (Format: TXT=36469 bytes) (Status: EXPERIMENTAL)

1889 RTP: A Transport Protocol for Real-Time Applications. Audio-Video Transport Working Group, H. Schulzrinne, S. Casner, R. Frederick & V. Jacobson. January 1996. (Format: TXT=188544 bytes) (Status: PROPOSED STANDARD)

1890 RTP Profile for Audio and Video Conferences with Minimal Control. Audio-Video Transport Working Group, H. Schulzrinne. January 1996. (Format: TXT=37509 bytes) (Status: PROPOSED STANDARD)

1891 SMTP Service Extension for Delivery Status Notifications. K. Moore. January 1996. (Format: TXT=65192 bytes) (Status: PROPOSED STANDARD)

1892 The Multipart/Report Content Type for the Reporting of Mail System Administrative Messages. G. Vaudreuil. January 1996. (Format: TXT=7800 bytes) (Status: PROPOSED STANDARD)

1893 Enhanced Mail System Status Codes. G. Vaudreuil. January 1996. (Format: TXT=28218 bytes) (Status: PROPOSED STANDARD)

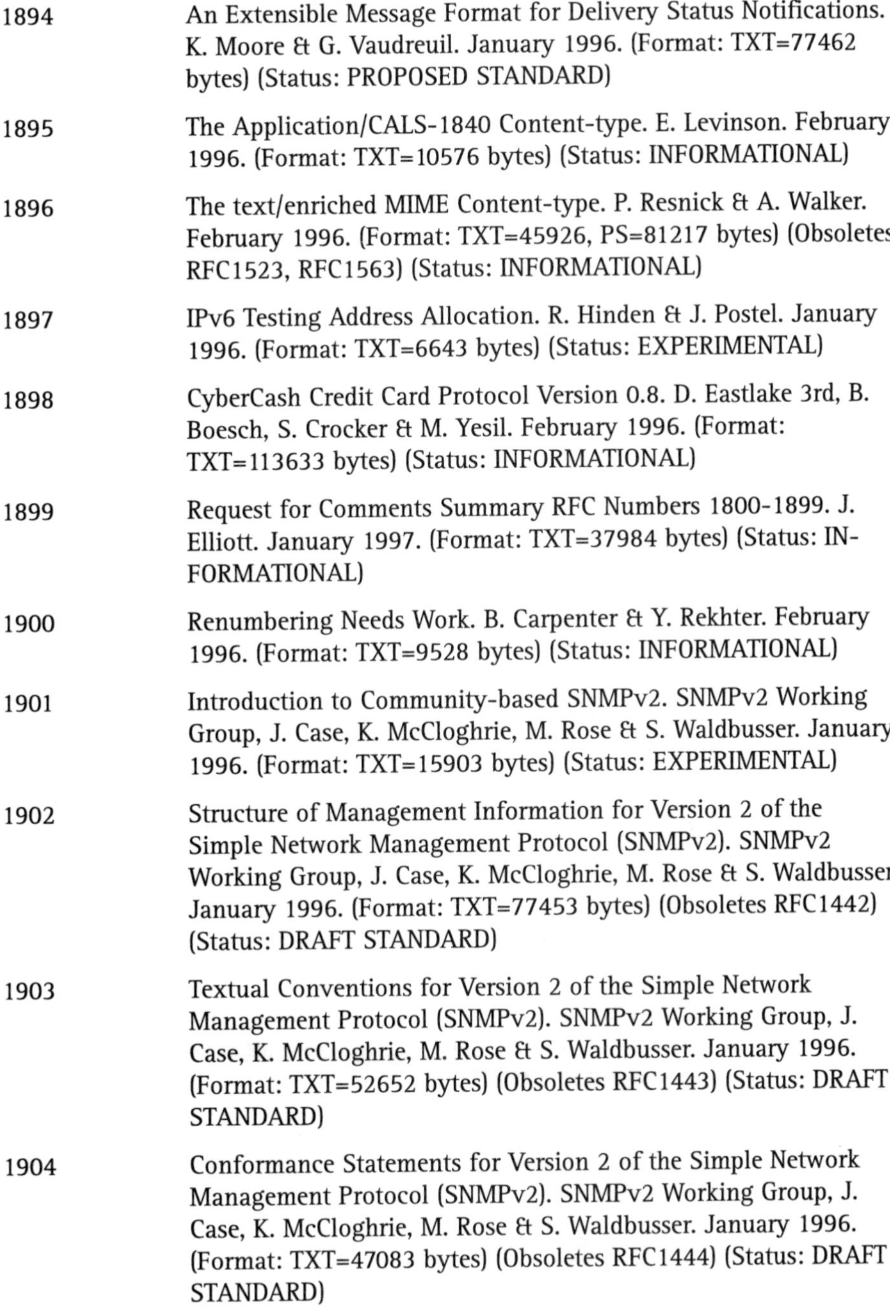

1894 An Extensible Message Format for Delivery Status Notifications. K. Moore & G. Vaudreuil. January 1996. (Format: TXT=77462 bytes) (Status: PROPOSED STANDARD)

1895 The Application/CALS-1840 Content-type. E. Levinson. February 1996. (Format: TXT=10576 bytes) (Status: INFORMATIONAL)

1896 The text/enriched MIME Content-type. P. Resnick & A. Walker. February 1996. (Format: TXT=45926, PS=81217 bytes) (Obsoletes RFC1523, RFC1563) (Status: INFORMATIONAL)

1897 IPv6 Testing Address Allocation. R. Hinden & J. Postel. January 1996. (Format: TXT=6643 bytes) (Status: EXPERIMENTAL)

1898 CyberCash Credit Card Protocol Version 0.8. D. Eastlake 3rd, B. Boesch, S. Crocker & M. Yesil. February 1996. (Format: TXT=113633 bytes) (Status: INFORMATIONAL)

1899 Request for Comments Summary RFC Numbers 1800-1899. J. Elliott. January 1997. (Format: TXT=37984 bytes) (Status: INFORMATIONAL)

1900 Renumbering Needs Work. B. Carpenter & Y. Rekhter. February 1996. (Format: TXT=9528 bytes) (Status: INFORMATIONAL)

1901 Introduction to Community-based SNMPv2. SNMPv2 Working Group, J. Case, K. McCloghrie, M. Rose & S. Waldbusser. January 1996. (Format: TXT=15903 bytes) (Status: EXPERIMENTAL)

1902 Structure of Management Information for Version 2 of the Simple Network Management Protocol (SNMPv2). SNMPv2 Working Group, J. Case, K. McCloghrie, M. Rose & S. Waldbusser. January 1996. (Format: TXT=77453 bytes) (Obsoletes RFC1442) (Status: DRAFT STANDARD)

1903 Textual Conventions for Version 2 of the Simple Network Management Protocol (SNMPv2). SNMPv2 Working Group, J. Case, K. McCloghrie, M. Rose & S. Waldbusser. January 1996. (Format: TXT=52652 bytes) (Obsoletes RFC1443) (Status: DRAFT STANDARD)

1904 Conformance Statements for Version 2 of the Simple Network Management Protocol (SNMPv2). SNMPv2 Working Group, J. Case, K. McCloghrie, M. Rose & S. Waldbusser. January 1996. (Format: TXT=47083 bytes) (Obsoletes RFC1444) (Status: DRAFT STANDARD)

1905 Protocol Operations for Version 2 of the Simple Network Management Protocol (SNMPv2). SNMPv2 Working Group, J. Case, K. McCloghrie, M. Rose & S. Waldbusser. January 1996. (Format: TXT=55526 bytes) (Obsoletes RFC1448) (Status: DRAFT STANDARD)

1906 Transport Mappings for Version 2 of the Simple Network Management Protocol (SNMPv2). SNMPv2 Working Group, J. Case, K. McCloghrie, M. Rose & S. Waldbusser. January 1996. (Format: TXT=27465 bytes) (Obsoletes RFC1449) (Status: DRAFT STANDARD)

1907 Management Information Base for Version 2 of the Simple Network Management Protocol (SNMPv2). SNMPv2 Working Group, J. Case, K. McCloghrie, M. Rose & S. Waldbusser. January 1996. (Format: TXT=34881 bytes) (Obsoletes RFC1450) (Status: DRAFT STANDARD)

1908 Coexistence between Version 1 and Version 2 of the Internet-standard Network Management Framework. SNMPv2 Working Group, J. Case, K. McCloghrie, M. Rose & S. Waldbusser. January 1996. (Format: TXT=21463 bytes) (Obsoletes RFC1452) (Status: DRAFT STANDARD)

1909 An Administrative Infrastructure for SNMPv2. K. McCloghrie. February 1996. (Format: TXT=45773 bytes) (Status: EXPERIMENTAL)

1910 User-based Security Model for SNMPv2. G. Waters. February 1996. (Format: TXT=98252 bytes) (Status: EXPERIMENTAL)

1911 Voice Profile for Internet Mail. G. Vaudreuil. February 1996. (Format: TXT=50242 bytes) (Obsoleted by RFC2421, RFC2422, RFC2423) (Status: EXPERIMENTAL)

1912 Common DNS Operational and Configuration Errors. D. Barr. February 1996. (Format: TXT=38252 bytes) (Obsoletes RFC1537) (Status: INFORMATIONAL)

1913 Architecture of the Whois++ Index Service. C. Weider, J. Fullton & S. Spero. February 1996. (Format: TXT=33743 bytes) (Status: PROPOSED STANDARD)

1914 How to Interact with a Whois++ Mesh. P. Faltstrom, R. Schoultz & C. Weider. February 1996. (Format: TXT=17842 bytes) (Status: PROPOSED STANDARD)

1915 Variance for The PPP Connection Control Protocol and The PPP Encryption Control Protocol. F. Kastenholz. February 1996. (Format: TXT=14347 bytes) (Also BCP0003) (Status: BEST CURRENT PRACTICE)

1916 Enterprise Renumbering: Experience and Information Solicitation. H. Berkowitz, P. Ferguson, W. Leland, & P. Nesser. February 1996. (Format: TXT=16117 bytes) (Status: INFORMATIONAL)

1917 An Appeal to the Internet Community to Return Unused IP Networks (Prefixes) to the IANA. P. Nesser II. February 1996. (Format: TXT=23623 bytes) (Also BCP0004) (Status: BEST CURRENT PRACTICE)

1918 Address Allocation for Private Internets. Y. Rekhter, B. Moskowitz, D. Karrenberg, G. J. de Groot & E. Lear. February 1996. (Format: TXT=22270 bytes) (Obsoletes RFC1627, RFC1597) (Also BCP0005) (Status: BEST CURRENT PRACTICE)

1919 Classical versus Transparent IP Proxies. M. Chatel. March 1996. (Format: TXT=87374 bytes) (Status: INFORMATIONAL)

1920 INTERNET OFFICIAL PROTOCOL STANDARDS. J. Postel. March 1996. (Format: TXT=91936 bytes) (Obsoletes RFC1780, RFC1720, RFC1800, RFC1880) (Obsoleted by RFC2000, RFC2200, RFC2300, RFC2109, STD0001, RFC2400) (Also STD0001) (Status: HISTORIC)

1921 TNVIP Protocol. J. Dujonc. March 1996. (Format: TXT=57475 bytes) (Status: INFORMATIONAL)

1922 Chinese Character Encoding for Internet Messages. HF. Zhu, DY. Hu, ZG. Wang, TC. Kao, WCH. Chang & M. Crispi. March 1996. (Format: TXT=50995 bytes) (Status: INFORMATIONAL)

1923 RIPv1 Applicability Statement for Historic Status. J. Halpern & S. Bradner. March 1996. (Format: TXT=5560 bytes) (Status: INFORMATIONAL)

1924 A Compact Representation of IPv6 Addresses. R. Elz. April 1996. (Format: TXT=10409 bytes) (Status: INFORMATIONAL)

1925 The Twelve Networking Truths. R. Callon. April 1996. (Format: TXT=4294 bytes) (Status: INFORMATIONAL)

1926 An Experimental Encapsulation of IP Datagrams on Top of ATM. J. Eriksson. April 1996. (Format: TXT=2969 bytes) (Status: INFORMATIONAL)

1927 Suggested Additional MIME Types for Associating Documents. C. Rogers. April 1996. (Format: TXT=5254 bytes) (Status: INFORMATIONAL)

1928 SOCKS Protocol Version 5. M. Leech, M. Ganis, Y. Lee, R. Kuris, D. Koblas & L. Jones. April 1996. (Format: TXT=19741 bytes) (Status: PROPOSED STANDARD)

1929 Username/Password Authentication for SOCKS V5. M. Leech. April 1996. (Format: TXT=3568 bytes) (Status: PROPOSED STANDARD)

1930 Guidelines for creation, selection, and registration of an Autonomous System (AS). J. Hawkinson, T. Bates. March 1996. (Format: TXT=22073 bytes) (Also BCP0006) (Status: BEST CURRENT PRACTICE)

1931 Dynamic RARP Extensions for Automatic Network Address Acquisition. D. Brownell. April 1996. (Format: TXT=27544 bytes) (Status: INFORMATIONAL)

1932 IP over ATM: A Framework Document. R. Cole, D. Shur, & C. Villamizar. April 1996. (Format: TXT=68031 bytes) (Status: INFORMATIONAL)

1933 Transition Mechanisms for IPv6 Hosts and Routers. R. Gilligan & E. Nordmark. April 1996. (Format: TXT=47005 bytes) (Status: PROPOSED STANDARD)

1934 Ascend's Multilink Protocol Plus (MP+). K. Smith. April 1996. (Format: TXT=87072 bytes) (Status: INFORMATIONAL)

1935 What is the Internet, Anyway?. J. Quarterman & S. Carl-Mitchell. April 1996. (Format: TXT=30369 bytes) (Status: INFORMATIONAL)

1936 Implementing the Internet Checksum in Hardware. J. Touch & B. Parham. April 1996. (Format: TXT=36618 bytes) (Status: INFORMATIONAL)

1937 "Local/Remote" Forwarding Decision in Switched Data Link Subnetworks. Y. Rekhter & D. Kandlur. May 1996. (Format: TXT=18302 bytes) (Status: INFORMATIONAL)

1938 A One-Time Password System. N. Haller & C. Metz. May 1996. (Format: TXT=44844 bytes) (Obsoleted by RFC2289) (Status: PROPOSED STANDARD)

1939 Post Office Protocol - Version 3. J. Myers & M. Rose. May 1996. (Format: TXT=47018 bytes) (Obsoletes RFC1725) (Updated by RFC1957) (Also STD0053) (Status: STANDARD)

1940 Source Demand Routing: Packet Format and Forwarding Specification (Version 1). D. Estrin, T. Li, Y. Rekhter, K. Varadhan, D. Zappala. May 1996. (Format: TXT=60858 bytes) (Status: INFORMATIONAL)

1941 Frequently Asked Questions for Schools. J. Sellers & J. Robichaux. May 1996. (Format: TXT=150980 bytes) (Obsoletes RFC1578) (Also FYI0022) (Status: INFORMATIONAL)

1942 HTML Tables. D. Raggett. May 1996. (Format: TXT=68705 bytes) (Status: EXPERIMENTAL)

1943 Building an X.500 Directory Service in the US. B. Jennings. May 1996. (Format: TXT=51266 bytes) (Status: INFORMATIONAL)

1944 Benchmarking Methodology for Network Interconnect Devices. S. Bradner & J. McQuaid. May 1996. (Format: TXT=66061 bytes) (Status: INFORMATIONAL)

1945 Hypertext Transfer Protocol – HTTP/1.0. T. Berners-Lee, R. Fielding & H. Frystyk. May 1996. (Format: TXT=137582 bytes) (Status: INFORMATIONAL)

1946 Native ATM Support for ST2+. S. Jackowski. May 1996. (Format: TXT=50430 bytes) (Status: INFORMATIONAL)

1947 Greek Character Encoding for Electronic Mail Messages. D. Spinellis. May 1996. (Format: TXT=14428 bytes) (Status: INFORMATIONAL)

1948 Defending Against Sequence Number Attacks. S. Bellovin. May 1996. (Format: TXT=13074 bytes) (Status: INFORMATIONAL)

1949 Scalable Multicast Key Distribution. A. Ballardie. May 1996. (Format: TXT=41853 bytes) (Status: EXPERIMENTAL)

1950 ZLIB Compressed Data Format Specification version 3.3. P. Deutsch & J-L. Gailly. May 1996. (Format: TXT=20502, PS=37768 bytes) (Status: INFORMATIONAL)

1951 DEFLATE Compressed Data Format Specification version 1.3. P. Deutsch. May 1996. (Format: TXT=36944, PS=57408 bytes) (Status: INFORMATIONAL)

1952 GZIP file format specification version 4.3. P. Deutsch. May 1996. (Format: TXT=25036, PS=43337 bytes) (Status: INFORMATIONAL)

1953 Ipsilon Flow Management Protocol Specification for IPv4 Version 1.0. P. Newman, W. Edwards, R. Hinden, E. Hoffman, F. Ching Liaw, T. Lyon & G. Minshall. May 1996. (Format: TXT=43749 bytes) (Status: INFORMATIONAL)

1954 Transmission of Flow Labelled IPv4 on ATM Data Links Ipsilon Version 1.0. P. Newman, W. Edwards, R. Hinden, E. Hoffman, F. Ching Liaw, T. Lyon & G. Minshall. May 1996. (Format: TXT=16075 bytes) (Status: INFORMATIONAL)

1955 New Scheme for Internet Routing and Addressing (ENCAPS) for IPNG. R. Hinden. June 1996. (Format: TXT=10115 bytes) (Status: INFORMATIONAL)

1956 Registration in the MIL Domain. D. Engebretson & R. Plzak. June 1996. (Format: TXT=2923 bytes) (Status: INFORMATIONAL)

1957 Some Observations on Implementations of the Post Office Protocol (POP3). R. Nelson. June 1996. (Format: TXT=2325 bytes) (Updates RFC1939) (Status: INFORMATIONAL)

1958 Architectural Principles of the Internet. B. Carpenter. June 1996. (Format: TXT=17345 bytes) (Status: INFORMATIONAL)

1959 An LDAP URL Format. T. Howes & M. Smith. June 1996. (Format: TXT=7243 bytes) (Status: PROPOSED STANDARD)

1960 A String Representation of LDAP Search Filters. T. Howes. June 1996. (Format: TXT=5288 bytes) (Obsoletes RFC1558) (Status: PROPOSED STANDARD)

1961 GSS-API Authentication Method for SOCKS Version 5. P. McMahon. June 1996. (Format: TXT=16036 bytes) (Status: PROPOSED STANDARD)

1962 The PPP Compression Control Protocol (CCP). D. Rand. June 1996. (Format: TXT=18005 bytes) (Updated by RFC2153) (Status: PROPOSED STANDARD)

1963 PPP Serial Data Transport Protocol (SDTP). K. Schneider & S. Venters. August 1996. (Format: TXT=38185 bytes) (Status: INFORMATIONAL)

1964 The Kerberos Version 5 GSS-API Mechanism. J. Linn. June 1996. (Format: TXT=47413 bytes) (Status: PROPOSED STANDARD)

1965 Autonomous System Confederations for BGP. P. Traina. June 1996. (Format: TXT=13575 bytes) (Status: EXPERIMENTAL)

1966 BGP Route Reflection An alternative to full mesh IBGP. T. Bates & R. Chandrasekeran. June 1996. (Format: TXT=14320 bytes) (Status: EXPERIMENTAL)

1967 PPP LZS-DCP Compression Protocol (LZS-DCP). K. Schneider & R. Friend. August 1996. (Format: TXT=40039 bytes) (Status: INFORMATIONAL)

1968 The PPP Encryption Control Protocol (ECP). G. Meyer. June 1996. (Format: TXT=20781 bytes) (Status: PROPOSED STANDARD)

1969 The PPP DES Encryption Protocol (DESE). K. Sklower & G. Meyer. June 1996. (Format: TXT=20383 bytes) (Obsoleted by RFC2419) (Status: INFORMATIONAL)

1970 Neighbor Discovery for IP Version 6 (IPv6). T. Narten, E. Nordmark & W. Simpson. August 1996. (Format: TXT=197632 bytes) (Status: PROPOSED STANDARD)

1971 IPv6 Stateless Address Autoconfiguration. S. Thomson & T. Narten. August 1996. (Format: TXT=56890 bytes) (Status: PROPOSED STANDARD)

1972 A Method for the Transmission of IPv6 Packets over Ethernet Networks. M. Crawford. August 1996. (Format: TXT=6353 bytes) (Status: PROPOSED STANDARD)

1973 PPP in Frame Relay. W. Simpson. June 1996. (Format: TXT=14780 bytes) (Status: PROPOSED STANDARD)

1974 PPP Stac LZS Compression Protocol. R. Friend & W. Simpson. August 1996. (Format: TXT=45267 bytes) (Status: INFORMATIONAL)

1975 PPP Magnalink Variable Resource Compression. D. Schremp, J. Black, J. Weiss. August 1996. (Format: TXT=8655 bytes) (Status: INFORMATIONAL)

1976 PPP for Data Compression in Data Circuit-Terminating Equipment (DCE). K. Schneider & S. Venters. August 1996. (Format: TXT=19781 bytes) (Status: INFORMATIONAL)

1977 PPP BSD Compression Protocol. V. Schryver. August 1996. (Format: TXT=50747 bytes) (Status: INFORMATIONAL)

1978 PPP Predictor Compression Protocol. D. Rand. August 1996. (Format: TXT=17424 bytes) (Status: INFORMATIONAL)

1979 PPP Deflate Protocol. J. Woods. August 1996. (Format: TXT=18803 bytes) (Status: INFORMATIONAL)

1980 A Proposed Extension to HTML : Client-Side Image Maps. J. Seidman. August 1996. (Format: TXT=13448 bytes) (Status: INFORMATIONAL)

1981 Path MTU Discovery for IP version 6. J. McCann, S. Deering & J. Mogul. August 1996. (Format: TXT=34088 bytes) (Status: PROPOSED STANDARD)

1982 Serial Number Arithmetic. R. Elz & R. Bush. August 1996. (Format: TXT=14440 bytes) (Updates RFC1034, RFC1035) (Status: PROPOSED STANDARD)

1983 Internet Users' Glossary. G. Malkin. August 1996. (Format: TXT=123008 bytes) (Obsoletes RFC1392) (Also FYI0018) (Status: INFORMATIONAL)

1984 IAB and IESG Statement on Cryptographic Technology and the Internet. IAB & IESG. August 1996. (Format: TXT=10738 bytes) (Status: INFORMATIONAL)

1985 SMTP Service Extension for Remote Message Queue Starting. J. De Winter. August 1996. (Format: TXT=14815 bytes) (Status: PROPOSED STANDARD)

1986 Experiments with a Simple File Transfer Protocol for Radio Links using Enhanced Trivial File Transfer Protocol (ETFTP). W. Polites, W. Wollman, D. Woo & R. Langan. August 1996. (Format: TXT=49772 bytes) (Status: EXPERIMENTAL)

1987 Ipsilon's General Switch Management Protocol Specification Version 1.1. P. Newman, W. Edwards, R. Hinden, E. Hoffman, F. Ching Liaw, T. Lyon & G. Minshall. August 1996. (Format: TXT=105821 bytes) (Updated by RFC2297) (Status: INFORMATIONAL)

1988 Conditional Grant of Rights to Specific Hewlett-Packard Patents In Conjunction With the Internet Engineering Task Force's Internet-Standard Network Management Framework. G. McAnally, D. Gilbert & J. Flick. August 1996. (Format: TXT=3821 bytes) (Status: INFORMATIONAL)

1989 PPP Link Quality Monitoring. W. Simpson. August 1996. (Format: TXT=29289 bytes) (Obsoletes RFC1333) (Status: DRAFT STANDARD)

1990 The PPP Multilink Protocol (MP). K. Sklower, B. Lloyd, G. McGregor, D. Carr & T. Coradetti. August 1996. (Format: TXT=53271 bytes) (Obsoletes RFC1717) (Status: DRAFT STANDARD)

1991 PGP Message Exchange Formats. D. Atkins, W. Stallings & P. Zimmermann. August 1996. (Format: TXT=46255 bytes) (Status: INFORMATIONAL)

1992 The Nimrod Routing Architecture. I. Castineyra, N. Chiappa, M. Steenstrup. August 1996. (Format: TXT=59848 bytes) (Status: INFORMATIONAL)

1993 PPP Gandalf FZA Compression Protocol. A. Barbir, D. Carr & W. Simpson. August 1996. (Format: TXT=9811 bytes) (Status: INFORMATIONAL)

1994 PPP Challenge Handshake Authentication Protocol (CHAP). W. Simpson. August 1996. (Format: TXT=24094 bytes) (Obsoletes RFC1334) (Status: DRAFT STANDARD)

1995 Incremental Zone Transfer in DNS. M. Ohta. August 1996. (Format: TXT=16810 bytes) (Updates RFC1035) (Status: PROPOSED STANDARD)

1996 A Mechanism for Prompt Notification of Zone Changes (DNS NOTIFY). P. Vixie. August 1996. (Format: TXT=15247 bytes) (Updates RFC1035) (Status: PROPOSED STANDARD)

1997 BGP Communities Attribute. R. Chandra, P. Traina & T. Li. August 1996. (Format: TXT=8275 bytes) (Status: PROPOSED STANDARD)

1998 An Application of the BGP Community Attribute in Multi-home Routing. E. Chen & T. Bates. August 1996. (Format: TXT=16953 bytes) (Status: INFORMATIONAL)

1999 Request for Comments Summary RFC Numbers 1900-1999. J. Elliott. January 1997. (Format: TXT=39819 bytes) (Status: INFORMATIONAL)

2000 INTERNET OFFICIAL PROTOCOL STANDARDS. J. Postel, Editor. February 1997. (Format: TXT=121356 bytes) (Obsoletes RFC1920, 1880, 1800, 1780, 1720, 1610, 1600, 1540, 1500, 1410, 1360, 1280, 1250, 1200, 1140, 1130, 1100, 1083) (Obsoleted by RFC2200, STD0001, RFC2300, RFC2400) (Also STD0001) (Status: HISTORIC)

2001 TCP Slow Start, Congestion Avoidance, Fast Retransmit, and Fast Recovery Algorithms. W. Stevens. January 1997. (Format: TXT=12981 bytes) (Status: PROPOSED STANDARD)

2002 IP Mobility Support. C. Perkins. October 1996. (Format: TXT=193103 bytes) (Updated by RFC2290) (Status: PROPOSED STANDARD)

2003 IP Encapsulation within IP. C. Perkins. October 1996. (Format: TXT=30291 bytes) (Status: PROPOSED STANDARD)

2004 Minimal Encapsulation within IP. C. Perkins. October 1996. (Format: TXT=12202 bytes) (Status: PROPOSED STANDARD)

2005 Applicability Statement for IP Mobility Support. J. Solomon. October 1996. (Format: TXT=10509 bytes) (Status: PROPOSED STANDARD)

2006 The Definitions of Managed Objects for IP Mobility Support using SMIv2. D. Cong, M. Hamlen, C. Perkins. October 1996. (Format: TXT=95030 bytes) (Status: PROPOSED STANDARD)

2007 Catalogue of Network Training Materials. J. Foster, M. Isaacs & M. Prior. October 1996. (Format: TXT=78941 bytes) (Also FYI0029) (Status: INFORMATIONAL)

2008 Implications of Various Address Allocation Policies for Internet Routing. Y. Rekhter, T. Li. October 1996. (Format: TXT=34717 bytes) (Also BCP0007) (Status: BEST CURRENT PRACTICE)

2009 GPS-Based Addressing and Routing. T. Imielinski, J. Navas. November 1996. (Format: TXT=66229 bytes) (Status: EXPERIMENTAL)

2010 Operational Criteria for Root Name Servers. B. Manning, P. Vixie. October 1996. (Format: TXT=14870 bytes) (Status: INFORMATIONAL)

2011 SNMPv2 Management Information Base for the Internet Protocol using SMIv2. K. McCloghrie. November 1996. (Format: TXT=31168 bytes) (Updates RFC1213) (Status: PROPOSED STANDARD)

2012 SNMPv2 Management Information Base for the Transmission Control Protocol using SMIv2. K. McCloghrie. November 1996. (Format: TXT=16792 bytes) (Updates RFC1213) (Status: PROPOSED STANDARD)

2013 SNMPv2 Management Information Base for the User Datagram Protocol using SMIv2. K. McCloghrie. November 1996. (Format: TXT=9333 bytes) (Updates RFC1213) (Status: PROPOSED STANDARD)

2014 IRTF Research Group Guidelines and Procedures. A. Weinrib, J. Postel. October 1996. (Format: TXT=27507 bytes) (Also BCP0008) (Status: BEST CURRENT PRACTICE)

2015 MIME Security with Pretty Good Privacy (PGP). M. Elkins. October 1996. (Format: TXT=14223 bytes) (Status: PROPOSED STANDARD)

2016 Uniform Resource Agents (URAs). L. Daigle, P. Deutsch, B. Heelan, C. Alpaugh, M. Maclachlan. October 1996. (Format: TXT=38355 bytes) (Status: EXPERIMENTAL)

2017 Definition of the URL MIME External-Body Access-Type. N. Freed, K. Moore, A. Cargille. October 1996. (Format: TXT=9000 bytes) (Status: PROPOSED STANDARD)

2018 TCP Selective Acknowledgement Options. M. Mathis, J. Mahdavi, S. Floyd, A. Romanow. October 1996. (Format: TXT=25671 bytes) (Status: PROPOSED STANDARD)

2019 Transmission of IPv6 Packets Over FDDI. M. Crawford. October 1996. (Format: TXT=12344 bytes) (Status: PROPOSED STANDARD)

2020 IEEE 802.12 Interface MIB. J. Flick. October 1996. (Format: TXT=72135 bytes) (Status: PROPOSED STANDARD)

2021 Remote Network Monitoring Management Information Base Version 2 using SMIv2. S. Waldbusser. January 1997. (Format: TXT=262223 bytes) (Status: PROPOSED STANDARD)

2022 Support for Multicast over UNI 3.0/3.1 based ATM Networks. G. Armitage. November 1996. (Format: TXT=189219 bytes) (Status: PROPOSED STANDARD)

2023 IP Version 6 over PPP. D. Haskin, E. Allen. October 1996. (Format: TXT=20275 bytes) (Status: PROPOSED STANDARD)

2024 Definitions of Managed Objects for Data Link Switching using SMIv2. D. Chen, P. Gayek, S. Nix. October 1996. (Format: TXT=173952 bytes) (Status: PROPOSED STANDARD)

2025 The Simple Public-Key GSS-API Mechanism (SPKM). C. Adams. October 1996. (Format: TXT=101692 bytes) (Status: PROPOSED STANDARD)

2026 The Internet Standards Process – Revision 3. S. Bradner. October 1996. (Format: TXT=86731 bytes) (Obsoletes RFC1602) (Also BCP0009) (Status: BEST CURRENT PRACTICE)

2027 IAB and IESG Selection, Confirmation, and Recall Process: Operation of the Nominating and Recall Committees. J. Galvin. October 1996. (Format: TXT=24207 bytes) (Obsoleted by BCP0010, RFC2282) (Also BCP0010) (Status: BEST CURRENT PRACTICE)

2028 The Organizations Involved in the IETF Standards Process. R. Hovey, S. Bradner. October 1996. (Format: TXT=13865 bytes) (Also BCP0011) (Status: BEST CURRENT PRACTICE)

2029 RTP Payload Format of Sun's CellB Video Encoding. M. Speer, D. Hoffman. October 1996. (Format: TXT=11216 bytes) (Status: PROPOSED STANDARD)

2030 Simple Network Time Protocol (SNTP) Version 4 for IPv4, IPv6 and OSI. D. Mills. October 1996. (Format: TXT=48620 bytes) (Obsoletes RFC1769) (Status: INFORMATIONAL)

2031 IETF-ISOC relationship. E. Huizer. October 1996. (Format: TXT=8816 bytes) (Status: INFORMATIONAL)

2032 RTP Payload Format for H.261 Video Streams. T. Turletti, C. Huitema. October 1996. (Format: TXT=27488 bytes) (Status: PROPOSED STANDARD)

2033 Local Mail Transfer Protocol. J. Myers. October 1996. (Format: TXT=14711 bytes) (Status: INFORMATIONAL)

2034 SMTP Service Extension for Returning Enhanced Error Codes. N. Freed. October 1996. (Format: TXT=10460 bytes) (Status: PROPOSED STANDARD)

2035 RTP Payload Format for JPEG-compressed Video. L. Berc, W. Fenner, R. Frederick, S. McCanne. October 1996. (Format: TXT=30079 bytes) (Status: PROPOSED STANDARD)

2036 Observations on the use of Components of the Class A Address Space within the Internet. G. Huston. October 1996. (Format: TXT=20743 bytes) (Status: INFORMATIONAL)

2037 Entity MIB using SMIv2. K. McCloghrie, A. Bierman. October 1996. (Format: TXT=74362 bytes) (Status: PROPOSED STANDARD)

2038 RTP Payload Format for MPEG1/MPEG2 Video. D. Hoffman, G. Fernando, V. Goyal. October 1996. (Format: TXT=23266 bytes) (Obsoleted by RFC2250) (Status: PROPOSED STANDARD)

2039 Applicability of Standards Track MIBs to Management of World Wide Web Servers. C. Kalbfleisch. November 1996. (Format: TXT=31966 bytes) (Status: INFORMATIONAL)

2040 The RC5, RC5-CBC, RC5-CBC-Pad, and RC5-CTS Algorithms. R. Baldwin, R. Rivest. October 1996. (Format: TXT=54598 bytes) (Status: INFORMATIONAL)

2041 Mobile Network Tracing. B. Noble, G. Nguyen, M. Satyanarayanan, R. Katz. December 1996. (Format: TXT=64688 bytes) (Status: INFORMATIONAL)

2042 Registering New BGP Attribute Types. B. Manning. January 1997. (Format: TXT=4001 bytes) (Status: INFORMATIONAL)

2043 The PPP SNA Control Protocol (SNACP). A. Fuqua. October 1996. (Format: TXT=13719 bytes) (Status: PROPOSED STANDARD)

2044 UTF-8, a transformation format of Unicode and ISO 10646. F. Yergeau. October 1996. (Format: TXT=11932 bytes) (Obsoleted by RFC2279) (Status: INFORMATIONAL)

2045 Multipurpose Internet Mail Extensions (MIME) Part One: Format of Internet Message Bodies. N. Freed & N. Borenstein. November 1996. (Format: TXT=72932 bytes) (Obsoletes RFC1521, RFC1522, RFC1590) (Updated by RFC2184, RFC2231) (Status: DRAFT STANDARD)

2046 Multipurpose Internet Mail Extensions (MIME) Part Two: Media Types. N. Freed & N. Borenstein. November 1996. (Format: TXT=105854 bytes) (Obsoletes RFC1521, RFC1522, RFC1590) (Status: DRAFT STANDARD)

2047 MIME (Multipurpose Internet Mail Extensions) Part Three: Message Header Extensions for Non-ASCII Text. K. Moore. November 1996. (Format: TXT=33262 bytes) (Obsoletes RFC1521, RFC1522, RFC1590) (Updated by RFC2184, RFC2231) (Status: DRAFT STANDARD)

2048 Multipurpose Internet Mail Extensions (MIME) Part Four: Registration Procedures. N. Freed, J. Klensin & J. Postel. November 1996. (Format: TXT=45033 bytes) (Obsoletes RFC1521, RFC1522, RFC1590) (Also BCP0013) (Status: BEST CURRENT PRACTICE)

2049 Multipurpose Internet Mail Extensions (MIME) Part Five: Conformance Criteria and Examples. N. Freed & N. Borenstein. November 1996. (Format: TXT=51207 bytes) (Obsoletes RFC1521, RFC1522, RFC1590) (Status: DRAFT STANDARD)

2050 INTERNET REGISTRY IP ALLOCATION GUIDELINES. K. Hubbard, M. Kosters, D. Conrad, D. Karrenberg, J. Postel. November 1996. (Format: TXT=28975 bytes) (Also BCP0012) (Status: BEST CURRENT PRACTICE)

2051 Definitions of Managed Objects for APPC using SMIv2. M. Allen, B. Clouston, Z. Kielczewski, W. Kwan, B. Moore. October 1996. (Format: TXT=239359 bytes) (Status: PROPOSED STANDARD)

2052 A DNS RR for specifying the location of services (DNS SRV). A. Gulbrandsen, P. Vixie. October 1996. (Format: TXT=19257 bytes) (Status: EXPERIMENTAL)

2053 The AM (Armenia) Domain. E. Der-Danieliantz. October 1996. (Format: TXT=4128 bytes) (Status: INFORMATIONAL)

2054 WebNFS Client Specification. B. Callaghan. October 1996. (Format: TXT=36354 bytes) (Status: INFORMATIONAL)

2055 WebNFS Server Specification. B. Callaghan. October 1996. (Format: TXT=20498 bytes) (Status: INFORMATIONAL)

2056 Uniform Resource Locators for Z39.50. R. Denenberg, J. Kunze, D. Lynch. November 1996. (Format: TXT=14204 bytes) (Status: PROPOSED STANDARD)

2057 Source Directed Access Control on the Internet. S. Bradner. November 1996. (Format: TXT=56664 bytes) (Status: INFORMATIONAL)

2058 Remote Authentication Dial In User Service (RADIUS). C. Rigney, A. Rubens, W. Simpson, S. Willens. January 1997. (Format: TXT=118880 bytes) (Obsoleted by RFC2138) (Status: PROPOSED STANDARD)

2059 RADIUS Accounting. C. Rigney. January 1997. (Format: TXT=44237 bytes) (Obsoleted by RFC2139) (Status: INFORMATIONAL)

2060 INTERNET MESSAGE ACCESS PROTOCOL - VERSION 4rev1. M. Crispin. December 1996. (Format: TXT=166513 bytes) (Obsoletes RFC1730) (Status: PROPOSED STANDARD)

2061 IMAP4 COMPATIBILITY WITH IMAP2BIS. M. Crispin. December 1996. (Format: TXT=5867 bytes) (Obsoletes RFC1730) (Status: INFORMATIONAL)

2062 Internet Message Access Protocol - Obsolete Syntax. M. Crispin. December 1996. (Format: TXT=14222 bytes) (Status: PROPOSED STANDARD)

2063 Traffic Flow Measurement: Architecture. N. Brownlee, C. Mills, G. Ruth. January 1997. (Format: TXT=89092 bytes) (Status: EXPERIMENTAL)

2064 Traffic Flow Measurement: Meter MIB. N. Brownlee. January 1997. (Format: TXT=67520 bytes) (Status: EXPERIMENTAL)

2065 Domain Name System Security Extensions. D. Eastlake, 3rd, C. Kaufman. January 1997. (Format: TXT=97718 bytes) (Updates RFC1034, RFC1035) (Status: PROPOSED STANDARD)

2066 TELNET CHARSET Option. R. Gellens. January 1997. (Format: TXT=26088 bytes) (Status: EXPERIMENTAL)

2067 IP over HIPPI. J. Renwick. January 1997. (Format: TXT=66702 bytes) (Status: DRAFT STANDARD)

2068 Hypertext Transfer Protocol – HTTP/1.1. R. Fielding, J. Gettys, J. Mogul, H. Frystyk, T. Berners-Lee. January 1997. (Format: TXT=378114 bytes) (Status: PROPOSED STANDARD)

2069 An Extension to HTTP : Digest Access Authentication. J. Franks, P. Hallam-Baker, J. Hostetler, P. Leach, A. Luotonen, E. Sink, L. Stewart. January 1997. (Format: TXT=41733 bytes) (Status: PROPOSED STANDARD)

2070 Internationalization of the Hypertext Markup Language. F. Yergeau, G. Nicol, G. Adams, M. Duerst. January 1997. (Format: TXT=91887 bytes) (Status: PROPOSED STANDARD)

2071 Network Renumbering Overview: Why would I want it and what is it anyway?. P. Ferguson, H. Berkowitz. January 1997. (Format: TXT=33218 bytes) (Status: INFORMATIONAL)

2072 Router Renumbering Guide. H. Berkowitz. January 1997. (Format: TXT=110591 bytes) (Status: INFORMATIONAL)

2073 An IPv6 Provider-Based Unicast Address Format. Y. Rekhter, P. Lothberg, R. Hinden, S. Deering, J. Postel. January 1997. (Format: TXT=15549 bytes) (Obsoleted by RFC2374) (Status: PROPOSED STANDARD)

2074 Remote Network Monitoring MIB Protocol Identifiers. A. Bierman, R. Iddon. January 1997. (Format: TXT=81262 bytes) (Status: PROPOSED STANDARD)

2075 IP Echo Host Service. C. Partridge. January 1997. (Format: TXT=12536 bytes) (Status: EXPERIMENTAL)

2076 Common Internet Message Headers. J. Palme. February 1997. (Format: TXT=47639 bytes) (Status: INFORMATIONAL)

2077 The Model Primary Content Type for Multipurpose Internet Mail Extensions. S. Nelson, C. Parks, Mitra. January 1997. (Format: TXT=30158 bytes) (Status: PROPOSED STANDARD)

2078 Generic Security Service Application Program Interface, Version 2. J. Linn. January 1997. (Format: TXT=185990 bytes) (Obsoletes RFC1508) (Status: PROPOSED STANDARD)

2079 Definition of an X.500 Attribute Type and an Object Class to Hold Uniform Resource Identifiers (URIs). M. Smith. January 1997. (Format: TXT=8757 bytes) (Status: PROPOSED STANDARD)

2080 RIPng for IPv6. G. Malkin, R. Minnear. January 1997. (Format: TXT=47534 bytes) (Status: PROPOSED STANDARD)

2081 RIPng Protocol Applicability Statement. G. Malkin. January 1997. (Format: TXT=6821 bytes) (Status: INFORMATIONAL)

2082 RIP-2 MD5 Authentication. F. Baker, R. Atkinson. January 1997. (Format: TXT=25436 bytes) (Status: PROPOSED STANDARD)

2083 PNG (Portable Network Graphics) Specification. T. Boutell. January 1997. (Format: TXT=242528 bytes) (Status: INFORMATIONAL)

2084 Considerations for Web Transaction Security. G. Bossert, S. Cooper, W. Drummond. January 1997. (Format: TXT=9022 bytes) (Status: INFORMATIONAL)

2085 HMAC-MD5 IP Authentication with Replay Prevention. M. Oehler, R. Glenn. February 1997. (Format: TXT=13399 bytes) (Status: PROPOSED STANDARD)

2086 IMAP4 ACL extension. J. Myers. January 1997. (Format: TXT=13925 bytes) (Status: PROPOSED STANDARD)

2087 IMAP4 QUOTA extension. J. Myers. January 1997. (Format: TXT=8542 bytes) (Status: PROPOSED STANDARD)

2088 IMAP4 non-synchronizing literals. J. Myers. January 1997. (Format: TXT=4052 bytes) (Status: PROPOSED STANDARD)

2089 V2ToV1 Mapping SNMPv2 onto SNMPv1 within a bi-lingual SNMP agent. B. Wijnen, D. Levi. January 1997. (Format: TXT=23814 bytes) (Status: INFORMATIONAL)

2090 TFTP Multicast Option. A. Emberson. February 1997. (Format: TXT=11857 bytes) (Status: EXPERIMENTAL)

2091 Triggered Extensions to RIP to Support Demand Circuits. G. Meyer, S. Sherry. January 1997. (Format: TXT=44835 bytes) (Status: PROPOSED STANDARD)

2092 Protocol Analysis for Triggered RIP. S. Sherry, G. Meyer. January 1997. (Format: TXT=10865 bytes) (Status: INFORMATIONAL)

2093 Group Key Management Protocol (GKMP) Specification. H. Harney, C. Muckenhirn. July 1997. (Format: TXT=48678 bytes) (Status: EXPERIMENTAL)

2094 Group Key Management Protocol (GKMP) Architecture. H. Harney, C. Muckenhirn. July 1997. (Format: TXT=53097 bytes) (Status: EXPERIMENTAL)

2095 IMAP/POP AUTHorize Extension for Simple Challenge/Response. J. Klensin, R. Catoe, P. Krumviede. January 1997. (Format: TXT=10446 bytes) (Obsoleted by RFC2195) (Status: PROPOSED STANDARD)

2096 IP Forwarding Table MIB. F. Baker. January 1997. (Format: TXT=35930 bytes) (Obsoletes RFC1354) (Status: PROPOSED STANDARD)

2097 The PPP NetBIOS Frames Control Protocol (NBFCP). G. Pall. January 1997. (Format: TXT=27104 bytes) (Status: PROPOSED STANDARD)

2098 Toshiba's Router Architecture Extensions for ATM : Overview. Y. Katsube, K. Nagami, H. Esaki. February 1997. (Format: TXT=43622 bytes) (Status: INFORMATIONAL)

2099 Request for Comments Summary RFC Numbers 2000-2099. J. Elliott. March 1997. (Format: TXT=40763 bytes) (Status: INFORMATIONAL)

2100 The Naming of Hosts. J. Ashworth. April 1997. (Format: TXT=4077 bytes) (Status: INFORMATIONAL)

2101 IPv4 Address Behaviour Today. B. Carpenter, J. Crowcroft, Y. Rekhter. February 1997. (Format: TXT=31407 bytes) (Status: INFORMATIONAL)

2102 Multicast Support for Nimrod : Requirements and Solution Approaches. R. Ramanathan. February 1997. (Format: TXT=50963 bytes) (Status: INFORMATIONAL)

2103 Mobility Support for Nimrod : Challenges and Solution Approaches. R. Ramanathan. February 1997. (Format: TXT=41352 bytes) (Status: INFORMATIONAL)

2104 HMAC: Keyed-Hashing for Message Authentication. H. Krawczyk, M. Bellare, R. Canetti. February 1997. (Format: TXT=22297 bytes) (Status: INFORMATIONAL)

2105 Cisco Systems' Tag Switching Architecture Overview. Y. Rekhter, B. Davie, D. Katz, E. Rosen, G. Swallow. February 1997. (Format: TXT=33013 bytes) (Status: INFORMATIONAL)

2106 Data Link Switching Remote Access Protocol. S. Chiang, J. Lee, H. Yasuda. February 1997. (Format: TXT=40819 bytes) (Obsoleted by RFC2114) (Status: INFORMATIONAL)

2107 Ascend Tunnel Management Protocol - ATMP. K. Hamzeh. February 1997. (Format: TXT=44300 bytes) (Status: INFORMATIONAL)

2108 Definitions of Managed Objects for IEEE 802.3 Repeater Devices using SMIv2. K. de Graaf, D. Romascanu, D. McMaster, K. McCloghrie. February 1997. (Format: TXT=166336 bytes) (Obsoletes RFC1516) (Status: PROPOSED STANDARD)

2109 HTTP State Management Mechanism. D. Kristol, L. Montulli. February 1997. (Format: TXT=43469 bytes) (Obsoletes RFC1920) (Status: PROPOSED STANDARD)

2110 MIME E-mail Encapsulation of Aggregate Documents, such as HTML (MHTML). J. Palme, A. Hopmann. March 1997. (Format: TXT=41961 bytes) (Status: PROPOSED STANDARD)

2111 Content-ID and Message-ID Uniform Resource Locators. E. Levinson. February 1997. (Format: TXT=9099 bytes) (Obsoleted by RFC2392) (Status: PROPOSED STANDARD)

2112 The MIME Multipart/Related Content-type. E. Levinson. February 1997. (Format: TXT=17052 bytes) (Obsoletes RFC1872) (Obsoleted by RFC2387) (Status: PROPOSED STANDARD)

2113 IP Router Alert Option. D. Katz. February 1997. (Format: TXT=7924 bytes) (Status: PROPOSED STANDARD)

2114 Data Link Switching Client Access Protocol. S. Chiang, J. Lee, H. Yasuda. February 1997. (Format: TXT=50872 bytes) (Obsoletes RFC2106) (Status: INFORMATIONAL)

2115 Management Information Base for Frame Relay DTEs Using SMIv2. C. Brown, F. Baker. September 1997. (Format: TXT=59950 bytes) (Obsoletes RFC1315) (Status: DRAFT STANDARD)

2116 X.500 Implementations Catalog-96. C. Apple, K. Rossen. April 1997. (Format: TXT=243994 bytes) (Obsoletes RFC1632) (Also FYI0011) (Status: INFORMATIONAL)

2117 Protocol Independent Multicast-Sparse Mode (PIM-SM): Protocol Specification. D. Estrin, D. Farinacci, A. Helmy, D. Thaler, S. Deering, M. Handley, V. Jacobson, C. Liu, P. Sharma, L. Wei. June 1997. (Format: TXT=151886 bytes) (Obsoleted by RFC2362) (Status: EXPERIMENTAL)

2118 Microsoft Point-To-Point Compression (MPPC) Protocol. G. Pall. March 1997. (Format: TXT=17443 bytes) (Status: INFORMATIONAL)

2119 Key words for use in RFCs to Indicate Requirement Levels. S. Bradner. March 1997. (Format: TXT=4723 bytes) (Also BCP0014) (Status: BEST CURRENT PRACTICE)

2120 Managing the X.500 Root Naming Context. D. Chadwick. March 1997. (Format: TXT=30773 bytes) (Status: EXPERIMENTAL)

2121 Issues affecting MARS Cluster Size. G. Armitage. March 1997. (Format: TXT=26781 bytes) (Status: INFORMATIONAL)

2122 VEMMI URL Specification. D. Mavrakis, H. Layec, K. Kartmann. March 1997. (Format: TXT=25043 bytes) (Status: PROPOSED STANDARD)

2123 Traffic Flow Measurement: Experiences with NeTraMet. N. Brownlee. March 1997. (Format: TXT=81874 bytes) (Status: INFORMATIONAL)

2124 Cabletron's Light-weight Flow Admission Protocol Specification Version 1.0. P. Amsden, J. Amweg, P. Calato, S. Bensley, G. Lyons. March 1997. (Format: TXT=47912 bytes) (Status: INFORMATIONAL)

2125 The PPP Bandwidth Allocation Protocol (BAP) / The PPP Bandwidth Allocation Control Protocol (BACP). C. Richards, K. Smith. March 1997. (Format: TXT=49213 bytes) (Status: PROPOSED STANDARD)

2126 ISO Transport Service on top of TCP (ITOT). Y. Pouffary, A. Young. March 1997. (Format: TXT=51032 bytes) (Status: PROPOSED STANDARD)

2127 ISDN Management Information Base using SMIv2. G. Roeck. March 1997. (Format: TXT=95994 bytes) (Status: PROPOSED STANDARD)

2128 Dial Control Management Information Base using SMIv2. G. Roeck. March 1997. (Format: TXT=66153 bytes) (Status: PROPOSED STANDARD)

2129 Toshiba's Flow Attribute Notification Protocol (FANP) Specification. K. Nagami, Y. Katsube, Y. Shobatake, A. Mogi, S. Matsuzawa, T. Jinmei, H. Esaki. April 1997. (Format: TXT=41137 bytes) (Status: INFORMATIONAL)

2130 The Report of the IAB Character Set Workshop held 29 February - 1 March, 1996. C. Weider, C. Preston, K. Simonsen, H. Alvestrand, R. Atkinson, M. Crispin, P. Svanberg. April 1997. (Format: TXT=63443 bytes) (Status: INFORMATIONAL)

2131 Dynamic Host Configuration Protocol. R. Droms. March 1997. (Format: TXT=113738 bytes) (Obsoletes RFC1541) (Status: DRAFT STANDARD)

2132 DHCP Options and BOOTP Vendor Extensions. S. Alexander, R. Droms. MArch 1997. (Format: TXT=63670 bytes) (Obsoletes RFC1533) (Status: DRAFT STANDARD)

2133 Basic Socket Interface Extensions for IPv6. R. Gilligan, S. Thomson, J. Bound, W. Stevens. April 1997. (Format: TXT=69737 bytes) (Status: INFORMATIONAL)

2134 Articles of Incorporation of Internet Society. ISOC Board of Trustees. April 1997. (Format: TXT=9131 bytes) (Status: INFORMATIONAL)

2135 Internet Society By-Laws. ISOC Board of Trustees. April 1997. (Format: TXT=20467 bytes) (Status: INFORMATIONAL)

2136 Dynamic Updates in the Domain Name System (DNS UPDATE). P. Vixie, Ed., S. Thomson, Y. Rekhter, J. Bound. April 1997. (Format: TXT=56354 bytes) (Updates RFC1035) (Status: PROPOSED STANDARD)

2137 Secure Domain Name System Dynamic Update. D. Eastlake. April 1997. (Format: TXT=24824 bytes) (Updates RFC1035) (Status: PROPOSED STANDARD)

2138 Remote Authentication Dial In User Service (RADIUS). C. Rigney, A. Rubens, W. Simpson, S. Willens. April 1997. (Format: TXT=120407 bytes) (Obsoletes RFC2058) (Status: PROPOSED STANDARD)

2139 RADIUS Accounting. C. Rigney. April 1997. (Format: TXT=44919 bytes) (Obsoletes RFC2059) (Status: INFORMATIONAL)

2140 TCP Control Block Interdependence. J. Touch. April 1997. (Format: TXT=26032 bytes) (Status: INFORMATIONAL)

2141 URN Syntax. R. Moats. May 1997. (Format: TXT=14077 bytes) (Status: PROPOSED STANDARD)

2142 Mailbox Names for Common Services, Roles and Functions. D. Crocker. May 1997. (Format: TXT=12195 bytes) (Status: PROPOSED STANDARD)

2143 Encapsulating IP with the Small Computer System Interface. B. Elliston. May 1997. (Format: TXT=10749 bytes) (Status: EXPERIMENTAL)

2144 The CAST-128 Encryption Algorithm. C. Adams. May 1997. (Format: TXT=37532 bytes) (Status: INFORMATIONAL)

2145 Use and Interpretation of HTTP Version Numbers. J. C. Mogul, R. Fielding, J. Gettys, H. Frystyk. May 1997. (Format: TXT=13659 bytes) (Status: INFORMATIONAL)

2146 U.S. Government Internet Domain Names. Federal Networking Council. May 1997. (Format: TXT=26564 bytes) (Obsoletes RFC1816) (Status: INFORMATIONAL)

2147 TCP and UDP over IPv6 Jumbograms. D. Borman. May 1997. (Format: TXT=1883 bytes) (Status: PROPOSED STANDARD)

2148 Deployment of the Internet White Pages Service. H. Alvestrand, P. Jurg. September 1997. (Format: TXT=31539 bytes) (Also BCP0015) (Status: BEST CURRENT PRACTICE)

2149 Multicast Server Architectures for MARS-based ATM multicasting. R. Talpade, M. Ammar. May 1997. (Format: TXT=42007 bytes) (Status: INFORMATIONAL)

2150 Humanities and Arts: Sharing Center Stage on the Internet. J. Max, W. Stickle. October 1997. (Format: TXT=154037 bytes) (Also FYI0031) (Status: INFORMATIONAL)

2151 A Primer On Internet and TCP/IP Tools and Utilities. G. Kessler, S. Shepard. June 1997. (Format: TXT=114130 bytes) (Obsoletes RFC1739) (Also FYI0030) (Status: INFORMATIONAL)

2152 UTF-7 A Mail-Safe Transformation Format of Unicode. D. Goldsmith, M. Davis. May 1997. (Format: TXT=28065 bytes) (Obsoletes RFC1642) (Status: INFORMATIONAL)

2153 PPP Vendor Extensions. W. Simpson. May 1997. (Format: TXT=10780 bytes) (Updates RFC1661, RFC1962) (Status: INFORMATIONAL)

2154 OSPF with Digital Signatures. S. Murphy, M. Badger, B. Wellington. June 1997. (Format: TXT=72701 bytes) (Status: EXPERIMENTAL)

2155 Definitions of Managed Objects for APPN using SMIv2. B. Clouston, B. Moore. June 1997. (Format: TXT=213809 bytes) (Status: PROPOSED STANDARD)

2156 MIXER (Mime Internet X.400 Enhanced Relay): Mapping between X.400 and RFC 822/MIME. S. Kille. January 1998. (Format: TXT=280385 bytes) (Obsoletes RFC0987, RFC1026, RFC1138, RFC1148, RFC1327, RFC1495) (Updates RFC0822) (Status: PROPOSED STANDARD)

2157 Mapping between X.400 and RFC-822/MIME Message Bodies. H. Alvestrand. January 1998. (Format: TXT=92554 bytes) (Status: PROPOSED STANDARD)

2158 X.400 Image Body Parts. H. Alvestrand. January 1998. (Format: TXT=5547 bytes) (Status: PROPOSED STANDARD)

2159 A MIME Body Part for FAX. H. Alvestrand. January 1998. (Format: TXT=11471 bytes) (Status: PROPOSED STANDARD)

2160 Carrying PostScript in X.400 and MIME. H. Alvestrand. January 1998. (Format: TXT=7059 bytes) (Status: PROPOSED STANDARD)

2161 A MIME Body Part for ODA. H. Alvestrand. January 1998. (Format: TXT=8009 bytes) (Status: EXPERIMENTAL)

2162 MaXIM-11 - Mapping between X.400 / Internet mail and Mail-11 mail. C. Allocchio. January 1998. (Format: TXT=58553 bytes) (Obsoletes RFC1405) (Status: EXPERIMENTAL)

2163 Using the Internet DNS to Distribute MIXER Conformant Global Address Mapping (MCGAM). C. Allocchio. January 1998. (Format: TXT=58789 bytes) (Obsoletes RFC1664) (Status: PROPOSED STANDARD)

2164 Use of an X.500/LDAP directory to support MIXER address mapping. S. Kille. January 1998. (Format: TXT=16701 bytes) (Obsoletes RFC1838) (Status: PROPOSED STANDARD)

2165 Service Location Protocol. J. Veizades, E. Guttman, C. Perkins, S. Kaplan. June 1997. (Format: TXT=169889 bytes) (Status: PROPOSED STANDARD)

2166 APPN Implementer's Workshop Closed Pages Document DLSw v2.0 Enhancements. D. Bryant, P. Brittain. June 1997. (Format: TXT=75527 bytes) (Status: INFORMATIONAL)

2167 Referral Whois (RWhois) Protocol V1.5. S. Williamson, M. Kosters, D. Blacka, J. Singh, K. Zeilstra. June 1997. (Format: TXT=136355 bytes) (Obsoletes RFC1714) (Status: INFORMATIONAL)

2168 Resolution of Uniform Resource Identifiers using the Domain Name System. R. Daniel, M. Mealling. June 1997. (Format: TXT=46528 bytes) (Status: EXPERIMENTAL)

2169 A Trivial Convention for using HTTP in URN Resolution. R. Daniel. June 1997. (Format: TXT=17763 bytes) (Status: EXPERIMENTAL)

2170 Application REQuested IP over ATM (AREQUIPA). W. Almesberger, J. Le Boudec, P. Oechslin. June 1997. (Format: TXT=22874 bytes) (Status: INFORMATIONAL)

2171 MAPOS - Multiple Access Protocol over SONET/SDH Version 1. K. Murakami, M. Maruyama. June 1997. (Format: TXT=17480 bytes) (Status: INFORMATIONAL)

2172 MAPOS Version 1 Assigned Numbers. M. Maruyama, K. Murakami. June 1997. (Format: TXT=4857 bytes) (Status: INFORMATIONAL)

2173 A MAPOS version 1 Extension - Node Switch Protocol. K. Murakami, M. Maruyama. June 1997. (Format: TXT=12251 bytes) (Status: INFORMATIONAL)

2174 A MAPOS version 1 Extension - Switch-Switch Protocol. K. Murakami, M. Maruyama. June 1997. (Format: TXT=47967 bytes) (Status: INFORMATIONAL)

2175 MAPOS 16 - Multiple Access Protocol over SONET/SDH with 16 Bit Addressing. K. Murakami, M. Maruyama. June 1997. (Format: TXT=11677 bytes) (Status: INFORMATIONAL)

2176 IPv4 over MAPOS Version 1. K. Murakami, M. Maruyama. June 1997. (Format: TXT=12305 bytes) (Status: INFORMATIONAL)

2177 IMAP4 IDLE command. B. Leiba. June 1997. (Format: TXT=6770 bytes) (Status: PROPOSED STANDARD)

2178 OSPF Version 2. J. Moy. July 1997. (Format: TXT=495866 bytes) (Obsoletes RFC1583) (Obsoleted by RFC2328) (Status: DRAFT STANDARD)

2179 Network Security For Trade Shows. A. Gwinn. July 1997. (Format: TXT=20690 bytes) (Status: INFORMATIONAL)

2180 IMAP4 Multi-Accessed Mailbox Practice. M. Gahrns. July 1997. (Format: TXT=24750 bytes) (Status: INFORMATIONAL)

2181 Clarifications to the DNS Specification. R. Elz, R. Bush. July 1997. (Format: TXT=36989 bytes) (Updates RFC1034, RFC1035, RFC1123) (Status: PROPOSED STANDARD)

2182 Selection and Operation of Secondary DNS Servers. R. Elz, R. Bush, S. Bradner, M. Patton. July 1997. (Format: TXT=27456 bytes) (Also BCP0016) (Status: BEST CURRENT PRACTICE)

2183 Communicating Presentation Information in Internet Messages: The Content-Disposition Header Field. R. Troost, S. Dorner, K. Moore. August 1997. (Format: TXT=23150 bytes) (Updates RFC1806) (Updated by RFC2184, RFC2231) (Status: PROPOSED STANDARD)

2184 MIME Parameter Value and Encoded Word Extensions: Character Sets, Languages, and Continuations. N. Freed, K. Moore. August 1997. (Format: TXT=17635 bytes) (Obsoletes RFC2184) (Obsoleted by RFC2184, RFC2231) (Updates RFC2045, RFC2047, RFC2183) (Status: PROPOSED STANDARD)

2185 Routing Aspects of IPv6 Transition. R. Callon, D. Haskin. September 1997. (Format: TXT=31281 bytes) (Status: INFORMATIONAL)

2186 Internet Cache Protocol (ICP), version 2. D. Wessels, K. Claffy. September 1997. (Format: TXT=18808 bytes) (Status: INFORMATIONAL)

2187 Application of Internet Cache Protocol (ICP), version 2. D. Wessels, K. Claffy. September 1997. (Format: TXT=51662 bytes) (Status: INFORMATIONAL)

2188 AT&T/Neda's Efficient Short Remote Operations (ESRO) Protocol Specification Version 1.2. M. Banan, M. Taylor, and J. Cheng. September 1997. (Format: TXT=118374 bytes) (Status: INFORMATIONAL)

2189 Core Based Trees (CBT version 2) Multicast Routing. A. Ballardie. September 1997. (Format: TXT=52043 bytes) (Status: EXPERIMENTAL)

2190 RTP Payload Format for H.263 Video Streams. C. Zhu. September 1997. (Format: TXT=26409 bytes) (Status: PROPOSED STANDARD)

2191 VENUS - Very Extensive Non-Unicast Service. G. Armitage. September 1997. (Format: TXT=31316 bytes) (Status: INFORMATIONAL)

2192 IMAP URL Scheme. C. Newman. September 1997. (Format: TXT=31426 bytes) (Status: PROPOSED STANDARD)

2193 IMAP4 Mailbox Referrals. M. Gahrns. September 1997. (Format: TXT=16248 bytes) (Status: PROPOSED STANDARD)

2194 Review of Roaming Implementations. B. Aboba, J. Lu, J. Alsop, J. Ding, W. Wang. September 1997. (Format: TXT=81533 bytes) (Status: INFORMATIONAL)

2195 IMAP/POP AUTHorize Extension for Simple Challenge/Response. J. Klensin, R. Catoe, P. Krumviede. September 1997. (Format: TXT=10468 bytes) (Obsoletes RFC2095) (Status: PROPOSED STANDARD)

2196 Site Security Handbook. B. Fraser. September 1997. (Format: TXT=191772 bytes) (Obsoletes RFC1244) (Also FYI0008) (Status: INFORMATIONAL)

2197 SMTP Service Extension for Command Pipelining. N. Freed. September 1997. (Format: TXT=15003 bytes) (Obsoletes RFC1854) (Status: DRAFT STANDARD)

2198 RTP Payload for Redundant Audio Data. C. Perkins, I. Kouvelas, O. Hodson, V. Hardman, M. Handley, J.C. Bolot, A. Vega-Garcia, S. Fosse-Parisis. September 1997. (Format: TXT=25166 bytes) (Status: PROPOSED STANDARD)

2199 Request for Comments Summary RFC Numbers 2100-2199. A. Ramos. January 1998. (Format: TXT=47664 bytes) (Status: INFORMATIONAL)

2200 INTERNET OFFICIAL PROTOCOL STANDARDS. J. Postel. June 1997. (Format: TXT=94506 bytes) (Obsoletes RFC2000, RFC1920, RFC1880, RFC1800, RFC1780, RFC1720, RFC1610, RFC1600, RFC1540, RFC1500, RFC1410, RFC1360, RFC1280, RFC1250, RFC1200, RFC1140, RFC1130, RFC1100, RFC1083) (Obsoleted by RFC2300, RFC2400, STD0001) (Also STD0001) (Status: STANDARD)

2201 Core Based Trees (CBT) Multicast Routing Architecture. A. Ballardie. September 1997. (Format: TXT=38040 bytes) (Status: EXPERIMENTAL)

2202 Test Cases for HMAC-MD5 and HMAC-SHA-1. P. Cheng, R. Glenn. September 1997. (Format: TXT=11945 bytes) (Status: INFORMATIONAL)

2203 RPCSEC_GSS Protocol Specification. M. Eisler, A. Chiu, L. Ling. September 1997. (Format: TXT=50937 bytes) (Status: PROPOSED STANDARD)

2204 ODETTE File Transfer Protocol. D. Nash. September 1997. (Format: TXT=151857 bytes) (Status: INFORMATIONAL)

2205 Resource ReSerVation Protocol (RSVP) – Version 1 Functional Specification. R. Braden, Ed., L. Zhang, S. Berson, S. Herzog, S. Jamin. September 1997. (Format: TXT=223974 bytes) (Status: PROPOSED STANDARD)

2206 RSVP Management Information Base using SMIv2. F. Baker, J. Krawczyk, A. Sastry. September 1997. (Format: TXT=112937 bytes) (Status: PROPOSED STANDARD)

2207 RSVP Extensions for IPSEC Data Flows. L. Berger, T. O'Malley. September 1997. (Format: TXT=30473 bytes) (Status: PROPOSED STANDARD)

2208 Resource ReSerVation Protocol (RSVP) – Version 1 Applicability Statement Some Guidelines on Deployment. A. Mankin, Ed., F. Baker, B. Braden, S. Bradner, M. O`Dell, A. Romanow, A. Weinrib, L. Zhang. September 1997. (Format: TXT=14289 bytes) (Status: INFORMATIONAL)

2209 Resource ReSerVation Protocol (RSVP) – Version 1 Message Processing Rules. R. Braden, L. Zhang. September 1997. (Format: TXT=51690 bytes) (Status: INFORMATIONAL)

2210 The Use of RSVP with IETF Integrated Services. J. Wroclawski. September 1997. (Format: TXT=77613 bytes) (Status: PROPOSED STANDARD)

2211 Specification of the Controlled-Load Network Element Service. J. Wroclawski. September 1997. (Format: TXT=46523 bytes) (Status: PROPOSED STANDARD)

2212 Specification of Guaranteed Quality of Service. S. Shenker, C. Partridge, R. Guerin. September 1997. (Format: TXT=52330 bytes) (Status: PROPOSED STANDARD)

2213 Integrated Services Management Information Base using SMIv2. F. Baker, J. Krawczyk, A. Sastry. September 1997. (Format: TXT=36147 bytes) (Status: PROPOSED STANDARD)

2214 Integrated Services Management Information Base Guaranteed Service Extensions using SMIv2. F. Baker, J. Krawczyk, A. Sastry. September 1997. (Format: TXT=15971 bytes) (Status: PROPOSED STANDARD)

2215 General Characterization Parameters for Integrated Service Network Elements. S. Shenker, J. Wroclawski. September 1997. (Format: TXT=39552 bytes) (Status: PROPOSED STANDARD)

2216 Network Element Service Specification Template. S. Shenker, J. Wroclawski. September 1997. (Format: TXT=53655 bytes) (Status: INFORMATIONAL)

2217 Telnet Com Port Control Option. G. Clark. October 1997. (Format: TXT=31664 bytes) (Status: EXPERIMENTAL)

2218 A Common Schema for the Internet White Pages Service. T. Genovese, B. Jennings. October 1997. (Format: TXT=16258 bytes) (Status: PROPOSED STANDARD)

2219 Use of DNS Aliases for Network Services. M. Hamilton, R. Wright. October 1997. (Format: TXT=17858 bytes) (Also BCP0017) (Status: BEST CURRENT PRACTICE)

2220 The Application/MARC Content-type. R. Guenther. October 1997. (Format: TXT=7025 bytes) (Status: INFORMATIONAL)

2221 IMAP4 Login Referrals. M. Gahrns. October 1997. (Format: TXT=9251 bytes) (Status: PROPOSED STANDARD)

2222 Simple Authentication and Security Layer (SASL). J. Myers. October 1997. (Format: TXT=35010 bytes) (Status: PROPOSED STANDARD)

2223 Instructions to RFC Authors. J. Postel, J. Reynolds. October 1997. (Format: TXT=37948 bytes) (Obsoletes RFC1543, RFC1111, RFC825) (Status: INFORMATIONAL)

2224 NFS URL Scheme. B. Callaghan. October 1997. (Format: TXT=22726 bytes) (Status: INFORMATIONAL)

2225 Classical IP and ARP over ATM. M. Laubach, J. Halpern. April 1998. (Format: TXT=65779 bytes) (Obsoletes RFC1626, RFC1577) (Status: PROPOSED STANDARD)

2226 IP Broadcast over ATM Networks. T. Smith, G. Armitage. October 1997. (Format: TXT=30661 bytes) (Status: PROPOSED STANDARD)

2227 Simple Hit-Metering and Usage-Limiting for HTTP. J. Mogul, P. Leach. October 1997. (Format: TXT=85127 bytes) (Status: PROPOSED STANDARD)

2228 FTP Security Extensions. M. Horowitz, S. Lunt. October 1997. (Format: TXT=58733 bytes) (Updates RFC0959) (Status: PROPOSED STANDARD)

2229 A Dictionary Server Protocol. R. Faith, B. Martin. October 1997. (Format: TXT=59551 bytes) (Status: INFORMATIONAL)

2230 Key Exchange Delegation Record for the DNS. R. Atkinson. October 1997. (Format: TXT=25563 bytes) (Status: INFORMATIONAL)

2231 MIME Parameter Value and Encoded Word Extensions: Character Sets, Languages, and Continuations. N. Freed, K. Moore. November 1997. (Format: TXT=19280 bytes) (Obsoletes RFC2184) (Updates RFC2045, RFC2047 RFC2183) (Status: PROPOSED STANDARD)

2232 Definitions of Managed Objects for DLUR using SMIv2. B. Clouston, B. Moore. November 1997. (Format: TXT=37955 bytes) (Status: PROPOSED STANDARD)

2233 The Interfaces Group MIB using SMIv2. K. McCloghrie, F. Kastenholz. November 1997. (Format: TXT=148033 bytes) (Obsoletes RFC1573) (Status: PROPOSED STANDARD)

2234 Augmented BNF for Syntax Specifications: ABNF. D. Crocker, Ed., P. Overell. November 1997. (Format: TXT=24265 bytes) (Status: PROPOSED STANDARD)

2235 Hobbes' Internet Timeline. R. Zakon. November 1997. (Format: TXT=43060 bytes) (Also FYI0032) (Status: INFORMATIONAL)

2236 Internet Group Management Protocol, Version 2. W. Fenner. November 1997. (Format: TXT=51048 bytes) (Updates RFC1112) (Status: PROPOSED STANDARD)

2237 Japanese Character Encoding for Internet Messages. K. Tamaru. November 1997. (Format: TXT=11628 bytes) (Status: INFORMATIONAL)

2238 Definitions of Managed Objects for HPR using SMIv2. B. Clouston, B. Moore. November 1997. (Format: TXT=65498 bytes) (Status: PROPOSED STANDARD)

2239 Definitions of Managed Objects for IEEE 802.3 Medium Attachment Units (MAUs) using SMIv2. K. de Graaf, D. Romascanu, D. McMaster, K. McCloghrie, S. Roberts. November 1997. (Format: TXT=80651 bytes) (Status: PROPOSED STANDARD)

2240 A Legal Basis for Domain Name Allocation. O. Vaughan. November 1997. (Format: TXT=13602 bytes) (Obsoleted by RFC2352) (Status: INFORMATIONAL)

2241 DHCP Options for Novell Directory Services. D. Provan. November 1997. (Format: TXT=8419 bytes) (Status: PROPOSED STANDARD)

2242 NetWare/IP Domain Name and Information. R. Droms, K. Fong. November 1997. (Format: TXT=10653 bytes) (Status: PROPOSED STANDARD)

2243 OTP Extended Responses. C. Metz. November 1997. (Format: TXT=19730 bytes) (Status: PROPOSED STANDARD)

2244 ACAP – Application Configuration Access Protocol. C. Newman, J. G. Myers. November 1997. (Format: TXT=154610 bytes) (Status: PROPOSED STANDARD)

2245 Anonymous SASL Mechanism. C. Newman. November 1997. (Format: TXT=9974 bytes) (Status: PROPOSED STANDARD)

2247 Using Domains in LDAP/X.500 Distinguished Names. S. Kille, M. Wahl, A. Grimstad, R. Huber, S. Sataluri. January 1998. (Format: TXT=12411 bytes) (Status: PROPOSED STANDARD)

2248 Network Services Monitoring MIB. N. Freed, S. Kille. January 1998. (Format: TXT=34107 bytes) (Obsoletes RFC1565) (Status: PROPOSED STANDARD)

2249 Mail Monitoring MIB. N. Freed, S. Kille. January 1998. (Format: TXT=52334 bytes) (Obsoletes RFC1566) (Status: PROPOSED STANDARD)

2250 RTP Payload Format for MPEG1/MPEG2 Video. D. Hoffman, G. Fernando, V. Goyal, M. Civanlar. January 1998. (Format: TXT=34293 bytes) (Obsoletes RFC2038) (Status: PROPOSED STANDARD)

2251 Lightweight Directory Access Protocol (v3). M. Wahl, T. Howes, S. Kille. December 1997. (Format: TXT=114488 bytes) (Status: PROPOSED STANDARD)

2252	Lightweight Directory Access Protocol (v3): Attribute Syntax Definitions. M. Wahl, A. Coulbeck, T. Howes, S. Kille. December 1997. (Format: TXT=60204 bytes) (Status: PROPOSED STANDARD)
2253	Lightweight Directory Access Protocol (v3): UTF-8 String Representation of Distinguished Names. M. Wahl, S. Kille, T. Howes. December 1997. (Format: TXT=18226 bytes) (Status: PROPOSED STANDARD)
2254	The String Representation of LDAP Search Filters. T. Howes. December 1997. (Format: TXT=13511 bytes) (Status: PROPOSED STANDARD)
2255	The LDAP URL Format. T. Howes, M. Smith. December 1997. (Format: TXT=20685 bytes) (Status: PROPOSED STANDARD)
2256	A Summary of the X.500(96) User Schema for use with LDAPv3. M. Wahl. December 1997. (Format: TXT=32377 bytes) (Status: PROPOSED STANDARD)
2257	Agent Extensibility (AgentX) Protocol Version 1. M. Daniele, B. Wijnen, D. Francisco. January 1998. (Format: TXT=177452 bytes) (Status: PROPOSED STANDARD)
2258	Internet Nomenclator Project. J. Ordille. January 1998. (Format: TXT=34871 bytes) (Status: INFORMATIONAL)
2259	Simple Nomenclator Query Protocol (SNQP). J. Elliott, J. Ordille. January 1998. (Format: TXT=58508 bytes) (Status: INFORMATIONAL)
2260	Scalable Support for Multi-homed Multi-provider Connectivity. T. Bates, Y. Rekhter. January 1998. (Format: TXT=28085 bytes) (Status: INFORMATIONAL)
2261	An Architecture for Describing SNMP Management Frameworks. D. Harrington, R. Presuhn, B. Wijnen. January 1998. (Format: TXT=128036 bytes) (Obsoleted by RFC2271) (Status: PROPOSED STANDARD)
2262	Message Processing and Dispatching for the Simple Network Management Protocol (SNMP). J. Case, D. Harrington, R. Presuhn, B. Wijnen. January 1998. (Format: TXT=88254 bytes) (Obsoleted by RFC2272) (Status: PROPOSED STANDARD)
2263	SNMPv3 Applications. D. Levi, P. Meyer, B. Stewart. January 1998. (Format: TXT=143493 bytes) (Obsoleted by RFC2273) (Status: PROPOSED STANDARD)

2264 User-based Security Model (USM) for version 3 of the Simple Network Management Protocol (SNMPv3). U. Blumenthal, B. Wijnen. January 1998. (Format: TXT=168759 bytes) (Obsoleted by RFC2274) (Status: PROPOSED STANDARD)

2265 View-based Access Control Model (VACM) for the Simple Network Management Protocol (SNMP). B. Wijnen, R. Presuhn, K. McCloghrie. January 1998. (Format: TXT=77807 bytes) (Obsoleted by RFC2275) (Status: PROPOSED STANDARD)

2266 Definitions of Managed Objects for IEEE 802.12 Repeater Devices. J. Flick. January 1998. (Format: TXT=134027 bytes) (Status: PROPOSED STANDARD)

2267 Network Ingress Filtering: Defeating Denial of Service Attacks which employ IP Source Address Spoofing. P. Ferguson, D. Senie. January 1998. (Format: TXT=21032 bytes) (Status: INFORMATIONAL)

2268 A Description of the RC2(r) Encryption Algorithm. R. Rivest. January 1998. (Format: TXT=19048 bytes) (Status: INFORMATIONAL)

2269 Using the MARS Model in non-ATM NBMA Networks. G. Armitage. January 1998. (Format: TXT=12094 bytes) (Status: INFORMATIONAL)

2270 Using a Dedicated AS for Sites Homed to a Single Provider. J. Stewart, T. Bates, R. Chandra, E. Chen. January 1998. (Format: TXT=12063 bytes) (Status: INFORMATIONAL)

2271 An Architecture for Describing SNMP Management Frameworks. D. Harrington, R. Presuhn, B. Wijnen. January 1998. (Format: TXT=128227 bytes) (Obsoletes RFC2261) (Status: PROPOSED STANDARD)

2272 Message Processing and Dispatching for the Simple Network Management Protocol (SNMP). J. Case, D. Harrington, R. Presuhn, B. Wijnen. January 1998. (Format: TXT=88445 bytes) (Obsoletes RFC2262) (Status: PROPOSED STANDARD)

2273 SNMPv3 Applications. D. Levi, P. Meyer, B. Stewart. January 1998. (Format: TXT=143754 bytes) (Obsoletes RFC2263) (Status: PROPOSED STANDARD)

2274 User-based Security Model (USM) for version 3 of the Simple Network Management Protocol (SNMPv3). U. Blumenthal, B. Wijnen. January 1998. (Format: TXT=168950 bytes) (Obsoletes RFC2264) (Status: PROPOSED STANDARD)

2275 View-based Access Control Model (VACM) for the Simple Network Management Protocol (SNMP). B. Wijnen, R. Presuhn, K. McCloghrie. January 1998. (Format: TXT=77998 bytes) (Obsoletes RFC2265) (Status: PROPOSED STANDARD)

2276 Architectural Principles of Uniform Resource Name Resolution. K. Sollins. January 1998. (Format: TXT=64811 bytes) (Status: INFORMATIONAL)

2277 IETF Policy on Character Sets and Languages. H. Alvestrand. January 1998. (Format: TXT=16622 bytes) (Also BCP0018) (Status: Best Current Practice)

2278 IANA Charset Registration Procedures. N. Freed, J. Postel. January 1998. (Format: TXT=18881 bytes) (Also BCP0019) (Status: Best Current Practice)

2279 UTF-8, a transformation format of ISO 10646. F. Yergeau. January 1998. (Format: TXT=21634 bytes) (Obsoletes RFC2044) (Status: PROPOSED STANDARD)

2280 Routing Policy Specification Language (RPSL). C. Alaettinoglu, T. Bates, E. Gerich, D. Karrenberg, D. Meyer, M. Terpstra, C. Villamizar. January 1998. (Format: TXT=114985 bytes) (Status: PROPOSED STANDARD)

2281 Cisco Hot Standby Router Protocol (HSRP). T. Li, B. Cole, P. Morton, D. Li. March 1998. (Format: TXT=35161 bytes) (Status: INFORMATIONAL)

2282 IAB and IESG Selection, Confirmation, and Recall Process: Operation of the Nominating and Recall Committees. J. Galvin. February 1998. (Format: TXT=29852 bytes) (Obsoletes RFC2027) (Also BCP0010) (Status: BEST CURRENT PRACTICE)

2283 Multiprotocol Extensions for BGP-4. T. Bates, R. Chandra, D. Katz, Y. Rekhter. February 1998. (Format: TXT=18946 bytes) (Status: PROPOSED STANDARD)

2284 PPP Extensible Authentication Protocol (EAP). L. Blunk, J. Vollbrecht. March 1998. (Format: TXT=29452 bytes) (Status: PROPOSED STANDARD)

2285 Benchmarking Terminology for LAN Switching Devices. R. Mandeville. February 1998. (Format: TXT=43130 bytes) (Status: INFORMATIONAL)

2286 Test Cases for HMAC-RIPEMD160 and HMAC-RIPEMD128. J. Kapp. February 1998. (Format: TXT=11849 bytes) (Status: INFORMATIONAL)

2287	Definitions of System-Level Managed Objects for Applications. C. Krupczak, J. Saperia. February 1998. (Format: TXT=98210 bytes) (Status: PROPOSED STANDARD)
2288	Using Existing Bibliographic Identifiers as Uniform Resource Names. C. Lynch, C. Preston, R. Daniel. February 1998. (Format: TXT=21628 bytes) (Status: INFORMATIONAL)
2289	A One-Time Password System. N. Haller, C. Metz, P. Nesser, M. Straw. February 1998. (Format: TXT=56495 bytes) (Obsoletes RFC1938) (Status: DRAFT STANDARD)
2290	Mobile-IPv4 Configuration Option for PPP IPCP. J. Solomon, S. Glass. February 1998. (Format: TXT=39421 bytes) (Updates RFC2002) (Status: PROPOSED STANDARD)
2291	Requirements for a Distributed Authoring and Versioning Protocol for the World Wide Web. J. Slein, F. Vitali, E. Whitehead, D. Durand. February 1998. (Format: TXT=44036 bytes) (Status: INFORMATIONAL)
2292	Advanced Sockets API for IPv6. W. Stevens, M. Thomas. February 1998. (Format: TXT=152077 bytes) (Status: INFORMATIONAL)
2293	Representing Tables and Subtrees in the X.500 Direct. S. Kille. March 1998. (Format: TXT=12539 bytes) (Obsoletes RFC1837) (Status: PROPOSED STANDARD)
2294	Representing the O/R Address hierarchy in the X.500 Directory Information Tree. S. Kille. March 1998. (Format: TXT=22059 bytes) (Obsoletes RFC1836) (Status: PROPOSED STANDARD)
2295	Transparent Content Negotiation in HTTP. K. Holtman, A. Mutz. March 1998. (Format: TXT=125130 bytes) (Status: EXPERIMENTAL)
2296	HTTP Remote Variant Selection Algorithm – RVSA/1.0. K. Holtman, A. Mutz. March 1998. (Format: TXT=26932 bytes) (Status: EXPERIMENTAL)
2297	Ipsilon's General Switch Management Protocol Specification Version 2.0. P. Newman, W. Edwards, R. Hinden, E. Hoffman, F. Ching Liaw, T. Lyon, G. Minshall. March 1998. (Format: TXT=280484 bytes) (Updates RFC1987) (Status: INFORMATIONAL)
2298	An Extensible Message Format for Message Disposition Notifications. R. Fajman. March 1998. (Format: TXT=62059 bytes) (Status: PROPOSED STANDARD)

2300 INTERNET OFFICIAL PROTOCOL STANDARDS. J. Postel. May 1998. (Format: TXT=128322 bytes) (Obsoletes RFC2200, RFC2000, RFC1920, RFC1880, RFC1800, RFC1780, RFC1720, RFC1610, RFC1600, RFC1540, RFC1500, RFC1410, RFC1360, RFC1280, RFC1250, RFC1200, RFC1140, RFC1130, RFC1100, RFC1083) (Obsoleted by RFC2400, STD0001) (Also STD0001) (Status: STANDARDS TRACK)

2301 File Format for Internet Fax. L. McIntyre, S. Zilles, R. Buckley, D. Venable, G. Parsons, J. Rafferty. March 1998. (Format: TXT=200525 bytes) (Status: PROPOSED STANDARD)

2302 Tag Image File Format (TIFF) - image/tiff MIME Sub-type Registration. G. Parsons, J. Rafferty, S. Zilles. March 1998. (Format: TXT=14375 bytes) (Status: PROPOSED STANDARD)

2303 Minimal PSTN address format in Internet Mail. C. Allocchio. March 1998. (Format: TXT=14625 bytes) (Status: PROPOSED STANDARD)

2304 Minimal FAX address format in Internet Mail. C. Allocchio. March 1998. (Format: TXT=13236 bytes) (Status: PROPOSED STANDARD)

2305 A Simple Mode of Facsimile Using Internet Mail. K. Toyoda, H. Ohno, J. Murai, D. Wing. March 1998. (Format: TXT=24624 bytes) (Status: PROPOSED STANDARD)

2306 Tag Image File Format (TIFF) - F Profile for Facsimile. G. Parsons, J. Rafferty. March 1998. (Format: TXT=59358 bytes) (Status: INFORMATIONAL)

2307 An Approach for Using LDAP as a Network Information Service. L. Howard. March 1998. (Format: TXT=41396 bytes) (Status: EXPERIMENTAL)

2308 Negative Caching of DNS Queries (DNS NCACHE). M. Andrews. March 1998. (Format: TXT=41428 bytes) (Obsoletes RFC1034) (Updates RFC1034, RFC1035) (Status: PROPOSED STANDARD)

2309 Recommendations on Queue Management and Congestion Avoidance in the Internet. B. Braden, D. Clark, J. Crowcroft, B. Davie, S. Deering, D. Estrin, S. Floyd, V. Jacobson, G. Minshall, C. Partridge, L. Peterson, K. Ramakrishnan, S. Shenker, J. Wroclawski, L. Zhang. April 1998. (Format: TXT=38079 bytes) (Status: INFORMATIONAL)

2310 The Safe Response Header Field. K. Holtman. April 1998. (Format: TXT=8091 bytes) (Status: EXPERIMENTAL)

2311 S/MIME Version 2 Message Specification. S. Dusse, P. Hoffman, B. Ramsdell, L. Lundblade, L. Repka. March 1998. (Format: TXT=70901 bytes) (Status: INFORMATIONAL)

2312 S/MIME Version 2 Certificate Handling. S. Dusse, P. Hoffman, B. Ramsdell, J. Weinstein. March 1998. (Format: TXT=39829 bytes) (Status: INFORMATIONAL)

2313 PKCS 1: RSA Encryption Version 1-5. B. Kaliski. March 1998. (Format: TXT=37777 bytes) (Status: INFORMATIONAL)

2314 PKCS 10: Certification Request Syntax Version 1-5. B. Kaliski. March 1998. (Format: TXT=15814 bytes) (Status: INFORMATIONAL)

2315 PKCS 7: Cryptographic Message Syntax Version 1-5. B. Kaliski. March 1998. (Format: TXT=69679 bytes) (Status: INFORMATIONAL)

2316 Report of the IAB Security Architecture Workshop. S. Bellovin. April 1998. (Format: TXT=19733 bytes) (Status: INFORMATIONAL)

2317 Classless IN-ADDR.ARPA delegation. H. Eidnes, G. de Groot, P. Vixie. March 1998. (Format: TXT=17744 bytes) (Also BCP0020) (Status: Best Current Practice)

2318 The text/css Media Type. H. Lie, B. Bos, C. Lilley. March 1998. (Format: TXT=7819 bytes) (Status: INFORMATIONAL)

2319 Ukrainian Character Set KOI8-U. KOI8-U Working Group. April 1998. (Format: TXT=18042 bytes) (Status: INFORMATIONAL)

2320 Definitions of Managed Objects for Classical IP and ARP Over ATM Using SMIv2 (IPOA-MIB). M. Greene, J. Luciani, K. White, T. Kuo. April 1998. (Format: TXT=102116 bytes) (Status: PROPOSED STANDARD)

2321 RITA – The Reliable Internetwork Troubleshooting Agent. A. Bressen. March 1998. (Format: TXT=12302 bytes) (Status: INFORMATIONAL)

2322 Management of IP numbers by peg-dhcp. K. van den Hout, A. Koopal, R. van Mook. March 1998. (Format: TXT=12665 bytes) (Status: INFORMATIONAL)

2323 IETF Identification and Security Guidelines. A. Ramos. March 1998. (Format: TXT=9257 bytes) (Status: INFORMATIONAL)

2324 Hyper Text Coffee Pot Control Protocol (HTCPCP/1.0). L. Masinter. March 1998. (Format: TXT=19610 bytes) (Status: INFORMATIONAL)

2325 Definitions of Managed Objects for Drip-Type Heated Beverage Hardware Devices using SMIv2. M. Slavitch. March 1998. (Format: TXT=12726 bytes) (Status: INFORMATIONAL)

2326 Real Time Streaming Protocol (RTSP). H. Schulzrinne, A. Rao, R. Lanphier. April 1998. (Format: TXT=195010 bytes) (Status: PROPOSED STANDARD)

2327 SDP: Session Description Protocol. M. Handley, V. Jacobson. April 1998. (Format: TXT=87096 bytes) (Status: PROPOSED STANDARD)

2328 OSPF Version 2. J. Moy. April 1998. (Format: TXT=447367 bytes) (Obsoletes RFC2178) (Also STD0054) (Status: STANDARD)

2329 OSPF Standardization Report. J. Moy. April 1998. (Format: TXT=15130 bytes) (Status: INFORMATIONAL)

2330 Framework for IP Performance Metrics. V. Paxson, G. Almes, J. Mahdavi, M. Mathis. May 1998. (Format: TXT=94387 bytes) (Status: INFORMATIONAL)

2331 ATM Signalling Support for IP over ATM - UNI Signalling 4.0 Update. M. Maher. April 1998. (Format: TXT=61119 bytes) (Status: PROPOSED STANDARD)

2332 NBMA Next Hop Resolution Protocol (NHRP). J. Luciani, D. Katz, D. Piscitello, B. Cole, N. Doraswamy. April 1998. (Format: TXT=126978 bytes) (Status: PROPOSED STANDARD)

2333 NHRP Protocol Applicability Statement. D. Cansever. April 1998. (Format: TXT=20164 bytes) (Status: PROPOSED STANDARD)

2334 Server Cache Synchronization Protocol (SCSP). J. Luciani, G. Armitage, J. Halpern, N. Doraswamy. April 1998. (Format: TXT=98161 bytes) (Status: PROPOSED STANDARD)

2335 A Distributed NHRP Service Using SCSP. J. Luciani. April 1998. (Format: TXT=14007 bytes) (Status: PROPOSED STANDARD)

2336 Classical IP to NHRP Transition. J. Luciani. July 1998. (Format: TXT=10500 bytes) (Status: INFORMATIONAL)

2337 Intra-LIS IP multicast among routers over ATM using Sparse Mode PIM. D. Farinacci, D. Meyer, Y. Rekhter. April 1998. (Format: TXT=16357 bytes) (Status: EXPERIMENTAL)

2338 Virtual Router Redundancy Protocol. S. Knight, D. Weaver, D. Whipple, R. Hinden, D. Mitzel, P. Hunt, P. Higginson, M. Shand, A. Lindem. April 1998. (Format: TXT=59871 bytes) (Status: PROPOSED STANDARD)

2339 An Agreement Between the Internet Society, the IETF, and Sun Microsystems, Inc. in the matter of NFS V.4 Protocols. The Internet Society, Sun Microsystems. May 1998. (Format: TXT=10745 bytes) (Status: INFORMATIONAL)

2340 Nortel's Virtual Network Switching (VNS) Overview. B. Jamoussi, D. Jamieson, D. Williston, S. Gabe. May 1998. (Format: TXT=30731 bytes) (Status: INFORMATIONAL)

2341 Cisco Layer Two Forwarding (Protocol) "L2F". A. Valencia, M. Littlewood, T. Kolar. May 1998. (Format: TXT=66592 bytes) (Status: HISTORIC)

2342 IMAP4 Namespace. M. Gahrns, C. Newman. May 1998. (Format: TXT=19489 bytes) (Status: PROPOSED STANDARD)

2343 RTP Payload Format for Bundled MPEG. M. Civanlar, G. Cash, B. Haskell. May 1998. (Format: TXT=16557 bytes) (Status: EXPERIMENTAL)

2344 Reverse Tunneling for Mobile IP. G. Montenegro. May 1998. (Format: TXT=39468 bytes) (Status: PROPOSED STANDARD)

2345 Domain Names and Company Name Retrieval. J. Klensin, T. Wolf, G. Oglesby. May 1998. (Format: TXT=29707 bytes) (Status: EXPERIMENTAL)

2346 Making Postscript and PDF International. J. Palme. May 1998. (Format: TXT=12382 bytes) (Status: INFORMATIONAL)

2347 TFTP Option Extension. G. Malkin, A. Harkin. May 1998. (Format: TXT=13060 bytes) (Obsoletes RFC1782) (Updates RFC1350) (Status: DRAFT STANDARD)

2348 TFTP Blocksize Option. G. Malkin, A. Harkin. May 1998. (Format: TXT=9515 bytes) (Obsoletes RFC1783) (Updates RFC1350) (Status: DRAFT STANDARD)

2349 TFTP Timeout Interval and Transfer Size Options. G. Malkin, A. Harkin. May 1998. (Format: TXT=7848 bytes) (Obsoletes RFC1784) (Updates RFC1350) (Status: DRAFT STANDARD)

2350 Expectations for Computer Security Incident Response. N. Brownlee, E. Guttman. June 1998. (Format: TXT=86545 bytes) (Also BCP0021) (Status: BEST CURRENT PRACTICE)

2351 Mapping of Airline Reservation, Ticketing, and Messaging Traffic over IP. A. Rober. May 1998. (Format: TXT=43440 bytes) (Status: INFORMATIONAL)

2352 A Convention For Using Legal Names as Domain Names. O. Vaughan. May 1998. (Format: TXT=16354 bytes) (Obsoletes RFC2240) (Status: INFORMATIONAL)

2353 APPN/HPR in IP Networks APPN Implementers' Workshop Closed Pages Document. G. Dudley. May 1998. (Format: TXT=116972 bytes) (Status: INFORMATIONAL)

2354 Options for Repair of Streaming Media. C. Perkins, O. Hodson. June 1998. (Format: TXT=28876 bytes) (Status: INFORMATIONAL)

2355 TN3270 Enhancements. B. Kelly. June 1998. (Format: TXT=89394 bytes) (Obsoletes RFC1647) (Status: DRAFT STANDARD)

2356 Sun's SKIP Firewall Traversal for Mobile IP. G. Montenegro, V. Gupta. June 1998. (Format: TXT=53198 bytes) (Status: INFORMATIONAL)

2357 IETF Criteria for Evaluating Reliable Multicast Transport and Application Protocols. A. Mankin, A. Romanow, S. Bradner, V. Paxson. June 1998. (Format: TXT=24130 bytes) (Obsoletes RFC1650) (Status: INFORMATIONAL)

2358 Definitions of Managed Objects for the Ethernet-like Interface Types. J. Flick, J. Johnson. June 1998. (Format: TXT=87891 bytes) (Obsoletes RFC1650) (Status: PROPOSED STANDARD)

2359 IMAP4 UIDPLUS extension. J. Myers. June 1998. (Format: TXT=10862 bytes) (Status: PROPOSED STANDARD)

2360 Guide for Internet Standards Writers. G. Scott. June 1998. (Format: TXT=47280 bytes) (Also BCP0022) (Status: BEST CURRENT PRACTICE)

2361 WAVE and AVI Codec Registries. E. Fleischman. June 1998. (Format: TXT=97796 bytes) (Status: INFORMATIONAL)

2362 Protocol Independent Multicast-Sparse Mode (PIM-SM): Protocol Specification. D. Estrin, D. Farinacci, A. Helmy, D. Thaler, S. Deering, M. Handley, V. Jacobson, C. Liu, P. Sharma, L. Wei. June 1998. (Format: TXT=159833 bytes) (Obsoletes RFC2117) (Status: EXPERIMENTAL)

2363 PPP Over FUNI. G. Gross, M. Kaycee, A. Li, A. Malis, J. Stephens. July 1998. (Format: TXT=22576 bytes) (Status: PROPOSED STANDARD)

2364 PPP Over AAL5. G. Gross, M. Kaycee, A. Li, A. Malis, J. Stephens. July 1998. (Format: TXT=23539 bytes) (Status: PROPOSED STANDARD)

2365 Administratively Scoped IP Multicast. D. Meyer. July 1998. (Format: TXT=17770 bytes) (Also BCP0023) (Status: BEST CURRENT PRACTICE)

2366 Definitions of Managed Objects for Multicast over UNI 3.0/3.1 based ATM Networks. C. Chung, M. Greene. July 1998. (Format: TXT=134312 bytes) (Obsoleted by RFC2417) (Status: PROPOSED STANDARD)

2367 PF_KEY Key Management API, Version 2. D. McDonald, C. Metz, B. Phan. July 1998. (Format: TXT=146754 bytes) (Status: INFORMATIONAL)

2368 The mailto URL scheme. P. Hoffman, L. Masinter, J. Zawinski. July 1998. (Format: TXT=16502 bytes) (Updates RFC1738, RFC1808) (Status: PROPOSED STANDARD)

2369 The Use of URLs as Meta-Syntax for Core Mail List Commands and their Transport through Message Header Fields. G. Neufeld, J. Baer. July 1998. (Format: TXT=30853 bytes) (Status: PROPOSED STANDARD)

2370 The OSPF Opaque LSA Option. R. Coltun. July 1998. (Format: TXT=33789 bytes) (Also RFC2328) (Status: PROPOSED STANDARD)

2371 Transaction Internet Protocol Version 3.0. J. Lyon, K. Evans, J. Klein. July 1998. (Format: TXT=71399 bytes) (Status: PROPOSED STANDARD)

2372 Transaction Internet Protocol - Requirements and Supplemental Information. K. Evans, J. Klein, J. Lyon. July 1998. (Format: TXT=53699 bytes) (Status: INFORMATIONAL)

2373 IP Version 6 Addressing Architecture. R. Hinden, S. Deering. July 1998. (Format: TXT=52526 bytes) (Obsoletes RFC1884) (Status: PROPOSED STANDARD)

2374 An IPv6 Aggregatable Global Unicast Address Format. R. Hinden, M. O'Dell, S. Deering. July 1998. (Format: TXT=25068 bytes) (Obsoletes RFC2073) (Status: PROPOSED STANDARD)

2375 IPv6 Multicast Address Assignments. R. Hinden, S. Deering. July 1998. (Format: TXT=14356 bytes) (Status: INFORMATIONAL)

2376 XML Media Types. E. Whitehead, M. Murata. July 1998. (Format: TXT=32143 bytes) (Status: INFORMATIONAL)

2377 Naming Plan for Internet Directory-Enabled Applications. A. Grimstad, R. Huber, S. Sataluri, M. Wahl. September 1998. (Format: TXT=38274 bytes) (Status: INFORMATIONAL)

2378 The CCSO Nameserver (Ph) Architecture. R. Hedberg, P. Pomes. August 1998. (Format: TXT=38960 bytes) (Status: INFORMATIONAL)

2379 RSVP over ATM Implementation Guidelines. L. Berger. August 1998. (Format: TXT=15174 bytes) (Also BCP0024) (Status: Best Current Practice)

2380 RSVP over ATM Implementation Requirements. L. Berger. August 1998. (Format: TXT=31234 bytes) (Status: PROPOSED STANDARD)

2381 Interoperation of Controlled-Load Service and Guaranteed Service with ATM. M. Garrett, M. Borden. August 1998. (Format: TXT=107299 bytes) (Status: PROPOSED STANDARD)

2382 A Framework for Integrated Services and RSVP over ATM. E. Crawley, L. Berger, S. Berson, F. Baker, M. Borden, J. Krawczyk. August 1998. (Format: TXT=73865 bytes) (Status: INFORMATIONAL)

2383 ST2+ over ATM Protocol Specification - UNI 3.1 Version. M. Suzuki. August 1998. (Format: TXT=99889 bytes) (Status: INFORMATIONAL)

2384 POP URL Scheme. R. Gellens. August 1998. (Format: TXT=13649 bytes) (Status: PROPOSED STANDARD)

2385 Protection of BGP Sessions via the TCP MD5 Signature Option. A. Heffernan. August 1998. (Format: TXT=12315 bytes) (Status: PROPOSED STANDARD)

2386 A Framework for QoS-based Routing in the Internet. E. Crawley, R. Nair, B. Rajagopalan, H. Sandick. August 1998. (Format: TXT=93459 bytes) (Status: INFORMATIONAL)

2387 The MIME Multipart/Related Content-type. E. Levinson. August 1998. (Format: TXT=18864 bytes) (Obsoletes RFC2112) (Status: PROPOSED STANDARD)

2388 Returning Values from Forms: multipart/form-data. L. Masinter. August 1998. (Format: TXT=16531 bytes) (Status: PROPOSED STANDARD)

2389 Feature negotiation mechanism for the File Transfer Protocol. P. Hethmon, R. Elz. August 1998. (Format: TXT=18536 bytes) (Also RFC0959) (Status: PROPOSED STANDARD)

2390 Inverse Address Resolution Protocol. T. Bradley, C. Brown, A. Malis. August 1998. (Format: TXT=20849 bytes) (Obsoletes RFC1293) (Status: DRAFT STANDARD)

2391 Load Sharing using IP Network Address Translation (LSNAT). P. Srisuresh, D. Gan. August 1998. (Format: TXT=44884 bytes) (Status: INFORMATIONAL)

2392 Content-ID and Message-ID Uniform Resource Locators. E. Levinson. August 1998. (Format: TXT=11141 bytes) (Obsoletes RFC2111) (Status: PROPOSED STANDARD)

2393 August 1998. (Not online)

2394 August 1998. (Not online)

2395 August 1998. (Not online)

2396 Uniform Resource Identifiers (URI): Generic Syntax. T. Berners-Lee, R. Fielding, L. Masinter. August 1998. (Format: TXT=83639 bytes) (Status: DRAFT STANDARD)

2397 The “data” URL scheme. L. Masinter. August 1998. (Format: TXT=9514 bytes) (Status: PROPOSED STANDARD)

2398 Some Testing Tools for TCP Implementors. S. Parker, C. Schmechel. August 1998. (Format: TXT=24107 bytes) (Obsoletes NONE) (Updates NONE) (Also NONE) (Status: INFORMATIONAL)

2399 August 1998. (Not online)

2400 INTERNET OFFICIAL PROTOCOL STANDARDS. J. Postel, J. Reynolds. September 1998. (Format: TXT=110969 bytes) (Obsoletes RFC2300, RFC2200, RFC2000, RFC1920, RFC1880, RFC1800, RFC1780, RFC1720, RFC1610, RFC1600, RFC1540, RFC1500, RFC1410, RFC1360, RFC1280, RFC1250, RFC1200, RFC1140, RFC1130, RFC1100, RFC1083) (Also STD0001) (Status: STANDARD)

2413 Dublin Core Metadata for Resource Discovery. S. Weibel, J. Kunze, C. Lagoze, M. Wolf. September 1998. (Format: TXT=15501 bytes) (Status: INFORMATIONAL)

2414 Increasing TCP's Initial Window. M. Allman, S. Floyd, C. Partridg. September 1998. (Format: TXT=32019 bytes) (Status: EXPERIMENTAL)

2415 Simulation Studies of Increased Initial TCP Window Size. K. Poduri, K. Nichols. September 1998. (Format: TXT=24205 bytes) (Status: INFORMATIONAL)

2416 When TCP Starts Up With Four Packets Into Only Three Buffers. T. Shepard, C. Partridge. September 1998. (Format: TXT=12663 bytes) (Status: INFORMATIONAL)

2417 Definitions of Managed Objects for Multicast over UNI 3.0/3.1 based ATM Networks. C. Chung, M. Greene. September 1998. (Format: TXT=134862 bytes) (Obsoletes RFC2366) (Status: PROPOSED STANDARD)

2418 IETF Working Group Guidelines and Procedures. S. Bradner. September 1998. (Format: TXT=62857 bytes) (Obsoletes RFC1603) (Also BCP0025) (Status: BEST CURRENT PRACTICE)

2419 The PPP DES Encryption Protocol, Version 2 (DESE-bis). K. Sklower, G. Meyer. September 1998. (Format: TXT=24414 bytes) (Obsoletes RFC1969) (Status: PROPOSED STANDARD)

2420 The PPP Triple-DES Encryption Protocol (3DESE). H. Kummert. September 1998. (Format: TXT=16729 bytes) (Status: PROPOSED STANDARD)

2421 Voice Profile for Internet Mail - version 2. G. Vaudreuil, G. Parsons. September 1998. (Format: TXT=123663 bytes) (Obsoletes RFC1911) (Status: PROPOSED STANDARD)

2422 Toll Quality Voice - 32 kbit/s ADPCM MIME Sub-type Registration. G. Vaudreuil, G. Parsons. September 1998. (Format: TXT=10157 bytes) (Obsoletes RFC1911) (Status: PROPOSED STANDARD)

2423 VPIM Voice Message MIME Sub-type Registration. G. Vaudreuil, G. Parsons. September 1998. (Format: TXT=10729 bytes) (Obsoletes RFC1911) (Status: PROPOSED STANDARD)

2424 Content Duration MIME Header Definition. G. Vaudreuil, G. Parsons. September 1998. (Format: TXT=7116 bytes) (Status: PROPOSED STANDARD)

2425 A MIME Content-Type for Directory Information. T. Howes, M. Smith, F. Dawson. September 1998. (Format: TXT=64478 bytes) (Status: PROPOSED STANDARD)

2426 vCard MIME Directory Profile. F. Dawson, T. Howes. September 1998. (Format: TXT=74646 bytes) (Status: PROPOSED STANDARD)

2427 Multiprotocol Interconnect over Frame Relay. C. Brown, A. Malis. September 1998. (Format: TXT=74671 bytes) (Obsoletes RFC1490, RFC1294) (Status: STANDARD)

2428 FTP Extensions for IPv6 and NATs. M. Allman, S. Ostermann, C. Metz. September 1998. (Format: TXT=16028 bytes) (Status: PROPOSED STANDARD)

2429 RTP Payload Format for the 1998 Version of ITU-T Rec. H.263 Video (H.263+). C. Bormann, L. Cline, G. Deisher, T. Gardos, C. Maciocco, D. Newell, J. Ott, G. Sullivan, S. Wenger, C. Zhu. October 1998. (Format: TXT=43166 bytes) (Status: PROPOSED STANDARD)

2430 DOC-ID: RA Provider Architecture for Differentiated Services and Traffic Engineering (PASTE)FC2429. T. Li, Y. Rekhter. October 1998. (Format: TXT=40148 bytes) (Status: INFORMATIONAL)

2431 RTP Payload Format for BT.656 Video Encoding. D. Tynan. October 1998. (Format: TXT=22323 bytes) (Status: PROPOSED STANDARD)

2432 Terminology for IP Multicast Benchmarking. K. Dubray. October 1998. (Format: TXT=29758 bytes) (Status: INFORMATIONAL)

2433 Microsoft PPP CHAP Extensions. G. Zorn, S. Cobb. October 1998. (Format: TXT=34502 bytes) (Status: INFORMATIONAL)

2434 Guidelines for Writing an IANA Considerations Section in RFCs. T. Narten, H. Alvestrand. October 1998. (Format: TXT=25092 bytes) (Also BCP0026) (Status: BEST CURRENT PRACTICE)

2435 RTP Payload Format for JPEG-compressed Video. L. Berc, W. Fenner, R. Frederick, S. McCanne, P. Stewart. October 1998. (Format: TXT=54173 bytes) (Obsoletes RFC2035) (Status: PROPOSED STANDARD)

2436 Collaboration between ISOC/IETF and ITU-T. R. Brett, S. Bradner, G. Parsons. October 1998. (Format: TXT=31154 bytes) (Status: INFORMATIONAL)

2437 PKCS #1: RSA Cryptography Specifications Version 2.0. B. Kaliski, J. Staddon. October 1998. (Format: TXT=73529 bytes) (Obsoletes RFC2313) (Status: INFORMATIONAL)

2438 Advancement of MIB specifications on the IETF Standards Track. M. O'Dell, H. Alvestrand, B. Wijnen, S. Bradner. October 1998. (Format: TXT=13633 bytes) (Also BCP0027) (Status: BEST CURRENT PRACTICE)

2439 BGP Route Flap Damping. C. Villamizar, R. Chandra, R. Govindan. November 1998. (Format: TXT=86376 bytes) (Status: PROPOSED STANDARD)

2440 OpenPGP Message Format. J. Callas, L. Donnerhacke, H. Finney, R. Thayer. November 1998. (Format: TXT=141371 bytes) (Status: PROPOSED STANDARD)

2441 Working with Jon, Tribute delivered at UCLA, October 30, 1998. D. Cohen. November 1998. (Format: TXT=11992 bytes) (Status: INFORMATIONAL)

2442 The Batch SMTP Media Type. N. Freed, D. Newman, J. Belissen, M. Hoy. November 1998. (Format: TXT=18384 bytes) (Status: INFORMATIONAL)

2443 A Distributed MARS Service Using SCSP. J. Luciani, A. Gallo. November 1998. (Format: TXT=41451 bytes) (Status: EXPERIMENTAL)

2444 The One-Time-Password SASL Mechanism. C. Newman. October 1998. (Format: TXT=13408 bytes) (Updates RFC2222) (Status: PROPOSED STANDARD)

2445 Internet Calendaring and Scheduling Core Object Specification (iCalendar). F. Dawson, D. Stenerson. November 1998. (Format: TXT=291838 bytes) (Status: PROPOSED STANDARD)

2446 iCalendar Transport-Independent Interoperability Protocol (iTIP) Scheduling Events, BusyTime, To-dos and Journal Entries. S. Silverberg, S. Mansour, F. Dawson, R. Hopson. November 1998. (Format: TXT=225964 bytes) (Status: PROPOSED STANDARD)

2447 iCalendar Message-Based Interoperability Protocol (iMIP). F. Dawson, S. Mansour, S. Silverberg. November 1998. (Format: TXT=33480 bytes) (Status: PROPOSED STANDARD)

2448 AT&T's Error Resilient Video Transmission Technique. M. Civanlar, G. Cash, B. Haskell. November 1998. (Format: TXT=14655 bytes) (Status: INFORMATIONAL)

2449 POP3 Extension Mechanism. R. Gellens, C. Newman, L. Lundblade. November 1998. (Format: TXT=36017 bytes) (Updates RFC1939) (Status: PROPOSED STANDARD)

2450 Proposed TLA and NLA Assignment Rule. R. Hinden. December 1998. (Format: TXT=24486 bytes) (Status: INFORMATIONAL)

2451 The ESP CBC-Mode Cipher Algorithms. R. Pereira, R. Adams. November 1998. (Format: TXT=26400 bytes) (Status: PROPOSED STANDARD)

2452 IP Version 6 Management Information Base for the Transmission Control Protocol. M. Daniele. December 1998. (Format: TXT=19066 bytes) (Status: PROPOSED STANDARD)

2453 RIP Version 2. G. Malkin. November 1998. (Format: TXT=98462 bytes) (Obsoletes RFC1388, RFC1723) (Updates RFC1723, RFC1388) (Also STD0056) (Status: STANDARD)

2454 IP Version 6 Management Information Base for the User Datagram Protocol. M. Daniele. December 1998. (Format: TXT=15862 bytes) (Status: PROPOSED STANDARD)

2455 Definitions of Managed Objects for APPN. B. Clouston, B. Moore. November 1998. (Format: TXT=251061 bytes) (Obsoletes RFC2155) (Status: PROPOSED STANDARD)

2456 Definitions of Managed Objects for APPN TRAPS. B. Clouston, B. Moore. November 1998. (Format: TXT=44023 bytes) (Status: PROPOSED STANDARD)

2457 Definitions of Managed Objects for Extended Border Node. B. Clouston, B. Moore. November 1998. (Format: TXT=54380 bytes) (Status: PROPOSED STANDARD)

2458 Toward the PSTN/Internet Inter-Networking–Pre-PINT Implementations. H. Lu, M. Krishnaswamy, L. Conroy, S. Bellovin, F. Burg, A., DeSimone, K. Tewani, P. Davidson, H. Schulzrinne, K. Vishwanathan. November 1998. (Format: TXT=139100 bytes) (Status: INFORMATIONAL)

2459 Internet X.509 Public Key Infrastructure Certificate and CRL Profile. R. Housley, W. Ford, W. Polk, D. Solo. January 1999. (Format: TXT=278438 bytes) (Status: PROPOSED STANDARD)

2460 Internet Protocol, Version 6 (IPv6) Specification. S. Deering, R. Hinden. December 1998. (Format: TXT=85490 bytes) (Obsoletes RFC1883) (Status: DRAFT STANDARD)

2461 Neighbor Discovery for IP Version 6 (IPv6). T. Narten, E. Nordmark, W. Simpson. December 1998. (Format: TXT=222516 bytes) (Obsoletes RFC1970) (Status: DRAFT STANDARD)

2462 IPv6 Stateless Address Autoconfiguration. S. Thomson, T. Narten. December 1998. (Format: TXT=61210 bytes) (Obsoletes RFC1971) (Status: DRAFT STANDARD)

2463 Internet Control Message Protocol (ICMPv6) for the Internet Protocol Version 6 (IPv6) Specification. A. Conta, S. Deering. December 1998. (Format: TXT=34190 bytes) (Obsoletes RFC1885) (Status: DRAFT STANDARD)

2464 Transmission of IPv6 Packets over Ethernet Networks. M. Crawford. December 1998. (Format: TXT=12725 bytes) (Obsoletes RFC1972) (Status: PROPOSED STANDARD)

2465 Management Information Base for IP Version 6: Textual Conventions and General Group. D. Haskin, S. Onishi. December 1998. (Format: TXT=77339 bytes) (Status: PROPOSED STANDARD)

2466 Management Information Base for IP Version 6: ICMPv6 Group. D. Haskin, S. Onishi. December 1998. (Format: TXT=27547 bytes) (Status: PROPOSED STANDARD)

2467 Transmission of IPv6 Packets over FDDI Networks. M. Crawford. December 1998. (Format: TXT=16028 bytes) (Obsoletes RFC2019) (Status: PROPOSED STANDARD)

2468 I REMEMBER IANA. V. Cerf. October 1998. (Format: TXT=8543 bytes) (Status: INFORMATIONAL)

2469 A Caution On The Canonical Ordering Of Link-Layer Addresses. T. Narten, C. Burton. December 1998. (Format: TXT=9948 bytes) (Status: INFORMATIONAL)

2470 Transmission of IPv6 Packets over Token Ring Networks. M. Crawford, T. Narten, S. Thomas. December 1998. (Format: TXT=21677 bytes) (Status: PROPOSED STANDARD)

2471 IPv6 Testing Address Allocation. R. Hinden, R. Fink, J. Postel (deceased). December 1998. (Format: TXT=8031 bytes) (Obsoletes RFC1897) (Status: EXPERIMENTAL)

2472 IP Version 6 over PPP. D. Haskin, E. Allen. December 1998. (Format: TXT=29696 bytes) (Obsoletes RFC2023) (Status: PROPOSED STANDARD)

2473 Generic Packet Tunneling in IPv6 Specification. A. Conta, S. Deering. December 1998. (Format: TXT=77956 bytes) (Status: PROPOSED STANDARD)

2474 Definition of the Differentiated Services Field (DS Field) in the IPv4 and IPv6 Headers. K. Nichols, S. Blake, F. Baker, D. Black. December 1998. (Format: TXT=50576 bytes) (Obsoletes RFC1455, RFC1349) (Updates RFC791, RFC1122, RFC1123, RFC1812) (Status: PROPOSED STANDARD)

2475 An Architecture for Differentiated Service. S. Blake, D. Black, M. Carlson, E. Davies, Z. Wang, W. Weiss. December 1998. (Format: TXT=94786 bytes) (Status: PROPOSED STANDARD)

2476 Message Submission. R. Gellens, J. Klensin. December 1998. (Format: TXT=30050 bytes) (Status: PROPOSED STANDARD)

2477 Criteria for Evaluating Roaming Protocols. B. Aboba, G. Zorn. December 1998. (Format: TXT=23530 bytes) (Status: INFORMATIONAL)

2478 The Simple and Protected GSS-API Negotiation Mechanism. E. Baize, D. Pinkas. December 1998. (Format: TXT=35581 bytes) (Status: PROPOSED STANDARD)

2479 Independent Data Unit Protection Generic Security Service Application Program Interface (IDUP-GSS-API). C. Adams. December 1998. (Format: TXT=156070 bytes) (Status: INFORMATIONAL)

2480 Gateways and MIME Security Multiparts. N. Freed. January 1999. (Format: TXT=11751 bytes) (Status: PROPOSED STANDARD)

2481 A Proposal to add Explicit Congestion Notification (ECN) to IP. K. Ramakrishnan, S. Floyd. January 1999. (Format: TXT=64559 bytes) (Status: EXPERIMENTAL)

2482 Language Tagging in Unicode Plain Text. K. Whistler, G. Adams. January 1999. (Format: TXT=27800 bytes) (Status: INFORMATIONAL)

2483 URI Resolution Services Necessary for URN Resolution. M. Mealling, R. Daniel, Jr.. January 199. (Format: TXT=30518 bytes) (Status: EXPERIMENTAL)

2484 PPP LCP Internationalization Configuration Option. G. Zorn. January 1999. (Format: TXT=8330 bytes) (Updates RFC2284, RFC1994, RFC1570) (Status: PROPOSED STANDARD)

2485 DHCP Option for The Open Group's User Authentication Protocol. S. Drach. January 1999. (Format: TXT=7205 bytes) (Status: PROPOSED STANDARD)

2486 The Network Access Identifier. B. Aboba, M. Beadles. January 1999. (Format: TXT=14261 bytes) (Status: PROPOSED STANDARD)

2487 SMTP Service Extension for Secure SMTP over TLS. P. Hoffman. January 1999. (Format: TXT=15120 bytes) (Status: PROPOSED STANDARD)

2488 Enhancing TCP Over Satellite Channels using Standard Mechanisms. M. Allman, D. Glover, L. Sanchez. January 1999. (Format: TXT=47857 bytes) (Also BCP0028) (Status: BEST CURRENT PRACTICE)

2489 Procedure for Defining New DHCP Options. R. Droms. January 1999. (Format: TXT=10484 bytes) (Also BCP0029) (Status: BEST CURRENT PRACTICE)

2490 A Simulation Model for IP Multicast with RSVP. M. Pullen, R. Malghan, L. Lavu, G. Duan, J. Ma, H. Nah. January 1999. (Format: TXT=74936, PS=1956365 bytes) (Status: INFORMATIONAL)

2491 IPv6 over Non-Broadcast Multiple Access (NBMA) networks. G. Armitage, P. Schulter, M. Jork, G. Harter. January 1999. (Format: TXT=100782 bytes) (Status: PROPOSED STANDARD)

2492 IPv6 over ATM Networks. G. Armitage, P. Schulter, M. Jork. January 1999. (Format: TXT=21199 bytes) (Status: PROPOSED STANDARD)

2493 Textual Conventions for MIB Modules Using Performance History Based on 15 Minute Intervals. K. Tesink, Ed.. January 1999. (Format: TXT=18749 bytes) (Status: PROPOSED STANDARD)

2494 Definitions of Managed Objects for the DS0 and DS0 Bundle Interface Type. D. Fowler, Ed.. January 1999. (Format: TXT=47208 bytes) (Status: PROPOSED STANDARD)

2495 Definitions of Managed Objects for the DS1, E1, DS2 and E2 Interface Types. D. Fowler, Ed.. January 1999. (Format: TXT=155560 bytes) (Status: PROPOSED STANDARD)

2496 Definitions of Managed Object for the DS3/E3 Interface Typ. D. Fowler, Ed.. January 1999. (Format: TXT=124251 bytes) (Status: PROPOSED STANDARD)

2497 Transmission of IPv6 Packets over ARCnet Networks. I. Souvatzis. January 1999. (Format: TXT=10304 bytes) (Also RFC1201) (Status: PROPOSED STANDARD)

2498 IPPM Metrics for Measuring Connectivity. J. Mahdavi, V. Paxson. January 1999. (Format: TXT=17869 bytes) (Status: EXPERIMENTAL)

2501 Mobile Ad hoc Networking (MANET): Routing Protocol Performance Issues and Evaluation Considerations. S. Corson, J. Macker. January 1999. (Format: TXT=28912 bytes) (Status: INFORMATIONAL)

2502 Limitations of Internet Protocol Suite for Distributed Simulation the Large Multicast Environment. M. Pullen, M. Myjak, C. Bouwens. February 1999. (Format: TXT=28190 bytes) (Status: INFORMATIONAL)

2503 MIME Types for Use with the ISO ILL Protocol. R. Moulton, M. Needleman. February 1999. (Format: TXT=9078 bytes) (Status: INFORMATIONAL)

2504 Users' Security Handbook. . Guttman, L. Leong, G. Malkin. February 1999. (Format: TXT=74036 bytes) (Also FYI0034) (Status: INFORMATIONAL)

2505 Anti-Spam Recommendations for SMTP MTAs. G. Lindberg. February 1999. (Format: TXT=53597 bytes) (Also BCP0030) (Status: BEST CURRENT PRACTICE)

2506 Media Feature Tag Registration Procedure. K. Holtman, A. Mutz, T. Hardie. March 1999. (Format: TXT=24892 bytes) (Also BCP0031) (Status: BEST CURRENT PRACTICE)

2507 IP Header Compression. M. Degermark, B. Nordgren, S. Pink. February 1999. (Format: TXT=106292 bytes) (Status: PROPOSED STANDARD)

2508 Compressing IP/UDP/RTP Headers for Low-Speed Serial Links. S. Casner, V. Jacobson. February 1999. (Format: TXT=60474 bytes) (Status: PROPOSED STANDARD)

2509 IP Header Compression over PPP. M. Engan, S. Casner, C. Bormann. February 1999. (Format: TXT=18676 bytes) (Status: PROPOSED STANDARD)

2510 Internet X.509 Public Key Infrastructure Certificate Management Protocols. C. Adams, S. Farrell. March 1999. (Format: TXT=158178 bytes) (Status: PROPOSED STANDARD)

2511 Internet X.509 Certificate Request Message Format. M. Myers, C. Adams, D. Solo, D. Kemp. March 1999. (Format: TXT=48278 bytes) (Status: PROPOSED STANDARD)

2512 Accounting Information for ATM Networks. K. McCloghrie, J. Heinanen, W. Greene, A. Prasad. February 1999. (Format: TXT=29119 bytes) (Status: PROPOSED STANDARD)

2513 Managed Objects for Controlling the Collection and Storage of Accounting Information for Connection-Oriented Networks. K. McCloghrie, J. Heinanen, W. Greene, A. Prasad. February 1999. (Format: TXT=60789 bytes) (Status: PROPOSED STANDARD)

2514 Definitions of Textual Conventions and OBJECT-IDENTITIES for ATM Management. M. Noto, E. Spiegel, K. Tesink. February 1999. (Format: TXT=37583 bytes) (Status: PROPOSED STANDARD)

2515 Definitions of Managed Objects for ATM Management. K. Tesink, Ed.. February 1999. (Format: TXT=179993 bytes) (Obsoletes RFC1695) (Status: PROPOSED STANDARD)

2516 Method for Transmitting PPP Over Ethernet (PPPoE). L. Mamakos, K. Lidl, J. Evarts, D. Carrel, D. Simone, R. Wheeler. February 1999. (Format: TXT=32537 bytes) (Status: INFORMATIONAL)

2517 Building Directories from DNS: Experiences from WWWSeeker. R. Moats, R. Huber. February 1999. (Format: TXT=14001 bytes) (Status: INFORMATIONAL)

2518 HTTP Extensions for Distributed Authoring – WEBDAV. Y. Goland, E. Whitehead, A. Faizi, S. Carter, D. Jensen. February 1999. (Format: TXT=202829 bytes) (Status: PROPOSED STANDARD)

2519 A Framework for Inter-Domain Route Aggregation. E. Chen, J. Stewart. February 1999. (Format: TXT=25394 bytes) (Status: INFORMATIONAL)

2520 NHRP with Mobile NHCs. J. Luciani, H. Suzuki, N. Doraswamy, D. Horton. February 1999. (Format: TXT=16763 bytes) (Status: EXPERIMENTAL)

2521 ICMP Security Failures Messages. P. Karn, W. Simpson. March 1999. (Format: TXT=14637 bytes) (Status: EXPERIMENTAL)

2522 Photuris: Session-Key Management Protocol. P. Karn, W. Simpson. March 1999. (Format: TXT=157224 bytes) (Status: EXPERIMENTAL)

2523 Photuris: Extended Schemes and Attributes. P. Karn, W. Simpson. March 1999. (Format: TXT=38166 bytes) (Status: EXPERIMENTAL)

2524 Neda's Efficient Mail Submission and Delivery (EMSD) Protocol Specification Version 1.3. M. Banan. February 1999. (Format: TXT=153171 bytes) (Status: INFORMATIONAL)

2525 Known TCP Implementation Problems. V. Paxson, M Allman, S. Dawson, W. Fenner, J. Griner, I. Heavens, K. Lahey, J. Semke, B. Volz. March 1999. (Format: TXT=137201 bytes) (Status: INFORMATIONAL)

2526 Reserved IPv6 Subnet Anycast Addresses. D. Johnson, S. Deering. March 1999. (Format: TXT=14555 bytes) (Status: PROPOSED STANDARD)

2527 Internet X.509 Public Key Infrastructure Certificate Policy and Certification Practices Framework. S. Chokhani, W. Ford. March 1999. (Format: TXT=91860 bytes) (Status: INFORMATIONAL)

2528 Internet X.509 Public Key Infrastructure Representation of Key Exchange Algorithm (KEA) Keys in Internet X.509 Public Key Infrastructure Certificates. R. Housley, W. Polk. March 1999. (Format: TXT=18273 bytes) (Status: INFORMATIONAL)

2529 Transmission of IPv6 over IPv4 Domains without Explicit Tunnels. B. Carpenter, C. Jung. March 1999. (Format: TXT=21049 bytes) (Status: PROPOSED STANDARD)

2534 Media Features for Display, Print, and Fax. L. Masinter, D. Wing, A. Mutz, K. Holtman. March 1999. (Format: TXT=15466 bytes) (Status: PROPOSED STANDARD)

2535 Domain Name System Security Extensions. D. Eastlake. March 1999. (Format: TXT=110958 bytes) (Updates RFC2181, RFC1035, RFC1034) (Status: PROPOSED STANDARD)

2536 DSA KEYs and SIGs in the Domain Name System (DNS). D. Eastlake. March 1999. (Format: TXT=11121 bytes) (Status: PROPOSED STANDARD)

2537 RSA/MD5 KEYs and SIGs in the Domain Name System (DNS). D. Eastlake. March 1999. (Format: TXT=10810 bytes) (Status: PROPOSED STANDARD)

2538 Storing Certificates in the Domain Name System (DNS). D. Eastlake, O. Gudmundsson. March 1999. (Format: TXT=19857 bytes) (Status: PROPOSED STANDARD)

2539 Storage of Diffie-Hellman Keys in the Domain Name System (DNS). D. Eastlake. March 1999. (Format: TXT=21049 bytes) (Status: PROPOSED STANDARD)

2540 Detached Domain Name System (DNS) Information. D. Eastlake. March 1999. (Format: TXT=12546 bytes) (Status: EXPERIMENTAL)

2541 DNS Security Operational Considerations. D. Eastlake. March 1999. (Format: TXT=14498 bytes) (Status: INFORMATIONAL)

2542 Terminology and Goals for Internet Fax. L. Masinter. March 1999. (Format: TXT=46372 bytes) (Status: INFORMATIONAL)

2543 SIP: Session Initiation Protocol. M. Handley, H. Schulzrinne, E. Schooler, J. Rosenberg. March 1999. (Format: TXT=338861 bytes) (Status: PROPOSED STANDARD)

2544	Benchmarking Methodology for Network Interconnect Devices. S. Bradner, J. McQuaid. March 1999. (Format: TXT=66688 bytes) (Obsoletes RFC1944) (Status: INFORMATIONAL)
2545	Use of BGP-4 Multiprotocol Extensions for IPv6 Inter-Domain Routing. P. Marques, F. Dupont. March 1999. (Format: TXT=10209 bytes) (Status: PROPOSED STANDARD)
2546	6Bone Routing Practice. A. Durand, B. Buclin. March 1999. (Format: TXT=17844 bytes) (Status: INFORMATIONAL)
2547	BGP/MPLS VPNs. E. Rosen, Y. Rekhter. March 1999. (Format: TXT=63270 bytes) (Status: INFORMATIONAL)
2548	Microsoft Vendor-specific RADIUS Attributes. G. Zorn. March 1999. (Format: TXT=80763 bytes) (Status: INFORMATIONAL)
2549	IP over Avian Carriers with Quality of Service. D. Waitzman. April-01-1999. (Format: TXT=9519 bytes) (Updates 1149) (Status: INFORMATIONAL)
2550	Y10K and Beyond. S. Glassman, M. Manasse, J. Mogul. April-01-1999. (Format: TXT=28011 bytes) (Status: INFORMATIONAL)
2551	The Roman Standards Process – Revision III. S. Bradner. April-01-1999. (Format: TXT=28054 bytes) (Status: INFORMATIONAL)
2552	Architecture for the Information Brokerage in the ACTS Project GAIA. M. Blinov, M. Bessonov, C. Clissmann. April 1999. (Format: TXT=65172 bytes) (Status: INFORMATIONAL)
2553	Basic Socket Interface Extensions for IPv6. R. Gilligan, S. Thomson, J. Bound, W. Stevens. March 1999. (Format: TXT=89215 bytes) (Status: INFORMATIONAL)
2554	SMTP Service Extension for Authentication. J. Myers. March 1999. (Format: TXT=20534 bytes) (Status: PROPOSED STANDARD)
2555	30 Years of RFCs. RFC Editor, et al.. Apr-07-1999. (Format: TXT=42902 bytes) (Status: INFORMATIONAL)
2556	OSI connectionless transport services on top of UDP Applicability Statement for Historic Status. S. Bradner. March 1999. (Format: TXT=5864 bytes) (Status: INFORMATIONAL)
2557	MIME Encapsulation of Aggregate Documents, such as HTML (MHTML). J. Palme, A. Hopmann, N. Shelness. March 1999. (Format: TXT=61854 bytes) (Obsoletes RFC2110) (Status: PROPOSED STANDARD)

2558 Definitions of Managed Objects for the SONET/SDH Interface Type. K. Tesink. March 1999. (Format: TXT=138550 bytes) (Obsoletes RFC1595) (Status: PROPOSED STANDARD)

2559 Internet X.509 Public Key Infrastructure Operational Protocols - LDAPv2. S. Boeyen, T. Howes, P. Richard. April 1999. (Format: TXT=22889 bytes) (Updates RFC1778) (Status: PROPOSED STANDARD)

2561 Base Definitions of Managed Objects for TN3270E Using SMIv2. K. White, R. Moore. April 1999. (Format: TXT=113705 bytes) (Status: PROPOSED STANDARD)

2562 Definitions of Protocol and Managed Objects for TN3270E Response Time Collection Using SMIv2 (TN3270E-RT-MIB). K. White, R. Moore. April 1999. (Format: TXT=110633 bytes) (Status: PROPOSED STANDARD)

2563 DHCP Option to Disable Stateless Auto-Configuration in IPv4 Clients. R. Troll. May 1999. (Format: TXT=17838 bytes) (Status: PROPOSED STANDARD)

2564 Application Management MIB. C. Kalbfleisch, C. Krupczak, R. Presuhn, J. Saperia. May 1999. (Format: TXT=183314 bytes) (Status: PROPOSED STANDARD)

2565 Internet Printing Protocol/1.0: Encoding and Transport. R. Herriot, Ed., S. Butler, P. Moore, R. Turner. April 1999. (Format: TXT=80439 bytes) (Status: EXPERIMENTAL)

2566 Internet Printing Protocol/1.0: Model and Semantics. R. deBry, T. Hastings, R. Herriot, S. Isaacson, P. Powell. April 1999. (Format: TXT=438887 bytes) (Status: EXPERIMENTAL)

2567 Design Goals for an Internet Printing Protocol. F. Wright. April 1999. (Format: TXT=90260 bytes) (Status: EXPERIMENTAL)

2568 Rationale for the Structure of the Model and Protocol for the Internet Printing Protocol. S. Zilles. April 1999. (Format: TXT=23547 bytes) (Status: EXPERIMENTAL)

2569 Mapping between LPD and IPP Protocols. R. Herriot, Ed., T. Hastings, N. Jacobs, J. Martin. April 1999. (Format: TXT=57886 bytes) (Status: EXPERIMENTAL)

2570 Introduction to Version 3 of the Internet-standard Network Management Framework. J. Case, R. Mundy, D. Partain, B. Stewart. April 1999. (Format: TXT=50381 bytes) (Status: INFORMATIONAL)

2571 An Architecture for Describing SNMP Management Frameworks. B. Wijnen, D. Harrington, R. Presuhn. April 1999. (Format: TXT=139260 bytes) (Obsoletes RFC2271) (Status: DRAFT STANDARD)

2572 Message Processing and Dispatching for the Simple Network Management Protocol (SNMP). J. Case, D. Harrington, R. Presuhn, B. Wijnen. April 1999. (Format: TXT=96035 bytes) (Obsoletes RFC2272) (Status: DRAFT STANDARD)

2573 SNMP Applications. D. Levi, P. Meyer, B. Stewart. April 1999. (Format: TXT=150427 bytes) (Obsoletes RFC2273) (Status: DRAFT STANDARD)

2574 User-based Security Model (USM) for version 3 of the Simple Network Management Protocol (SNMPv3). U. Blumenthal, B. Wijnen. April 1999. (Format: TXT=190755 bytes) (Obsoletes RFC2274) (Status: DRAFT STANDARD)

2575 View-based Access Control Model (VACM) for the Simple Network Management Protocol (SNMP). B. Wijnen, R. Presuhn, K. McCloghrie. April 1999. (Format: TXT=79642 bytes) (Obsoletes RFC2275) (Status: DRAFT STANDARD)

2577 FTP Security Considerations. M. Allman, S. Ostermann. May 1999. (Format: TXT=17870 bytes) (Status: INFORMATIONAL)

2578 Structure of Management Information Version 2 (SMIv2). K. McCloghrie, D. Perkins, J. Schoenwaelder. April 1999. (Format: TXT=89712 bytes) (Obsoletes RFC1902) (Also STD0058) (Status: STANDARD)

2579 Textual Conventions for SMIv2. K. McCloghrie, D. Perkins, J. Schoenwaelder. April 1999. (Format: TXT=59039 bytes) (Obsoletes RFC1903) (Also STD0058) (Status: STANDARD)

2580 Conformance Statements for SMIv2. K. McCloghrie, D. Perkins, J. Schoenwaelder. April 1999. (Format: TXT=54253 bytes) (Obsoletes RFC1904) (Also STD0058) (Status: STANDARD)

2581 TCP Congestion Control. M. Allman, V. Paxson, W. Stevens. April 1999. (Format: TXT=31351 bytes) (Obsoletes RFC2001) (Status: PROPOSED STANDARD)

2582 The NewReno Modification to TCP's Fast Recovery Algorithm. S. Floyd, T. Henderson. April 1999. (Format: TXT=29393 bytes) (Status: EXPERIMENTAL)

2583 Guidelines for Next Hop Client (NHC) Developers. R. Carlson, L. Winkler. May 1999. (Format: TXT=21338 bytes) (Status: INFORMATIONAL)

Appendix E

Acronyms and Abbreviations

A

A	ampere
AARP	AppleTalk Address Resolution Protocol
ABP	alternate bipolar
ACK	acknowledgement
ACS	asynchronous communication server
ACTLU	activate logical unit
ACTPU	activate physical unit
ADSP	AppleTalk Data Stream Protocol
AEP	AppleTalk Echo Protocol
AFI	authority and format identifier
AFP	AppleTalk Filing Protocol
AFRP	ARCNET Fragmentation Protocol
AGS	asynchronous gateway server
AH	authentication header
AI	artificial intelligence
AMI	alternate mark inversion
AMT	address mapping table
ANSI	American National Standards Institute
API	applications program interface
APPC	Advanced Program-to-Program Communication
ARE	all routes explorer

ARI	address recognized indicator bit
ARM	administrative runtime module
ARP	Address Resolution Protocol
ARPA	Advanced Research Projects Agency
ARPANET	Advanced Research Projects Agency Network
ASCE	Association Control Service Element
ASCII	American Standard Code for Information Interchange
ASN.1	Abstract Syntax Notation One
ASP	AppleTalk Session Protocol
ATM	Asynchronous Transfer Mode
ATP	AppleTalk Transaction Protocol
AUP	acceptable use policy
AVM	administrative view module

B

B8ZS	bipolar with 8 ZERO substitution
BC	block check
BER	Basic Encoding Rules
BIOS	Basic Input/Output System
BITNET	Because It's Time NETwork
BIU	basic information unit
BOC	Bell Operating Company
BOFL	Breath of Life
BOOTP	Bootstrap Protocol
BPDU	bridge protocol data unit
bps	bits per second
BPV	bipolar violations
BRI	basic rate interface
BSC	binary synchronous communication
BSD	Berkeley Software Distribution

BTU	basic transmission unit
BUI	browser user interface

C

CATNIP	Common Architecture for Next Generation Internet Protocol
CCIS	common channel interoffice signaling
CCITT	International Telegraph and Telephone Consultative Committee
CCR	commitment, concurrency, and recovery
CICS	customer information communication system
CIDR	classless interdomain routing
CLNP	Connectionless Network Protocol
CLNS	Connectionless-mode Network Services
CLTP	Connectionless Transport Protocol
CMIP	Common Management Information Protocol
CMIS	Common Management Information Service
CMISE	Common Management Information Service Element
CMOL	CMIP on IEEE 802.2 Logical Link Control
CMOT	Common Management Information Protocol over TCP/IP
CONS	Connection-mode Network Services
CORBA	Common Object Request Broker Architecture
COS	Corporation for Open Systems
CPE	customer premises equipment
CPE	convergence protocol entity
CRC	cyclic redundancy check
CREN	The Corporation for Research and Educational Networking
CRS	configuration report server
CSMA/CD	Carrier Sense Multiple Access with Collision Detection
CSNET	computer+science network
CSU	channel service unit
CTERM	Command Terminal Protocol

D

DA	destination address
DAP	Data Access Protocol
DARPA	Defense Advanced Research Projects Agency
DAT	duplicate address test
DCA	Defense Communications Agency
DCC	Data Country Code
DCE	data circuit-terminating equipment
DDCMP	Digital Data Communications Message Protocol
DDN	Defense Data Network
DDP	Datagram Delivery Protocol
DECmcc	DEC Management Control Center
DEMPR	DEC multiport repeater
DHCP	Dynamic Host Configuration Protocol
DIX	DEC, Intel, and Xerox
DL	data link
DLC	data link control
DMA	direct memory access
DMI	Desktop Management Interface
DMTF	Desktop Management Task Force
DNIC	Data Network Identification Code
DNS	Domain Name System
DOD	Department of Defense
DPA	demand protocol architecture
DRP	DECnet Routing Protocol
DSAP	destination service access point
DSU	data service unit
DSU/CSU	Data service unit/channel service unit
DTE	data terminal equipment
DTR	data terminal ready

E

EBCDIC	Extended Binary Coded Decimal Interchange Code
ECL	End Communication layer
ECSA	Exchange Carriers Standards Association
EDI	electronic data interchange
EGA	enhanced graphics array
EGP	Exterior Gateway Protocol
EIA	Electronic Industries Association
ELAP	EtherTalk Link Access Protocol
EOT	end of transmission
ESF	extended superframe format
ES-IS	End System to Intermediate System Protocol
ESP	encapsulating security payload

F

FAL	file access listener
FAT	file access table
FCC	Federal Communications Commission
FCI	frame copied indicator bit
FCS	frame check sequence
FDDI	fiber data distributed interface
FDM	frequency division multiplexing
FID	format identifer
FIPS	Federal Information Processing Standard
FM	function management
FMD	function management data
FT1	fractional T1
FTAM	File Transfer Access and Management
FTP	File Transfer Protocol

G

G	giga-
GB	gigabyte
GHz	gigahertz
GOSIP	Government OSI profile
GUI	graphical user interface

H

HA	hardware address
HDLC	high-level data link control
HEMS	high-level entity management system
HLLAPI	High-level language API
HMMO	Hypermedia Managed Object
HMOM	Hypermedia Object Manager
HMMP	Hypermedia Management Protocol
HMMS	Hypermedia Management Schema
HTML	Hypertext Markup Language
HTTP	Hypertext Transfer Protocol
Hz	hertz

I

IAB	Internet Activities Board
IANA	Internet Assigned Numbers Authority
ICD	international code designator
ICMP	Internet Control Message Protocol
ICP	Internet Control Protocol
IDI	initial domain indicator
IDP	Internetwork Datagram Protocol
IDRP	Inter Domain Routing Protocol
IEEE	Institute of Electrical and Electronics Engineers

IETF	Internet Engineering Task Force
I/G	individual/group
IGMP	Internet Group Management Protocol
IGP	Interior Gateway Protocol
IGRP	Internet Gateway Routing Protocol
IMPS	interface message processors
I/O	input/output
IOC	inter-office channel
IP	Internet Protocol
IPng	Internet Protocol, next generation
IPv6	Internet Protocol, version 6
IPv6CP	Internet Protocol version 6 Control Protocol
IPC	Interprocess Communications Protocol
IPX	Internetwork Packet Exchange Protocol
IR	Internet router
IRTF	Internet Research Task Force
ISAKMP	Internet Secure Association Key Management Protocol
ISDN	Integrated Services Digital Network
IS-IS	Intermediate System to Intermediate System Protocol
ISN	initial sequence number
ISO	International Organization for Standardization
ISODE	ISO Development Environment
ITU	International Telecommunication Union
IXC	inter-exchange carrier

J

JDBC	Java Database Connectivity
JMAPI	Java Management Application Programming Interface

K

K	kilo bits per second
KHz	kilohertz

L

LAA	locally administered address
LAN	local area network
LAP	link access procedure
LAPB	Link Access Procedure Balanced
LAPD	Link Access Procedure D Channel
LAT	Local Area Transport
LATA	local access transport area
LAVC	local area VAX cluster
LCP	Link Control Protocol
LDAP	Lightweight Directory Access Protocol
LEC	local exchange carrier
LEN	length
LF	largest frame
LLAP	LocalTalk Link Access Protocol
LLC	Logical Link Control
LME	layer management entity
LMI	layer management interface
LMMP	LAN/MAN Management Protocol
LMMPE	LAN/MAN Management Protocol Entity
LMMS	LAN/MAN Management Service
LMMU	LAN/MAN Management User
LPP	Lightweight Presentation Protocol
LSB	least significant bit
LSL	Link Support layer

M

MAC	medium access control
MAN	metropolitan area network
Mbps	megabits per second
MHS	message handling service
MHz	megahertz
MIB	management information base
MILNET	MILitary NETwork
MIOX	Multiprotocol Interconnect over X.25
MIPS	millions instructions per second
MIS	management information systems
MLID	multiple link interface driver
MNP	Microcom Networking Protocol
MOP	Maintenance Operations Protocol
MSAU	multistation access unit
MSB	most significant bit
MSS	maximum segment size
MTA	message transfer agent
MTBF	mean time between failures
MTTR	mean time to repair
MTU	maximum transmission unit
MUX	multiplex, multiplexor

N

NACS	NetWare Asynchronous Communications Server
NAK	negative acknowledgement
NASI	NetWare Asynchronous Service Interface
NAU	network addressable unit
NAUN	nearest active upstream neighbor
NBP	Name Binding Protocol

NCP	Network Control Program
NCP	Network Control Protocol
NCP	NetWare Core Protocol
NCSI	network communications services interface
NDIS	Network Driver Interface Standard
NetBEUI	NetBIOS Extended User Interface
NetBIOS	Network Basic Input/Output System
NFS	Network File System
NIC	network information center
NIC	network interface card
NICE	network information and control exchange
NIS	names information socket
NIST	National Institute of Standards and Technology
NLA	next-level aggregation identifier
NLM	netware loadable module
NMS	network management station
NOC	network operations center
NOS	network operating system
NSAP	Network Service Access Point
NSF	National Science Foundation
NSP	Network Services Protocol
NT	network termination

O

OCI	optical carrier, level 1
ODI	Open Data Link Interface
OID	object identifier
OIM	OSI Internet management
OSF	Open Software Foundation
OSI	Open Systems Interconnection

OSI-RM Open Systems Interconnection Reference Model

OSPF Open Shortest Path First

P

PA protocol address

PABX private automatic branch exchange

PAD packet assembler and disassembler

PAP Printer Access Protocol

PBX private branch exchange

PCI protocol control information

PCM pulse code modulation

PDN public data network

PDU protocol data unit

PEP Packet Exchange Protocol

PLEN protocol length

PMTU path maximum transmission unit

POP point of presence

POSIX Portable Operating System Interface-UNIX

POTS plain old telephone service

PPP Point-to-Point Protocol

PSN packet switch node

PSP presentation services process

PSPDN packet switched public data network

PTP point-to-point

PUC Public Utility Commission

R

RARP Reverse Address Resolution Protocol

RBOC Regional Bell Operating Company

RC routing control

RD	route descriptor
RFC	request for comments
RFS	remote file system
RH	request/response header
RI	routing information
RII	route information indicator
RIP	Routing Information Protocol
RJE	remote job entry
ROSE	Remote Operations Service Element
RMI	Remote Method Invocation
RMON	remote monitoring
RPC	remote procedure call
RPS	ring parameter server
RSX	Realtime Resource-Sharing eXecutive
RT	routing type
RU	request/response unit

S

SA	source address
SA	security association
SABME	set asynchronous balanced mode extended
SAP	service access point
SAP	Service Advertising Protocol
SCS	system communication services
SDLC	Synchronous Data Link Control
SDN	software defined network
SEQ	sequence
SGMP	Simple Gateway Management Protocol
SIPP	Simple Internet Protocol Plus
S/L	strict/loose bits

SLA	site-level aggregation identifier
SLIP	Serial Line IP
SMB	server message block
SMDS	Switched Multimegabit Data Service
SMI	structure of management information
SMI	system management interface
SMTP	Simple Mail Transfer Protocol
SNA	System Network Architecture
SNADS	Systems Network Architecture Distribution Services
SNAP	sub-network access protocol
SNMP	Simple Network Management Protocol
SOH	start of header
SONET	Synchronous Optical Network
SPI	security parameters index
SPP	Sequenced Packet Protocol
SPX	Sequenced Packet Exchange protocol
SR	source routing
SRF	specifically routed frame
SRI	Stanford Research Institute
SRT	source routing transparent
SSAP	source service access point
STE	spanning tree explorer
SUA	stored upstream address
SVC	switched virtual circuit

T

TB	terabyte
TCP	Transmission Control Protocol
TCP/IP	Transmission Control Protocol/Internet Protocol
TDM	time division multiplexing

TELNET	Telecommunications Network Protocol
TFTP	Trivial File Transfer Protocol
TH	transmission header
TLA	top-level aggregation identifier
TLAP	TokenTalk Link Access Protocol
TLI	Transport Layer Interface
TLV	Type-Length-Value encoding
TP	Transport Protocol
TSR	terminate-and-stay resident
TTL	time to live
TUBA	TCP/UDP with Bigger Addresses

U

UA	unnumbered acknowledgement
UA	user agent
UDP	User Datagram Protocol
U/L	universal/local
ULP	Upper Layer Protocols
UNMA	unified network management architecture
UT	universal time
UTP	unshielded twisted pair
UUCP	UNIX to UNIX copy program

V

V	volt
VAN	value added network
VAP	value-added process
VARP	VINES Address Resolution Protocol
VFRP	VINES Fragmentation Protocol
VGA	video graphics array

VICP	VINES Internet Control Protocol
VINES	Virtual Networking System
VIP	VINES Internet Protocol
VIPC	VINES Interprocess Communications
VLSI	very large-scale integration
VMS	virtual memory system
VRTP	VINES Routing Update Protocol
VSPP	VINES Sequenced Packet Protocol
VT	virtual terminal

W

WAN	wide area network
WBEM	Web-based Enterprise Management
WIN	window

X

X	External data representation
XID	exchange identification
XMP	X/Open Management Protocol
XNS	Xerox Network System

Z

ZIP	Zone Information Protocol
ZIS	Zone Information Socket
ZIT	Zone Information Table

Appendix F

Trademarks

PostScript is a trademark of Adobe Systems.

Apple, the Apple logo, AppleShare, AppleTalk, Apple IIGS, EtherTalk, LaserWriter, LocalTalk, Macintosh, and TokenTalk are registered trademarks; and APDA, Finder, Image Writer, and Quickdraw are trademarks of Apple Computer, Inc.

Banyan, the Banyan logo, and VINES are registered trademarks of Banyan Systems Inc.; and StreetTalk, VANGuard and NetRPC are trademarks of Banyan Systems, Inc.

COMPAQ DEC, DECnet, LanWORKS, LAT, LAVC, Mailbus, Message Router, MicroVAX, MOP, Rdb, ThinWire, Ultrix, VAX, VAX Cluster, and VMS Mail are trademarks, and Ethernet is a registered trademark of COMPAQ Computer Corporation.

IP Library and IP Technologies Library are trademarks, and DigiNet is a registered trademark of Digital Network Corporation.

HP is a trademark of the Hewlett-Packard Company.

Intel and Ethernet are registered trademarks of Intel Corporation.

Dispatcher/SMTP and WatchTower are trademarks of Intercon Systems Corporation.

AS/400, DISOSS, IBM PC LAN, PC/AT, PC/XT, PROFS, SNA, SNADS, System/370, System/38, 3270 Display Station, DB2, ESCON, MicroChannel, VMS/ESA, MVS/SP, MVS/XA, Netbios, SAA, System View, VM/ESA, VM/XA, VSE/ESA, and VTAM are trademarks of International Business Machines Corporation; and AIX, AT, IBM, NetView, OS/2, OS/400, and PS/2 are registered trademarks of International Business Machines Corporation.

X and X Window System are trademarks of the Massachusetts Institute of Technology.

Microsoft, MS-DOS, and LAN Manager are registered trademarks of, and Windows NT is a trademark of Microsoft Corporation.

OnNet, is a trademark of, and PC/TCP and FTP Software are registered trademarks of NetManage, Inc.

Sniffer Analyzer is a trademark of Network Associates, Inc.

C Network Compiler, C Network Compiler/386, IPX, NACS, NetWare, NetWare C Interface for DOS, NetWare for VMS, NetWare MHS, NetWare RPC, NetWare SQL, NetWare System Call for DOS, NetWare 386, NLM, Novell, Portable NetWare, RX-Net, SFT, SPX, Transaction Tracking System, VAP, and Xtrieve Plus are trademarks and Novell, NetWire, Btrieve, and XQL are registered trademarks of Novell, Inc.

Proteon and proNET are registered trademarks of Open Route Networks, Inc.

Prime is a trademark of Prime Computer Inc.

4.2BSD and 4.3BSD are trademarks of the Regents of the University of California.

Retix is a trademark of Retix.

MultiNet is a trademark of TGV, Inc.

SMC is a registered trademark of Standard Microsystems Corporation.

Network File System, NFS, Open Network Computing, ONC, SPARC, Sun, SunOS, TOPS, and PC-NIFS are trademarks of Sun Microsystems, Inc.

Symbolics and CHAOSnet are trademarks of Symbolics, Inc.

3COM is a registered trademark of 3Com Corporation.

Ungerman Bass is a trademark of Ungerman-Bass, Inc.

Xerox, PUP, Clearinghouse, Interpress, Interscript, NS, XNS, and Open Look are trademarks, and Ethernet and Xerox are registered trademarks of Xerox Corporation.

UNIX is a registered trademark, licensed exclusively through X/Open Company, Ltd.

All other trademarks are the property of their respective owners.

Appendix G

Addresses of Standards Organizations

ANSI STANDARDS

American National Standards Institute
11 West 42nd Street, 13th Floor
New York, NY 10036
Telephone (212) 642-4900
Sales Department (212) 642-4980
www.ansi.org

ATIS PUBLICATIONS

Alliance for Telecommunications Industry Solutions
(formerly the Exchange Carriers Standards Association)
1200 G Street NW, Suite 500
Washington, DC 20005
Tel: (202) 628-6380
Fax: (202) 393-5453
www.atis.org

AT&T PUBLICATIONS

Lucent Technologies
P.O. Box 19901
Indianapolis, IN 46219
Tel: (317) 322-6557 or (888) 582-3688
Fax: (800) 566-9568
www.lucent.com

BELLCORE STANDARDS

Telecordia Technologies, Inc.
Information Management Services
8 Corporate Place, Room 3A-184
Piscataway, NJ 08854-4156
Tel: (908) 699-5800 or (800) 521-2673
Fax: (908) 336-2559
www.bellcore.com

CSA STANDARDS

Canadian Standards Association
178 Rexdale Boulevard
Etobicoke, ONT M9W 1R3
Canada
Tel: (416) 747-4363 or (800) 463-6727
Fax: (416) 747-2473
www.csa.ca

DISA STANDARDS

Defense Information Systems Agency
w▾ww.itsi.disa.mil

DOD STANDARDS

DoD Network Information Center
Boeing Corporation
7990 Boeing Court, M/S CV-50
Vienna, VA 22183-7000
Tel: (703) 821-6266 or (800) 365-3642
Fax: (703) 821-6161
`www.nic.mil`

ECMA STANDARDS

European Computer Manufacturers Association
114 Rue de Rhone
CH-1204 Geneva
Switzerland
Tel: 41 22 849 60 00
Fax: 41 22 849 60 01
E-mail: helpdesk@ecma.ch
`www.ecma.ch`

EIA STANDARDS

Electronic Industries Association
2500 Wilson Boulevard
Arlington, VA 22201
Tel: (703) 907-7500
Fax: (703) 907-7501
`www.eia.org`

ETSI STANDARDS

European Telecommunications Standards Institute
ETSI Publications Office
Sophia Antipolis Cedex
France
Tel: 33 (0) 492 94 42 41
Fax: 33 (0) 493 95 81 33
E-mail: anja.mulder@etsi.fr
`www.etsi.fr`

FEDERAL INFORMATION PROCESSING STANDARDS (FIPS)

U.S. Department of Commerce
National Technical Information Service (NTIS)
5285 Port Royal Road
Springfield, VA 22161
Tel: (703) 605-6000 or (800) 553-6847
Fax: (703) 605-6900
`www.ntis.gov`

IEC STANDARDS

International Electrotechnical Commission
Central Office
3, rue de Verenbe
P.O. Box 131
1211 Geneva 20
Switzerland
Tel: 41 22 919 02 11
Fax: 41 22 919 03 00
E-mail: dn@iec.ch
`www.hike.te.chiba-u.ac.jp/ikeda/IEC`

IEEE STANDARDS

Institute of Electrical and Electronics Engineers
445 Hoes Lane
P.O. Box 1331
Piscataway, NJ 08855-1331
Tel: (732) 981-0060 or (800) 678-4333
Fax: (732) 981-0538
`www.ieee.org`

INTERNET STANDARDS

Internet Society International
12020 Sunrise Valley Drive, Suite 210
Reston, VA 20191-3429
Tel: (703) 648-9888
Fax: (703) 648-9887
E-mail: isoc@isoc.org
`www.isoc.org`

ISO STANDARDS

International Organization for Standardization
1, Rue de Varembe'
Case postale 56
CH-1211 Geneva 20
Switzerland
Tel: 41 22 749 0111
Fax: 41 22 733 3430
E-mail: central@isocs.iso.ch
`www.iso.ch`

ITU STANDARDS

International Telecommunications Union
Information Services Department
Place des Nations
1211 Geneva 20
Switzerland
Tel: 41 22 730 5111
E-mail: helpdesk@itu.ch
`www.itu.ch`

NATIONAL INSTITUTE OF STANDARDS AND TECHNOLOGY

Technology Building 820
NIST N, Room B-562
Gaithersburg, MD 20899
Tel: (301) 975-2000
Fax: (301) 948 6213
`www.nist.gov`

WWW STANDARDS

World Wide Web Consortium
Massachusetts Institute of Technology
Laboratory for Computer Science
545 Technology Square Bldg. NE 43, Room 358
Cambridge, MA 02139
Tel: (617) 253-2613
Fax: (617) 258-5999
E-mail: www-request@w3.org
`www.w3.org`

MANY OF THE ABOVE STANDARDS MAY BE PURCHASED FROM:

GLOBAL ENGINEERING DOCUMENTS

15 Inverness Way East
Englewood, CO 80112
Tel: (303) 790-0600 or (800) 854-7179
Fax: (303) 397-2740
`www.global.ihs.com`

PHILLIPS BUSINESS INFORMATION, INC.

1201 Seven Locks Road, Suite #300
Potomac, MD 20854
Tel: (301) 424-3338 or (800) 777-5006
Fax: (301) 309-3847
E-mail:
clientservices.pbi@phillips.com
`www.phillips.com`

Index

Symbols & Numbers

A

B

C

D

E

I

J

K

L

M

N

O

P

Q

R

T

V

W

X

Y

Z

Other

IDG BOOKS WORLDWIDE, INC. END-USER LICENSE AGREEMENT

READ THIS. You should carefully read these terms and conditions before opening the software packet(s) included with this book ("Book"). This is a license agreement ("Agreement") between you and IDG Books Worldwide, Inc. ("IDGB"). By opening the accompanying software packet(s), you acknowledge that you have read and accept the following terms and conditions. If you do not agree and do not want to be bound by such terms and conditions, promptly return the Book and the unopened software packet(s) to the place you obtained them for a full refund.

1. **License Grant.** IDGB grants to you (either an individual or entity) a nonexclusive license to use one copy of the enclosed software program(s) (collectively, the "Software") solely for your own personal or business purposes on a single computer (whether a standard computer or a workstation component of a multiuser network). The Software is in use on a computer when it is loaded into temporary memory (RAM) or installed into permanent memory (hard disk, CD-ROM, or other storage device). IDGB reserves all rights not expressly granted herein.
2. **Ownership.** The author of this book is the owner of all right, title, and interest, including copyright, in and to the compilation of the Software recorded on the disk(s) or CD-ROM ("Software Media"). Copyright to the individual programs recorded on the Software Media is owned by the author or other authorized copyright owner of each program. Ownership of the Software and all proprietary rights relating thereto remain with author and author's licensors. The author's ownership does not extend to or include any works on the CD-ROM owned by the Internet Society () or any third party, and the restrictions of this Agreement do not apply to those works.
3. **Restrictions On Use and Transfer.**
   - (a) You may only (i) make one copy of the Software for backup or archival purposes, or (ii) transfer the Software to a single hard disk, provided that you keep the original for backup or archival purposes. You may not (i) rent or lease the Software, (ii) copy or reproduce the Software through a LAN or other network system or through any computer subscriber system or bulletin-board system, or (iii) modify, adapt, or create derivative works based on the Software.
   - (b) You may not reverse engineer, decompile, or disassemble the Software. You may transfer the Software and user documentation on a permanent basis, provided that the transferee agrees to accept the terms and conditions of this Agreement and you retain no copies. If the Software is an update or has been updated, any transfer must include the most recent update and all prior versions.
4. **Restrictions On Use of Individual Programs.** You must follow the individual requirements and restrictions detailed for each individual program in Appendix A of this Book. These limitations are also contained in the individual license agreements recorded on the Software Media. These limitations may include a requirement that after using the program for a specified period of time, the user must pay a registration fee or discontinue use. By opening the Software packet(s), you will be agreeing to abide by the licenses and restrictions for these individual programs that are detailed in Appendix A and on the Software Media. None of the material on the Software Media or in this Book may ever be redistributed, in original or modified form, for commercial purposes.
5. **Limited Warranty.**
   - (a) IDGB warrants that the Software Media is free from defects in materials and workmanship under normal use for a period of sixty (60) days from the date of purchase

of this Book. If IDGB receives notification within the warranty period of defects in materials or workmanship, IDGB will replace the defective Software Media.

(b) **IDGB AND THE AUTHOR OF THE BOOK DISCLAIM ALL OTHER WARRANTIES, EXPRESS OR IMPLIED, INCLUDING WITHOUT LIMITATION IMPLIED WARRANTIES OF MERCHANTABILITY AND FITNESS FOR A PARTICULAR PURPOSE, WITH RESPECT TO THE SOFTWARE, THE PROGRAMS, THE SOURCE CODE, THE WORKS OF THE INTERNET SOCIETY OR OF ANY OTHER THIRD PARTY CONTAINED THEREIN, AND/OR THE TECHNIQUES DESCRIBED IN THIS BOOK. IDGB DOES NOT WARRANT THAT THE FUNCTIONS CONTAINED IN THE SOFTWARE WILL MEET YOUR REQUIREMENTS OR THAT THE OPERATION OF THE SOFTWARE WILL BE ERROR FREE.**

(c) This limited warranty gives you specific legal rights, and you may have other rights that vary from jurisdiction to jurisdiction.

6. **Remedies.**

(a) IDGB's and author's entire liability and your exclusive remedy for defects in materials and workmanship shall be limited to replacement of the Software Media, which may be returned to IDGB with a copy of your receipt at the following address: Software Media Fulfillment Department, Attn.: *Troubleshooting TCP/IP, 3e*, IDG Books Worldwide, Inc., 7260 Shadeland Station, Ste. 100, Indianapolis, IN 46256, or call 1-800-762-2974. Please allow three to four weeks for delivery. This Limited Warranty is void if failure of the Software Media has resulted from accident, abuse, or misapplication. Any replacement Software Media will be warranted for the remainder of the original warranty period or thirty (30) days, whichever is longer.

(b) In no event shall IDGB or the author be liable for any damages whatsoever (including without limitation damages for loss of business profits, business interruption, loss of business information, or any other pecuniary loss) arising from the use of or inability to use the Book or the Software, even if IDGB or the author have been advised of the possibility of such damages.

(c) Because some jurisdictions do not allow the exclusion or limitation of liability for consequential or incidental damages, the above limitation or exclusion may not apply to you.

7. **U.S. Government Restricted Rights.** Use, duplication, or disclosure of the Software by the U.S. Government is subject to restrictions stated in paragraph (c)(1)(ii) of the Rights in Technical Data and Computer Software clause of DFARS 252.227-7013, and in subparagraphs (a) through (d) of the Commercial Computer – Restricted Rights clause at FAR 52.227-19, and in similar clauses in the NASA FAR supplement, when applicable.

8. **General.** This Agreement constitutes the entire understanding of the parties and revokes and supersedes all prior agreements, oral or written, between them and may not be modified or amended except in a writing signed by both parties hereto that specifically refers to this Agreement. This Agreement shall take precedence over any other documents that may be in conflict herewith. If any one or more provisions contained in this Agreement are held by any court or tribunal to be invalid, illegal, or otherwise unenforceable, each and every other provision shall remain in full force and effect.

CD-ROM Installation Instructions

To install the CD-ROM, insert the disk into the CD-ROM drive on your computer. You can access the contents of the CD-ROM through Windows Explorer, or by opening My Computer on the desktop.

The CD-ROM contains a collection of public domain Internet documents, from the Internet Architecture Board (IAB), Internet Engineering Task Force (IETF), Internet Research Group (IRG), and other Internet-related organizations. For a list of categories and subdirectories, please see Appendix A.

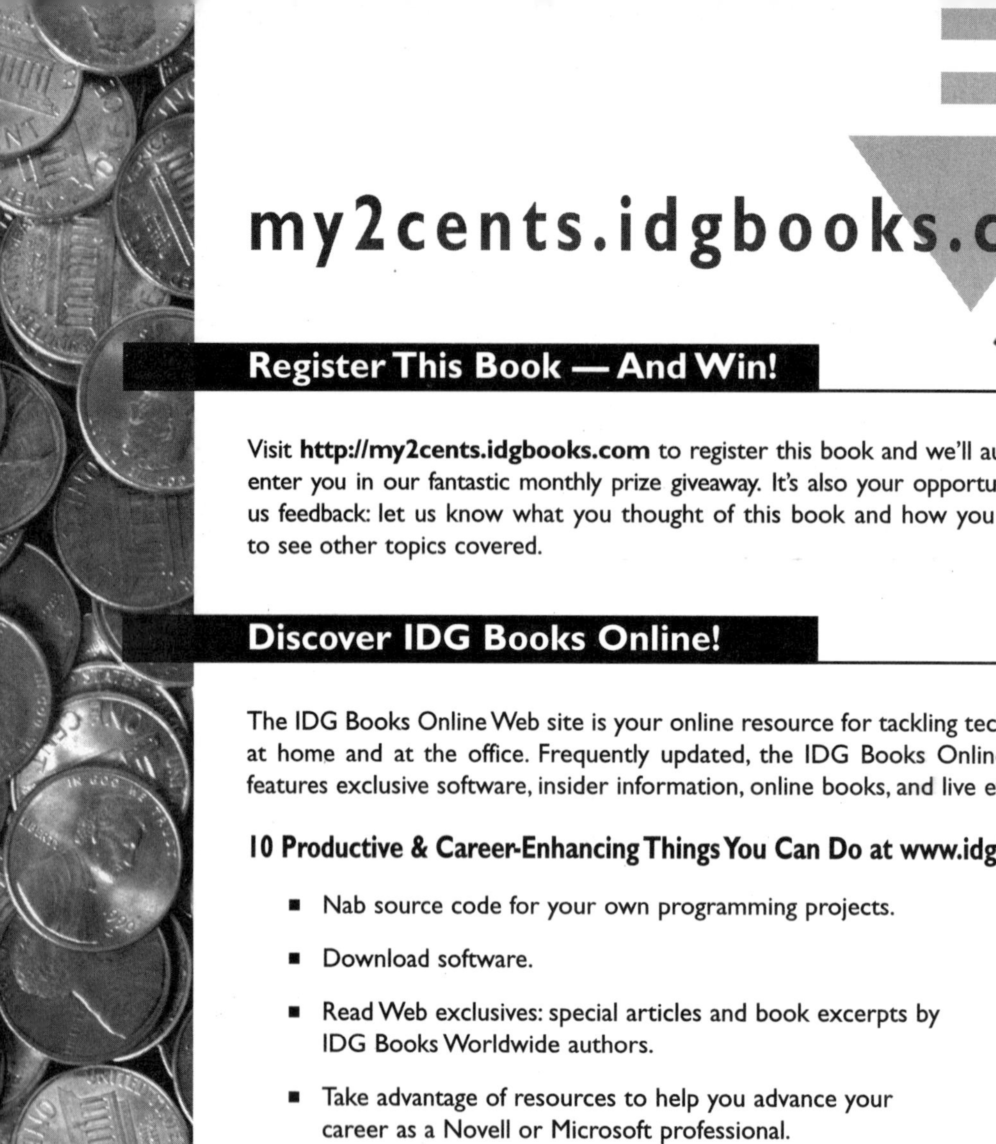

my2cents.idgbooks.com

Register This Book — And Win!

Visit **http://my2cents.idgbooks.com** to register this book and we'll automatically enter you in our fantastic monthly prize giveaway. It's also your opportunity to give us feedback: let us know what you thought of this book and how you would like to see other topics covered.

Discover IDG Books Online!

The IDG Books Online Web site is your online resource for tackling technology — at home and at the office. Frequently updated, the IDG Books Online Web site features exclusive software, insider information, online books, and live events!

10 Productive & Career-Enhancing Things You Can Do at www.idgbooks.com

- Nab source code for your own programming projects.
- Download software.
- Read Web exclusives: special articles and book excerpts by IDG Books Worldwide authors.
- Take advantage of resources to help you advance your career as a Novell or Microsoft professional.
- Buy IDG Books Worldwide titles or find a convenient bookstore that carries them.
- Register your book and win a prize.
- Chat live online with authors.
- Sign up for regular e-mail updates about our latest books.
- Suggest a book you'd like to read or write.
- Give us your 2¢ about our books and about our Web site.

You say you're not on the Web yet? It's easy to get started with IDG Books' *Discover the Internet,* available at local retailers everywhere.